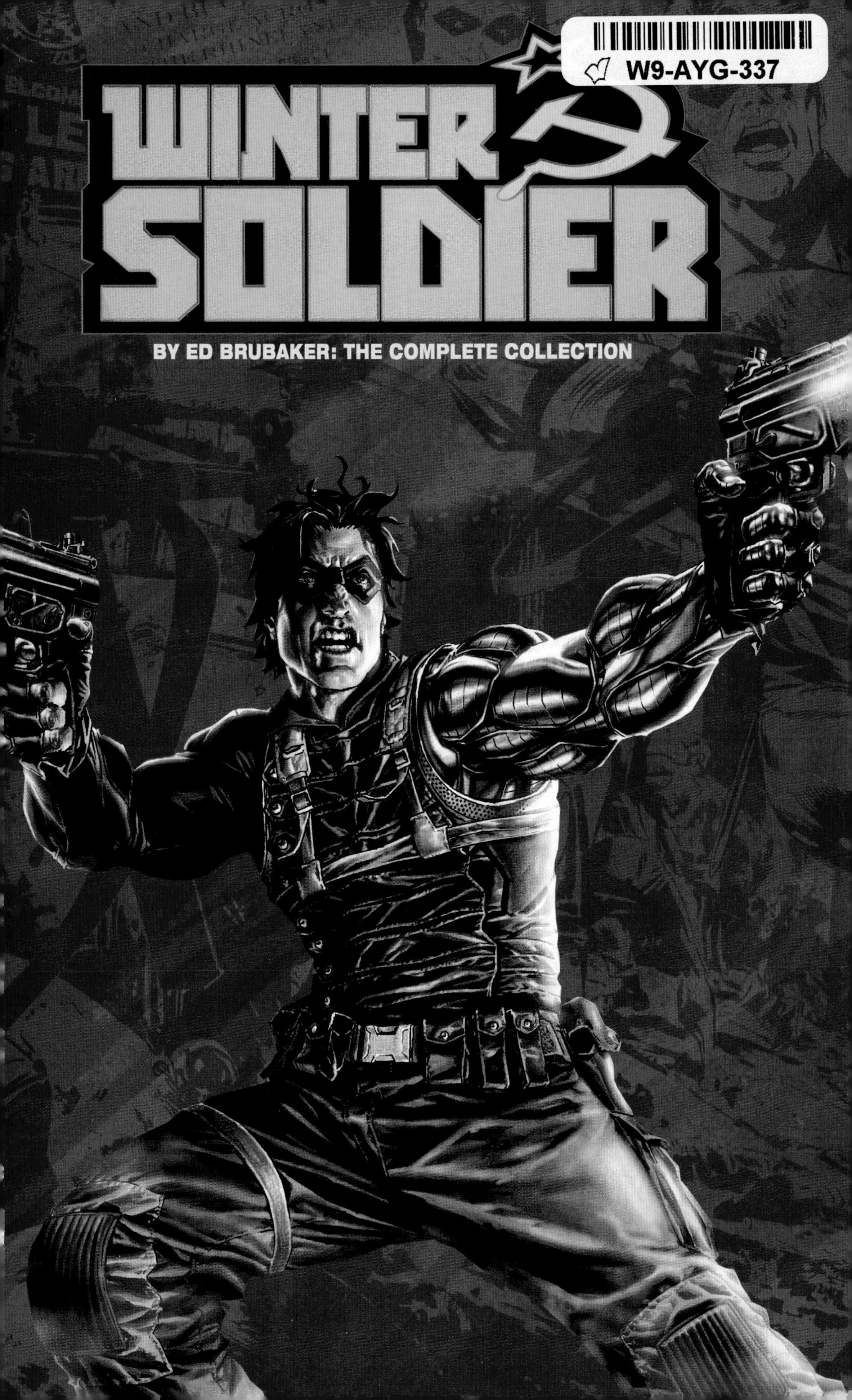
WINTER SOLDIER
BY ED BRUBAKER: THE COMPLETE COLLECTION

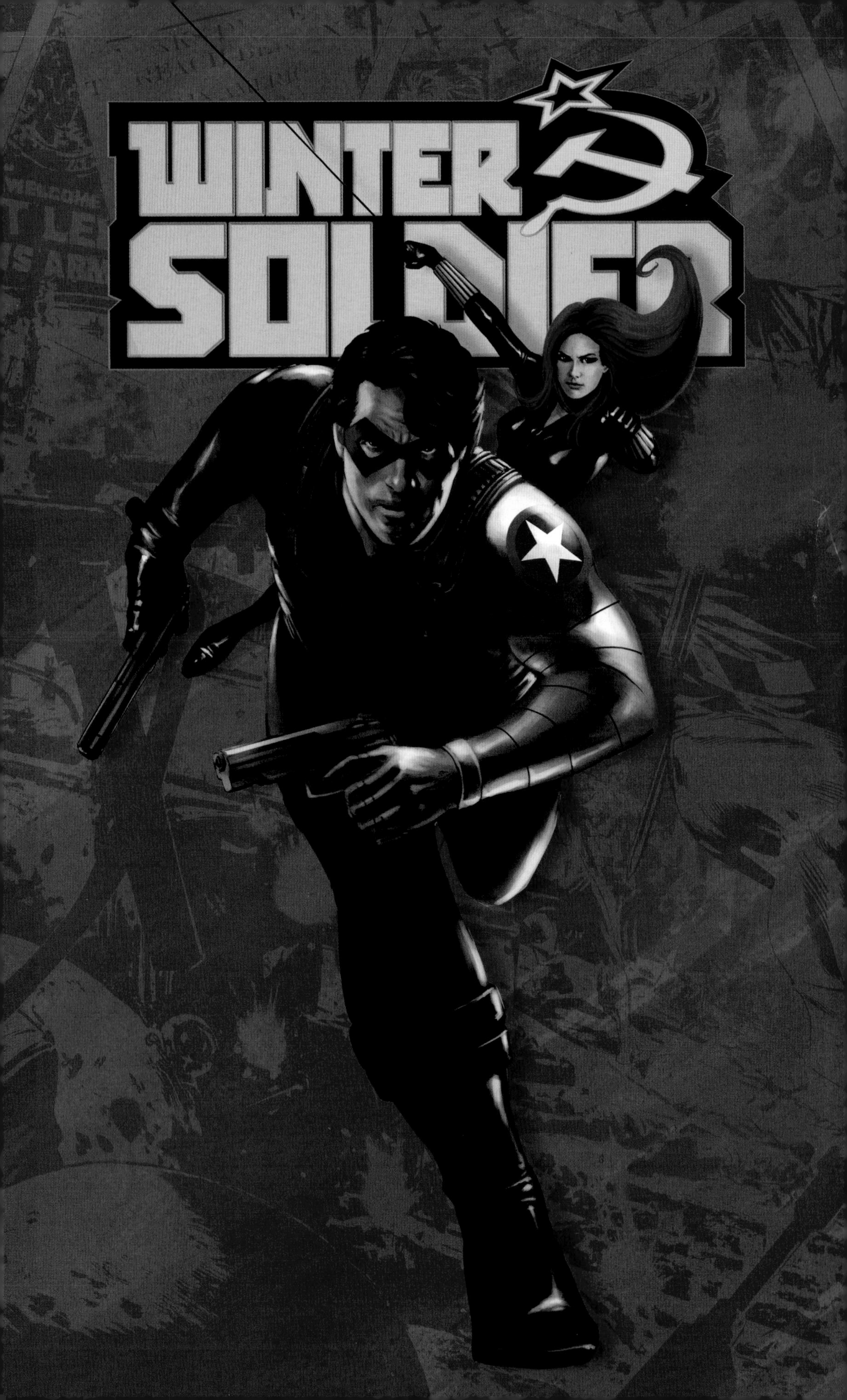
WINTER
SOLDIER

WRITER **ED BRUBAKER**

ISSUES #1-5 & FEAR ITSELF #7.1: CAPTAIN AMERICA

PENCILER **BUTCH GUICE**
INKERS, #3-5 **STEFANO GAUDIANO, BRIAN THIES & TOM PALMER**
COLOR ARTISTS **BETTIE BREITWEISER WITH JORDIE BELLAIRE** (#3) **& MATTHEW WILSON** (#4)
COVER ART **LEE BERMEJO** (#1-5) **& BUTCH GUICE** (FEAR ITSELF #7.1)

ISSUES #6-9

PENCILER **MICHAEL LARK**
INKERS **BRIAN THIES WITH STEFANO GAUDIANO**
COLOR ARTISTS **BETTIE BREITWEISER WITH MITCH BREITWEISER** (#8)
COVER ART **STEVE EPTING**

ISSUES #10-14

PENCILER **BUTCH GUICE**
INKERS **BUTCH GUICE** (#10) **& BRIAN THIES** (#11-14)
COLOR ARTISTS **BETTIE BREITWEISER** (#10-12 & #14) **& JORDIE BELLAIRE** (#13-14)
COVER ART **STEVE EPTING** (#10-13) **& DANIEL ACUÑA** (#14)

LETTERER **JOE CARAMAGNA**
ASSISTANT EDITORS **JOHN DENNING & JAKE THOMAS**
EDITOR **LAUREN SANKOVITCH**
EXECUTIVE EDITOR **TOM BREVOORT**

COLLECTION EDITOR **SARAH BRUNSTAD**
ASSOCIATE MANAGING EDITOR **ALEX STARBUCK**
EDITORS, SPECIAL PROJECTS **MARK D. BEAZLEY & JENNIFER GRÜNWALD**
SENIOR EDITOR, SPECIAL PROJECTS **JEFF YOUNGQUIST**
SVP OF PRINT & DIGITAL PUBLISHING SALES **DAVID GABRIEL**
BOOK DESIGN **JEFF POWELL & NELSON RIBEIRO**

EDITOR IN CHIEF **AXEL ALONSO**
CHIEF CREATIVE OFFICER **JOE QUESADA**
PUBLISHER **DAN BUCKLEY**
EXECUTIVE PRODUCER **ALAN FINE**

WINTER SOLDIER BY ED BRUBAKER: THE COMPLETE COLLECTION. Contains material originally published in magazine form as FEAR ITSELF #7.1: CAPTAIN AMERICA and WINTER SOLDIER #1-14. First printing 2014. ISBN# 978-0-7851-9065-3. Published by MARVEL WORLDWIDE, INC., a subsidiary of MARVEL ENTERTAINMENT, LLC. OFFICE OF PUBLICATION: 135 West 50th Street, New York, NY 10020. Printed in the U.S.A. ALAN FINE, EVP - Office of the President, Marvel Worldwide, Inc. and EVP & CMO Marvel Characters B.V.; DAN BUCKLEY, Publisher & President - Print, Animation & Digital Divisions; JOE QUESADA, Chief Creative Officer; TOM BREVOORT, SVP of Publishing; DAVID BOGART, SVP of Operations & Procurement, Publishing; C.B. CEBULSKI, SVP of Creator & Content Development; DAVID GABRIEL, SVP Print, Sales & Marketing; JIM O'KEEFE, VP of Operations & Logistics; DAN CARR, Executive Director of Publishing Technology; SUSAN CRESPI, Editorial Operations Manager; ALEX MORALES, Publishing Operations Manager; STAN LEE, Chairman Emeritus. For information regarding advertising in Marvel Comics or on Marvel.com, please contact Niza Disla, Director of Marvel Partnerships, at ndisla@marvel.com. For Marvel subscription inquiries, please call 800-217-9158. **Manufactured between 7/18/2014 and 8/25/2014 by QUAD/GRAPHICS, VERSAILLES, KY, USA.**

10 9 8 7 6 5 4 3 2 1

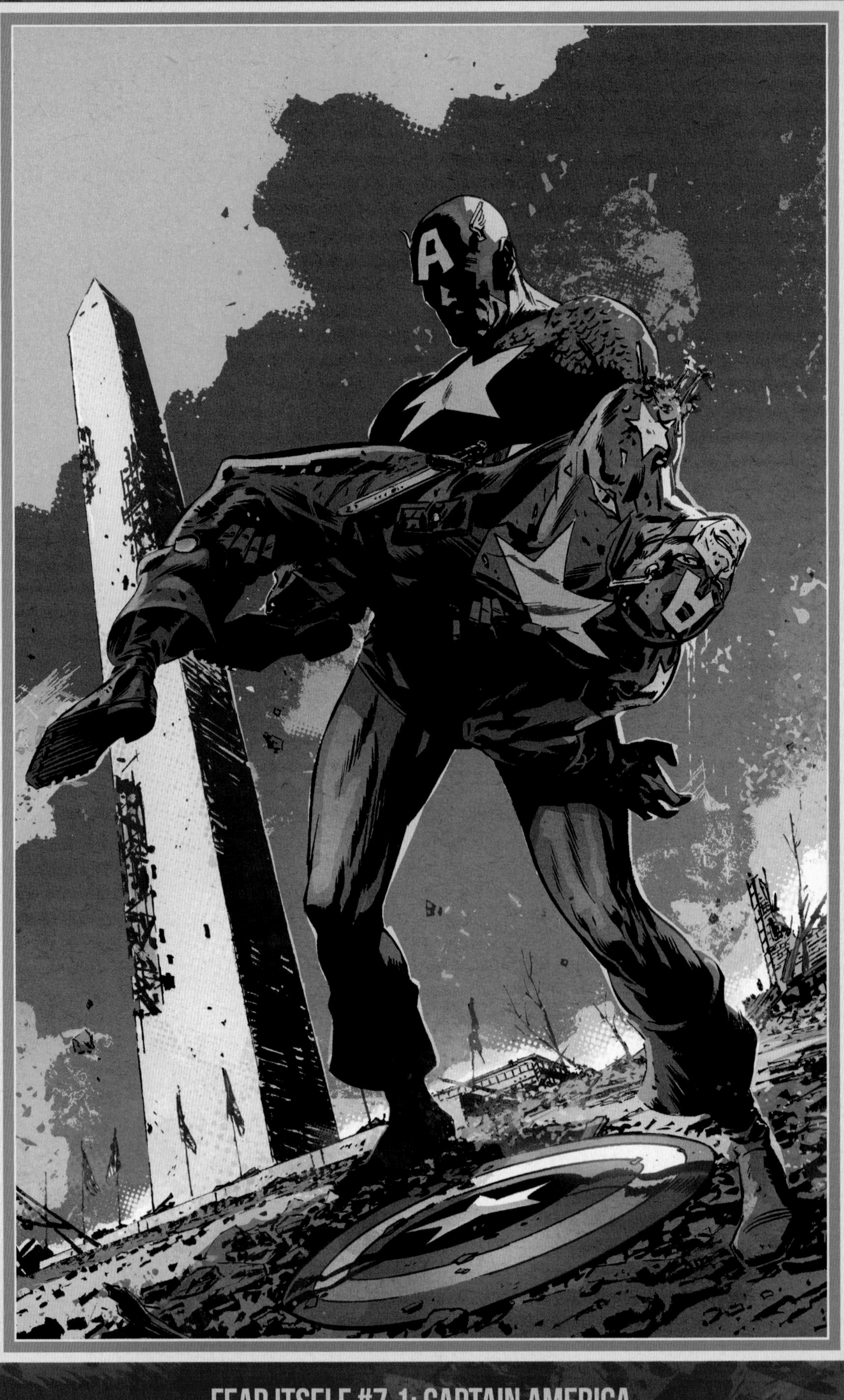

FEAR ITSELF #7.1: CAPTAIN AMERICA

FEAR ITSELF

CHAPTER 7.1: CAPTAIN AMERICA

A time of uncertainty and fear grips the world.

Sin, daughter of the Red Skull, has released the mysterious Serpent from entombment at the bottom of the Marianas Trench. The Serpent's mystic hammer empowers Sin, transforming her into his herald, Skadi.

The Serpent summons his Worthy, causing seven additional hammers to fall from the heavens and strike all over the world. Each hammer transforms its destined wielder into an unstoppable engine of destruction to rampage in the Serpent's name.

Withdrawing from Earth, Odin and the Asgardians begin preparations to burn the planet in order to destroy the Serpent. When Thor attempts to intercede, the Serpent reveals to him that he is Odin's brother, the true, exiled King of Asgard, and that Thor is fated to fall in battle with him.

In a last-ditch attempt to fend off the Serpent's army from the World Tree in Broxton, Tony Stark forges a set of weapons made of enchanted uru metal to even the odds for the Avengers. The heroes manage to hold the enemy at bay long enough for Thor to defeat the Serpent, take nine steps and die in his father's arms.

In the aftermath, the Avengers tend to the wounded and mourn their losses, including one of the early casualties of the Serpent's deadly campaign, the current Captain America, Bucky Barnes.

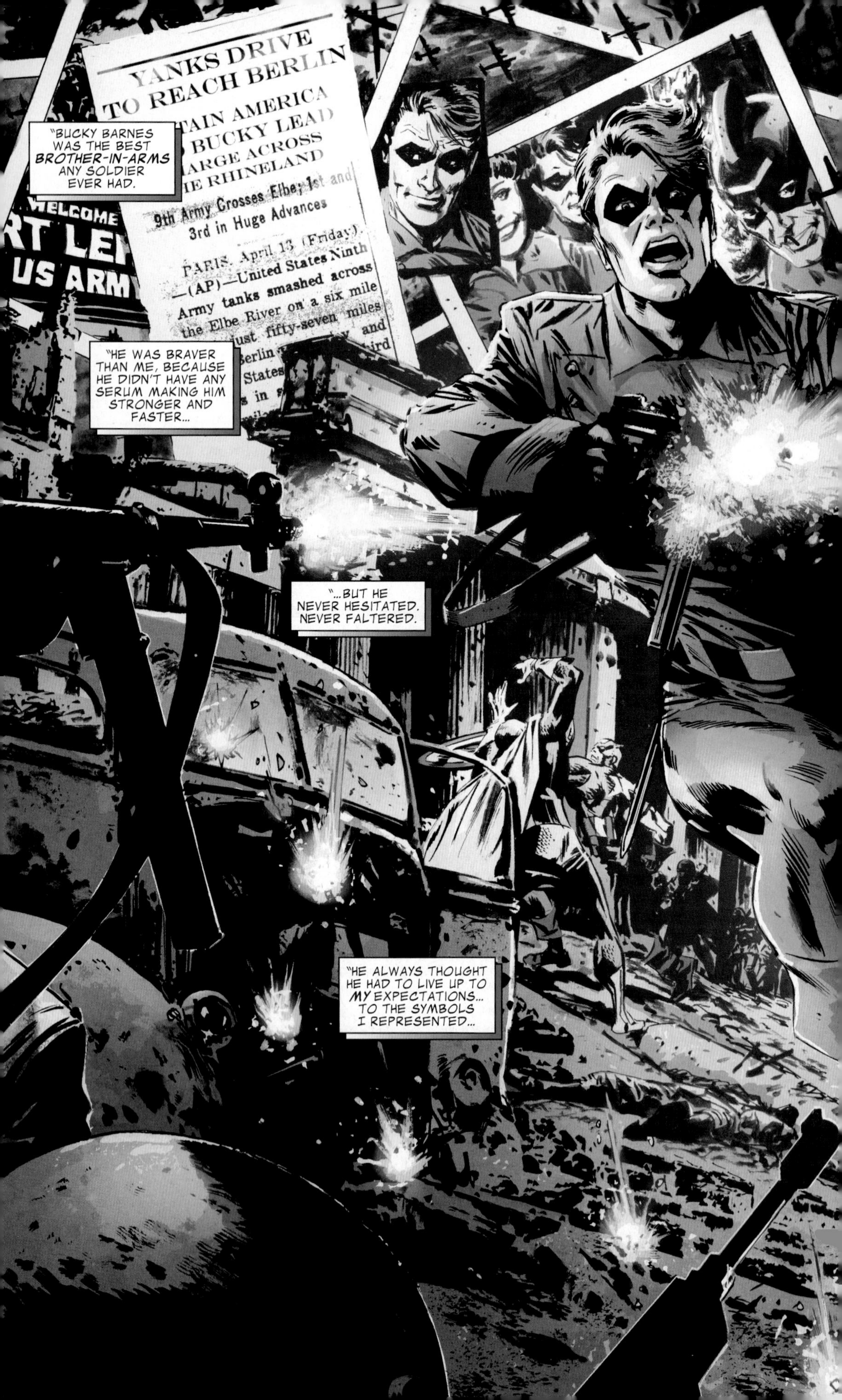
YANKS DRIVE TO REACH BERLIN
TAIN AMERICA
BUCKY LEAD
ARGE ACROSS
IE RHINELAND
9th Army Crosses Elbe; 1st and
3rd in Huge Advances
PARIS, April 13 (Friday)
—(AP)—United States Ninth
Army tanks smashed across
the Elbe River on a six mile
WELCOME
US ARMY
"BUCKY BARNES WAS THE BEST *BROTHER-IN-ARMS* ANY SOLDIER EVER HAD.
"HE WAS BRAVER THAN ME, BECAUSE HE DIDN'T HAVE ANY SERUM MAKING HIM STRONGER AND FASTER...
"...BUT HE NEVER HESITATED. NEVER FALTERED.
"HE ALWAYS THOUGHT HE HAD TO LIVE UP TO *MY* EXPECTATIONS... TO THE SYMBOLS I REPRESENTED...

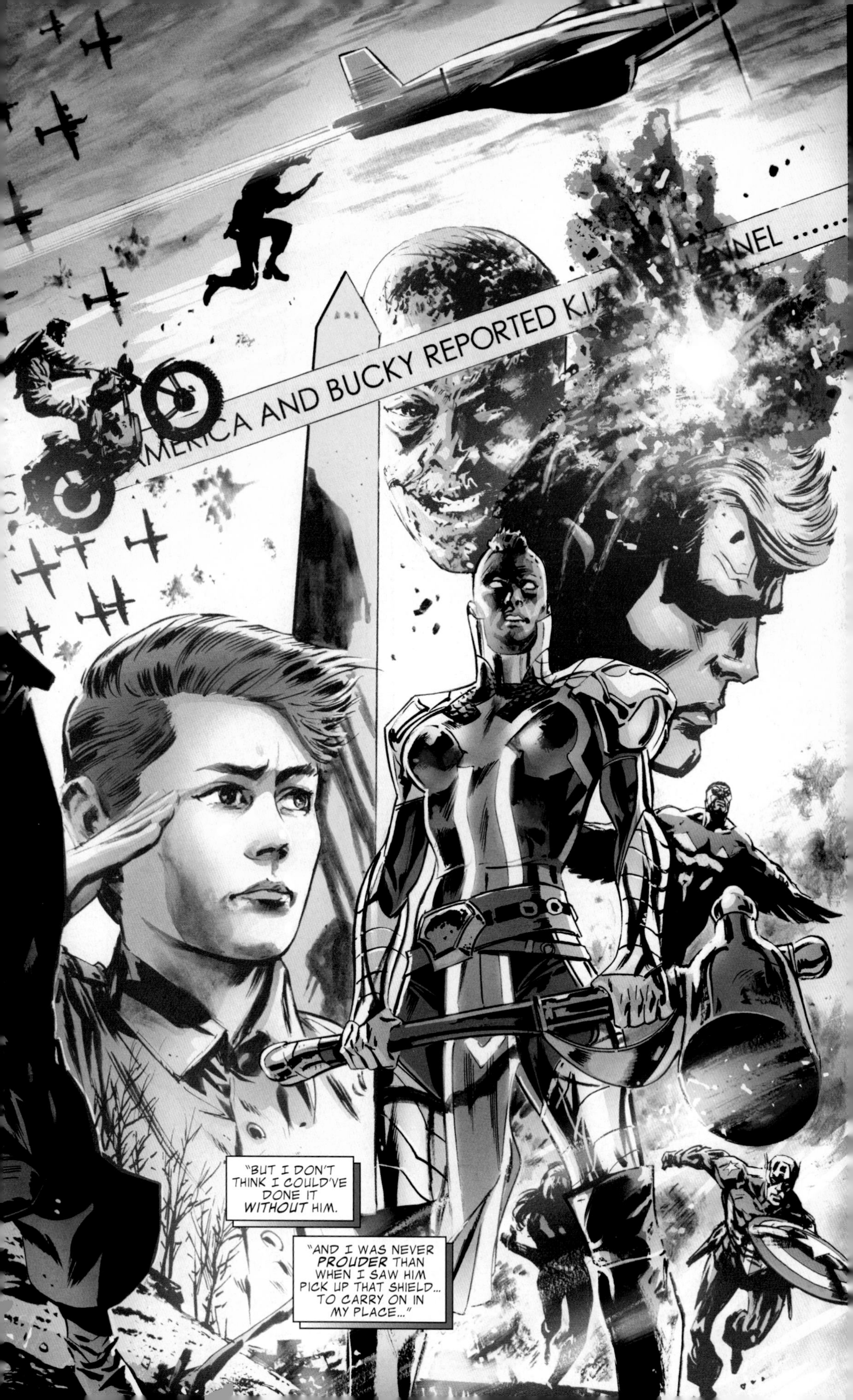
AMERICA AND BUCKY REPORTED K.I.A.
"BUT I DON'T THINK I COULD'VE DONE IT **WITHOUT** HIM.
"AND I WAS NEVER **PROUDER** THAN WHEN I SAW HIM PICK UP THAT SHIELD... TO CARRY ON IN MY PLACE..."

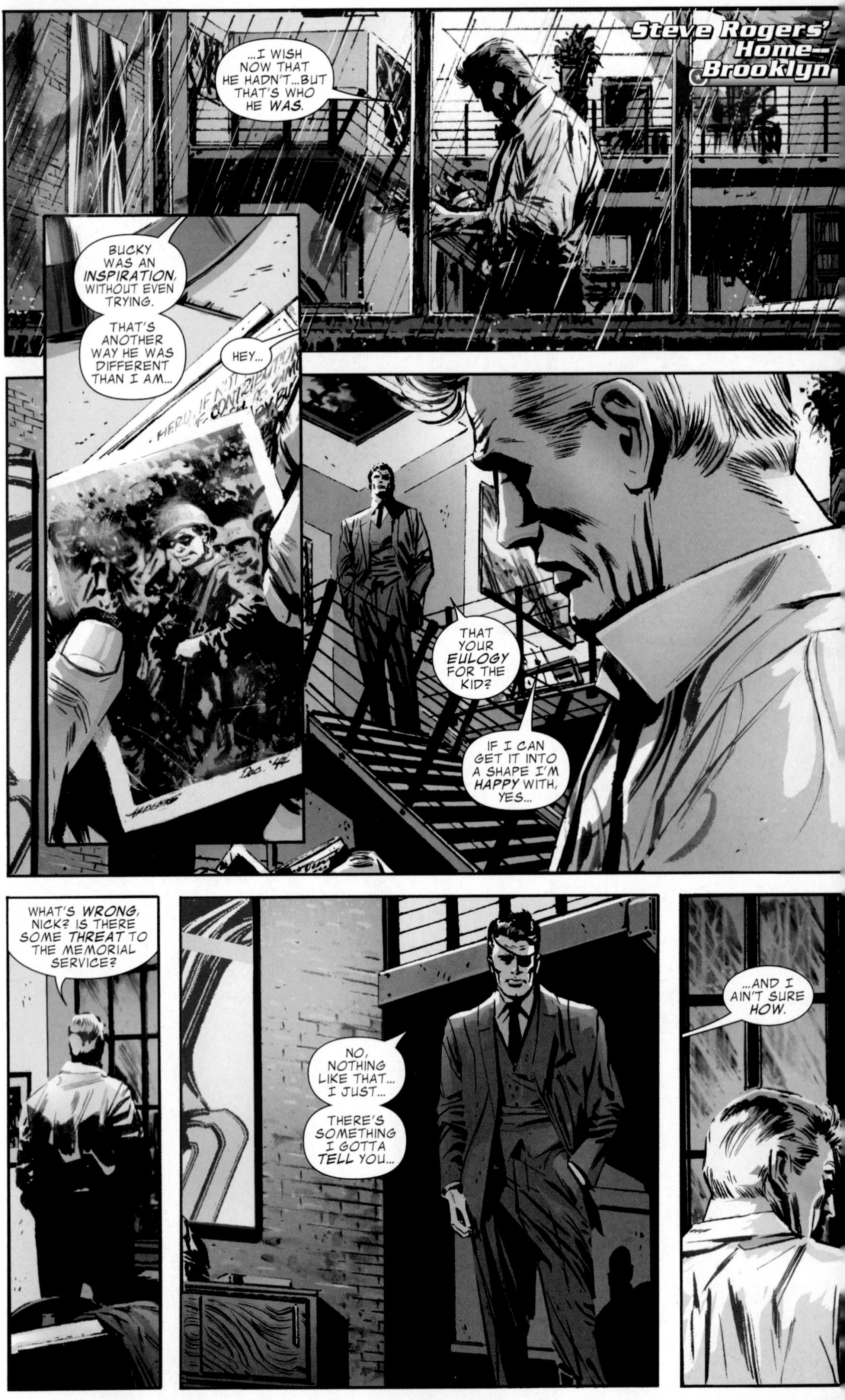
Steve Rogers' Home—Brooklyn
...I WISH NOW THAT HE HADN'T...BUT THAT'S WHO HE WAS.
BUCKY WAS AN INSPIRATION, WITHOUT EVEN TRYING.
THAT'S ANOTHER WAY HE WAS DIFFERENT THAN I AM...
HEY...
THAT YOUR EULOGY FOR THE KID?
IF I CAN GET IT INTO A SHAPE I'M HAPPY WITH, YES...
Dec. '44
WHAT'S WRONG, NICK? IS THERE SOME THREAT TO THE MEMORIAL SERVICE?
NO, NOTHING LIKE THAT... I JUST...
THERE'S SOMETHING I GOTTA TELL YOU...
...AND I AIN'T SURE HOW.

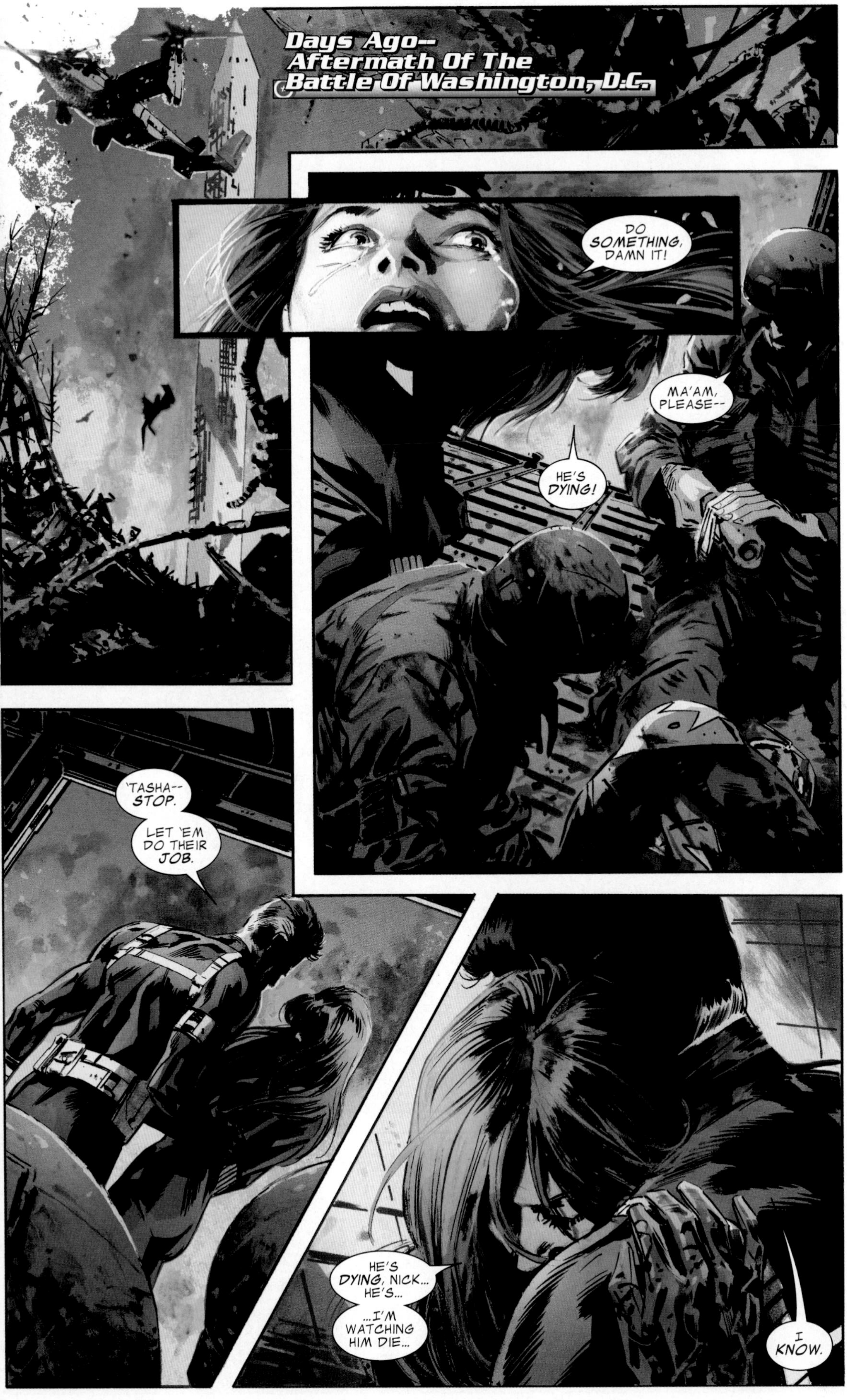
Days Ago--
Aftermath Of The
Battle Of Washington, D.C.
DO SOMETHING, DAMN IT!
MA'AM, PLEASE--
HE'S DYING!
'TASHA-- STOP.
LET 'EM DO THEIR JOB.
HE'S DYING, NICK... HE'S...
...I'M WATCHING HIM DIE...
I KNOW.

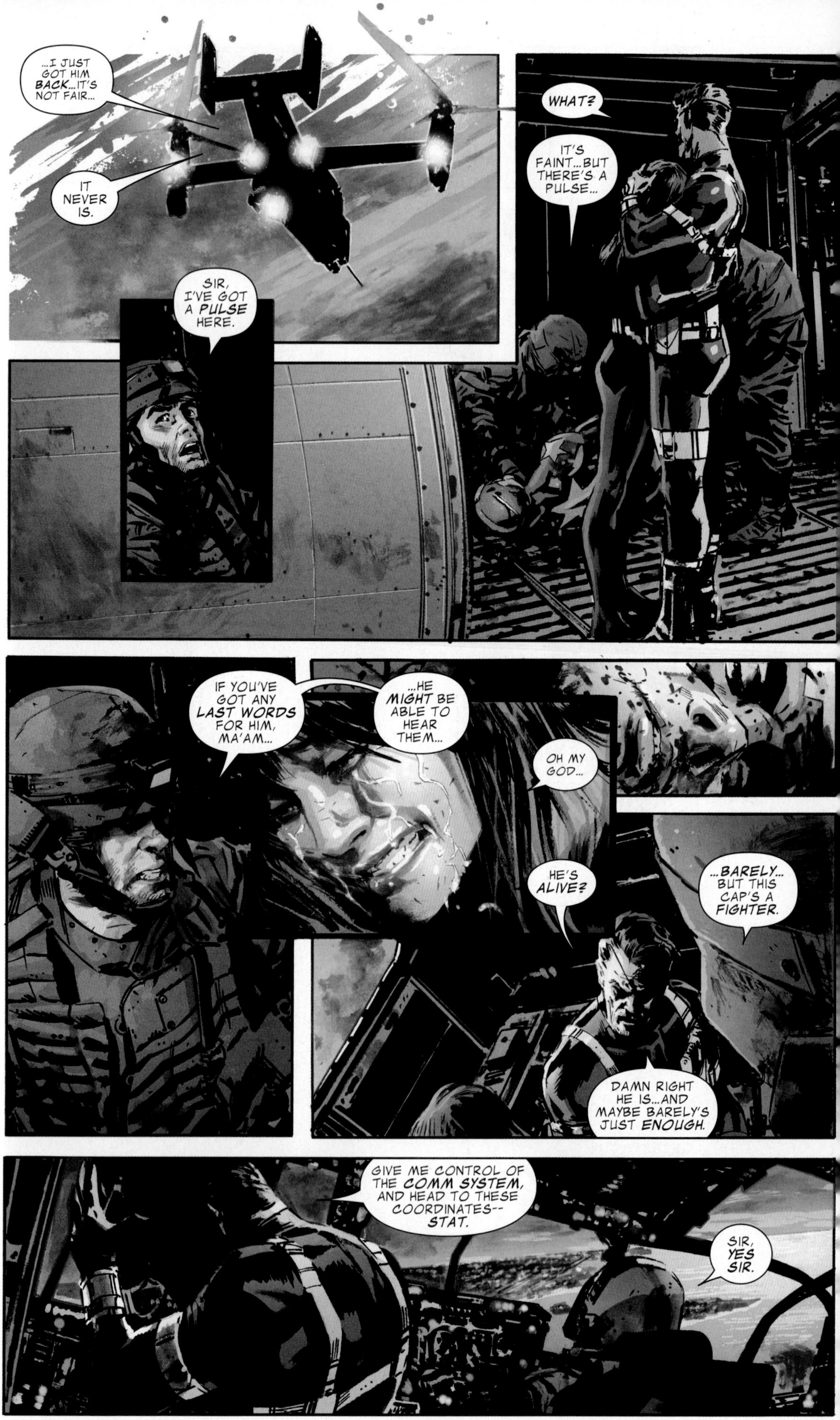

...I JUST GOT HIM BACK...IT'S NOT FAIR...
IT NEVER IS.
WHAT?
IT'S FAINT...BUT THERE'S A PULSE...
SIR, I'VE GOT A PULSE HERE.
IF YOU'VE GOT ANY LAST WORDS FOR HIM, MA'AM...
...HE MIGHT BE ABLE TO HEAR THEM...
OH MY GOD...
HE'S ALIVE?
...BARELY... BUT THIS CAP'S A FIGHTER.
DAMN RIGHT HE IS...AND MAYBE BARELY'S JUST ENOUGH.
GIVE ME CONTROL OF THE COMM SYSTEM, AND HEAD TO THESE COORDINATES-- STAT.
SIR, YES SIR.

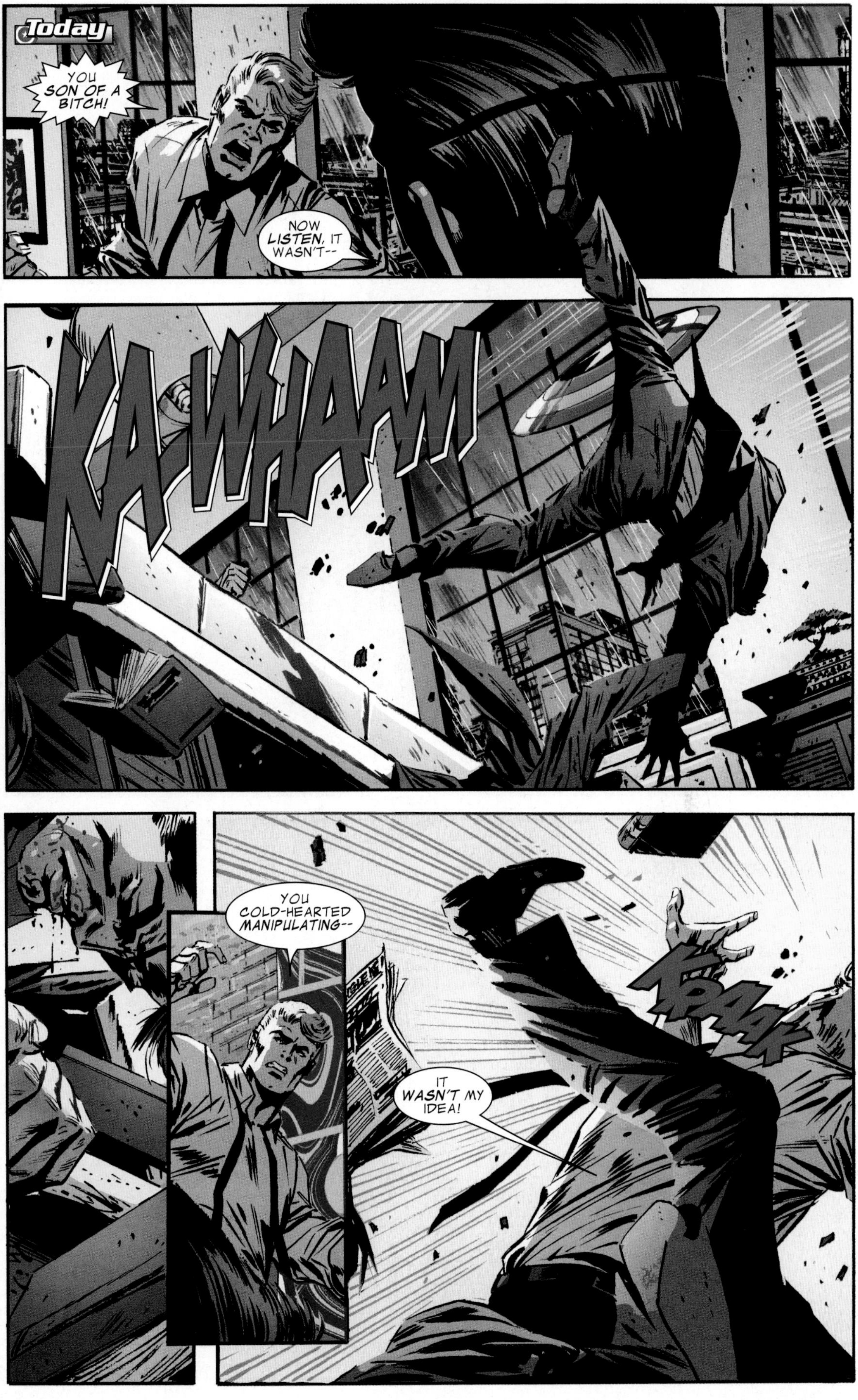
Today
YOU SON OF A BITCH!
NOW LISTEN, IT WASN'T--
KA-WHAAM
YOU COLD-HEARTED MANIPULATING--
KRAAK
IT WASN'T MY IDEA!

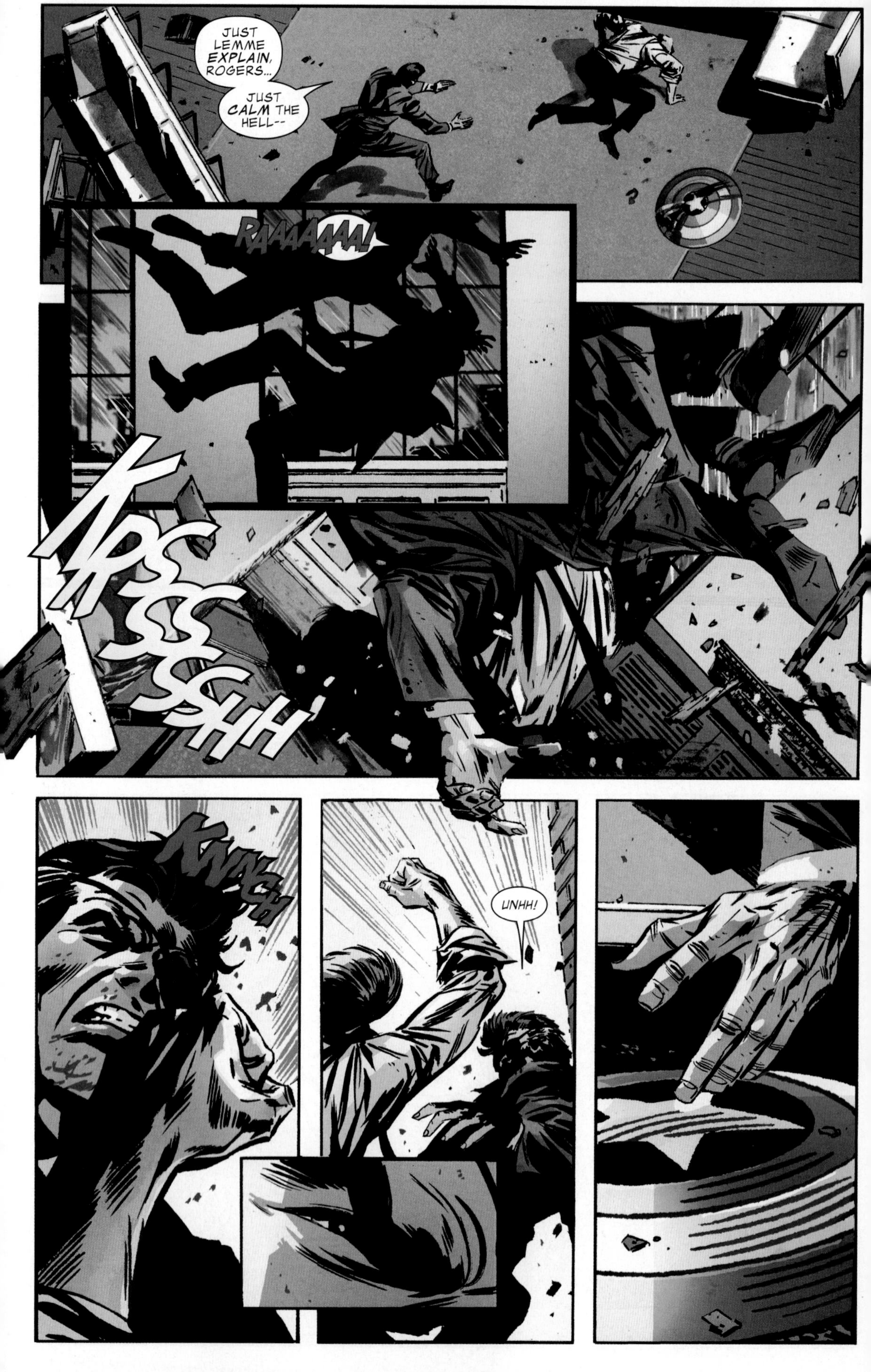
JUST LEMME EXPLAIN, ROGERS...
JUST CALM THE HELL--
RAAAAAAA!
KRSSSSHH
KNNCH
UNHH!

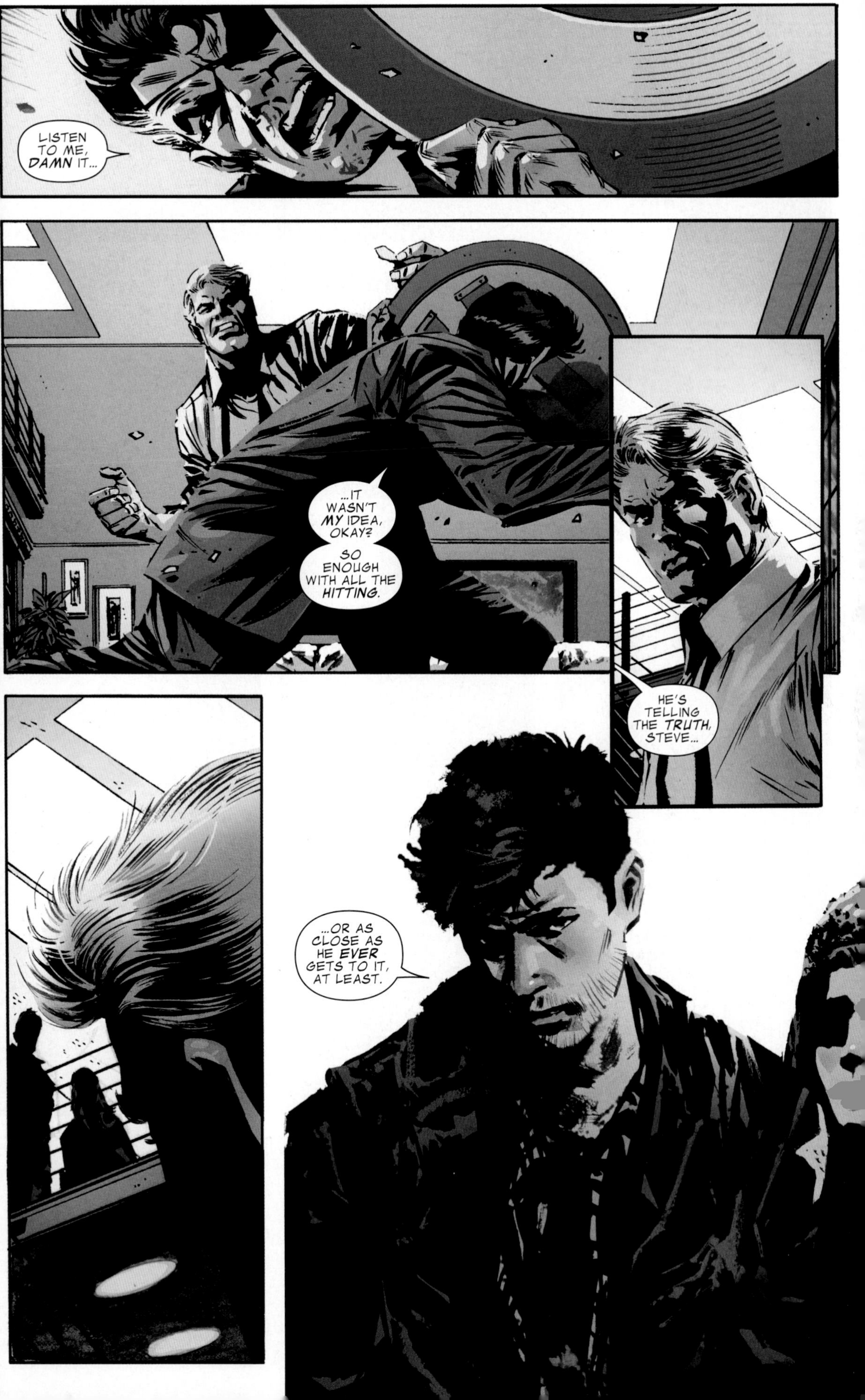
LISTEN TO ME, DAMN IT...
...IT WASN'T MY IDEA, OKAY?
SO ENOUGH WITH ALL THE HITTING.
HE'S TELLING THE TRUTH, STEVE...
...OR AS CLOSE AS HE EVER GETS TO IT, AT LEAST.

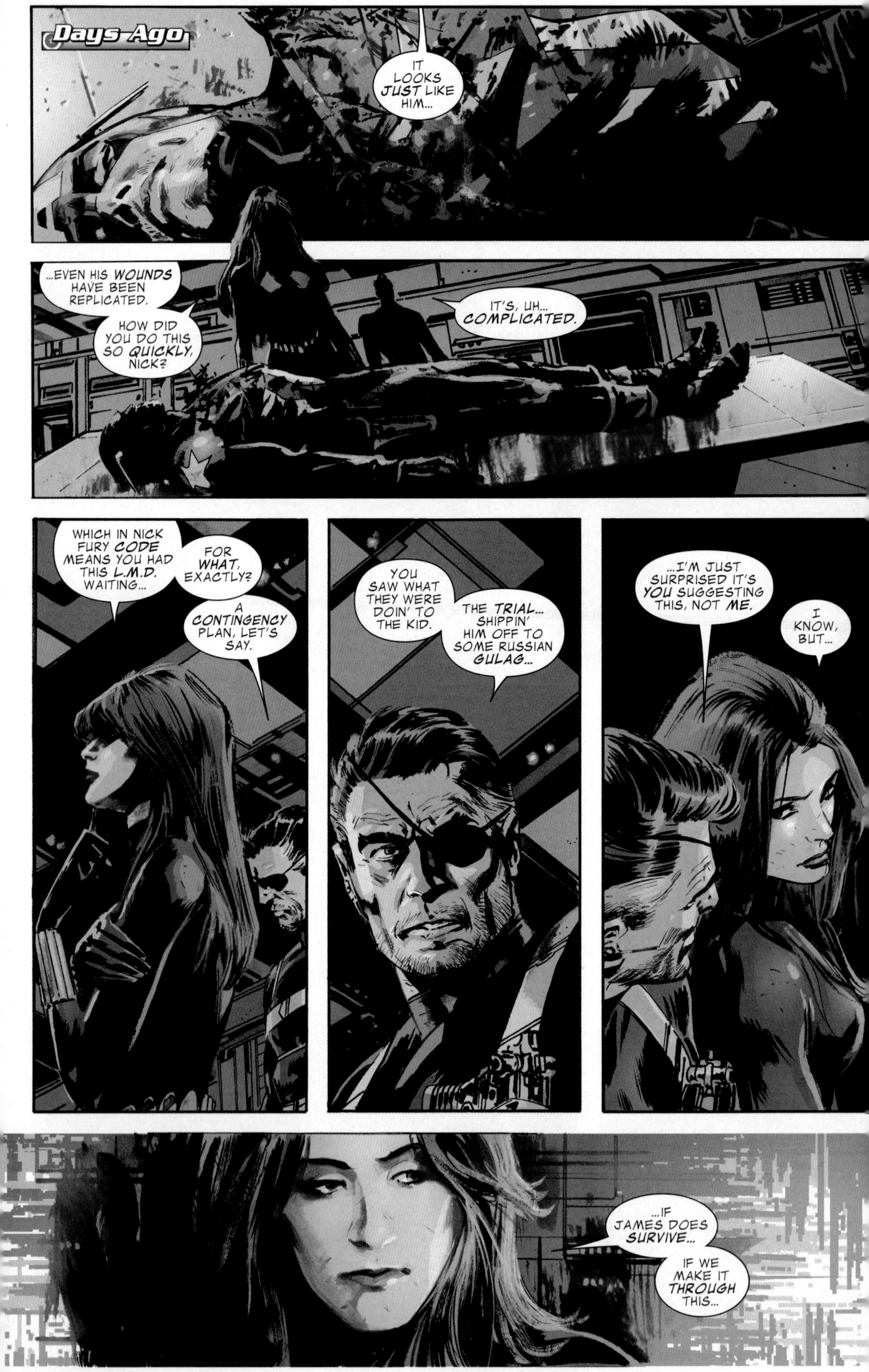
Days Ago
IT LOOKS JUST LIKE HIM...
...EVEN HIS WOUNDS HAVE BEEN REPLICATED.
HOW DID YOU DO THIS SO QUICKLY, NICK?
IT'S, UH... COMPLICATED.
WHICH IN NICK FURY CODE MEANS YOU HAD THIS L.M.D. WAITING...
FOR WHAT, EXACTLY?
A CONTINGENCY PLAN, LET'S SAY.
YOU SAW WHAT THEY WERE DOIN' TO THE KID.
THE TRIAL... SHIPPIN' HIM OFF TO SOME RUSSIAN GULAG...
...I'M JUST SURPRISED IT'S YOU SUGGESTING THIS, NOT ME.
I KNOW, BUT...
...IF JAMES DOES SURVIVE...
IF WE MAKE IT THROUGH THIS...

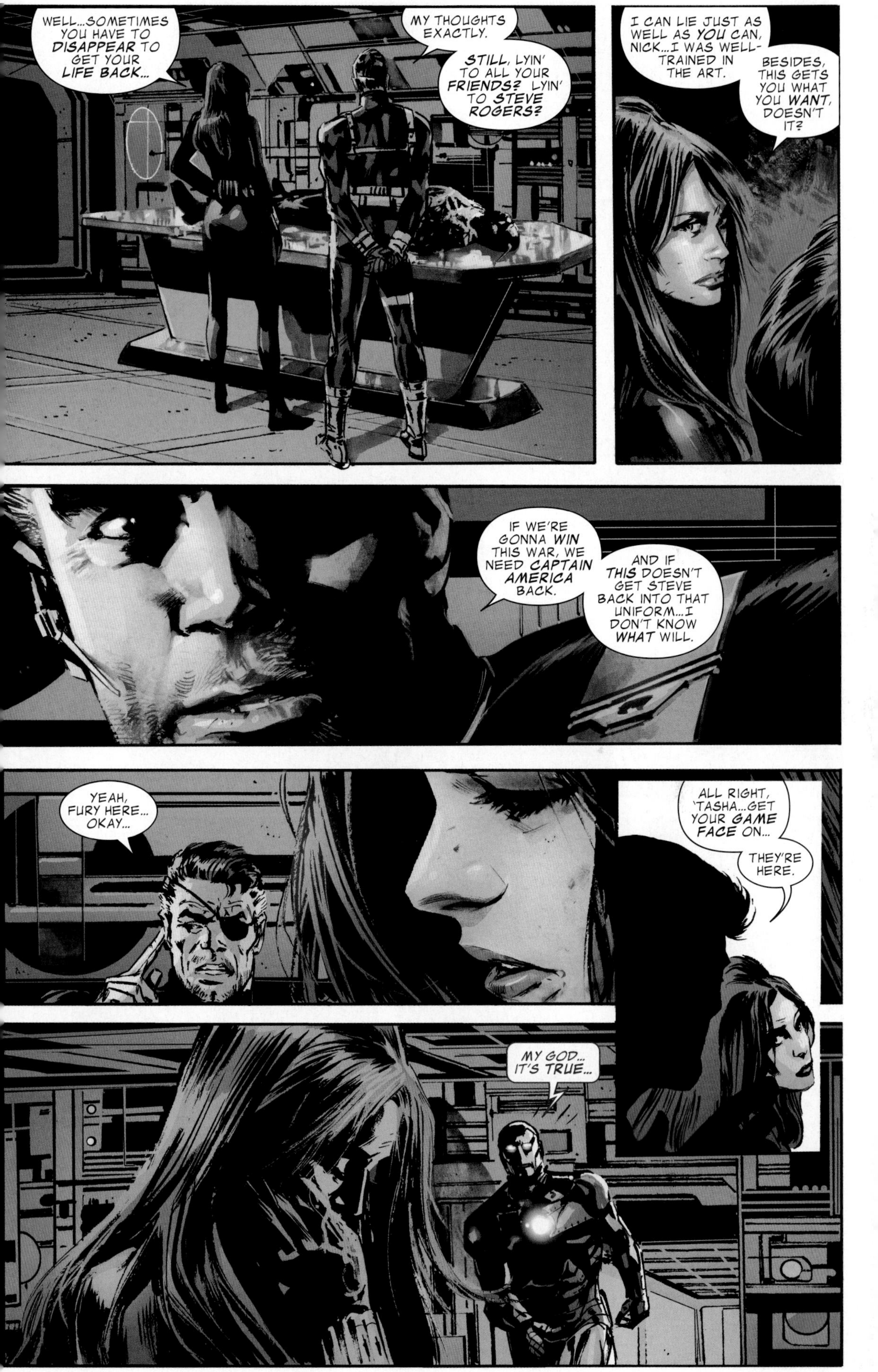
WELL...SOMETIMES YOU HAVE TO DISAPPEAR TO GET YOUR LIFE BACK...
MY THOUGHTS EXACTLY.
STILL, LYIN' TO ALL YOUR FRIENDS? LYIN' TO STEVE ROGERS?
I CAN LIE JUST AS WELL AS YOU CAN, NICK...I WAS WELL-TRAINED IN THE ART.
BESIDES, THIS GETS YOU WHAT YOU WANT, DOESN'T IT?
IF WE'RE GONNA WIN THIS WAR, WE NEED CAPTAIN AMERICA BACK.
AND IF THIS DOESN'T GET STEVE BACK INTO THAT UNIFORM...I DON'T KNOW WHAT WILL.
YEAH, FURY HERE... OKAY...
ALL RIGHT, 'TASHA...GET YOUR GAME FACE ON...
THEY'RE HERE.
MY GOD... IT'S TRUE...

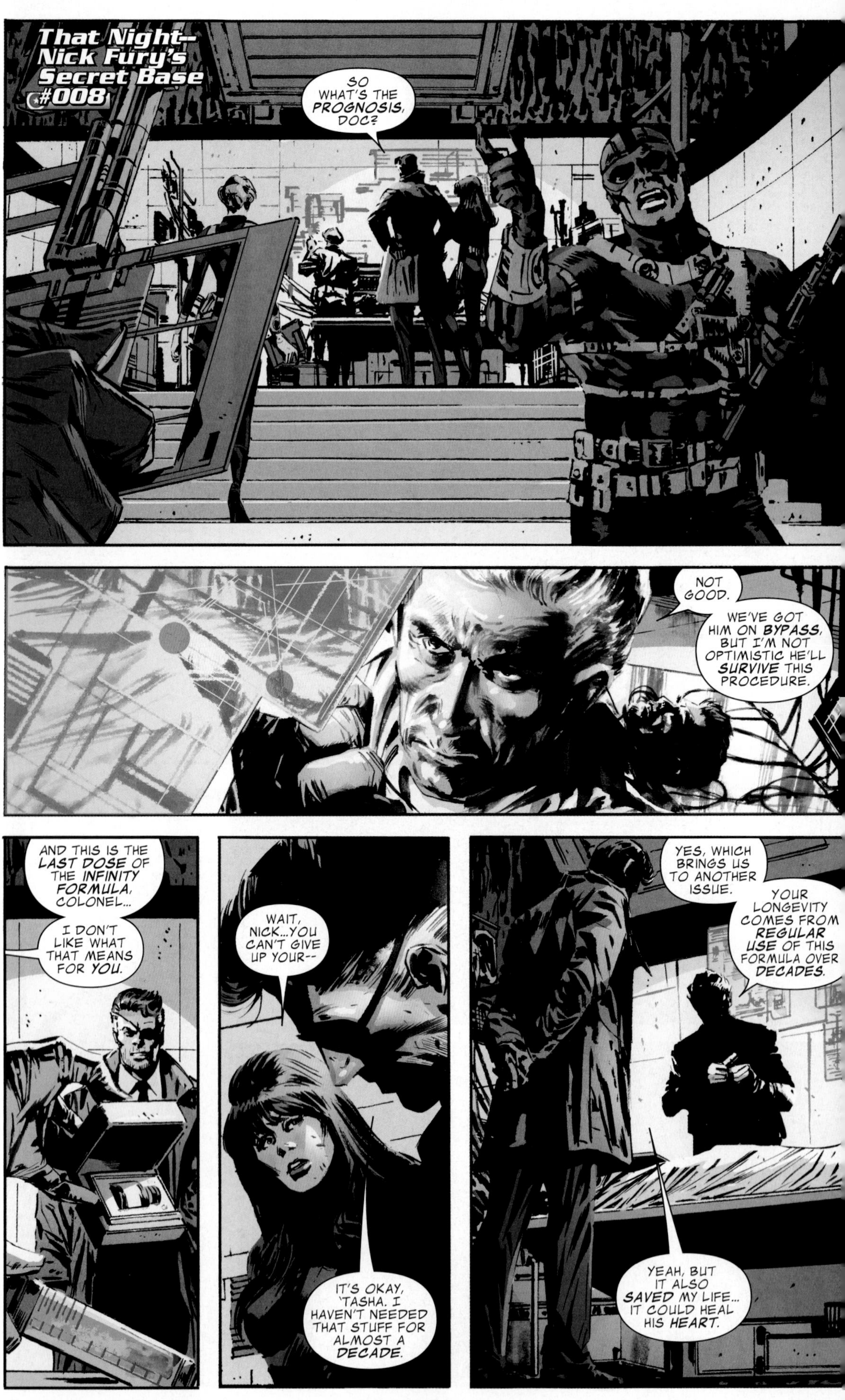
That Night--
Nick Fury's
Secret Base
#008
SO WHAT'S THE PROGNOSIS, DOC?
NOT GOOD.
WE'VE GOT HIM ON BYPASS, BUT I'M NOT OPTIMISTIC HE'LL SURVIVE THIS PROCEDURE.
AND THIS IS THE LAST DOSE OF THE INFINITY FORMULA, COLONEL...
I DON'T LIKE WHAT THAT MEANS FOR YOU.
WAIT, NICK...YOU CAN'T GIVE UP YOUR--
IT'S OKAY, 'TASHA. I HAVEN'T NEEDED THAT STUFF FOR ALMOST A DECADE.
YES, WHICH BRINGS US TO ANOTHER ISSUE.
YOUR LONGEVITY COMES FROM REGULAR USE OF THIS FORMULA OVER DECADES.
YEAH, BUT IT ALSO SAVED MY LIFE... IT COULD HEAL HIS HEART.

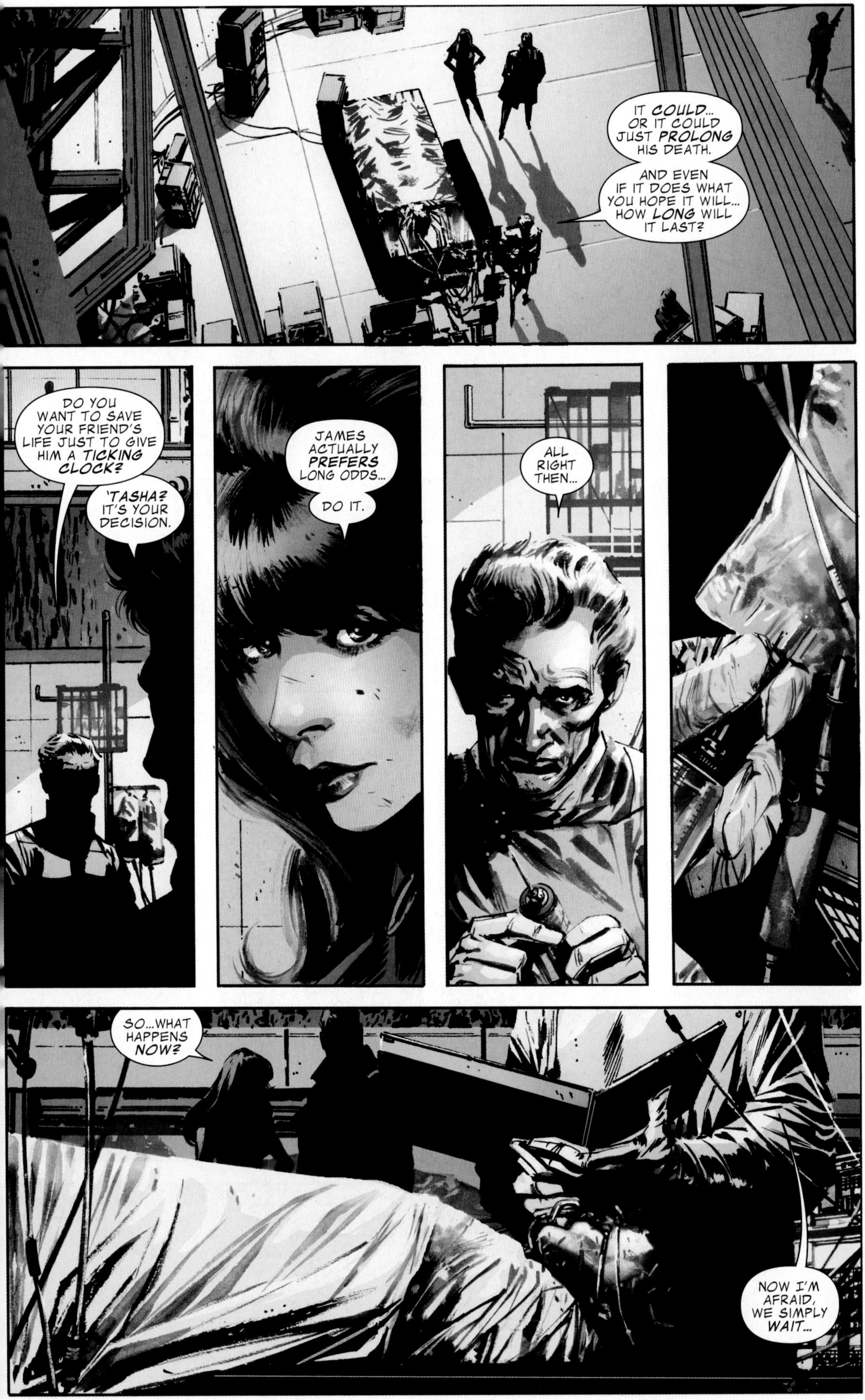
IT COULD... OR IT COULD JUST PROLONG HIS DEATH.
AND EVEN IF IT DOES WHAT YOU HOPE IT WILL... HOW LONG WILL IT LAST?
DO YOU WANT TO SAVE YOUR FRIEND'S LIFE JUST TO GIVE HIM A TICKING CLOCK?
'TASHA? IT'S YOUR DECISION.
JAMES ACTUALLY PREFERS LONG ODDS...
DO IT.
ALL RIGHT THEN...
SO...WHAT HAPPENS NOW?
NOW I'M AFRAID, WE SIMPLY WAIT...

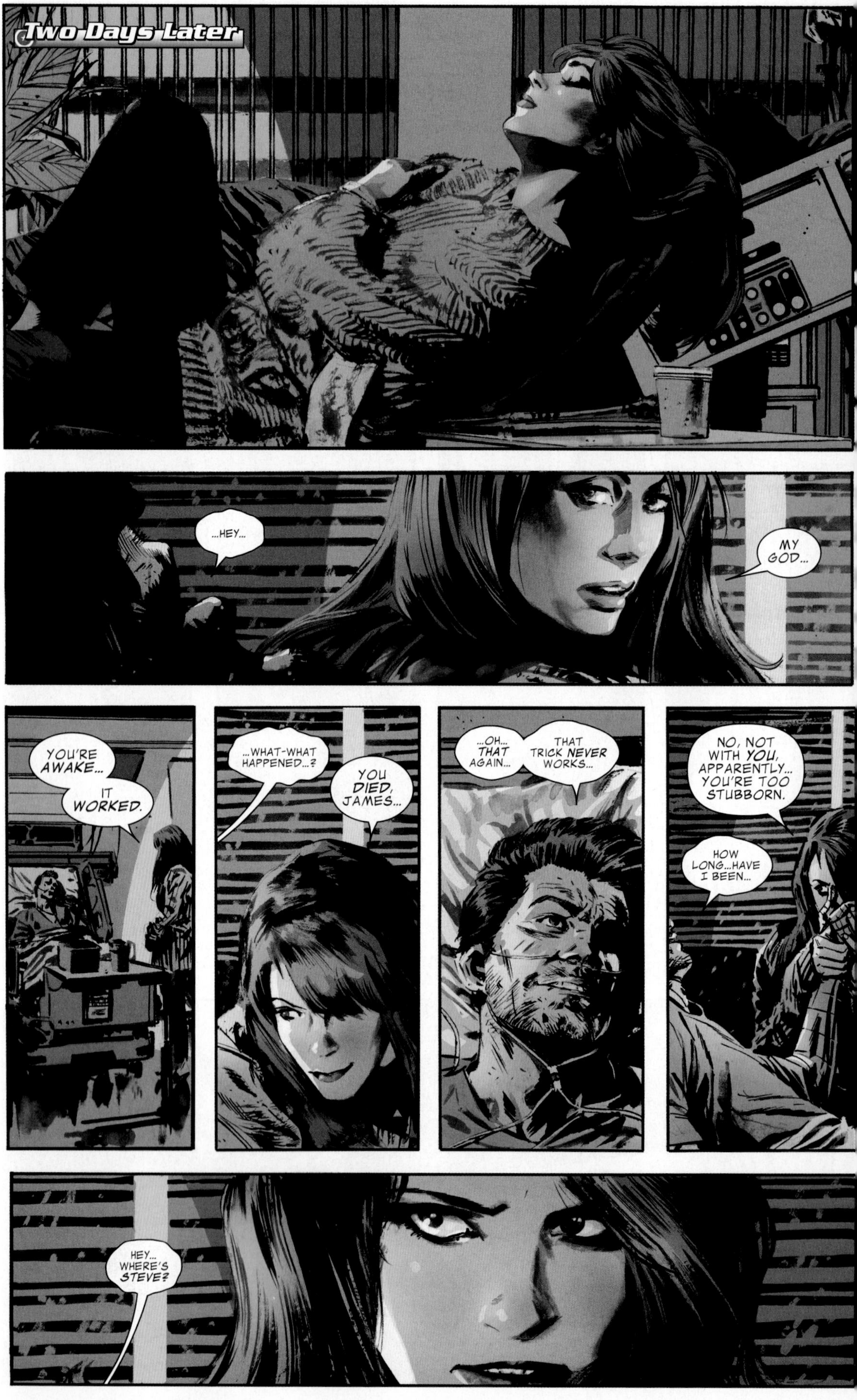
Two Days Later
...HEY...
MY GOD...
YOU'RE AWAKE...
IT WORKED.
...WHAT-WHAT HAPPENED...?
YOU DIED, JAMES...
...OH... THAT AGAIN...
THAT TRICK NEVER WORKS...
NO, NOT WITH YOU, APPARENTLY... YOU'RE TOO STUBBORN.
HOW LONG...HAVE I BEEN...
HEY... WHERE'S STEVE?

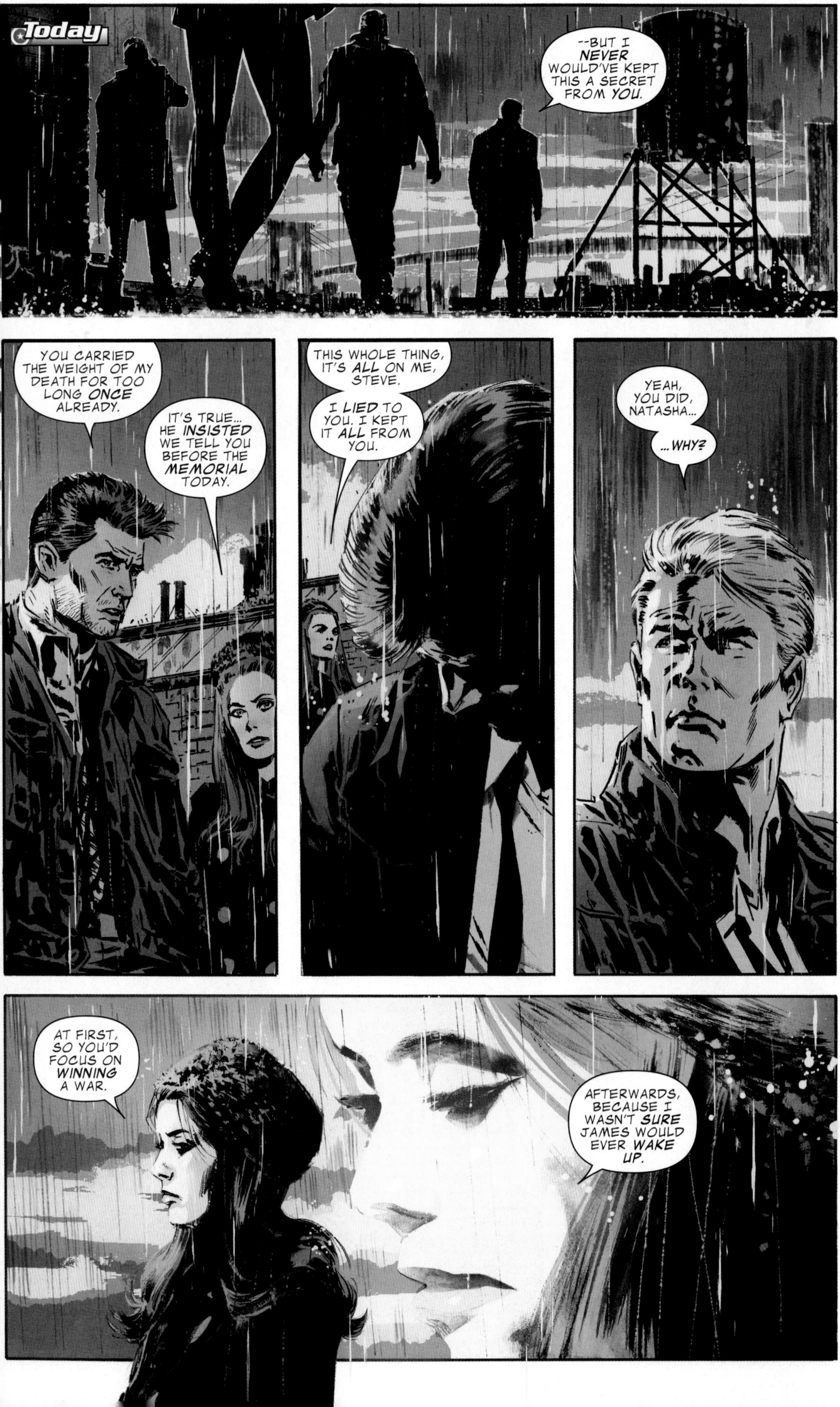
Today
--BUT I NEVER WOULD'VE KEPT THIS A SECRET FROM YOU.
YOU CARRIED THE WEIGHT OF MY DEATH FOR TOO LONG ONCE ALREADY.
IT'S TRUE... HE INSISTED WE TELL YOU BEFORE THE MEMORIAL TODAY.
THIS WHOLE THING, IT'S ALL ON ME, STEVE.
I LIED TO YOU. I KEPT IT ALL FROM YOU.
YEAH, YOU DID, NATASHA...
...WHY?
AT FIRST, SO YOU'D FOCUS ON WINNING A WAR.
AFTERWARDS, BECAUSE I WASN'T SURE JAMES WOULD EVER WAKE UP.

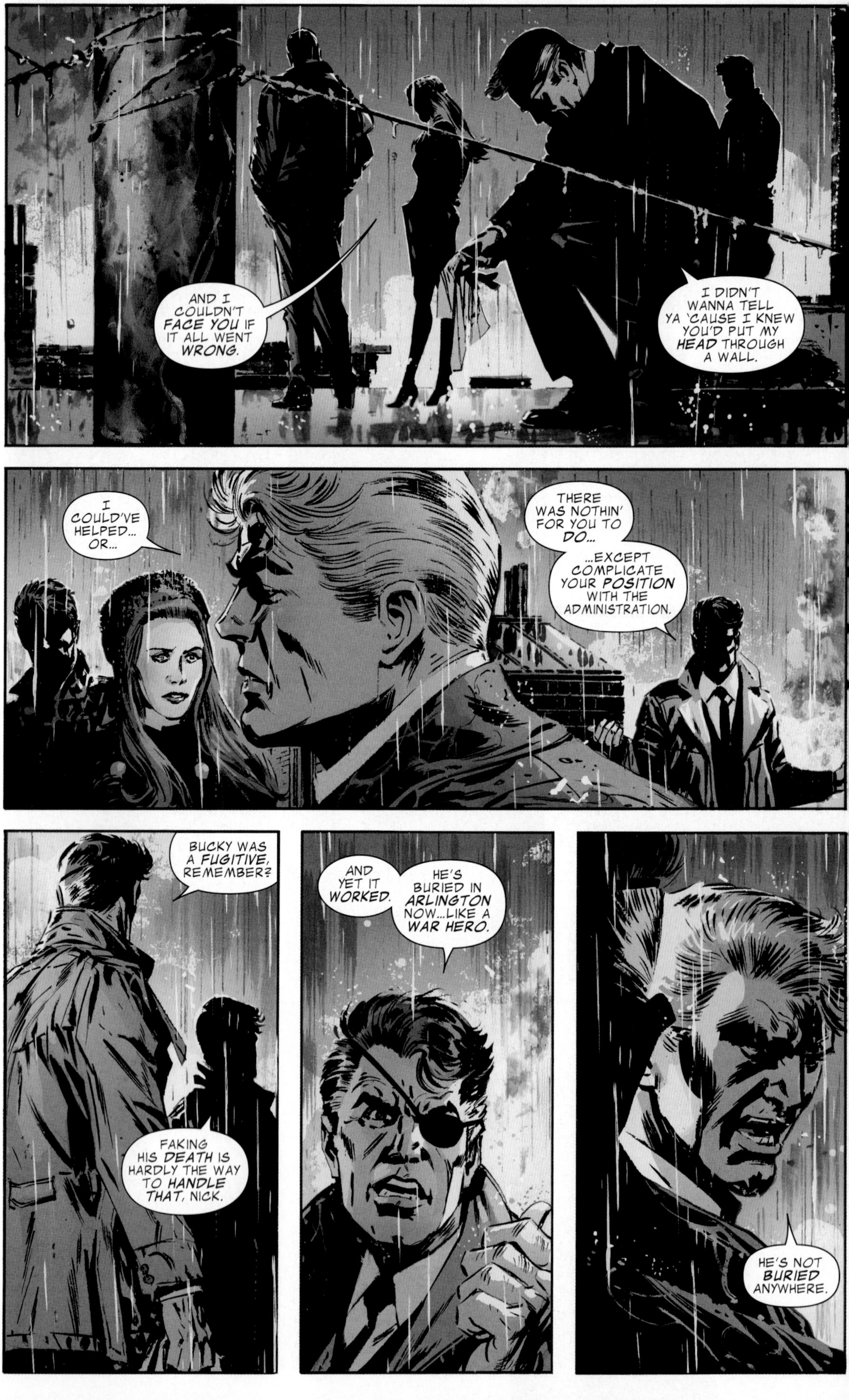
AND I COULDN'T FACE YOU IF IT ALL WENT WRONG.
I DIDN'T WANNA TELL YA 'CAUSE I KNEW YOU'D PUT MY HEAD THROUGH A WALL.
I COULD'VE HELPED... OR...
THERE WAS NOTHIN' FOR YOU TO DO...
...EXCEPT COMPLICATE YOUR POSITION WITH THE ADMINISTRATION.
BUCKY WAS A FUGITIVE, REMEMBER?
FAKING HIS DEATH IS HARDLY THE WAY TO HANDLE THAT, NICK.
AND YET IT WORKED.
HE'S BURIED IN ARLINGTON NOW...LIKE A WAR HERO.
HE'S NOT BURIED ANYWHERE.

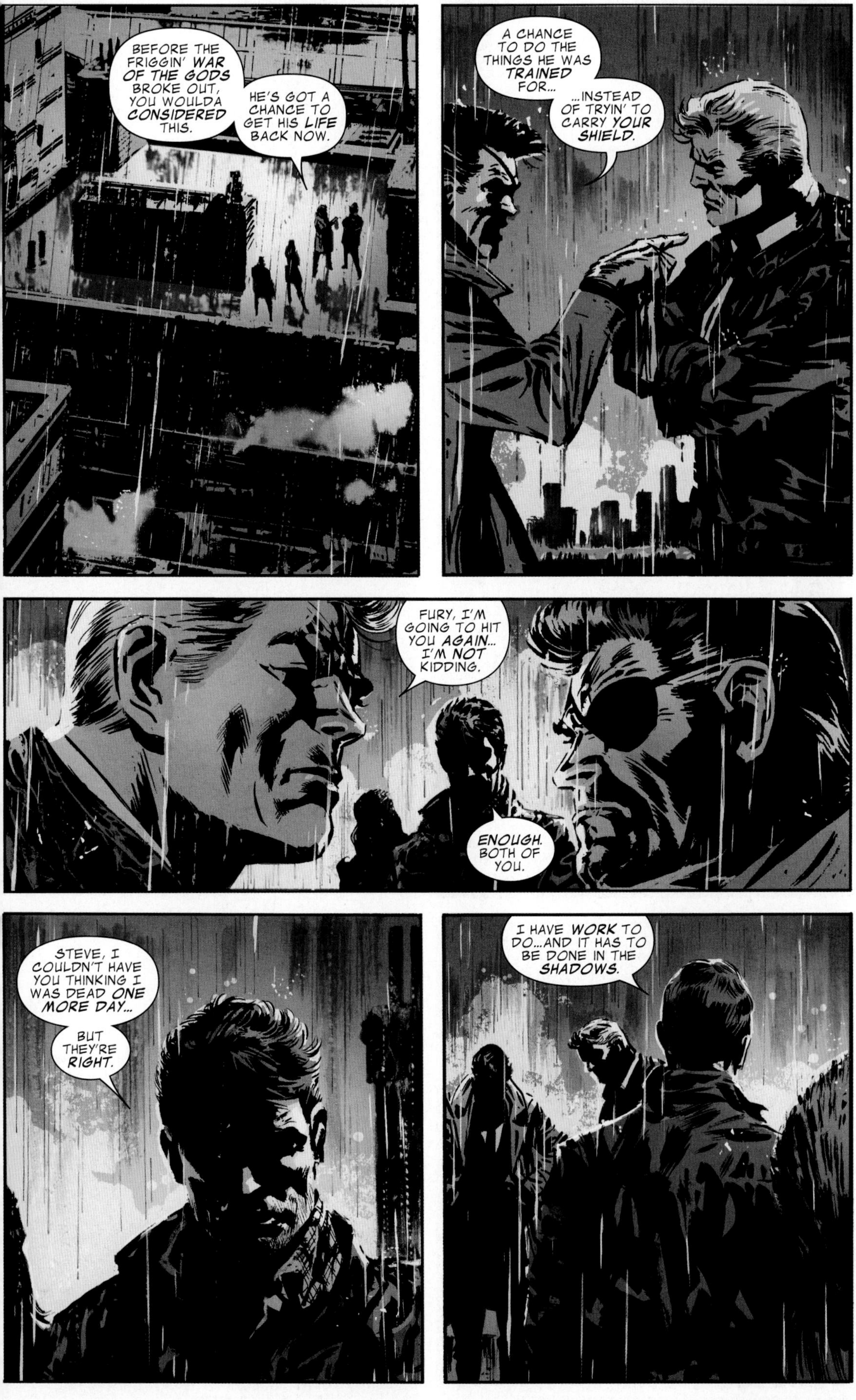
BEFORE THE FRIGGIN' WAR OF THE GODS BROKE OUT, YOU WOULDA CONSIDERED THIS.
HE'S GOT A CHANCE TO GET HIS LIFE BACK NOW.
A CHANCE TO DO THE THINGS HE WAS TRAINED FOR...
...INSTEAD OF TRYIN' TO CARRY YOUR SHIELD.
FURY, I'M GOING TO HIT YOU AGAIN... I'M NOT KIDDING.
ENOUGH. BOTH OF YOU.
STEVE, I COULDN'T HAVE YOU THINKING I WAS DEAD ONE MORE DAY...
BUT THEY'RE RIGHT.
I HAVE WORK TO DO...AND IT HAS TO BE DONE IN THE SHADOWS.

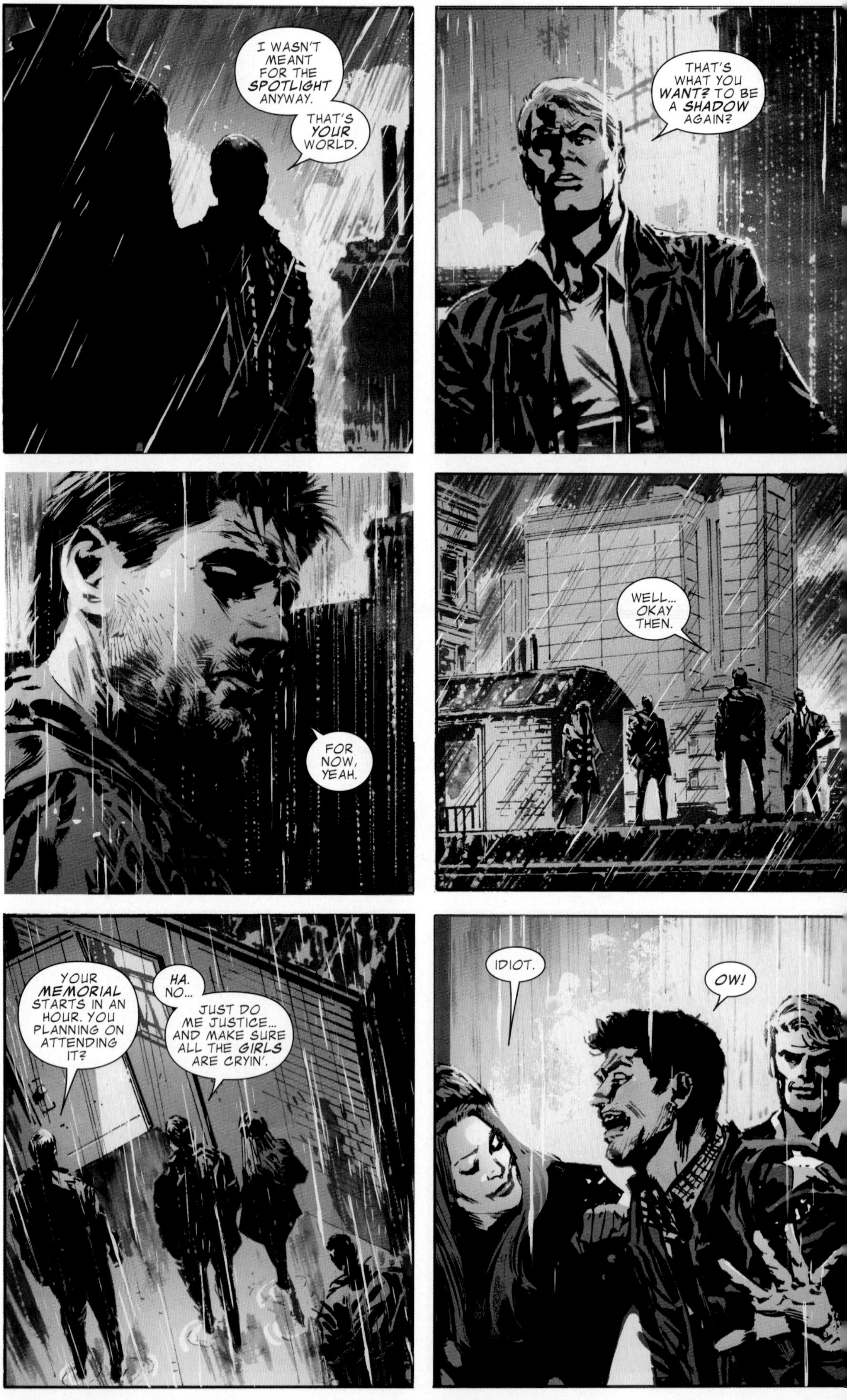

I WASN'T MEANT FOR THE SPOTLIGHT ANYWAY.
THAT'S YOUR WORLD.
THAT'S WHAT YOU WANT? TO BE A SHADOW AGAIN?
FOR NOW, YEAH.
WELL... OKAY THEN.
YOUR MEMORIAL STARTS IN AN HOUR. YOU PLANNING ON ATTENDING IT?
HA. NO...
JUST DO ME JUSTICE... AND MAKE SURE ALL THE GIRLS ARE CRYIN'.
IDIOT.
OW!

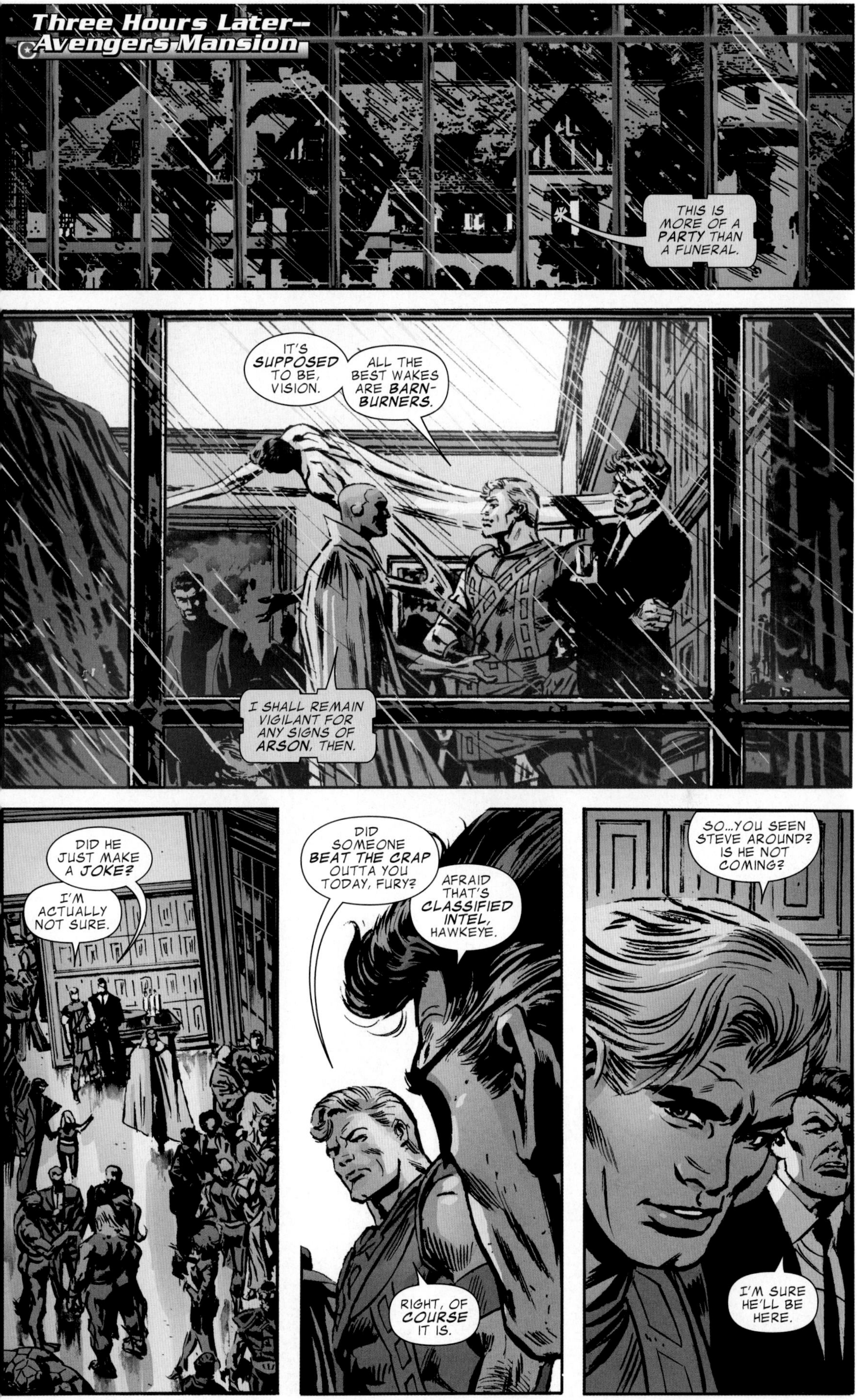
Three Hours Later--
Avengers Mansion
THIS IS MORE OF A PARTY THAN A FUNERAL.
IT'S SUPPOSED TO BE, VISION.
ALL THE BEST WAKES ARE BARN-BURNERS.
I SHALL REMAIN VIGILANT FOR ANY SIGNS OF ARSON, THEN.
DID HE JUST MAKE A JOKE?
I'M ACTUALLY NOT SURE.
DID SOMEONE BEAT THE CRAP OUTTA YOU TODAY, FURY?
AFRAID THAT'S CLASSIFIED INTEL, HAWKEYE.
RIGHT, OF COURSE IT IS.
SO...YOU SEEN STEVE AROUND? IS HE NOT COMING?
I'M SURE HE'LL BE HERE.

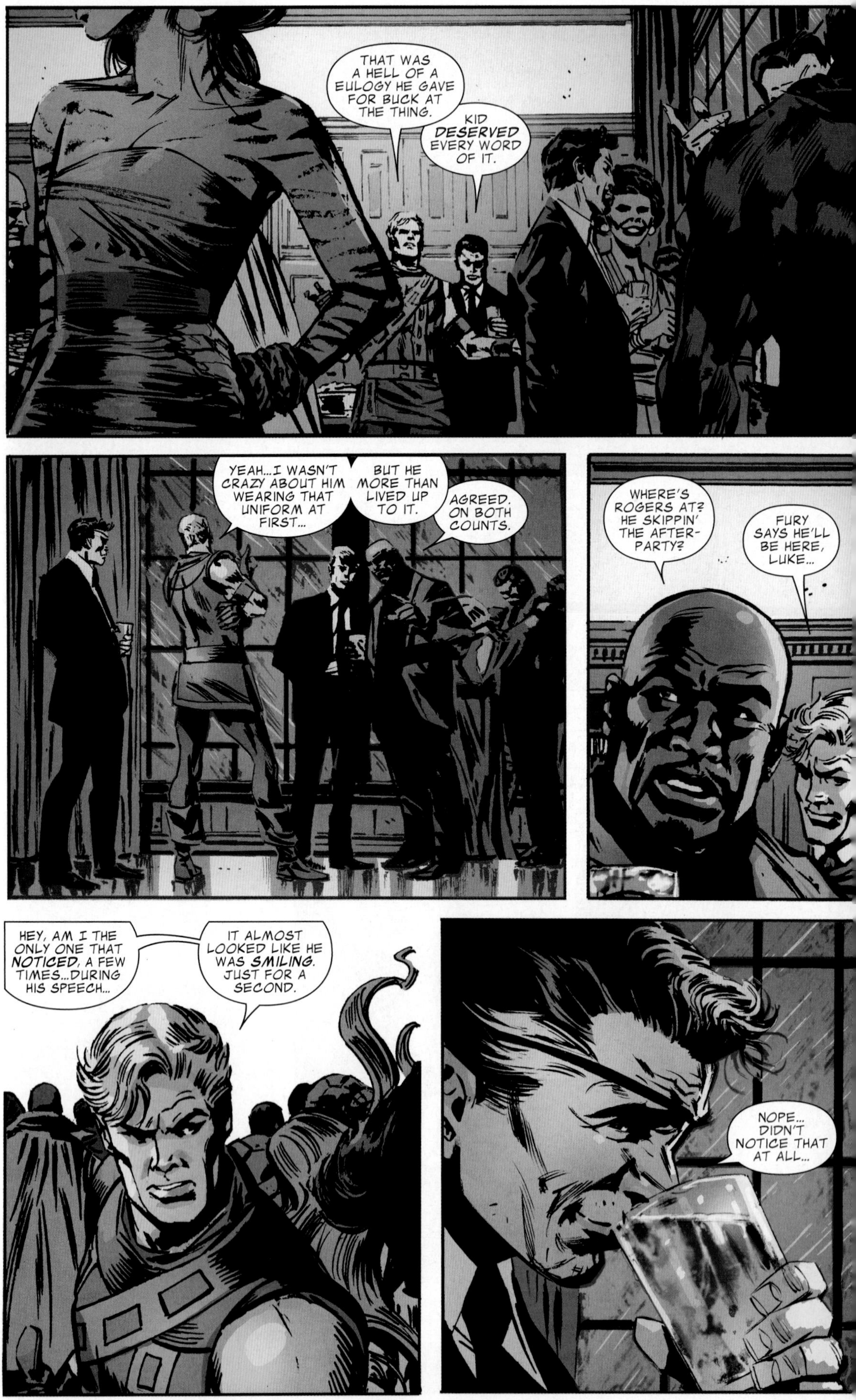
THAT WAS A HELL OF A EULOGY HE GAVE FOR BUCK AT THE THING.
KID DESERVED EVERY WORD OF IT.
YEAH...I WASN'T CRAZY ABOUT HIM WEARING THAT UNIFORM AT FIRST...
BUT HE MORE THAN LIVED UP TO IT.
AGREED. ON BOTH COUNTS.
WHERE'S ROGERS AT? HE SKIPPIN' THE AFTER-PARTY?
FURY SAYS HE'LL BE HERE, LUKE...
HEY, AM I THE ONLY ONE THAT NOTICED, A FEW TIMES...DURING HIS SPEECH...
IT ALMOST LOOKED LIKE HE WAS SMILING. JUST FOR A SECOND.
NOPE... DIDN'T NOTICE THAT AT ALL...

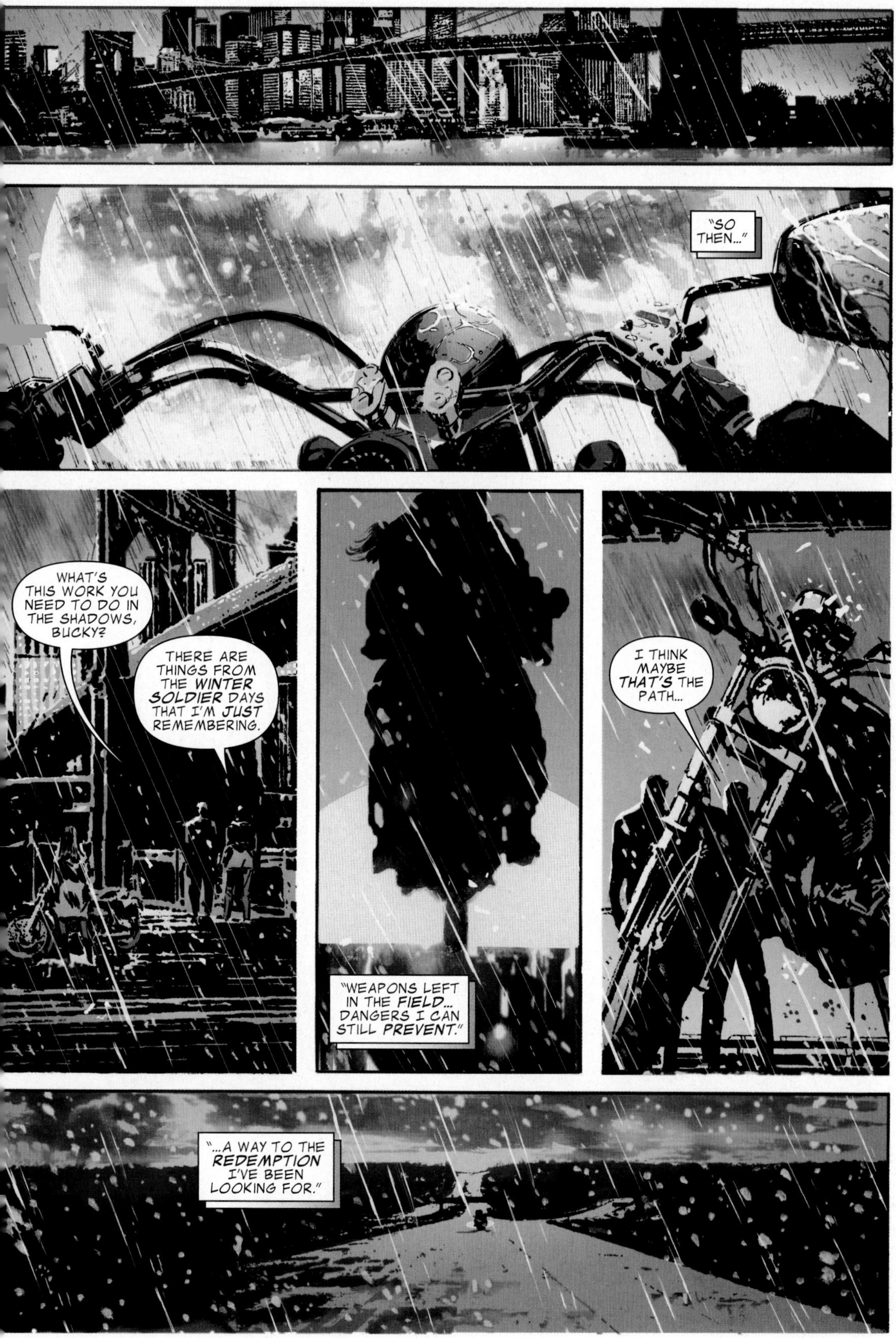
"SO THEN..."
WHAT'S THIS WORK YOU NEED TO DO IN THE SHADOWS, BUCKY?
THERE ARE THINGS FROM THE WINTER SOLDIER DAYS THAT I'M JUST REMEMBERING.
"WEAPONS LEFT IN THE FIELD... DANGERS I CAN STILL PREVENT."
I THINK MAYBE THAT'S THE PATH...
"...A WAY TO THE REDEMPTION I'VE BEEN LOOKING FOR."

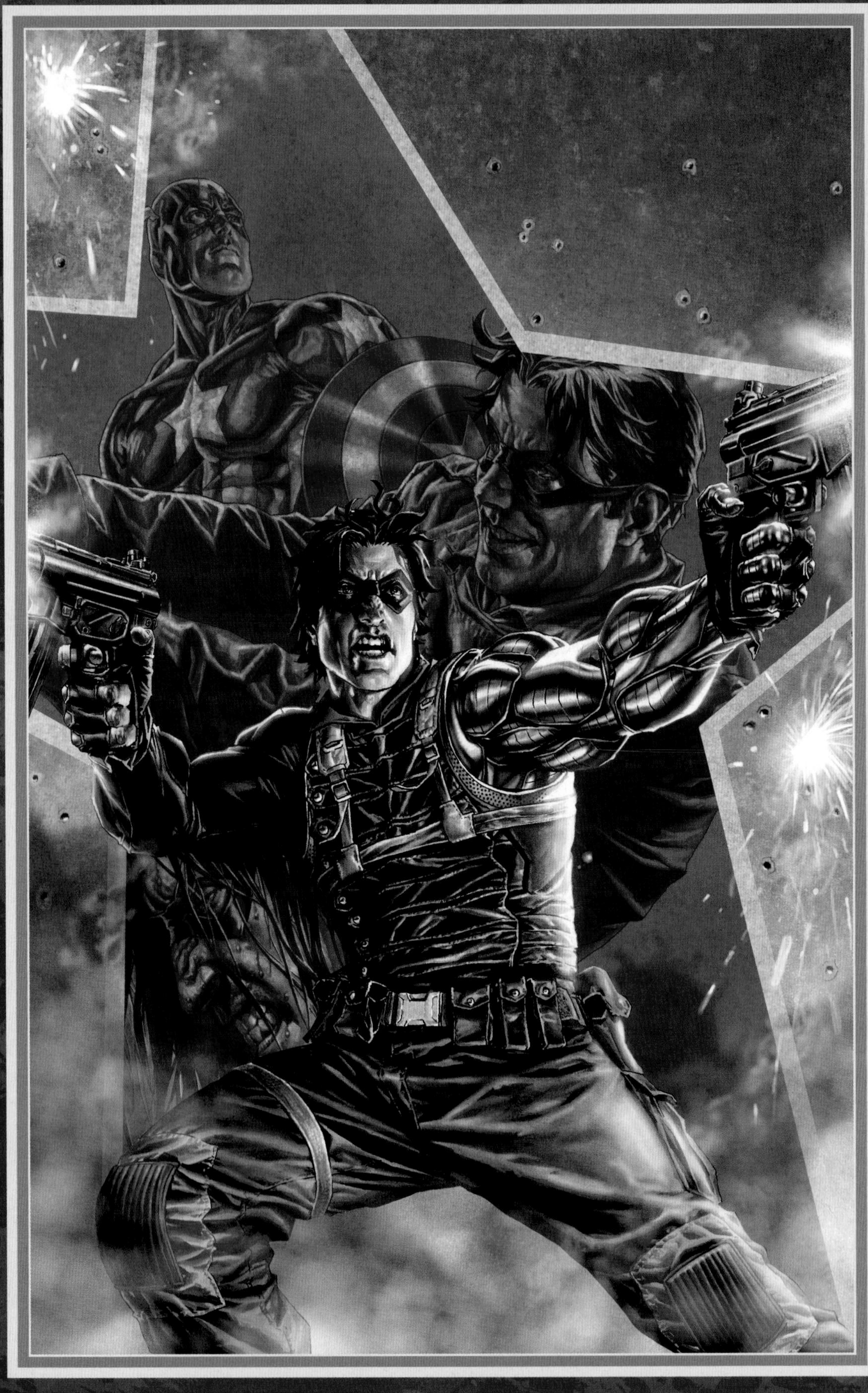

ONE

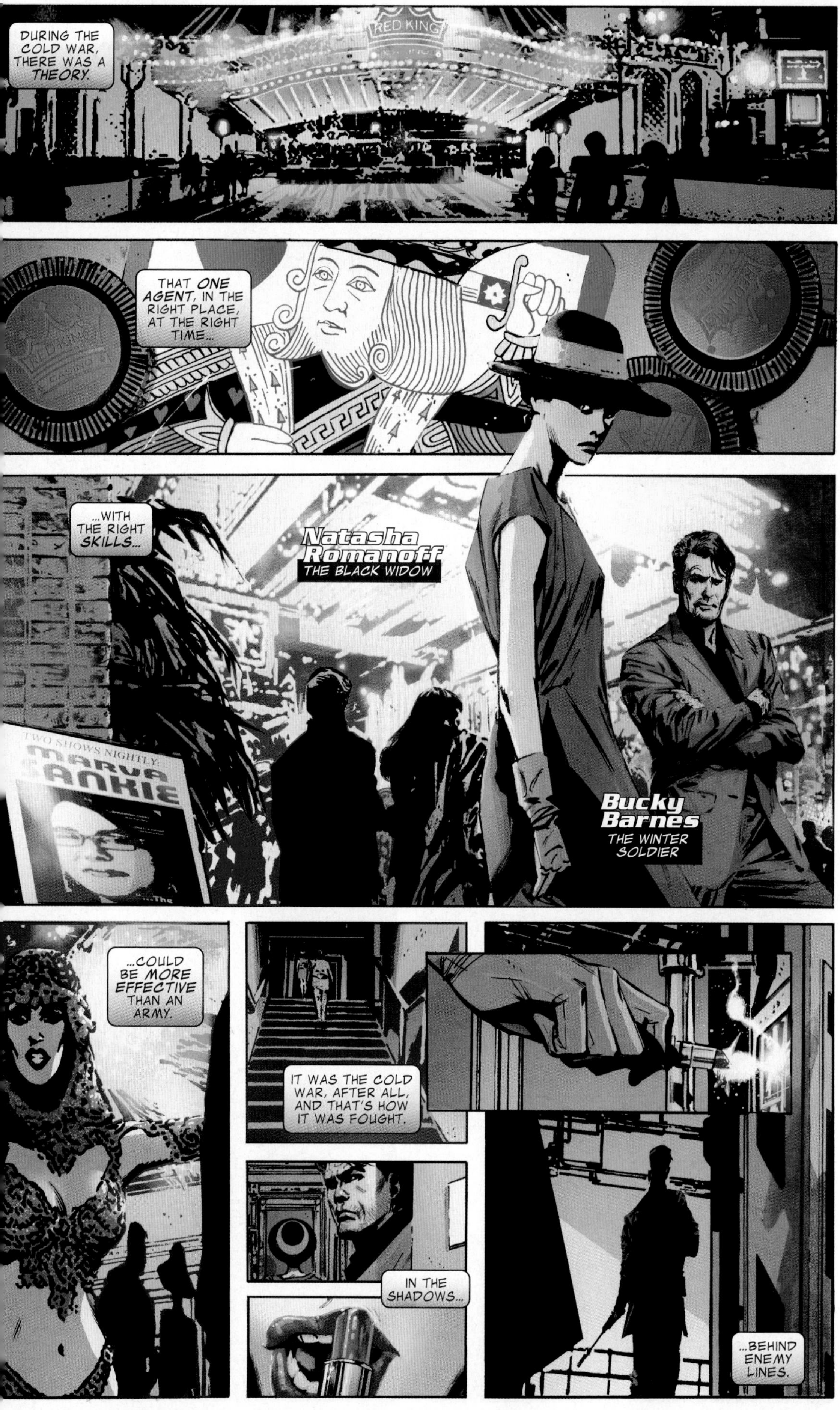

RED KING
DURING THE COLD WAR, THERE WAS A THEORY.
THAT ONE AGENT, IN THE RIGHT PLACE, AT THE RIGHT TIME...
RED KING CASINO
...WITH THE RIGHT SKILLS...
Natasha Romanoff
THE BLACK WIDOW
Bucky Barnes
THE WINTER SOLDIER
TWO SHOWS NIGHTLY:
MARVA SANKIE
...COULD BE MORE EFFECTIVE THAN AN ARMY.
IT WAS THE COLD WAR, AFTER ALL, AND THAT'S HOW IT WAS FOUGHT.
IN THE SHADOWS...
...BEHIND ENEMY LINES.

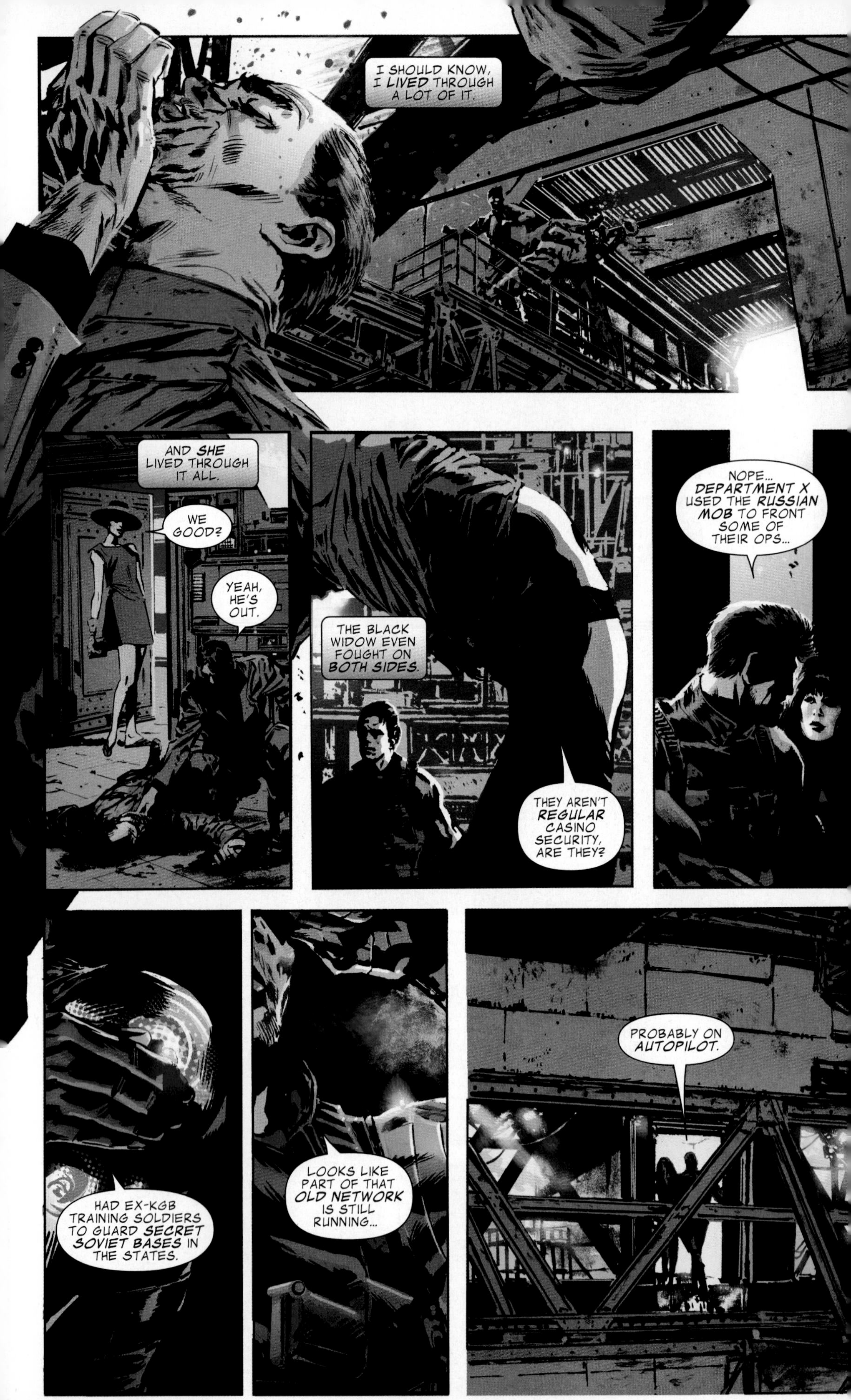

I SHOULD KNOW, I LIVED THROUGH A LOT OF IT.
AND SHE LIVED THROUGH IT ALL.
WE GOOD?
YEAH, HE'S OUT.
THE BLACK WIDOW EVEN FOUGHT ON BOTH SIDES.
THEY AREN'T REGULAR CASINO SECURITY, ARE THEY?
NOPE... DEPARTMENT X USED THE RUSSIAN MOB TO FRONT SOME OF THEIR OPS...
HAD EX-KGB TRAINING SOLDIERS TO GUARD SECRET SOVIET BASES IN THE STATES.
LOOKS LIKE PART OF THAT OLD NETWORK IS STILL RUNNING...
PROBABLY ON AUTOPILOT.

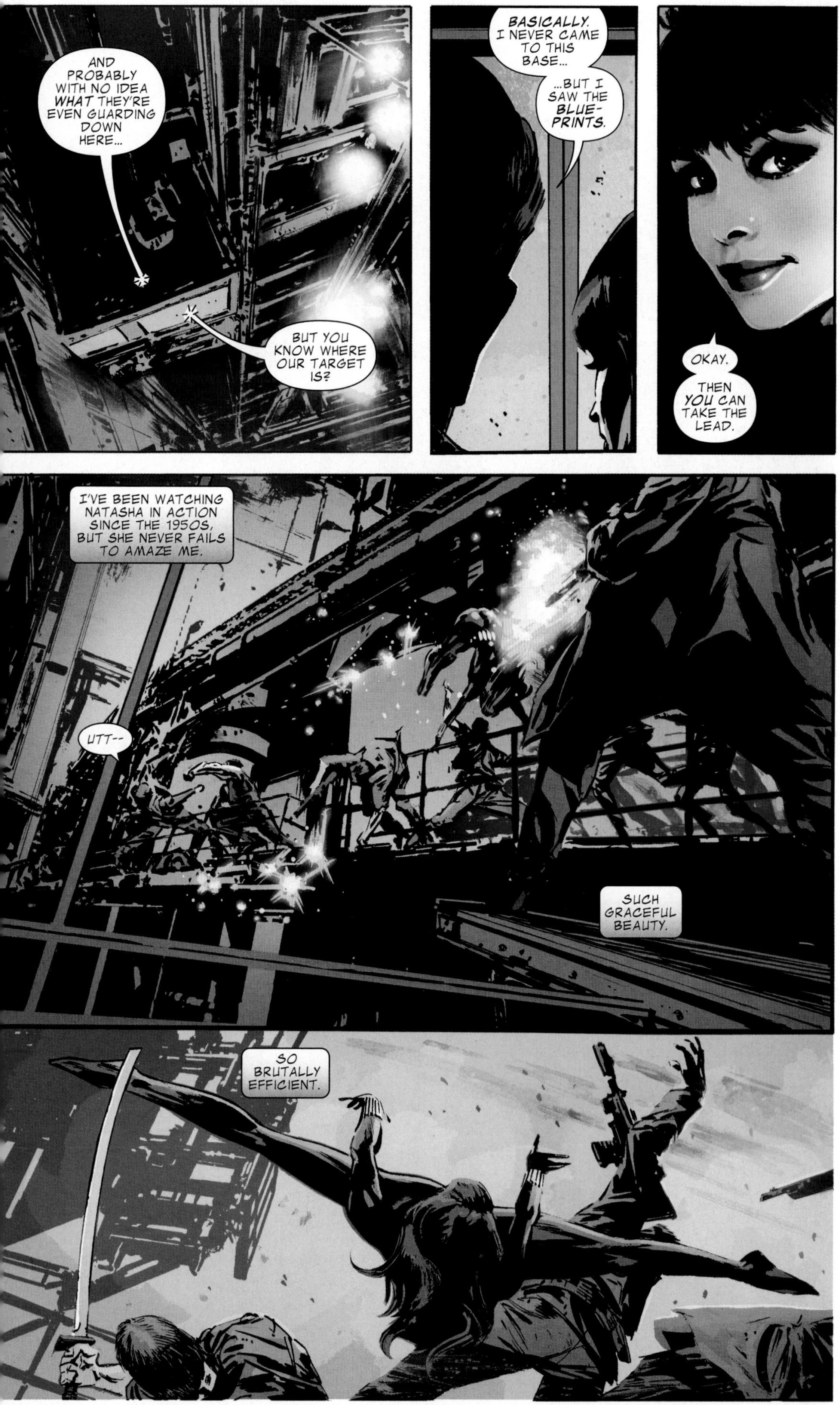
AND PROBABLY WITH NO IDEA WHAT THEY'RE EVEN GUARDING DOWN HERE...
BUT YOU KNOW WHERE OUR TARGET IS?
BASICALLY. I NEVER CAME TO THIS BASE...
...BUT I SAW THE BLUE-PRINTS.
OKAY.
THEN YOU CAN TAKE THE LEAD.
I'VE BEEN WATCHING NATASHA IN ACTION SINCE THE 1950S, BUT SHE NEVER FAILS TO AMAZE ME.
UTT--
SUCH GRACEFUL BEAUTY.
SO BRUTALLY EFFICIENT.

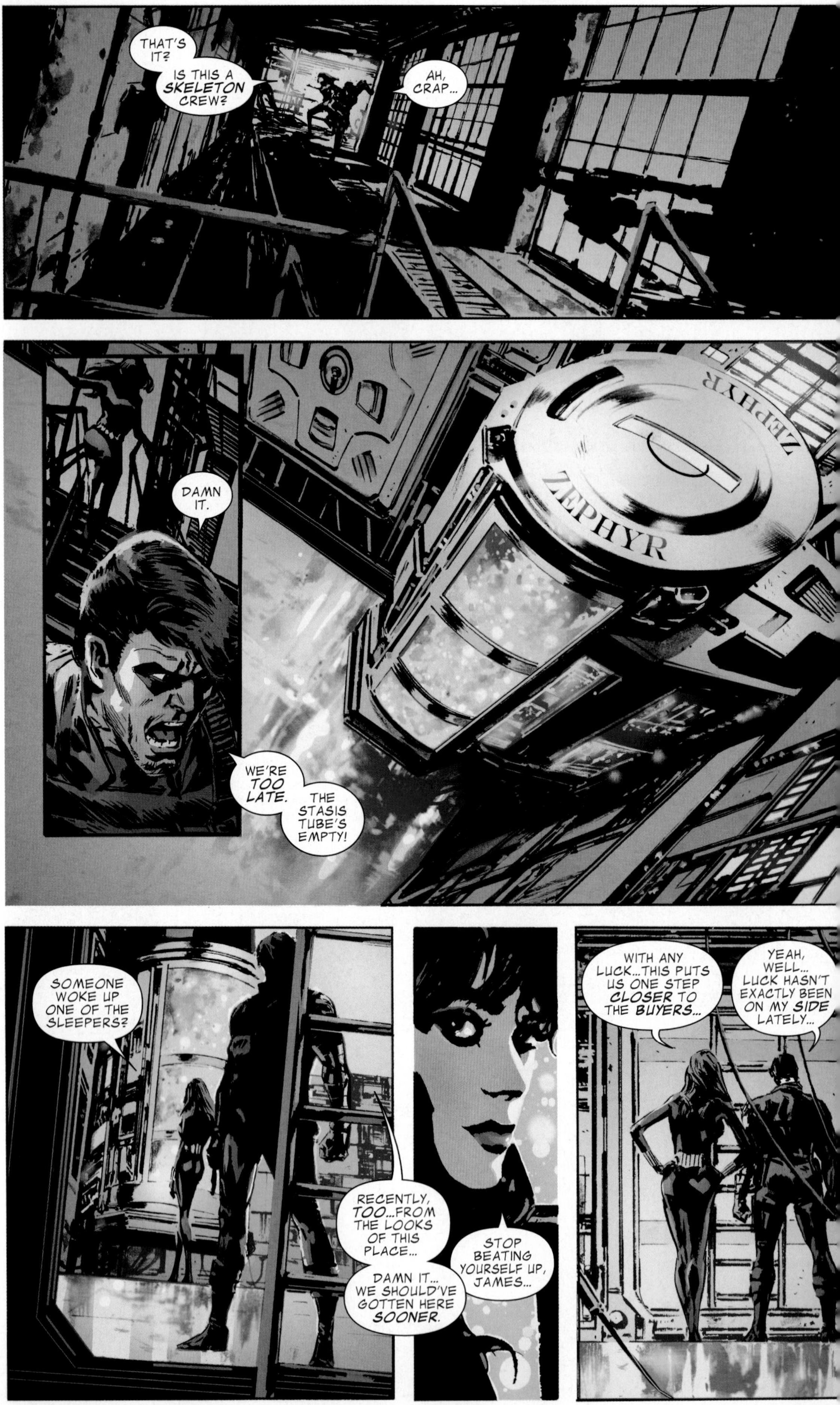
THAT'S IT?
IS THIS A SKELETON CREW?
AH, CRAP...
DAMN IT.
WE'RE TOO LATE.
THE STASIS TUBE'S EMPTY!
ZEPHYR
ZEPHYR
SOMEONE WOKE UP ONE OF THE SLEEPERS?
RECENTLY, TOO...FROM THE LOOKS OF THIS PLACE...
DAMN IT... WE SHOULD'VE GOTTEN HERE SOONER.
STOP BEATING YOURSELF UP, JAMES...
WITH ANY LUCK...THIS PUTS US ONE STEP CLOSER TO THE BUYERS...
YEAH, WELL... LUCK HASN'T EXACTLY BEEN ON MY SIDE LATELY...

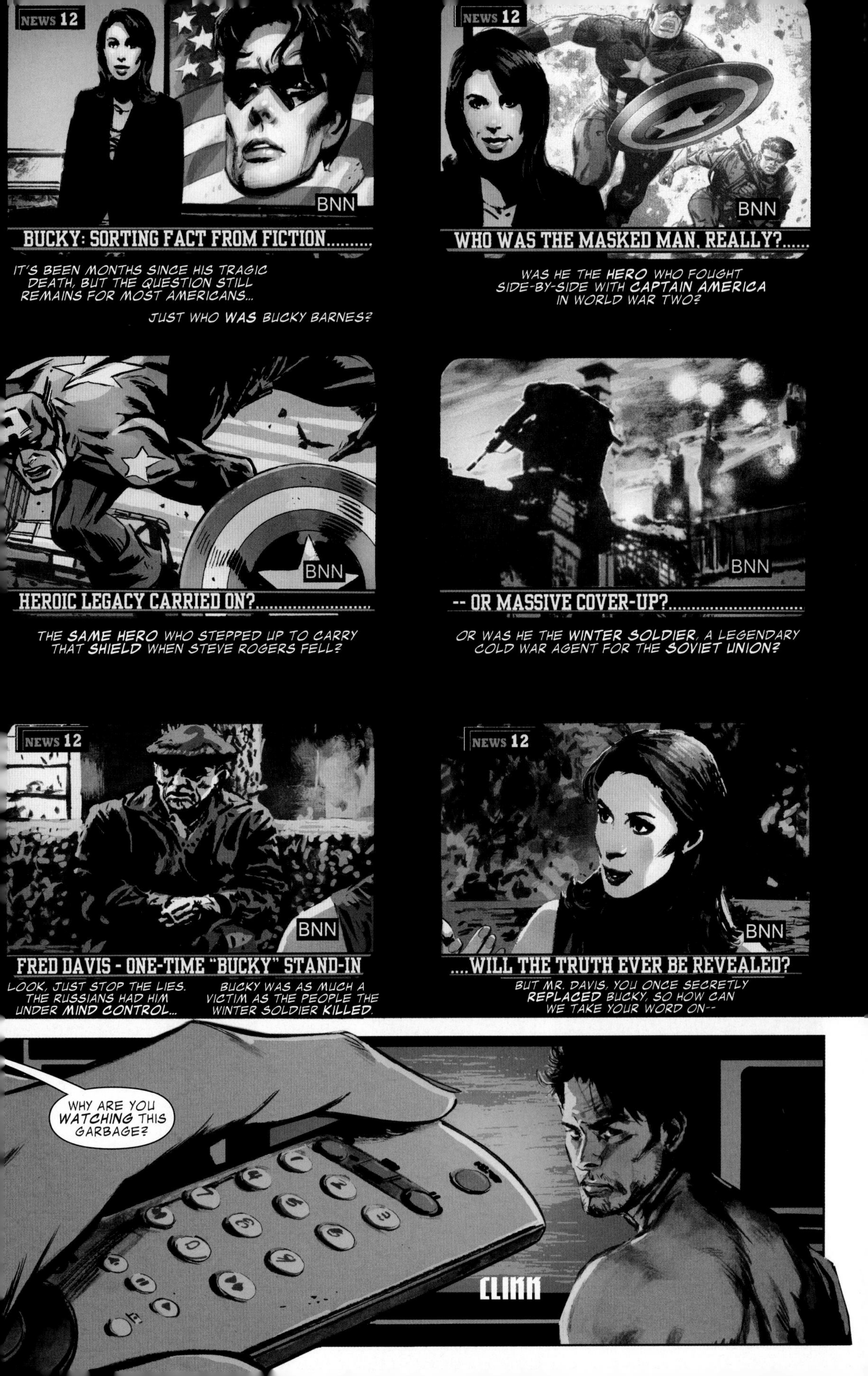
NEWS 12
BNN
BUCKY: SORTING FACT FROM FICTION..........
IT'S BEEN MONTHS SINCE HIS TRAGIC DEATH, BUT THE QUESTION STILL REMAINS FOR MOST AMERICANS...
JUST WHO WAS BUCKY BARNES?
NEWS 12
BNN
WHO WAS THE MASKED MAN, REALLY?......
WAS HE THE HERO WHO FOUGHT SIDE-BY-SIDE WITH CAPTAIN AMERICA IN WORLD WAR TWO?
BNN
HEROIC LEGACY CARRIED ON?......................
THE SAME HERO WHO STEPPED UP TO CARRY THAT SHIELD WHEN STEVE ROGERS FELL?
BNN
-- OR MASSIVE COVER-UP?..........................
OR WAS HE THE WINTER SOLDIER, A LEGENDARY COLD WAR AGENT FOR THE SOVIET UNION?
NEWS 12
BNN
FRED DAVIS - ONE-TIME "BUCKY" STAND-IN
LOOK, JUST STOP THE LIES. THE RUSSIANS HAD HIM UNDER MIND CONTROL...
BUCKY WAS AS MUCH A VICTIM AS THE PEOPLE THE WINTER SOLDIER KILLED.
NEWS 12
BNN
....WILL THE TRUTH EVER BE REVEALED?
BUT MR. DAVIS, YOU ONCE SECRETLY REPLACED BUCKY, SO HOW CAN WE TAKE YOUR WORD ON--
WHY ARE YOU WATCHING THIS GARBAGE?
CLINK

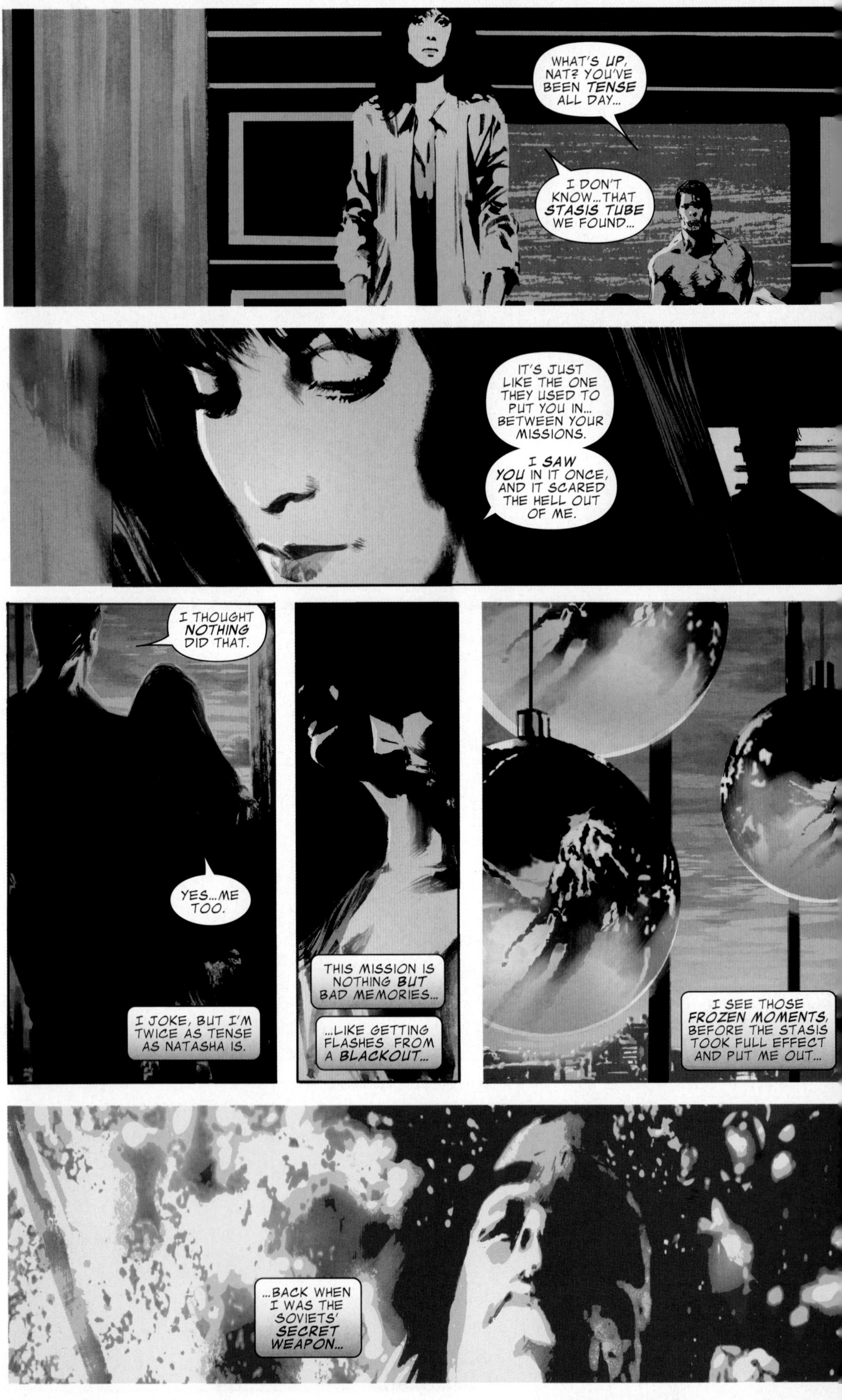
WHAT'S UP, NAT? YOU'VE BEEN TENSE ALL DAY...
I DON'T KNOW...THAT STASIS TUBE WE FOUND...
IT'S JUST LIKE THE ONE THEY USED TO PUT YOU IN... BETWEEN YOUR MISSIONS.
I SAW YOU IN IT ONCE, AND IT SCARED THE HELL OUT OF ME.
I THOUGHT NOTHING DID THAT.
YES...ME TOO.
I JOKE, BUT I'M TWICE AS TENSE AS NATASHA IS.
THIS MISSION IS NOTHING BUT BAD MEMORIES...
...LIKE GETTING FLASHES FROM A BLACKOUT...
I SEE THOSE FROZEN MOMENTS, BEFORE THE STASIS TOOK FULL EFFECT AND PUT ME OUT...
...BACK WHEN I WAS THE SOVIETS' SECRET WEAPON...

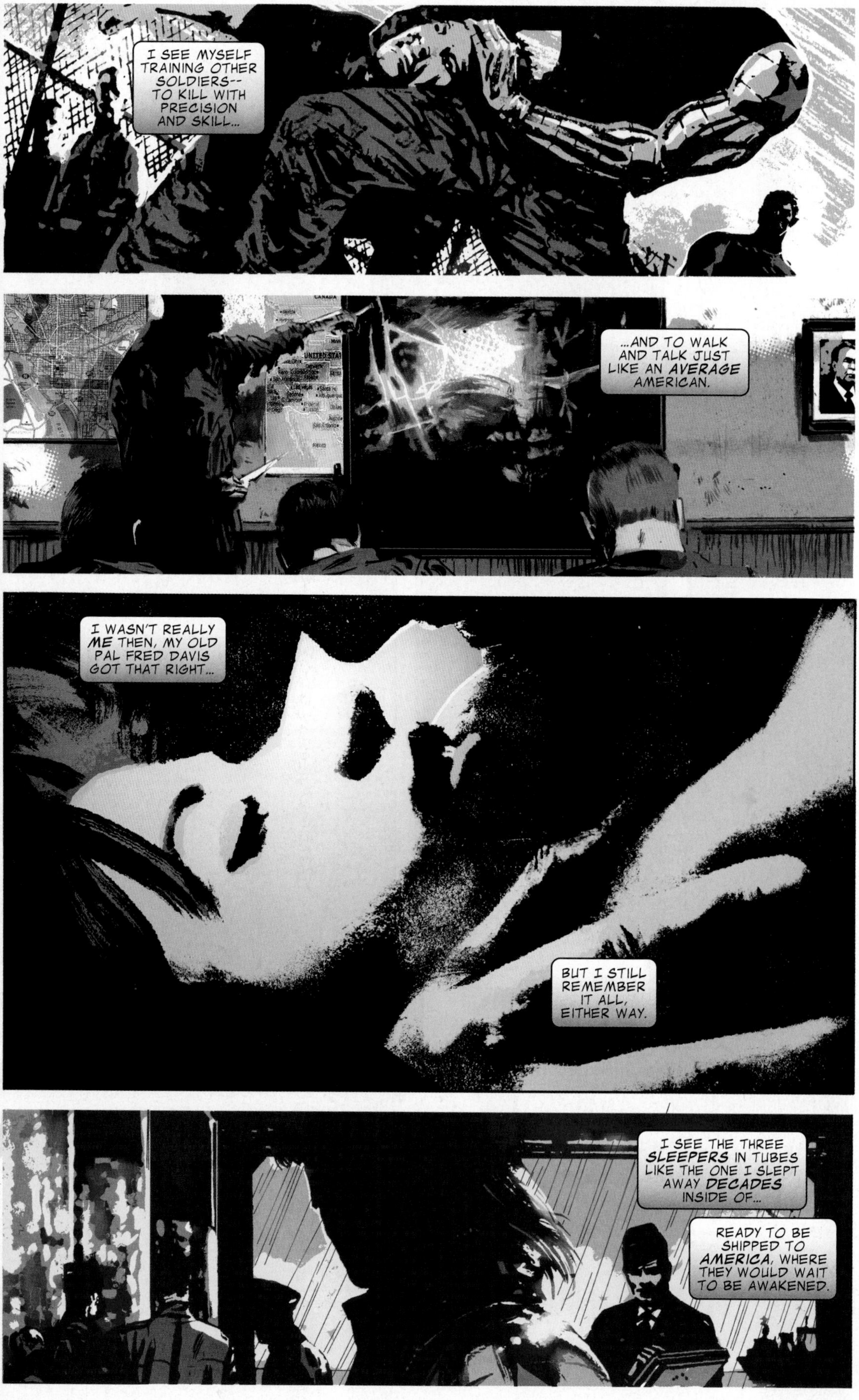
I SEE MYSELF TRAINING OTHER SOLDIERS-- TO KILL WITH PRECISION AND SKILL...
...AND TO WALK AND TALK JUST LIKE AN AVERAGE AMERICAN.
I WASN'T REALLY ME THEN, MY OLD PAL FRED DAVIS GOT THAT RIGHT...
BUT I STILL REMEMBER IT ALL, EITHER WAY.
I SEE THE THREE SLEEPERS IN TUBES LIKE THE ONE I SLEPT AWAY DECADES INSIDE OF...
READY TO BE SHIPPED TO AMERICA, WHERE THEY WOULD WAIT TO BE AWAKENED.

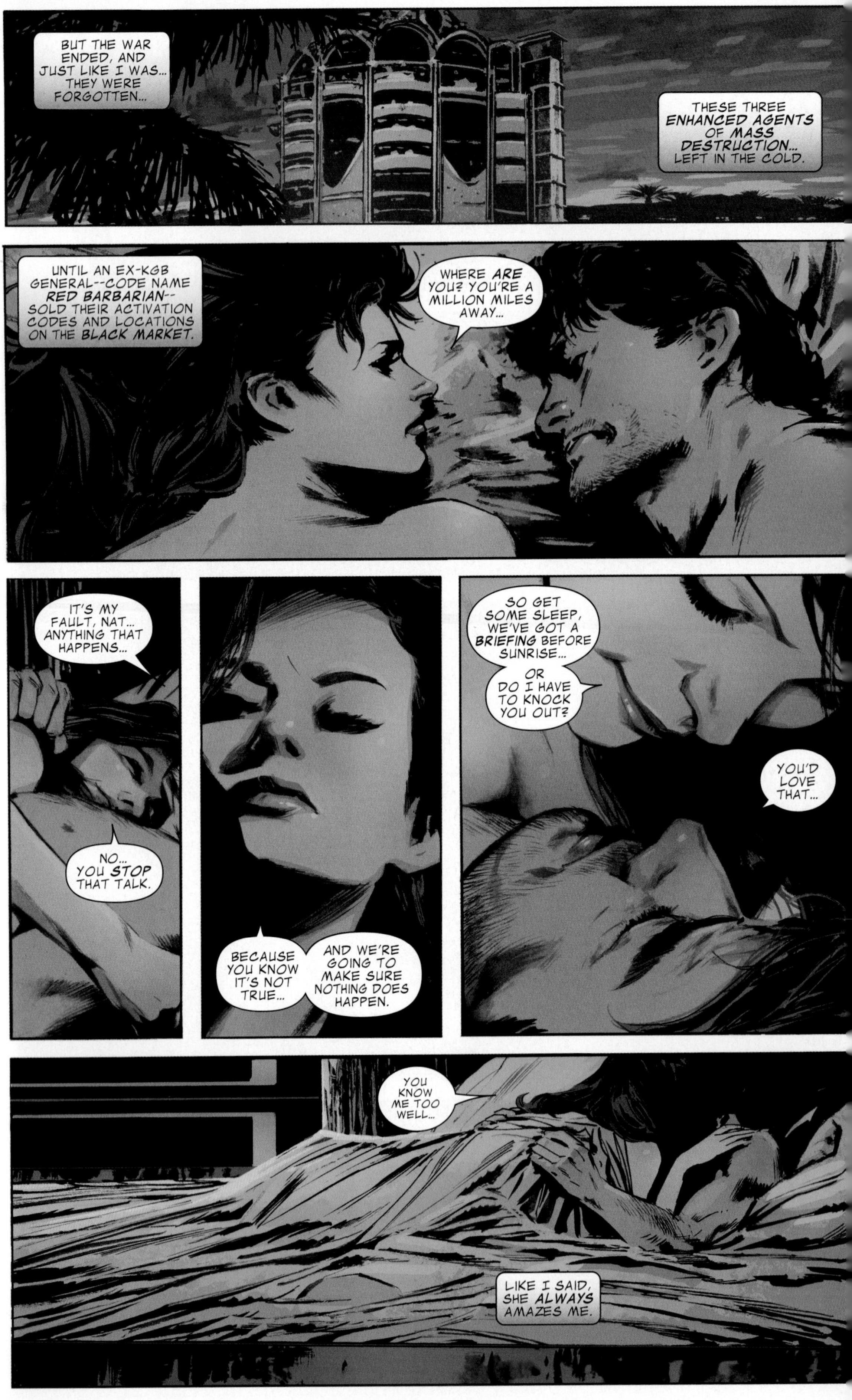

BUT THE WAR ENDED, AND JUST LIKE I WAS... THEY WERE FORGOTTEN...
THESE THREE ENHANCED AGENTS OF MASS DESTRUCTION... LEFT IN THE COLD.
UNTIL AN EX-KGB GENERAL--CODE NAME RED BARBARIAN--SOLD THEIR ACTIVATION CODES AND LOCATIONS ON THE BLACK MARKET.
WHERE ARE YOU? YOU'RE A MILLION MILES AWAY...
IT'S MY FAULT, NAT... ANYTHING THAT HAPPENS...
NO... YOU STOP THAT TALK.
BECAUSE YOU KNOW IT'S NOT TRUE...
AND WE'RE GOING TO MAKE SURE NOTHING DOES HAPPEN.
SO GET SOME SLEEP, WE'VE GOT A BRIEFING BEFORE SUNRISE...
OR DO I HAVE TO KNOCK YOU OUT?
YOU'D LOVE THAT...
YOU KNOW ME TOO WELL...
LIKE I SAID, SHE ALWAYS AMAZES ME.

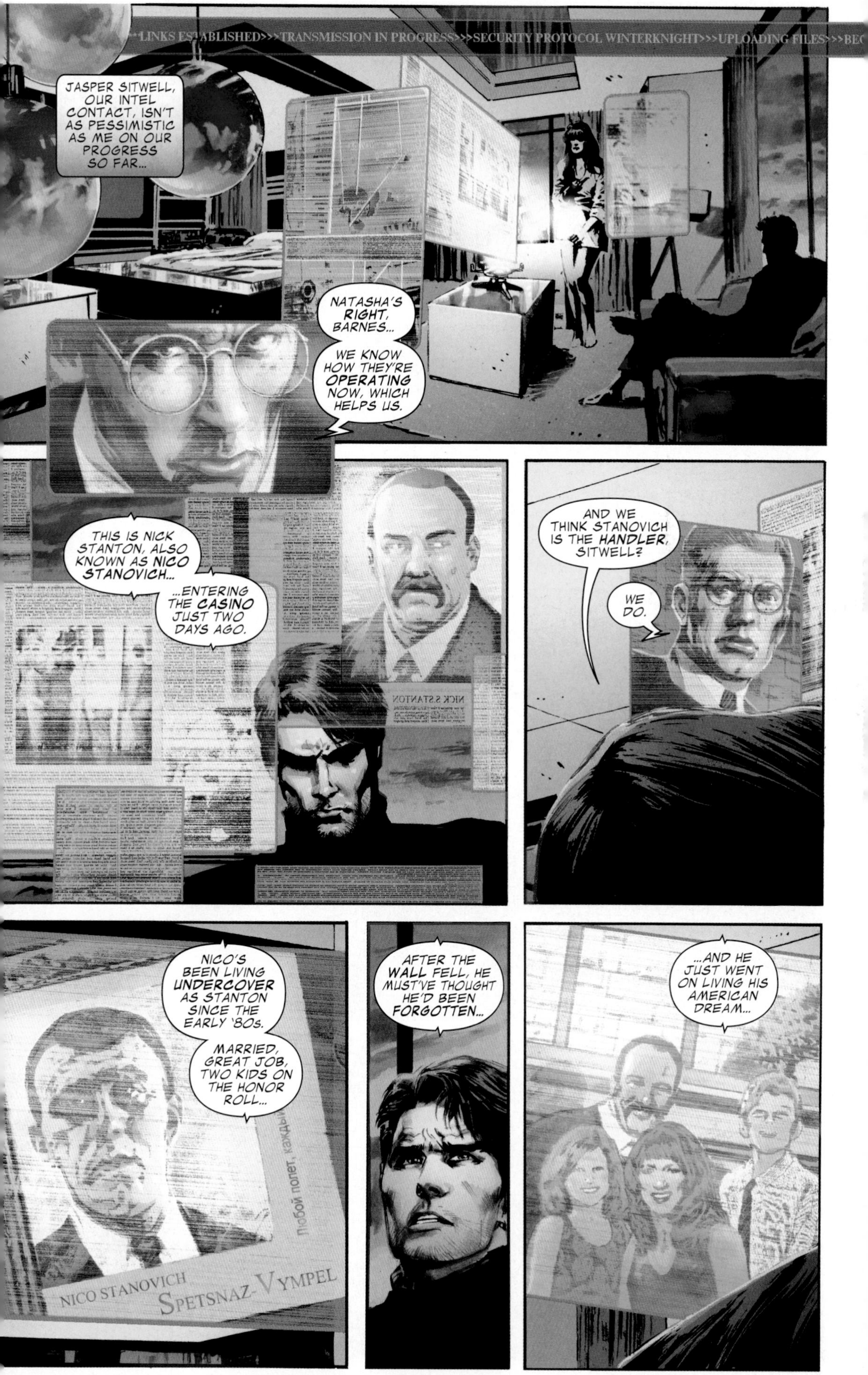
**LINKS ESTABLISHED>>>TRANSMISSION IN PROGRESS>>>SECURITY PROTOCOL WINTERKNIGHT>>>UPLOADING FILES>>>BE
JASPER SITWELL, OUR INTEL CONTACT, ISN'T AS PESSIMISTIC AS ME ON OUR PROGRESS SO FAR...
NATASHA'S RIGHT, BARNES...
WE KNOW HOW THEY'RE OPERATING NOW, WHICH HELPS US.
THIS IS NICK STANTON, ALSO KNOWN AS NICO STANOVICH...
...ENTERING THE CASINO JUST TWO DAYS AGO.
NICK STANTON
AND WE THINK STANOVICH IS THE HANDLER, SITWELL?
WE DO.
NICO'S BEEN LIVING UNDERCOVER AS STANTON SINCE THE EARLY '80s.
MARRIED, GREAT JOB, TWO KIDS ON THE HONOR ROLL...
Любой полет, каждый
NICO STANOVICH
SPETSNAZ-VYMPEL
AFTER THE WALL FELL, HE MUST'VE THOUGHT HE'D BEEN FORGOTTEN...
...AND HE JUST WENT ON LIVING HIS AMERICAN DREAM...

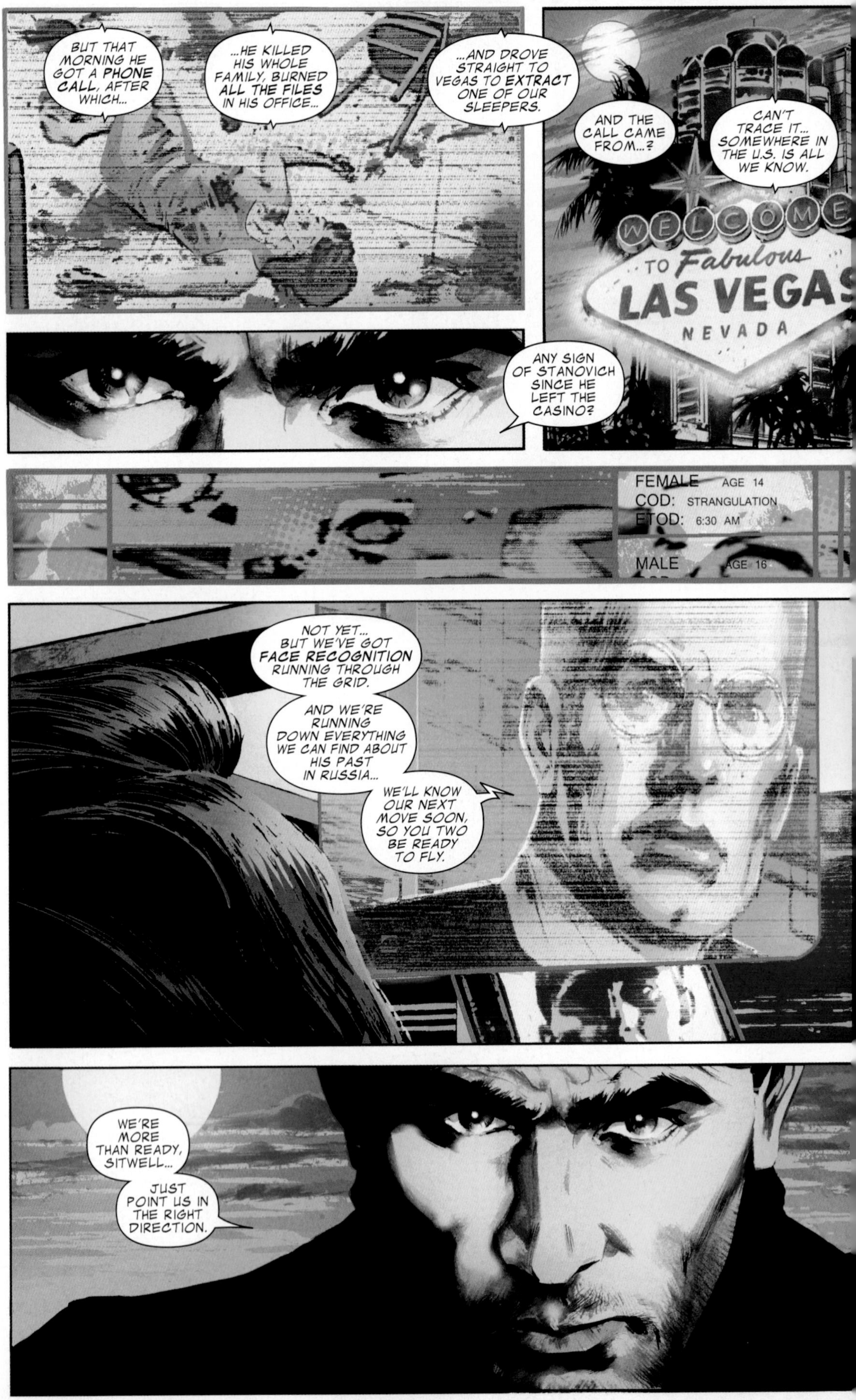
BUT THAT MORNING HE GOT A PHONE CALL, AFTER WHICH...
...HE KILLED HIS WHOLE FAMILY, BURNED ALL THE FILES IN HIS OFFICE...
...AND DROVE STRAIGHT TO VEGAS TO EXTRACT ONE OF OUR SLEEPERS.
AND THE CALL CAME FROM...?
CAN'T TRACE IT... SOMEWHERE IN THE U.S. IS ALL WE KNOW.
WELCOME TO Fabulous LAS VEGAS NEVADA
ANY SIGN OF STANOVICH SINCE HE LEFT THE CASINO?
FEMALE AGE 14
COD: STRANGULATION
ETOD: 6:30 AM
MALE AGE 16
NOT YET... BUT WE'VE GOT FACE RECOGNITION RUNNING THROUGH THE GRID.
AND WE'RE RUNNING DOWN EVERYTHING WE CAN FIND ABOUT HIS PAST IN RUSSIA...
WE'LL KNOW OUR NEXT MOVE SOON, SO YOU TWO BE READY TO FLY.
WE'RE MORE THAN READY, SITWELL...
JUST POINT US IN THE RIGHT DIRECTION.

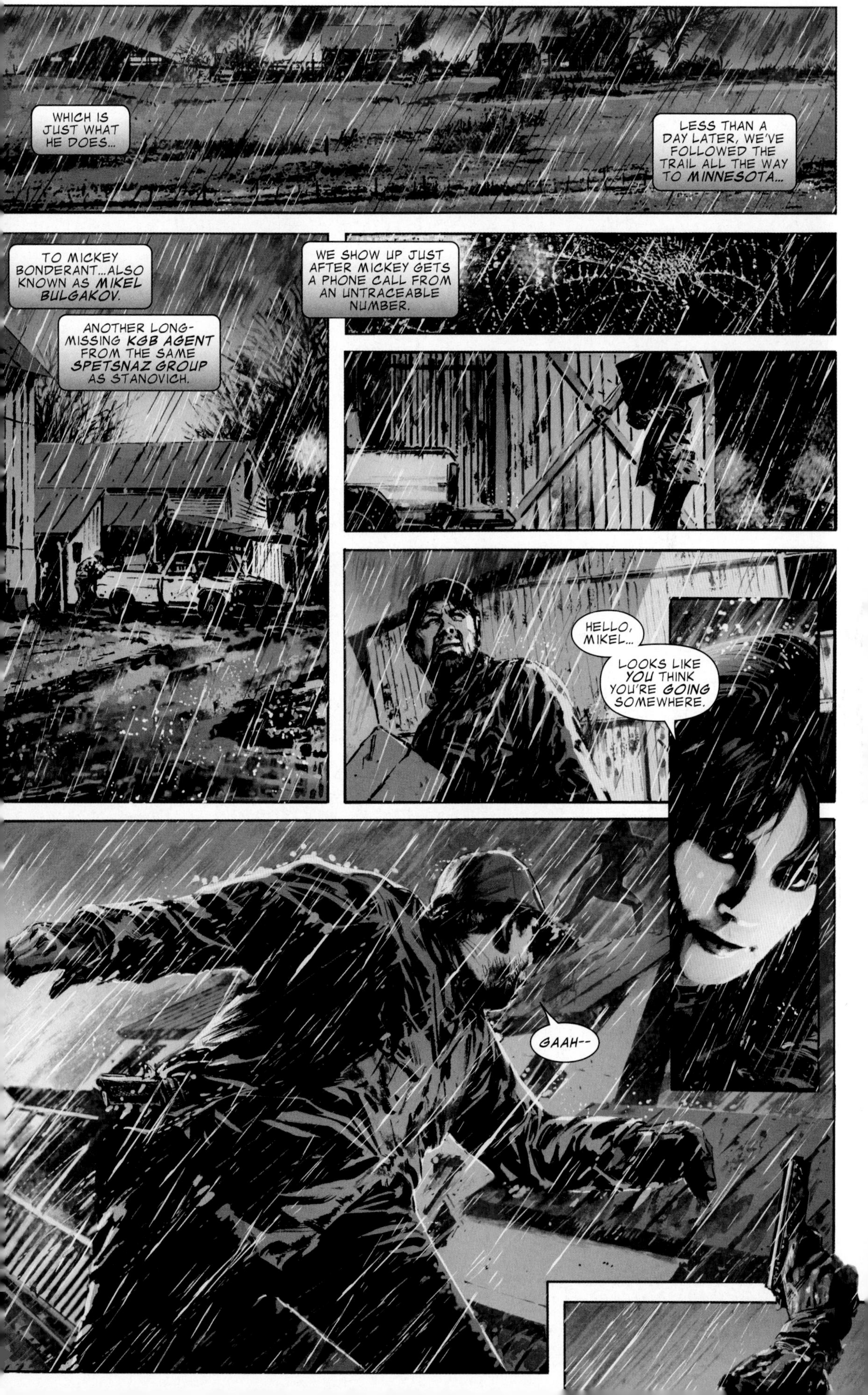
WHICH IS JUST WHAT HE DOES...
LESS THAN A DAY LATER, WE'VE FOLLOWED THE TRAIL ALL THE WAY TO MINNESOTA...
TO MICKEY BONDERANT...ALSO KNOWN AS MIKEL BULGAKOV.
ANOTHER LONG-MISSING KGB AGENT FROM THE SAME SPETSNAZ GROUP AS STANOVICH.
WE SHOW UP JUST AFTER MICKEY GETS A PHONE CALL FROM AN UNTRACEABLE NUMBER.
HELLO, MIKEL...
LOOKS LIKE YOU THINK YOU'RE GOING SOMEWHERE.
GAAH--

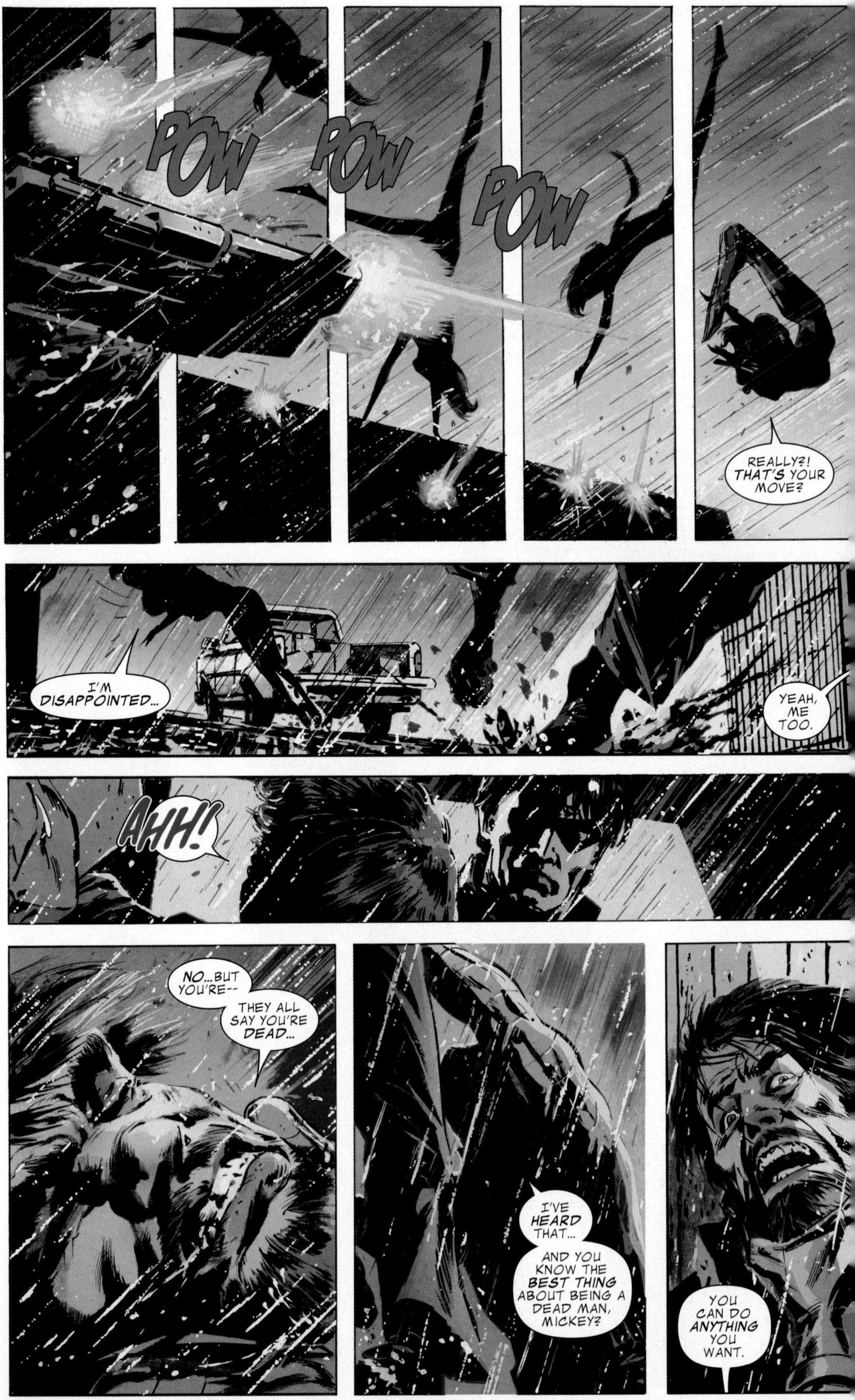
POW
POW
POW
REALLY?! THAT'S YOUR MOVE?
I'M DISAPPOINTED...
YEAH, ME TOO.
AHH!
NO...BUT YOU'RE--
THEY ALL SAY YOU'RE DEAD...
I'VE HEARD THAT...
AND YOU KNOW THE BEST THING ABOUT BEING A DEAD MAN, MICKEY?
YOU CAN DO ANYTHING YOU WANT.

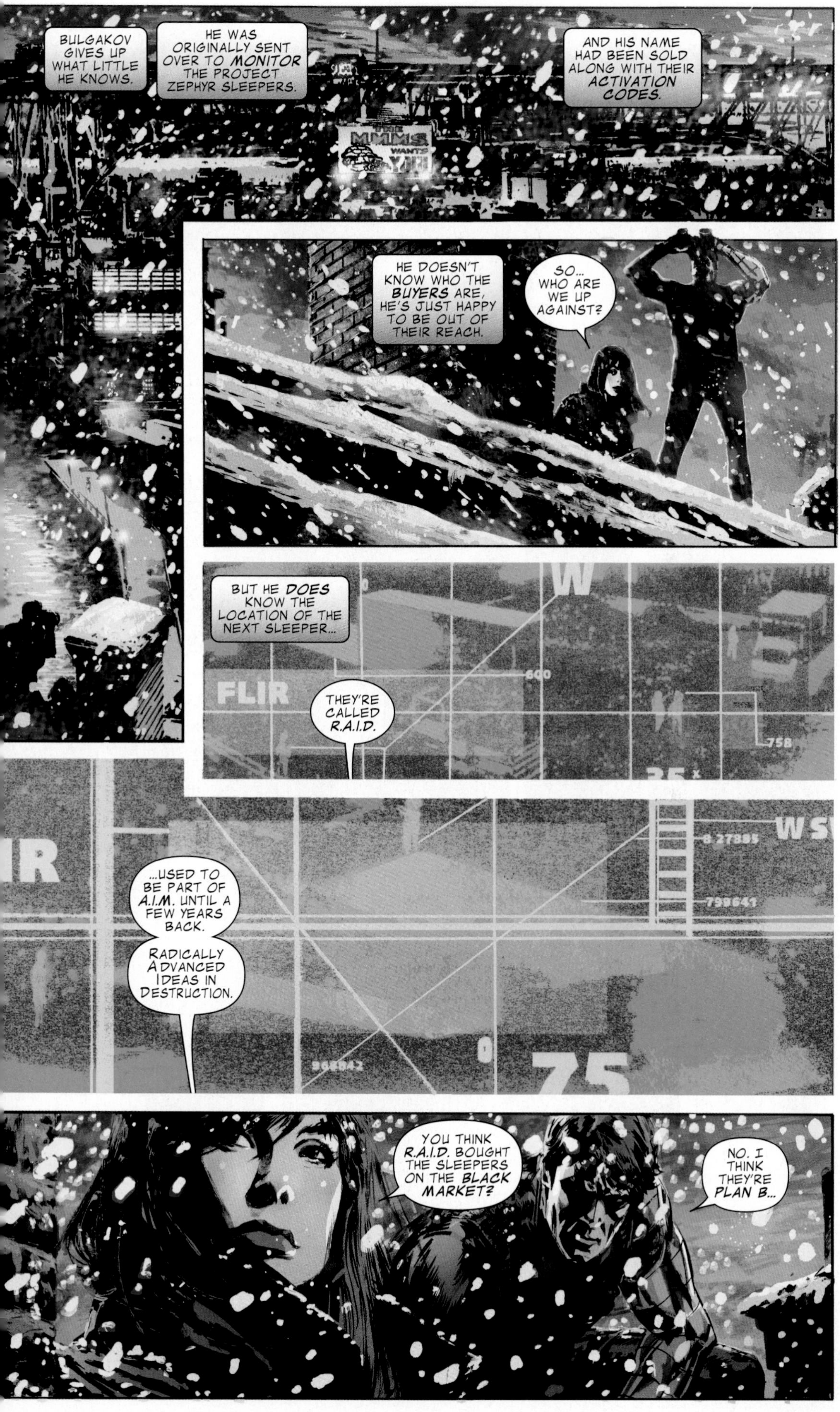

BULGAKOV GIVES UP WHAT LITTLE HE KNOWS.
HE WAS ORIGINALLY SENT OVER TO MONITOR THE PROJECT ZEPHYR SLEEPERS.
AND HIS NAME HAD BEEN SOLD ALONG WITH THEIR ACTIVATION CODES.
HE DOESN'T KNOW WHO THE BUYERS ARE, HE'S JUST HAPPY TO BE OUT OF THEIR REACH.
SO... WHO ARE WE UP AGAINST?
BUT HE DOES KNOW THE LOCATION OF THE NEXT SLEEPER...
FLIR
600
THEY'RE CALLED R.A.I.D.
758
W
...USED TO BE PART OF A.I.M. UNTIL A FEW YEARS BACK.
RADICALLY ADVANCED IDEAS IN DESTRUCTION.
8.27895
799641
75
YOU THINK R.A.I.D. BOUGHT THE SLEEPERS ON THE BLACK MARKET?
NO. I THINK THEY'RE PLAN B...

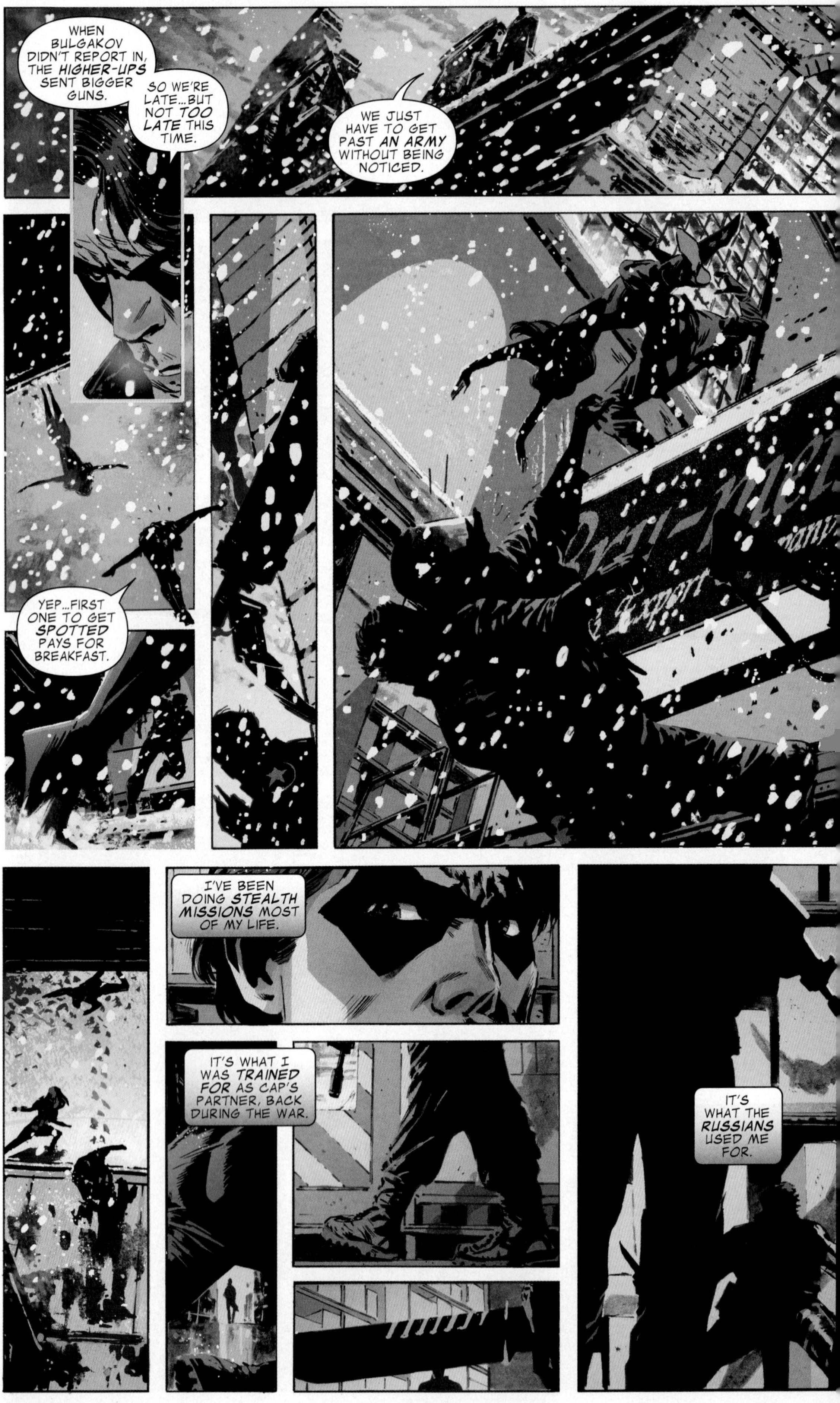
WHEN BULGAKOV DIDN'T REPORT IN, THE HIGHER-UPS SENT BIGGER GUNS.
SO WE'RE LATE...BUT NOT TOO LATE THIS TIME.
WE JUST HAVE TO GET PAST AN ARMY WITHOUT BEING NOTICED.
YEP...FIRST ONE TO GET SPOTTED PAYS FOR BREAKFAST.
I'VE BEEN DOING STEALTH MISSIONS MOST OF MY LIFE.
IT'S WHAT I WAS TRAINED FOR AS CAP'S PARTNER, BACK DURING THE WAR.
IT'S WHAT THE RUSSIANS USED ME FOR.

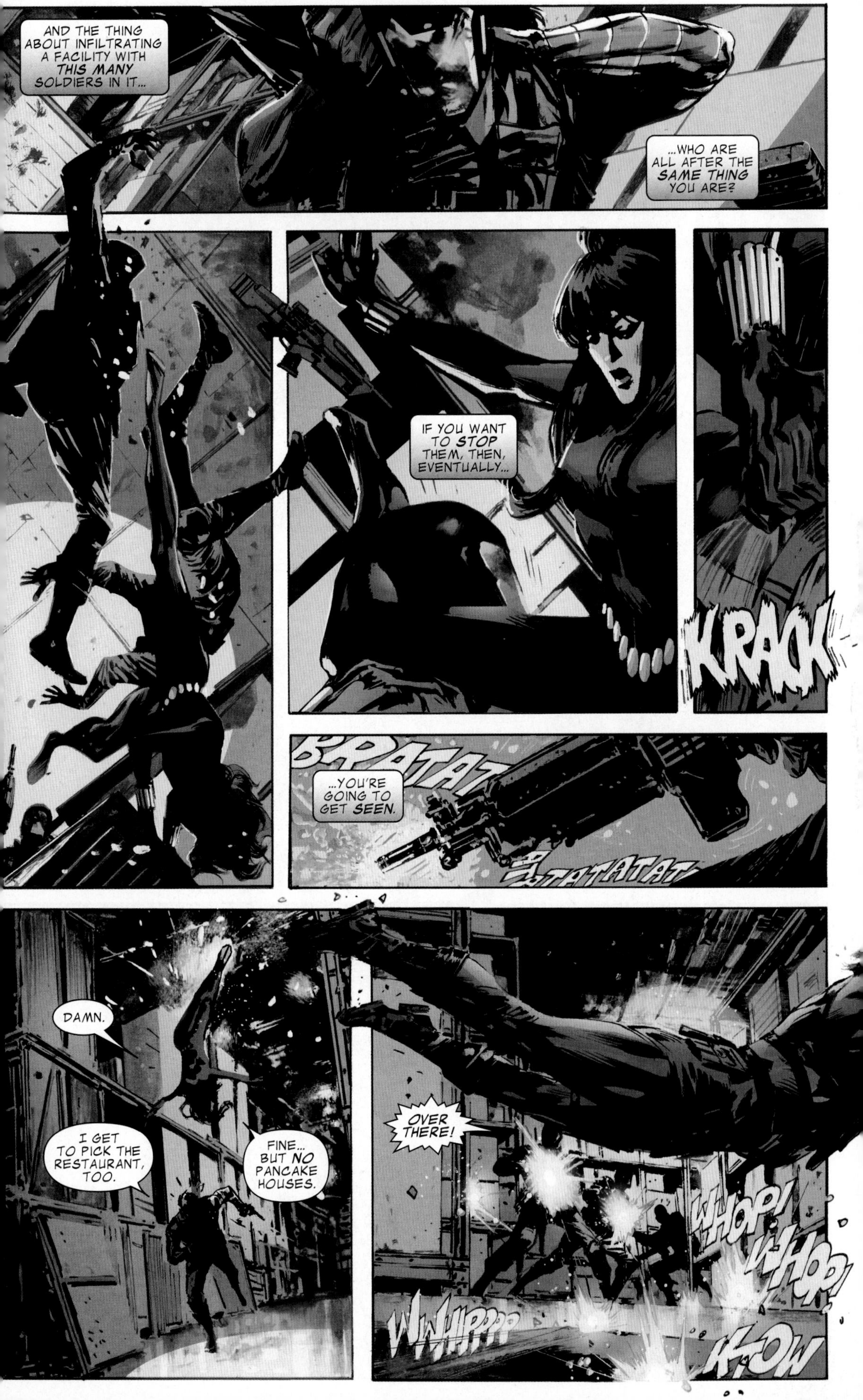

AND THE THING ABOUT INFILTRATING A FACILITY WITH THIS MANY SOLDIERS IN IT...
...WHO ARE ALL AFTER THE SAME THING YOU ARE?
IF YOU WANT TO STOP THEM, THEN, EVENTUALLY...
KRACK
BRATATAT
...YOU'RE GOING TO GET SEEN.
BRATATATATAT
DAMN.
I GET TO PICK THE RESTAURANT, TOO.
FINE... BUT NO PANCAKE HOUSES.
OVER THERE!
WHOP! WHOP!
WHIPPPP
KTOW

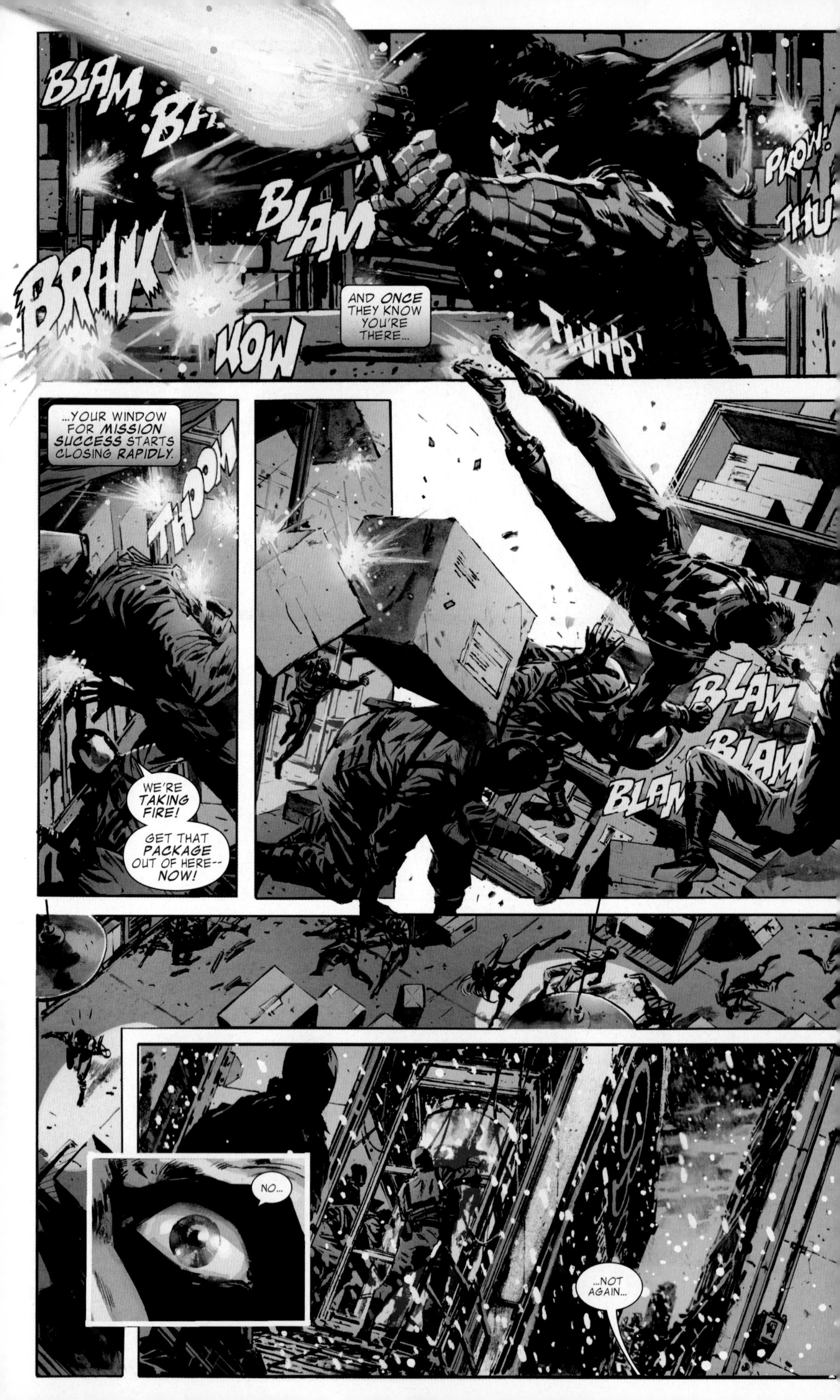
BLAM
BAM
BLAM
BRAK
KOW
AND ONCE THEY KNOW YOU'RE THERE...
TWHIP!
PKOW!
...YOUR WINDOW FOR MISSION SUCCESS STARTS CLOSING RAPIDLY.
THOOM
WE'RE TAKING FIRE!
GET THAT PACKAGE OUT OF HERE-- NOW!
BLAM
BLAM
BLAM
NO...
...NOT AGAIN...

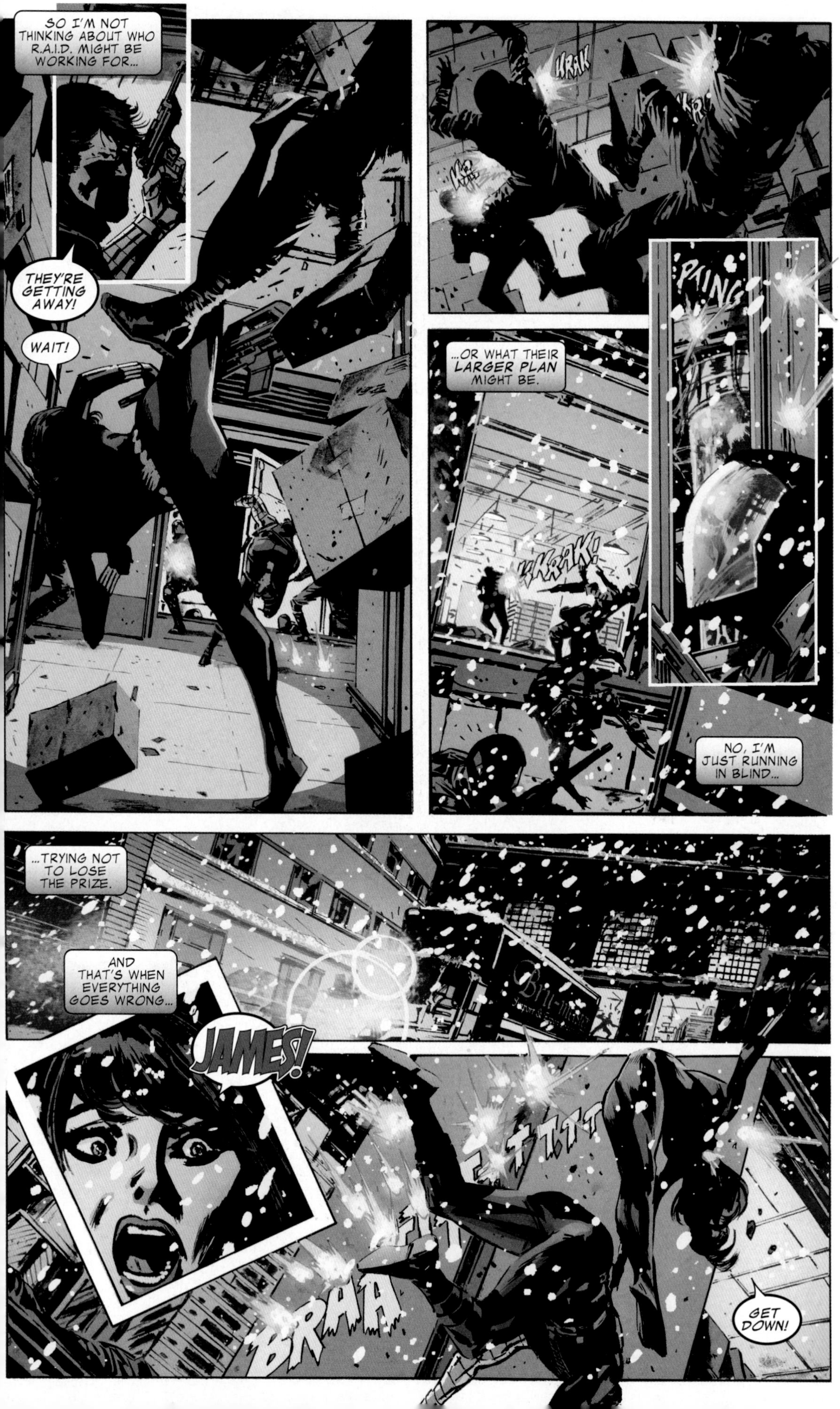
SO I'M NOT THINKING ABOUT WHO R.A.I.D. MIGHT BE WORKING FOR...
THEY'RE GETTING AWAY!
WAIT!
KRAK
...OR WHAT THEIR LARGER PLAN MIGHT BE.
PAING
KRAK!
NO, I'M JUST RUNNING IN BLIND...
...TRYING NOT TO LOSE THE PRIZE.
AND THAT'S WHEN EVERYTHING GOES WRONG...
JAMES!
BRAA
GET DOWN!

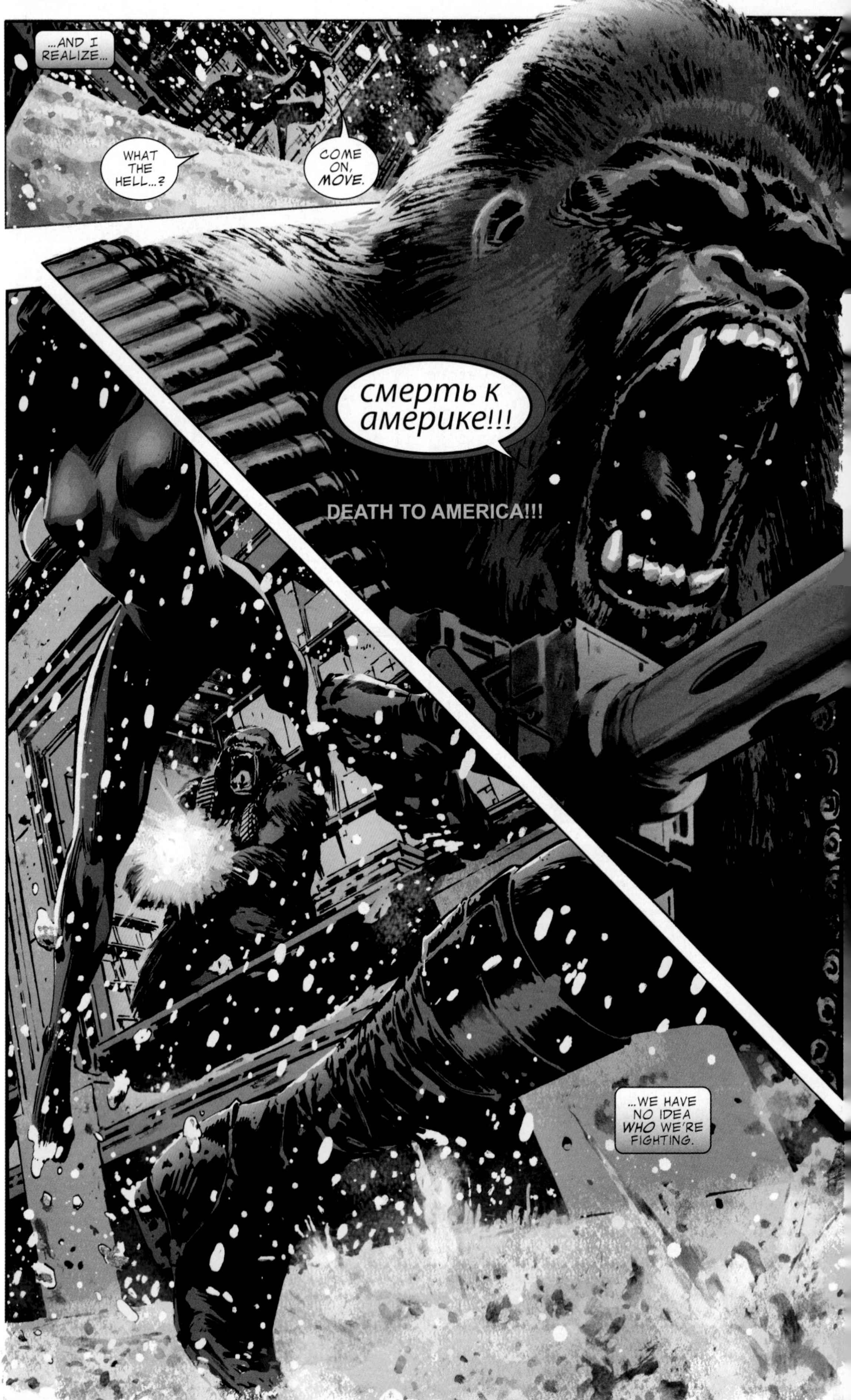
...AND I REALIZE...
WHAT THE HELL...?
COME ON, MOVE.
смерть к америке!!!
DEATH TO AMERICA!!!
...WE HAVE NO IDEA WHO WE'RE FIGHTING.

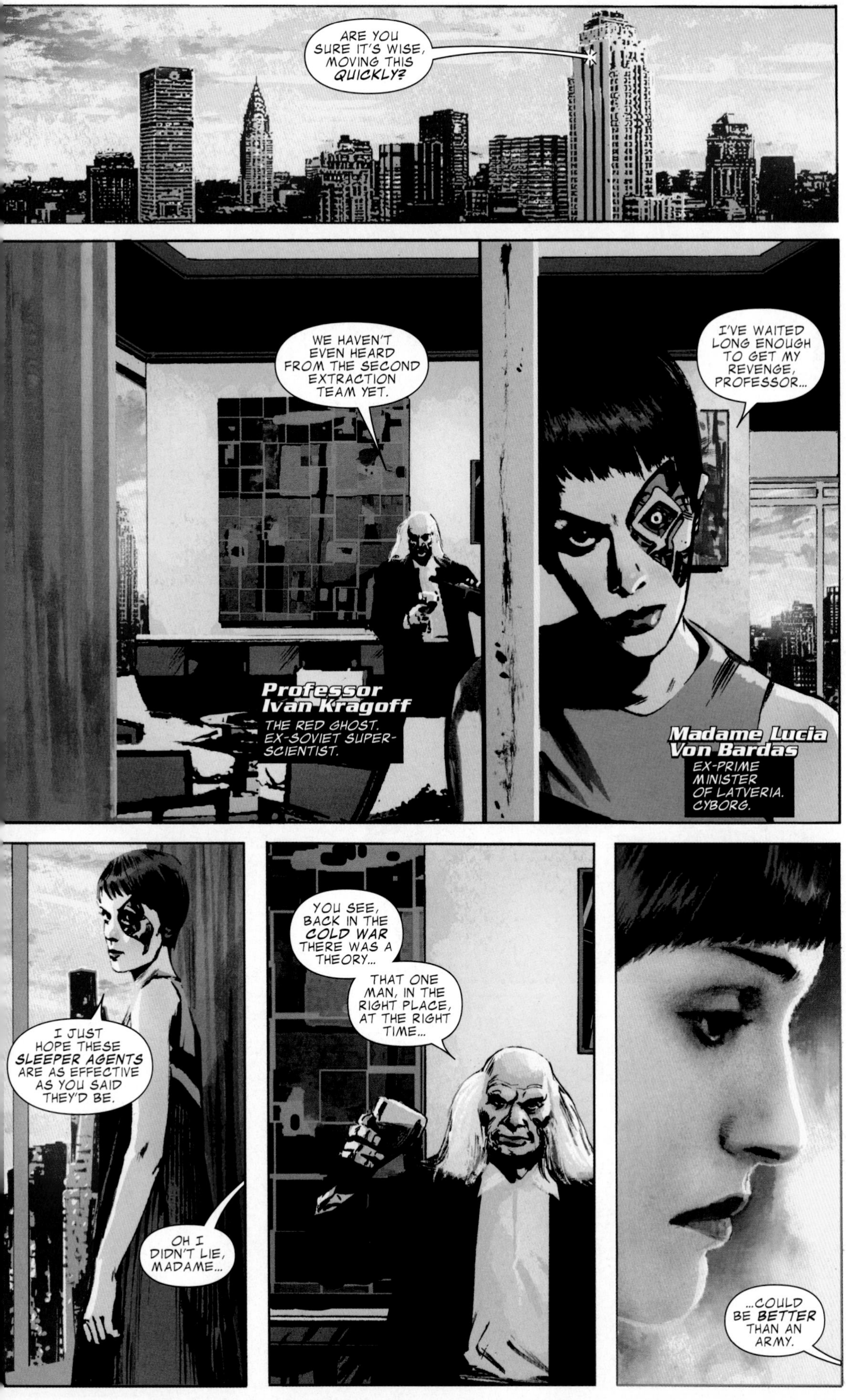
ARE YOU SURE IT'S WISE, MOVING THIS QUICKLY?
WE HAVEN'T EVEN HEARD FROM THE SECOND EXTRACTION TEAM YET.
I'VE WAITED LONG ENOUGH TO GET MY REVENGE, PROFESSOR...
Professor Ivan Kragoff
THE RED GHOST. EX-SOVIET SUPER-SCIENTIST.
Madame Lucia Von Bardas
EX-PRIME MINISTER OF LATVERIA. CYBORG.
I JUST HOPE THESE SLEEPER AGENTS ARE AS EFFECTIVE AS YOU SAID THEY'D BE.
OH I DIDN'T LIE, MADAME...
YOU SEE, BACK IN THE COLD WAR THERE WAS A THEORY...
THAT ONE MAN, IN THE RIGHT PLACE, AT THE RIGHT TIME...
...COULD BE BETTER THAN AN ARMY.

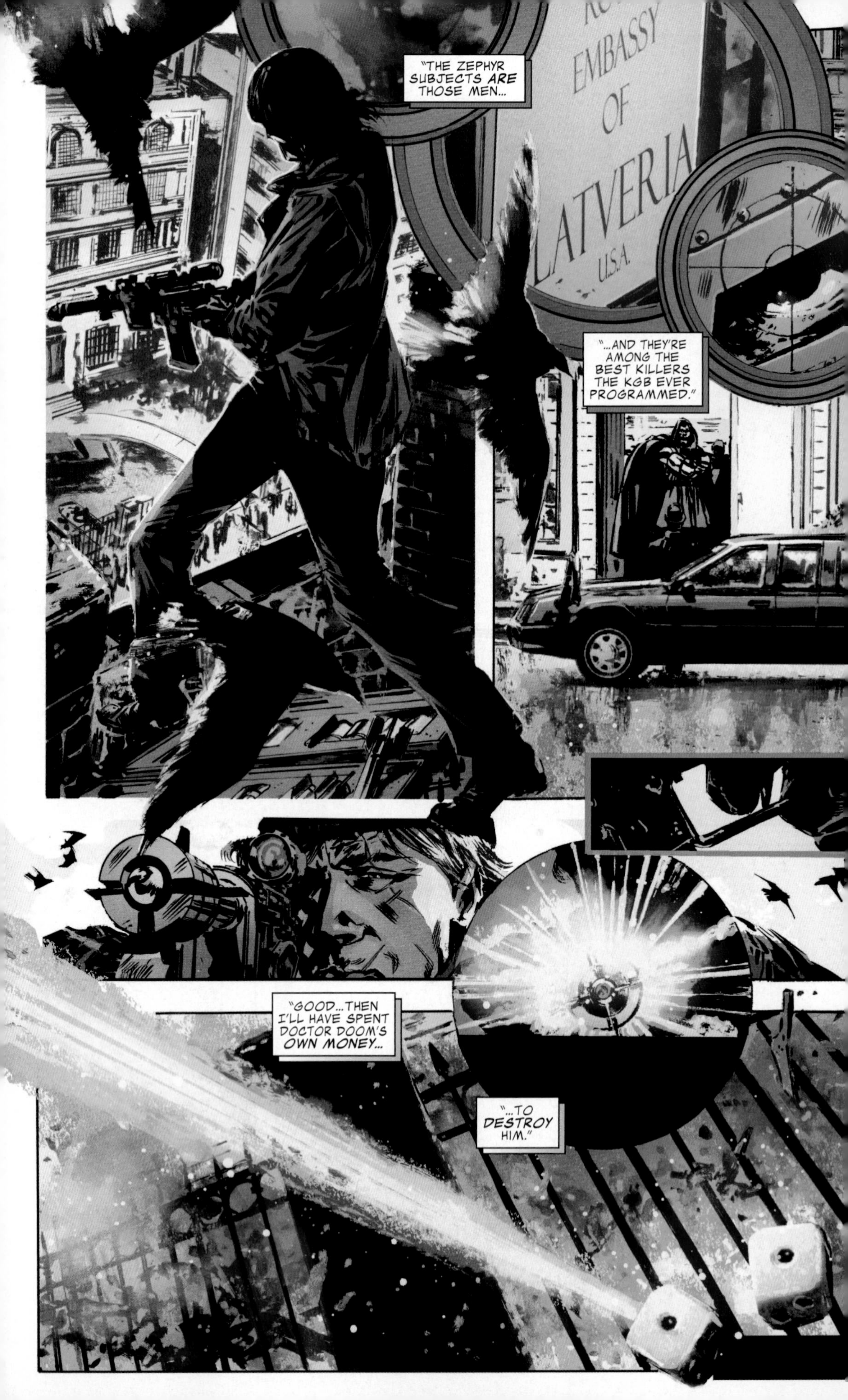

"THE ZEPHYR SUBJECTS ARE THOSE MEN...
EMBASSY OF LATVERIA U.S.A.
"...AND THEY'RE AMONG THE BEST KILLERS THE KGB EVER PROGRAMMED."
"GOOD...THEN I'LL HAVE SPENT DOCTOR DOOM'S OWN MONEY...
"...TO DESTROY HIM."

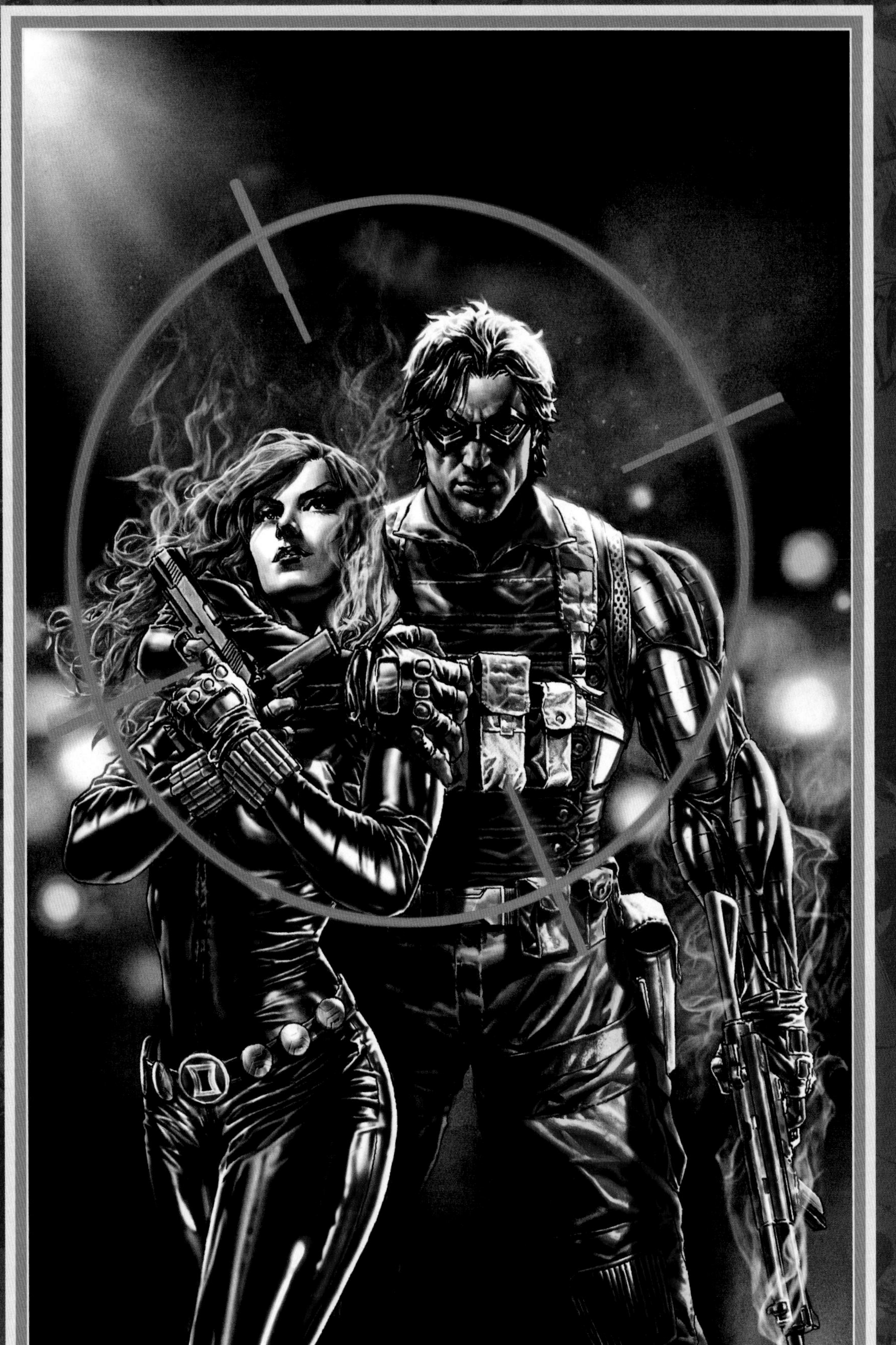

TWO

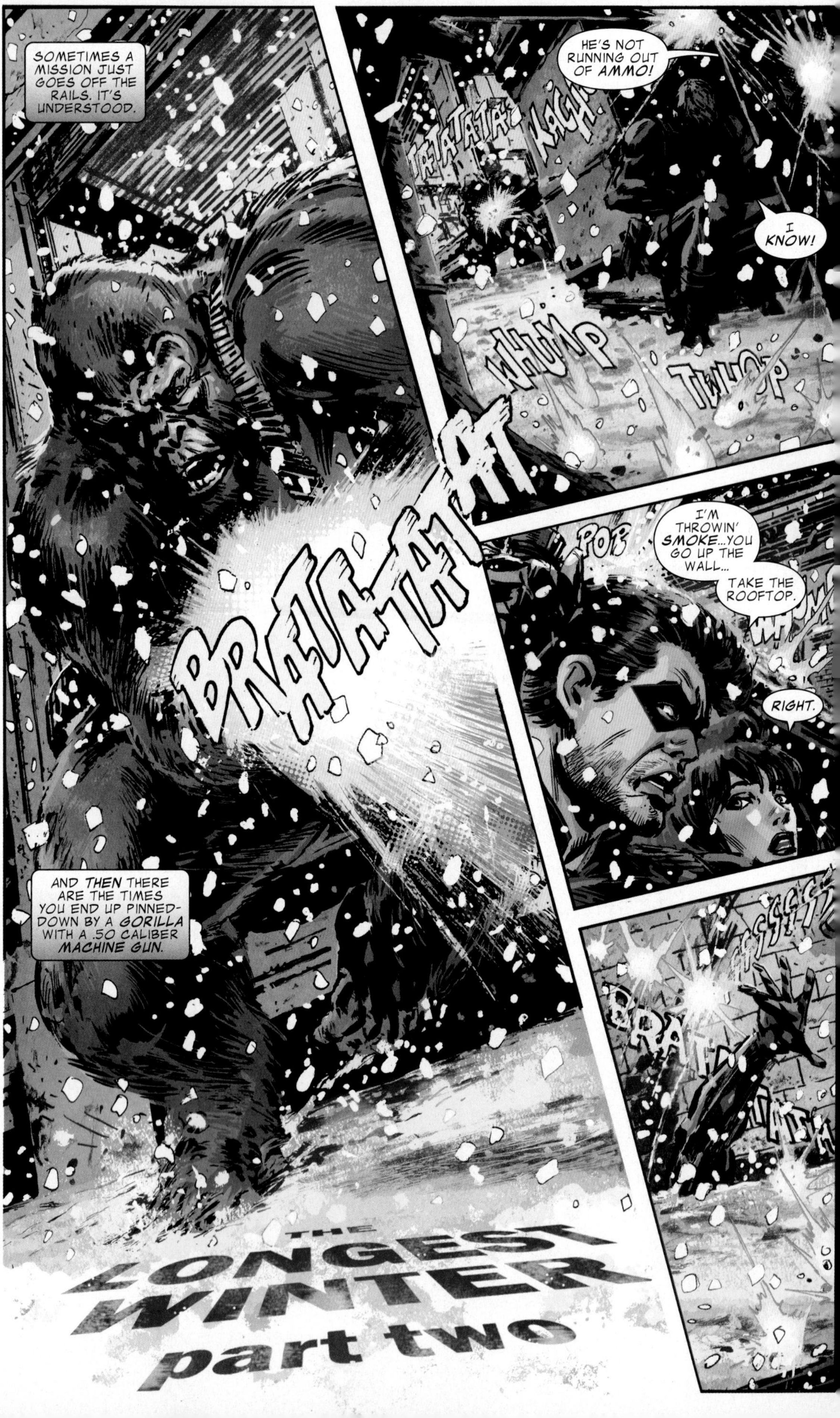
SOMETIMES A MISSION JUST GOES OFF THE RAILS. IT'S UNDERSTOOD.
HE'S NOT RUNNING OUT OF AMMO!
I KNOW!
WHUMP
THWOP
BRATATATAT
I'M THROWIN' SMOKE...YOU GO UP THE WALL...
TAKE THE ROOFTOP.
POP
RIGHT.
AND THEN THERE ARE THE TIMES YOU END UP PINNED-DOWN BY A GORILLA WITH A .50 CALIBER MACHINE GUN.
THE LONGEST WINTER part two

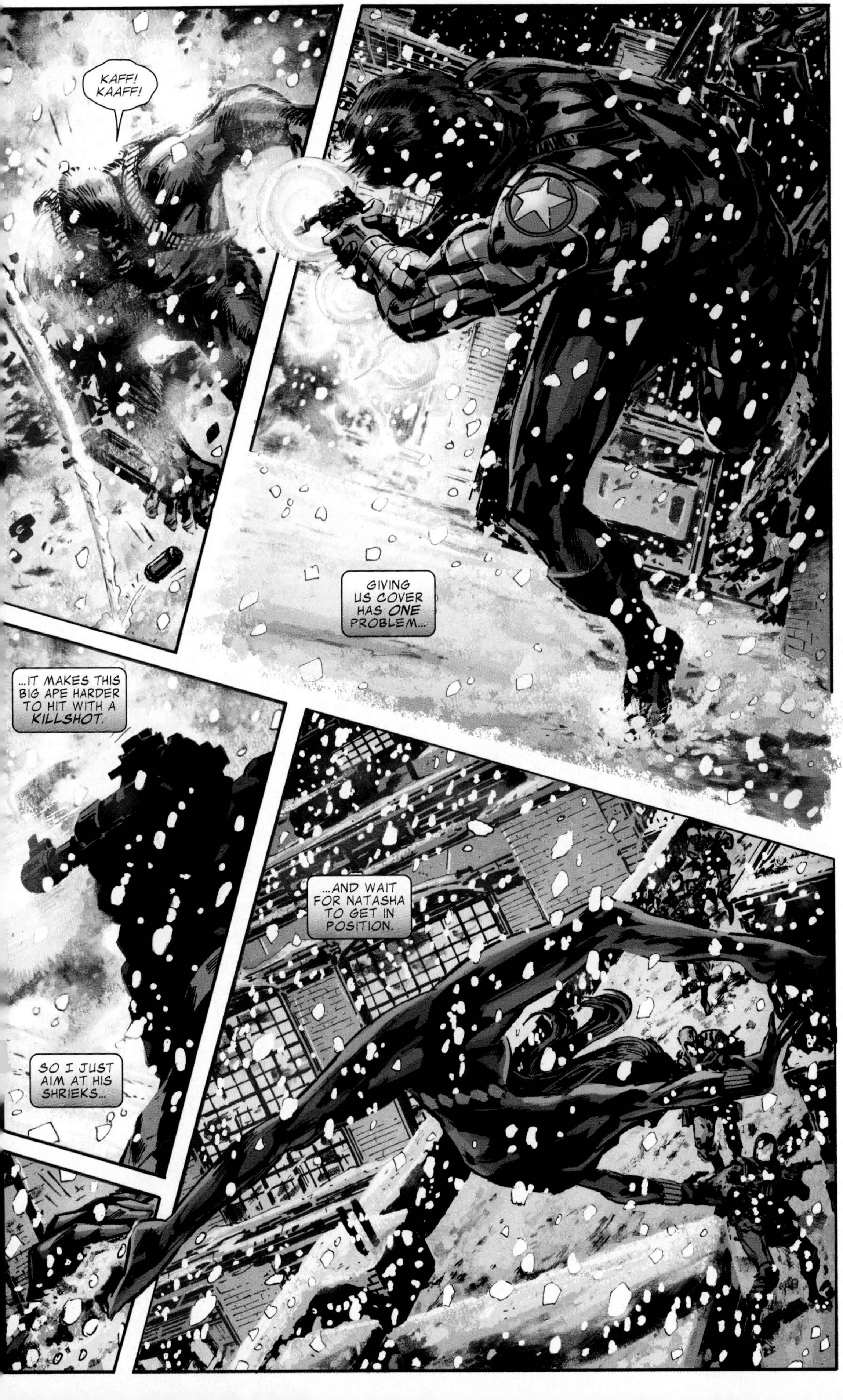
KAFF! KAAFF!
GIVING US COVER HAS ONE PROBLEM...
...IT MAKES THIS BIG APE HARDER TO HIT WITH A KILLSHOT.
SO I JUST AIM AT HIS SHRIEKS...
...AND WAIT FOR NATASHA TO GET IN POSITION.

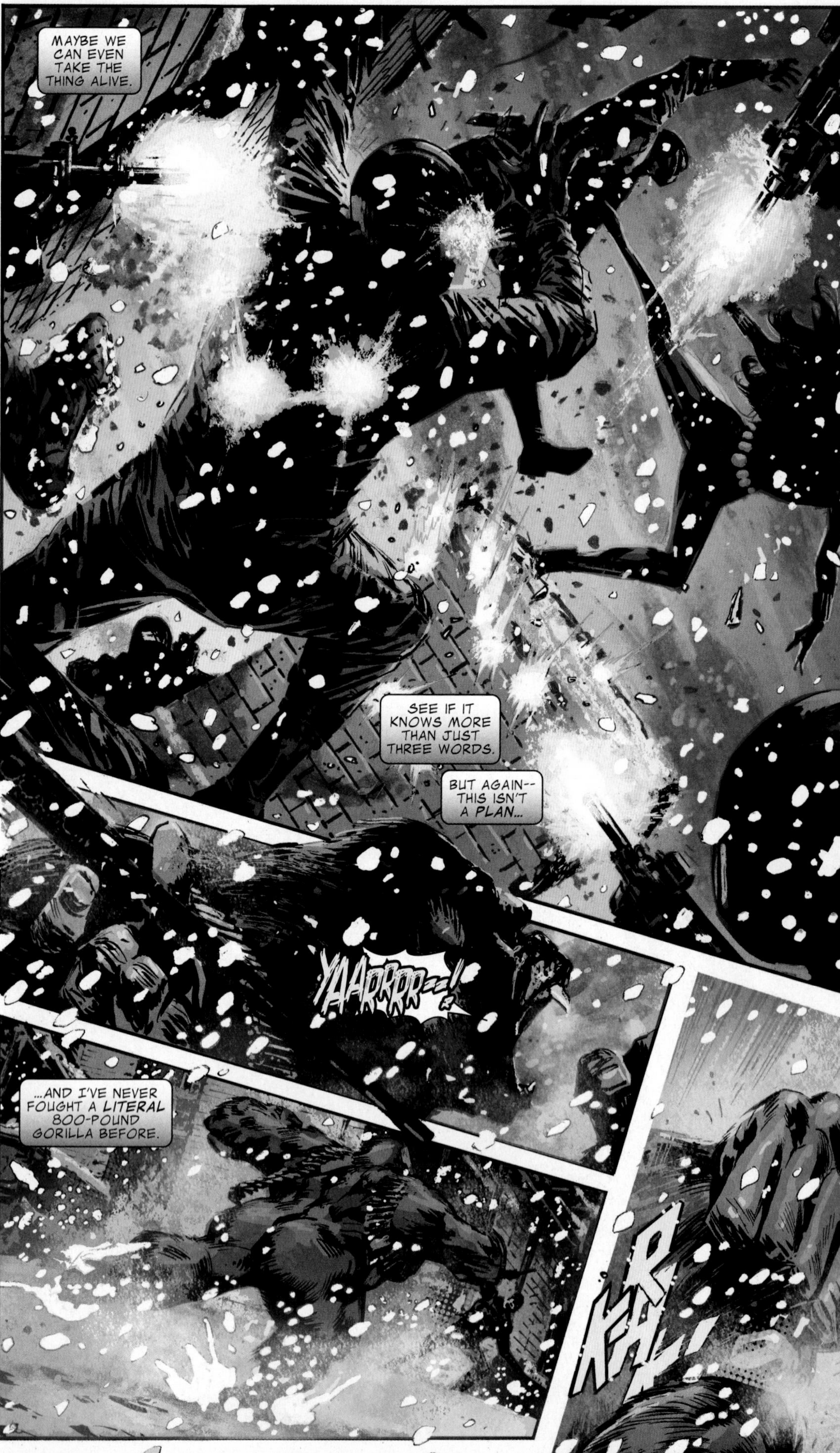
MAYBE WE CAN EVEN TAKE THE THING ALIVE.
SEE IF IT KNOWS MORE THAN JUST THREE WORDS.
BUT AGAIN-- THIS ISN'T A PLAN...
YAARRRR--!
...AND I'VE NEVER FOUGHT A LITERAL 800-POUND GORILLA BEFORE.

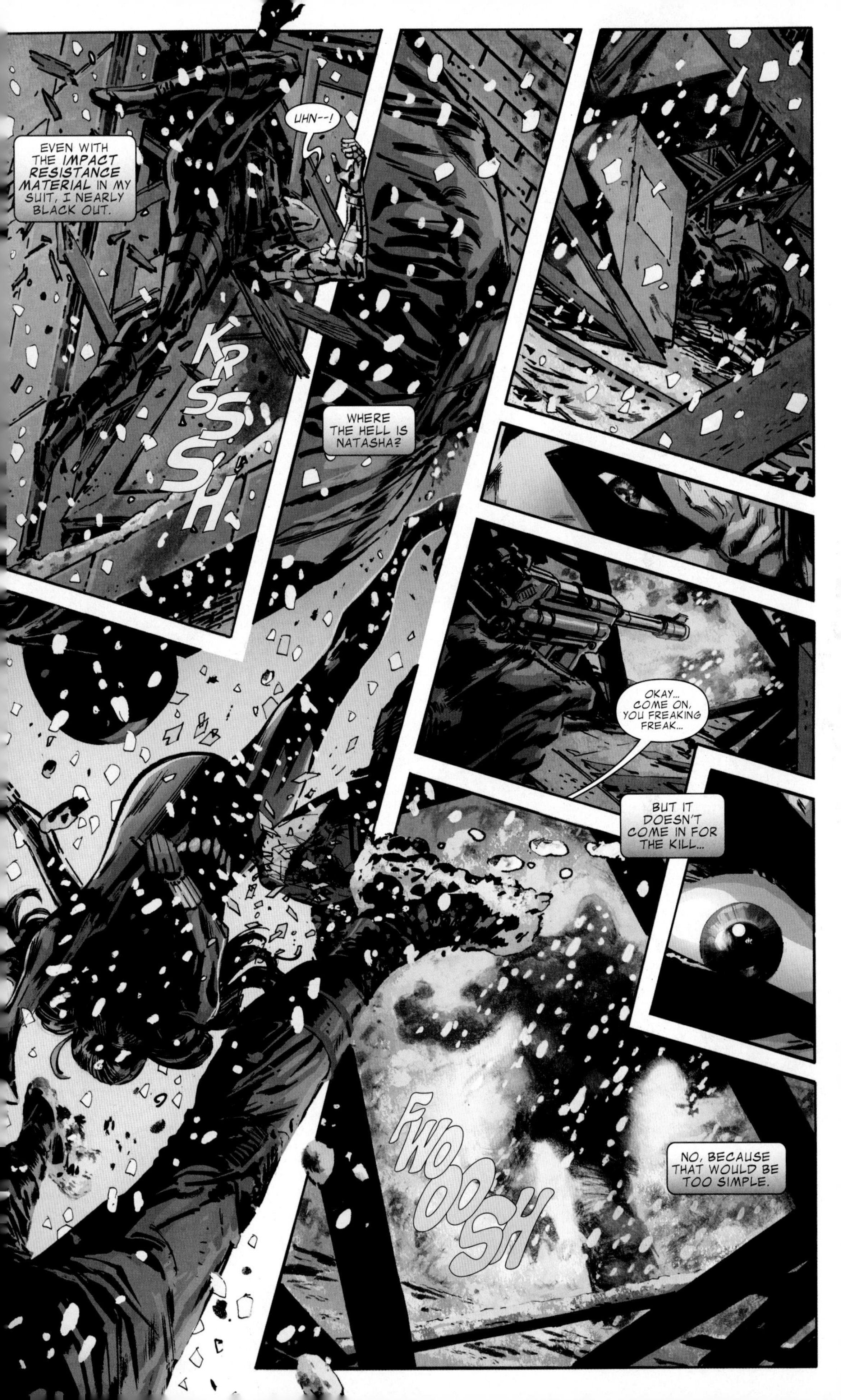

EVEN WITH THE IMPACT RESISTANCE MATERIAL IN MY SUIT, I NEARLY BLACK OUT.
UHN--!
KRSSSH
WHERE THE HELL IS NATASHA?
OKAY... COME ON, YOU FREAKING FREAK...
BUT IT DOESN'T COME IN FOR THE KILL...
FWOOOSH
NO, BECAUSE THAT WOULD BE TOO SIMPLE.

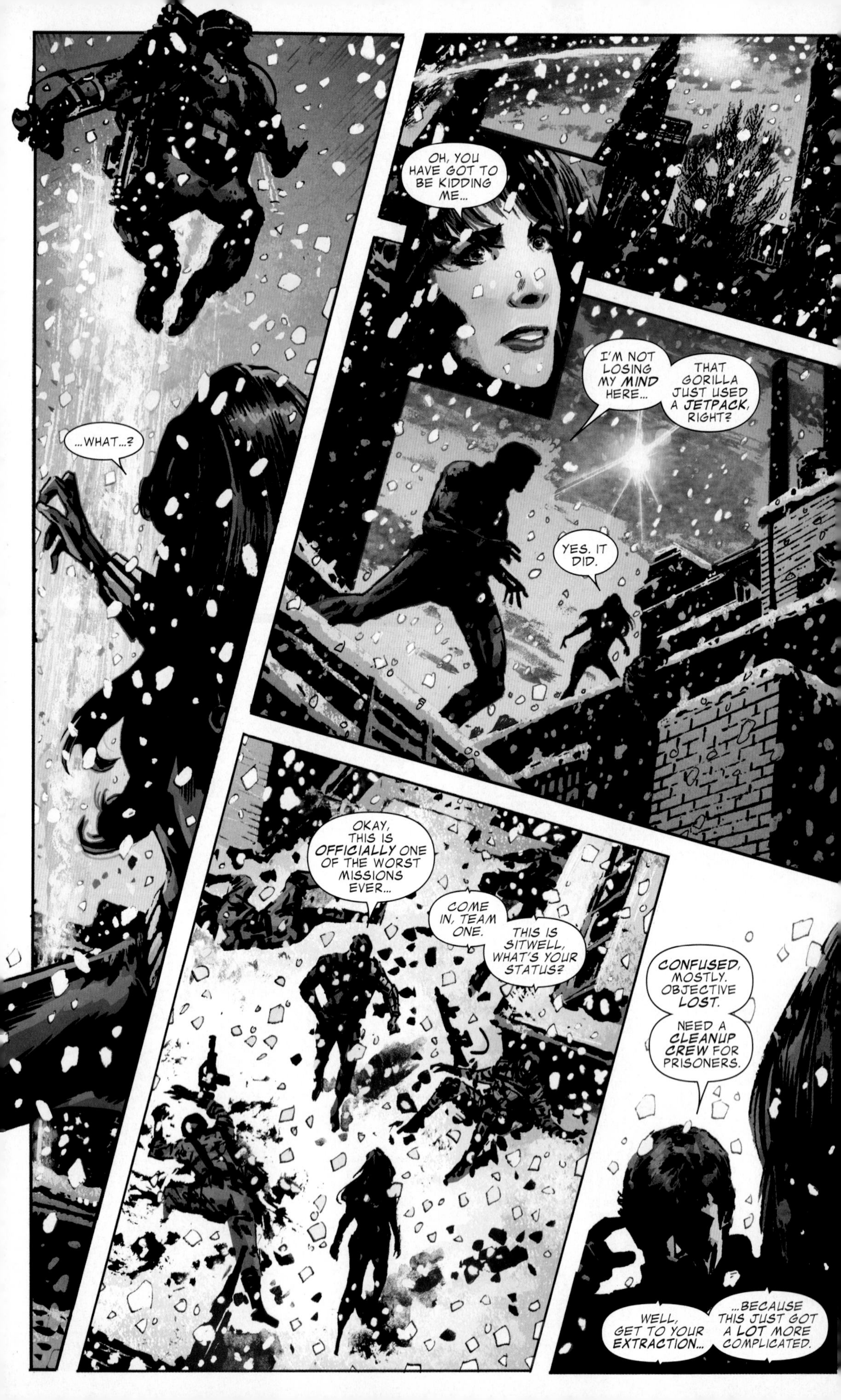

...WHAT...?
OH, YOU HAVE GOT TO BE KIDDING ME...
I'M NOT LOSING MY MIND HERE...
THAT GORILLA JUST USED A JETPACK, RIGHT?
YES. IT DID.
OKAY, THIS IS OFFICIALLY ONE OF THE WORST MISSIONS EVER...
COME IN, TEAM ONE.
THIS IS SITWELL, WHAT'S YOUR STATUS?
CONFUSED, MOSTLY. OBJECTIVE LOST.
NEED A CLEANUP CREW FOR PRISONERS.
WELL, GET TO YOUR EXTRACTION...
...BECAUSE THIS JUST GOT A LOT MORE COMPLICATED.

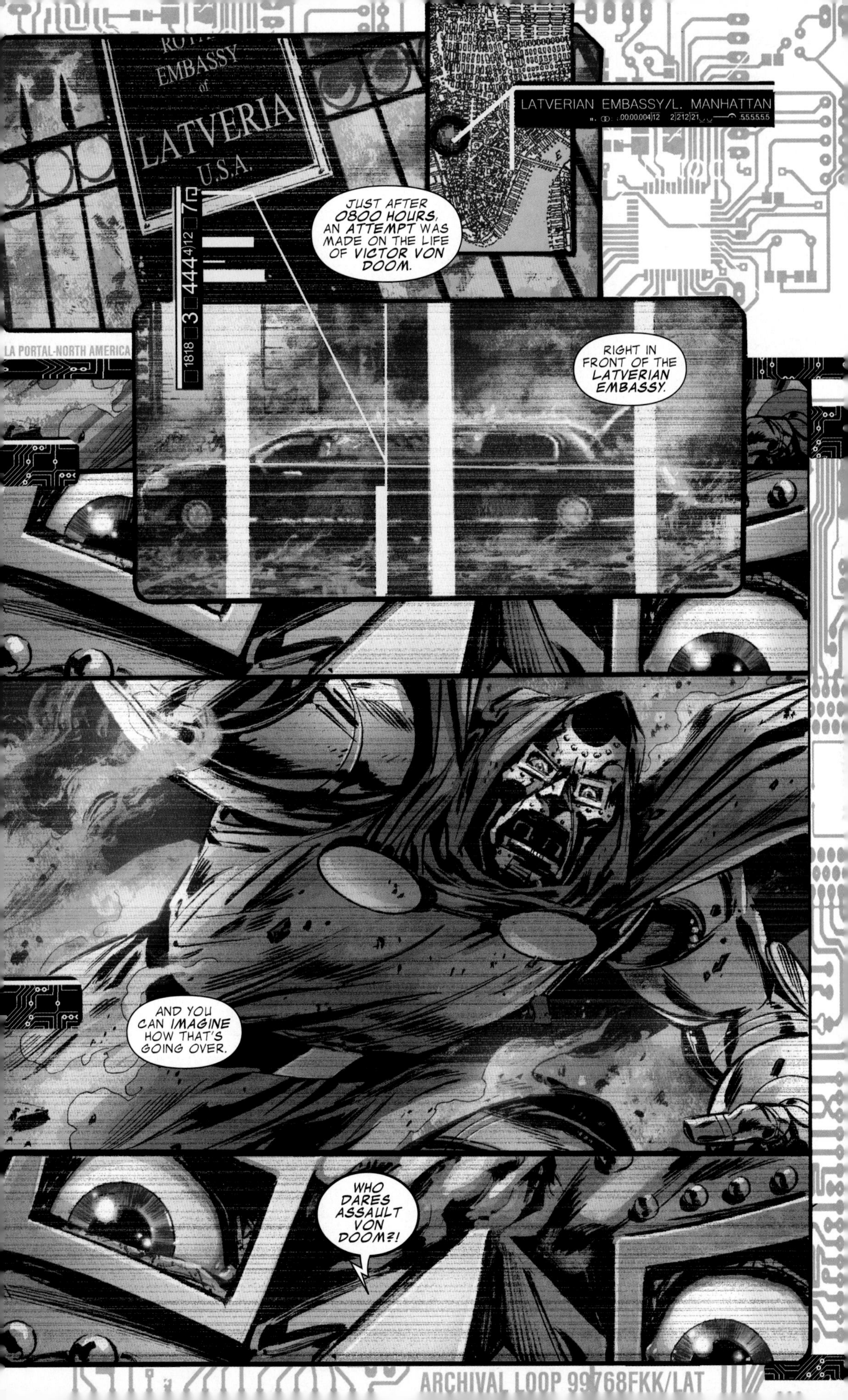

ROYAL EMBASSY of LATVERIA U.S.A.
LATVERIAN EMBASSY/L. MANHATTAN
JUST AFTER 0800 HOURS, AN ATTEMPT WAS MADE ON THE LIFE OF VICTOR VON DOOM.
LA PORTAL-NORTH AMERICA
RIGHT IN FRONT OF THE LATVERIAN EMBASSY.
AND YOU CAN IMAGINE HOW THAT'S GOING OVER.
WHO DARES ASSAULT VON DOOM?!
ARCHIVAL LOOP 99768FKK/LAT

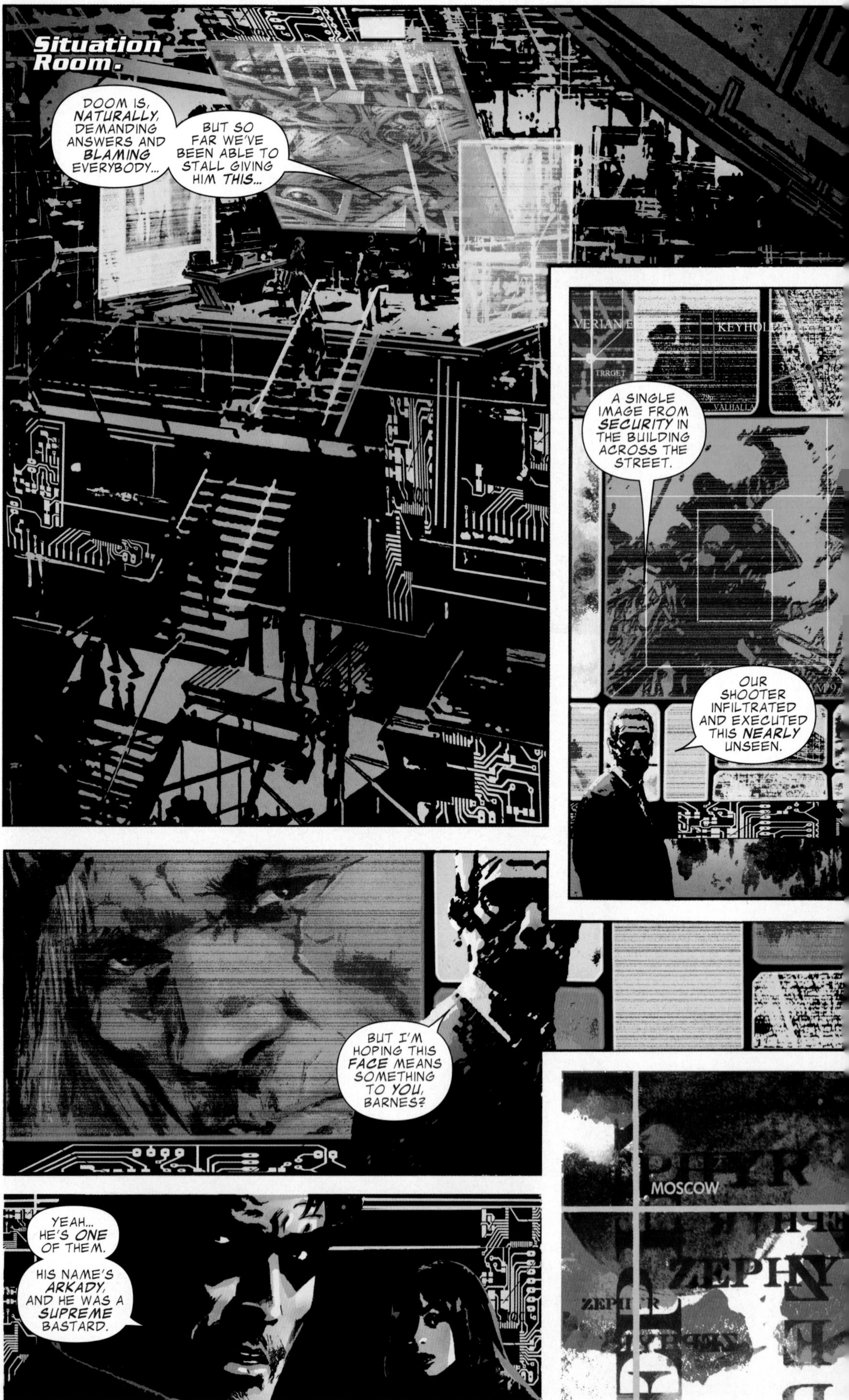
Situation Room.
DOOM IS, NATURALLY, DEMANDING ANSWERS AND BLAMING EVERYBODY...
BUT SO FAR WE'VE BEEN ABLE TO STALL GIVING HIM THIS...
VERIAN
KEYHOLE
TRRGET
VALHALLA
A SINGLE IMAGE FROM SECURITY IN THE BUILDING ACROSS THE STREET.
OUR SHOOTER INFILTRATED AND EXECUTED THIS NEARLY UNSEEN.
BUT I'M HOPING THIS FACE MEANS SOMETHING TO YOU, BARNES?
MOSCOW
ZEPHY
YEAH... HE'S ONE OF THEM.
HIS NAME'S ARKADY, AND HE WAS A SUPREME BASTARD.

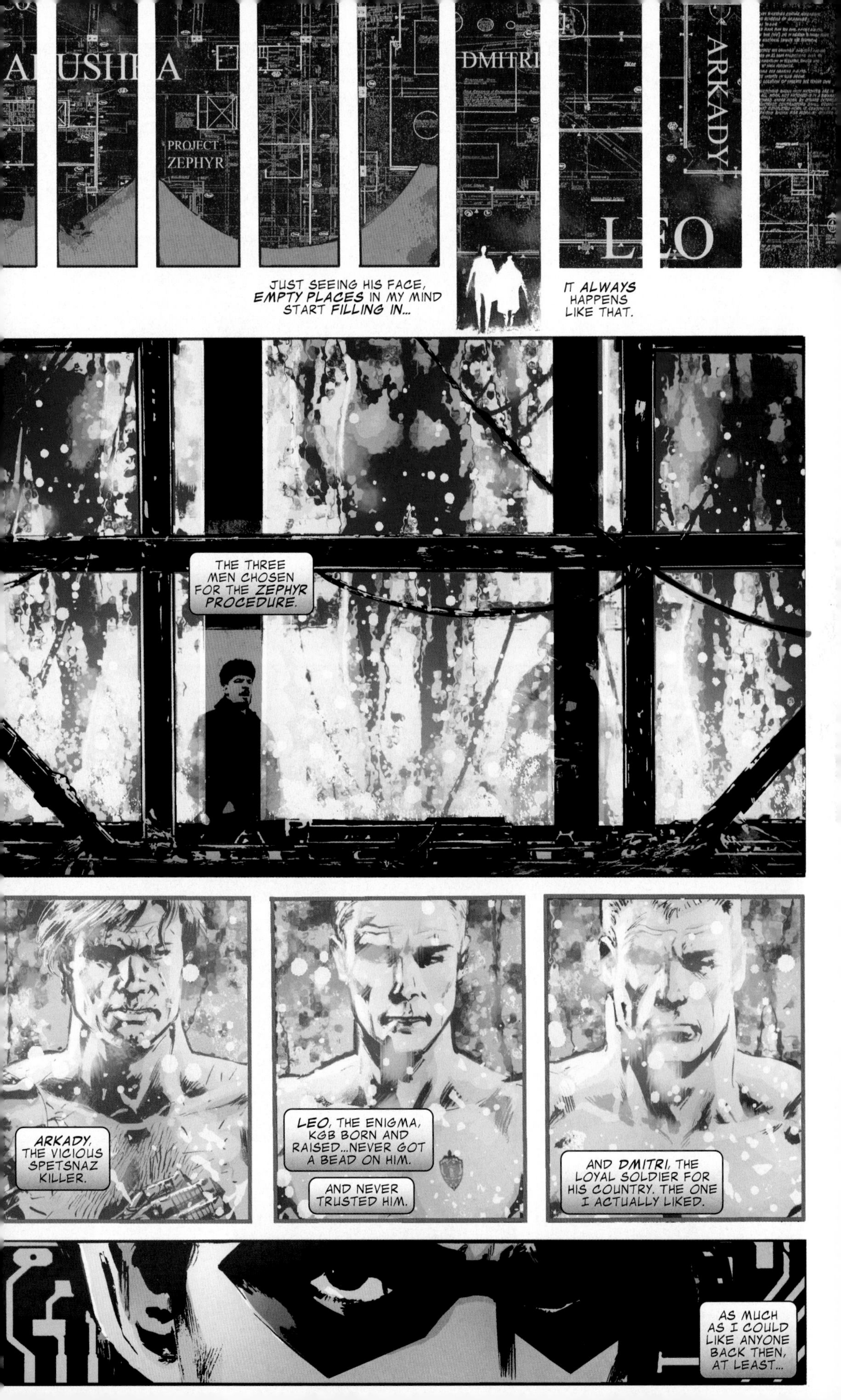

AKUSHKA
PROJECT ZEPHYR
DMITRI
ARKADY
LEO
JUST SEEING HIS FACE, EMPTY PLACES IN MY MIND START FILLING IN...
IT ALWAYS HAPPENS LIKE THAT.
THE THREE MEN CHOSEN FOR THE ZEPHYR PROCEDURE.
ARKADY, THE VICIOUS SPETSNAZ KILLER.
LEO, THE ENIGMA, KGB BORN AND RAISED...NEVER GOT A BEAD ON HIM.
AND NEVER TRUSTED HIM.
AND DMITRI, THE LOYAL SOLDIER FOR HIS COUNTRY. THE ONE I ACTUALLY LIKED.
AS MUCH AS I COULD LIKE ANYONE BACK THEN, AT LEAST...

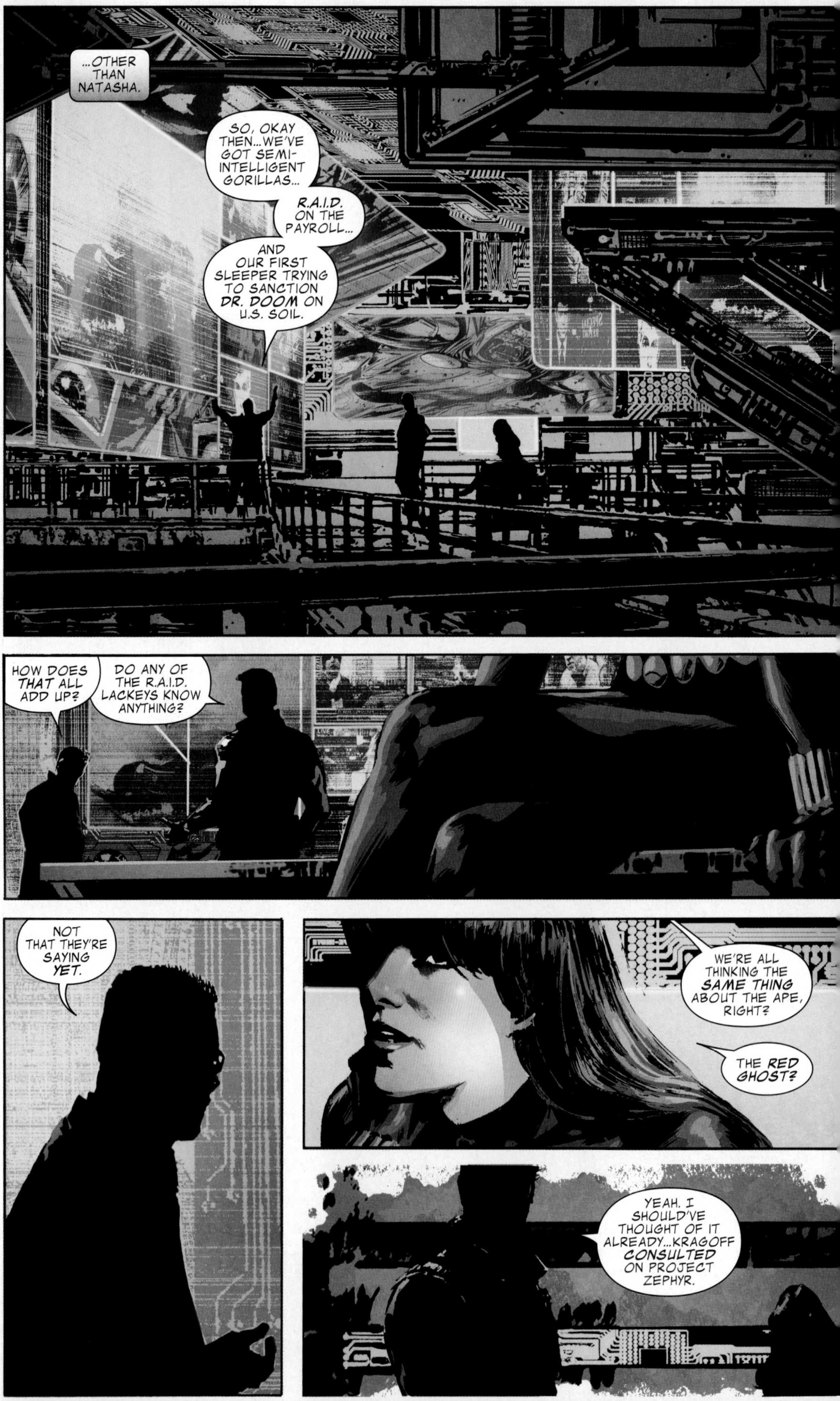
...OTHER THAN NATASHA.
SO, OKAY THEN...WE'VE GOT SEMI-INTELLIGENT GORILLAS...
R.A.I.D. ON THE PAYROLL...
AND OUR FIRST SLEEPER TRYING TO SANCTION DR. DOOM ON U.S. SOIL.
HOW DOES THAT ALL ADD UP?
DO ANY OF THE R.A.I.D. LACKEYS KNOW ANYTHING?
NOT THAT THEY'RE SAYING YET.
WE'RE ALL THINKING THE SAME THING ABOUT THE APE, RIGHT?
THE RED GHOST?
YEAH. I SHOULD'VE THOUGHT OF IT ALREADY...KRAGOFF CONSULTED ON PROJECT ZEPHYR.

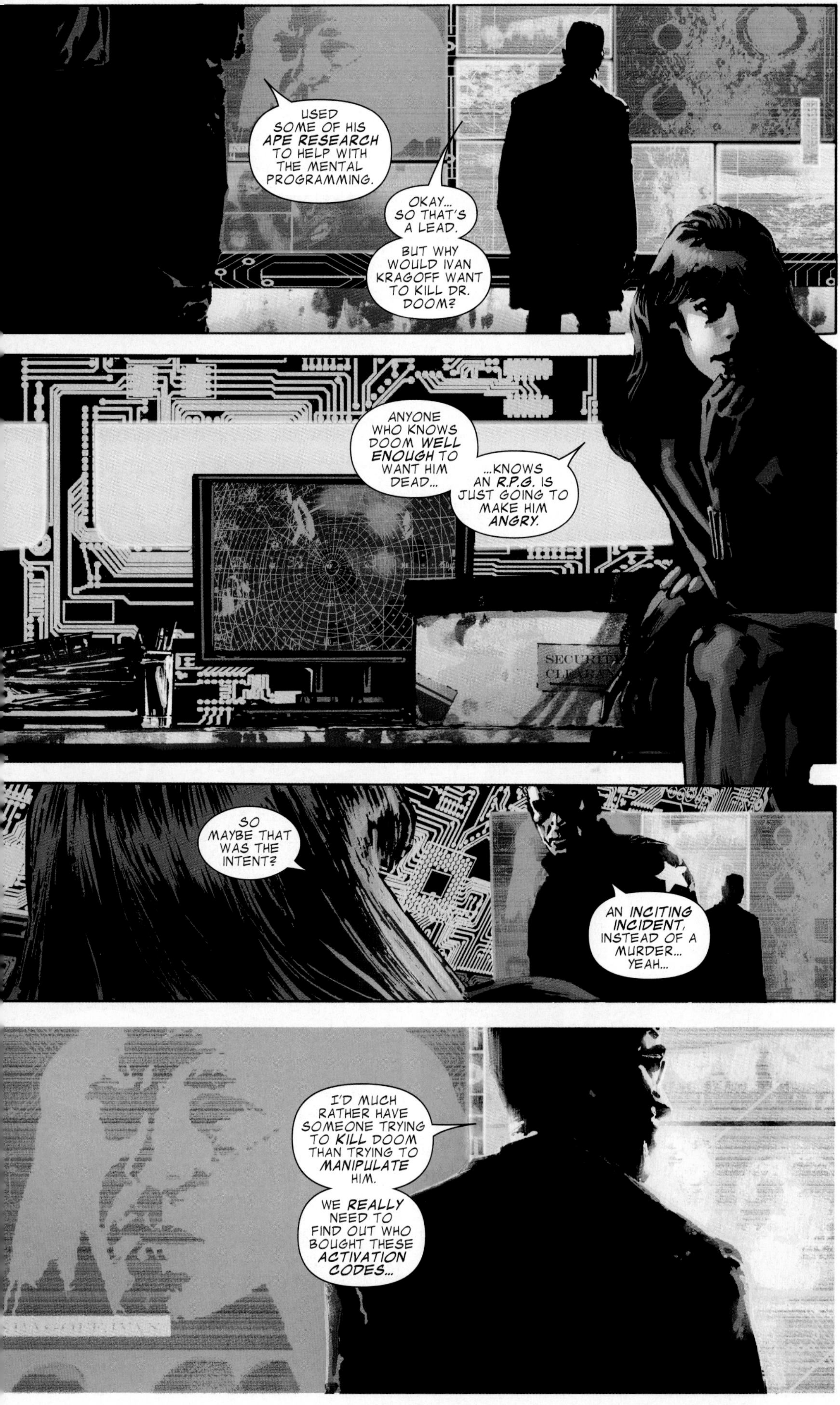

USED SOME OF HIS APE RESEARCH TO HELP WITH THE MENTAL PROGRAMMING.
OKAY... SO THAT'S A LEAD.
BUT WHY WOULD IVAN KRAGOFF WANT TO KILL DR. DOOM?
ANYONE WHO KNOWS DOOM WELL ENOUGH TO WANT HIM DEAD...
...KNOWS AN R.P.G. IS JUST GOING TO MAKE HIM ANGRY.
SO MAYBE THAT WAS THE INTENT?
AN INCITING INCIDENT, INSTEAD OF A MURDER... YEAH...
I'D MUCH RATHER HAVE SOMEONE TRYING TO KILL DOOM THAN TRYING TO MANIPULATE HIM.
WE REALLY NEED TO FIND OUT WHO BOUGHT THESE ACTIVATION CODES...

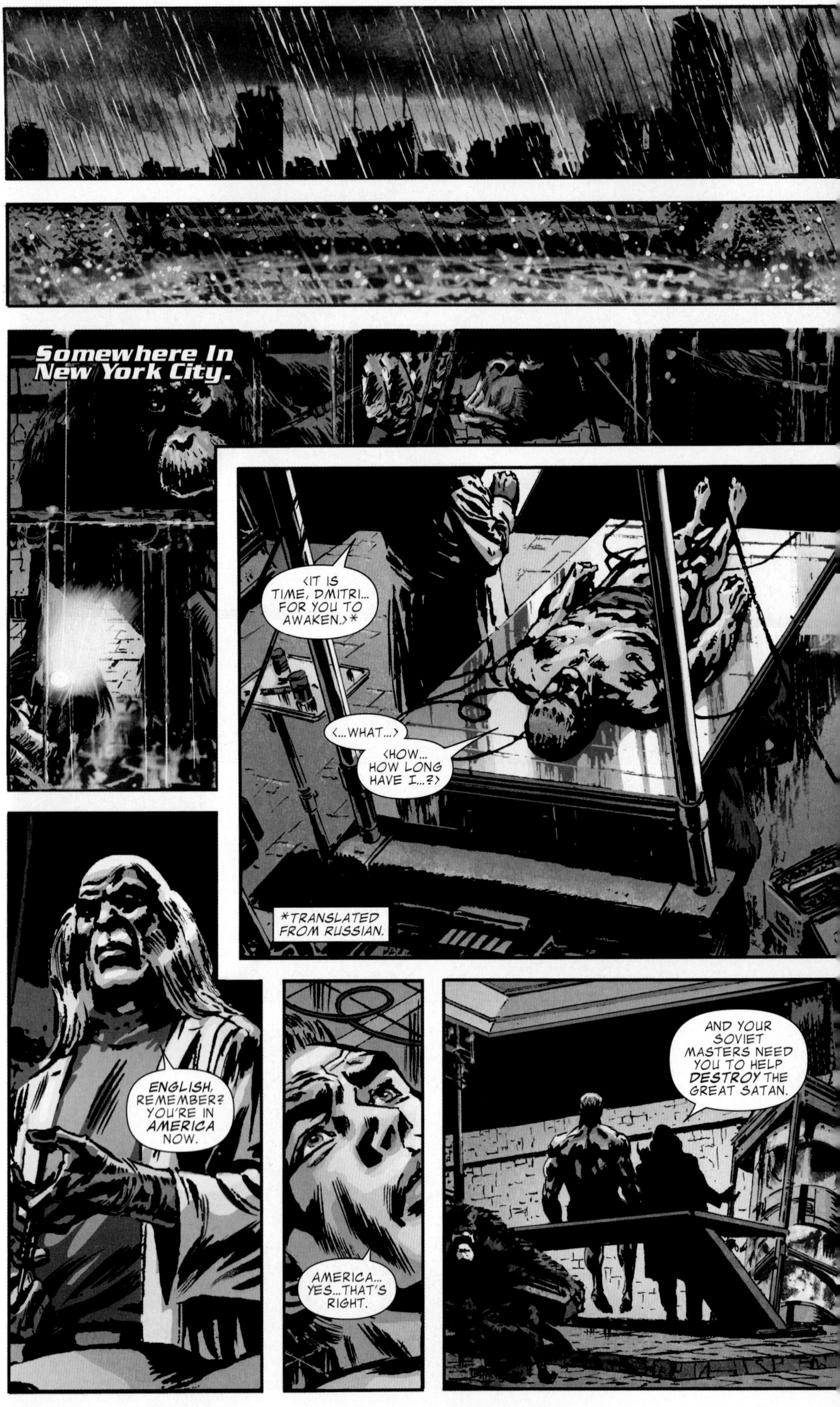
Somewhere In New York City.
<IT IS TIME, DMITRI... FOR YOU TO AWAKEN.>*
<...WHAT...>
<HOW... HOW LONG HAVE I...?>
*TRANSLATED FROM RUSSIAN.
ENGLISH, REMEMBER? YOU'RE IN AMERICA NOW.
AMERICA... YES...THAT'S RIGHT.
AND YOUR SOVIET MASTERS NEED YOU TO HELP DESTROY THE GREAT SATAN.

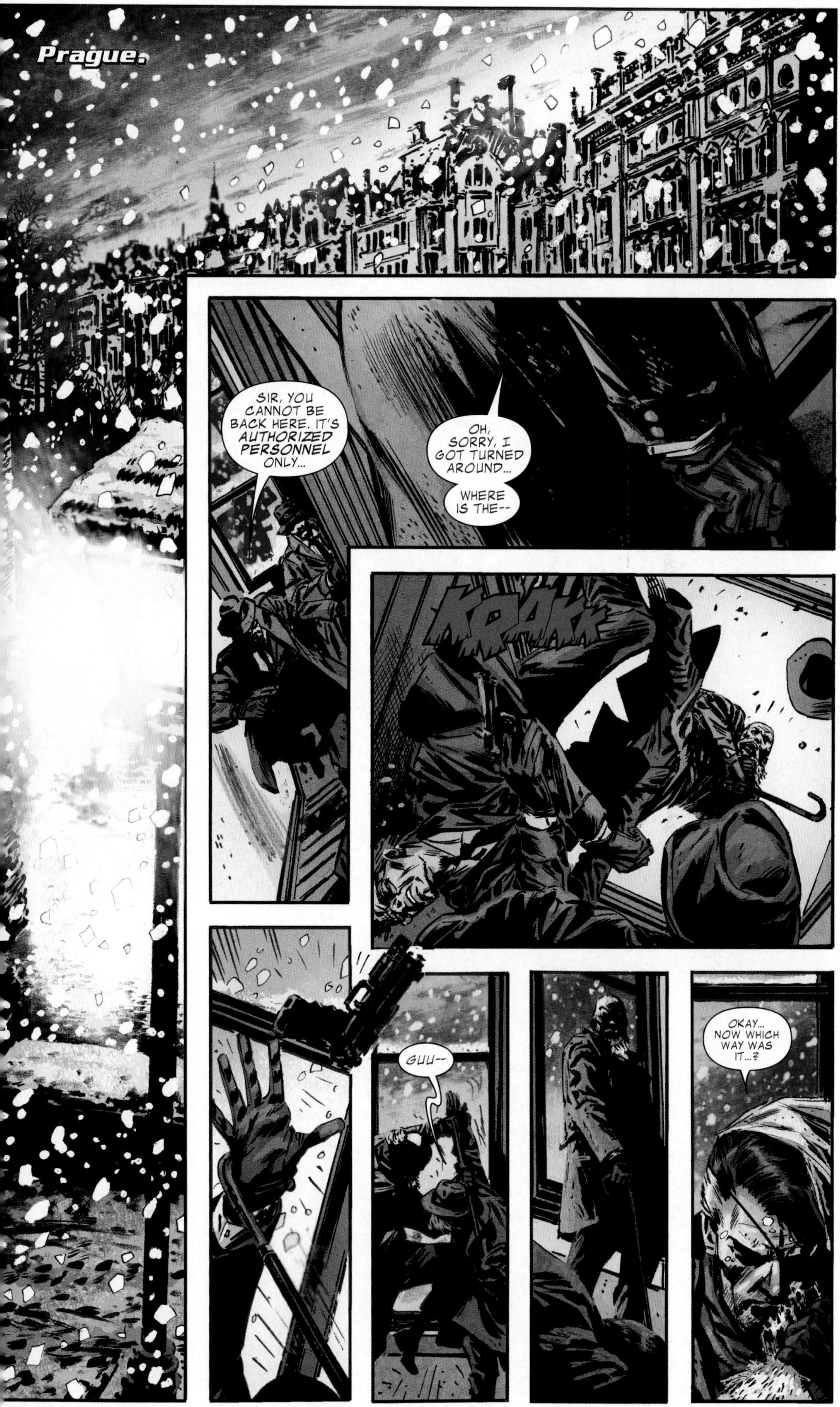
Prague.
SIR, YOU CANNOT BE BACK HERE. IT'S AUTHORIZED PERSONNEL ONLY...
OH, SORRY, I GOT TURNED AROUND...
WHERE IS THE--
KRAKK
GUU--
OKAY... NOW WHICH WAY WAS IT...?

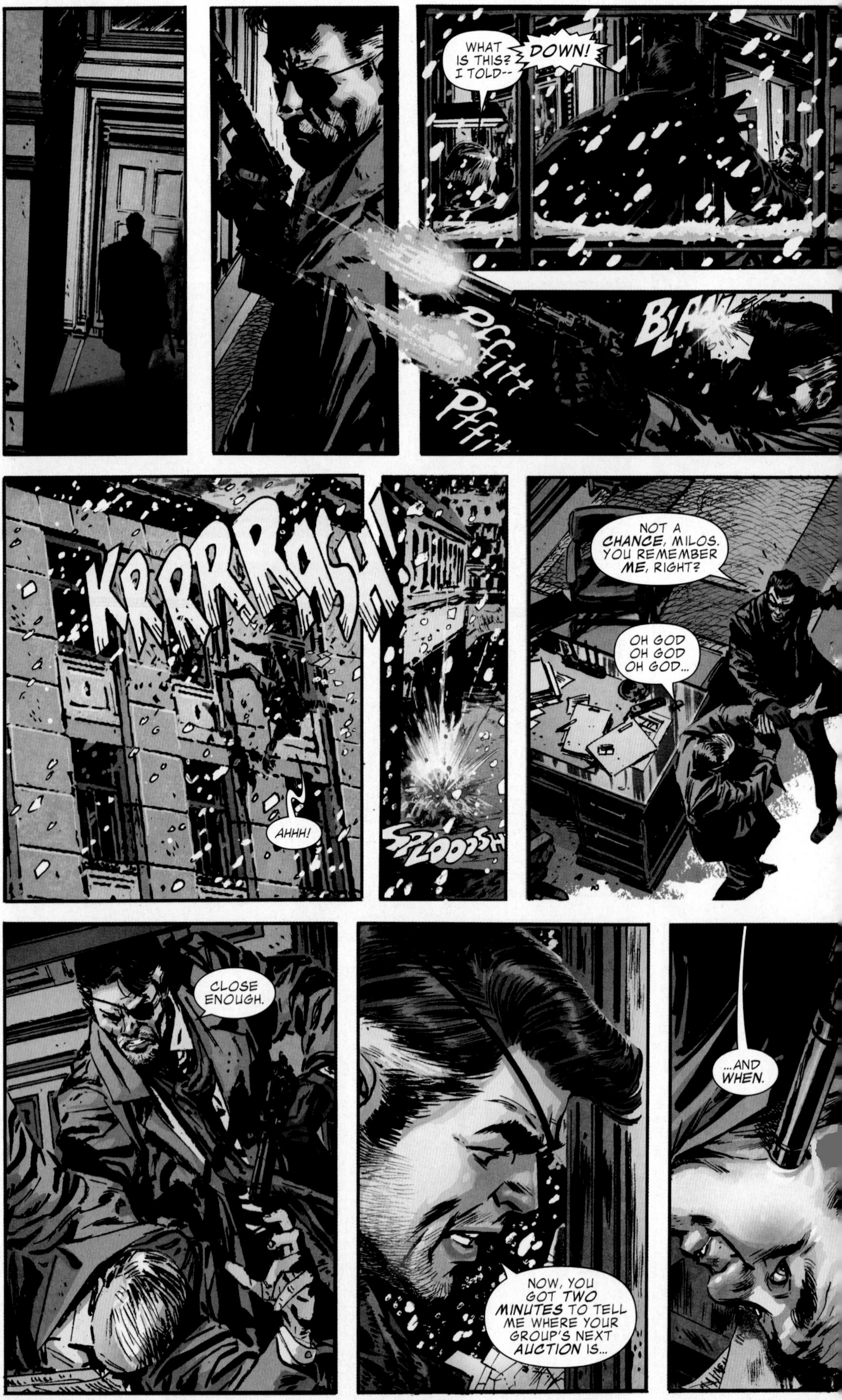

WHAT IS THIS? I TOLD--
DOWN!
PFFITT
PFFITT
BLAM
KRRRRASH!
AHHH!
SPLOOOSH
NOT A CHANCE, MILOS. YOU REMEMBER ME, RIGHT?
OH GOD OH GOD OH GOD...
CLOSE ENOUGH.
NOW, YOU GOT TWO MINUTES TO TELL ME WHERE YOUR GROUP'S NEXT AUCTION IS...
...AND WHEN.

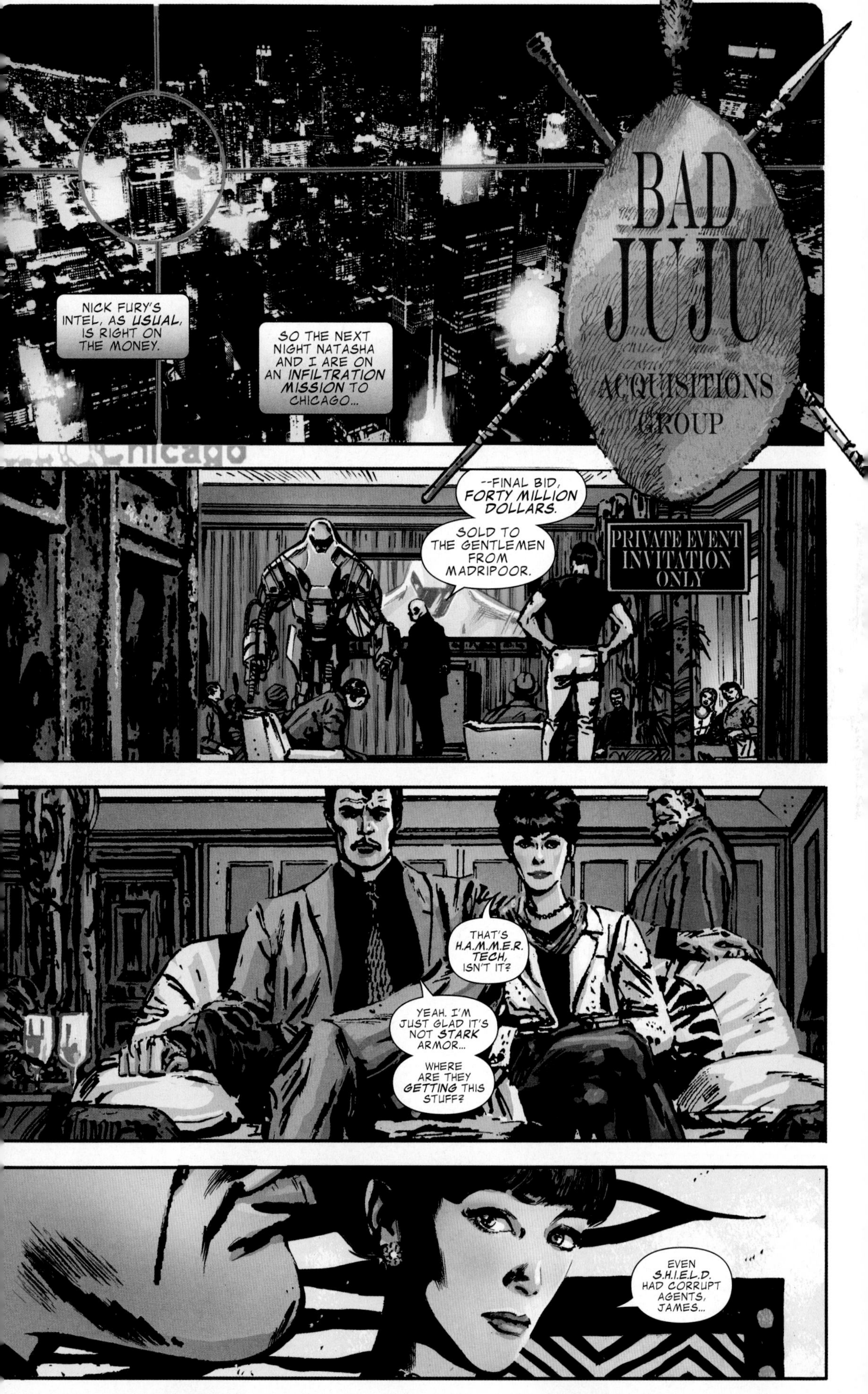

BAD JUJU ACQUISITIONS GROUP
NICK FURY'S INTEL, AS USUAL, IS RIGHT ON THE MONEY.
SO THE NEXT NIGHT NATASHA AND I ARE ON AN INFILTRATION MISSION TO CHICAGO...
--FINAL BID, FORTY MILLION DOLLARS.
SOLD TO THE GENTLEMEN FROM MADRIPOOR.
PRIVATE EVENT INVITATION ONLY
THAT'S H.A.M.M.E.R. TECH, ISN'T IT?
YEAH. I'M JUST GLAD IT'S NOT STARK ARMOR...
WHERE ARE THEY GETTING THIS STUFF?
EVEN S.H.I.E.L.D. HAD CORRUPT AGENTS, JAMES...

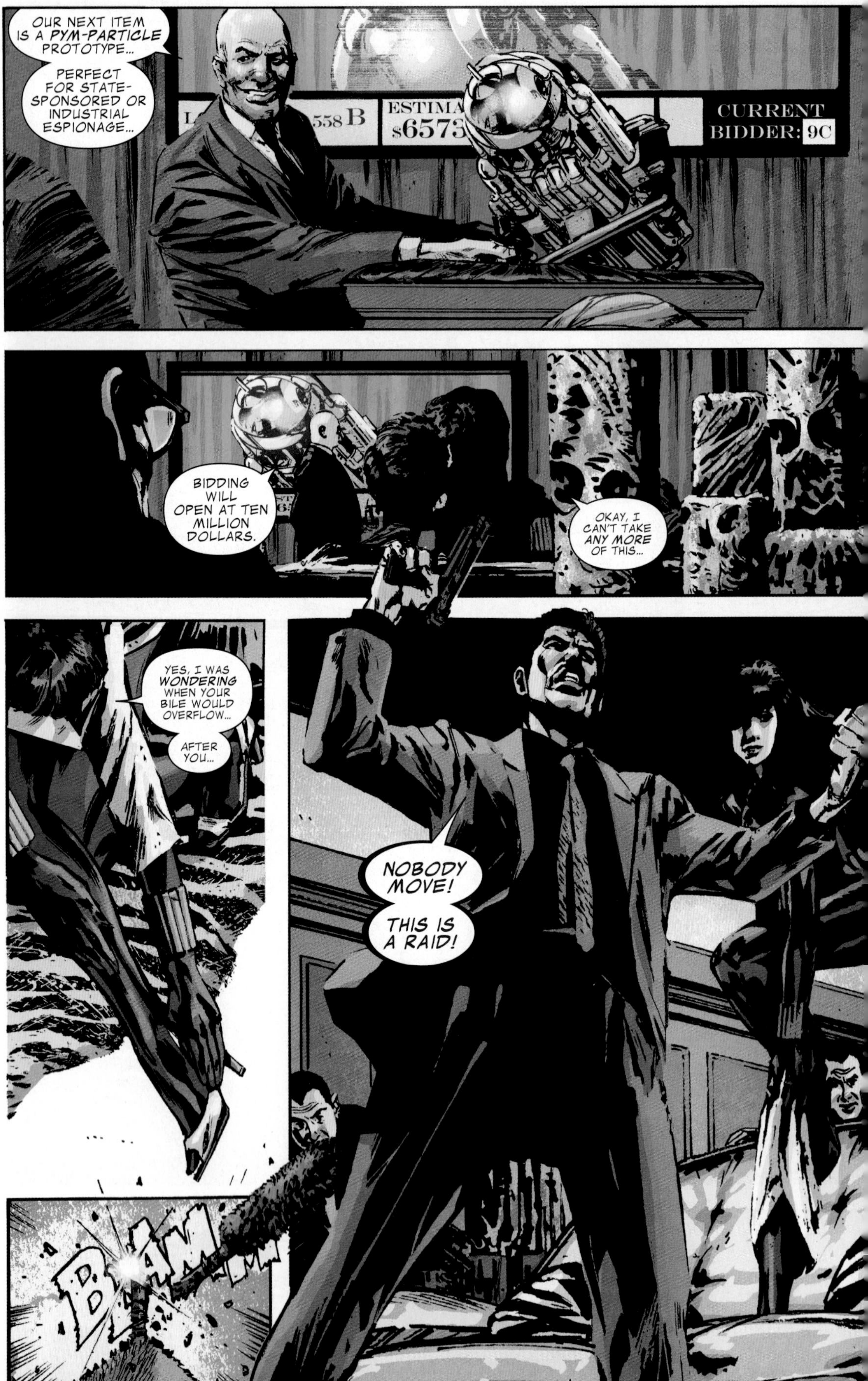

OUR NEXT ITEM IS A PYM-PARTICLE PROTOTYPE...
PERFECT FOR STATE-SPONSORED OR INDUSTRIAL ESPIONAGE...
558 B
ESTIMA
$6573
CURRENT BIDDER: 9C
BIDDING WILL OPEN AT TEN MILLION DOLLARS.
OKAY, I CAN'T TAKE ANY MORE OF THIS...
YES, I WAS WONDERING WHEN YOUR BILE WOULD OVERFLOW...
AFTER YOU...
...
NOBODY MOVE!
THIS IS A RAID!
BDAM

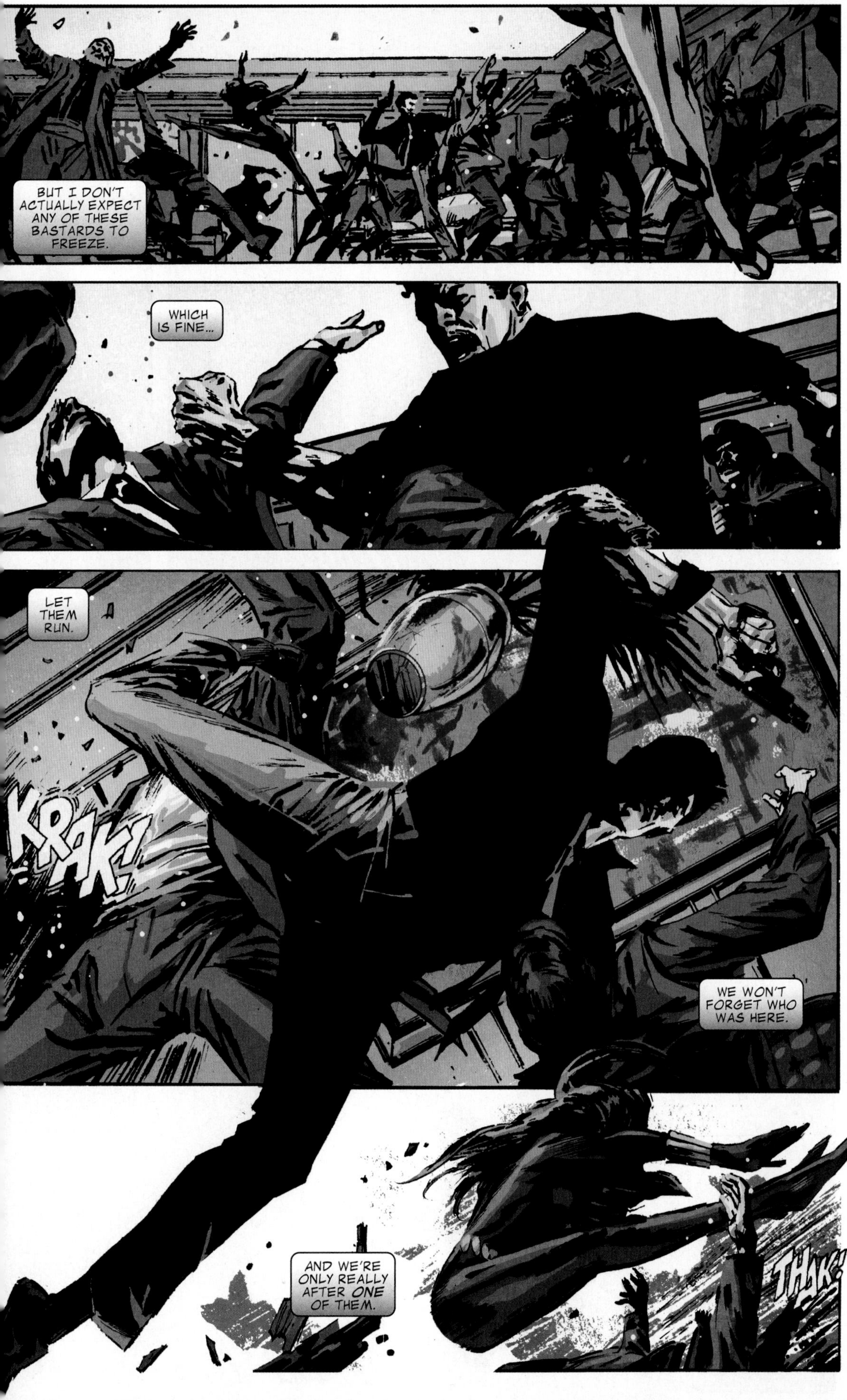
BUT I DON'T ACTUALLY EXPECT ANY OF THESE BASTARDS TO FREEZE.
WHICH IS FINE...
LET THEM RUN.
KRAK!
WE WON'T FORGET WHO WAS HERE.
AND WE'RE ONLY REALLY AFTER ONE OF THEM.
THAK!

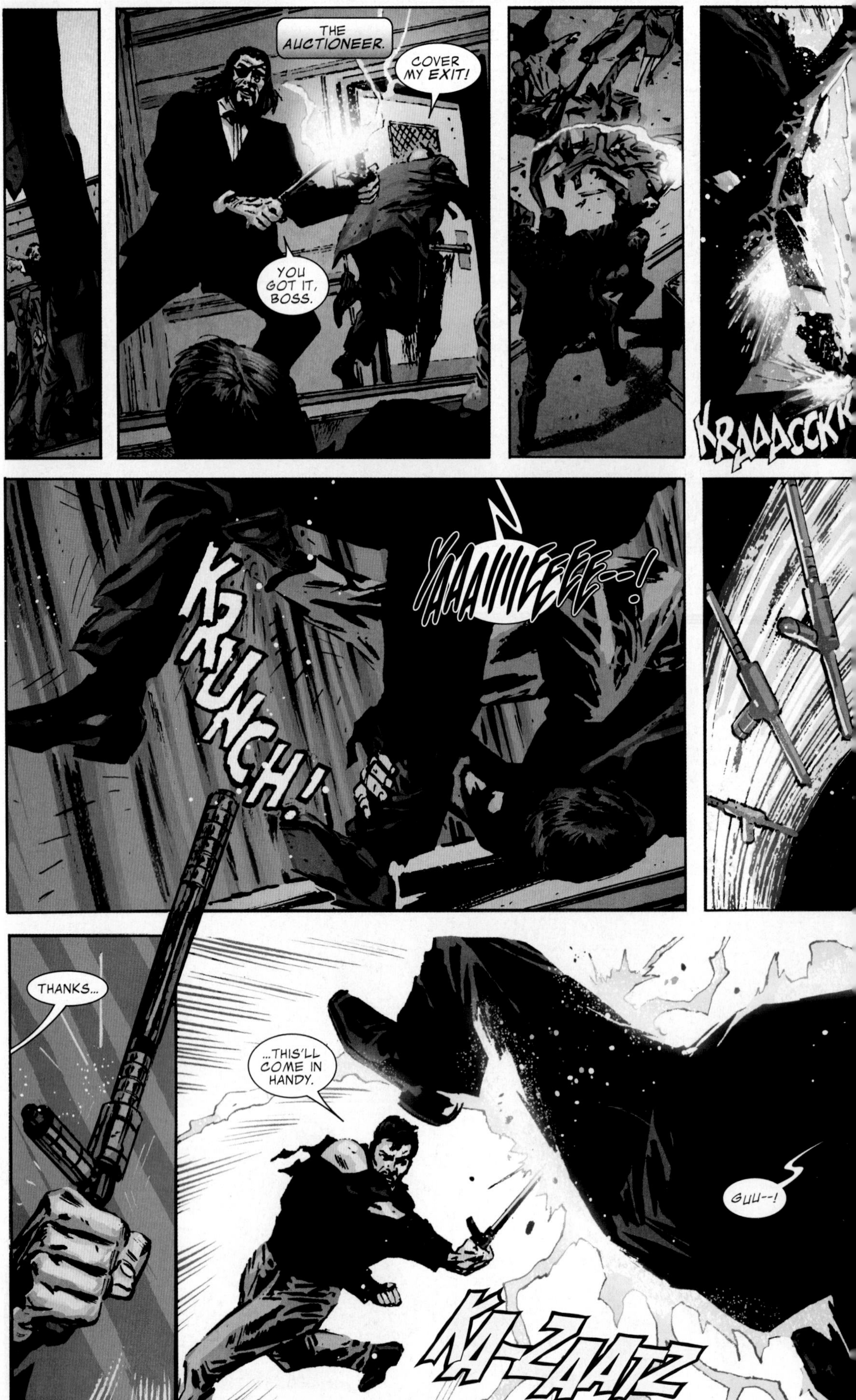
THE AUCTIONEER.
COVER MY EXIT!
YOU GOT IT, BOSS.
KRAAACCKK
KRUNCH!
YAAAIIIEEEE--!
THANKS...
...THIS'LL COME IN HANDY.
GUU--!
KA-ZAATZ

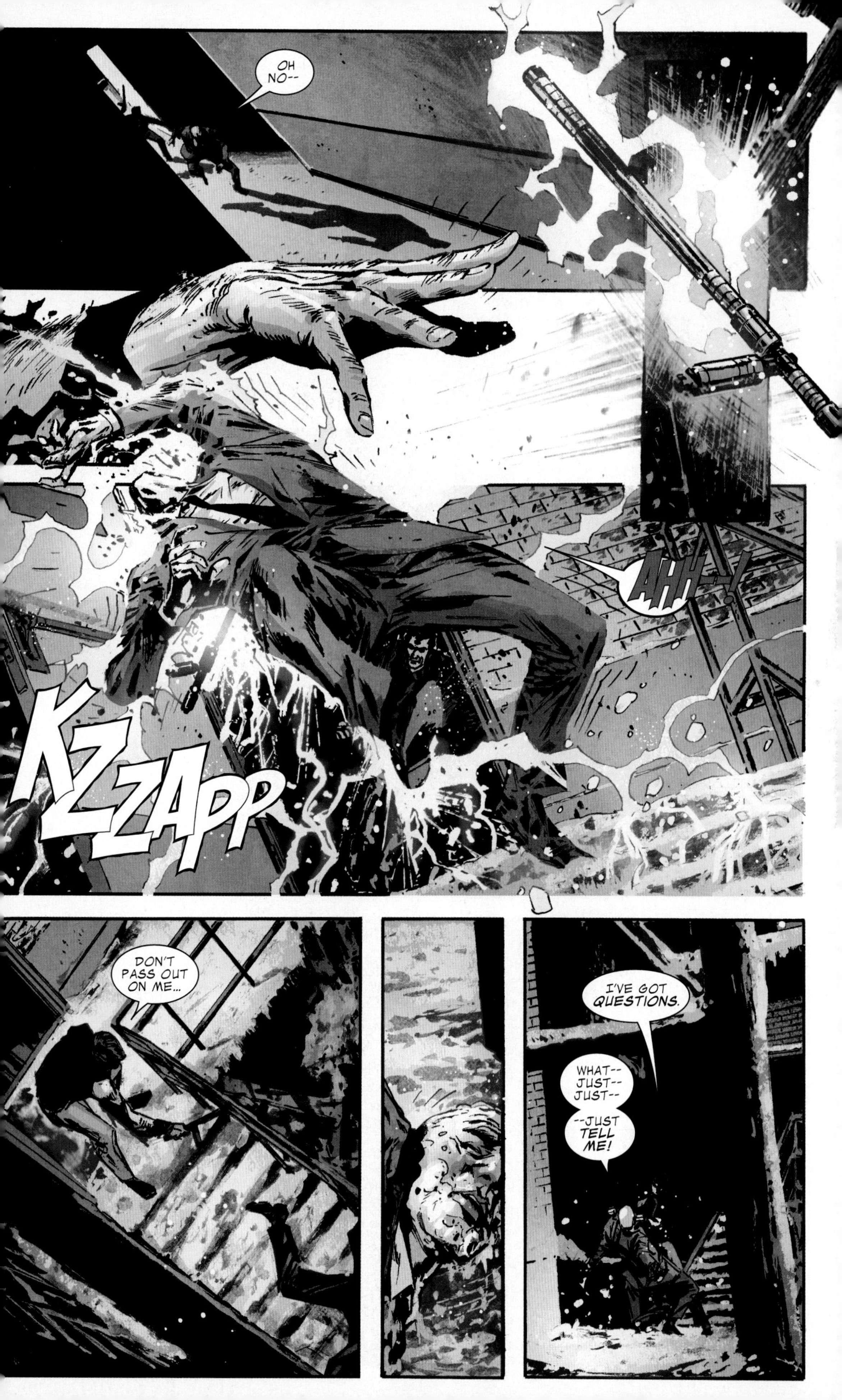
OH NO--
AHH--!!
KZZAPP
DON'T PASS OUT ON ME...
I'VE GOT QUESTIONS.
WHAT-- JUST-- JUST--
--JUST TELL ME!

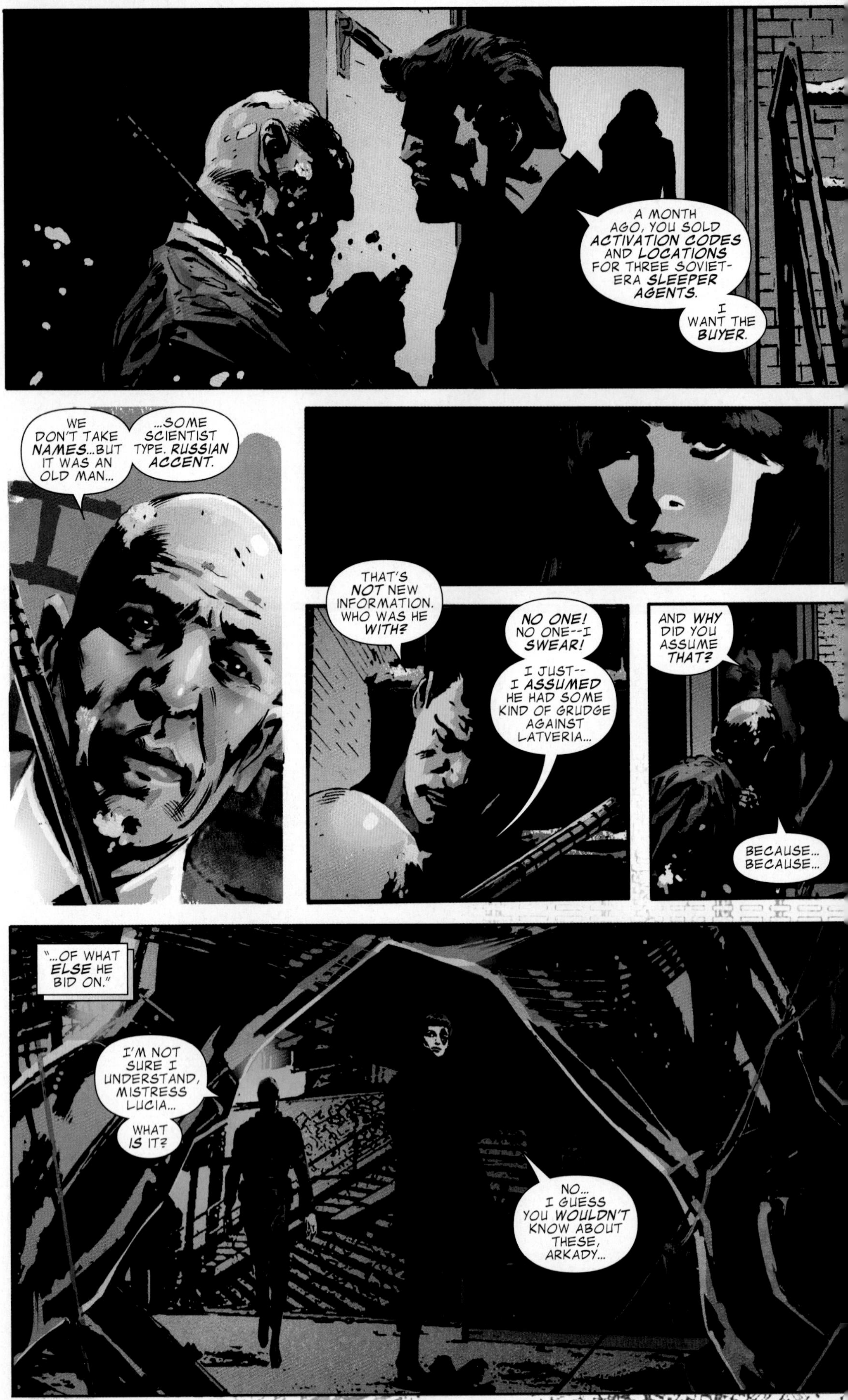
A MONTH AGO, YOU SOLD ACTIVATION CODES AND LOCATIONS FOR THREE SOVIET-ERA SLEEPER AGENTS.
I WANT THE BUYER.
WE DON'T TAKE NAMES...BUT IT WAS AN OLD MAN...
...SOME SCIENTIST TYPE. RUSSIAN ACCENT.
THAT'S NOT NEW INFORMATION. WHO WAS HE WITH?
NO ONE! NO ONE--I SWEAR!
I JUST-- I ASSUMED HE HAD SOME KIND OF GRUDGE AGAINST LATVERIA...
AND WHY DID YOU ASSUME THAT?
BECAUSE... BECAUSE...
"...OF WHAT ELSE HE BID ON."
I'M NOT SURE I UNDERSTAND, MISTRESS LUCIA...
WHAT IS IT?
NO... I GUESS YOU WOULDN'T KNOW ABOUT THESE, ARKADY...

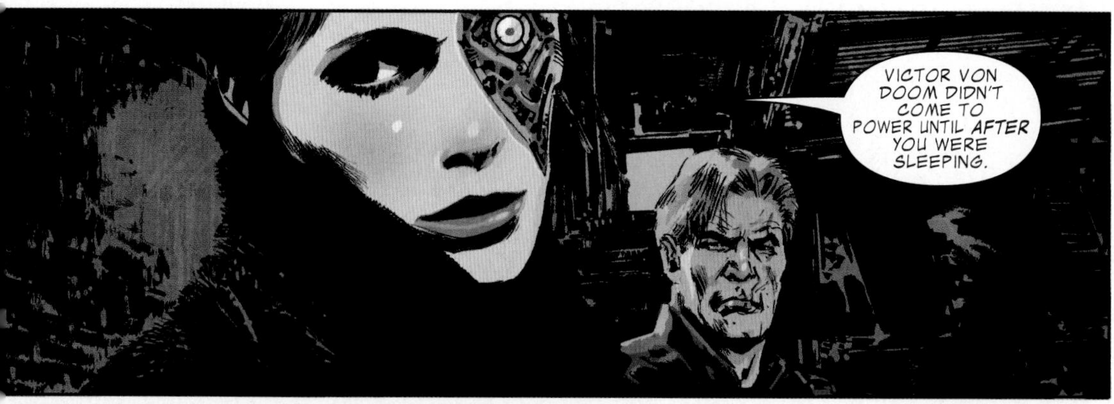
VICTOR VON DOOM DIDN'T COME TO POWER UNTIL AFTER YOU WERE SLEEPING.

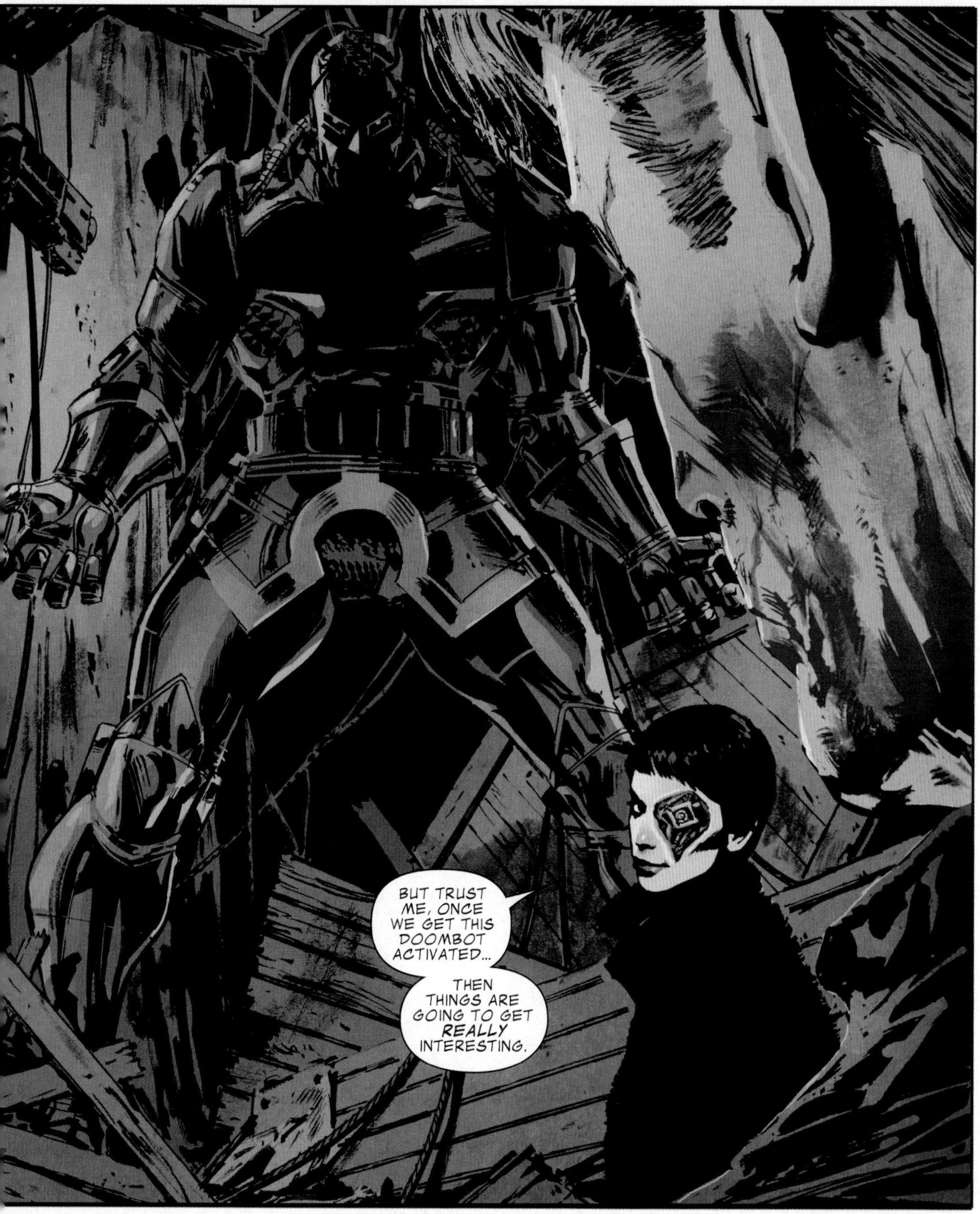
BUT TRUST ME, ONCE WE GET THIS DOOMBOT ACTIVATED...
THEN THINGS ARE GOING TO GET REALLY INTERESTING.

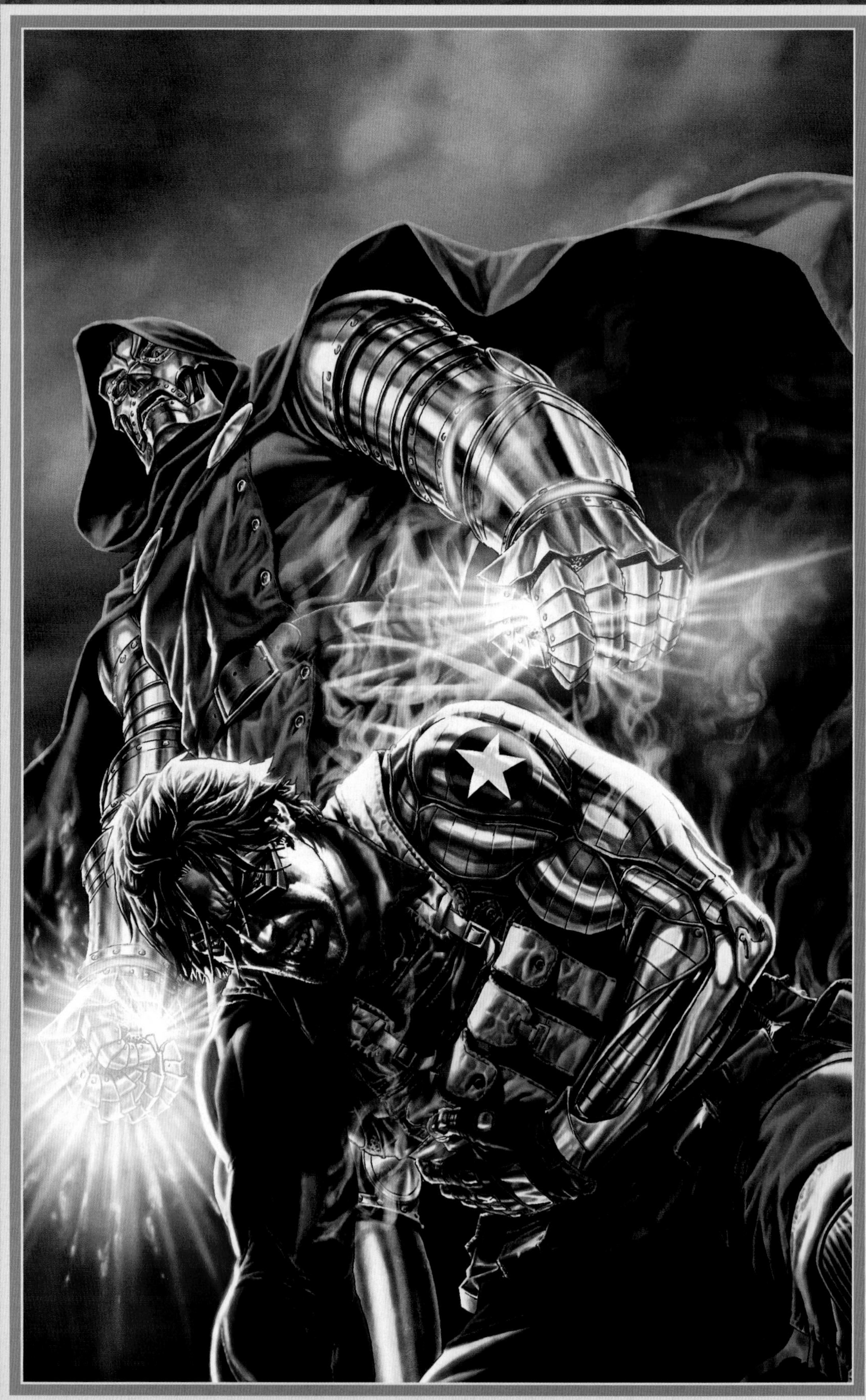

THREE

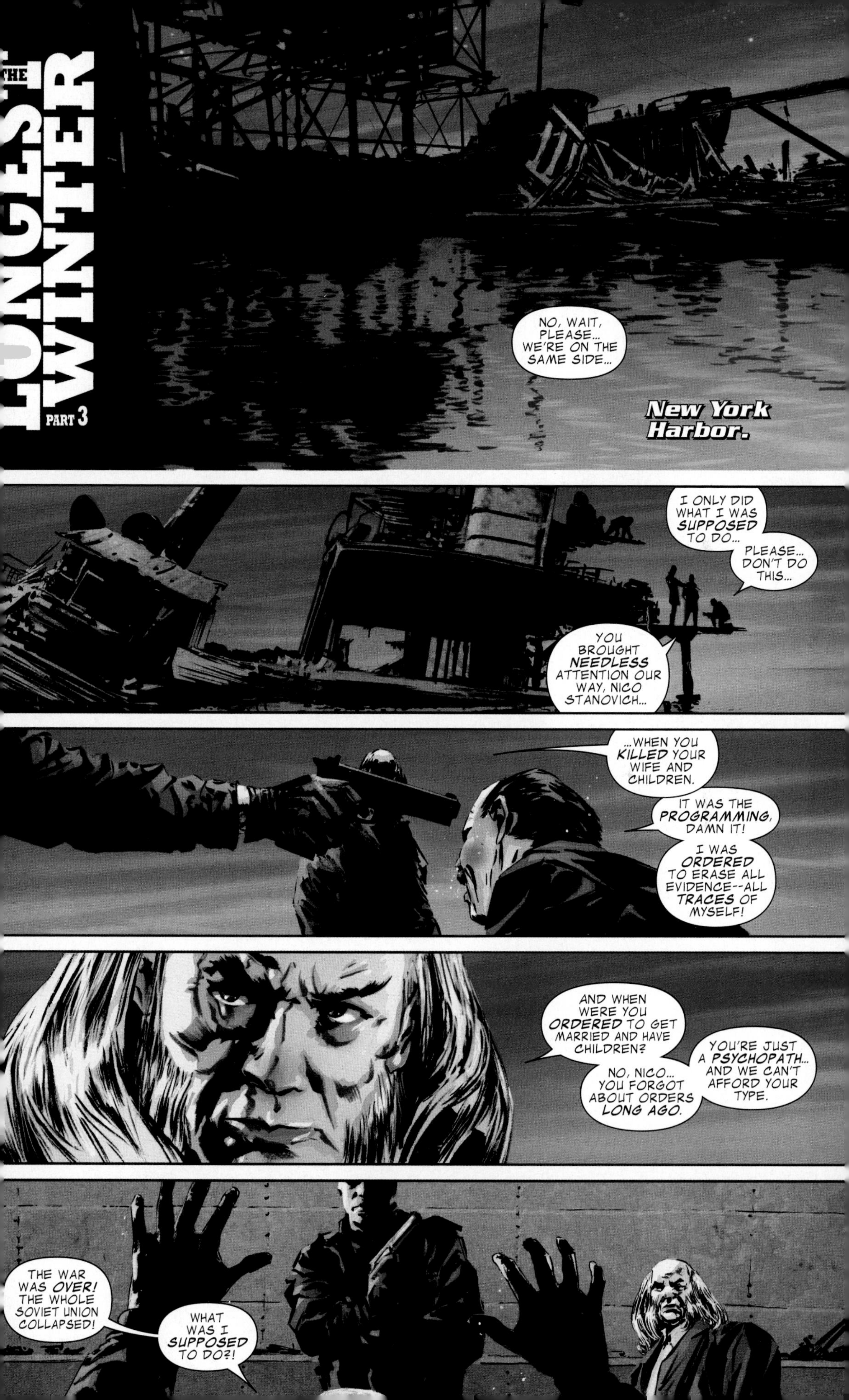
THE LONGEST WINTER
PART 3
NO, WAIT, PLEASE... WE'RE ON THE SAME SIDE...
New York Harbor.
I ONLY DID WHAT I WAS SUPPOSED TO DO...
PLEASE... DON'T DO THIS...
YOU BROUGHT NEEDLESS ATTENTION OUR WAY, NICO STANOVICH...
...WHEN YOU KILLED YOUR WIFE AND CHILDREN.
IT WAS THE PROGRAMMING, DAMN IT!
I WAS ORDERED TO ERASE ALL EVIDENCE--ALL TRACES OF MYSELF!
AND WHEN WERE YOU ORDERED TO GET MARRIED AND HAVE CHILDREN?
NO, NICO... YOU FORGOT ABOUT ORDERS LONG AGO.
YOU'RE JUST A PSYCHOPATH... AND WE CAN'T AFFORD YOUR TYPE.
THE WAR WAS OVER! THE WHOLE SOVIET UNION COLLAPSED!
WHAT WAS I SUPPOSED TO DO?!

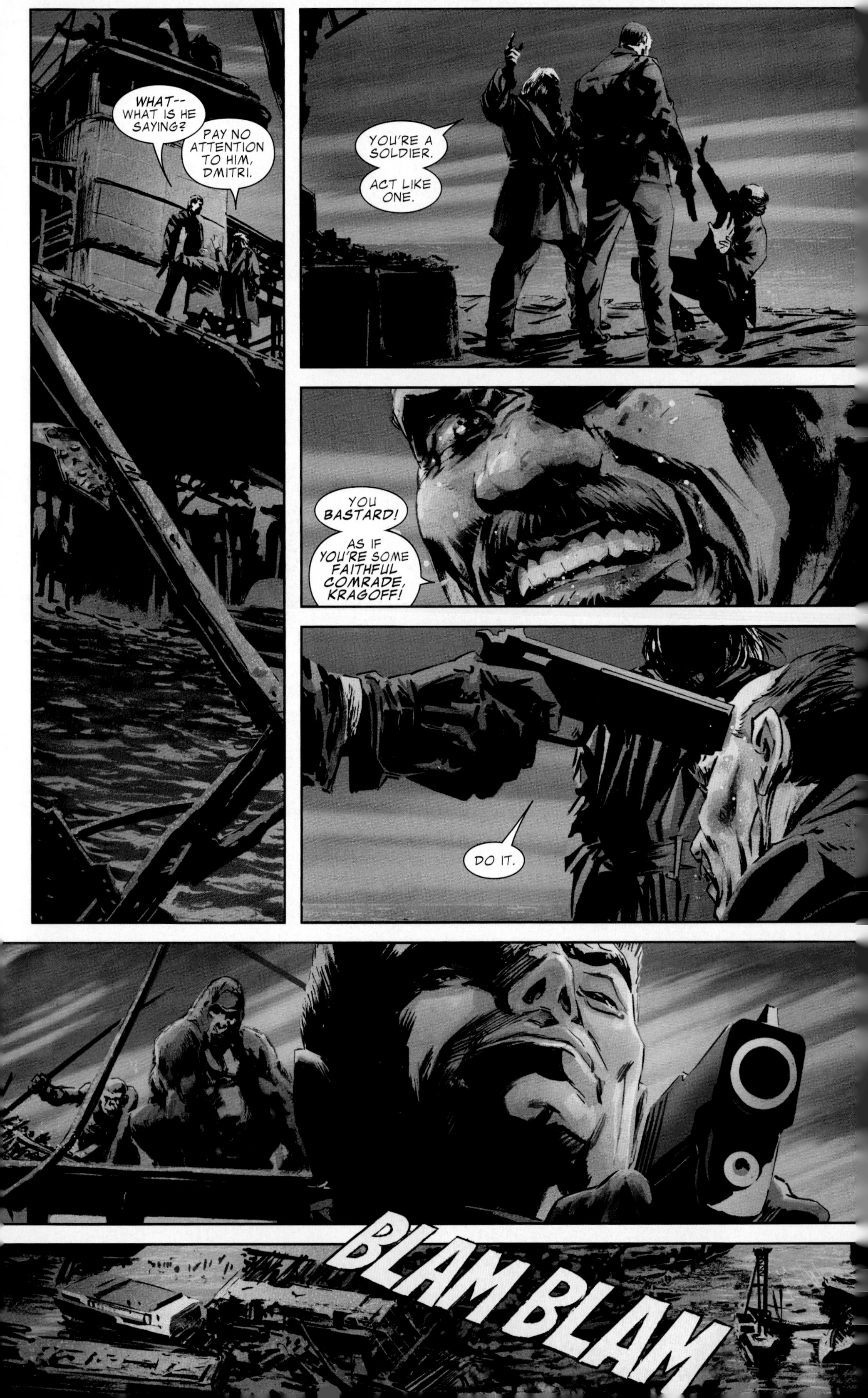
WHAT--
WHAT IS HE SAYING?
PAY NO ATTENTION TO HIM, DMITRI.
YOU'RE A SOLDIER.
ACT LIKE ONE.
YOU BASTARD!
AS IF YOU'RE SOME FAITHFUL COMRADE, KRAGOFF!
DO IT.
BLAM BLAM

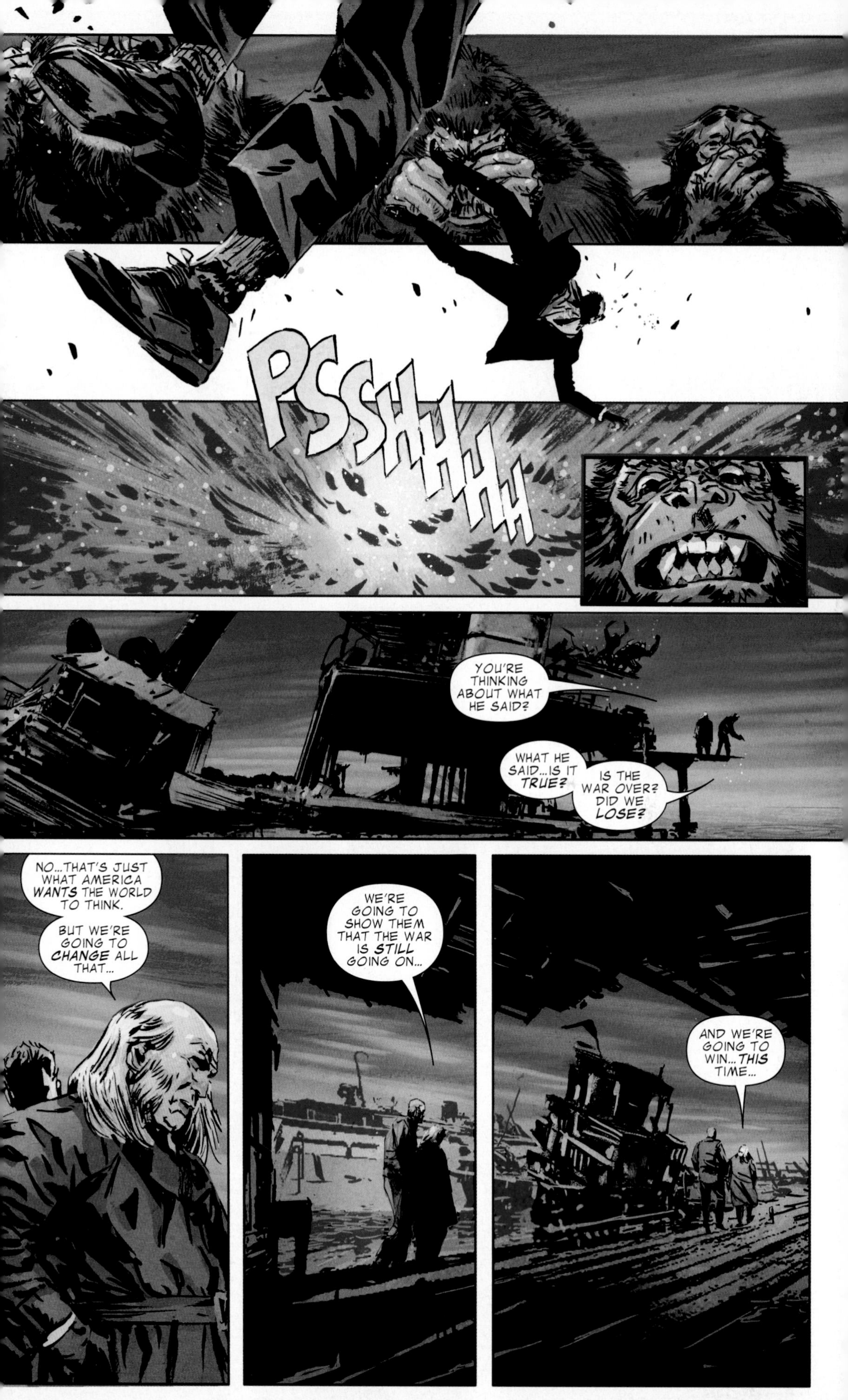
PSSHHHHH
YOU'RE THINKING ABOUT WHAT HE SAID?
WHAT HE SAID...IS IT TRUE?
IS THE WAR OVER? DID WE LOSE?
NO...THAT'S JUST WHAT AMERICA WANTS THE WORLD TO THINK.
BUT WE'RE GOING TO CHANGE ALL THAT...
WE'RE GOING TO SHOW THEM THAT THE WAR IS STILL GOING ON...
AND WE'RE GOING TO WIN...THIS TIME...

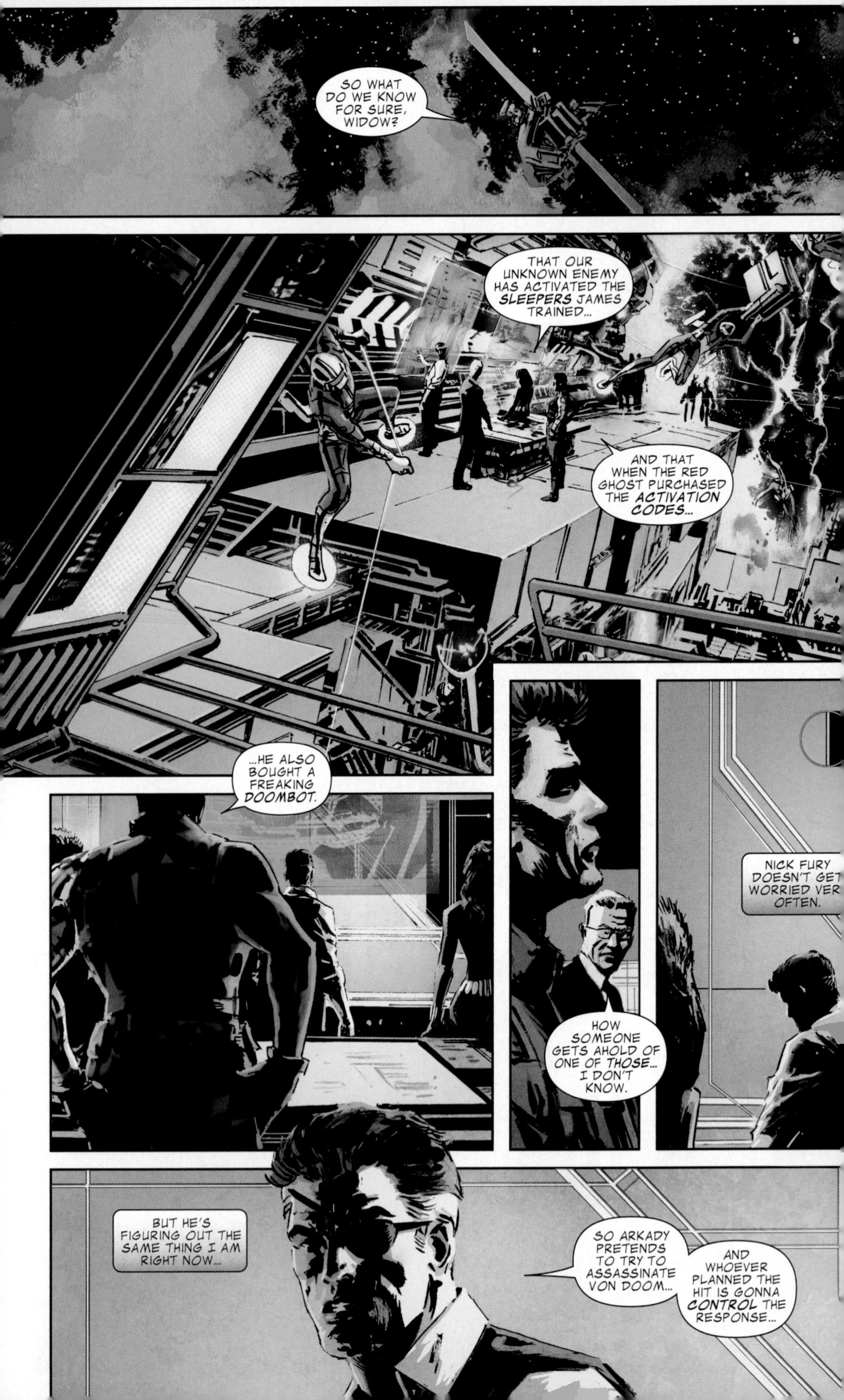
SO WHAT DO WE KNOW FOR SURE, WIDOW?
THAT OUR UNKNOWN ENEMY HAS ACTIVATED THE SLEEPERS JAMES TRAINED...
AND THAT WHEN THE RED GHOST PURCHASED THE ACTIVATION CODES...
...HE ALSO BOUGHT A FREAKING DOOMBOT.
HOW SOMEONE GETS AHOLD OF ONE OF THOSE... I DON'T KNOW.
NICK FURY DOESN'T GET WORRIED VER OFTEN.
BUT HE'S FIGURING OUT THE SAME THING I AM RIGHT NOW...
SO ARKADY PRETENDS TO TRY TO ASSASSINATE VON DOOM...
AND WHOEVER PLANNED THE HIT IS GONNA CONTROL THE RESPONSE...

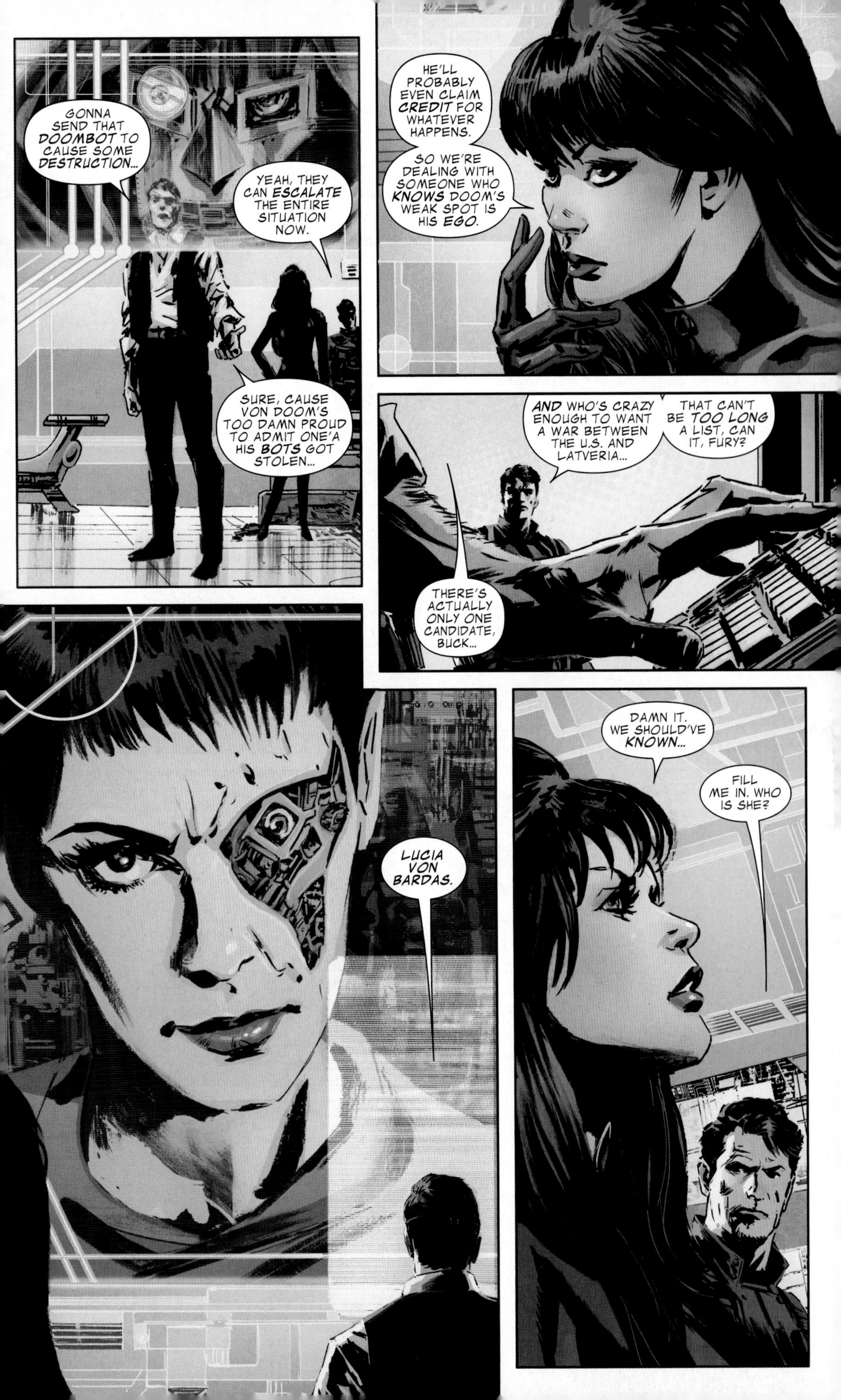
GONNA SEND THAT DOOMBOT TO CAUSE SOME DESTRUCTION...
YEAH, THEY CAN ESCALATE THE ENTIRE SITUATION NOW.
SURE, CAUSE VON DOOM'S TOO DAMN PROUD TO ADMIT ONE'A HIS BOTS GOT STOLEN...
HE'LL PROBABLY EVEN CLAIM CREDIT FOR WHATEVER HAPPENS.
SO WE'RE DEALING WITH SOMEONE WHO KNOWS DOOM'S WEAK SPOT IS HIS EGO.
AND WHO'S CRAZY ENOUGH TO WANT A WAR BETWEEN THE U.S. AND LATVERIA...
THAT CAN'T BE TOO LONG A LIST, CAN IT, FURY?
THERE'S ACTUALLY ONLY ONE CANDIDATE, BUCK...
LUCIA VON BARDAS.
DAMN IT. WE SHOULD'VE KNOWN...
FILL ME IN. WHO IS SHE?

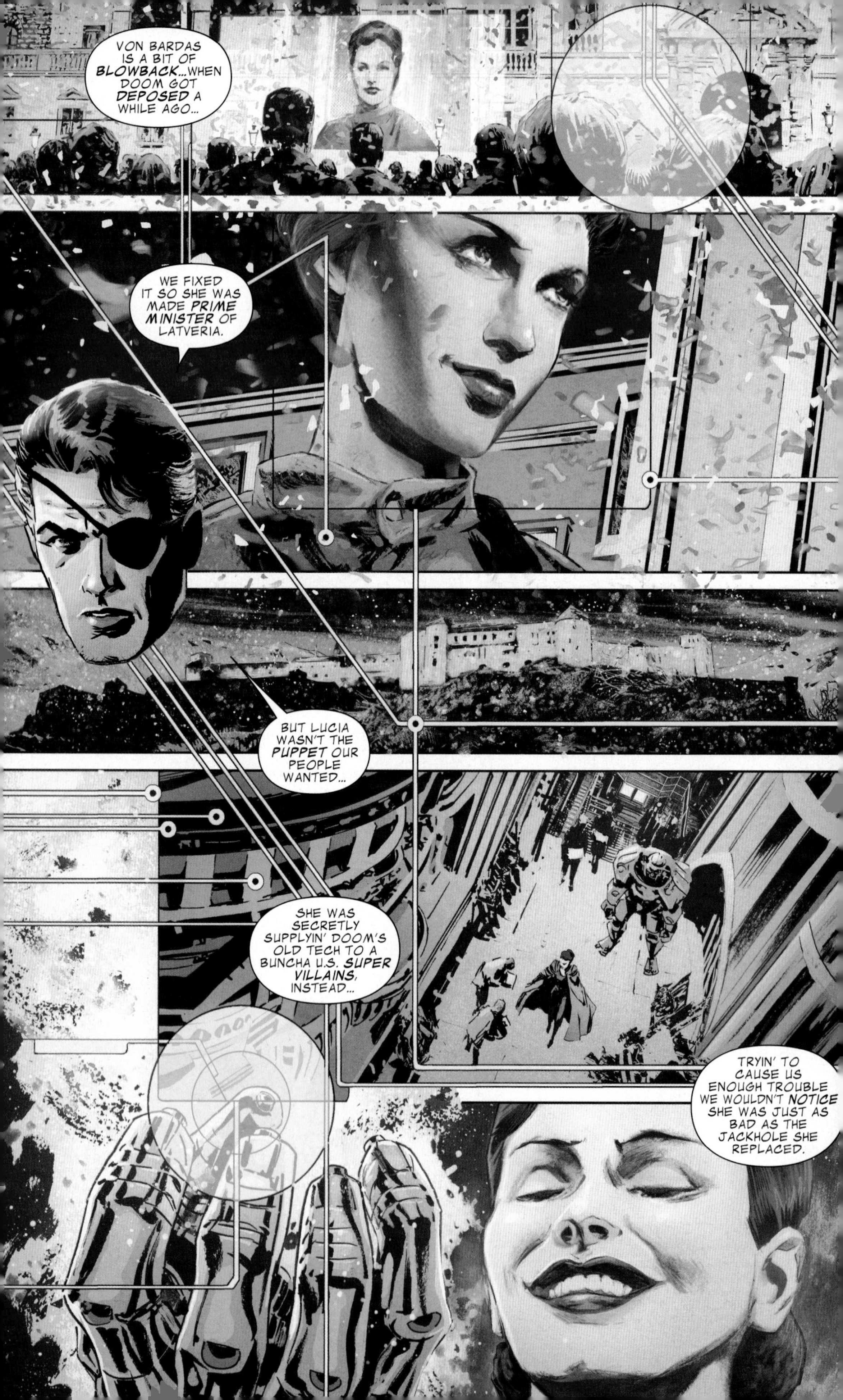

VON BARDAS IS A BIT OF BLOWBACK...WHEN DOOM GOT DEPOSED A WHILE AGO...
WE FIXED IT SO SHE WAS MADE PRIME MINISTER OF LATVERIA.
BUT LUCIA WASN'T THE PUPPET OUR PEOPLE WANTED...
SHE WAS SECRETLY SUPPLYIN' DOOM'S OLD TECH TO A BUNCHA U.S. SUPER VILLAINS, INSTEAD...
TRYIN' TO CAUSE US ENOUGH TROUBLE WE WOULDN'T NOTICE SHE WAS JUST AS BAD AS THE JACKHOLE SHE REPLACED.

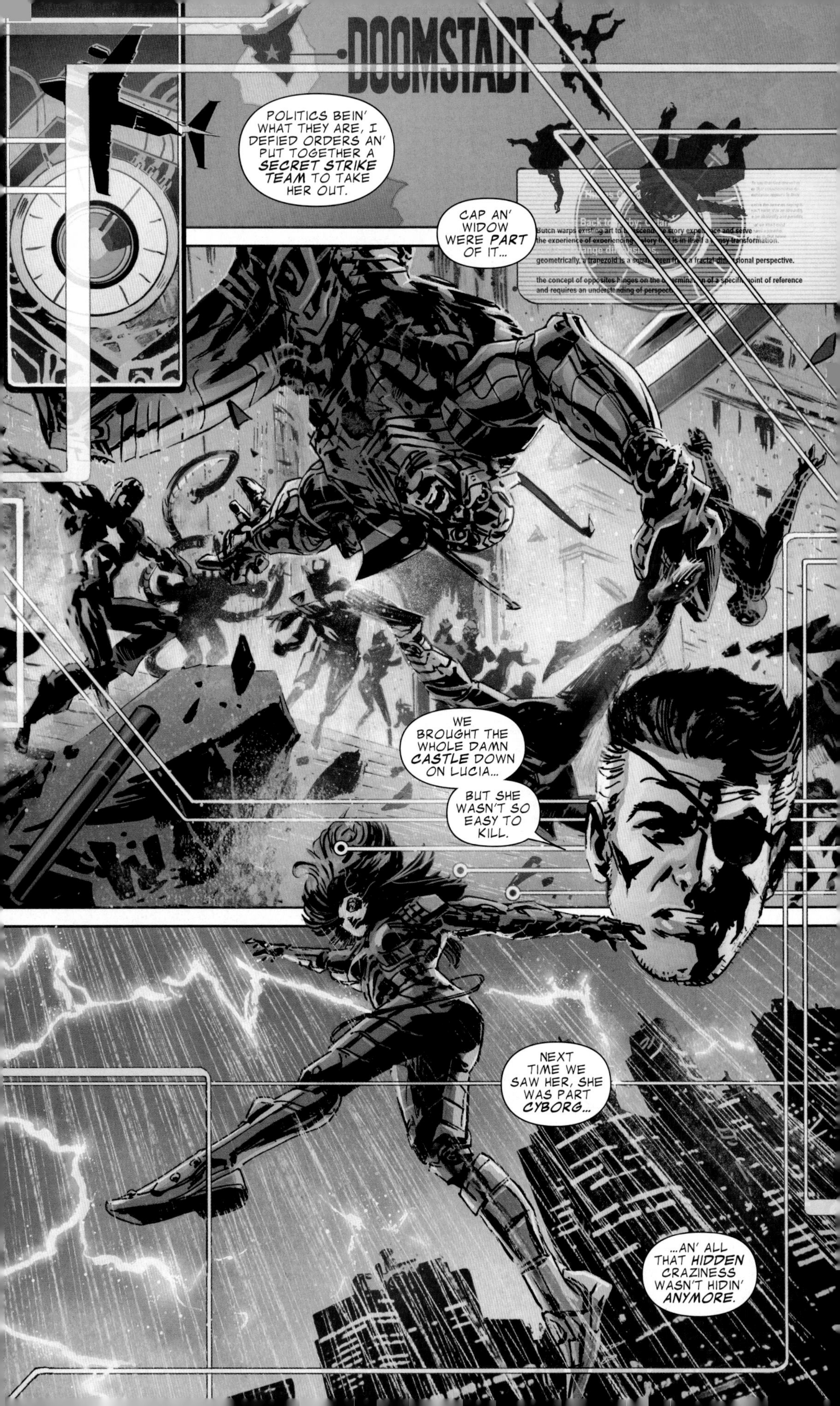
DOOMSTADT
POLITICS BEIN' WHAT THEY ARE, I DEFIED ORDERS AN' PUT TOGETHER A SECRET STRIKE TEAM TO TAKE HER OUT.
CAP AN' WIDOW WERE PART OF IT...
WE BROUGHT THE WHOLE DAMN CASTLE DOWN ON LUCIA...
BUT SHE WASN'T SO EASY TO KILL.
NEXT TIME WE SAW HER, SHE WAS PART CYBORG...
...AN' ALL THAT HIDDEN CRAZINESS WASN'T HIDIN' ANYMORE.

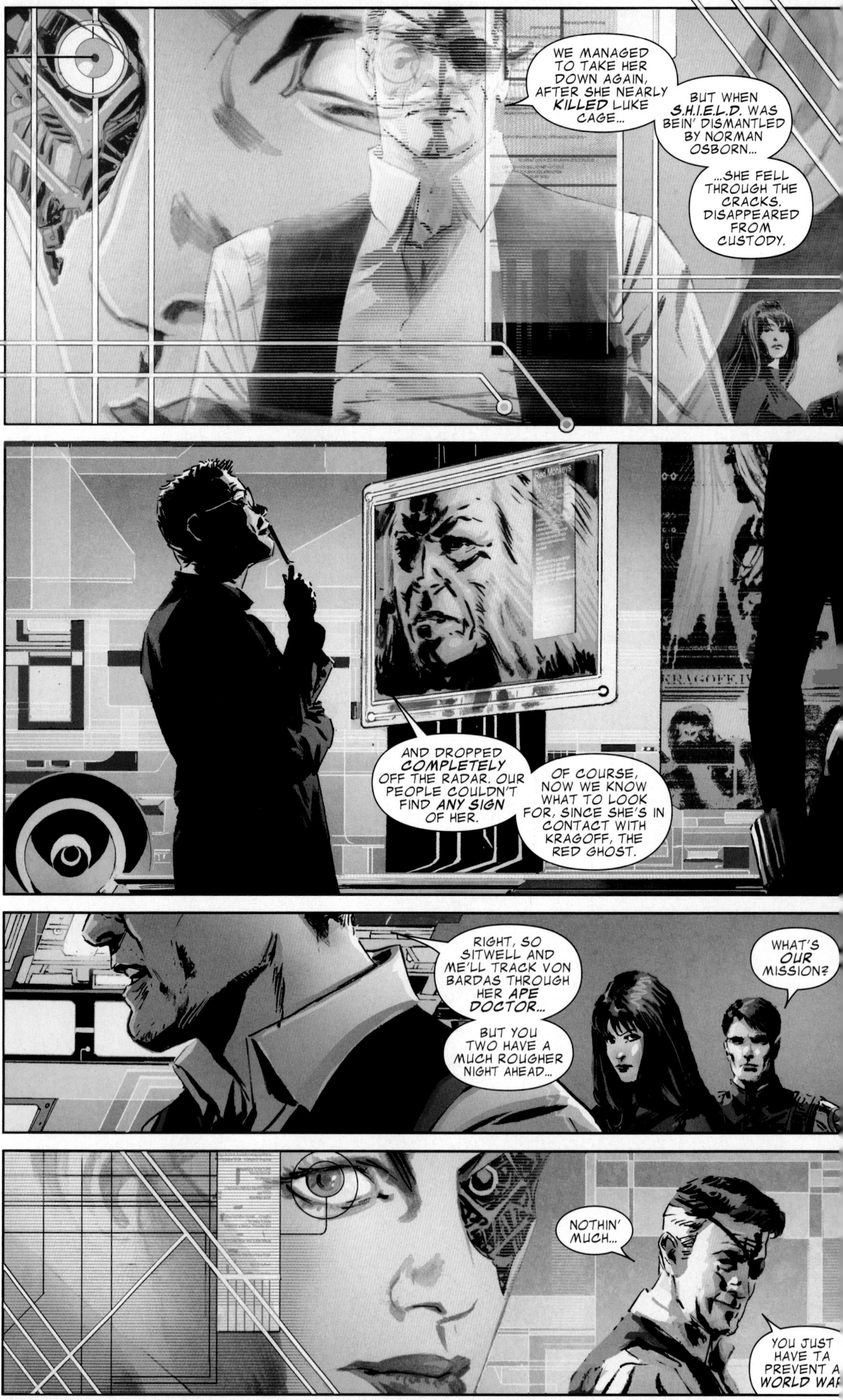
WE MANAGED TO TAKE HER DOWN AGAIN, AFTER SHE NEARLY KILLED LUKE CAGE...
BUT WHEN S.H.I.E.L.D. WAS BEIN' DISMANTLED BY NORMAN OSBORN...
...SHE FELL THROUGH THE CRACKS. DISAPPEARED FROM CUSTODY.
Red Monkeys
AND DROPPED COMPLETELY OFF THE RADAR. OUR PEOPLE COULDN'T FIND ANY SIGN OF HER.
OF COURSE, NOW WE KNOW WHAT TO LOOK FOR, SINCE SHE'S IN CONTACT WITH KRAGOFF, THE RED GHOST.
RIGHT, SO SITWELL AND ME'LL TRACK VON BARDAS THROUGH HER APE DOCTOR...
BUT YOU TWO HAVE A MUCH ROUGHER NIGHT AHEAD...
WHAT'S OUR MISSION?
NOTHIN' MUCH...
YOU JUST HAVE TA PREVENT A WORLD WA

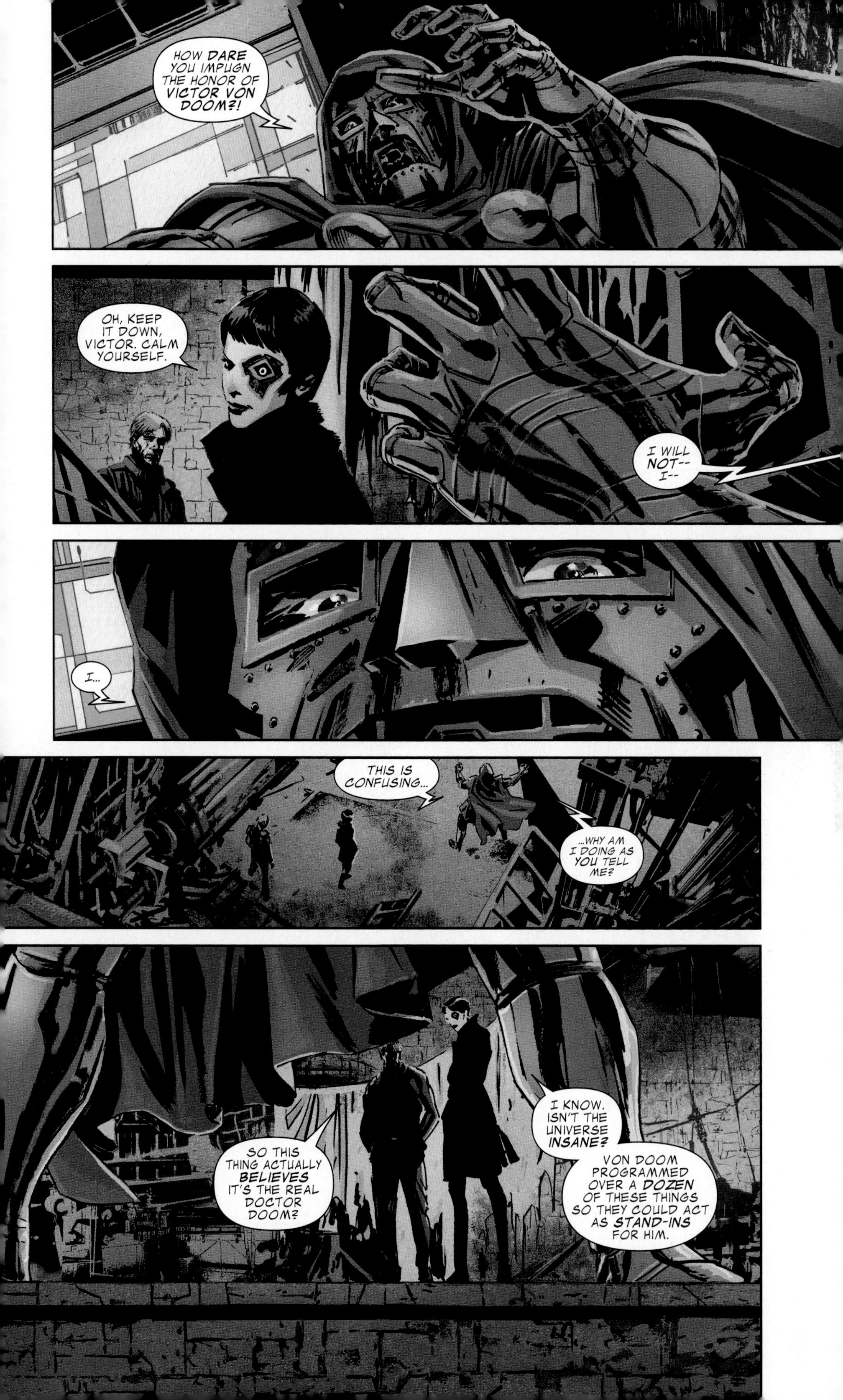
HOW DARE YOU IMPUGN THE HONOR OF VICTOR VON DOOM?!
OH, KEEP IT DOWN, VICTOR. CALM YOURSELF.
I WILL NOT-- I--
I...
THIS IS CONFUSING...
...WHY AM I DOING AS YOU TELL ME?
SO THIS THING ACTUALLY BELIEVES IT'S THE REAL DOCTOR DOOM?
I KNOW. ISN'T THE UNIVERSE INSANE?
VON DOOM PROGRAMMED OVER A DOZEN OF THESE THINGS SO THEY COULD ACT AS STAND-INS FOR HIM.

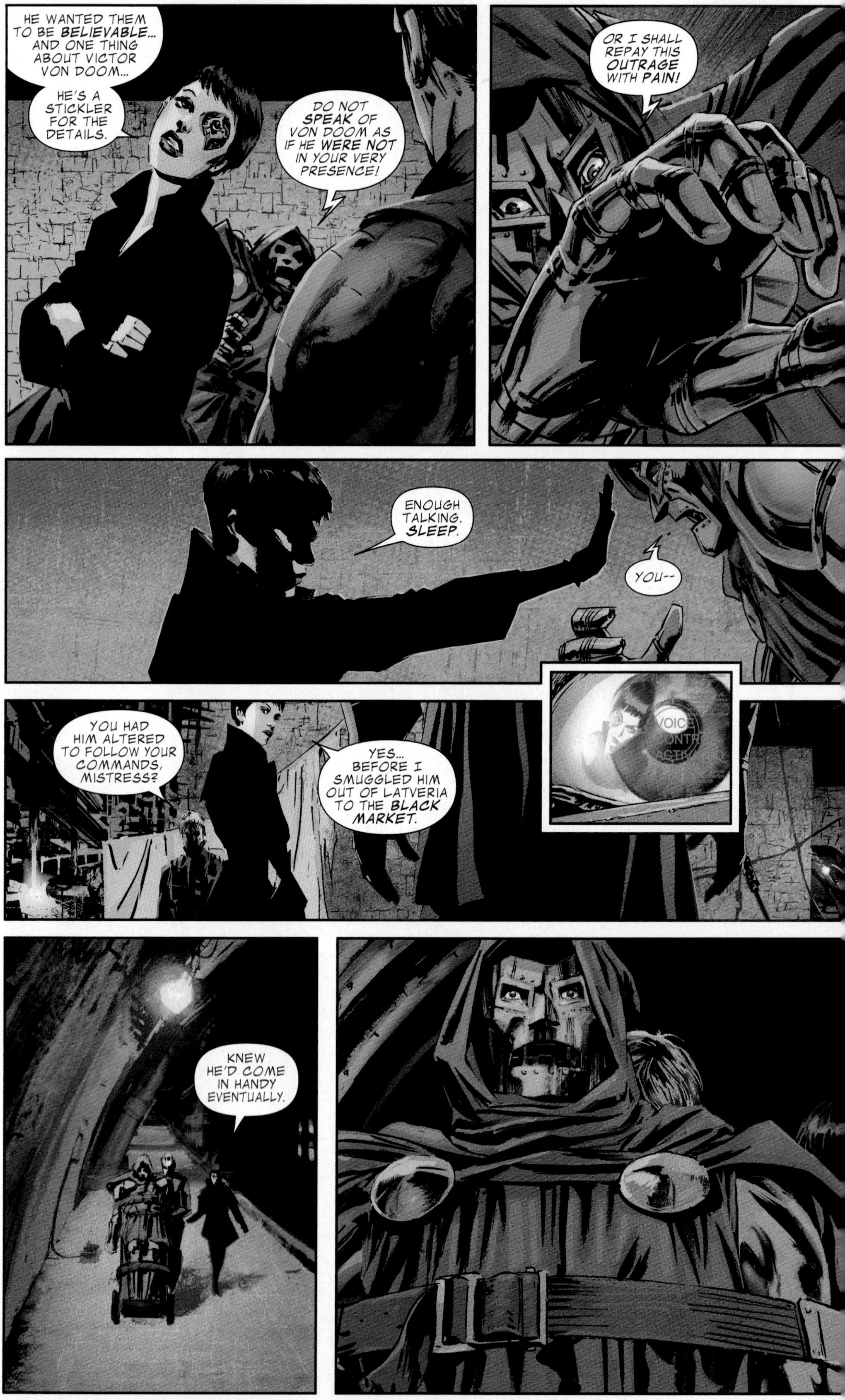

HE WANTED THEM TO BE BELIEVABLE... AND ONE THING ABOUT VICTOR VON DOOM...
HE'S A STICKLER FOR THE DETAILS.
DO NOT SPEAK OF VON DOOM AS IF HE WERE NOT IN YOUR VERY PRESENCE!
OR I SHALL REPAY THIS OUTRAGE WITH PAIN!
ENOUGH TALKING. SLEEP.
YOU--
VOICE CONTR ACTIV
YOU HAD HIM ALTERED TO FOLLOW YOUR COMMANDS, MISTRESS?
YES... BEFORE I SMUGGLED HIM OUT OF LATVERIA TO THE BLACK MARKET.
KNEW HE'D COME IN HANDY EVENTUALLY.

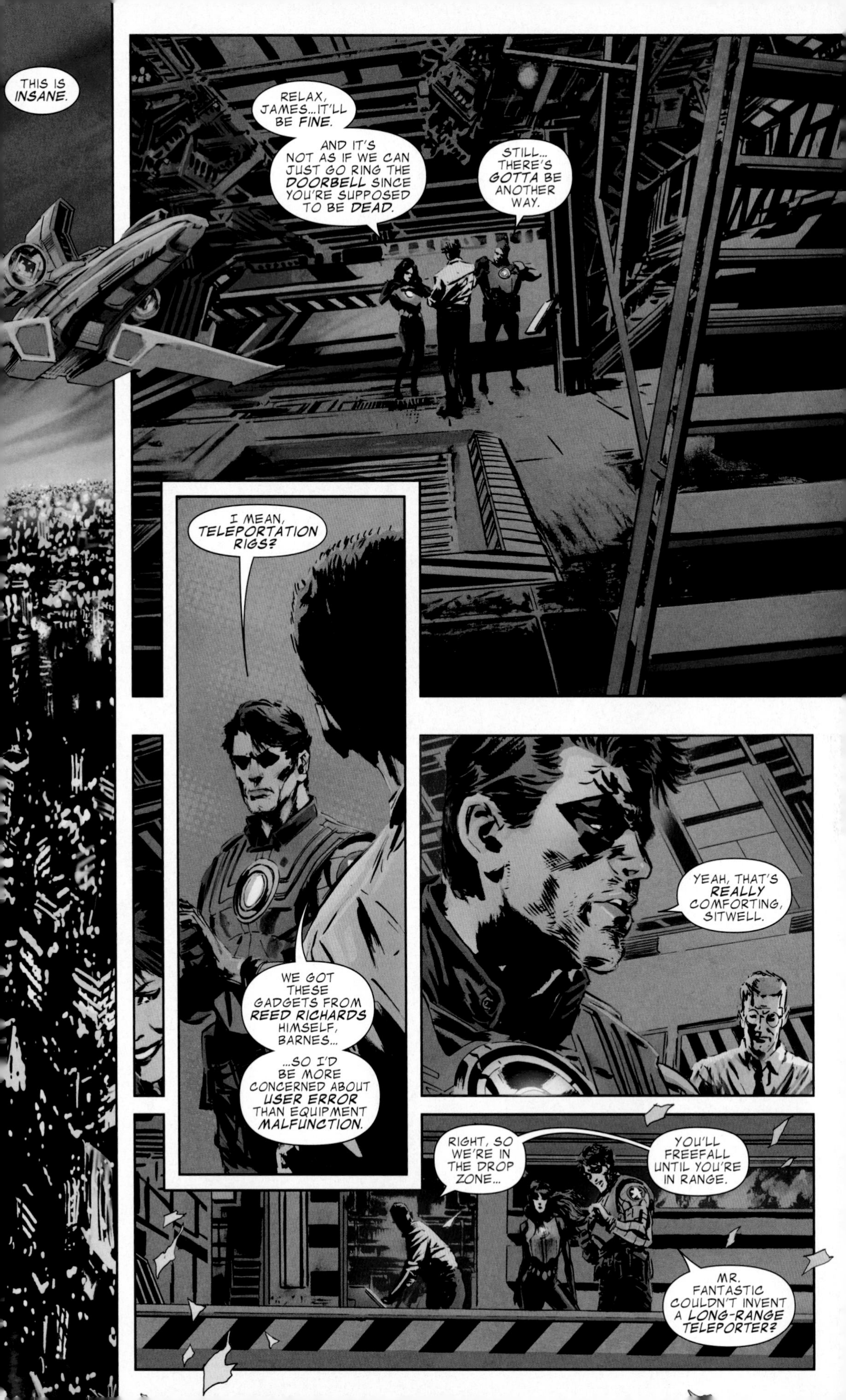

THIS IS INSANE.
RELAX, JAMES...IT'LL BE FINE.
AND IT'S NOT AS IF WE CAN JUST GO RING THE DOORBELL SINCE YOU'RE SUPPOSED TO BE DEAD.
STILL... THERE'S GOTTA BE ANOTHER WAY.
I MEAN, TELEPORTATION RIGS?
WE GOT THESE GADGETS FROM REED RICHARDS HIMSELF, BARNES...
...SO I'D BE MORE CONCERNED ABOUT USER ERROR THAN EQUIPMENT MALFUNCTION.
YEAH, THAT'S REALLY COMFORTING, SITWELL.
RIGHT, SO WE'RE IN THE DROP ZONE...
YOU'LL FREEFALL UNTIL YOU'RE IN RANGE.
MR. FANTASTIC COULDN'T INVENT A LONG-RANGE TELEPORTER?

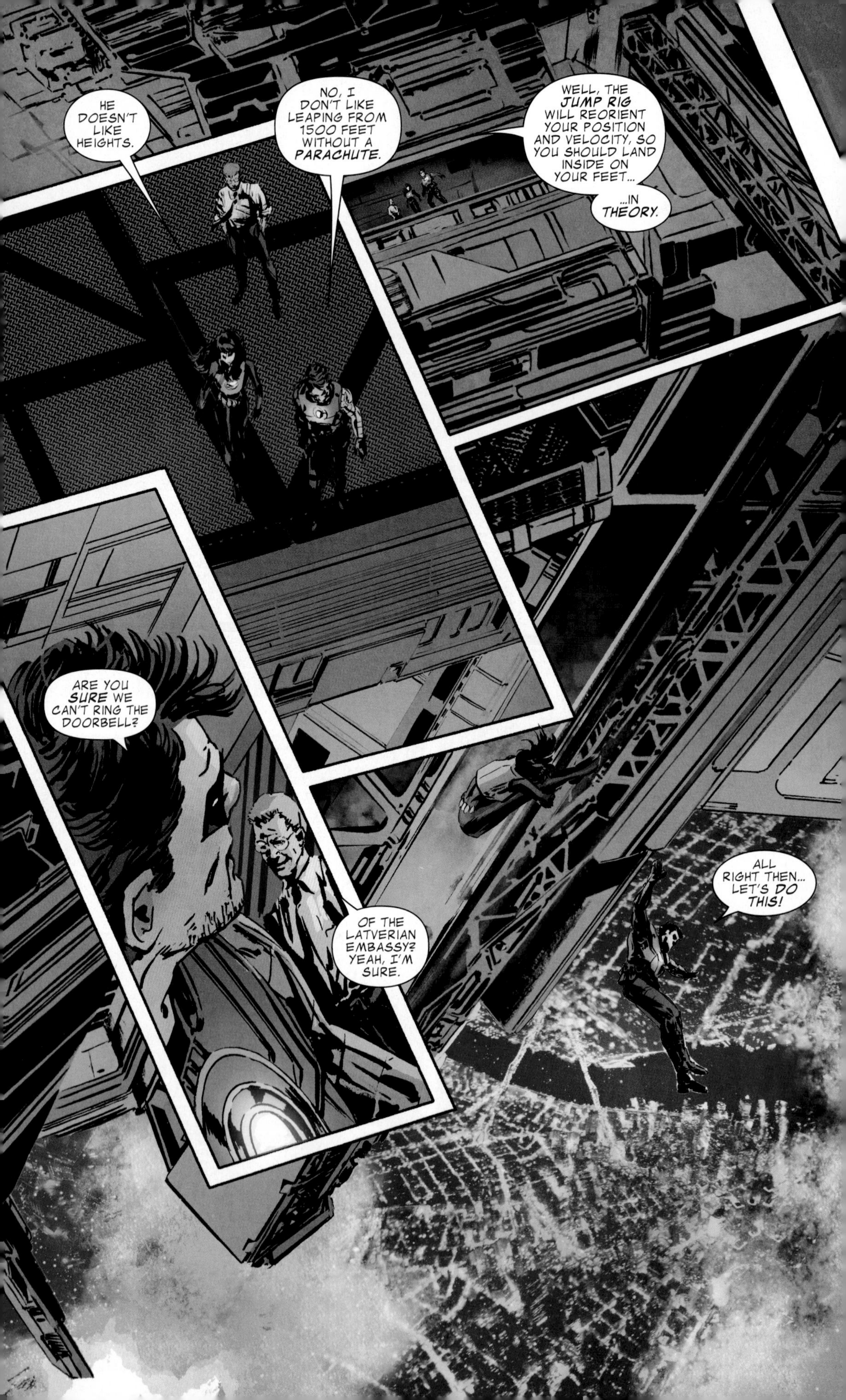
HE DOESN'T LIKE HEIGHTS.
NO, I DON'T LIKE LEAPING FROM 1500 FEET WITHOUT A PARACHUTE.
WELL, THE JUMP RIG WILL REORIENT YOUR POSITION AND VELOCITY, SO YOU SHOULD LAND INSIDE ON YOUR FEET...
...IN THEORY.
ARE YOU SURE WE CAN'T RING THE DOORBELL?
OF THE LATVERIAN EMBASSY? YEAH, I'M SURE.
ALL RIGHT THEN... LET'S DO THIS!

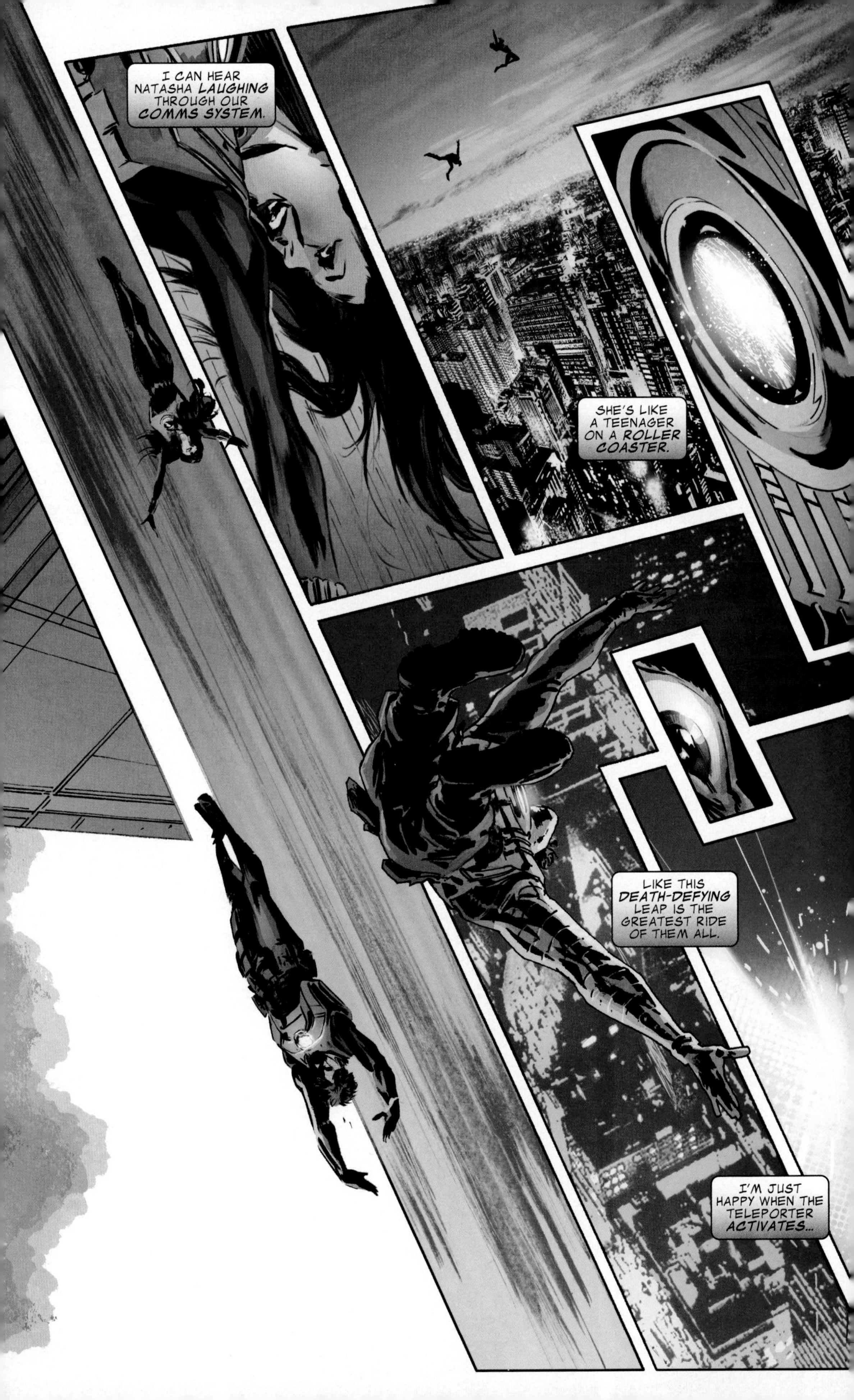
I CAN HEAR NATASHA LAUGHING THROUGH OUR COMMS SYSTEM.
SHE'S LIKE A TEENAGER ON A ROLLER COASTER.
LIKE THIS DEATH-DEFYING LEAP IS THE GREATEST RIDE OF THEM ALL.
I'M JUST HAPPY WHEN THE TELEPORTER ACTIVATES...

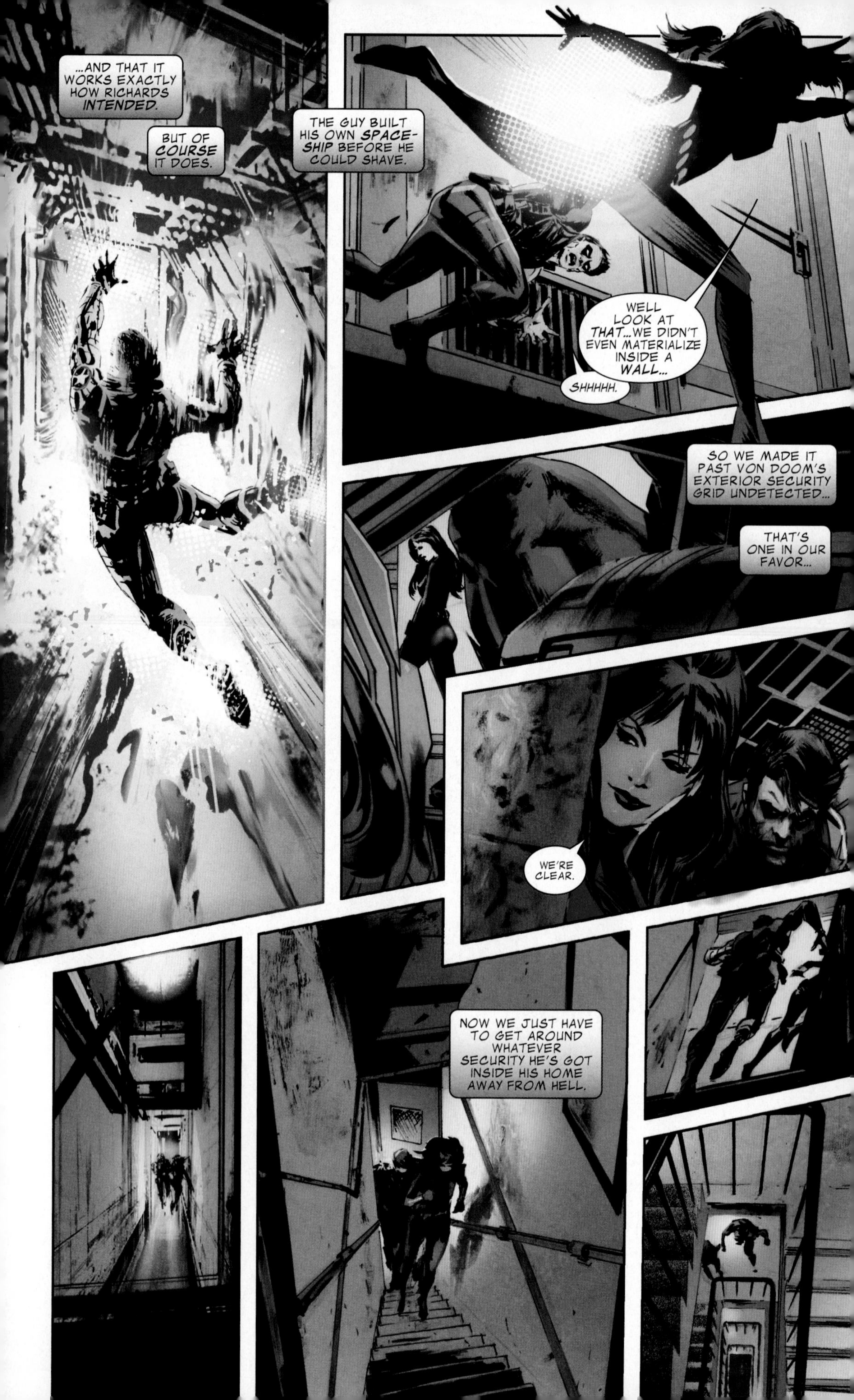
...AND THAT IT WORKS EXACTLY HOW RICHARDS INTENDED.
BUT OF COURSE IT DOES.
THE GUY BUILT HIS OWN SPACE-SHIP BEFORE HE COULD SHAVE.
WELL LOOK AT THAT...WE DIDN'T EVEN MATERIALIZE INSIDE A WALL...
SHHHHH.
SO WE MADE IT PAST VON DOOM'S EXTERIOR SECURITY GRID UNDETECTED...
THAT'S ONE IN OUR FAVOR...
WE'RE CLEAR.
NOW WE JUST HAVE TO GET AROUND WHATEVER SECURITY HE'S GOT INSIDE HIS HOME AWAY FROM HELL.

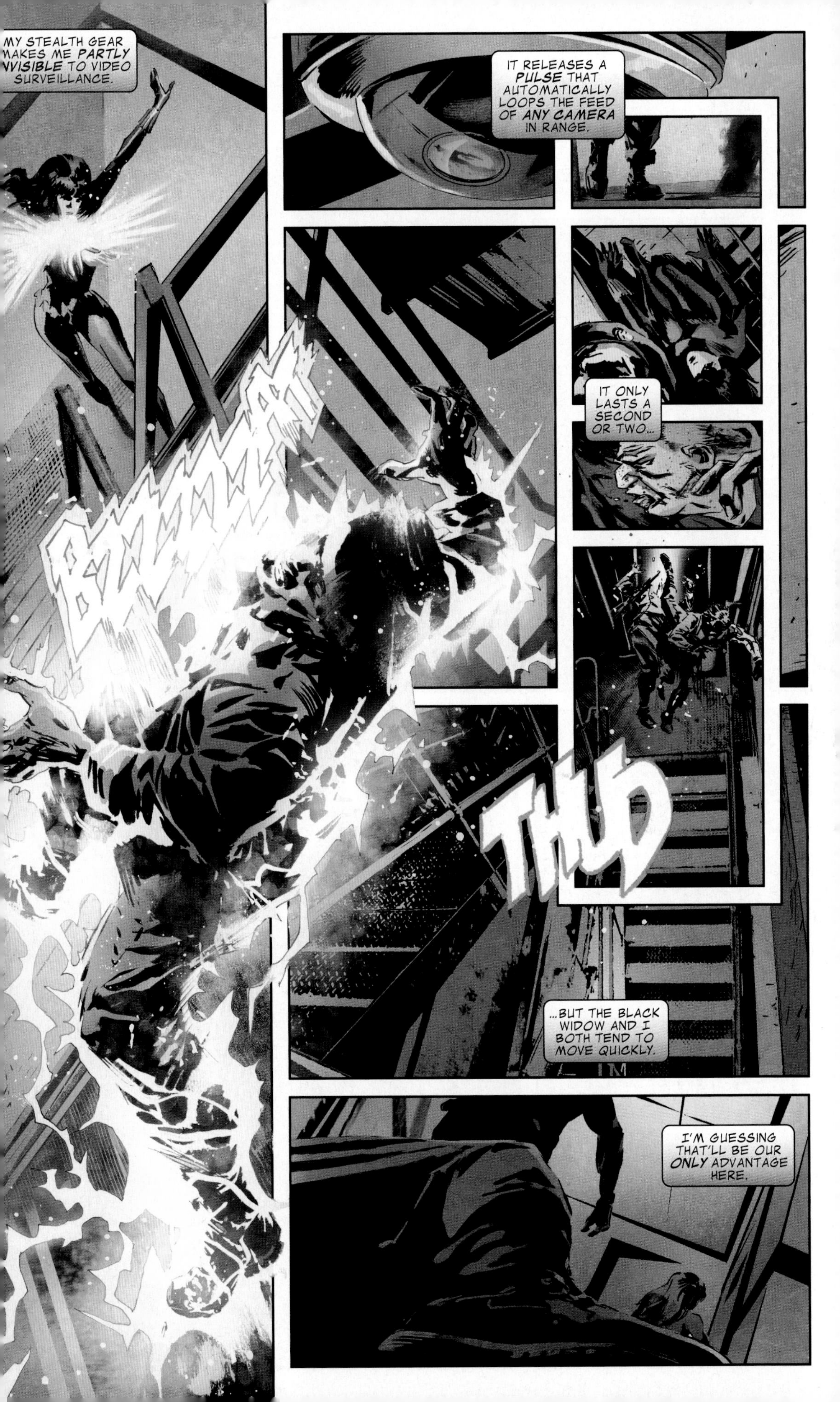
MY STEALTH GEAR MAKES ME PARTLY INVISIBLE TO VIDEO SURVEILLANCE.
IT RELEASES A PULSE THAT AUTOMATICALLY LOOPS THE FEED OF ANY CAMERA IN RANGE.
IT ONLY LASTS A SECOND OR TWO...
THUD
...BUT THE BLACK WIDOW AND I BOTH TEND TO MOVE QUICKLY.
I'M GUESSING THAT'LL BE OUR ONLY ADVANTAGE HERE.

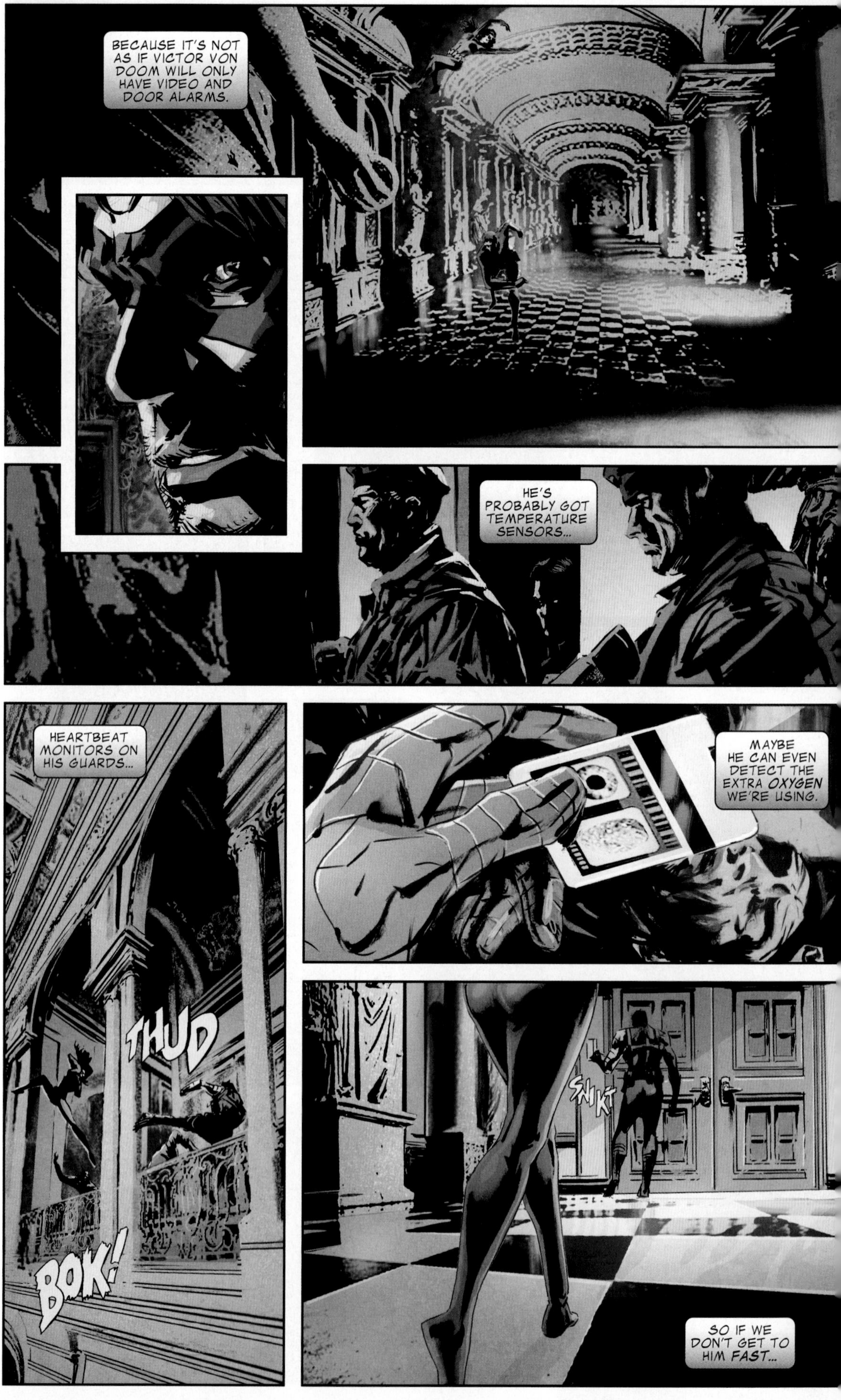
BECAUSE IT'S NOT AS IF VICTOR VON DOOM WILL ONLY HAVE VIDEO AND DOOR ALARMS.
HE'S PROBABLY GOT TEMPERATURE SENSORS...
HEARTBEAT MONITORS ON HIS GUARDS...
THUD
BOK!
MAYBE HE CAN EVEN DETECT THE EXTRA OXYGEN WE'RE USING.
SNIKT
SO IF WE DON'T GET TO HIM FAST...

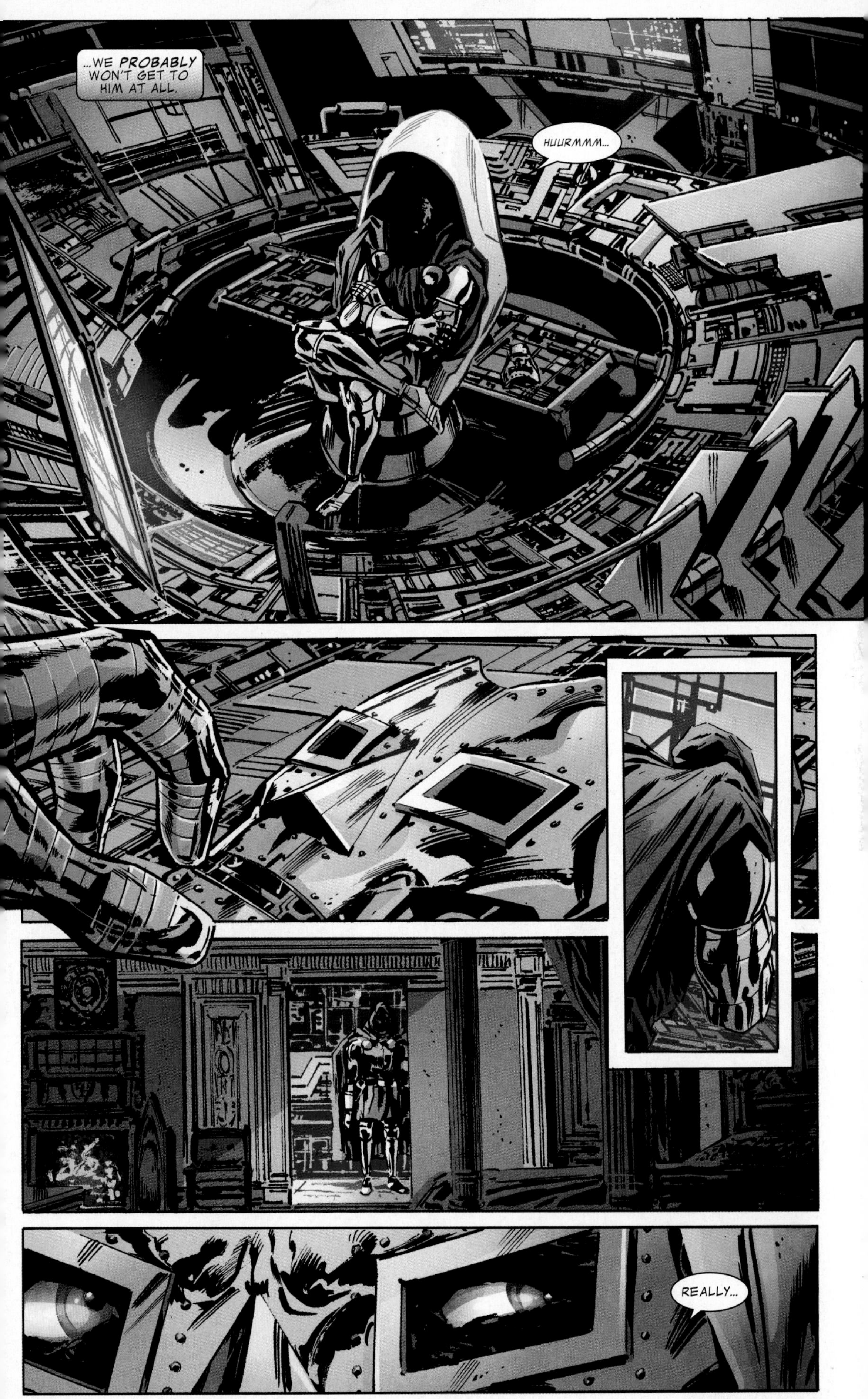
...WE PROBABLY WON'T GET TO HIM AT ALL.
HUURMMM...
REALLY...

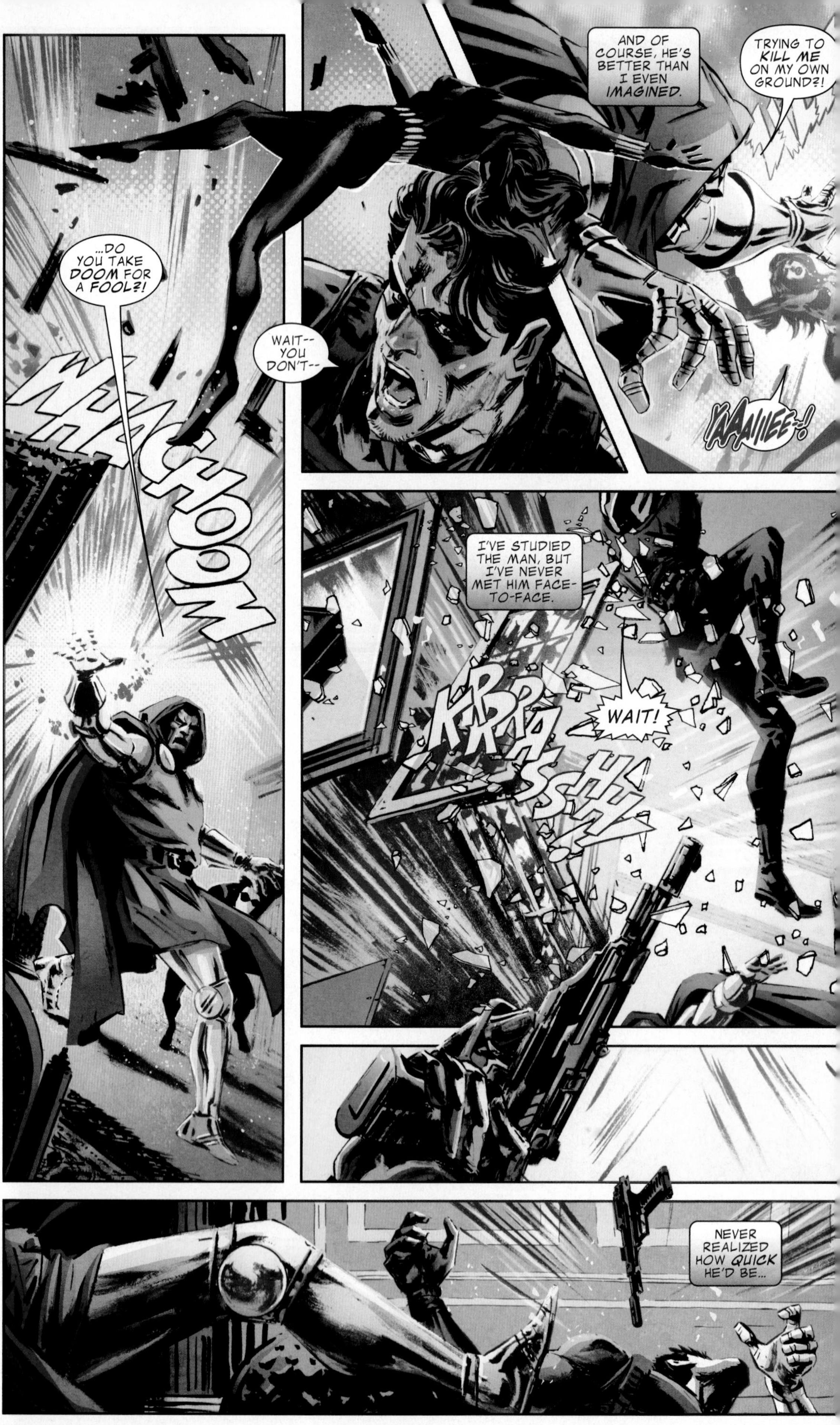

...DO YOU TAKE DOOM FOR A FOOL?!
WHACHOOM
AND OF COURSE, HE'S BETTER THAN I EVEN IMAGINED.
TRYING TO KILL ME ON MY OWN GROUND?!
WAIT-- YOU DON'T--
YAAAIIIEE--!
I'VE STUDIED THE MAN, BUT I'VE NEVER MET HIM FACE-TO-FACE.
KRRASSHH
WAIT!
NEVER REALIZED HOW QUICK HE'D BE...

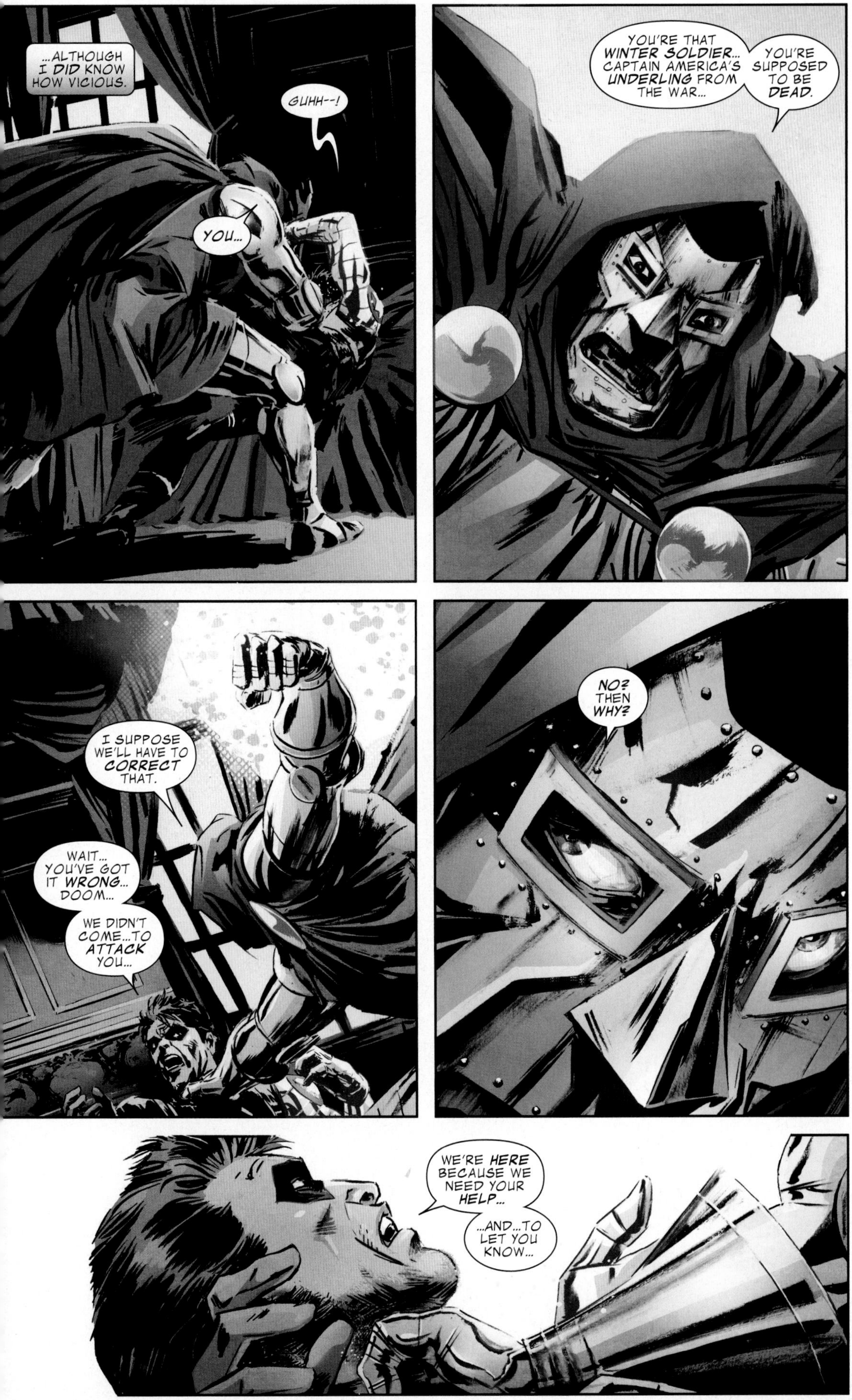

...ALTHOUGH I DID KNOW HOW VICIOUS.
GUHH--!
YOU...
YOU'RE THAT WINTER SOLDIER... CAPTAIN AMERICA'S UNDERLING FROM THE WAR...
YOU'RE SUPPOSED TO BE DEAD.
I SUPPOSE WE'LL HAVE TO CORRECT THAT.
WAIT... YOU'VE GOT IT WRONG... DOOM...
WE DIDN'T COME...TO ATTACK YOU...
NO? THEN WHY?
WE'RE HERE BECAUSE WE NEED YOUR HELP...
...AND...TO LET YOU KNOW...

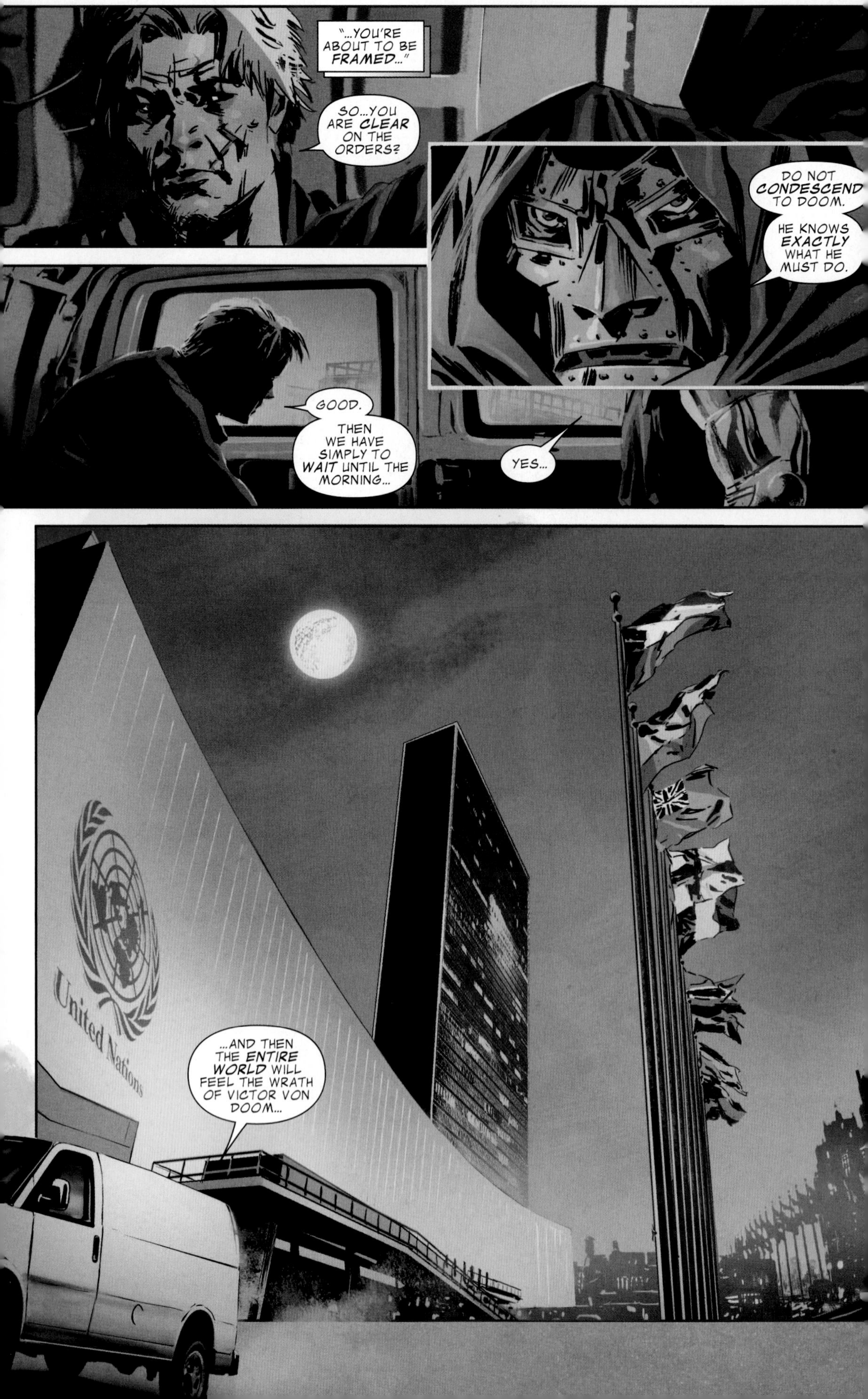
"...YOU'RE ABOUT TO BE FRAMED..."
SO...YOU ARE CLEAR ON THE ORDERS?
DO NOT CONDESCEND TO DOOM.
HE KNOWS EXACTLY WHAT HE MUST DO.
GOOD.
THEN WE HAVE SIMPLY TO WAIT UNTIL THE MORNING...
YES...
United Nations
...AND THEN THE ENTIRE WORLD WILL FEEL THE WRATH OF VICTOR VON DOOM...

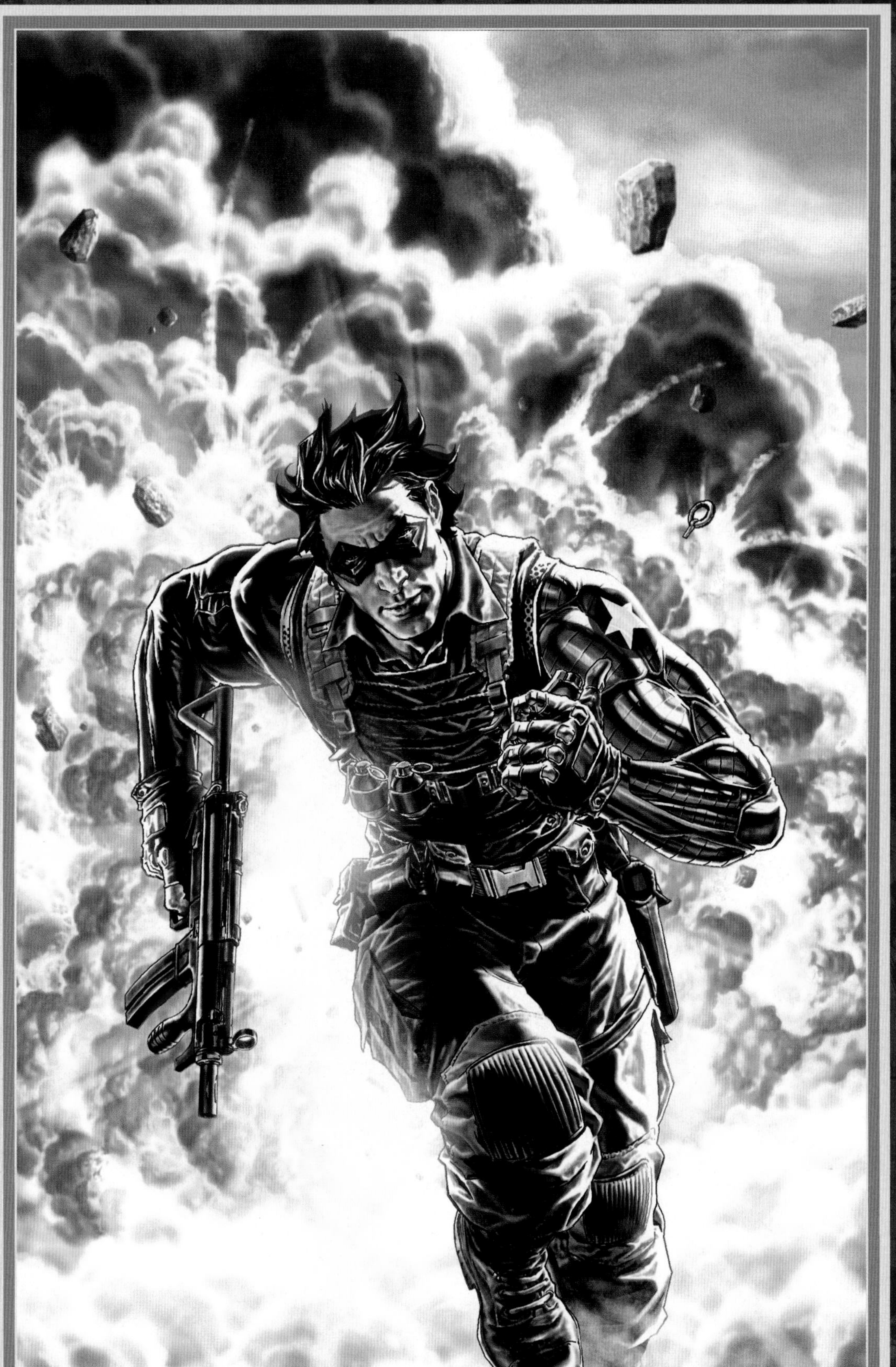

FOUR

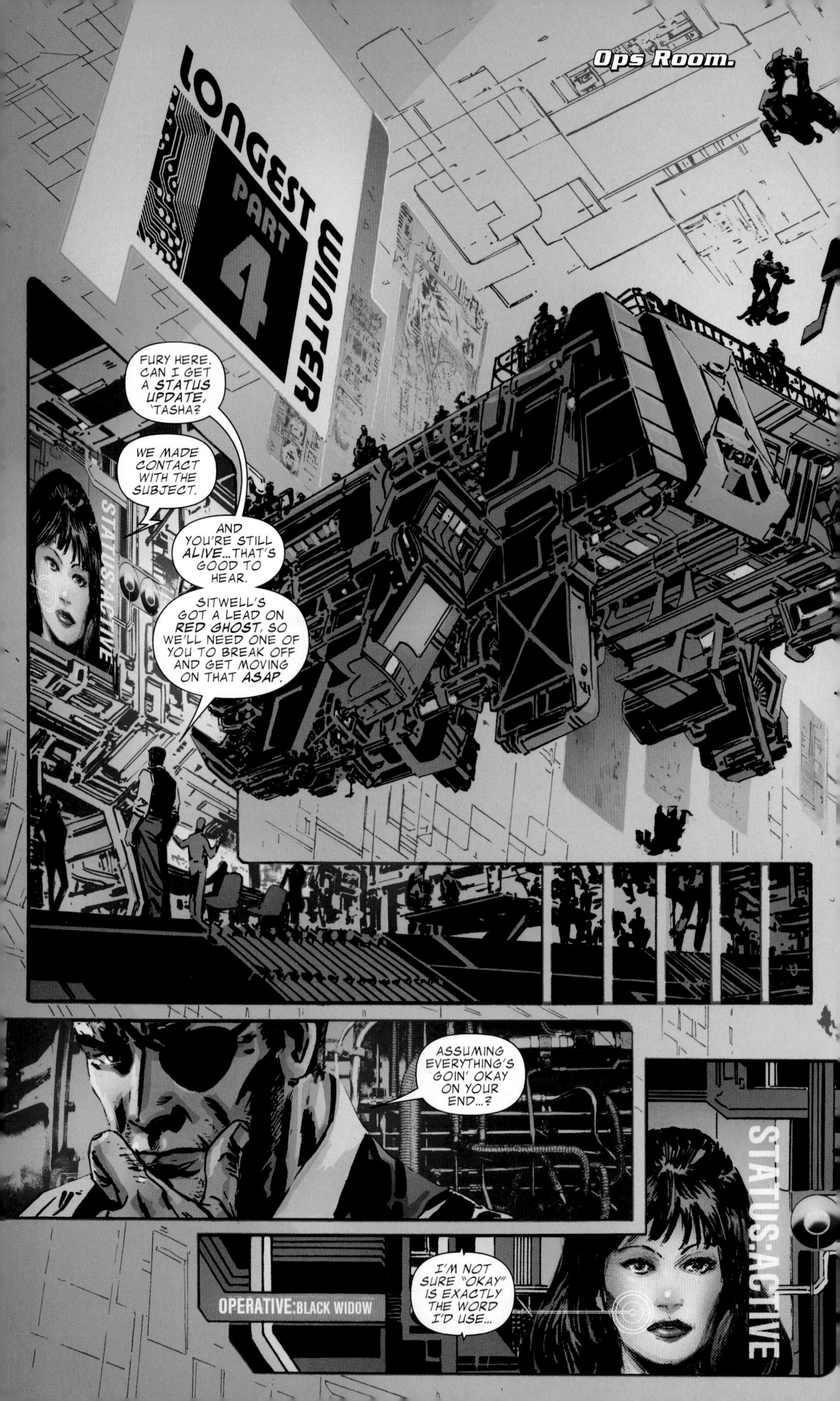

Ops Room.
LONGEST WINTER
PART 4
FURY HERE. CAN I GET A STATUS UPDATE, 'TASHA?
WE MADE CONTACT WITH THE SUBJECT.
STATUS:ACTIVE
AND YOU'RE STILL ALIVE...THAT'S GOOD TO HEAR.
SITWELL'S GOT A LEAD ON RED GHOST, SO WE'LL NEED ONE OF YOU TO BREAK OFF AND GET MOVING ON THAT ASAP.
ASSUMING EVERYTHING'S GOIN' OKAY ON YOUR END...?
STATUS:ACTIVE
OPERATIVE:BLACK WIDOW
I'M NOT SURE "OKAY" IS EXACTLY THE WORD I'D USE...

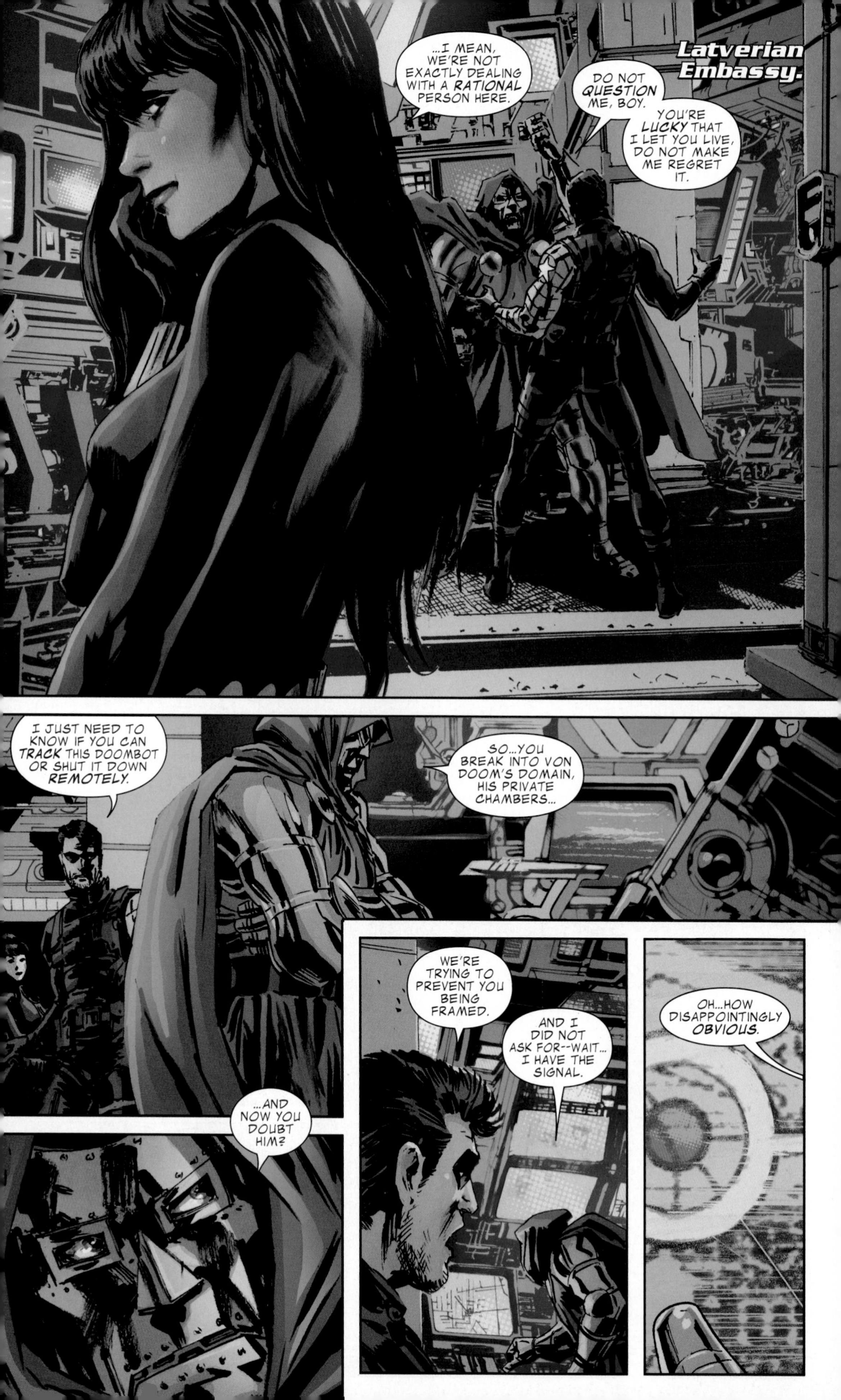
Latverian Embassy.
...I MEAN, WE'RE NOT EXACTLY DEALING WITH A RATIONAL PERSON HERE.
DO NOT QUESTION ME, BOY.
YOU'RE LUCKY THAT I LET YOU LIVE, DO NOT MAKE ME REGRET IT.
I JUST NEED TO KNOW IF YOU CAN TRACK THIS DOOMBOT OR SHUT IT DOWN REMOTELY.
SO...YOU BREAK INTO VON DOOM'S DOMAIN, HIS PRIVATE CHAMBERS...
...AND NOW YOU DOUBT HIM?
WE'RE TRYING TO PREVENT YOU BEING FRAMED.
AND I DID NOT ASK FOR--WAIT... I HAVE THE SIGNAL.
OH...HOW DISAPPOINTINGLY OBVIOUS.

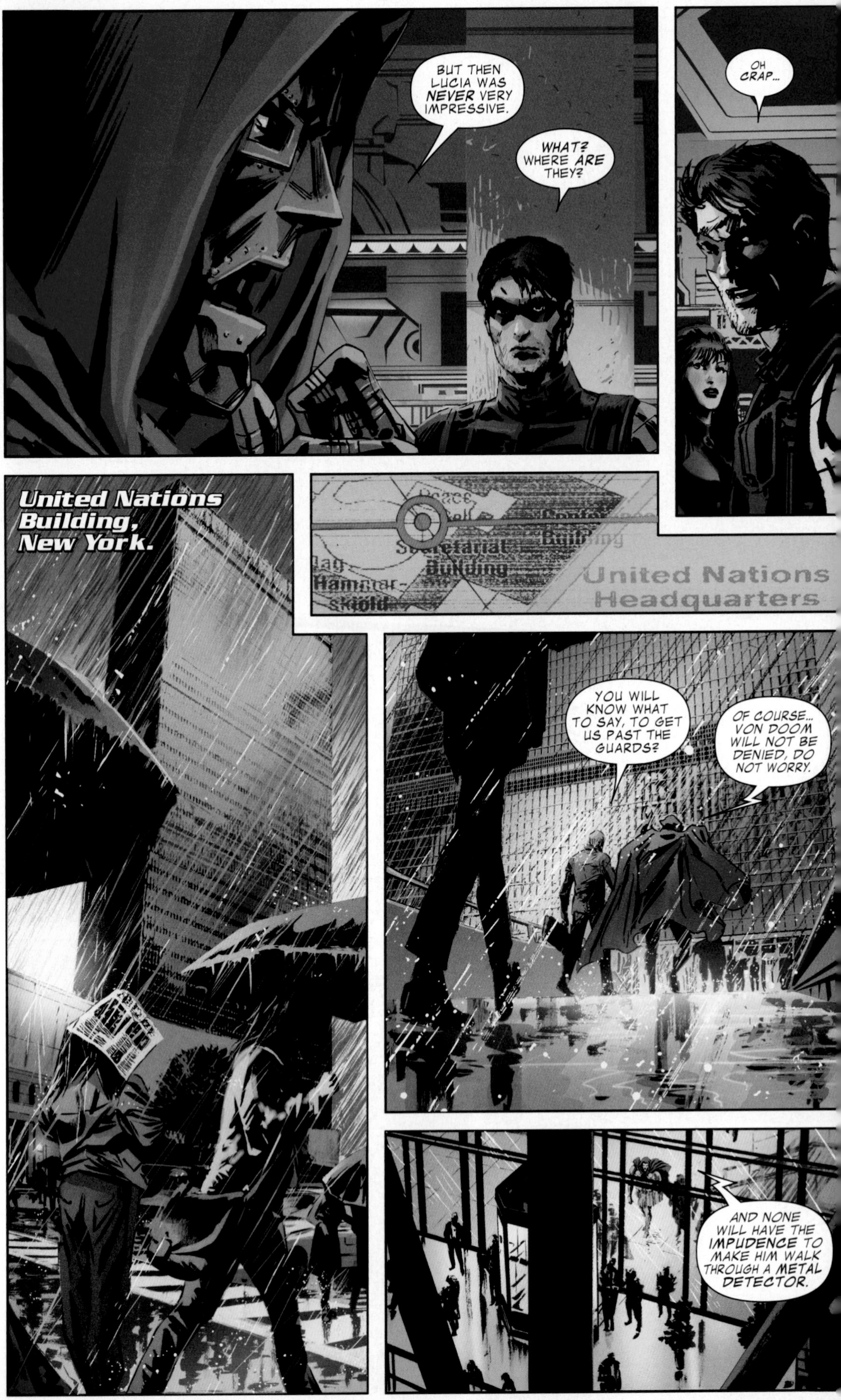
BUT THEN LUCIA WAS NEVER VERY IMPRESSIVE.
WHAT? WHERE ARE THEY?
OH CRAP...
United Nations Building, New York.
United Nations Headquarters
Secretariat Building
YOU WILL KNOW WHAT TO SAY, TO GET US PAST THE GUARDS?
OF COURSE... VON DOOM WILL NOT BE DENIED, DO NOT WORRY.
AND NONE WILL HAVE THE IMPUDENCE TO MAKE HIM WALK THROUGH A METAL DETECTOR.

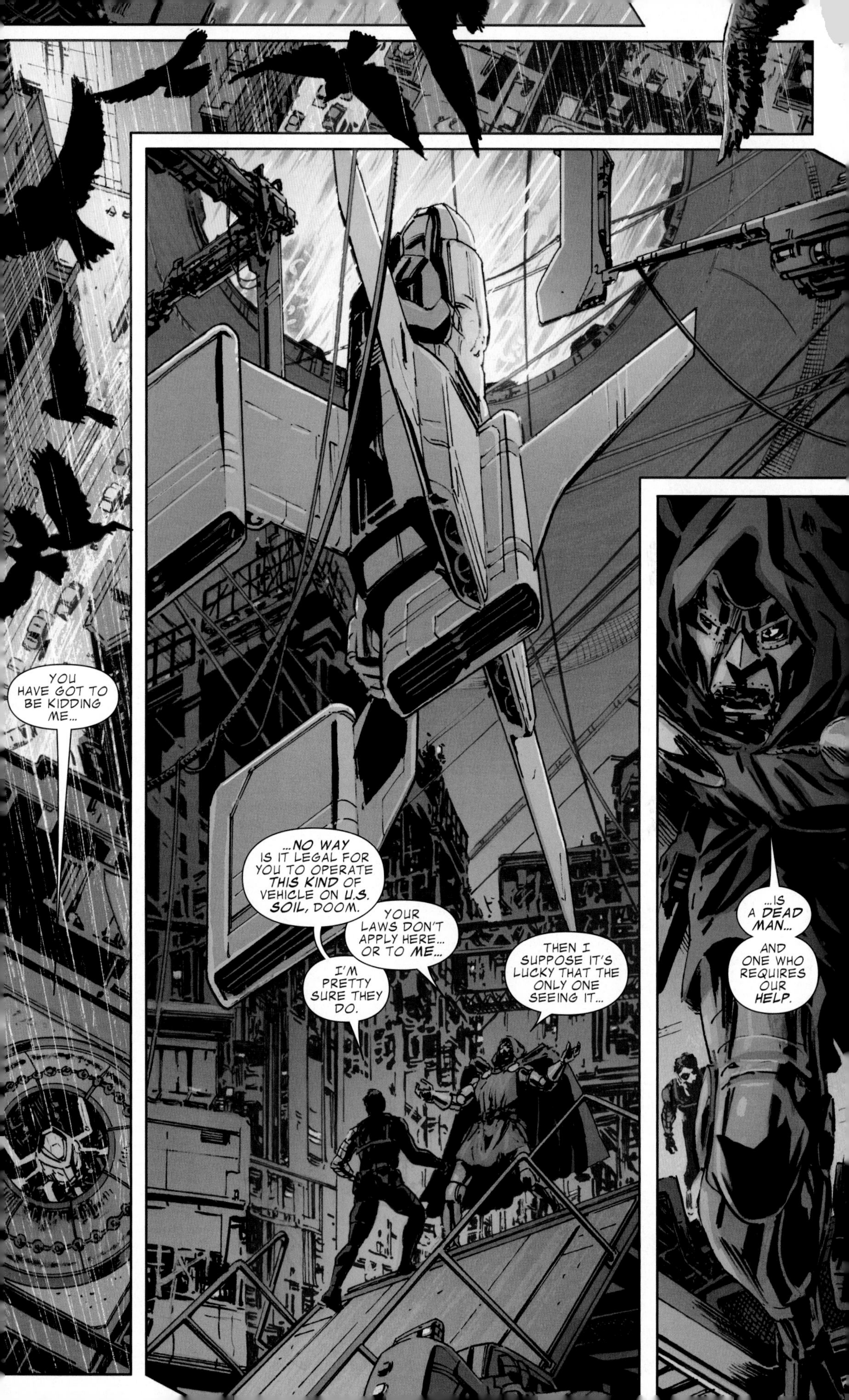
YOU HAVE GOT TO BE KIDDING ME...
...NO WAY IS IT LEGAL FOR YOU TO OPERATE THIS KIND OF VEHICLE ON U.S. SOIL, DOOM.
YOUR LAWS DON'T APPLY HERE... OR TO ME...
I'M PRETTY SURE THEY DO.
THEN I SUPPOSE IT'S LUCKY THAT THE ONLY ONE SEEING IT...
...IS A DEAD MAN...
AND ONE WHO REQUIRES OUR HELP.

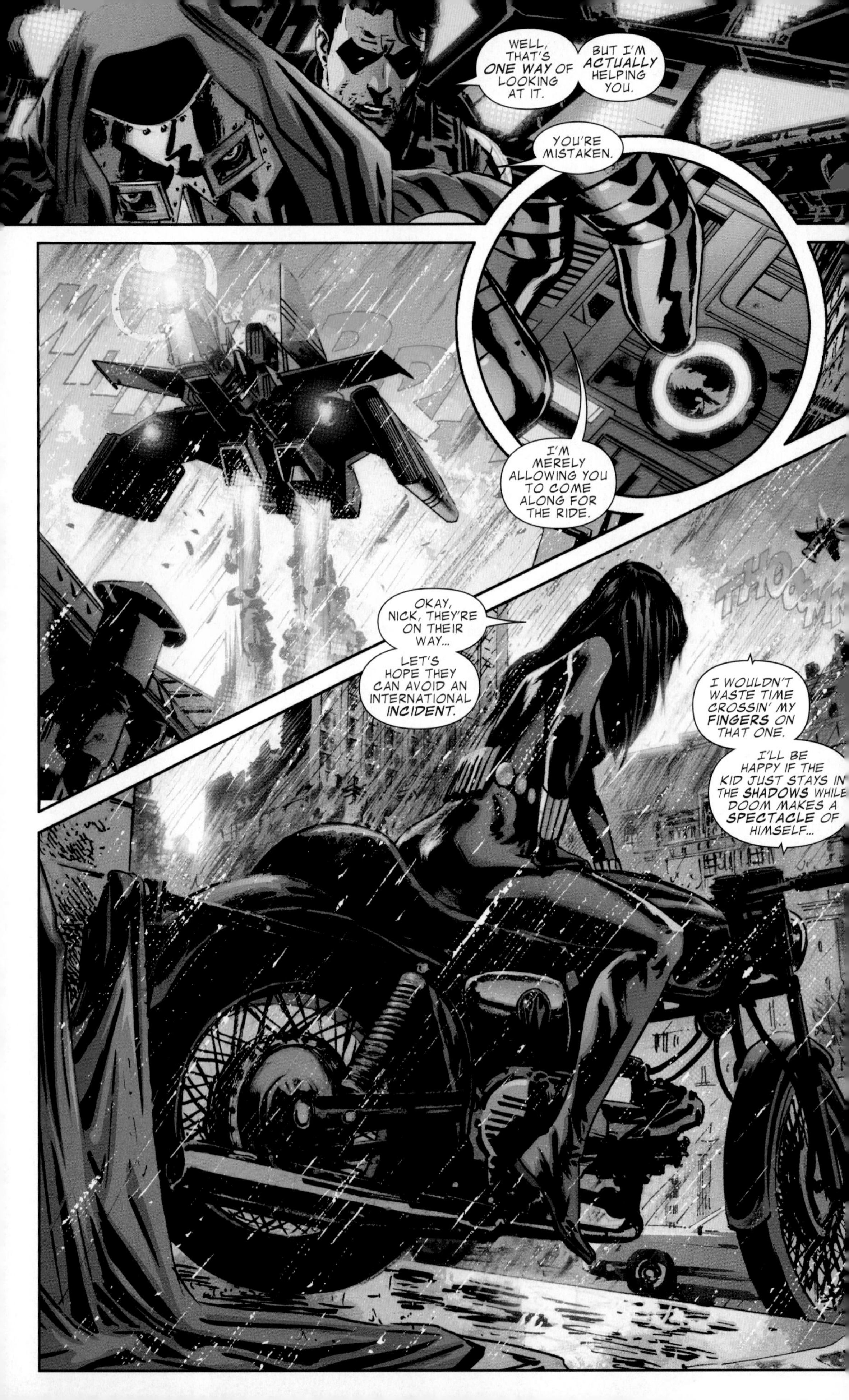
WELL, THAT'S ONE WAY OF LOOKING AT IT.
BUT I'M ACTUALLY HELPING YOU.
YOU'RE MISTAKEN.
I'M MERELY ALLOWING YOU TO COME ALONG FOR THE RIDE.
OKAY, NICK, THEY'RE ON THEIR WAY...
LET'S HOPE THEY CAN AVOID AN INTERNATIONAL INCIDENT.
I WOULDN'T WASTE TIME CROSSIN' MY FINGERS ON THAT ONE.
I'LL BE HAPPY IF THE KID JUST STAYS IN THE SHADOWS WHILE DOOM MAKES A SPECTACLE OF HIMSELF...

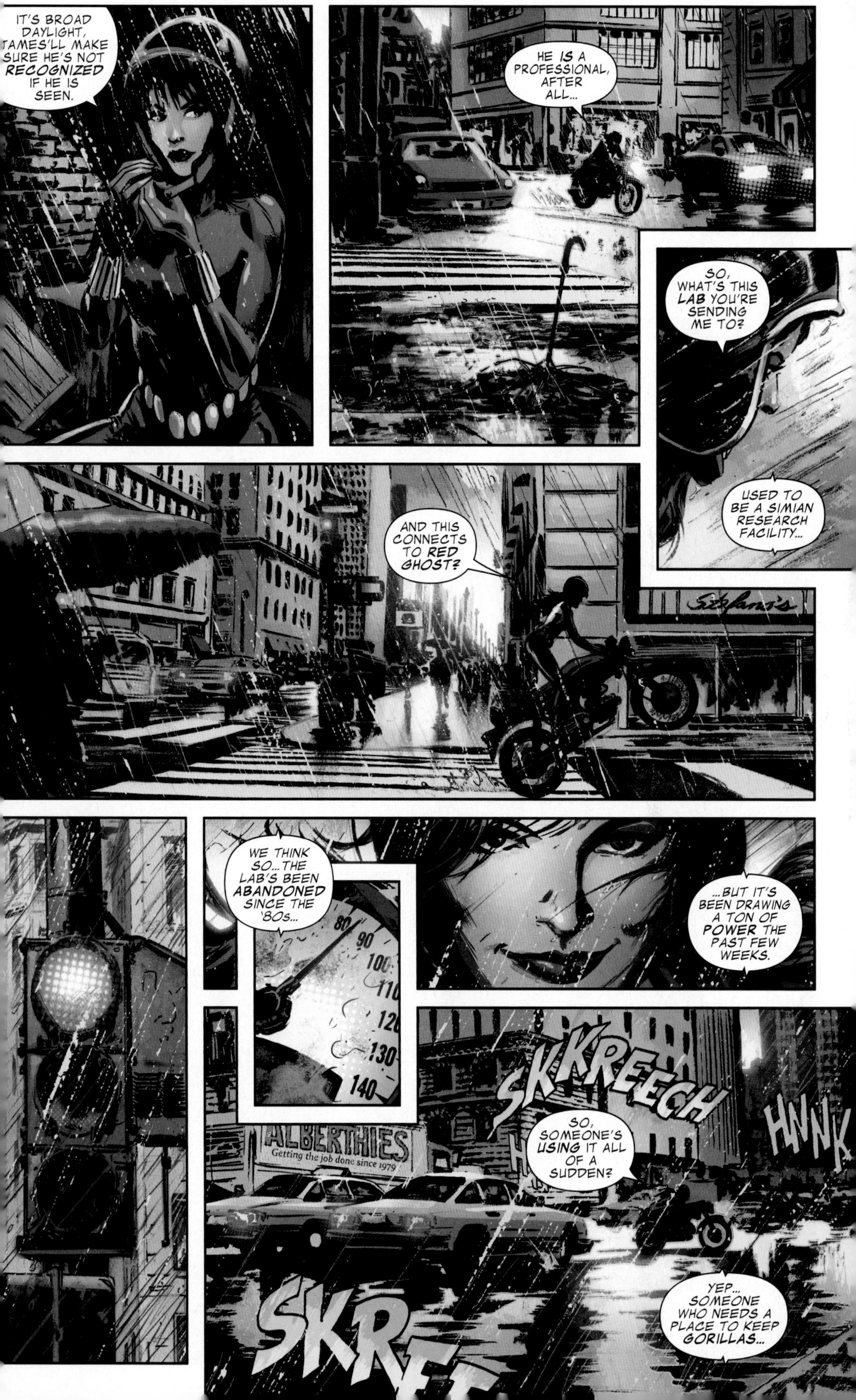
IT'S BROAD DAYLIGHT, JAMES'LL MAKE SURE HE'S NOT RECOGNIZED IF HE IS SEEN.
HE IS A PROFESSIONAL, AFTER ALL...
SO, WHAT'S THIS LAB YOU'RE SENDING ME TO?
USED TO BE A SIMIAN RESEARCH FACILITY...
AND THIS CONNECTS TO RED GHOST?
WE THINK SO... THE LAB'S BEEN ABANDONED SINCE THE '80s...
...BUT IT'S BEEN DRAWING A TON OF POWER THE PAST FEW WEEKS.
SKKREECH
HNNK
ALBERTHIES
Getting the job done since 1979
SO, SOMEONE'S USING IT ALL OF A SUDDEN?
YEP... SOMEONE WHO NEEDS A PLACE TO KEEP GORILLAS...

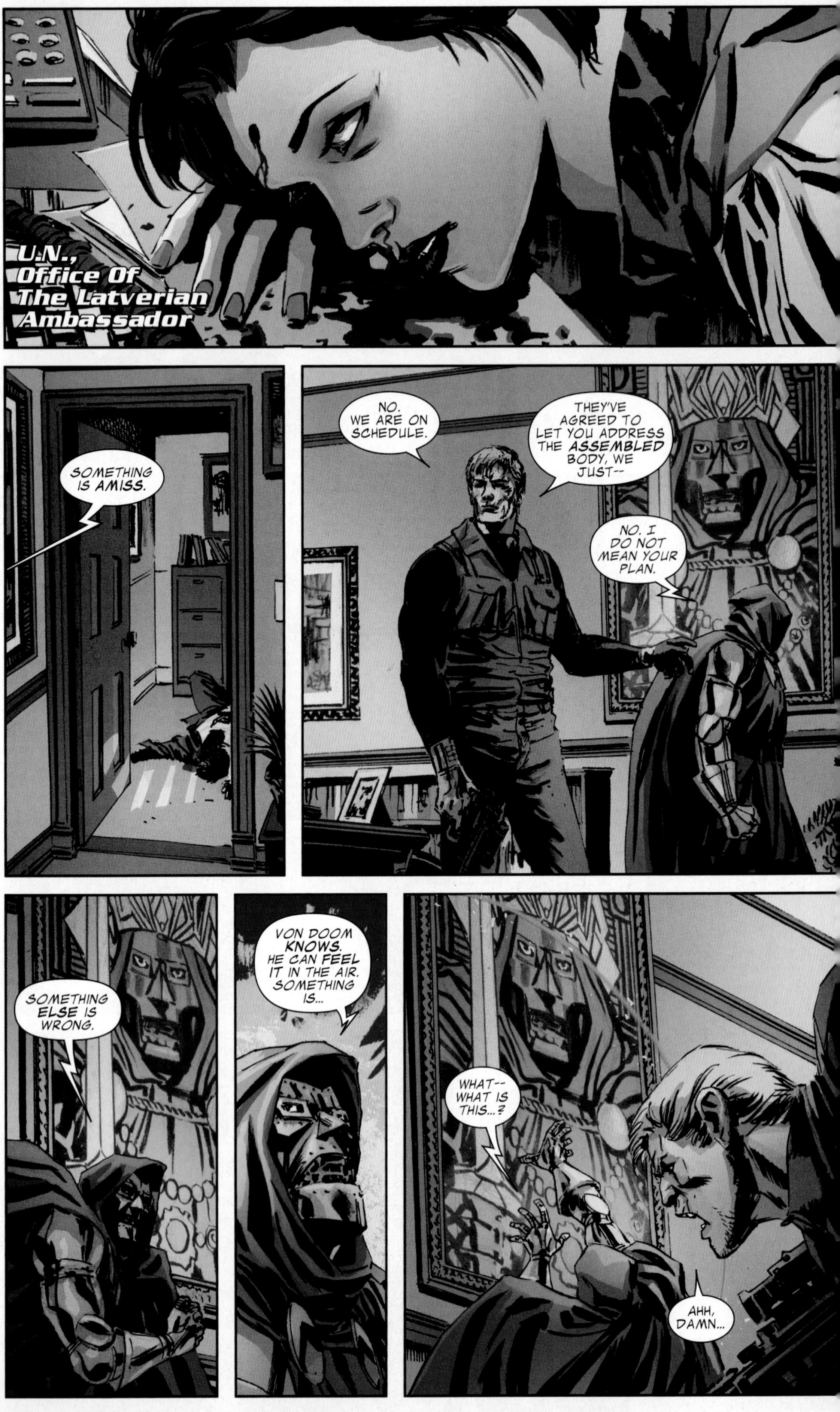
U.N., Office Of The Latverian Ambassador
SOMETHING IS AMISS.
NO. WE ARE ON SCHEDULE.
THEY'VE AGREED TO LET YOU ADDRESS THE ASSEMBLED BODY, WE JUST--
NO. I DO NOT MEAN YOUR PLAN.
SOMETHING ELSE IS WRONG.
VON DOOM KNOWS. HE CAN FEEL IT IN THE AIR. SOMETHING IS...
WHAT-- WHAT IS THIS...?
AHH, DAMN...

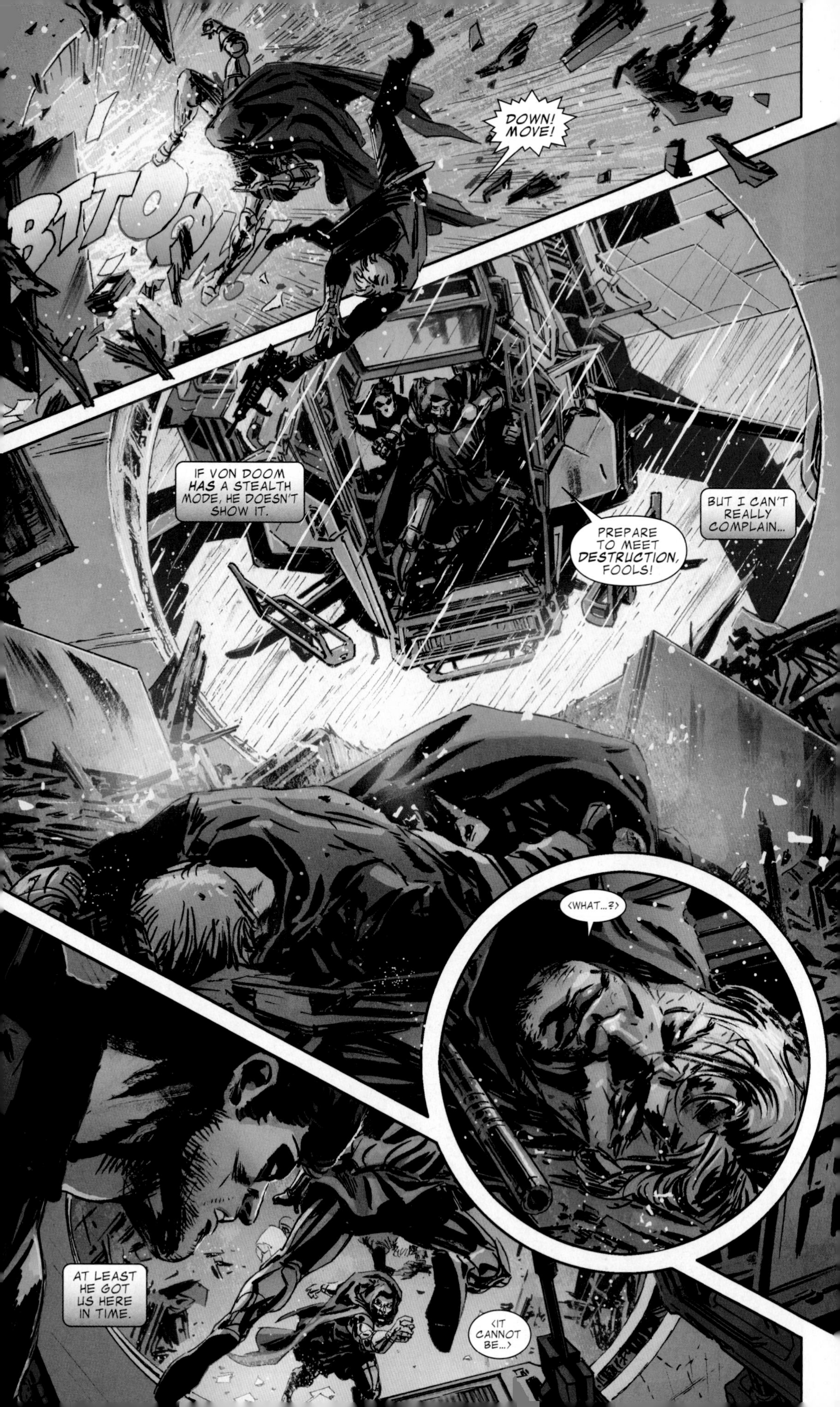
DOWN! MOVE!
IF VON DOOM HAS A STEALTH MODE, HE DOESN'T SHOW IT.
PREPARE TO MEET DESTRUCTION, FOOLS!
BUT I CAN'T REALLY COMPLAIN...
<WHAT...?>
AT LEAST HE GOT US HERE IN TIME.
<IT CANNOT BE...>

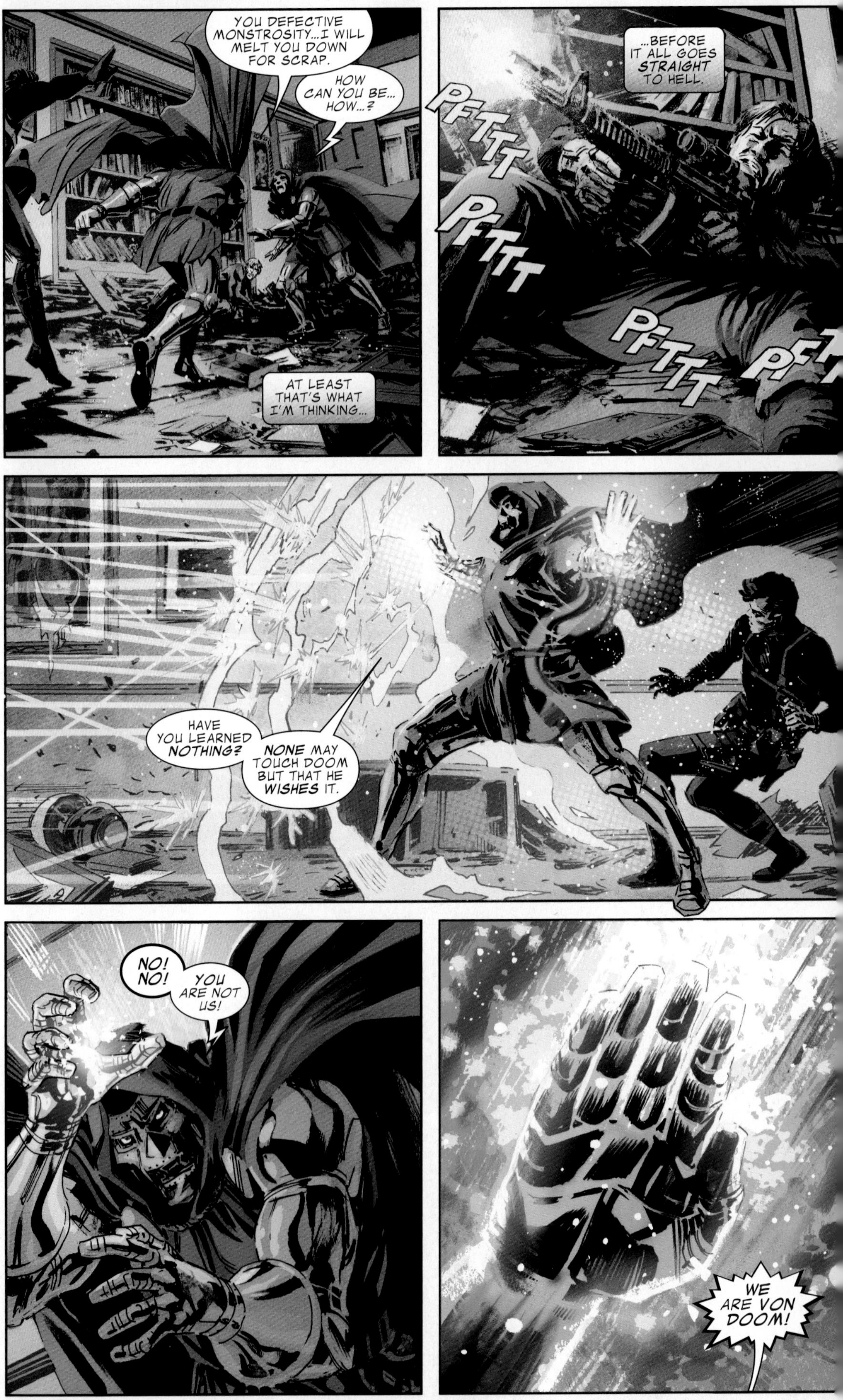
YOU DEFECTIVE MONSTROSITY...I WILL MELT YOU DOWN FOR SCRAP.
HOW CAN YOU BE... HOW...?
AT LEAST THAT'S WHAT I'M THINKING...
...BEFORE IT ALL GOES STRAIGHT TO HELL.
PFTTTT
PFTTTT
PFTTTT
HAVE YOU LEARNED NOTHING?
NONE MAY TOUCH DOOM BUT THAT HE WISHES IT.
NO! NO!
YOU ARE NOT US!
WE ARE VON DOOM!

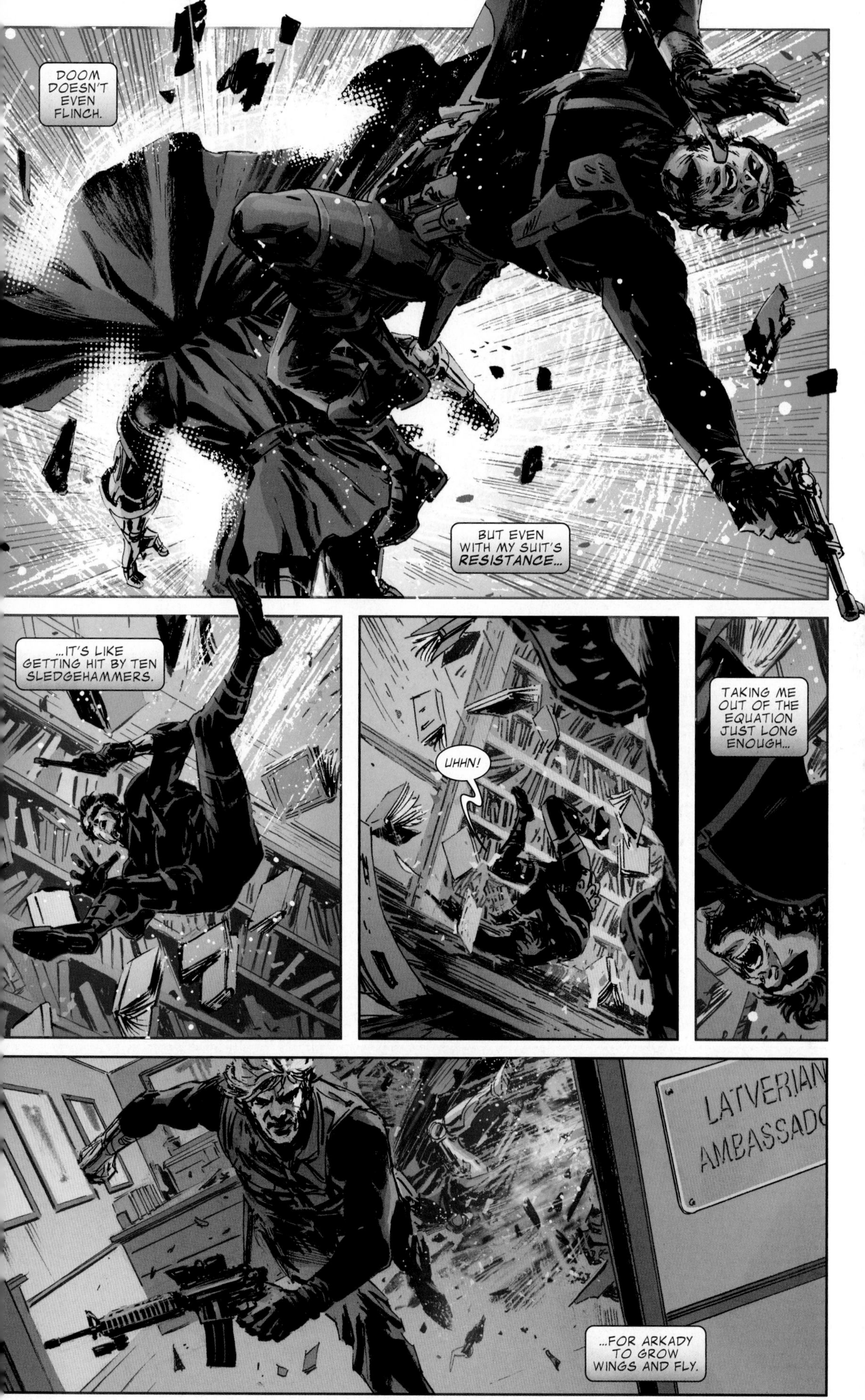
DOOM DOESN'T EVEN FLINCH.
BUT EVEN WITH MY SUIT'S RESISTANCE...
...IT'S LIKE GETTING HIT BY TEN SLEDGEHAMMERS.
UHHN!
TAKING ME OUT OF THE EQUATION JUST LONG ENOUGH...
LATVERIAN AMBASSADO
...FOR ARKADY TO GROW WINGS AND FLY.

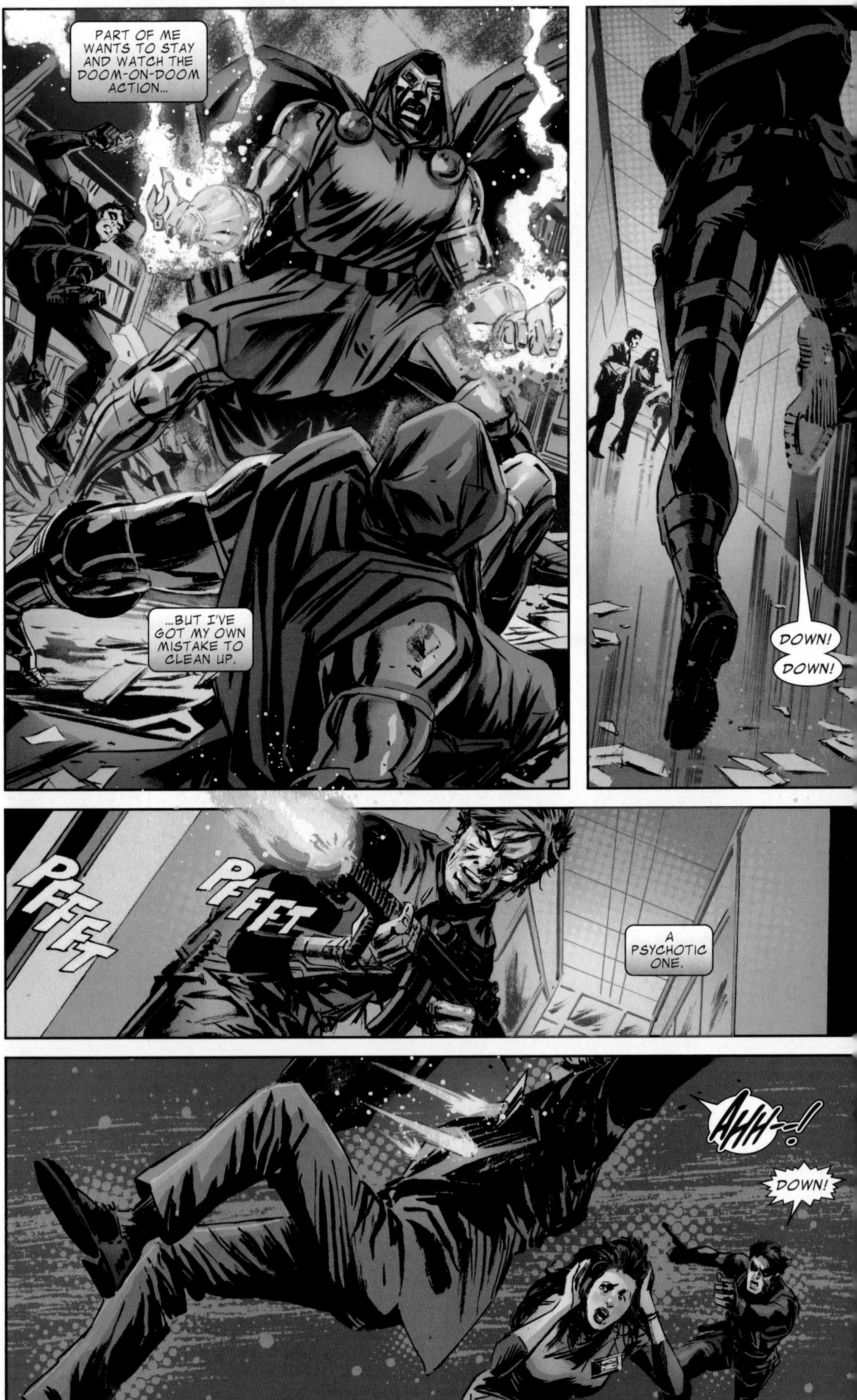
PART OF ME WANTS TO STAY AND WATCH THE DOOM-ON-DOOM ACTION...
...BUT I'VE GOT MY OWN MISTAKE TO CLEAN UP.
DOWN!
DOWN!
PFFFT
PFFFT
A PSYCHOTIC ONE.
AHH--!
DOWN!

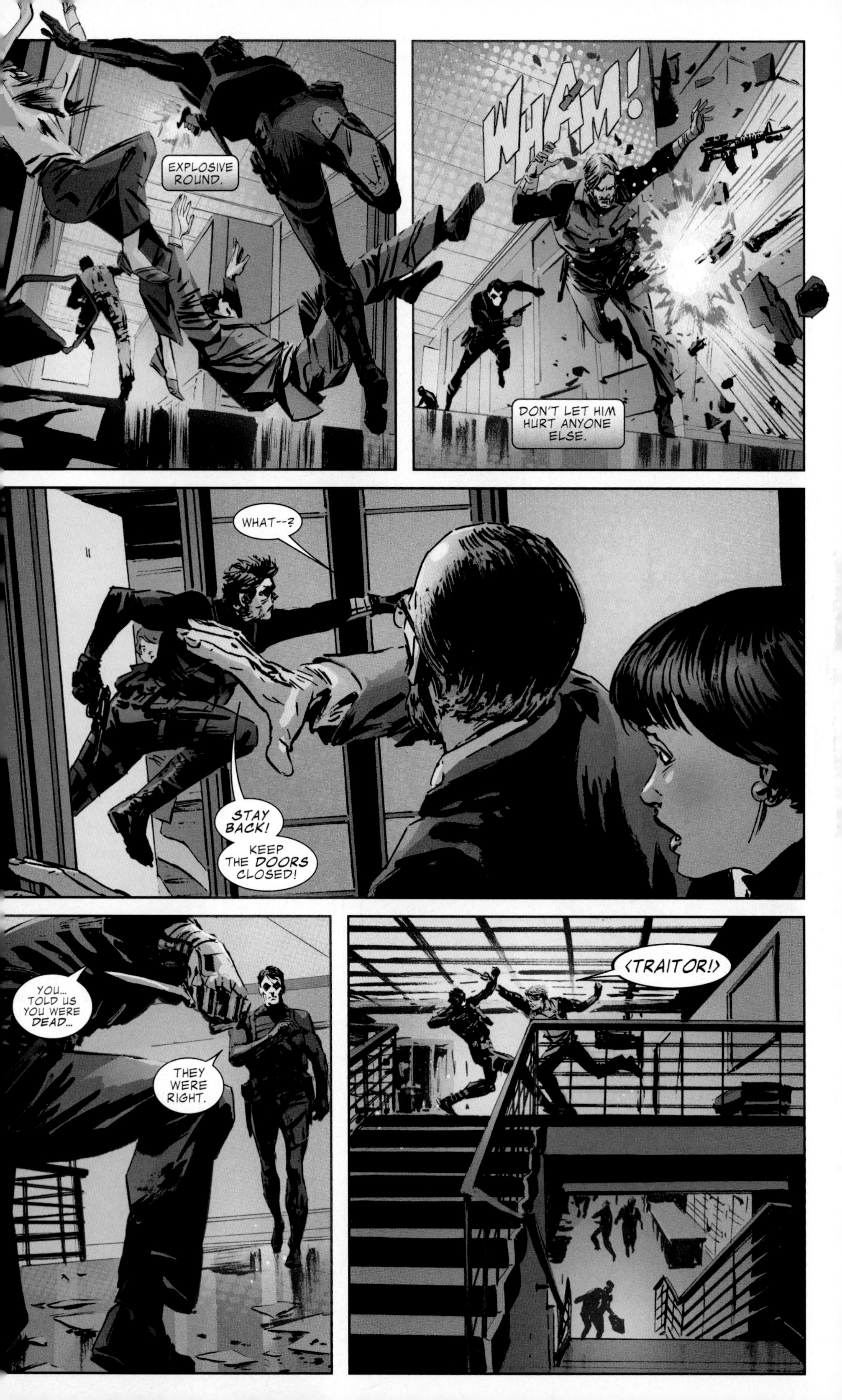
EXPLOSIVE ROUND.
WHAM!
DON'T LET HIM HURT ANYONE ELSE.
WHAT--?
STAY BACK!
KEEP THE DOORS CLOSED!
YOU... TOLD US YOU WERE DEAD...
THEY WERE RIGHT.
<TRAITOR!>

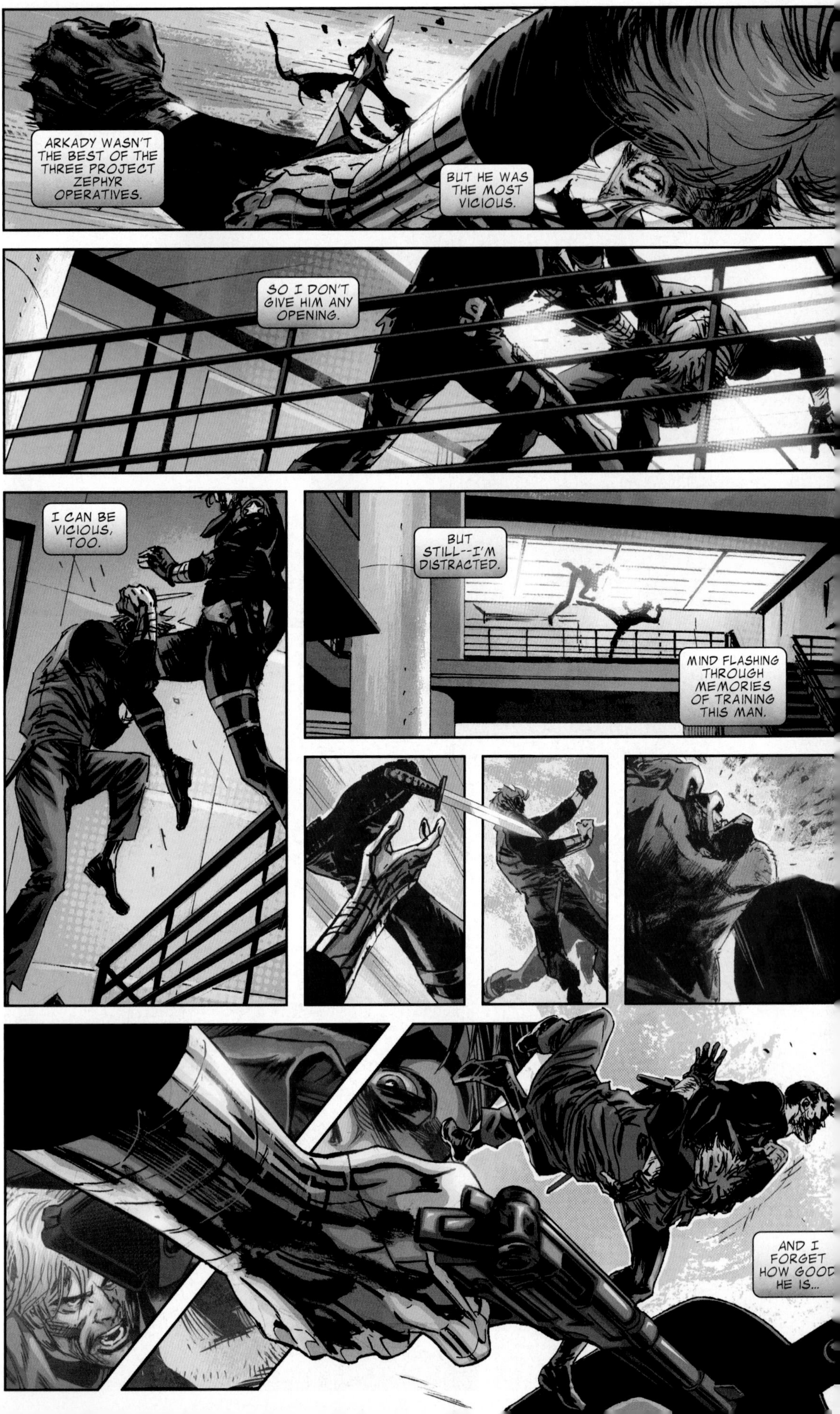
ARKADY WASN'T THE BEST OF THE THREE PROJECT ZEPHYR OPERATIVES.
BUT HE WAS THE MOST VICIOUS.
SO I DON'T GIVE HIM ANY OPENING.
I CAN BE VICIOUS, TOO.
BUT STILL--I'M DISTRACTED.
MIND FLASHING THROUGH MEMORIES OF TRAINING THIS MAN.
AND I FORGET HOW GOOD HE IS...

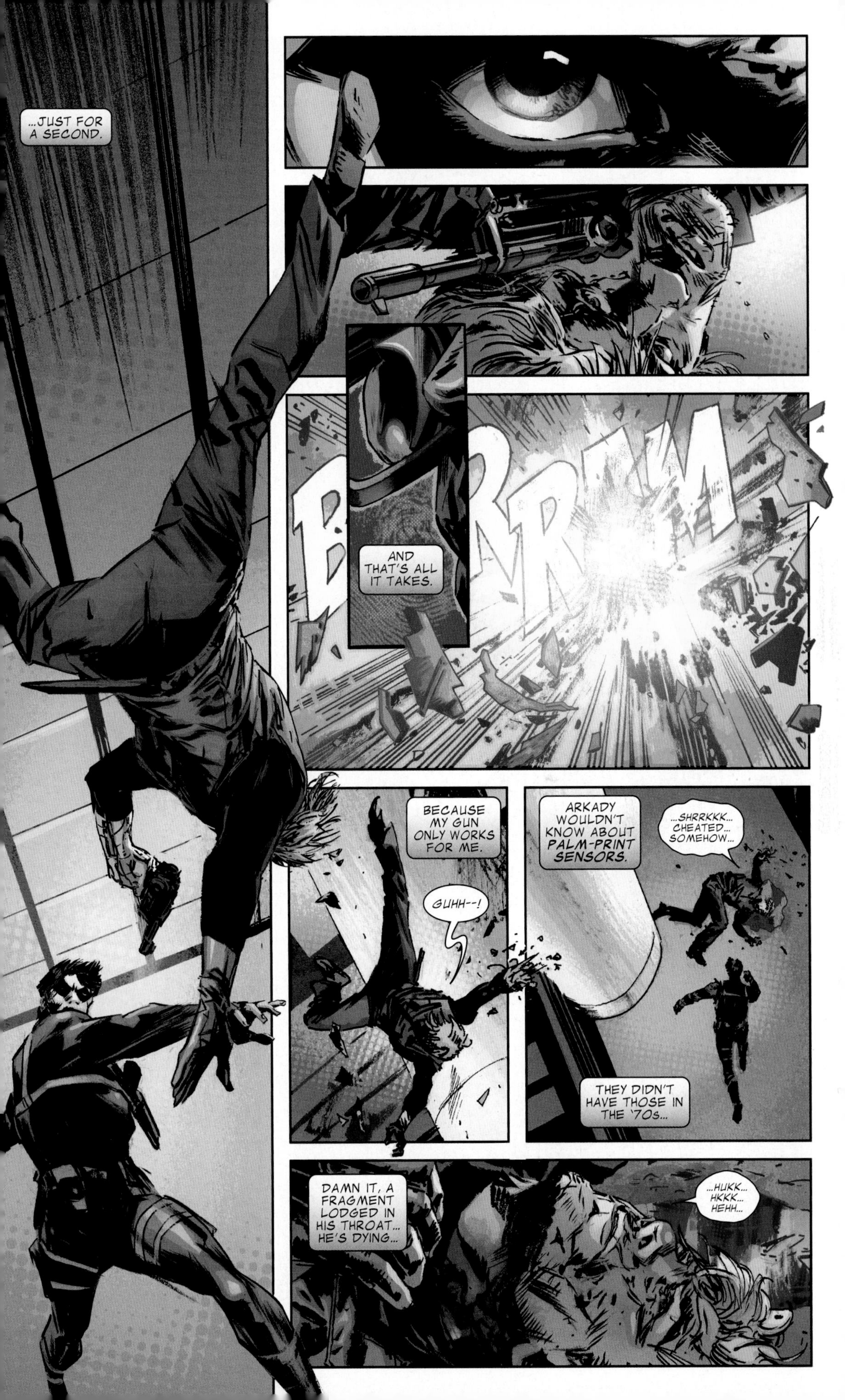
...JUST FOR A SECOND.
AND THAT'S ALL IT TAKES.
BRRRM
BECAUSE MY GUN ONLY WORKS FOR ME.
GUHH--!
ARKADY WOULDN'T KNOW ABOUT PALM-PRINT SENSORS.
...SHRRKKK... CHEATED... SOMEHOW...
THEY DIDN'T HAVE THOSE IN THE '70s...
DAMN IT, A FRAGMENT LODGED IN HIS THROAT... HE'S DYING...
...HUKK... HKKK... HEHH...

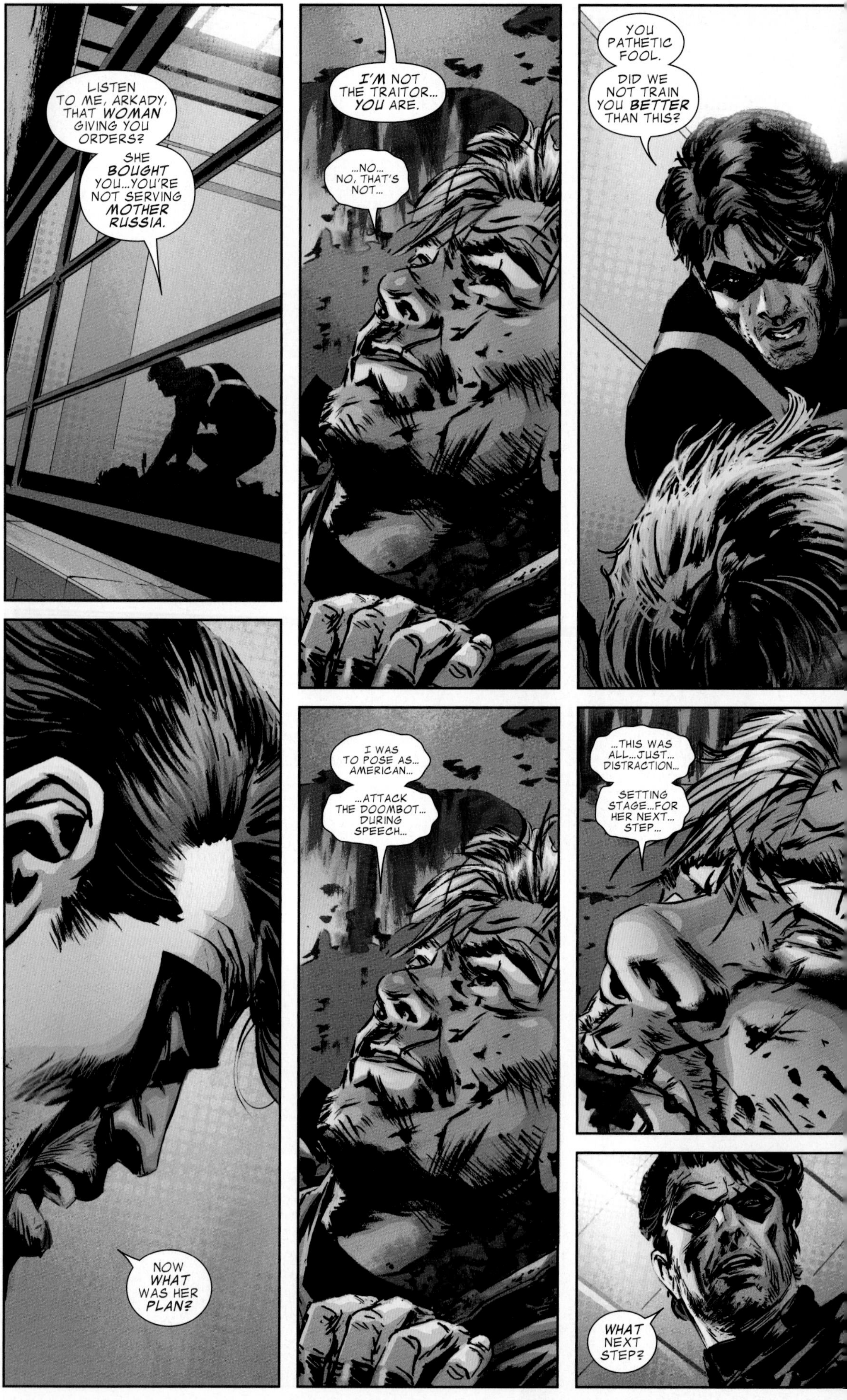
LISTEN TO ME, ARKADY, THAT WOMAN GIVING YOU ORDERS?
SHE BOUGHT YOU...YOU'RE NOT SERVING MOTHER RUSSIA.
I'M NOT THE TRAITOR... YOU ARE.
...NO... NO, THAT'S NOT...
YOU PATHETIC FOOL.
DID WE NOT TRAIN YOU BETTER THAN THIS?
NOW WHAT WAS HER PLAN?
I WAS TO POSE AS... AMERICAN...
...ATTACK THE DOOMBOT... DURING SPEECH...
...THIS WAS ALL...JUST... DISTRACTION...
SETTING STAGE...FOR HER NEXT... STEP...
WHAT NEXT STEP?

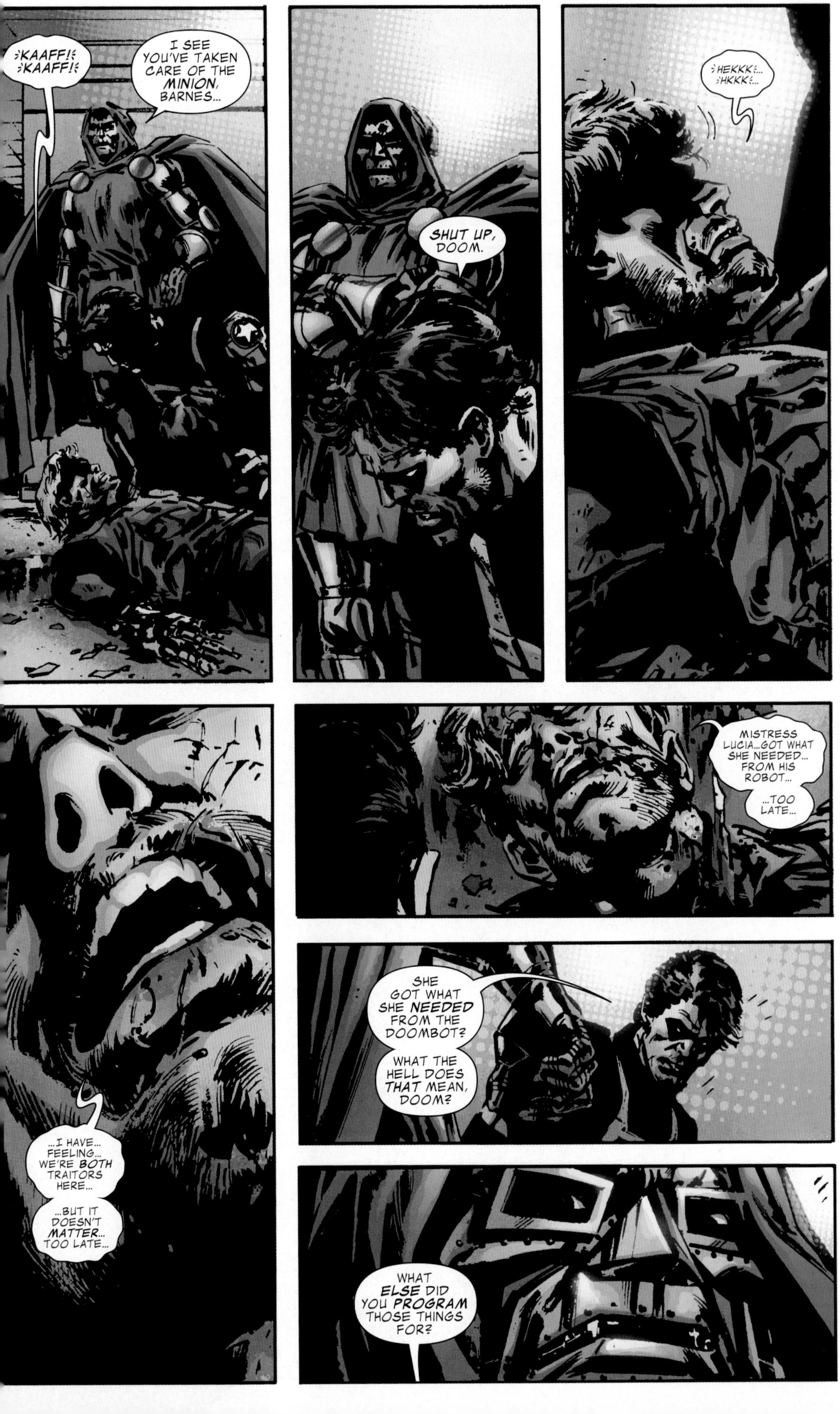
KAAFF! KAAFF!
I SEE YOU'VE TAKEN CARE OF THE MINION, BARNES...
SHUT UP, DOOM.
HEKKK... HKKK...
...I HAVE... FEELING... WE'RE BOTH TRAITORS HERE...
...BUT IT DOESN'T MATTER... TOO LATE...
MISTRESS LUCIA...GOT WHAT SHE NEEDED... FROM HIS ROBOT...
...TOO LATE...
SHE GOT WHAT SHE NEEDED FROM THE DOOMBOT?
WHAT THE HELL DOES THAT MEAN, DOOM?
WHAT ELSE DID YOU PROGRAM THOSE THINGS FOR?

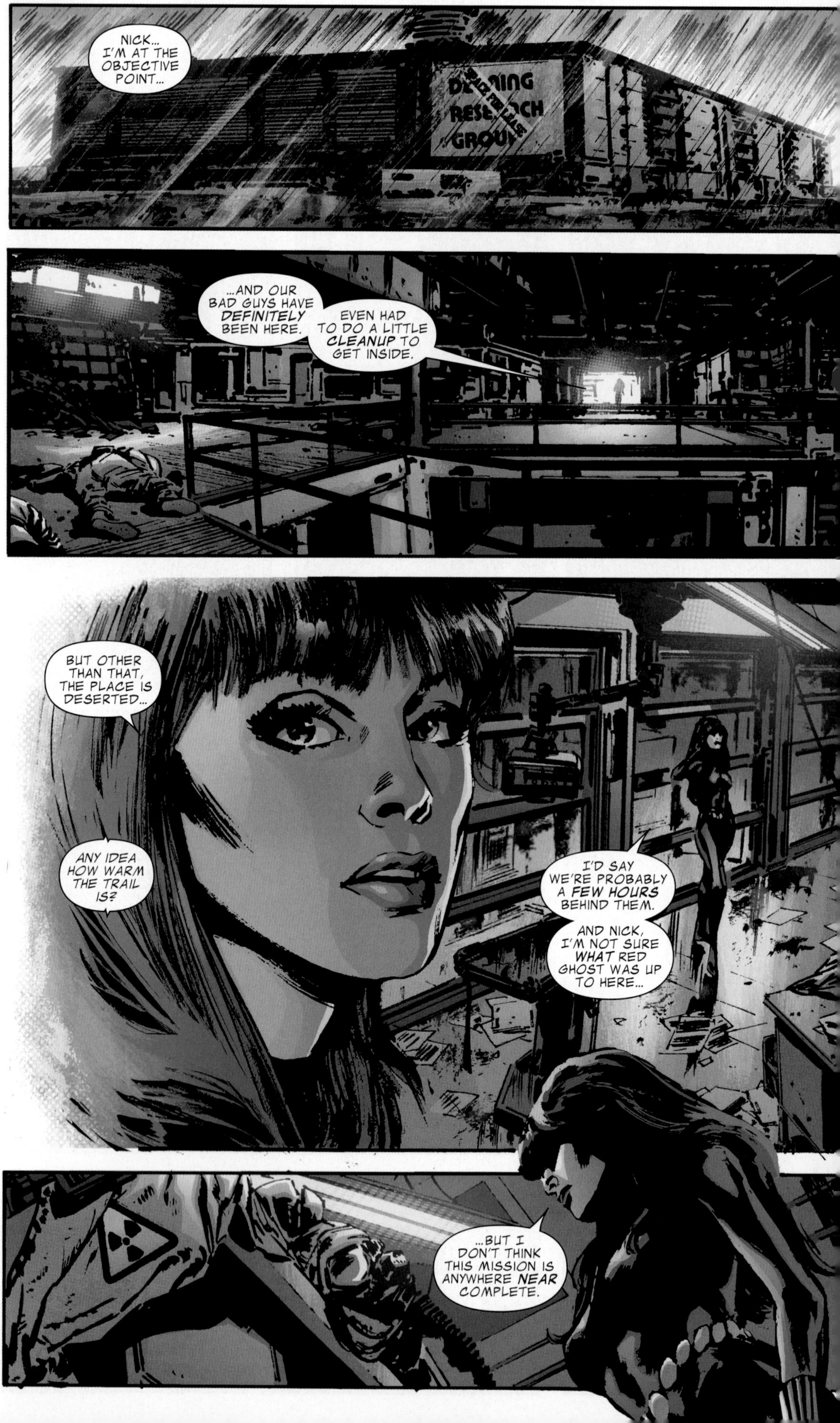
NICK... I'M AT THE OBJECTIVE POINT...
...AND OUR BAD GUYS HAVE DEFINITELY BEEN HERE.
EVEN HAD TO DO A LITTLE CLEANUP TO GET INSIDE.
BUT OTHER THAN THAT, THE PLACE IS DESERTED...
ANY IDEA HOW WARM THE TRAIL IS?
I'D SAY WE'RE PROBABLY A FEW HOURS BEHIND THEM.
AND NICK, I'M NOT SURE WHAT RED GHOST WAS UP TO HERE...
...BUT I DON'T THINK THIS MISSION IS ANYWHERE NEAR COMPLETE.

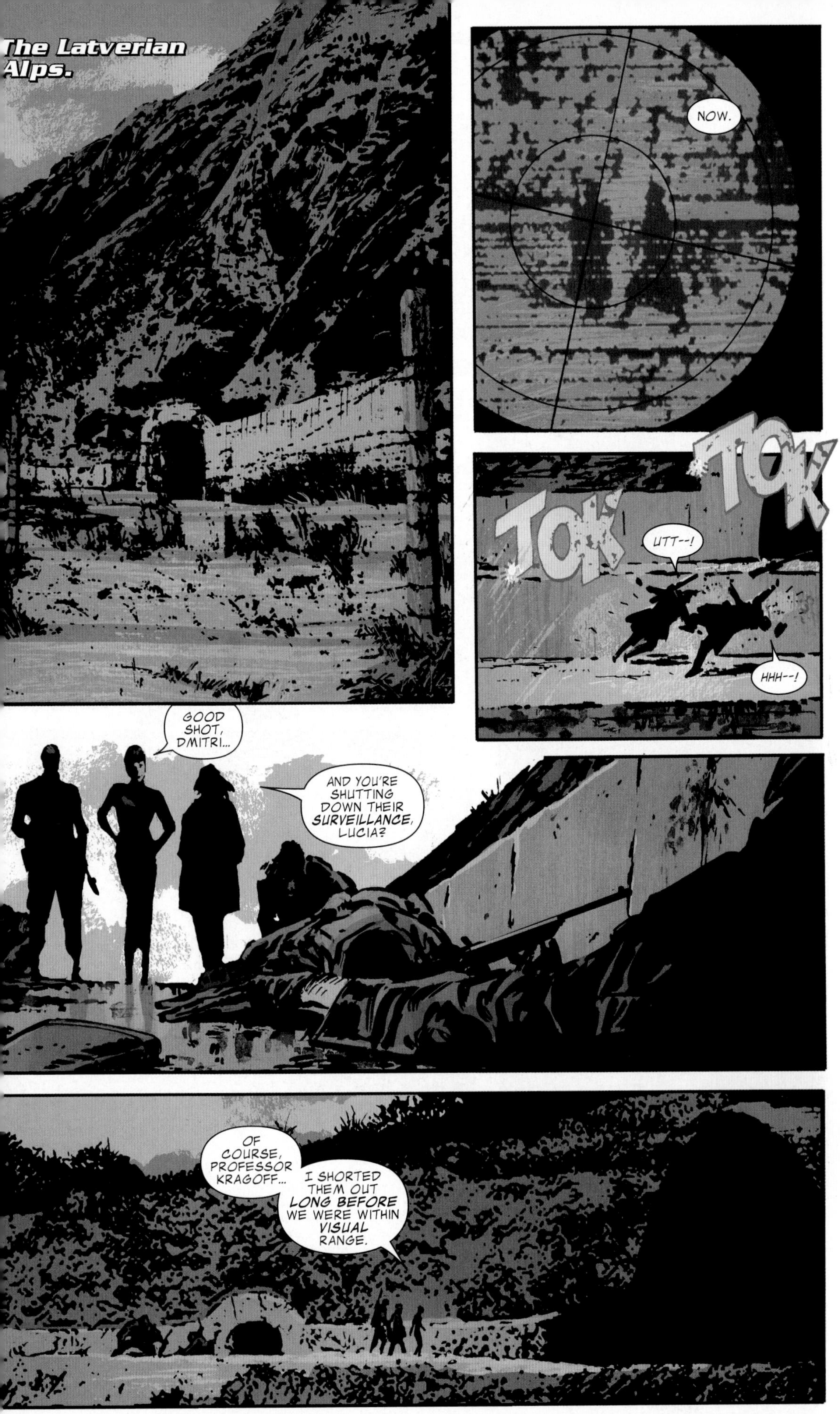
The Latverian Alps.
NOW.
TOK
TOK
UTT--!
HHH--!
GOOD SHOT, DMITRI...
AND YOU'RE SHUTTING DOWN THEIR SURVEILLANCE, LUCIA?
OF COURSE, PROFESSOR KRAGOFF...
I SHORTED THEM OUT LONG BEFORE WE WERE WITHIN VISUAL RANGE.

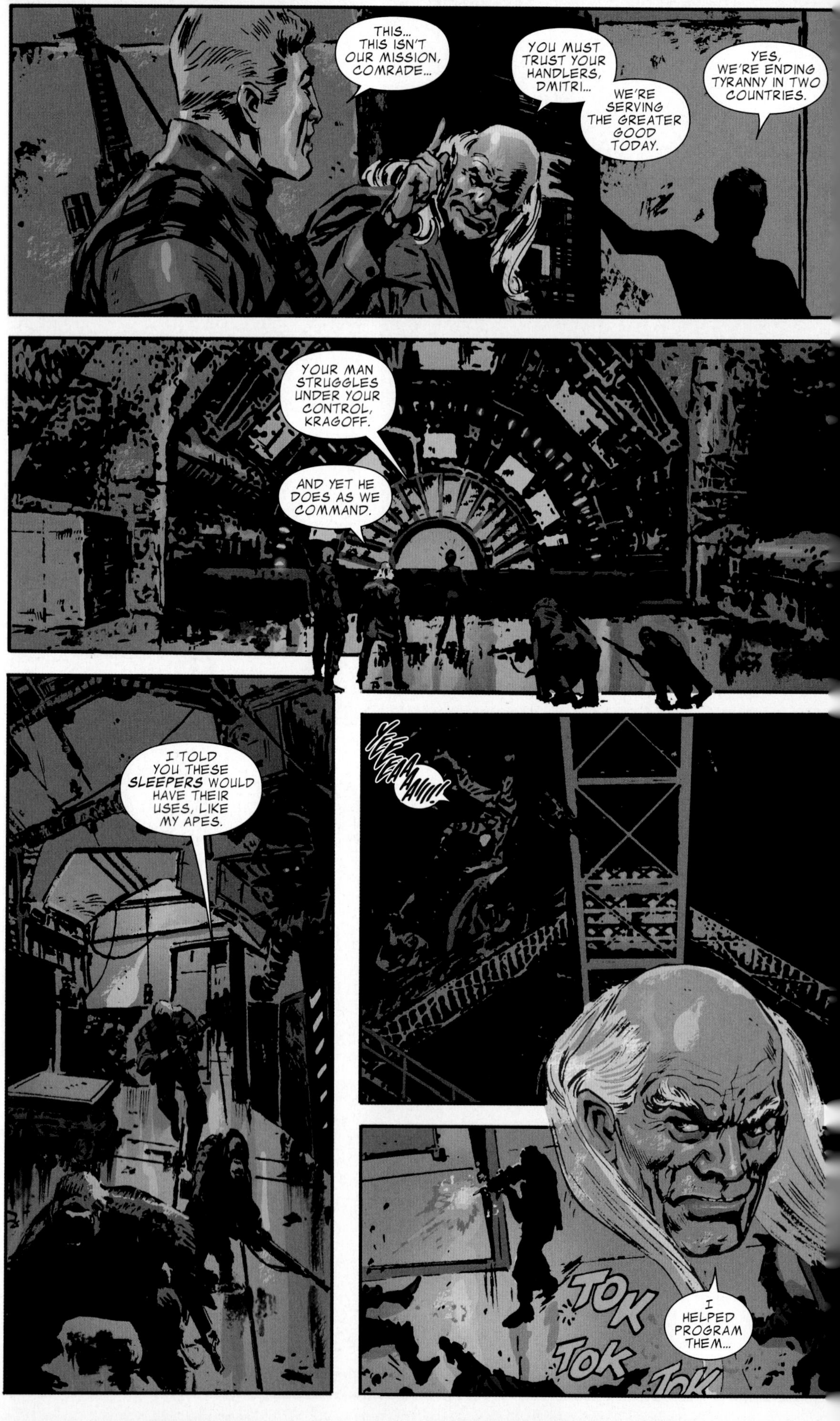

THIS... THIS ISN'T OUR MISSION, COMRADE...
YOU MUST TRUST YOUR HANDLERS, DMITRI...
WE'RE SERVING THE GREATER GOOD TODAY.
YES, WE'RE ENDING TYRANNY IN TWO COUNTRIES.
YOUR MAN STRUGGLES UNDER YOUR CONTROL, KRAGOFF.
AND YET HE DOES AS WE COMMAND.
I TOLD YOU THESE SLEEPERS WOULD HAVE THEIR USES, LIKE MY APES.
YEEEAAAAAIII!
TOK
TOK
TOK
I HELPED PROGRAM THEM...

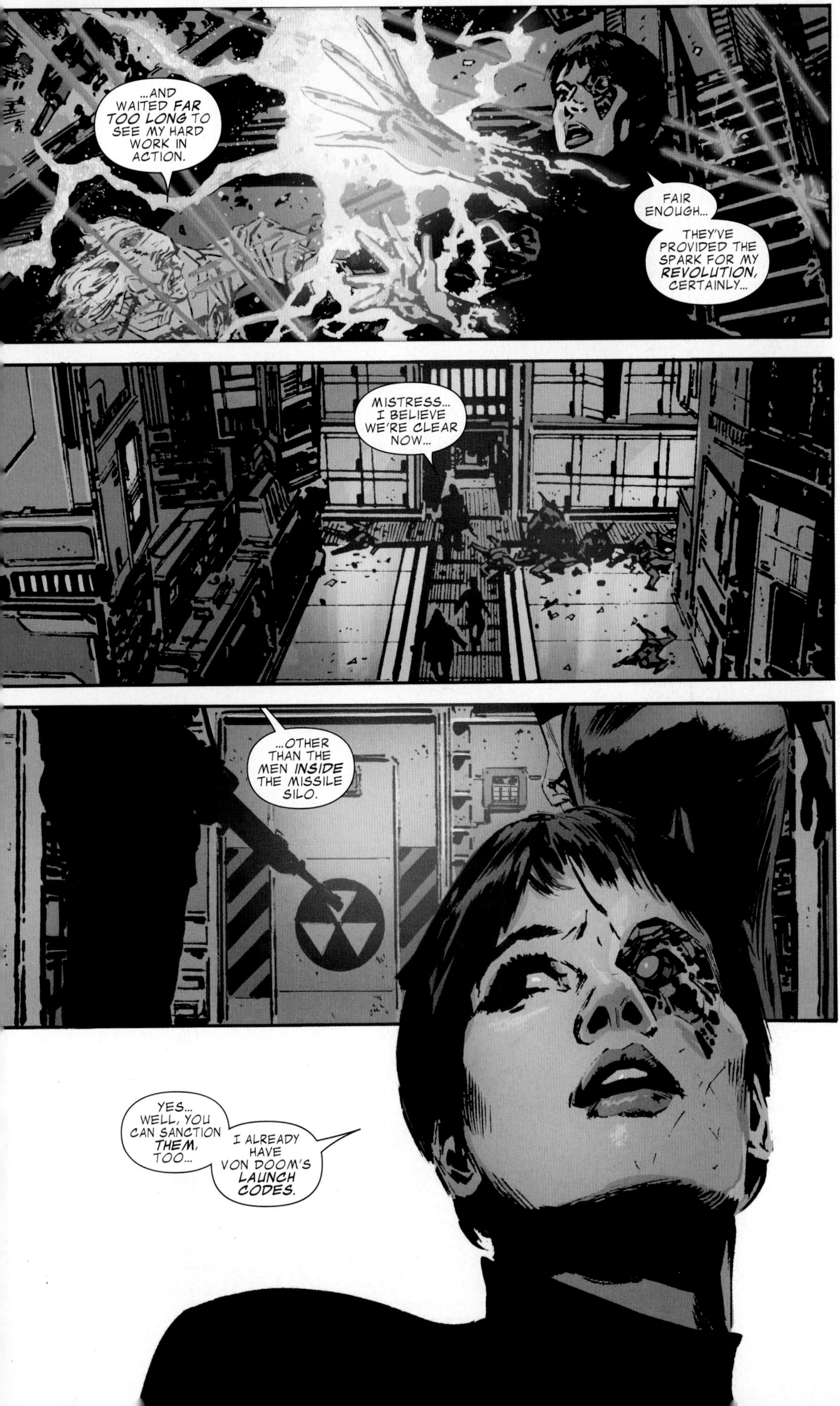
...AND WAITED FAR TOO LONG TO SEE MY HARD WORK IN ACTION.
FAIR ENOUGH...
THEY'VE PROVIDED THE SPARK FOR MY REVOLUTION, CERTAINLY...
MISTRESS... I BELIEVE WE'RE CLEAR NOW...
...OTHER THAN THE MEN INSIDE THE MISSILE SILO.
YES... WELL, YOU CAN SANCTION THEM, TOO...
I ALREADY HAVE VON DOOM'S LAUNCH CODES.

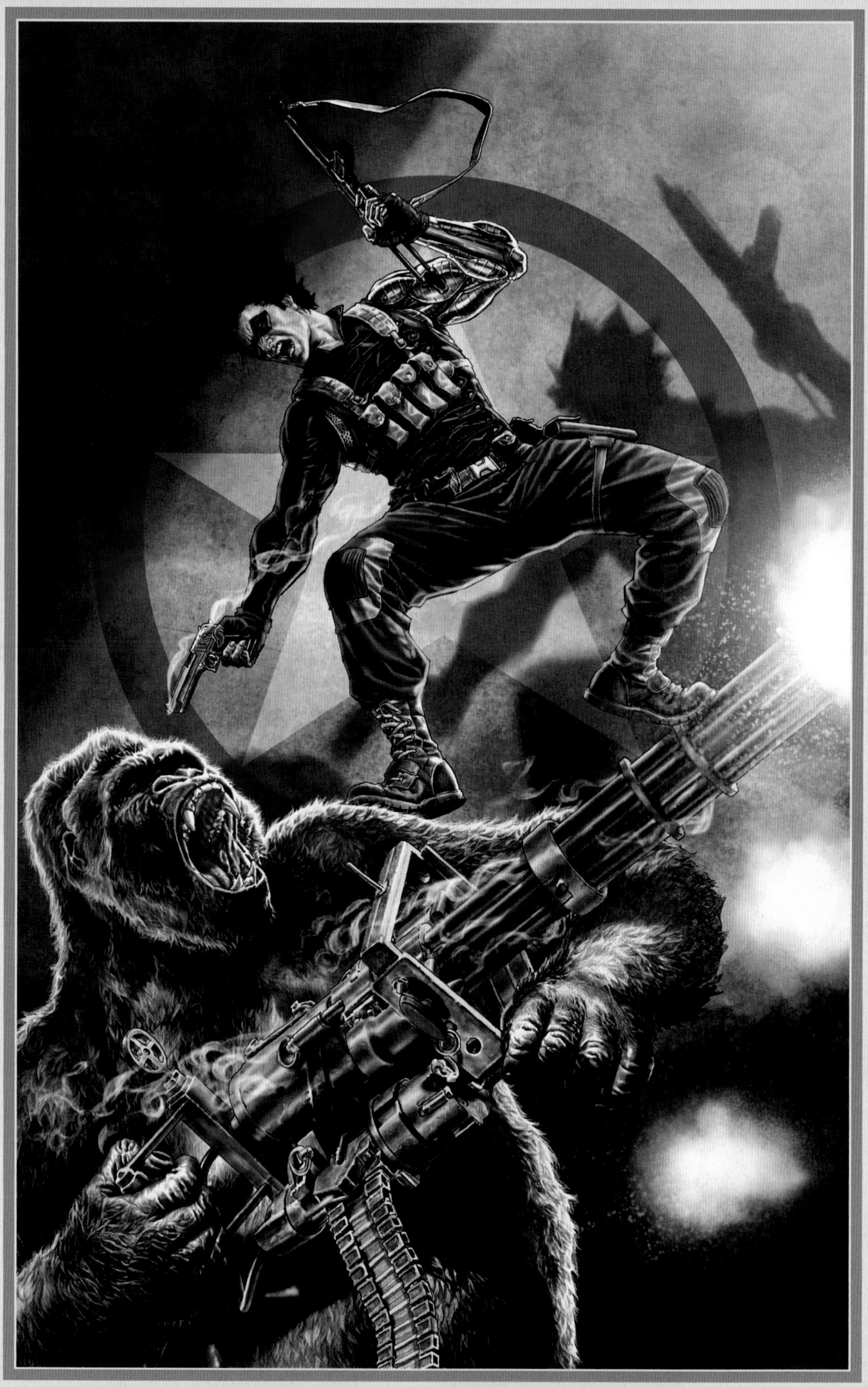

FIVE

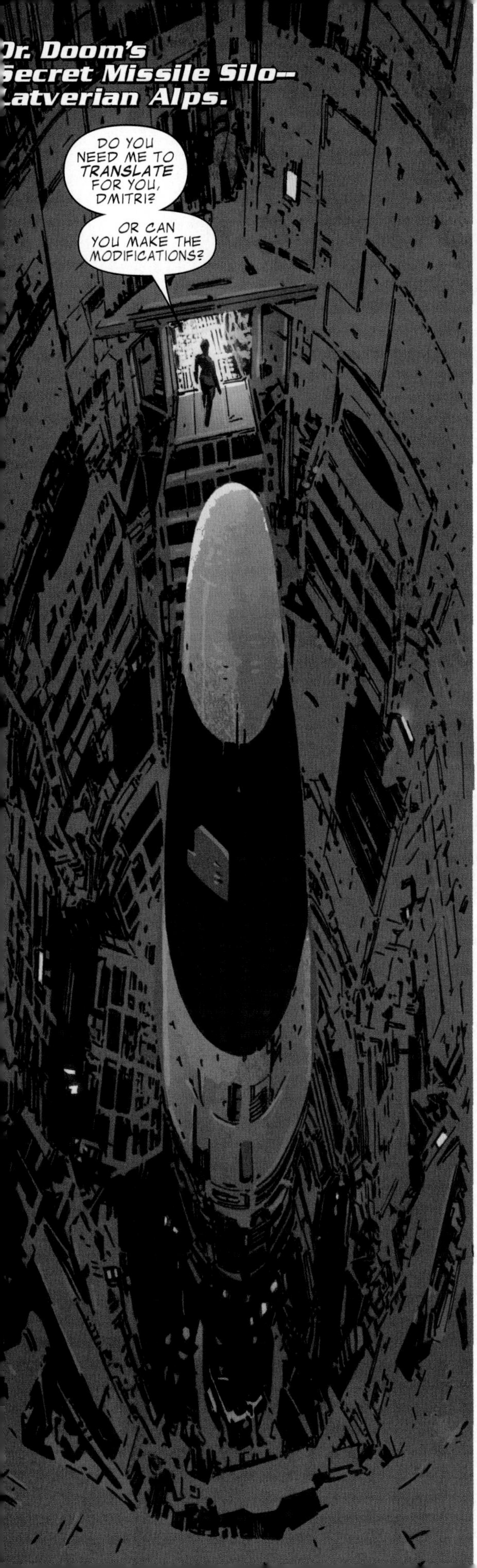
Dr. Doom's
Secret Missile Silo--
Latverian Alps.
DO YOU NEED ME TO *TRANSLATE* FOR YOU, DMITRI?
OR CAN YOU MAKE THE MODIFICATIONS?

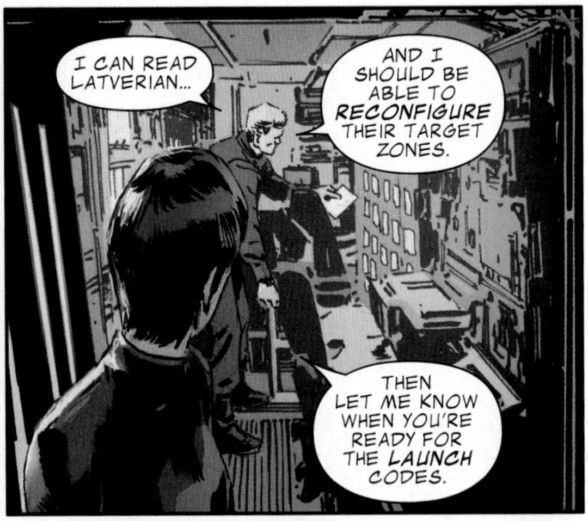
I CAN READ LATVERIAN...
AND I SHOULD BE ABLE TO *RECONFIGURE* THEIR TARGET ZONES.
THEN LET ME KNOW WHEN YOU'RE READY FOR THE *LAUNCH* CODES.

THE LONGEST WINTER

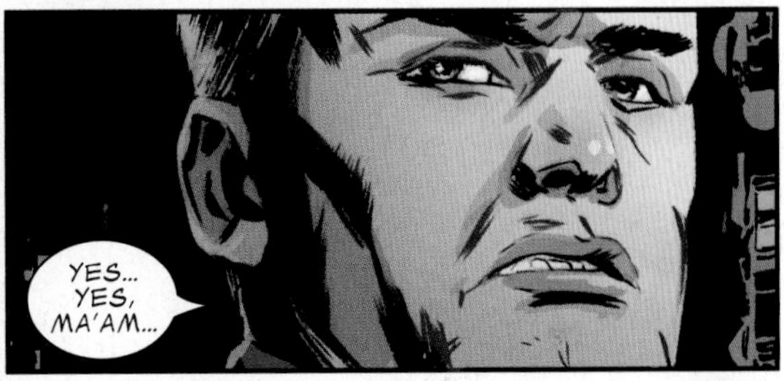
YES... YES, MA'AM...

PART 5 OF 5

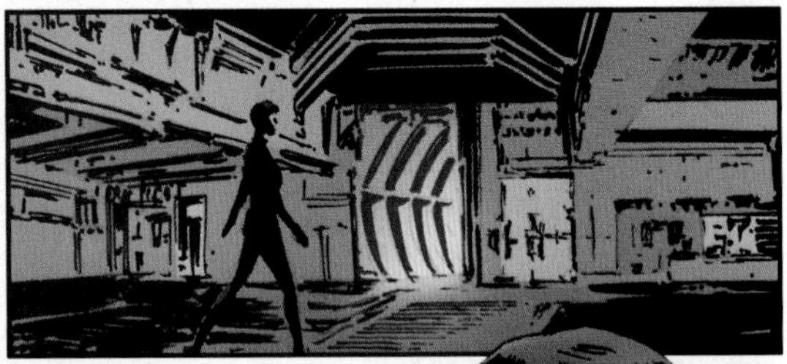

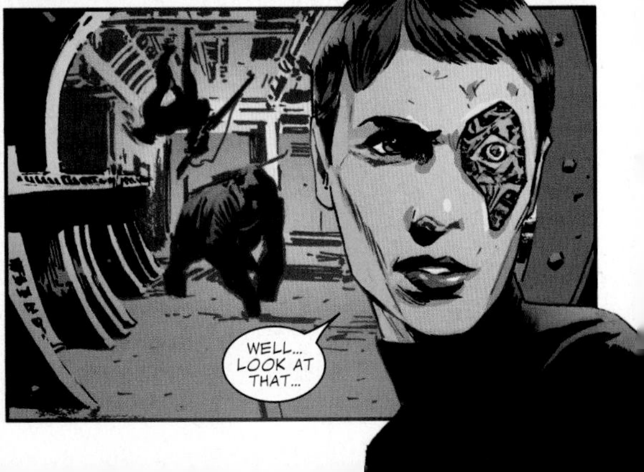
WELL... LOOK AT THAT...

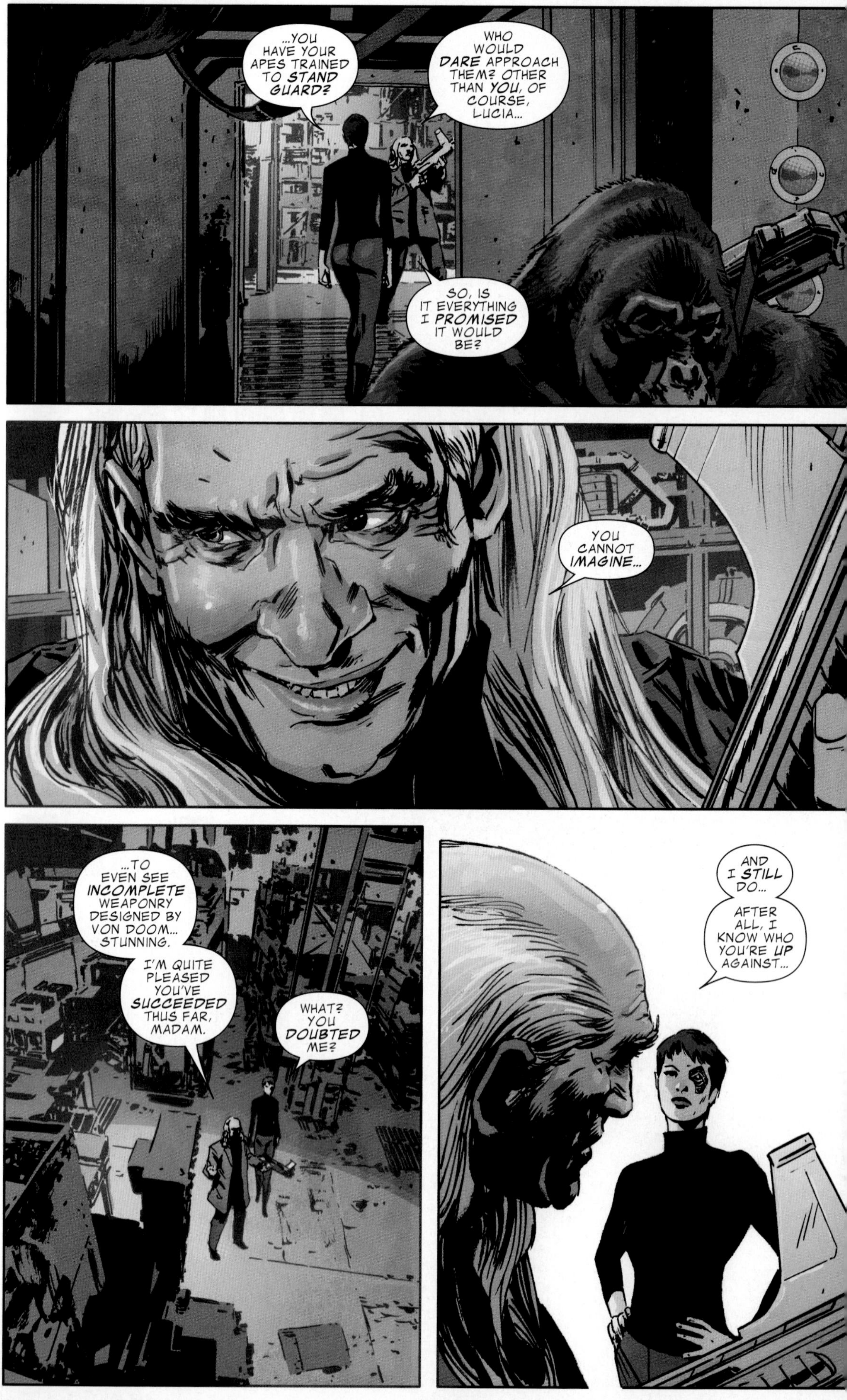
...YOU HAVE YOUR APES TRAINED TO STAND GUARD?
WHO WOULD DARE APPROACH THEM? OTHER THAN YOU, OF COURSE, LUCIA...
SO, IS IT EVERYTHING I PROMISED IT WOULD BE?
YOU CANNOT IMAGINE...
...TO EVEN SEE INCOMPLETE WEAPONRY DESIGNED BY VON DOOM... STUNNING.
I'M QUITE PLEASED YOU'VE SUCCEEDED THUS FAR, MADAM.
WHAT? YOU DOUBTED ME?
AND I STILL DO...
AFTER ALL, I KNOW WHO YOU'RE UP AGAINST...

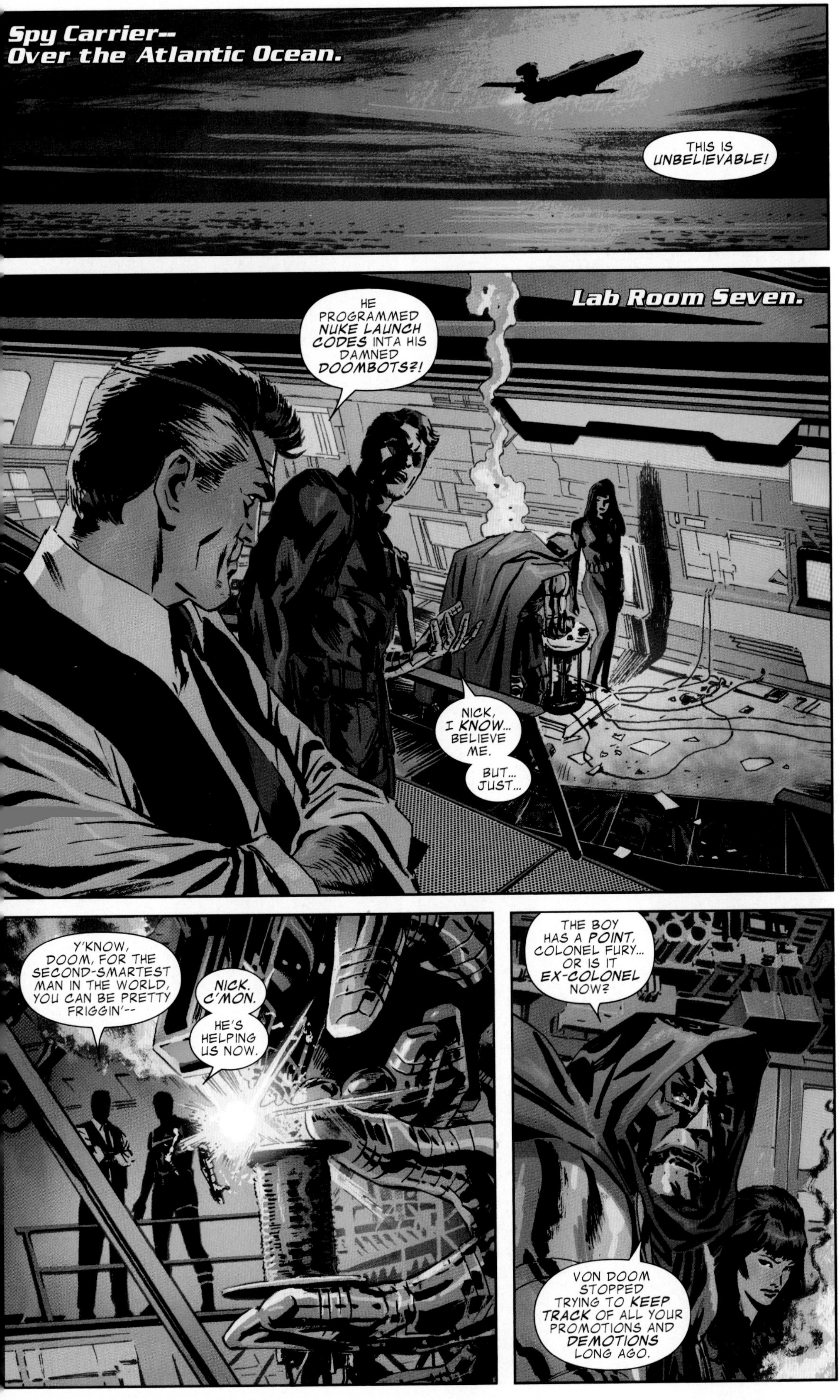
Spy Carrier--
Over the Atlantic Ocean.
THIS IS UNBELIEVABLE!
Lab Room Seven.
HE PROGRAMMED NUKE LAUNCH CODES INTA HIS DAMNED DOOMBOTS?!
NICK, I KNOW... BELIEVE ME.
BUT... JUST...
Y'KNOW, DOOM, FOR THE SECOND-SMARTEST MAN IN THE WORLD, YOU CAN BE PRETTY FRIGGIN'--
NICK. C'MON.
HE'S HELPING US NOW.
THE BOY HAS A POINT, COLONEL FURY... OR IS IT EX-COLONEL NOW?
VON DOOM STOPPED TRYING TO KEEP TRACK OF ALL YOUR PROMOTIONS AND DEMOTIONS LONG AGO.

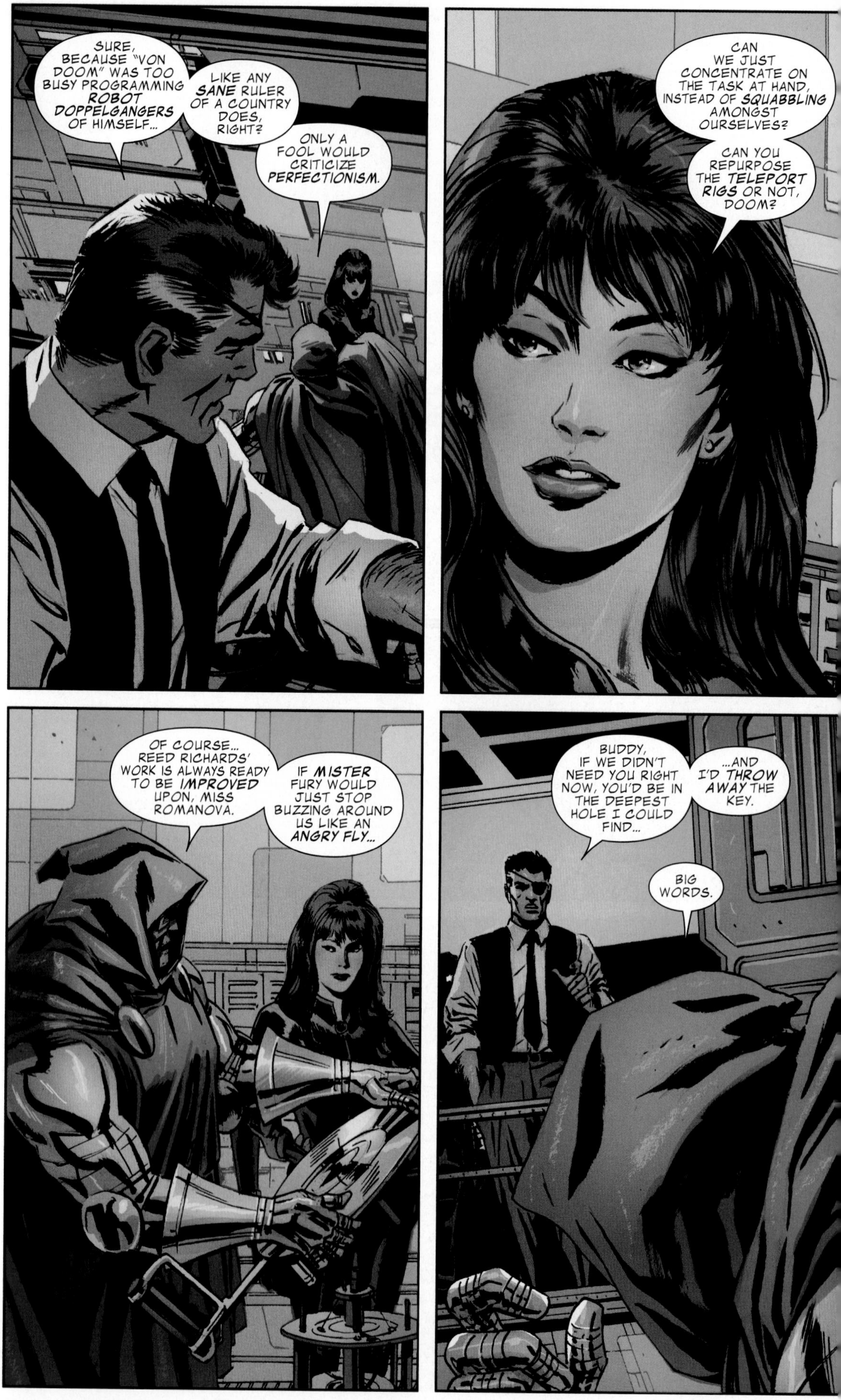

SURE, BECAUSE "VON DOOM" WAS TOO BUSY PROGRAMMING ROBOT DOPPELGANGERS OF HIMSELF...
LIKE ANY SANE RULER OF A COUNTRY DOES, RIGHT?
ONLY A FOOL WOULD CRITICIZE PERFECTIONISM.
CAN WE JUST CONCENTRATE ON THE TASK AT HAND, INSTEAD OF SQUABBLING AMONGST OURSELVES?
CAN YOU REPURPOSE THE TELEPORT RIGS OR NOT, DOOM?
OF COURSE... REED RICHARDS' WORK IS ALWAYS READY TO BE IMPROVED UPON, MISS ROMANOVA.
IF MISTER FURY WOULD JUST STOP BUZZING AROUND US LIKE AN ANGRY FLY...
BUDDY, IF WE DIDN'T NEED YOU RIGHT NOW, YOU'D BE IN THE DEEPEST HOLE I COULD FIND...
...AND I'D THROW AWAY THE KEY.
BIG WORDS.

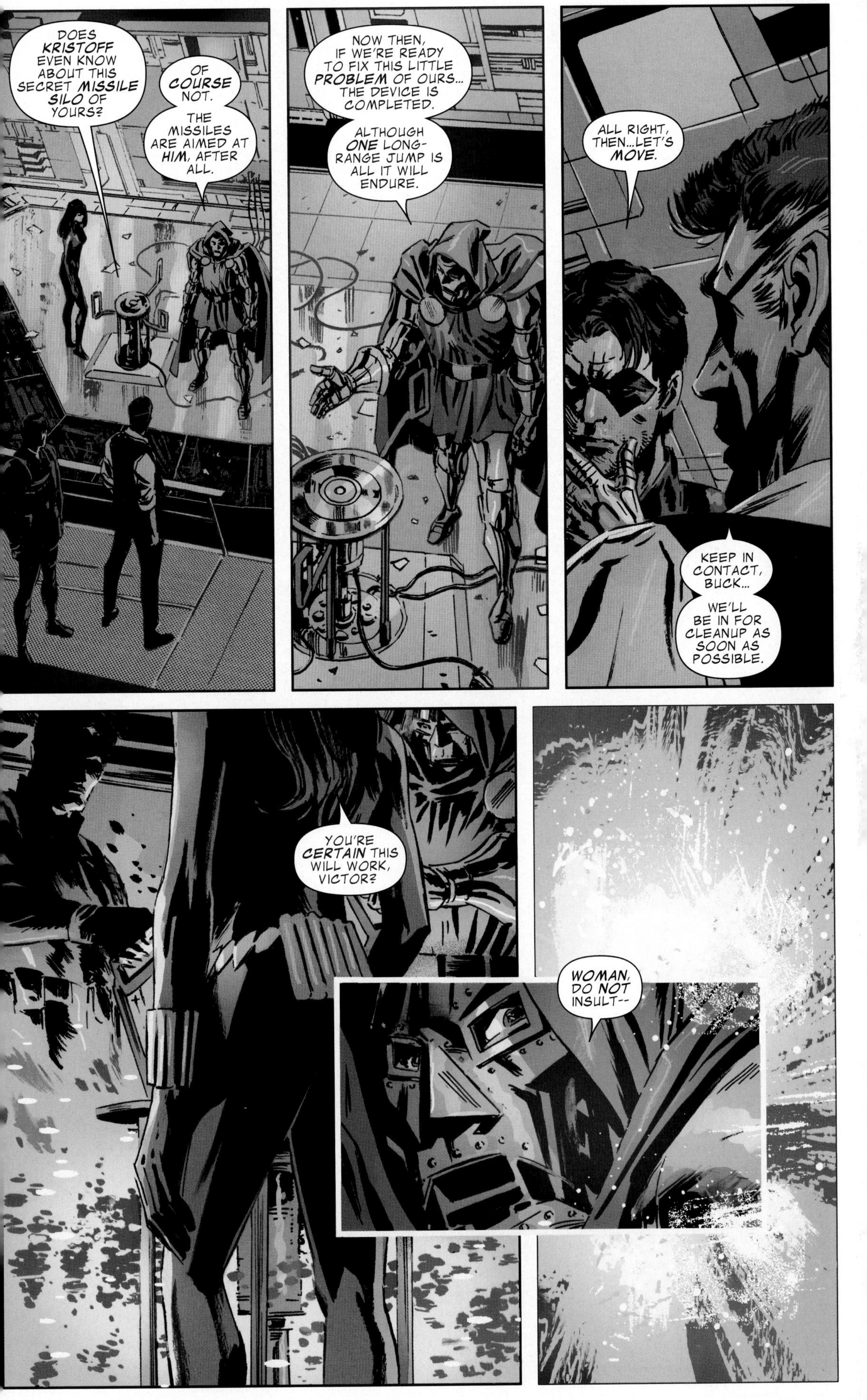
DOES KRISTOFF EVEN KNOW ABOUT THIS SECRET MISSILE SILO OF YOURS?
OF COURSE NOT.
THE MISSILES ARE AIMED AT HIM, AFTER ALL.
NOW THEN, IF WE'RE READY TO FIX THIS LITTLE PROBLEM OF OURS... THE DEVICE IS COMPLETED.
ALTHOUGH ONE LONG-RANGE JUMP IS ALL IT WILL ENDURE.
ALL RIGHT, THEN...LET'S MOVE.
KEEP IN CONTACT, BUCK...
WE'LL BE IN FOR CLEANUP AS SOON AS POSSIBLE.
YOU'RE CERTAIN THIS WILL WORK, VICTOR?
WOMAN, DO NOT INSULT--

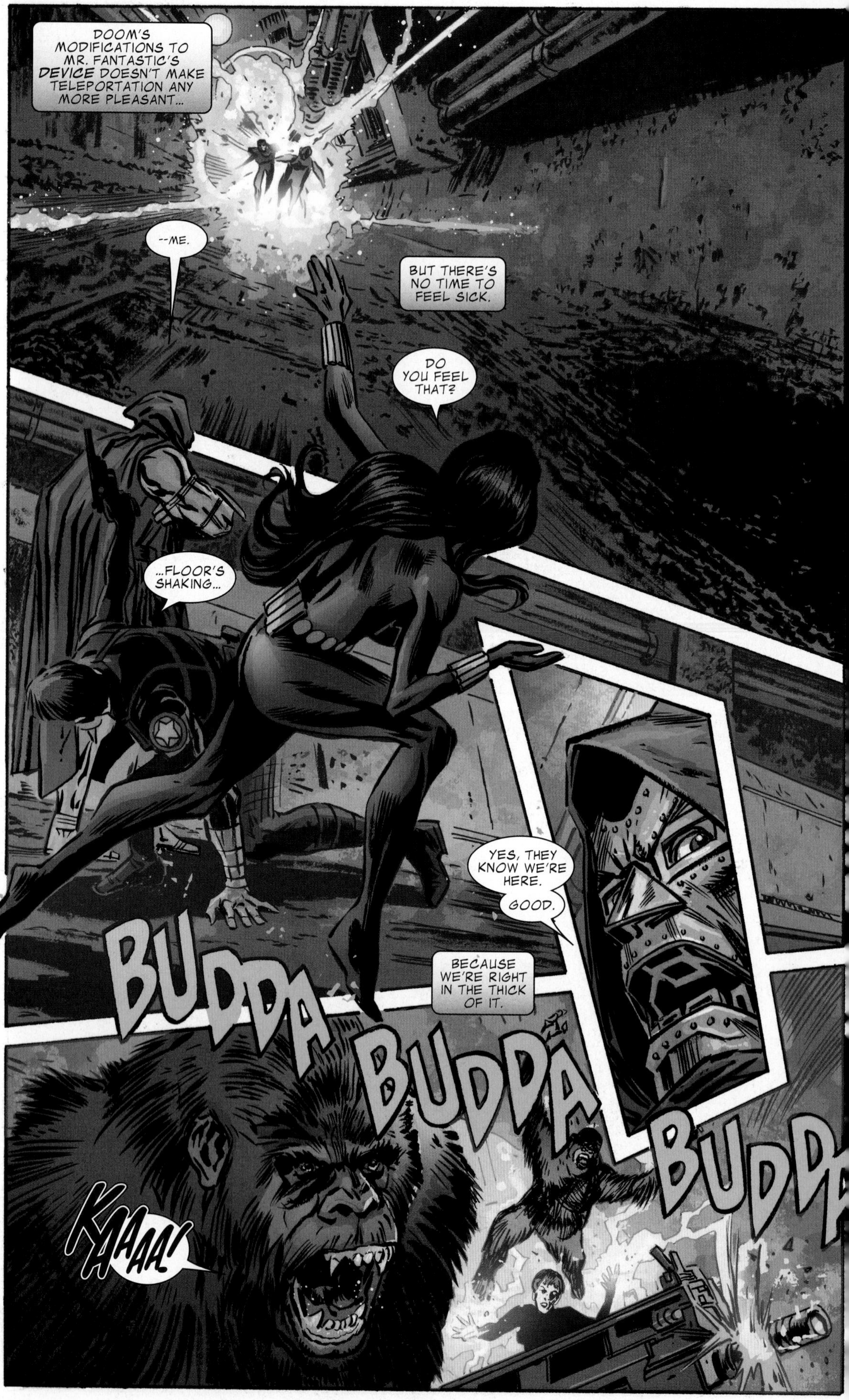
DOOM'S MODIFICATIONS TO MR. FANTASTIC'S DEVICE DOESN'T MAKE TELEPORTATION ANY MORE PLEASANT...
--ME.
BUT THERE'S NO TIME TO FEEL SICK.
DO YOU FEEL THAT?
...FLOOR'S SHAKING...
YES, THEY KNOW WE'RE HERE.
GOOD.
BECAUSE WE'RE RIGHT IN THE THICK OF IT.
BUDDA
BUDDA
BUDDA
KAAAAA!

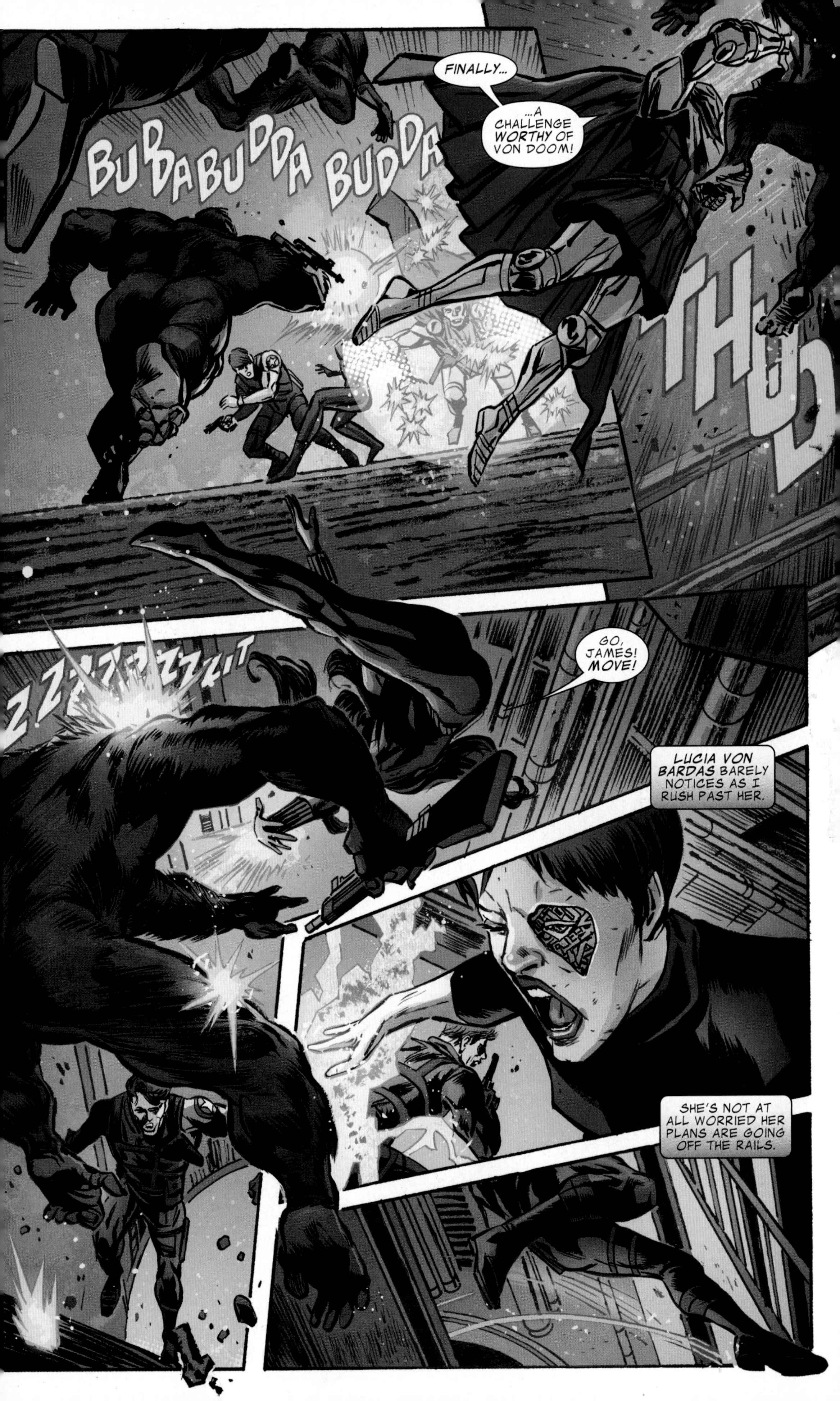
FINALLY...
...A CHALLENGE WORTHY OF VON DOOM!
BUBBABUDDA BUDDA
THUD
ZZZZZZZKIT
GO, JAMES! MOVE!
LUCIA VON BARDAS BARELY NOTICES AS I RUSH PAST HER.
SHE'S NOT AT ALL WORRIED HER PLANS ARE GOING OFF THE RAILS.

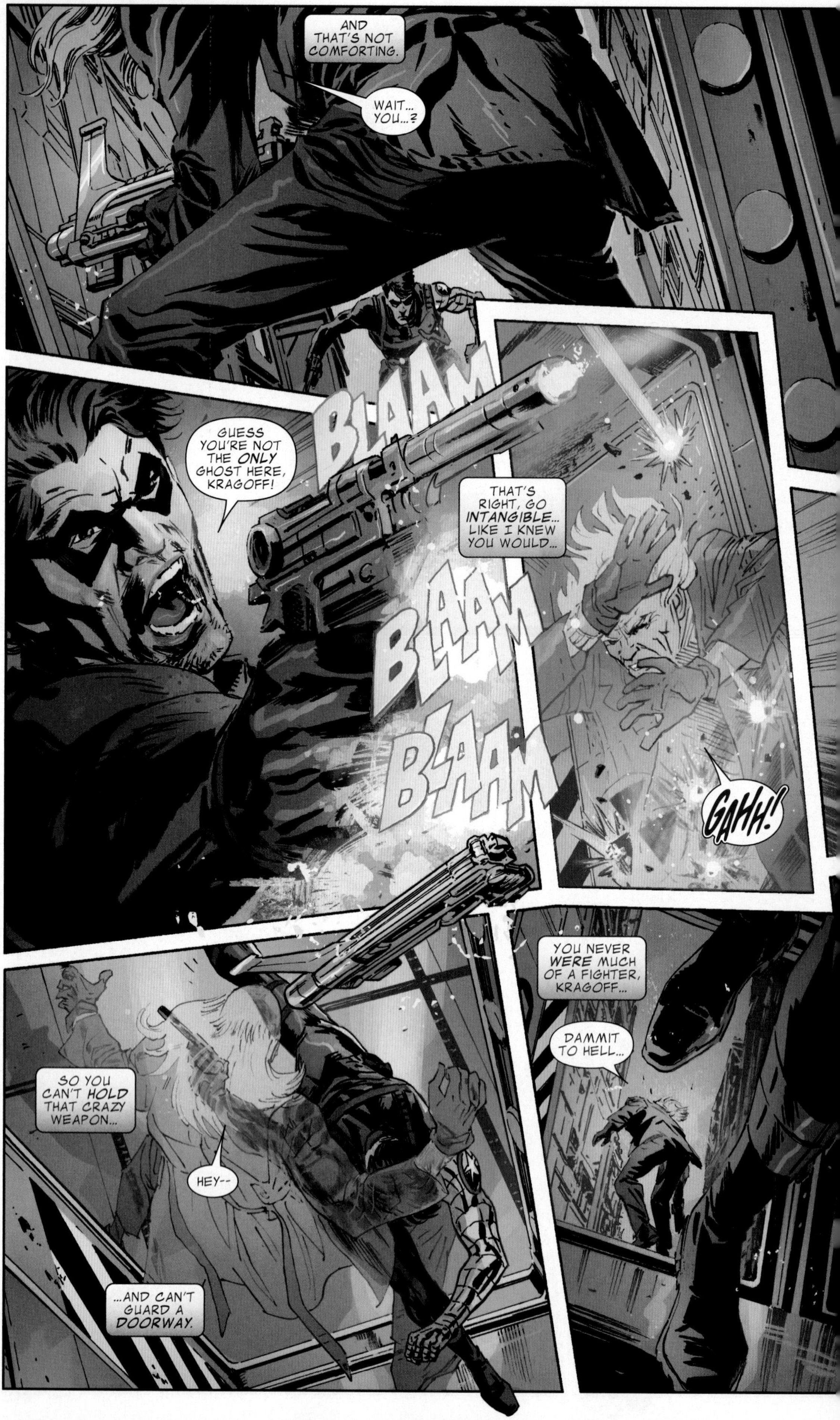

AND THAT'S NOT COMFORTING.
WAIT... YOU...?
BLAAM
GUESS YOU'RE NOT THE ONLY GHOST HERE, KRAGOFF!
THAT'S RIGHT, GO INTANGIBLE... LIKE I KNEW YOU WOULD...
BLAAM
BLAAM
GAHH!
SO YOU CAN'T HOLD THAT CRAZY WEAPON...
HEY--
...AND CAN'T GUARD A DOORWAY.
YOU NEVER WERE MUCH OF A FIGHTER, KRAGOFF...
DAMMIT TO HELL...

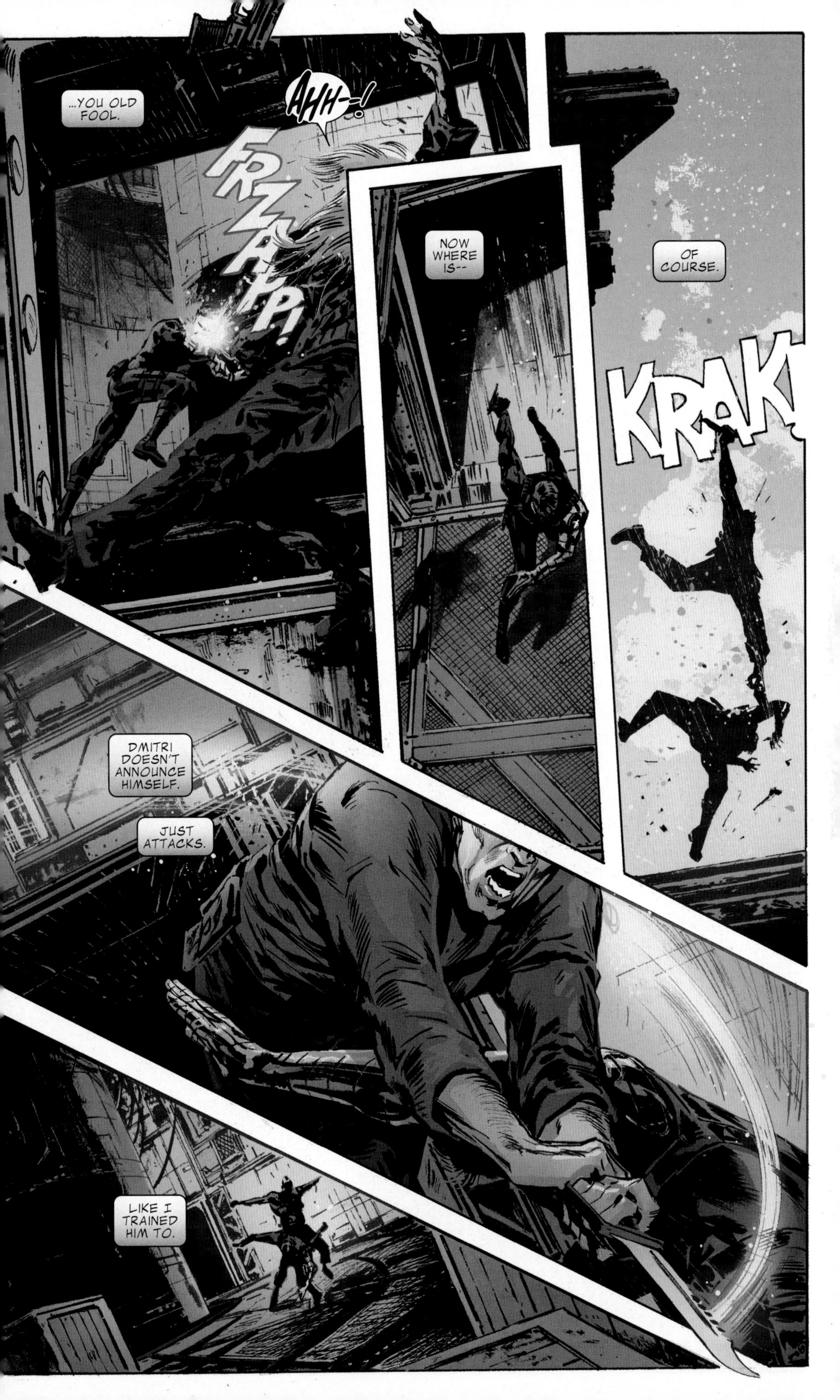
...YOU OLD FOOL.
AHH--!
FRZZAPP!
NOW WHERE IS--
OF COURSE.
KRAK
DMITRI DOESN'T ANNOUNCE HIMSELF.
JUST ATTACKS.
LIKE I TRAINED HIM TO.

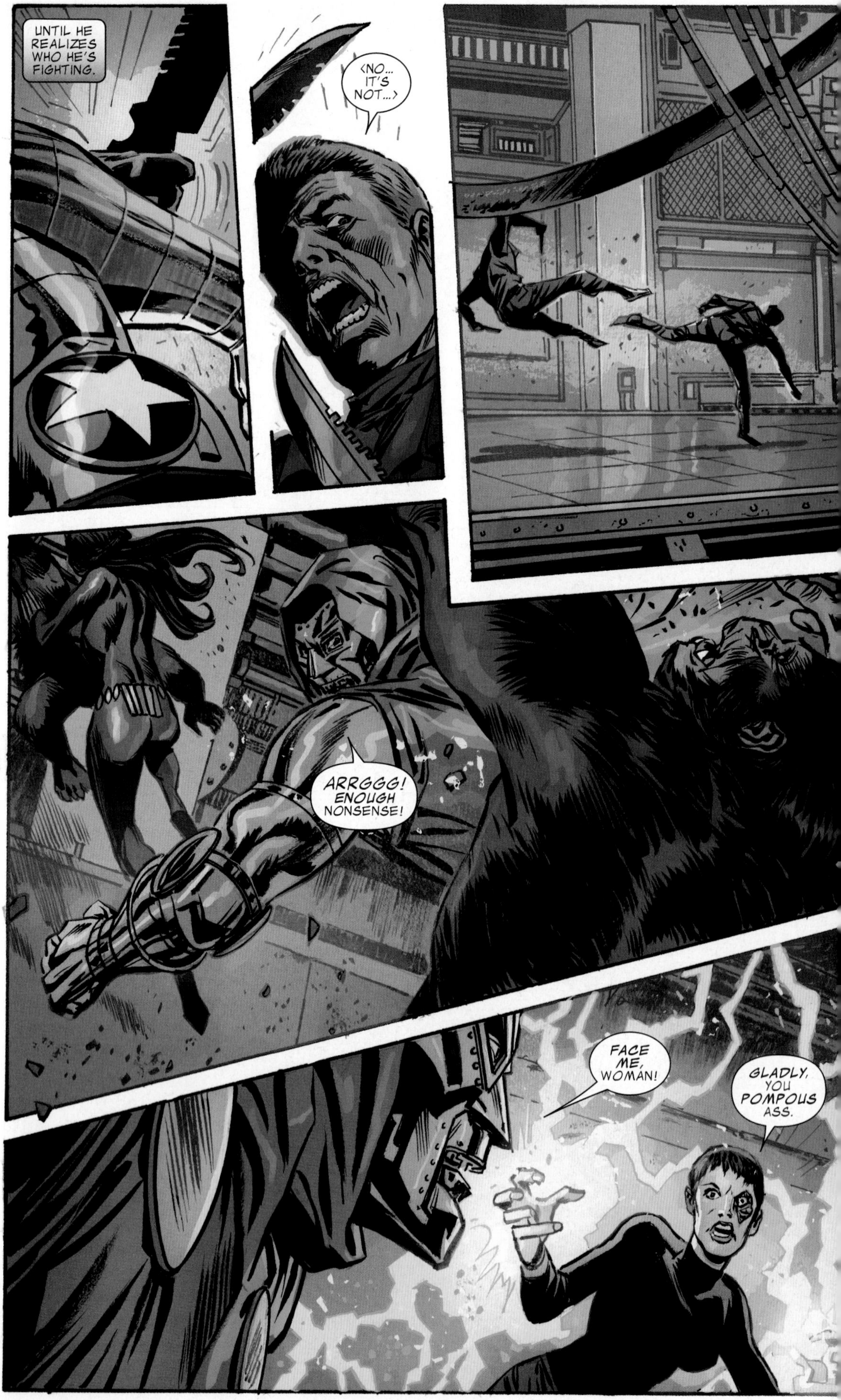

UNTIL HE REALIZES WHO HE'S FIGHTING.
<NO... IT'S NOT...>
ARRGGG! ENOUGH NONSENSE!
FACE ME, WOMAN!
GLADLY, YOU POMPOUS ASS.

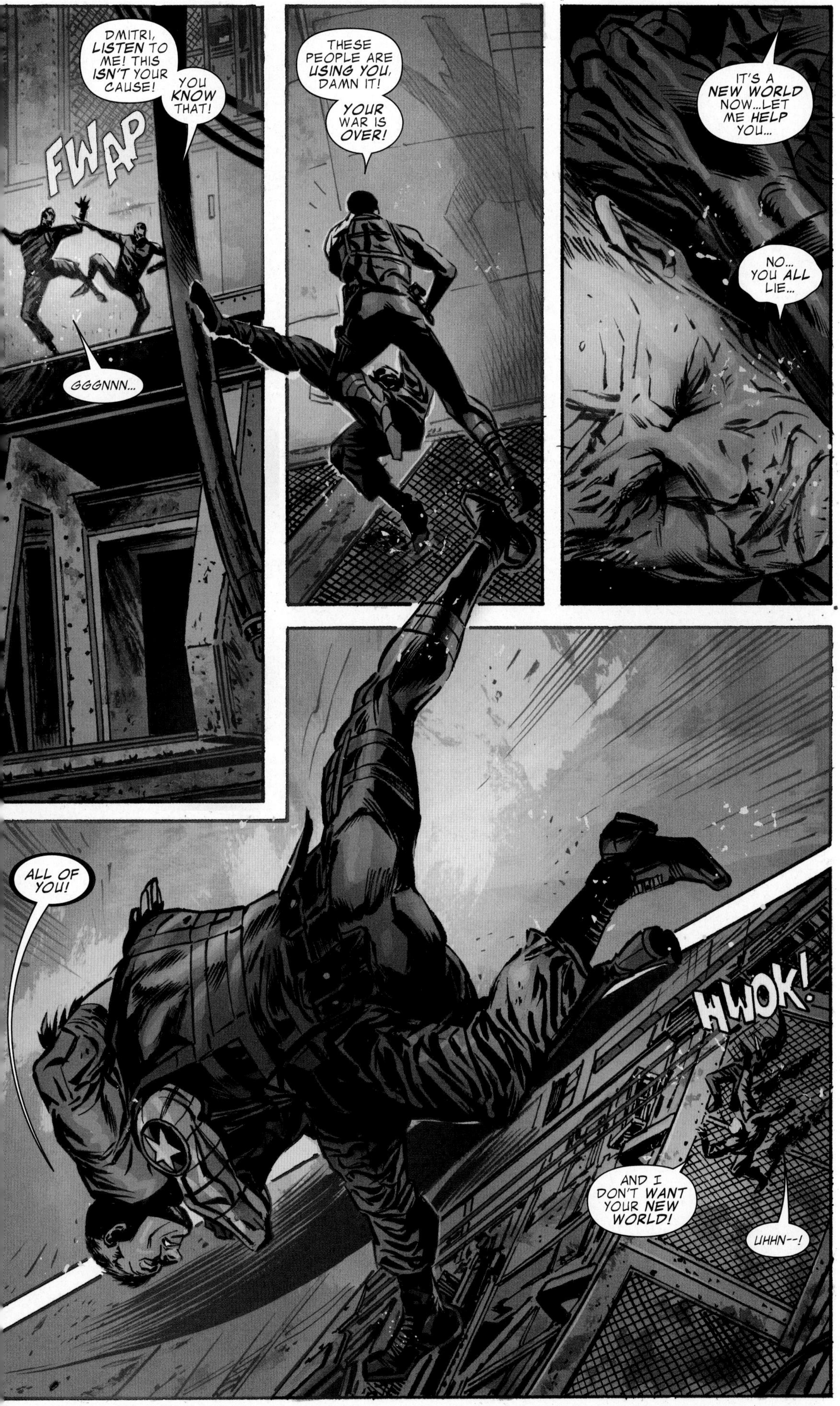
DMITRI, LISTEN TO ME! THIS ISN'T YOUR CAUSE!
YOU KNOW THAT!
FWAP
GGGNNN...
THESE PEOPLE ARE USING YOU, DAMN IT!
YOUR WAR IS OVER!
IT'S A NEW WORLD NOW...LET ME HELP YOU...
NO... YOU ALL LIE...
ALL OF YOU!
HWOK!
AND I DON'T WANT YOUR NEW WORLD!
UHHN--!

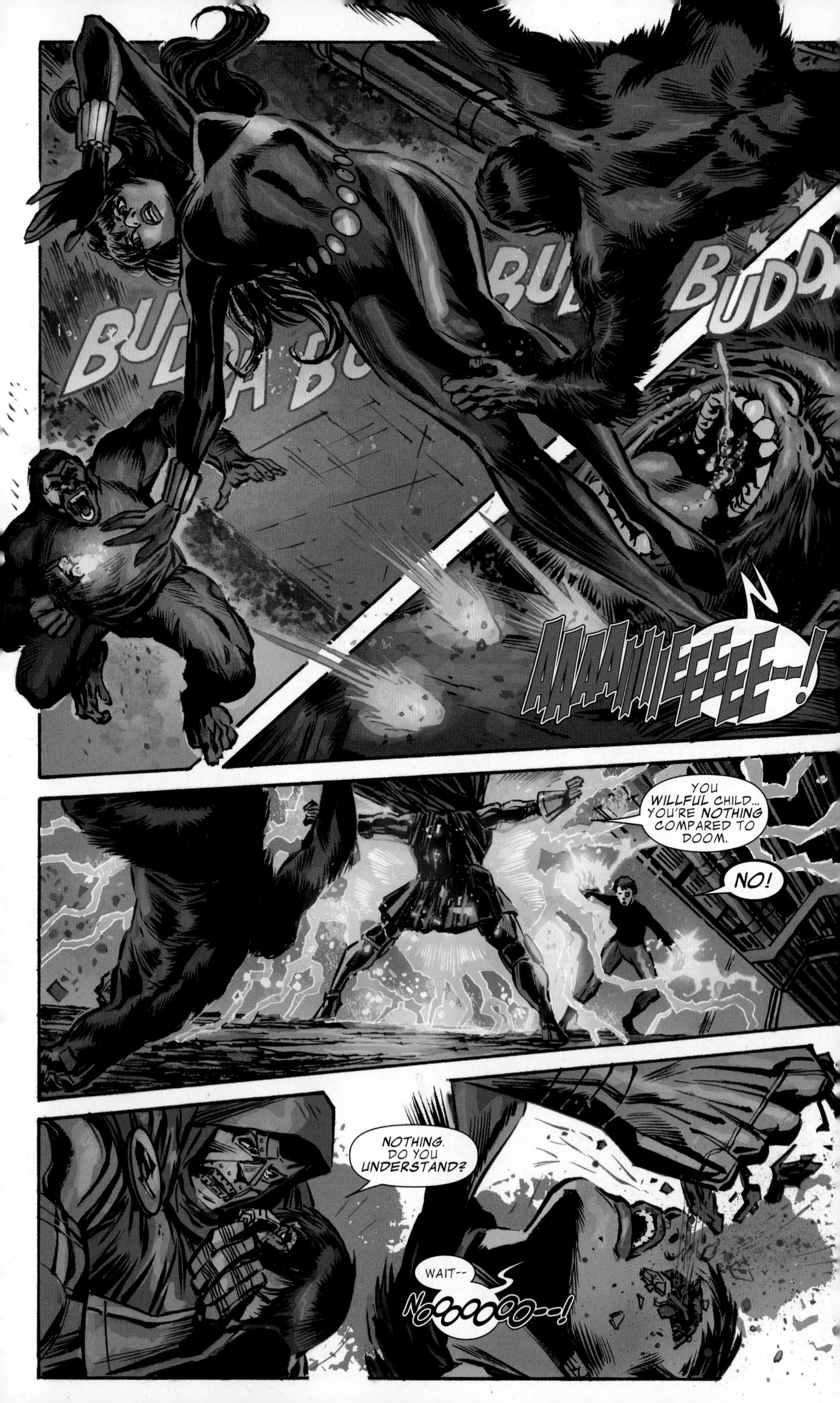

BUDDA BUDDA
BUDDA BUDDA
AAAAIIIIEEEEE--!
YOU WILLFUL CHILD... YOU'RE NOTHING COMPARED TO DOOM.
NO!
NOTHING. DO YOU UNDERSTAND?
WAIT--
NOOOOOOO--!

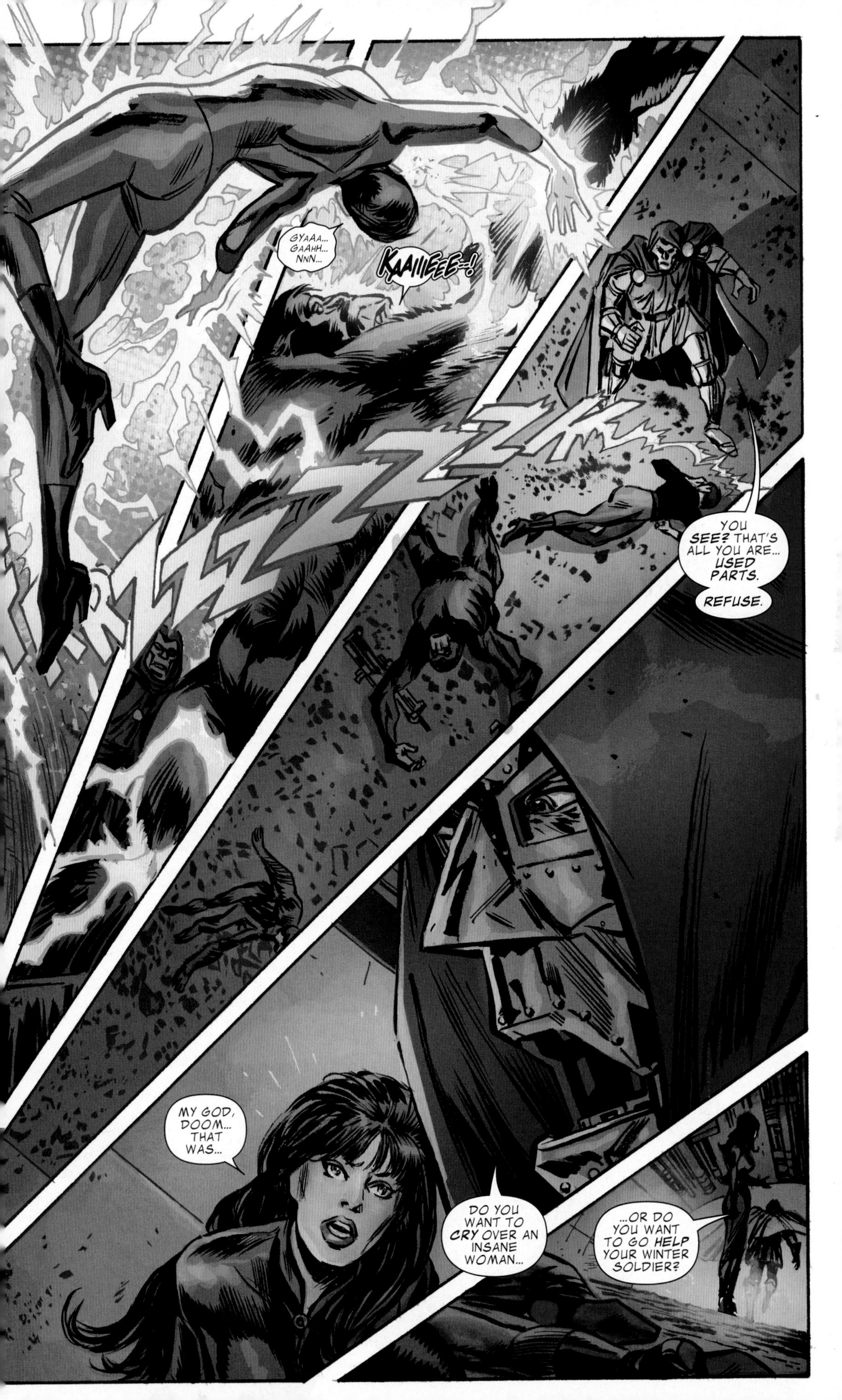
GYAAA... GAAHH... NNN...
KAAIIIEEE--!
YOU SEE? THAT'S ALL YOU ARE... USED PARTS.
REFUSE.
MY GOD, DOOM... THAT WAS...
DO YOU WANT TO CRY OVER AN INSANE WOMAN...
...OR DO YOU WANT TO GO HELP YOUR WINTER SOLDIER?

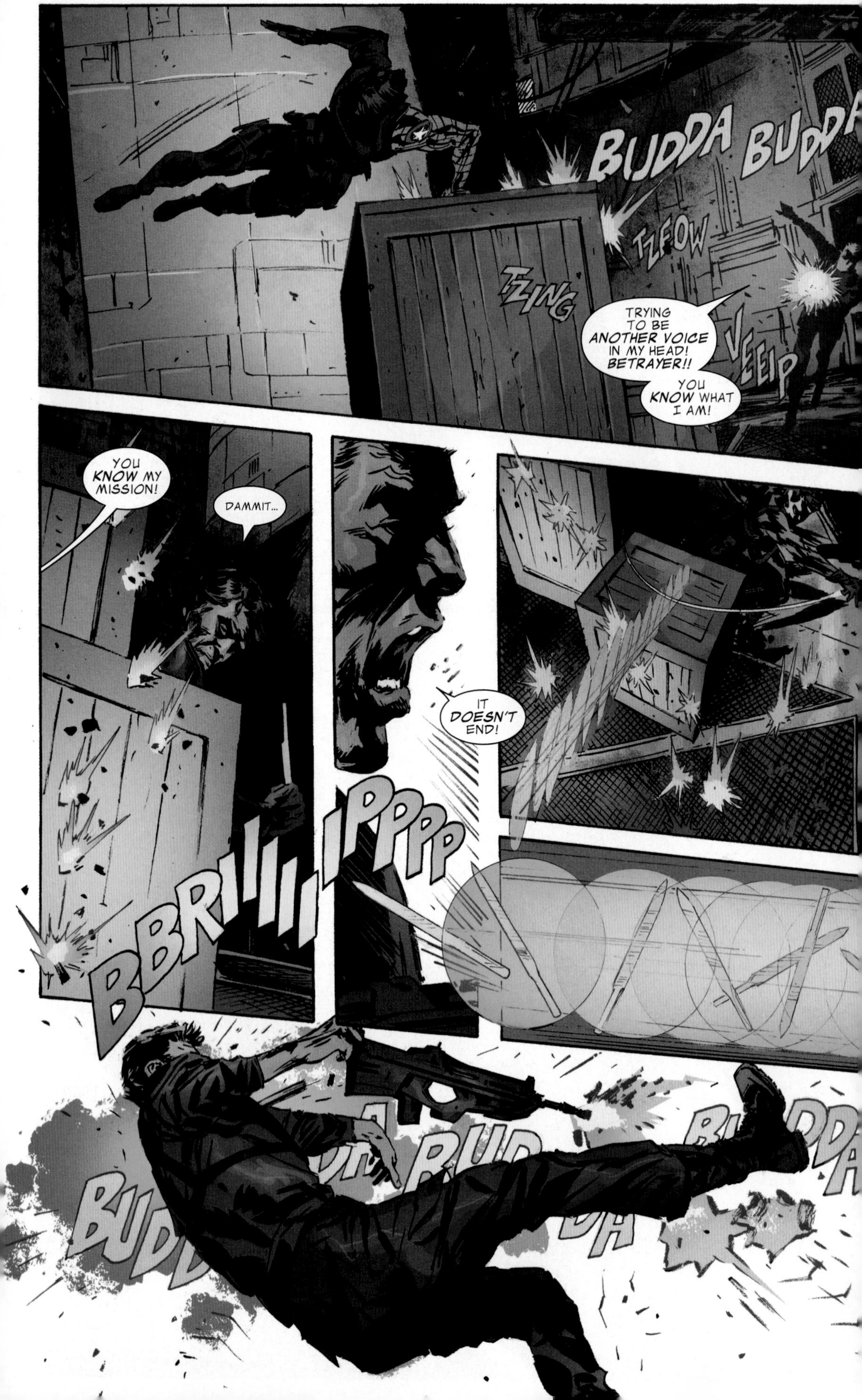
BUDDA BUDDA
TZFOW
TZING
TRYING TO BE ANOTHER VOICE IN MY HEAD! BETRAYER!!
YOU KNOW WHAT I AM!
VEEIP
YOU KNOW MY MISSION!
DAMMIT...
IT DOESN'T END!
BBRIIIIIIPPPP
BUDDA BUDDA BUDDA

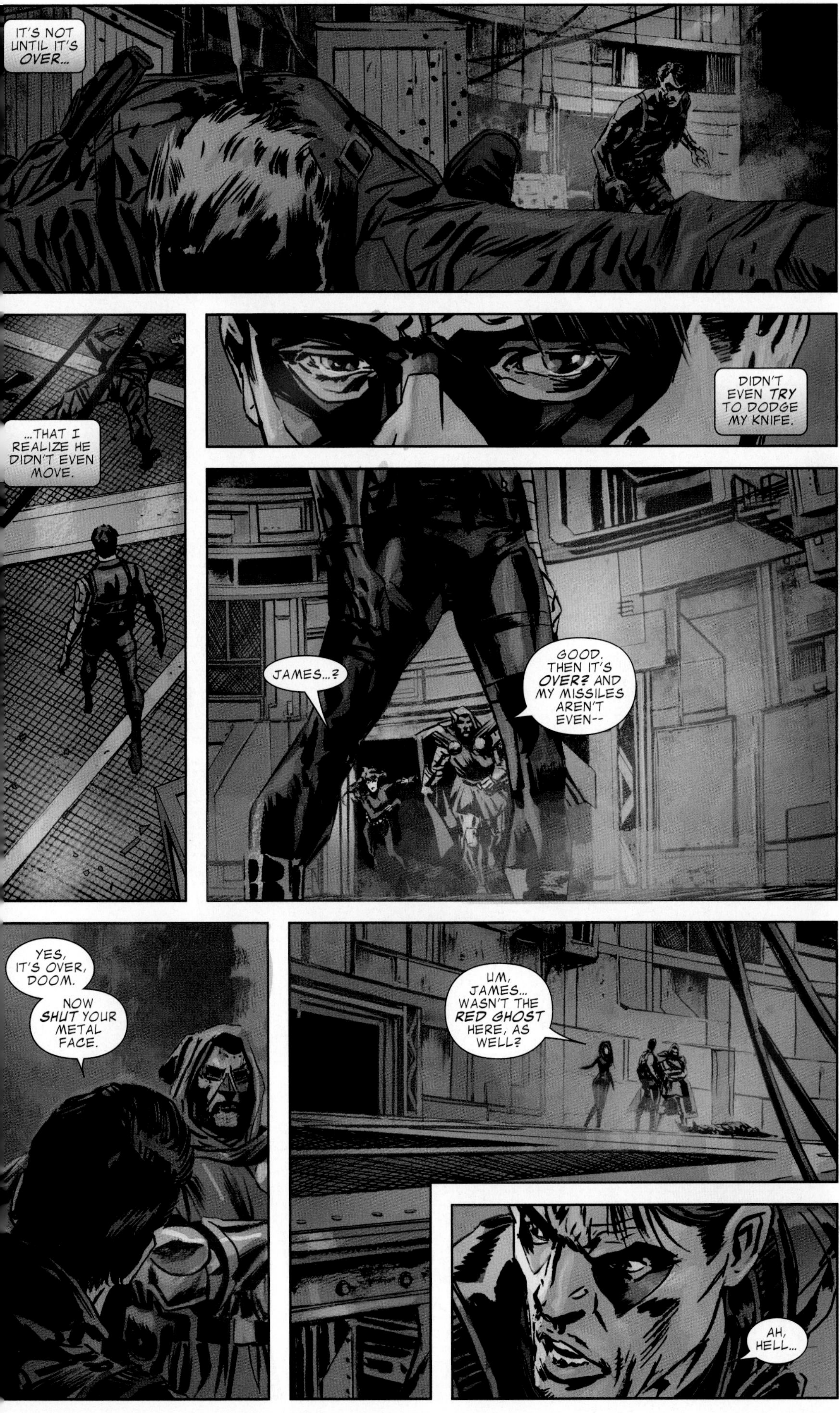
IT'S NOT UNTIL IT'S OVER...
...THAT I REALIZE HE DIDN'T EVEN MOVE.
DIDN'T EVEN TRY TO DODGE MY KNIFE.
JAMES...?
GOOD. THEN IT'S OVER? AND MY MISSILES AREN'T EVEN--
YES, IT'S OVER, DOOM.
NOW SHUT YOUR METAL FACE.
UM, JAMES... WASN'T THE RED GHOST HERE, AS WELL?
AH, HELL...

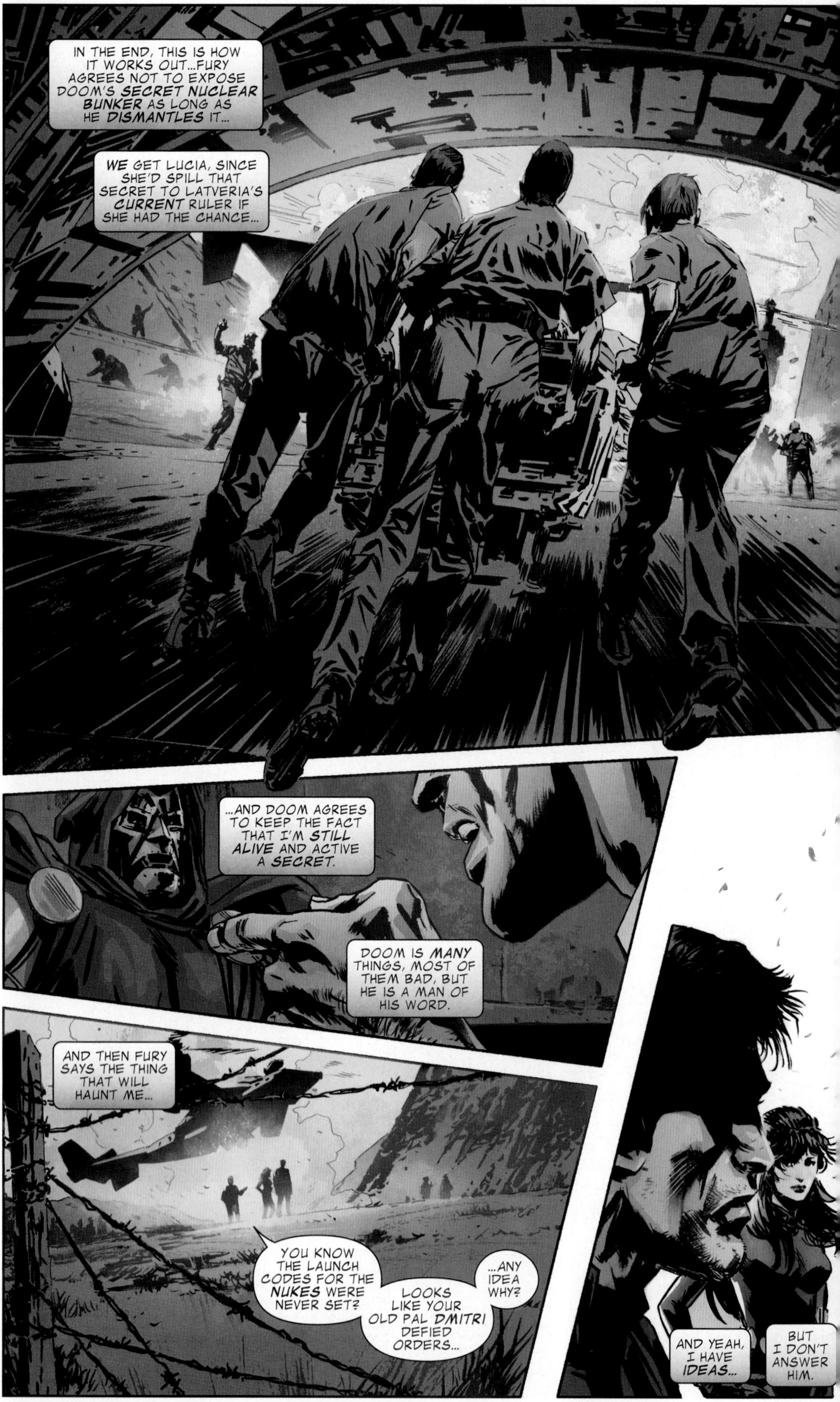
IN THE END, THIS IS HOW IT WORKS OUT...FURY AGREES NOT TO EXPOSE DOOM'S SECRET NUCLEAR BUNKER AS LONG AS HE DISMANTLES IT...
WE GET LUCIA, SINCE SHE'D SPILL THAT SECRET TO LATVERIA'S CURRENT RULER IF SHE HAD THE CHANCE...
...AND DOOM AGREES TO KEEP THE FACT THAT I'M STILL ALIVE AND ACTIVE A SECRET.
DOOM IS MANY THINGS, MOST OF THEM BAD, BUT HE IS A MAN OF HIS WORD.
AND THEN FURY SAYS THE THING THAT WILL HAUNT ME...
YOU KNOW THE LAUNCH CODES FOR THE NUKES WERE NEVER SET?
LOOKS LIKE YOUR OLD PAL DMITRI DEFIED ORDERS...
...ANY IDEA WHY?
AND YEAH, I HAVE IDEAS...
BUT I DON'T ANSWER HIM.

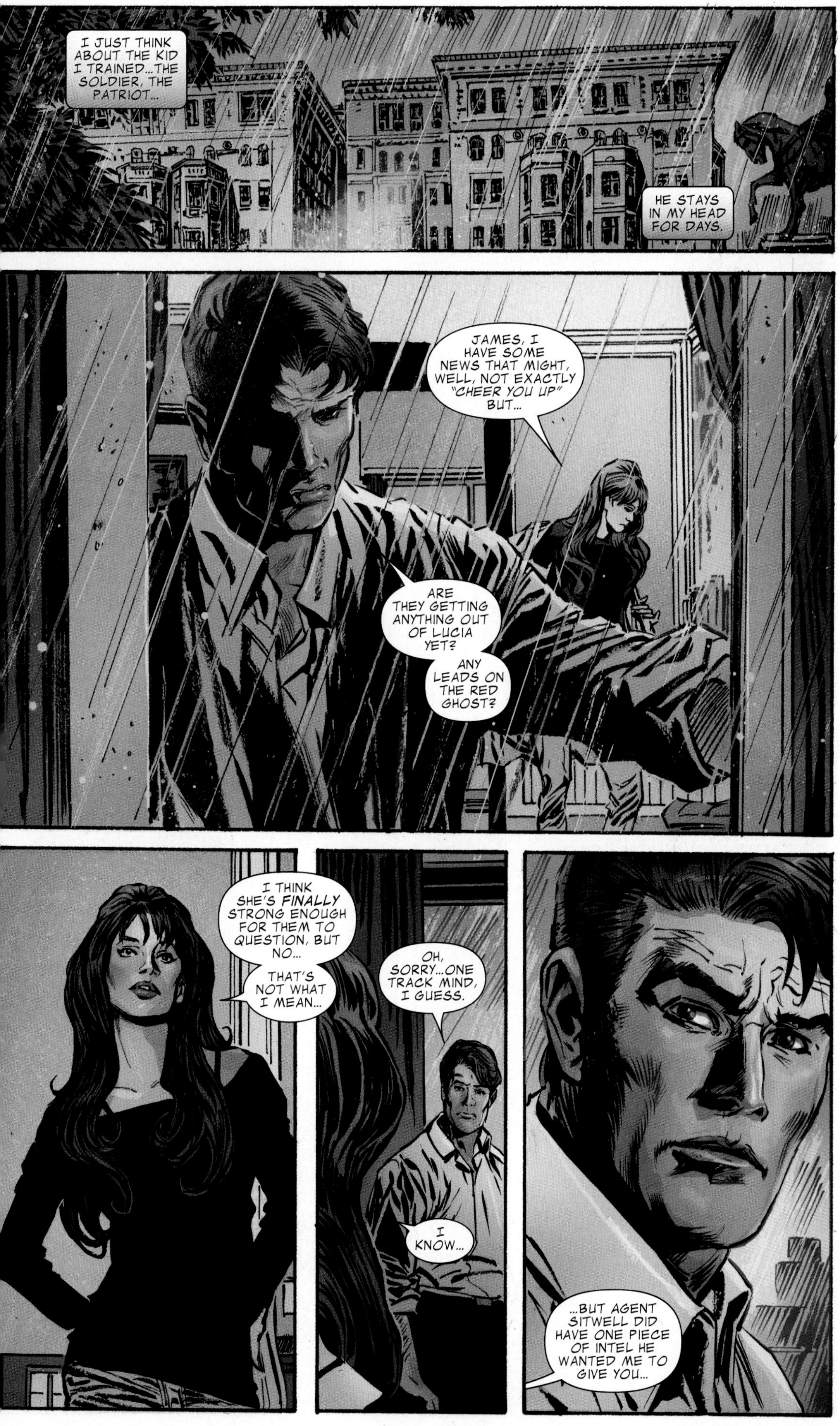

I JUST THINK ABOUT THE KID I TRAINED...THE SOLDIER, THE PATRIOT...
HE STAYS IN MY HEAD FOR DAYS.
JAMES, I HAVE SOME NEWS THAT MIGHT, WELL, NOT EXACTLY "CHEER YOU UP" BUT...
ARE THEY GETTING ANYTHING OUT OF LUCIA YET?
ANY LEADS ON THE RED GHOST?
I THINK SHE'S FINALLY STRONG ENOUGH FOR THEM TO QUESTION, BUT NO...
THAT'S NOT WHAT I MEAN...
OH, SORRY...ONE TRACK MIND, I GUESS.
I KNOW...
...BUT AGENT SITWELL DID HAVE ONE PIECE OF INTEL HE WANTED ME TO GIVE YOU...

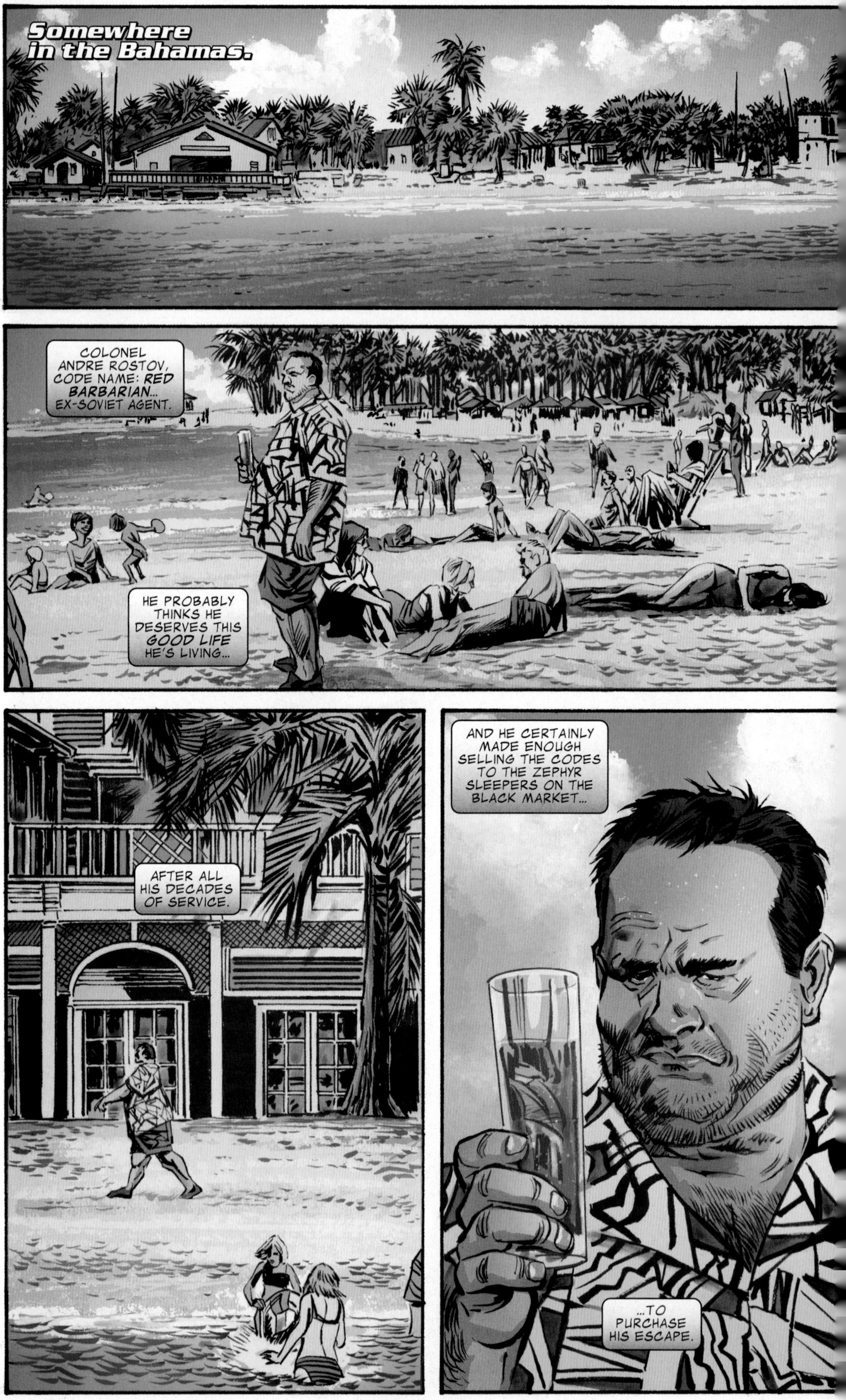
Somewhere in the Bahamas.
COLONEL ANDRE ROSTOV, CODE NAME: RED BARBARIAN... EX-SOVIET AGENT.
HE PROBABLY THINKS HE DESERVES THIS GOOD LIFE HE'S LIVING...
AFTER ALL HIS DECADES OF SERVICE.
AND HE CERTAINLY MADE ENOUGH SELLING THE CODES TO THE ZEPHYR SLEEPERS ON THE BLACK MARKET...
...TO PURCHASE HIS ESCAPE.

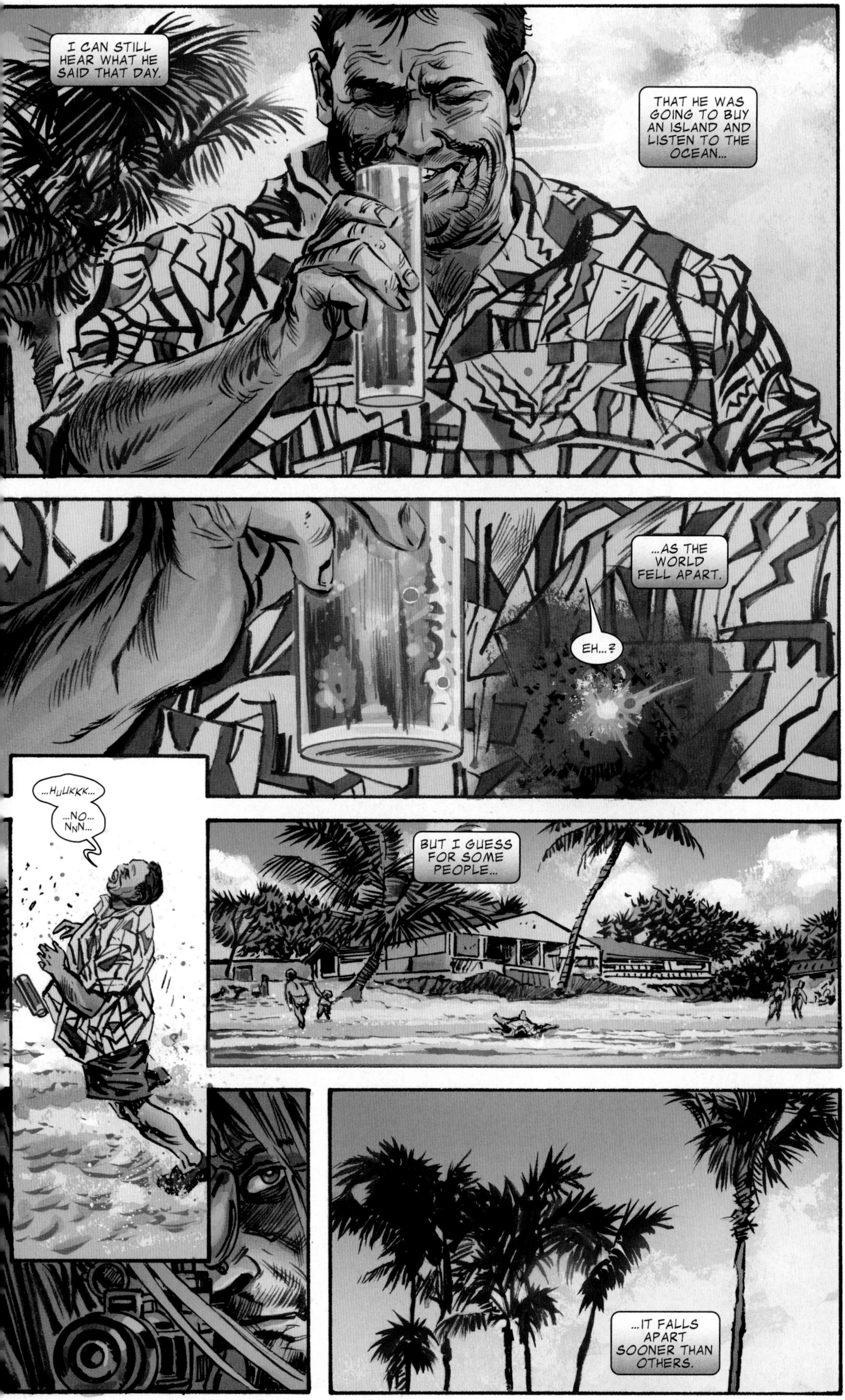
I CAN STILL HEAR WHAT HE SAID THAT DAY.
THAT HE WAS GOING TO BUY AN ISLAND AND LISTEN TO THE OCEAN...
...AS THE WORLD FELL APART.
EH...?
...HUUKKK...
...NO... NNN...
BUT I GUESS FOR SOME PEOPLE...
...IT FALLS APART SOONER THAN OTHERS.

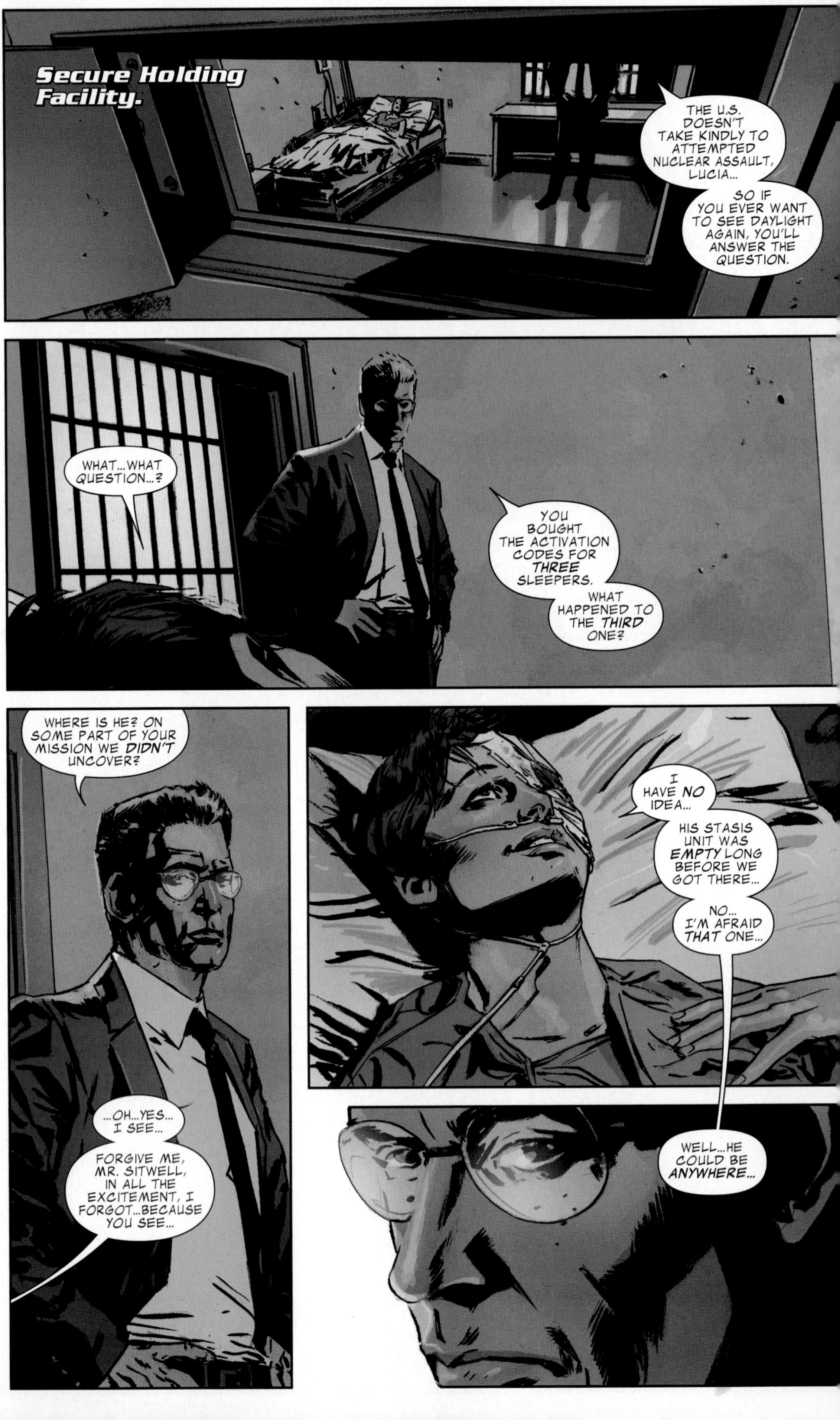
Secure Holding Facility.
THE U.S. DOESN'T TAKE KINDLY TO ATTEMPTED NUCLEAR ASSAULT, LUCIA...
SO IF YOU EVER WANT TO SEE DAYLIGHT AGAIN, YOU'LL ANSWER THE QUESTION.
WHAT...WHAT QUESTION...?
YOU BOUGHT THE ACTIVATION CODES FOR THREE SLEEPERS.
WHAT HAPPENED TO THE THIRD ONE?
WHERE IS HE? ON SOME PART OF YOUR MISSION WE DIDN'T UNCOVER?
I HAVE NO IDEA...
HIS STASIS UNIT WAS EMPTY LONG BEFORE WE GOT THERE...
NO... I'M AFRAID THAT ONE...
WELL...HE COULD BE ANYWHERE...
...OH...YES... I SEE...
FORGIVE ME, MR. SITWELL, IN ALL THE EXCITEMENT, I FORGOT...BECAUSE YOU SEE...

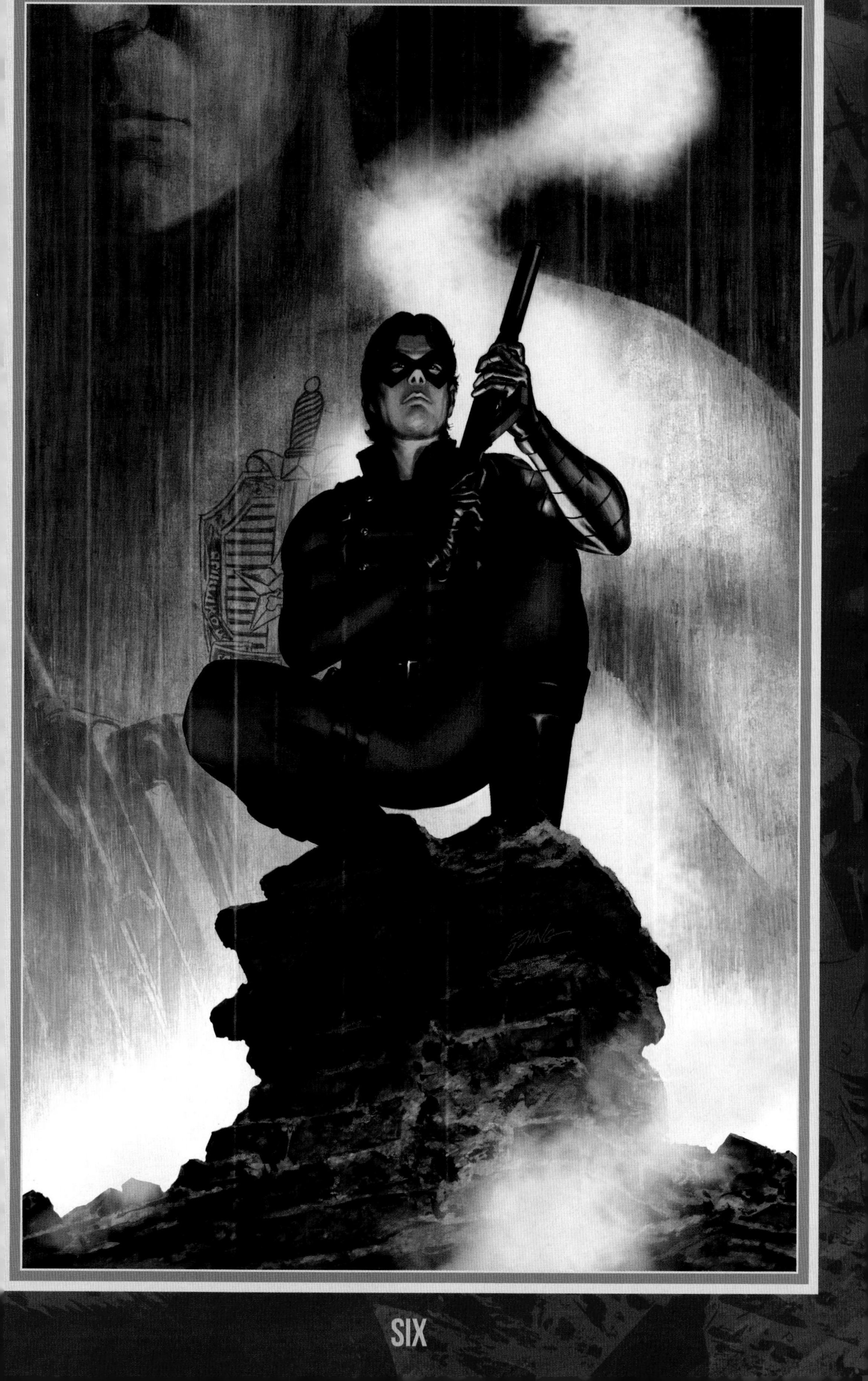

SIX

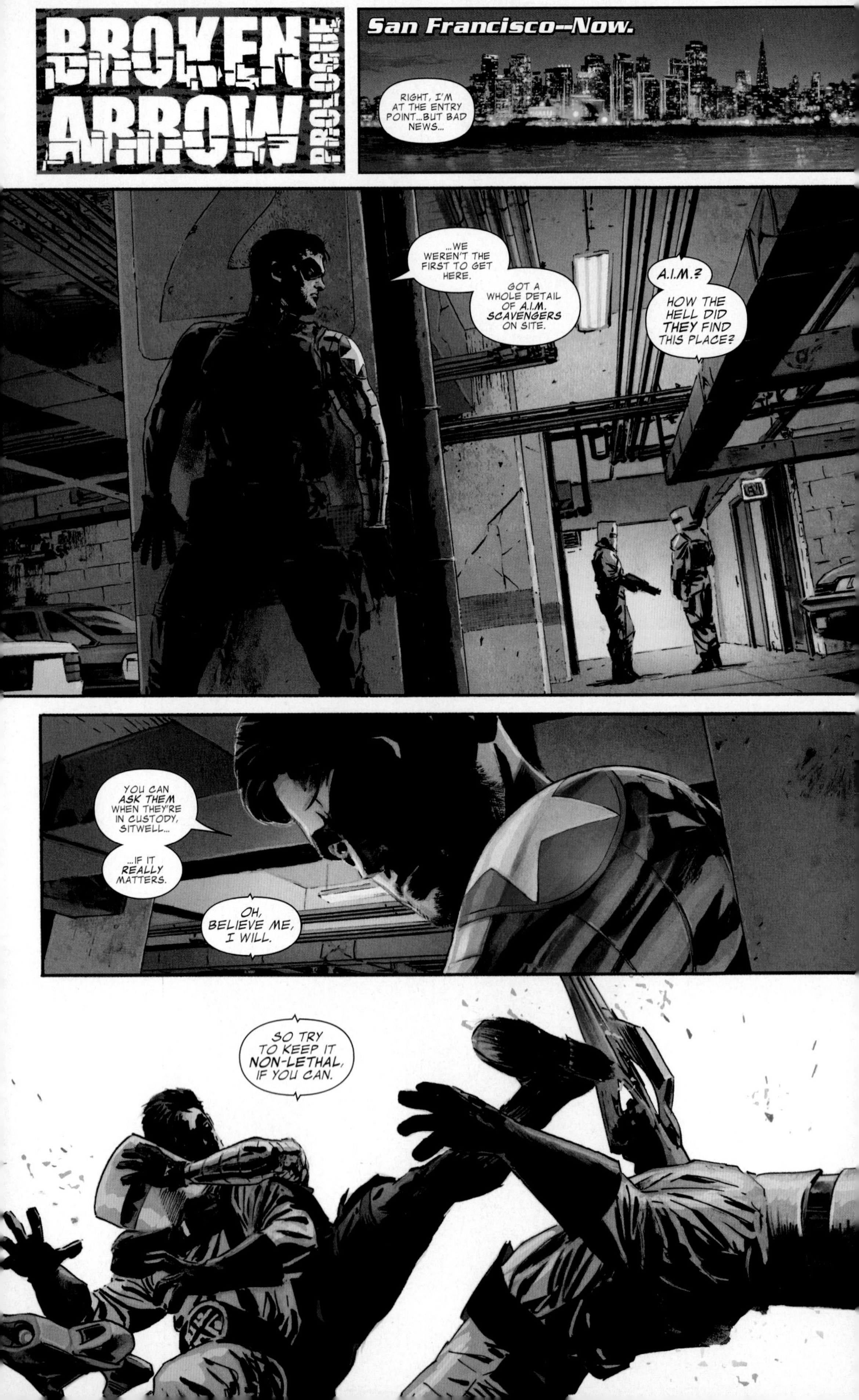

BROKEN ARROW
PROLOGUE
San Francisco--Now.
RIGHT, I'M AT THE ENTRY POINT...BUT BAD NEWS...
...WE WEREN'T THE FIRST TO GET HERE.
GOT A WHOLE DETAIL OF A.I.M. SCAVENGERS ON SITE.
A.I.M.?
HOW THE HELL DID THEY FIND THIS PLACE?
YOU CAN ASK THEM WHEN THEY'RE IN CUSTODY, SITWELL...
...IF IT REALLY MATTERS.
OH, BELIEVE ME, I WILL.
SO TRY TO KEEP IT NON-LETHAL, IF YOU CAN.

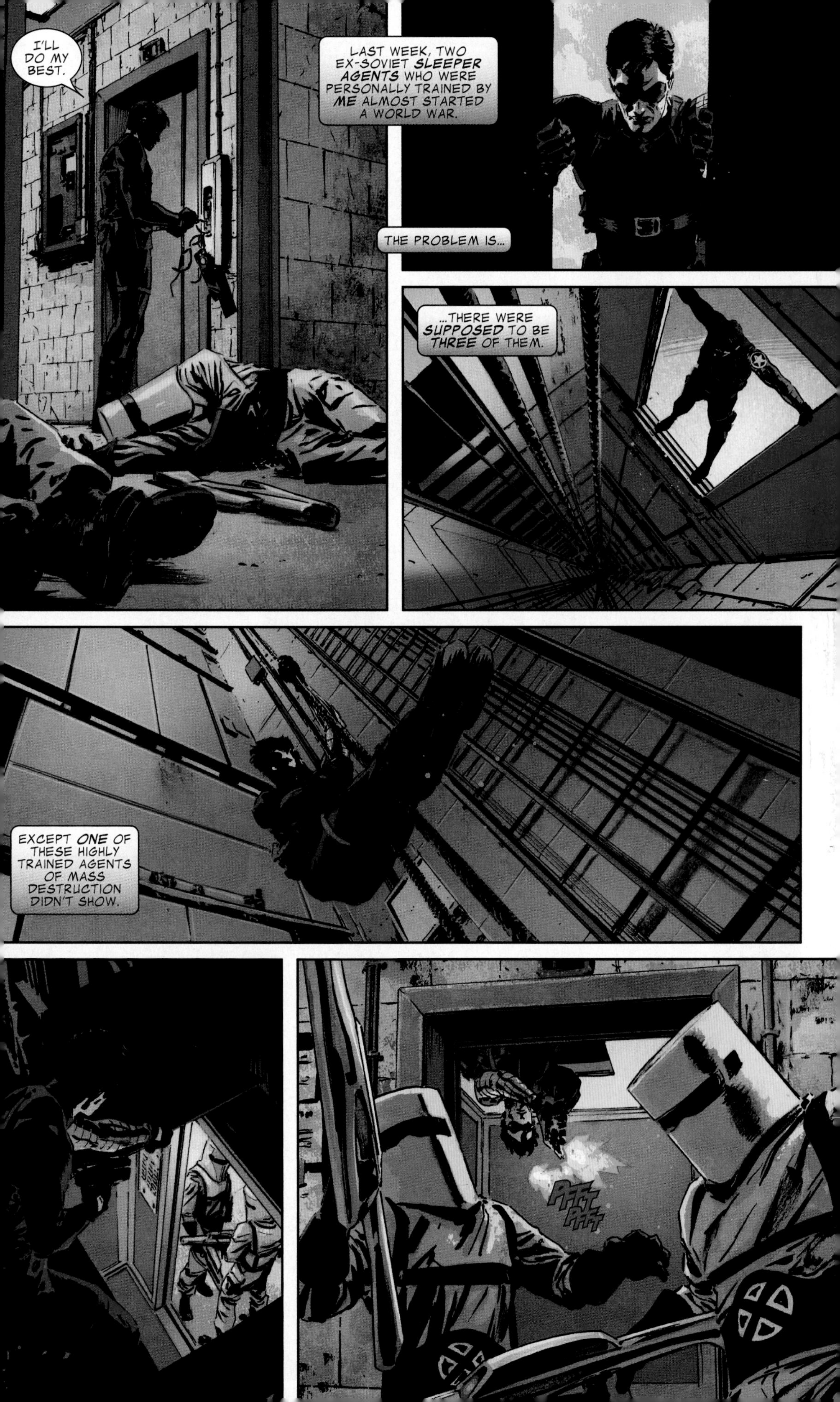
I'LL DO MY BEST.
LAST WEEK, TWO EX-SOVIET SLEEPER AGENTS WHO WERE PERSONALLY TRAINED BY ME ALMOST STARTED A WORLD WAR.
THE PROBLEM IS...
...THERE WERE SUPPOSED TO BE THREE OF THEM.
EXCEPT ONE OF THESE HIGHLY TRAINED AGENTS OF MASS DESTRUCTION DIDN'T SHOW.
PFFT PFFT

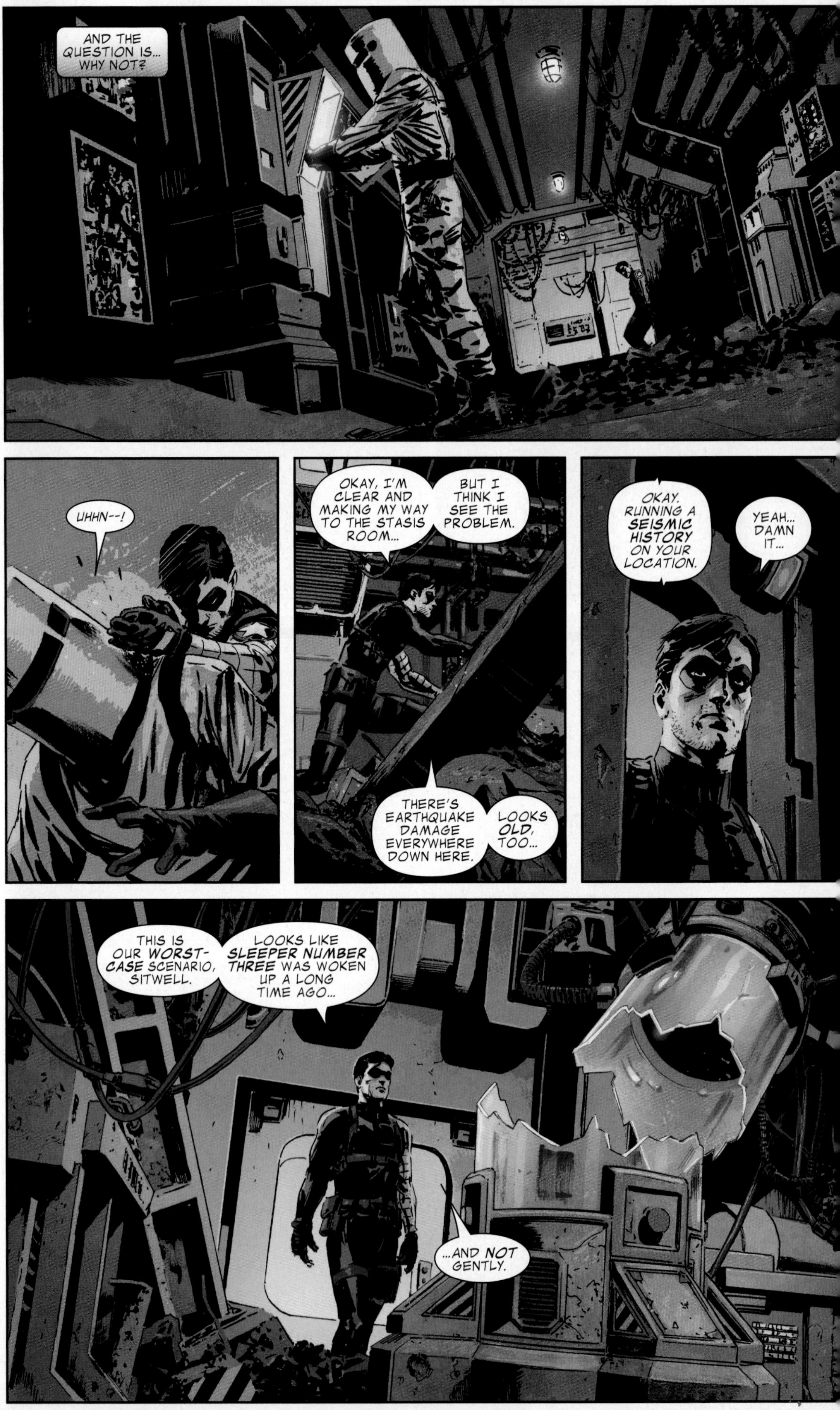
AND THE QUESTION IS... WHY NOT?
UHHN--!
OKAY, I'M CLEAR AND MAKING MY WAY TO THE STASIS ROOM...
BUT I THINK I SEE THE PROBLEM.
THERE'S EARTHQUAKE DAMAGE EVERYWHERE DOWN HERE.
LOOKS OLD, TOO...
OKAY. RUNNING A SEISMIC HISTORY ON YOUR LOCATION.
YEAH... DAMN IT...
THIS IS OUR WORST-CASE SCENARIO, SITWELL.
LOOKS LIKE SLEEPER NUMBER THREE WAS WOKEN UP A LONG TIME AGO...
...AND NOT GENTLY.

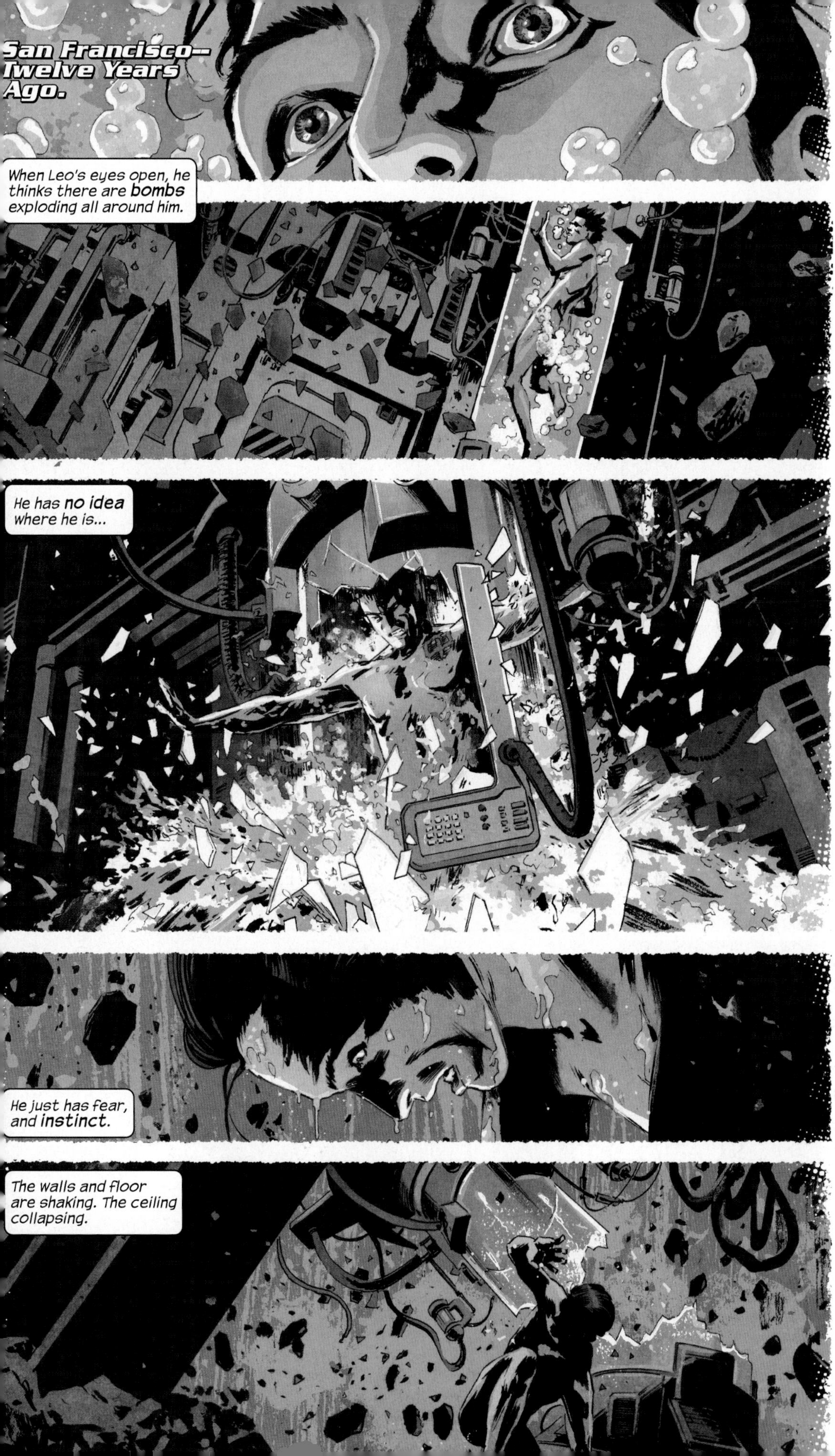
San Francisco--
Twelve Years
Ago.
When Leo's eyes open, he thinks there are bombs exploding all around him.
He has no idea where he is...
He just has fear, and instinct.
The walls and floor are shaking. The ceiling collapsing.

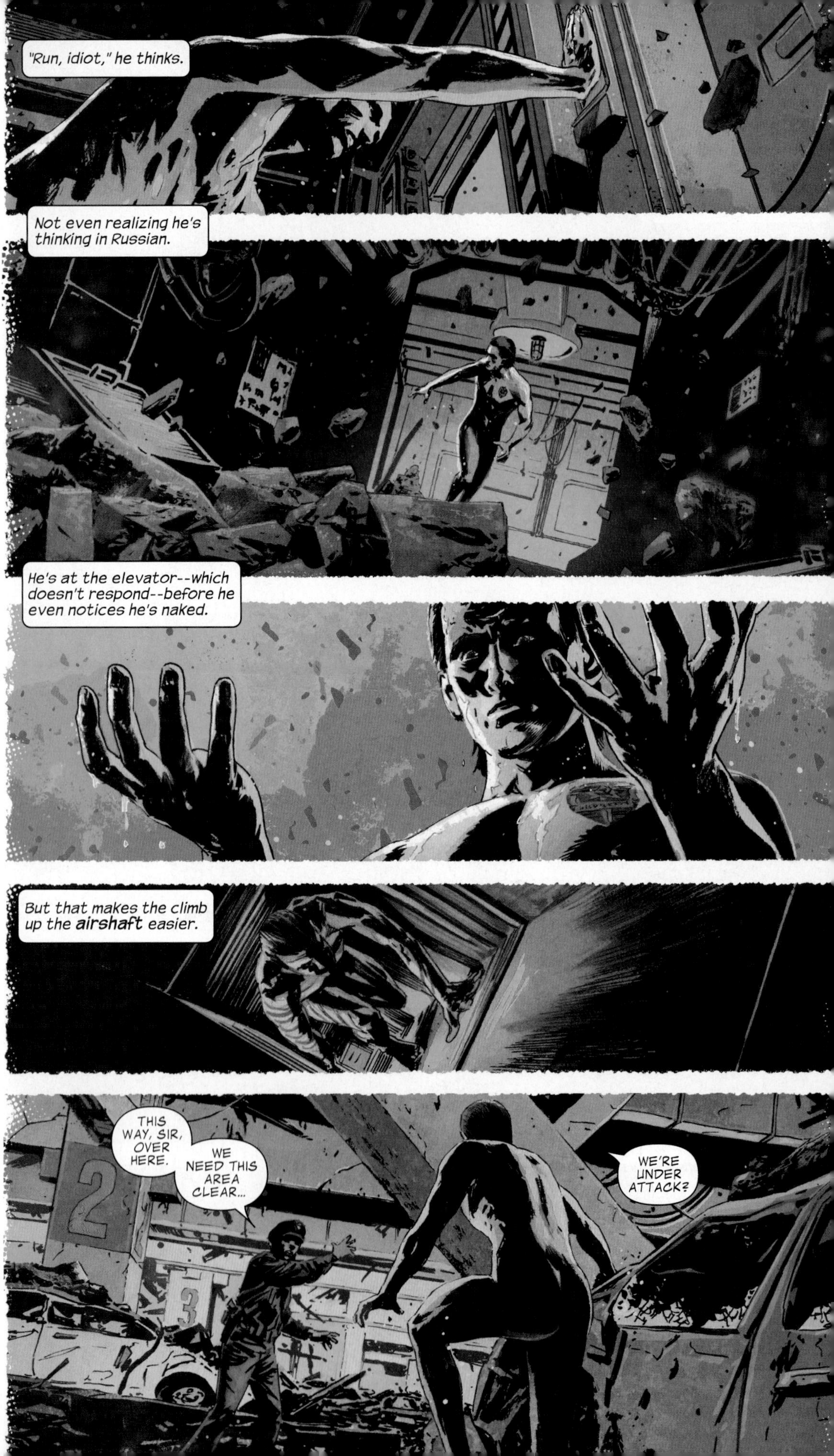
"Run, idiot," he thinks.
Not even realizing he's thinking in Russian.
He's at the elevator--which doesn't respond--before he even notices he's naked.
But that makes the climb up the airshaft easier.
THIS WAY, SIR, OVER HERE.
WE NEED THIS AREA CLEAR...
WE'RE UNDER ATTACK?

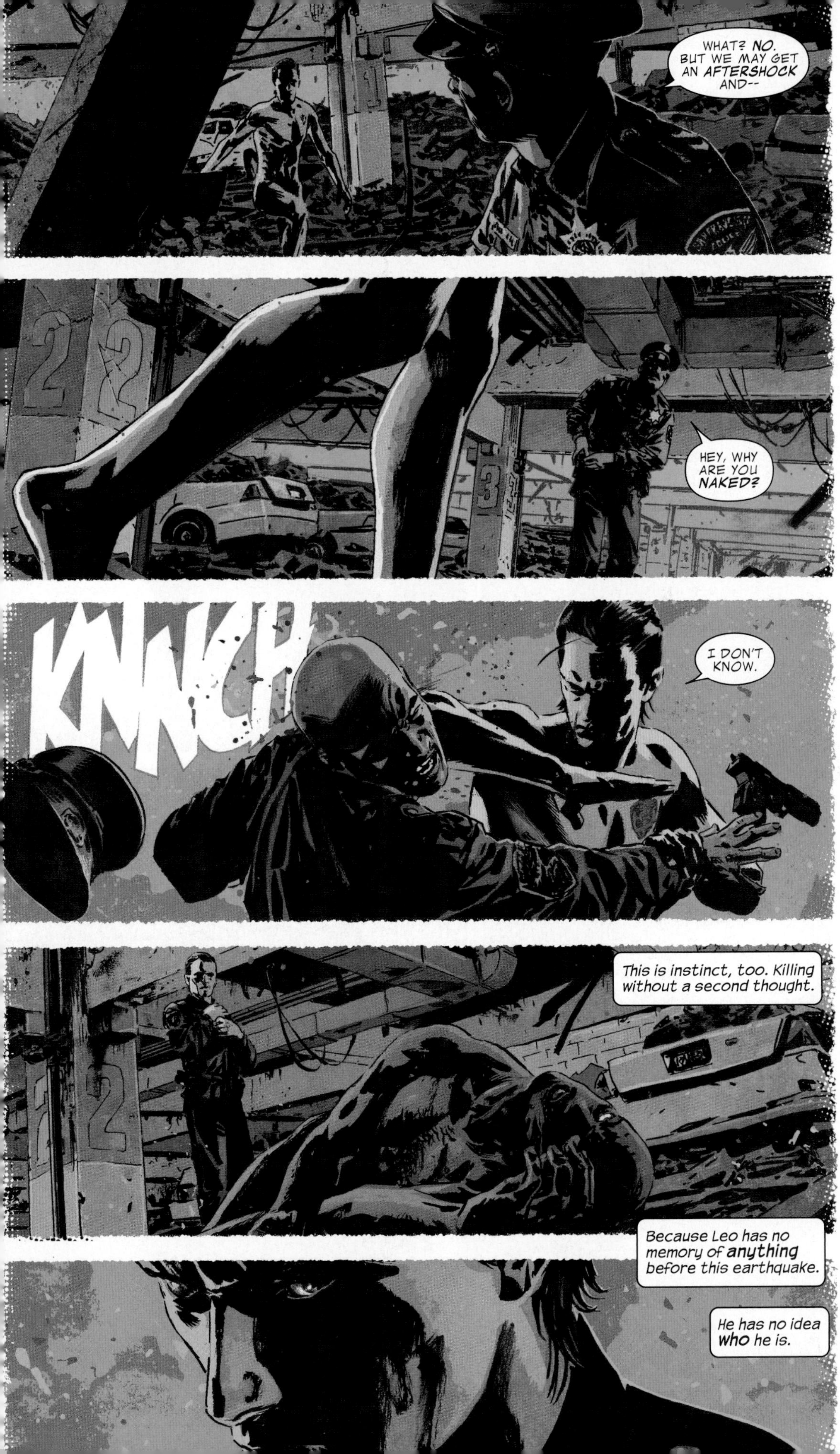
WHAT? NO. BUT WE MAY GET AN AFTERSHOCK AND--
HEY, WHY ARE YOU NAKED?
KNNCH
I DON'T KNOW.
This is instinct, too. Killing without a second thought.
Because Leo has no memory of anything before this earthquake.
He has no idea who he is.

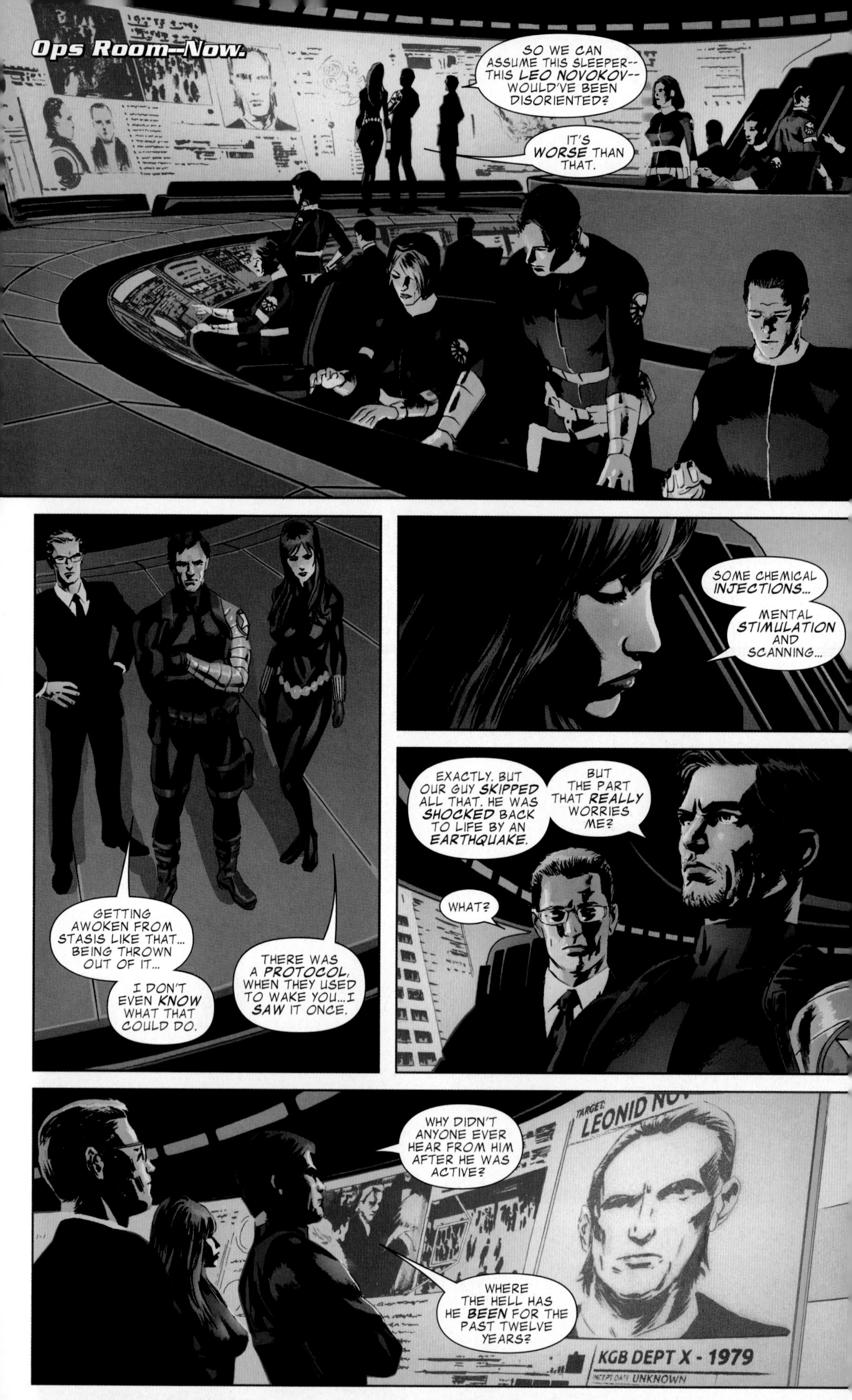
Ops Room--Now.
SO WE CAN ASSUME THIS SLEEPER-- THIS LEO NOVOKOV-- WOULD'VE BEEN DISORIENTED?
IT'S WORSE THAN THAT.
GETTING AWOKEN FROM STASIS LIKE THAT... BEING THROWN OUT OF IT...
I DON'T EVEN KNOW WHAT THAT COULD DO.
THERE WAS A PROTOCOL, WHEN THEY USED TO WAKE YOU...I SAW IT ONCE.
SOME CHEMICAL INJECTIONS...
MENTAL STIMULATION AND SCANNING...
EXACTLY. BUT OUR GUY SKIPPED ALL THAT. HE WAS SHOCKED BACK TO LIFE BY AN EARTHQUAKE.
BUT THE PART THAT REALLY WORRIES ME?
WHAT?
WHY DIDN'T ANYONE EVER HEAR FROM HIM AFTER HE WAS ACTIVE?
WHERE THE HELL HAS HE BEEN FOR THE PAST TWELVE YEARS?
TARGET:
KGB DEPT X - 1979
UNKNOWN

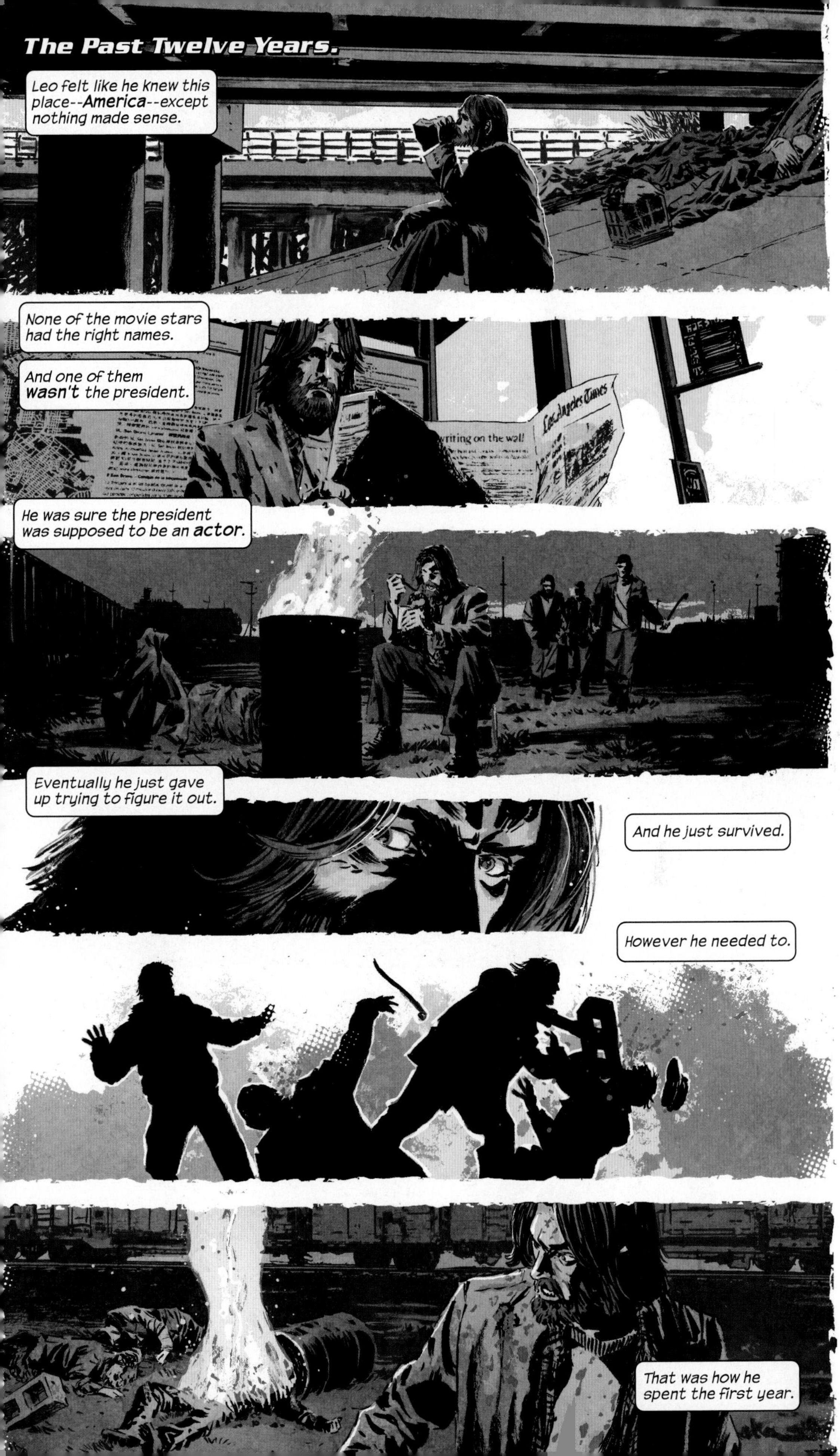
The Past Twelve Years.
Leo felt like he knew this place--America--except nothing made sense.
None of the movie stars had the right names.
And one of them wasn't the president.
Los Angeles Times
writing on the wall
He was sure the president was supposed to be an actor.
Eventually he just gave up trying to figure it out.
And he just survived.
However he needed to.
That was how he spent the first year.

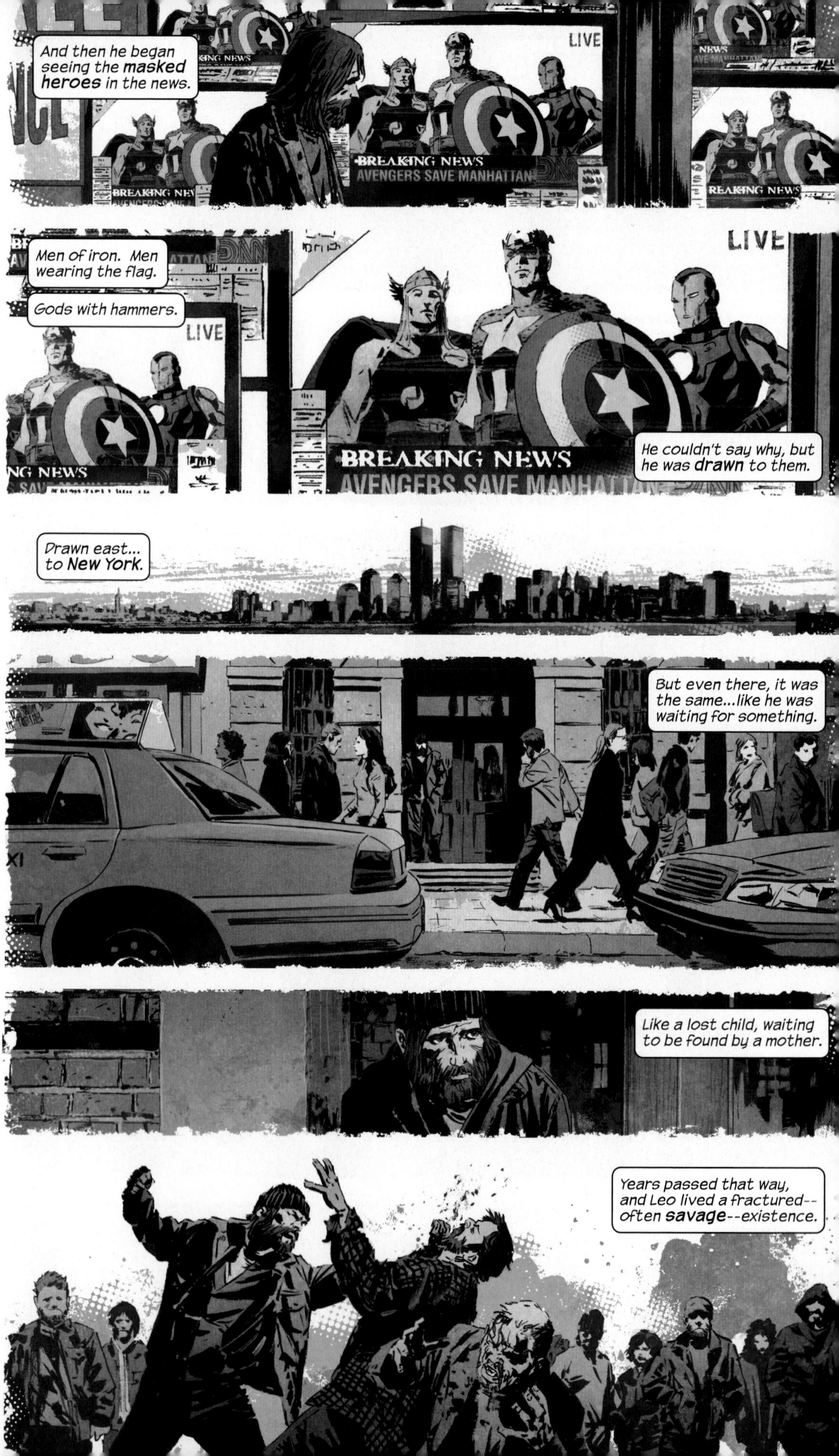
And then he began seeing the masked heroes in the news.
LIVE
BREAKING NEWS
AVENGERS SAVE MANHATTAN
Men of iron. Men wearing the flag.
Gods with hammers.
LIVE
LIVE
BREAKING NEWS
AVENGERS SAVE MANHATTAN
He couldn't say why, but he was drawn to them.
Drawn east... to New York.
But even there, it was the same...like he was waiting for something.
Like a lost child, waiting to be found by a mother.
Years passed that way, and Leo lived a fractured--often savage--existence.

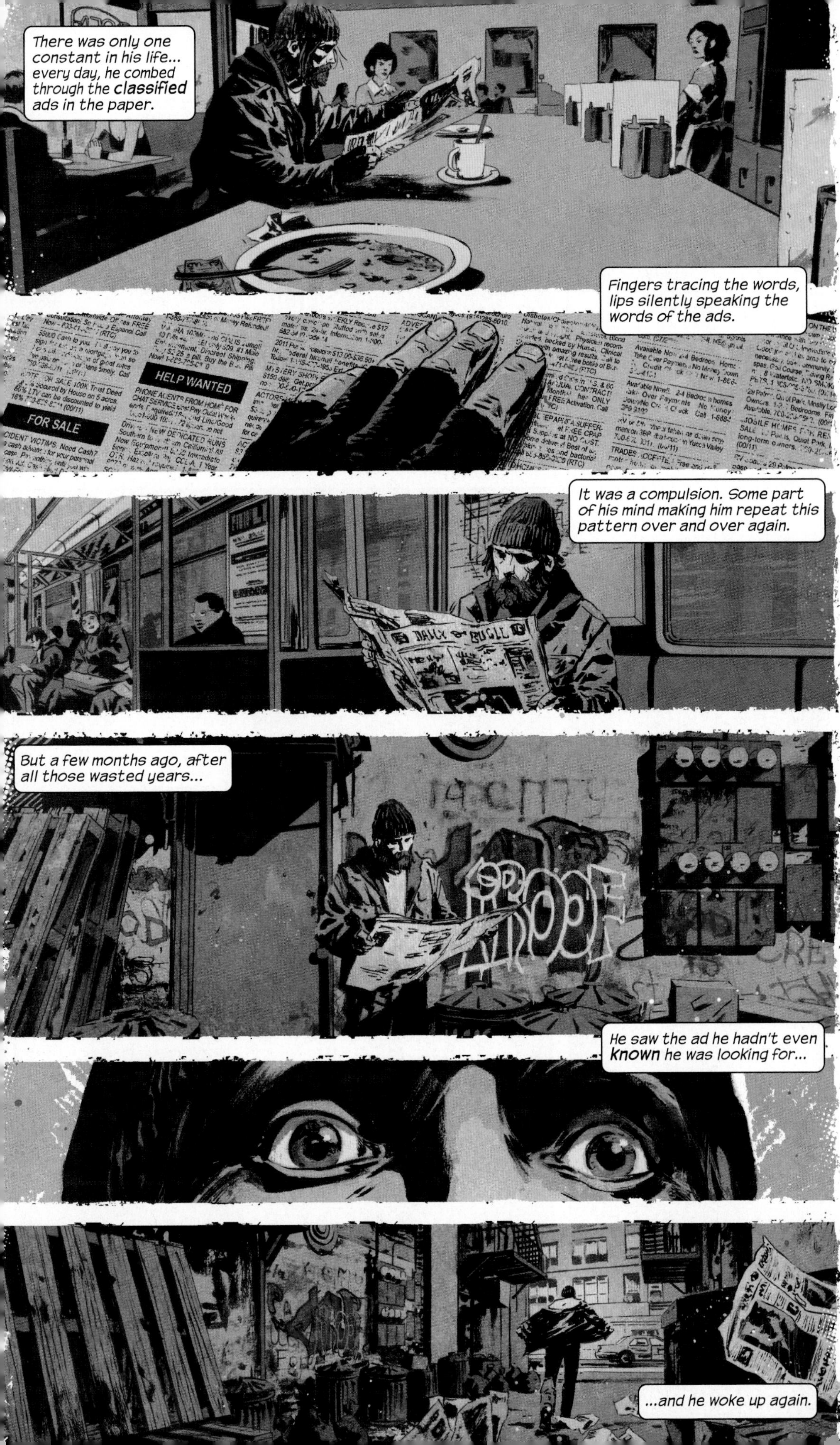
There was only one constant in his life... every day, he combed through the classified ads in the paper.
Fingers tracing the words, lips silently speaking the words of the ads.
HELP WANTED
FOR SALE
It was a compulsion. Some part of his mind making him repeat this pattern over and over again.
But a few months ago, after all those wasted years...
He saw the ad he hadn't even known he was looking for...
...and he woke up again.

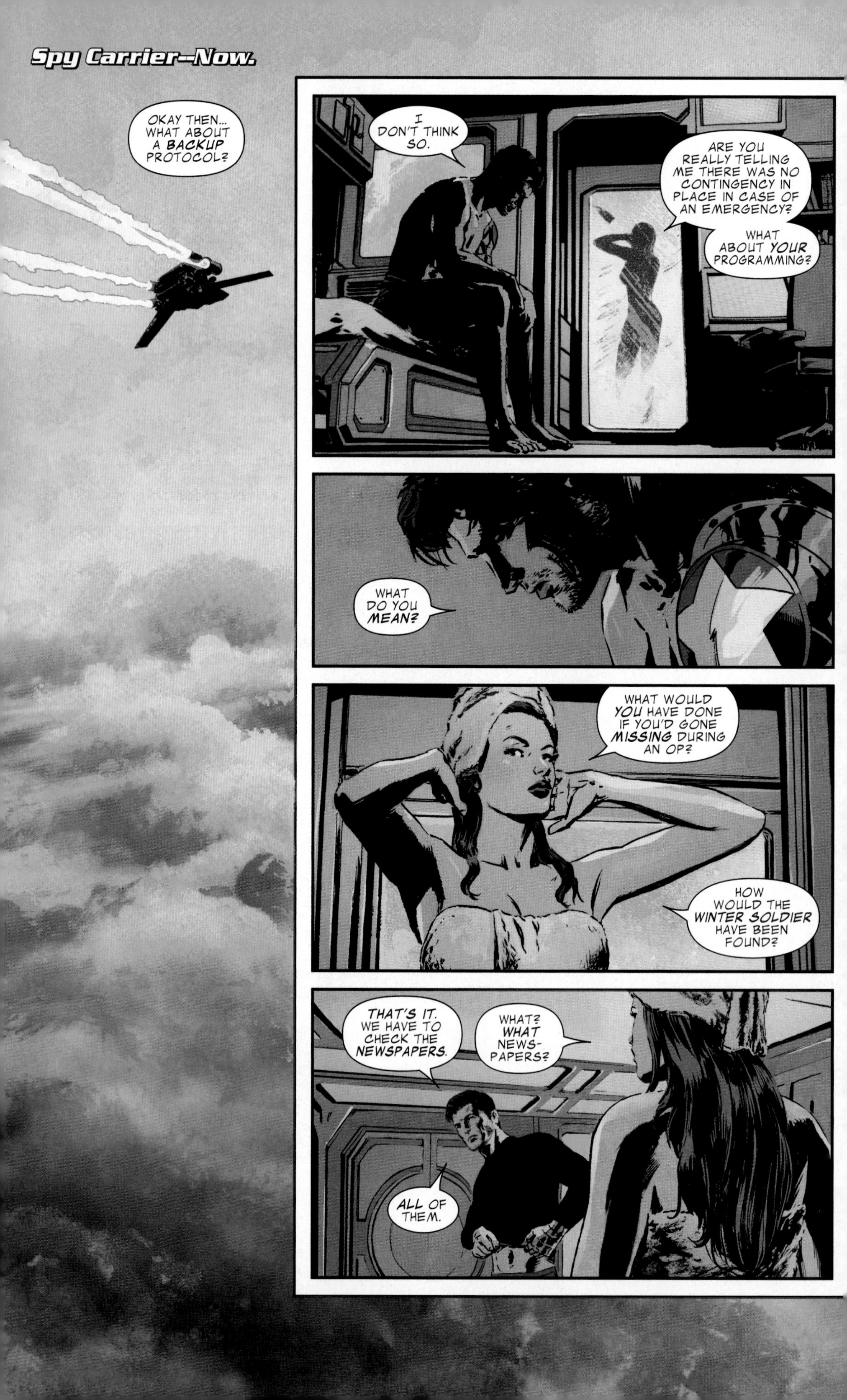
Spy Carrier--Now.
OKAY THEN... WHAT ABOUT A BACKUP PROTOCOL?
I DON'T THINK SO.
ARE YOU REALLY TELLING ME THERE WAS NO CONTINGENCY IN PLACE IN CASE OF AN EMERGENCY?
WHAT ABOUT YOUR PROGRAMMING?
WHAT DO YOU MEAN?
WHAT WOULD YOU HAVE DONE IF YOU'D GONE MISSING DURING AN OP?
HOW WOULD THE WINTER SOLDIER HAVE BEEN FOUND?
THAT'S IT. WE HAVE TO CHECK THE NEWSPAPERS.
WHAT? WHAT NEWS-PAPERS?
ALL OF THEM.

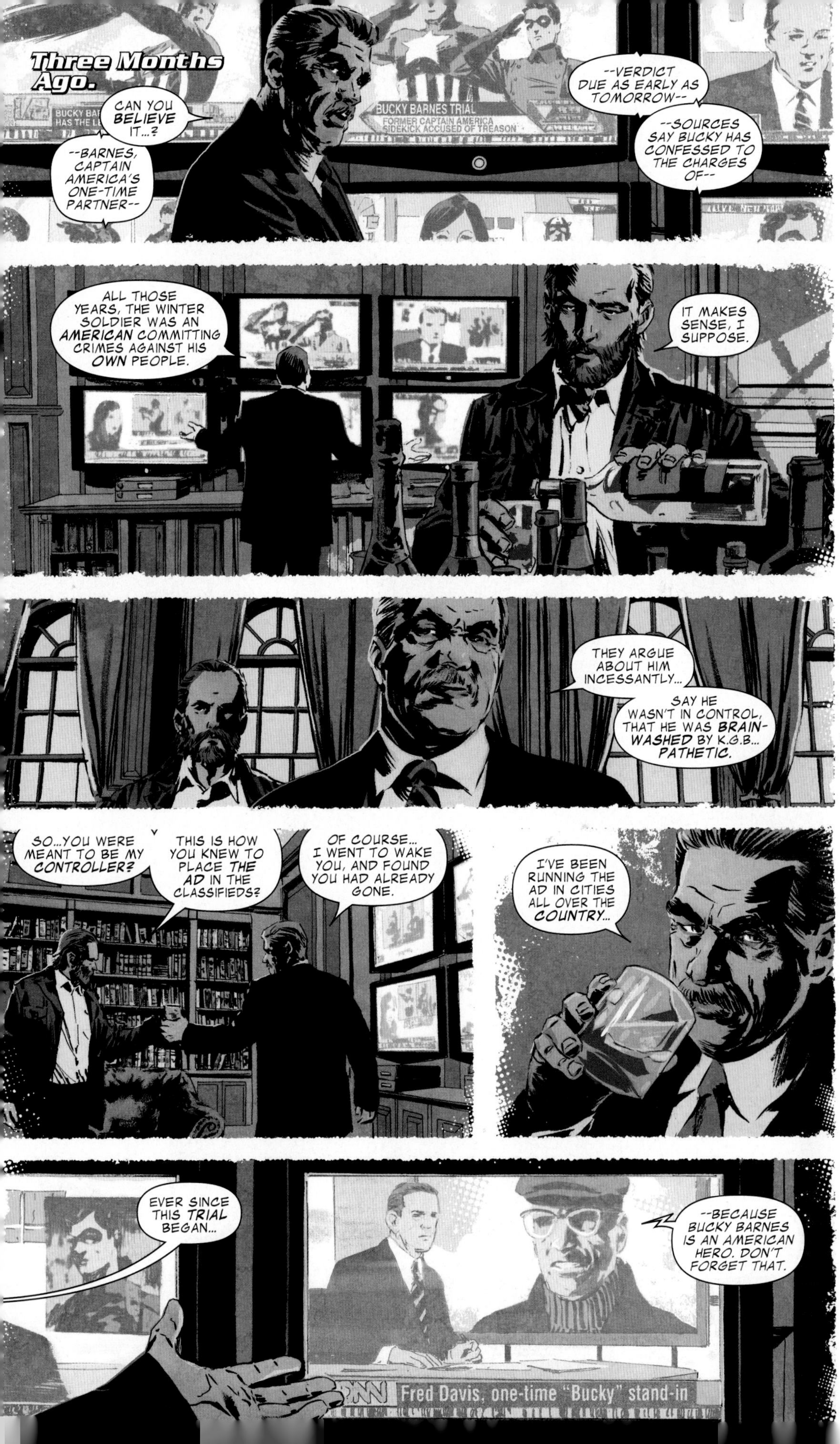
Three Months Ago.
CAN YOU BELIEVE IT...?
--BARNES, CAPTAIN AMERICA'S ONE-TIME PARTNER--
BUCKY BARNES TRIAL
FORMER CAPTAIN AMERICA SIDEKICK ACCUSED OF TREASON
--VERDICT DUE AS EARLY AS TOMORROW--
--SOURCES SAY BUCKY HAS CONFESSED TO THE CHARGES OF--
ALL THOSE YEARS, THE WINTER SOLDIER WAS AN AMERICAN COMMITTING CRIMES AGAINST HIS OWN PEOPLE.
IT MAKES SENSE, I SUPPOSE.
THEY ARGUE ABOUT HIM INCESSANTLY...
SAY HE WASN'T IN CONTROL, THAT HE WAS BRAIN-WASHED BY K.G.B... PATHETIC.
SO...YOU WERE MEANT TO BE MY CONTROLLER?
THIS IS HOW YOU KNEW TO PLACE THE AD IN THE CLASSIFIEDS?
OF COURSE... I WENT TO WAKE YOU, AND FOUND YOU HAD ALREADY GONE.
I'VE BEEN RUNNING THE AD IN CITIES ALL OVER THE COUNTRY...
EVER SINCE THIS TRIAL BEGAN...
--BECAUSE BUCKY BARNES IS AN AMERICAN HERO. DON'T FORGET THAT.
Fred Davis, one-time "Bucky" stand-in

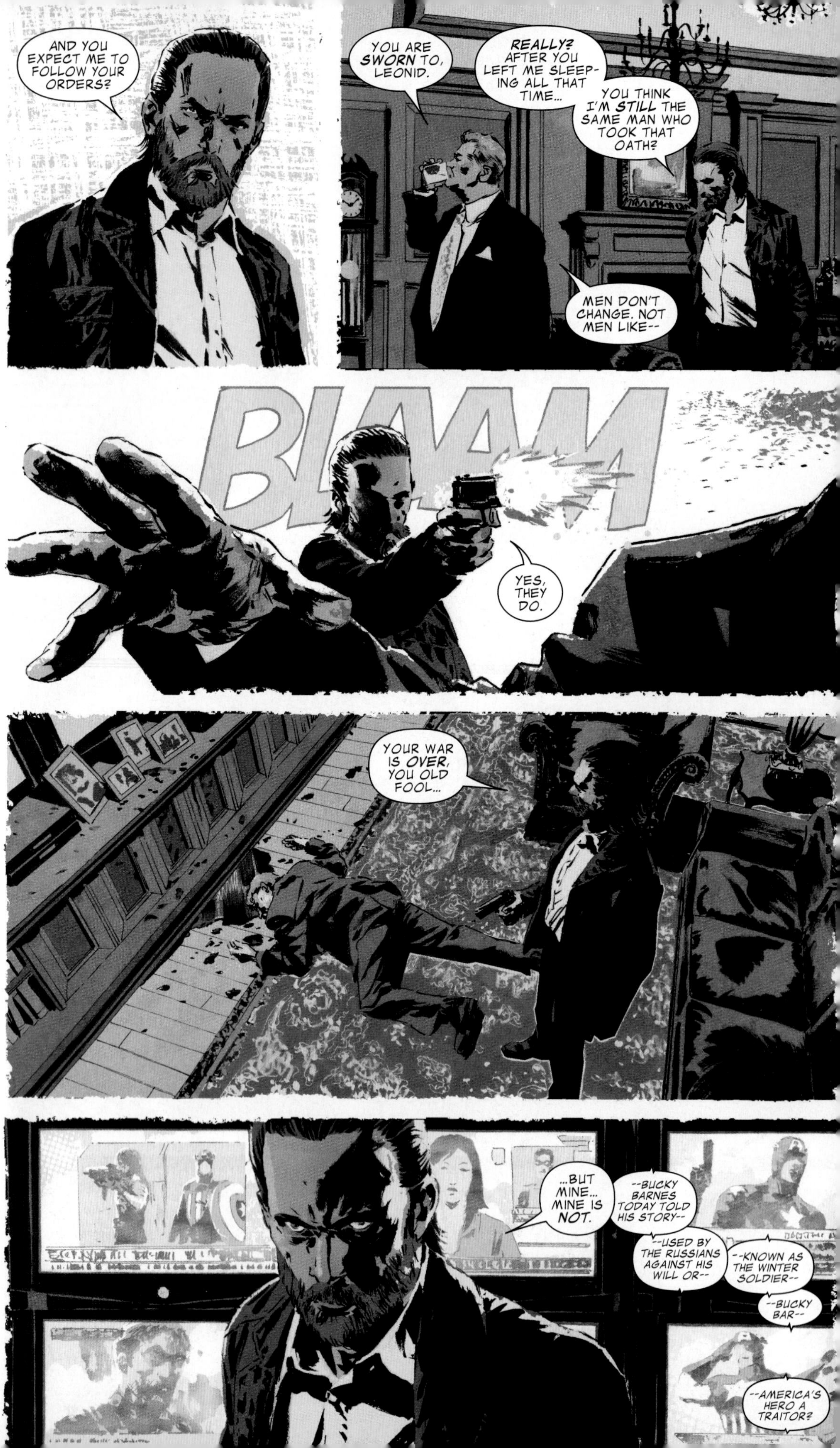
AND YOU EXPECT ME TO FOLLOW YOUR ORDERS?
YOU ARE SWORN TO, LEONID.
REALLY? AFTER YOU LEFT ME SLEEPING ALL THAT TIME...
YOU THINK I'M STILL THE SAME MAN WHO TOOK THAT OATH?
MEN DON'T CHANGE. NOT MEN LIKE--
BLAAM
YES, THEY DO.
YOUR WAR IS OVER, YOU OLD FOOL...
...BUT MINE... MINE IS NOT.
--BUCKY BARNES TODAY TOLD HIS STORY--
--USED BY THE RUSSIANS AGAINST HIS WILL OR--
--KNOWN AS THE WINTER SOLDIER--
--BUCKY BAR--
--AMERICA'S HERO A TRAITOR?

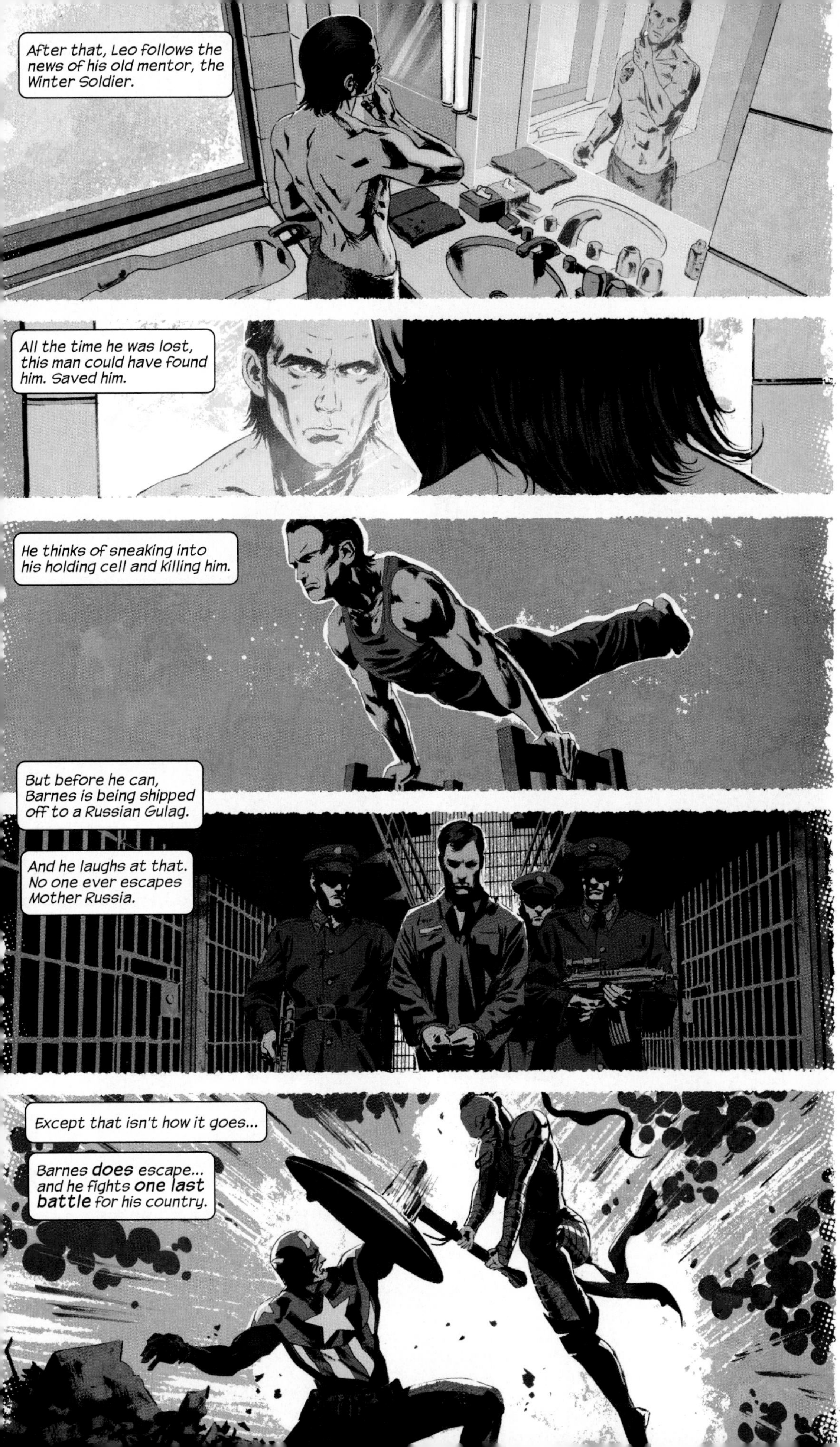
After that, Leo follows the news of his old mentor, the Winter Soldier.
All the time he was lost, this man could have found him. Saved him.
He thinks of sneaking into his holding cell and killing him.
But before he can, Barnes is being shipped off to a Russian Gulag.
And he laughs at that. No one ever escapes Mother Russia.
Except that isn't how it goes...
Barnes **does** escape... and he fights **one last battle** for his country.

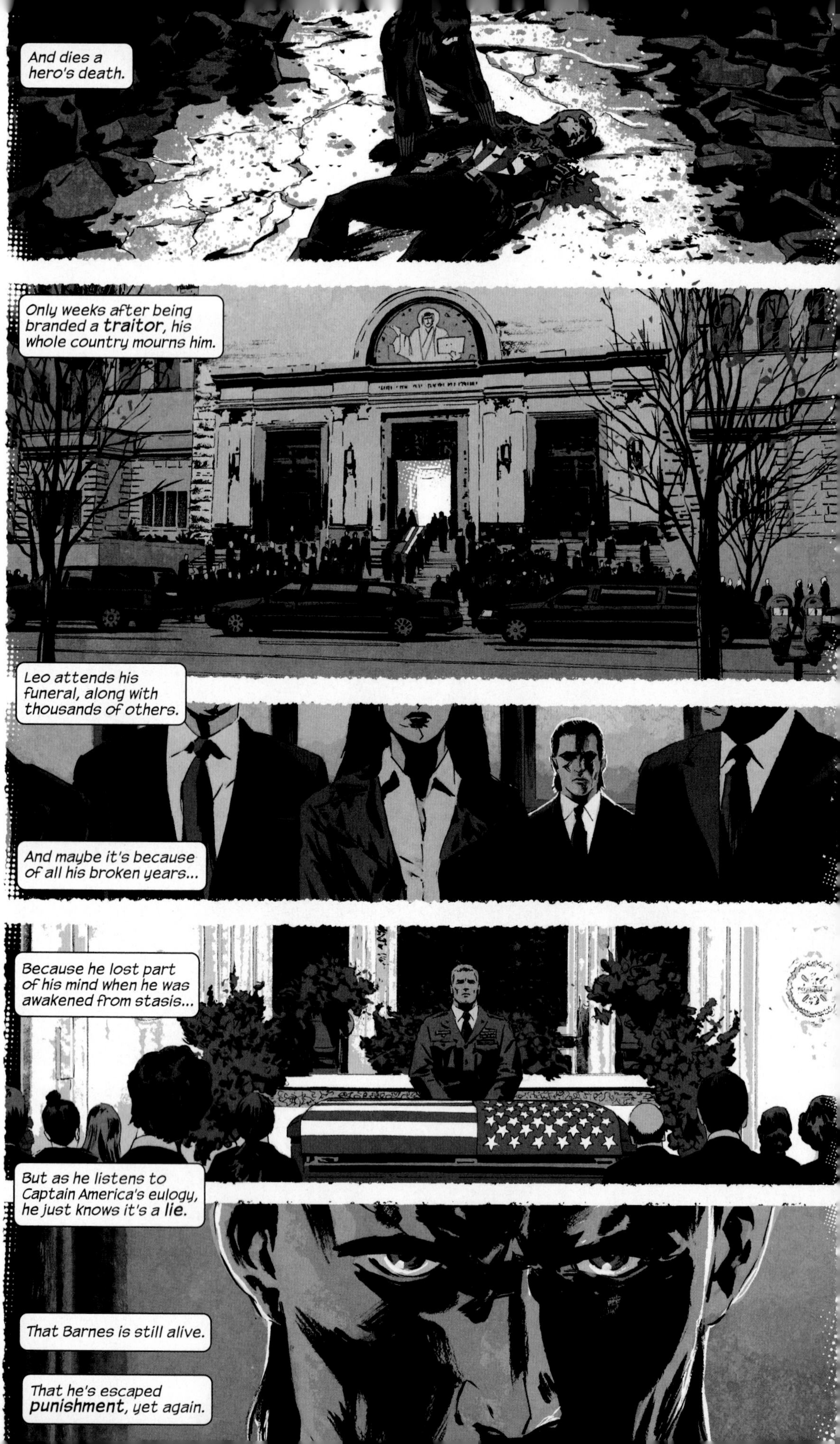
And dies a hero's death.
Only weeks after being branded a **traitor**, his whole country mourns him.
Leo attends his funeral, along with thousands of others.
And maybe it's because of all his broken years...
Because he lost part of his mind when he was awakened from stasis...
But as he listens to Captain America's eulogy, he just knows it's a **lie**.
That Barnes is still alive.
That he's escaped **punishment**, yet again.

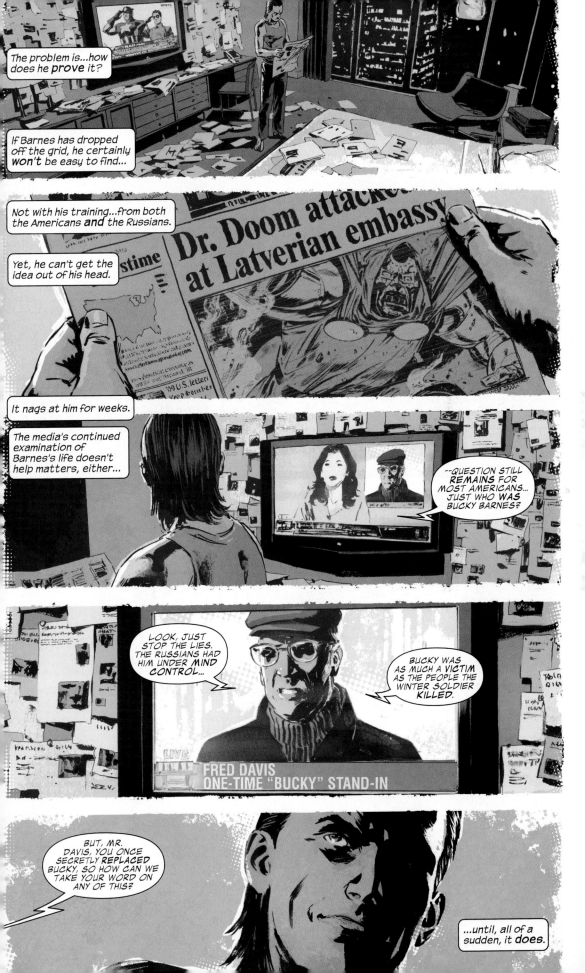

The problem is...how does he **prove** it?

If Barnes has dropped off the grid, he certainly **won't** be easy to find...

Not with his training...from both the Americans **and** the Russians.

Yet, he can't get the idea out of his head.

Dr. Doom attacked at Latverian embassy

It nags at him for weeks.

The media's continued examination of Barnes's life doesn't help matters, either...

--QUESTION STILL **REMAINS** FOR MOST AMERICANS... JUST WHO **WAS** BUCKY BARNES?

LOOK, JUST STOP THE LIES. THE RUSSIANS HAD HIM UNDER **MIND** CONTROL...

BUCKY WAS AS MUCH A VICTIM AS THE PEOPLE THE WINTER SOLDIER KILLED.

FRED DAVIS
ONE-TIME "BUCKY" STAND-IN

BUT, MR. DAVIS, YOU ONCE SECRETLY **REPLACED** BUCKY, SO HOW CAN WE TAKE YOUR WORD ON ANY OF THIS?

...until, all of a sudden, it **does**.

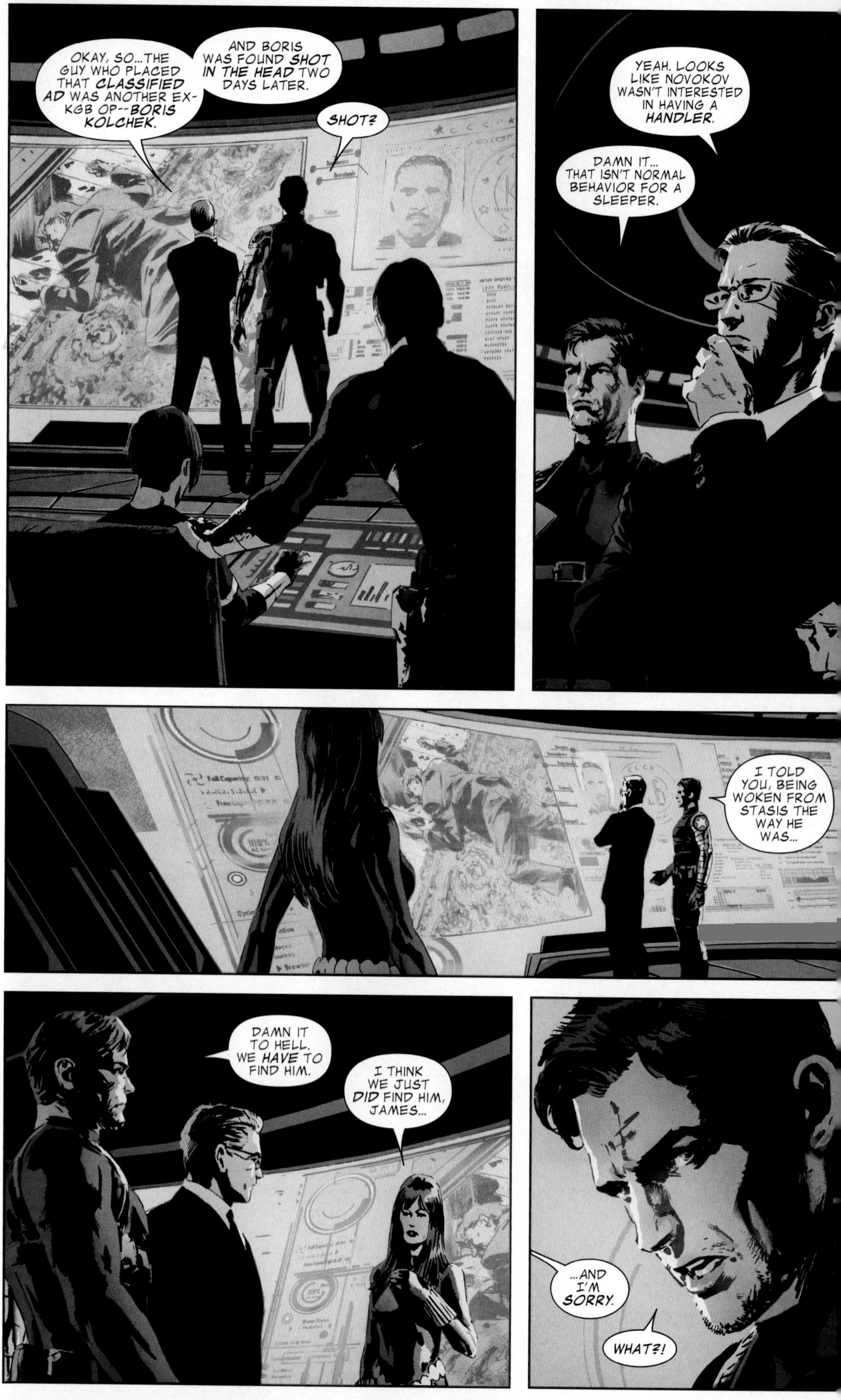

OKAY, SO...THE GUY WHO PLACED THAT **CLASSIFIED AD** WAS ANOTHER EX-KGB OP--**BORIS KOLCHEK.**
AND BORIS WAS FOUND **SHOT IN THE HEAD** TWO DAYS LATER.
SHOT?
YEAH. LOOKS LIKE NOVOKOV WASN'T INTERESTED IN HAVING A **HANDLER**.
DAMN IT... THAT ISN'T NORMAL BEHAVIOR FOR A SLEEPER.
I TOLD YOU, BEING WOKEN FROM STASIS THE WAY HE WAS...
DAMN IT TO HELL. WE **HAVE** TO FIND HIM.
I THINK WE JUST **DID** FIND HIM, JAMES...
...AND I'M **SORRY**.
WHAT?!

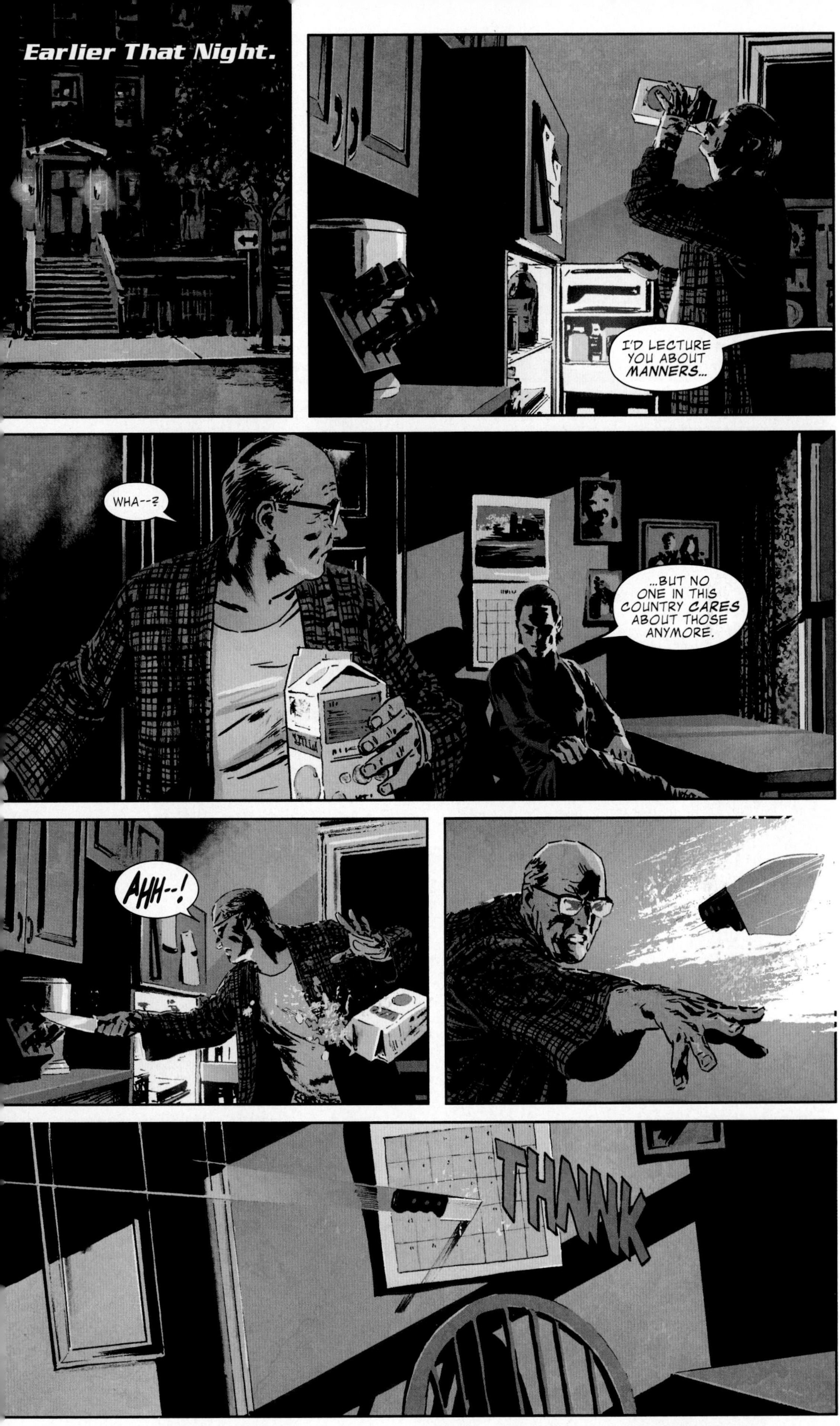
Earlier That Night.
I'D LECTURE YOU ABOUT MANNERS...
WHA--?
...BUT NO ONE IN THIS COUNTRY CARES ABOUT THOSE ANYMORE.
AHH--!
THNNK

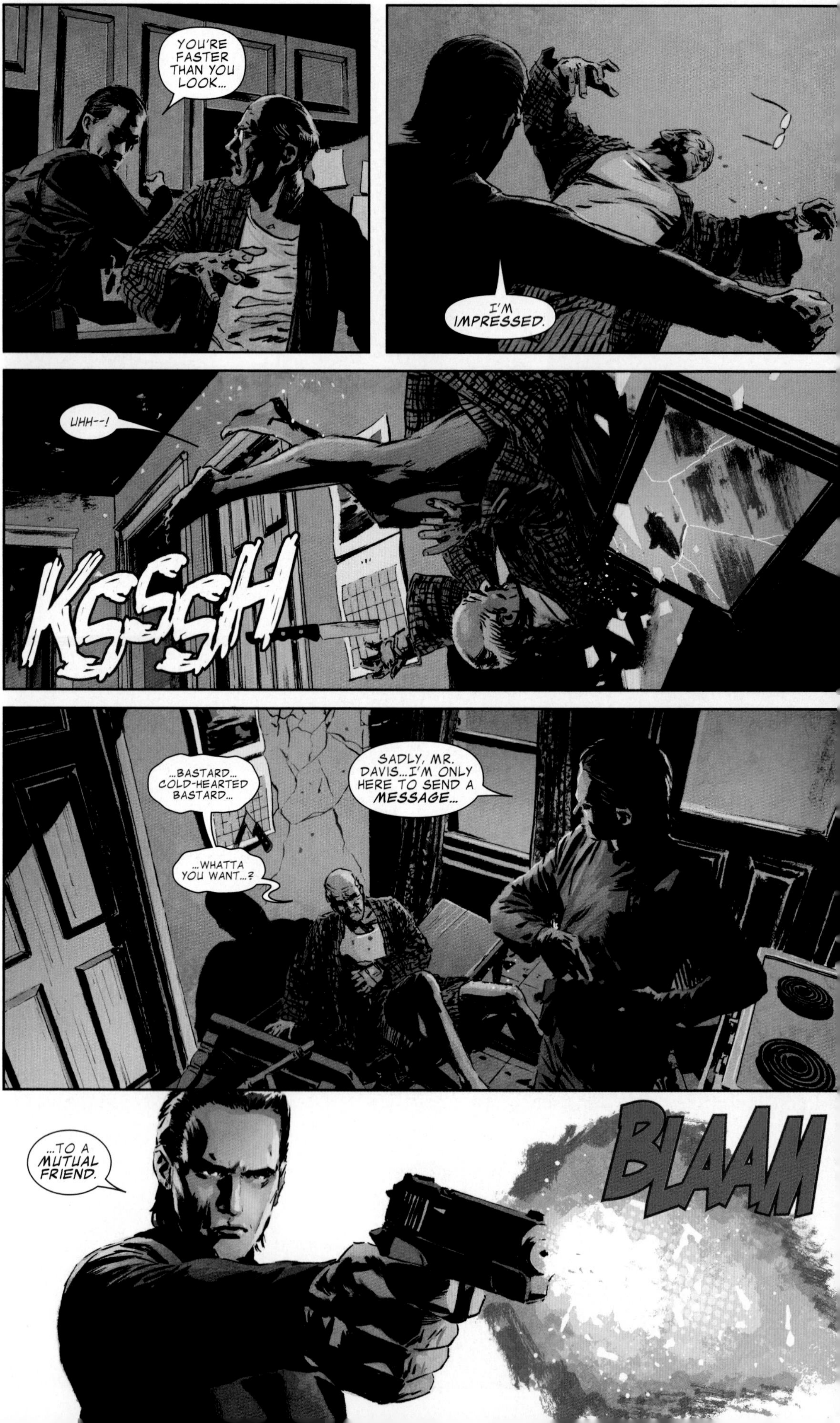

YOU'RE FASTER THAN YOU LOOK...
I'M IMPRESSED.
UHH--!
KSSSH
...BASTARD... COLD-HEARTED BASTARD...
...WHATTA YOU WANT...?
SADLY, MR. DAVIS...I'M ONLY HERE TO SEND A MESSAGE...
...TO A MUTUAL FRIEND.
BLAAM

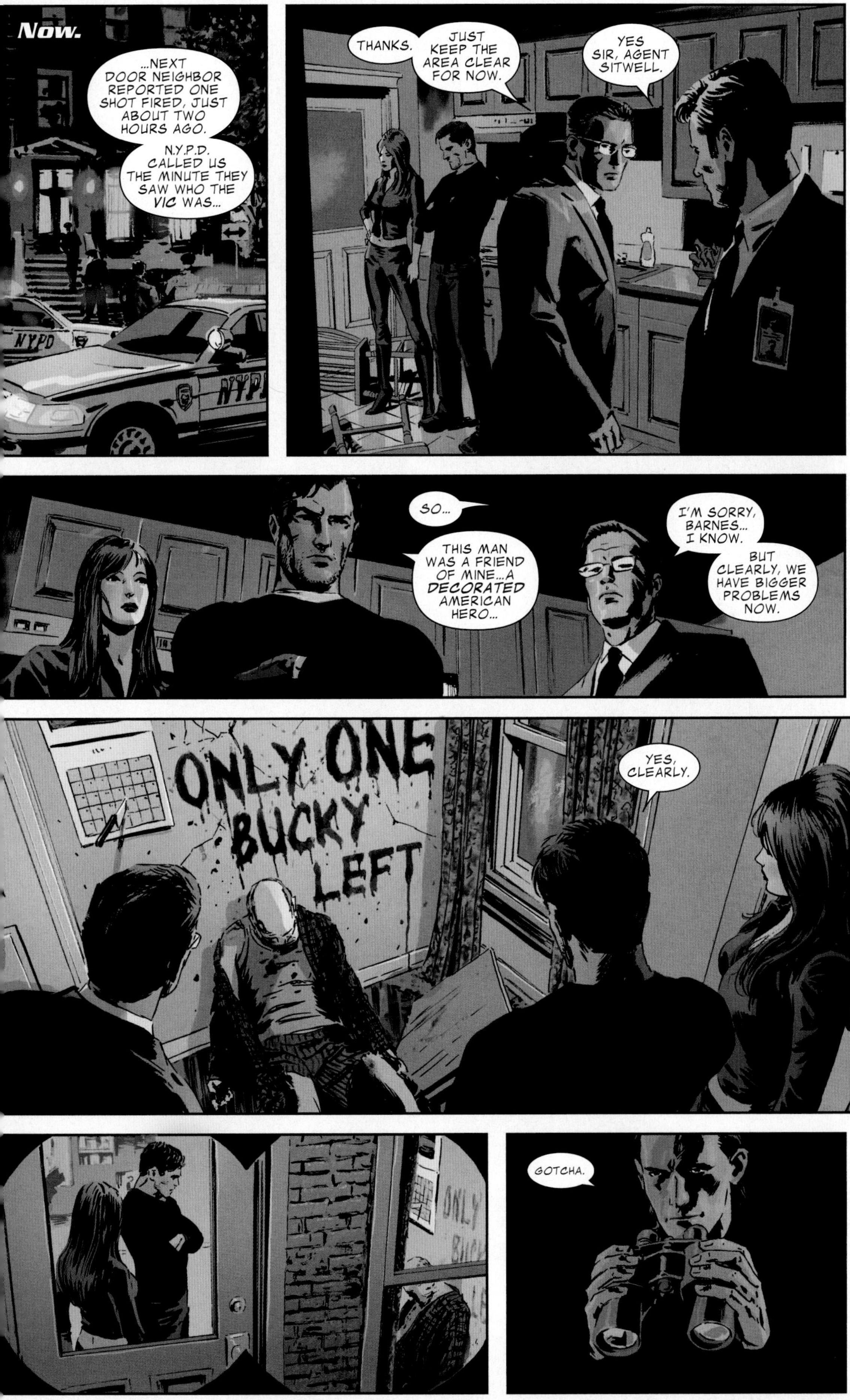
Now.
...NEXT DOOR NEIGHBOR REPORTED ONE SHOT FIRED, JUST ABOUT TWO HOURS AGO.
N.Y.P.D. CALLED US THE MINUTE THEY SAW WHO THE VIC WAS...
NYPD
THANKS.
JUST KEEP THE AREA CLEAR FOR NOW.
YES SIR, AGENT SITWELL.
SO...
THIS MAN WAS A FRIEND OF MINE...A DECORATED AMERICAN HERO...
I'M SORRY, BARNES... I KNOW.
BUT CLEARLY, WE HAVE BIGGER PROBLEMS NOW.
ONLY ONE BUCKY LEFT
YES, CLEARLY.
GOTCHA.

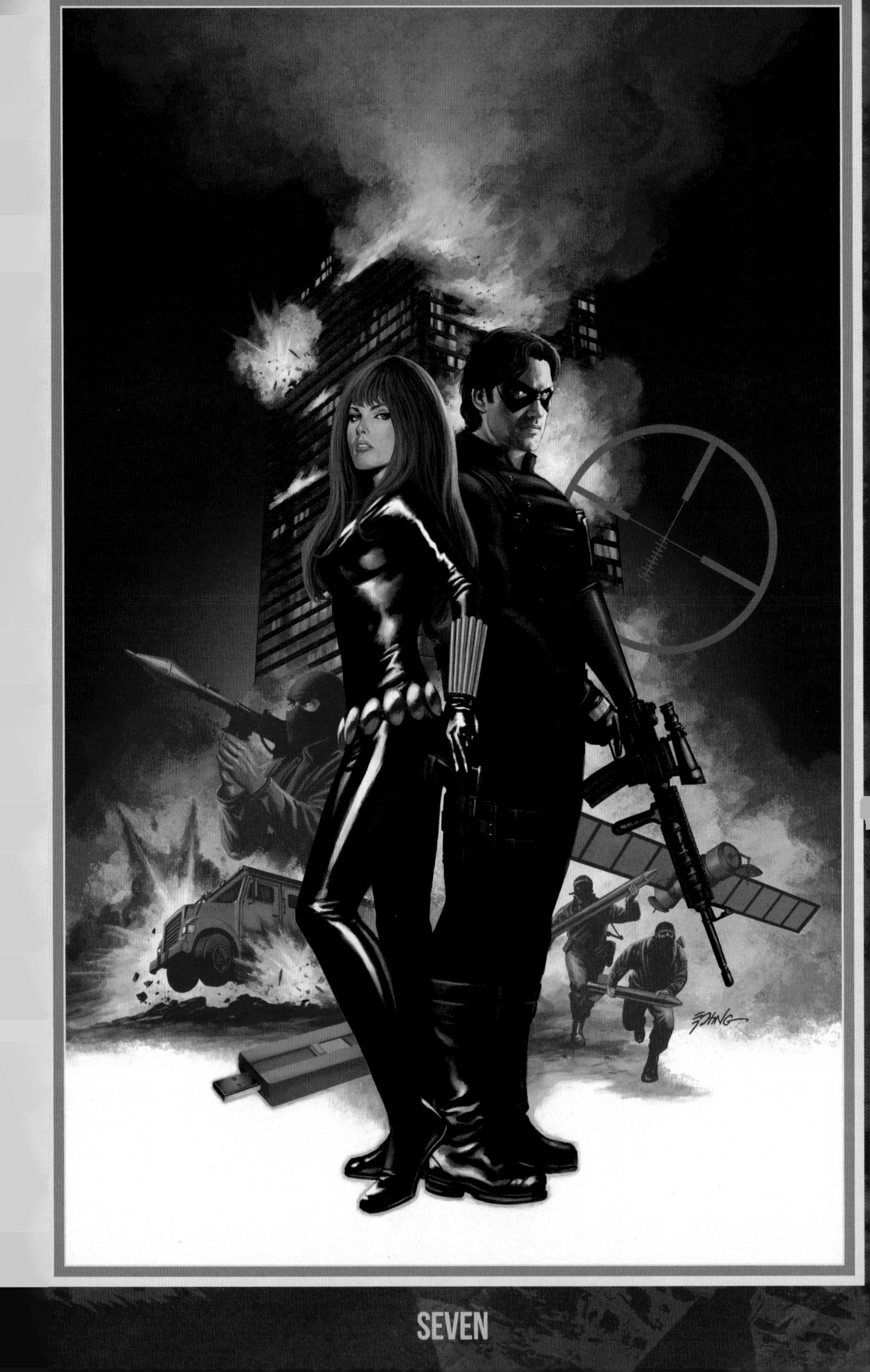

SEVEN

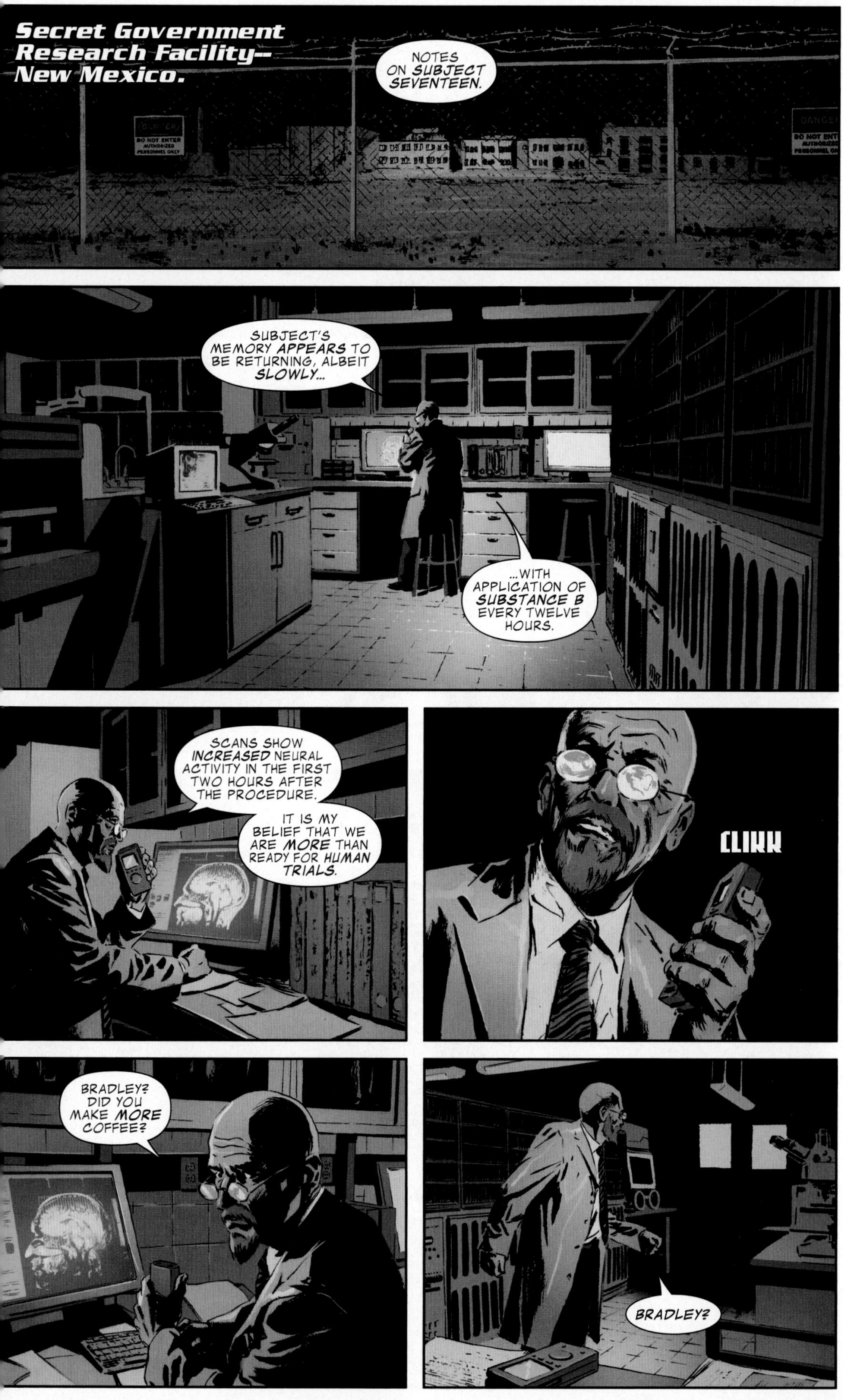
Secret Government Research Facility-- New Mexico.
NOTES ON SUBJECT SEVENTEEN.
DANGER DO NOT ENTER AUTHORIZED PERSONNEL ONLY
SUBJECT'S MEMORY APPEARS TO BE RETURNING, ALBEIT SLOWLY...
...WITH APPLICATION OF SUBSTANCE B EVERY TWELVE HOURS.
SCANS SHOW INCREASED NEURAL ACTIVITY IN THE FIRST TWO HOURS AFTER THE PROCEDURE.
IT IS MY BELIEF THAT WE ARE MORE THAN READY FOR HUMAN TRIALS.
CLIKK
BRADLEY? DID YOU MAKE MORE COFFEE?
BRADLEY?

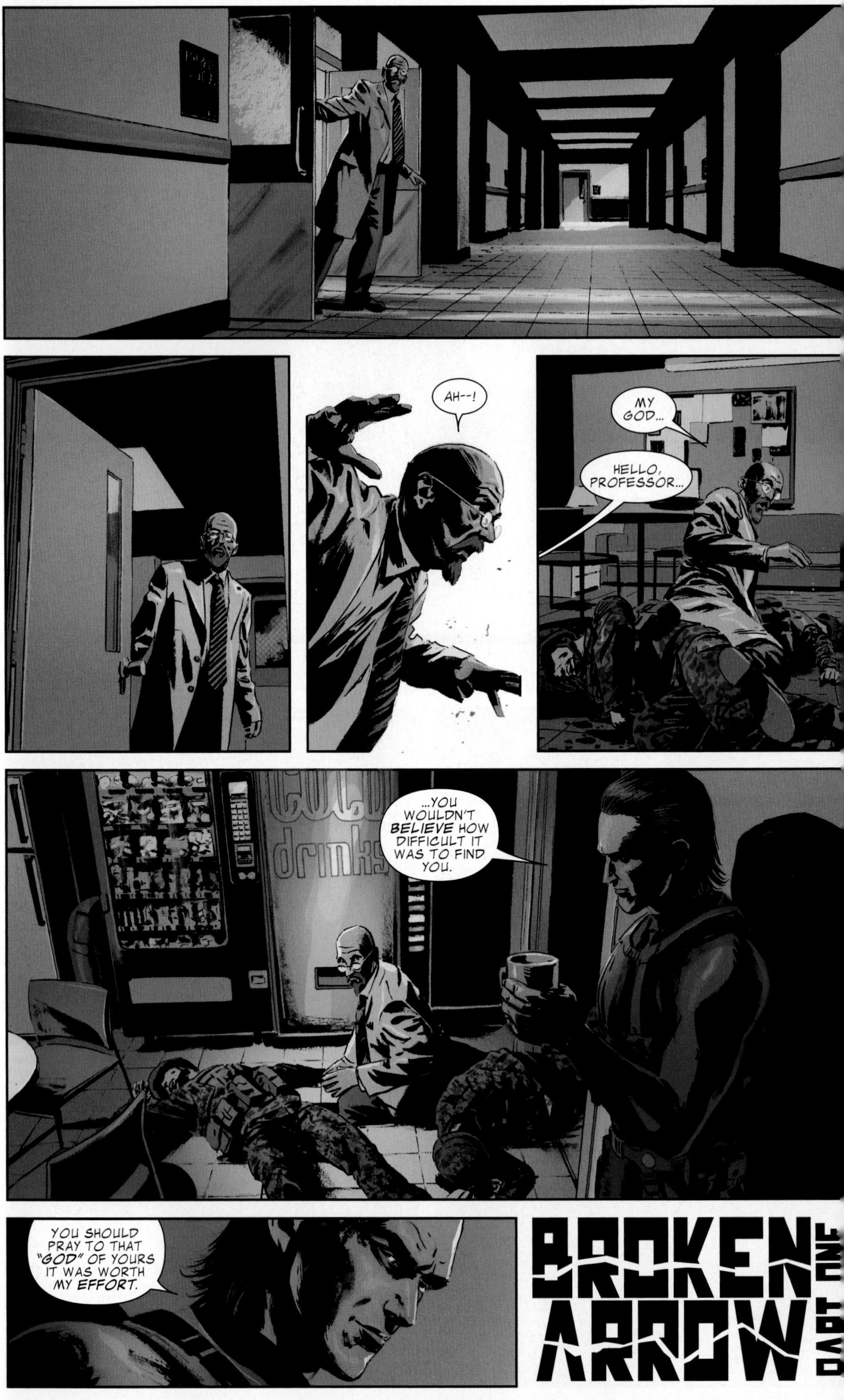
AH--!
MY GOD...
HELLO, PROFESSOR...
drinks
...YOU WOULDN'T BELIEVE HOW DIFFICULT IT WAS TO FIND YOU.
YOU SHOULD PRAY TO THAT "GOD" OF YOURS IT WAS WORTH MY EFFORT.
BROKEN ARROW
PART ONE

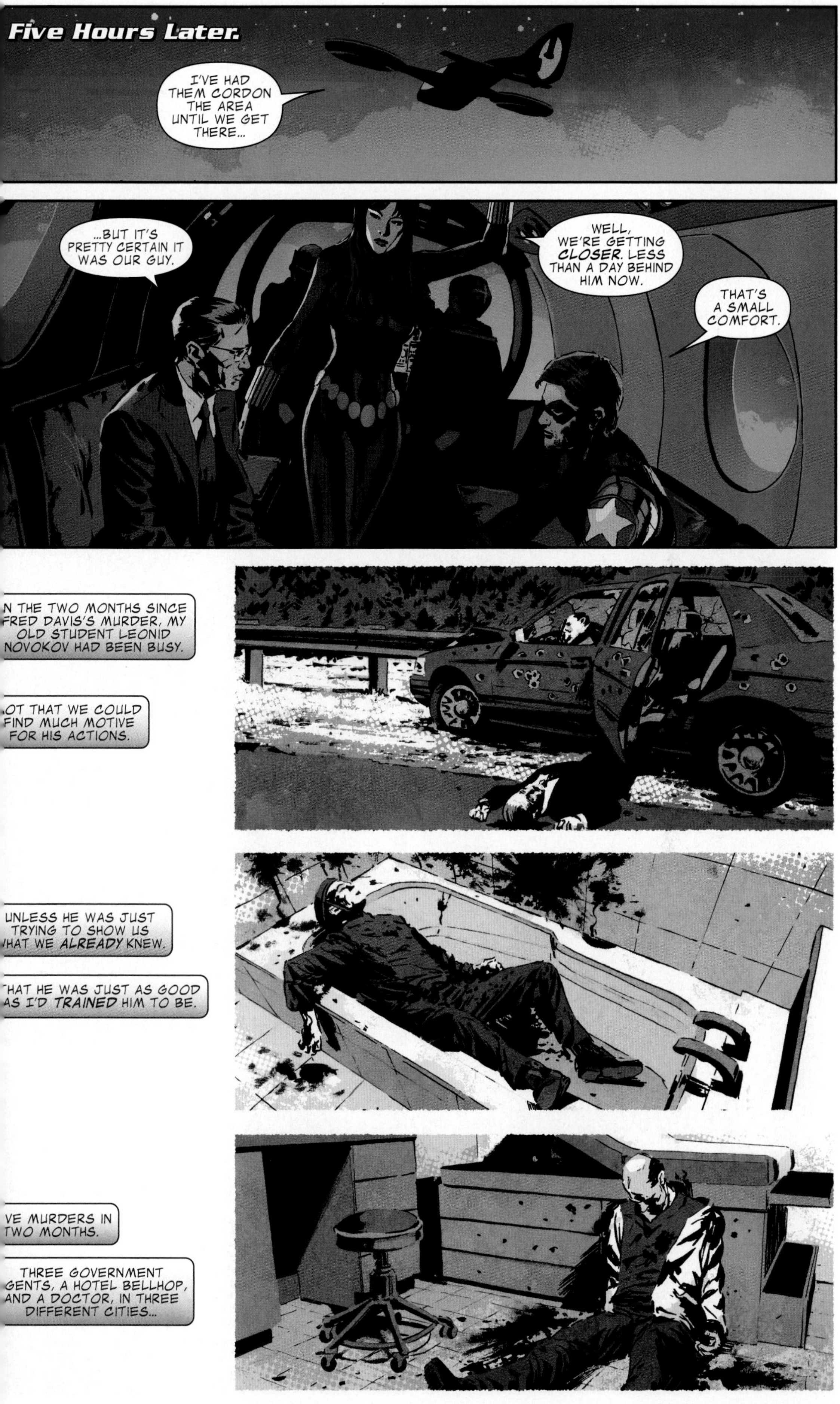
Five Hours Later.
I'VE HAD THEM CORDON THE AREA UNTIL WE GET THERE...
...BUT IT'S PRETTY CERTAIN IT WAS OUR GUY.
WELL, WE'RE GETTING CLOSER. LESS THAN A DAY BEHIND HIM NOW.
THAT'S A SMALL COMFORT.
N THE TWO MONTHS SINCE FRED DAVIS'S MURDER, MY OLD STUDENT LEONID NOVOKOV HAD BEEN BUSY.
OT THAT WE COULD FIND MUCH MOTIVE FOR HIS ACTIONS.
UNLESS HE WAS JUST TRYING TO SHOW US HAT WE ALREADY KNEW.
THAT HE WAS JUST AS GOOD AS I'D TRAINED HIM TO BE.
VE MURDERS IN TWO MONTHS.
THREE GOVERNMENT GENTS, A HOTEL BELLHOP, AND A DOCTOR, IN THREE DIFFERENT CITIES...

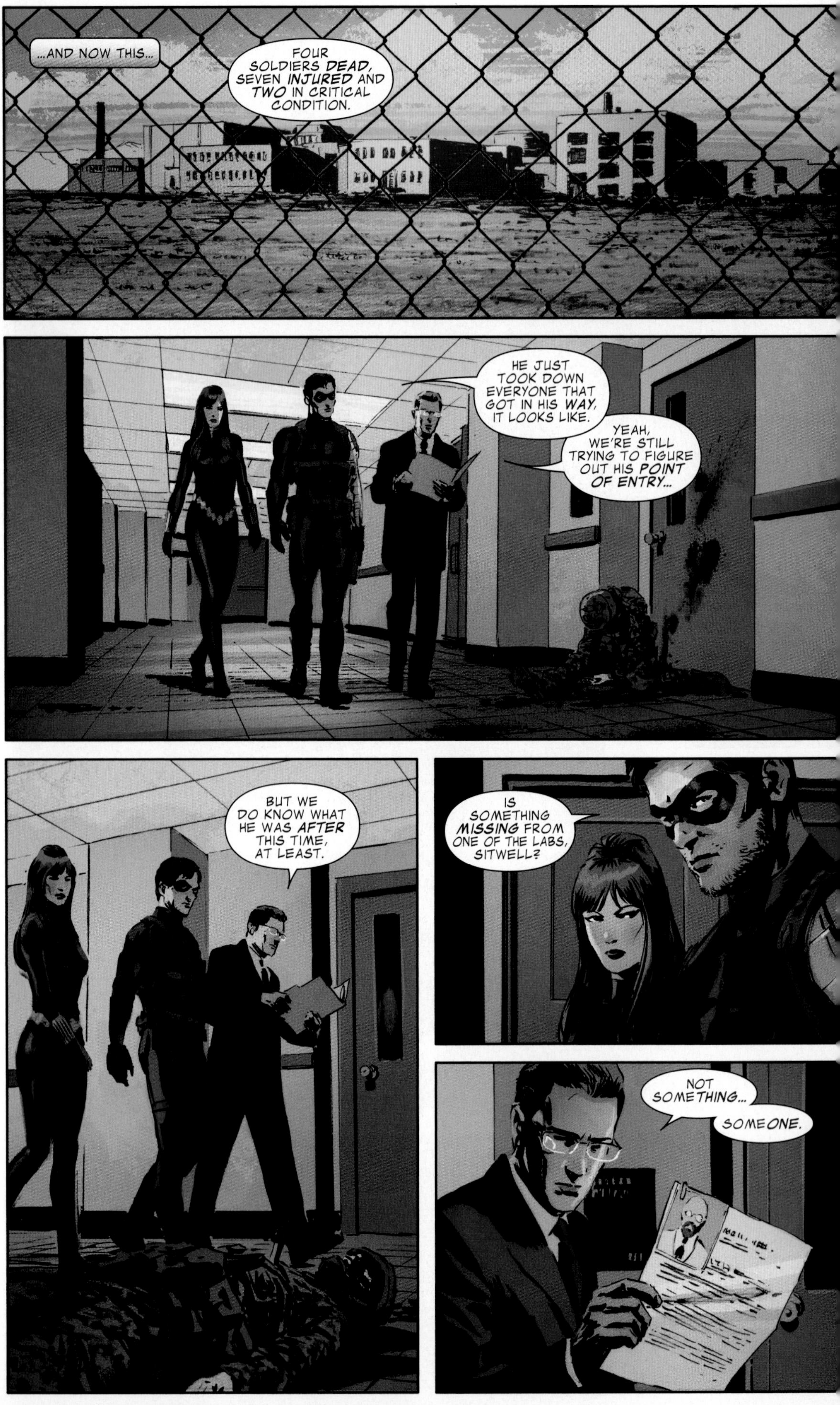
...AND NOW THIS...
FOUR SOLDIERS DEAD, SEVEN INJURED AND TWO IN CRITICAL CONDITION.
HE JUST TOOK DOWN EVERYONE THAT GOT IN HIS WAY, IT LOOKS LIKE.
YEAH, WE'RE STILL TRYING TO FIGURE OUT HIS POINT OF ENTRY...
BUT WE DO KNOW WHAT HE WAS AFTER THIS TIME, AT LEAST.
IS SOMETHING MISSING FROM ONE OF THE LABS, SITWELL?
NOT SOMETHING...
SOMEONE.

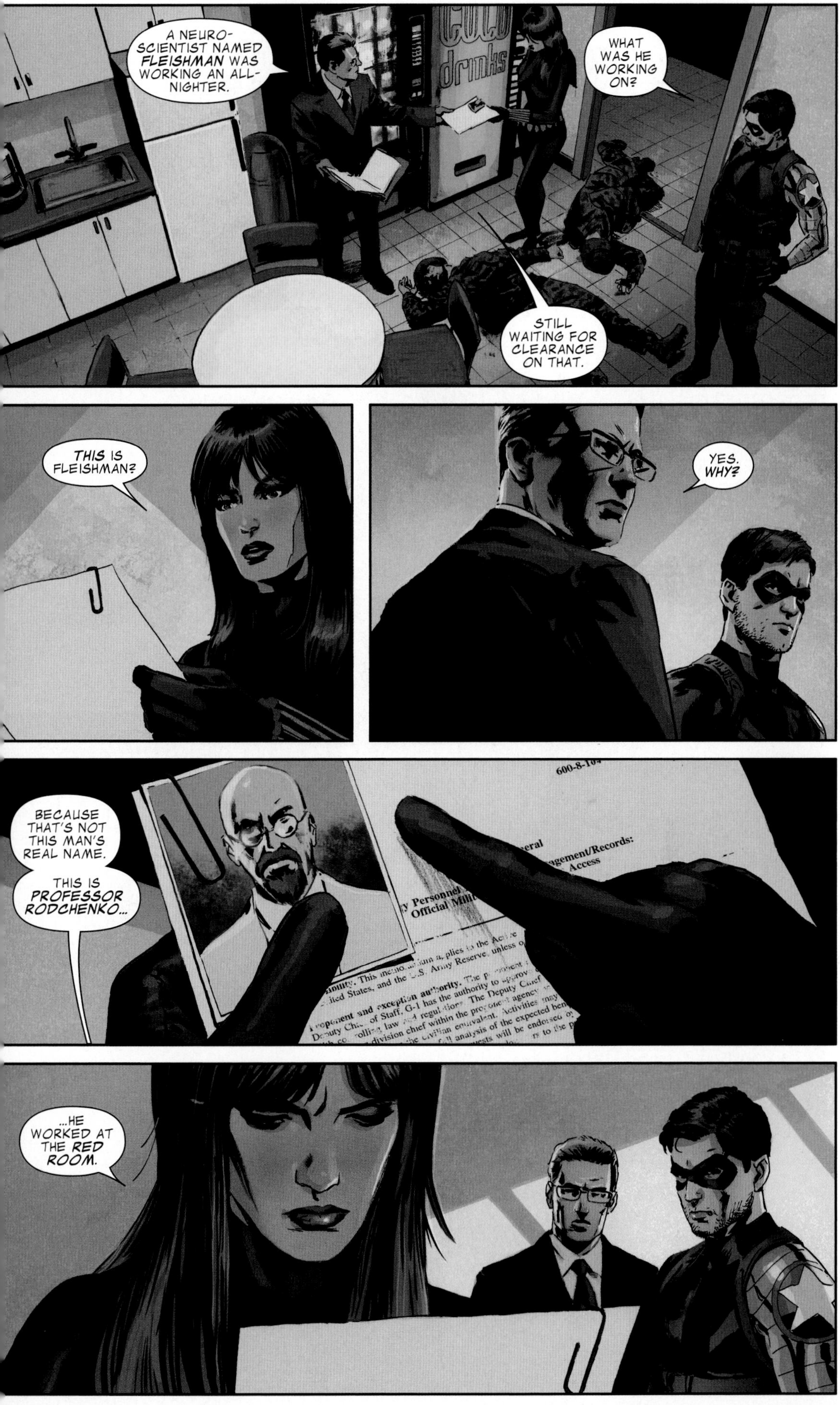
A NEURO-SCIENTIST NAMED FLEISHMAN WAS WORKING AN ALL-NIGHTER.
WHAT WAS HE WORKING ON?
STILL WAITING FOR CLEARANCE ON THAT.
THIS IS FLEISHMAN?
YES. WHY?
BECAUSE THAT'S NOT THIS MAN'S REAL NAME.
THIS IS PROFESSOR RODCHENKO...
600-8-104
...HE WORKED AT THE RED ROOM.

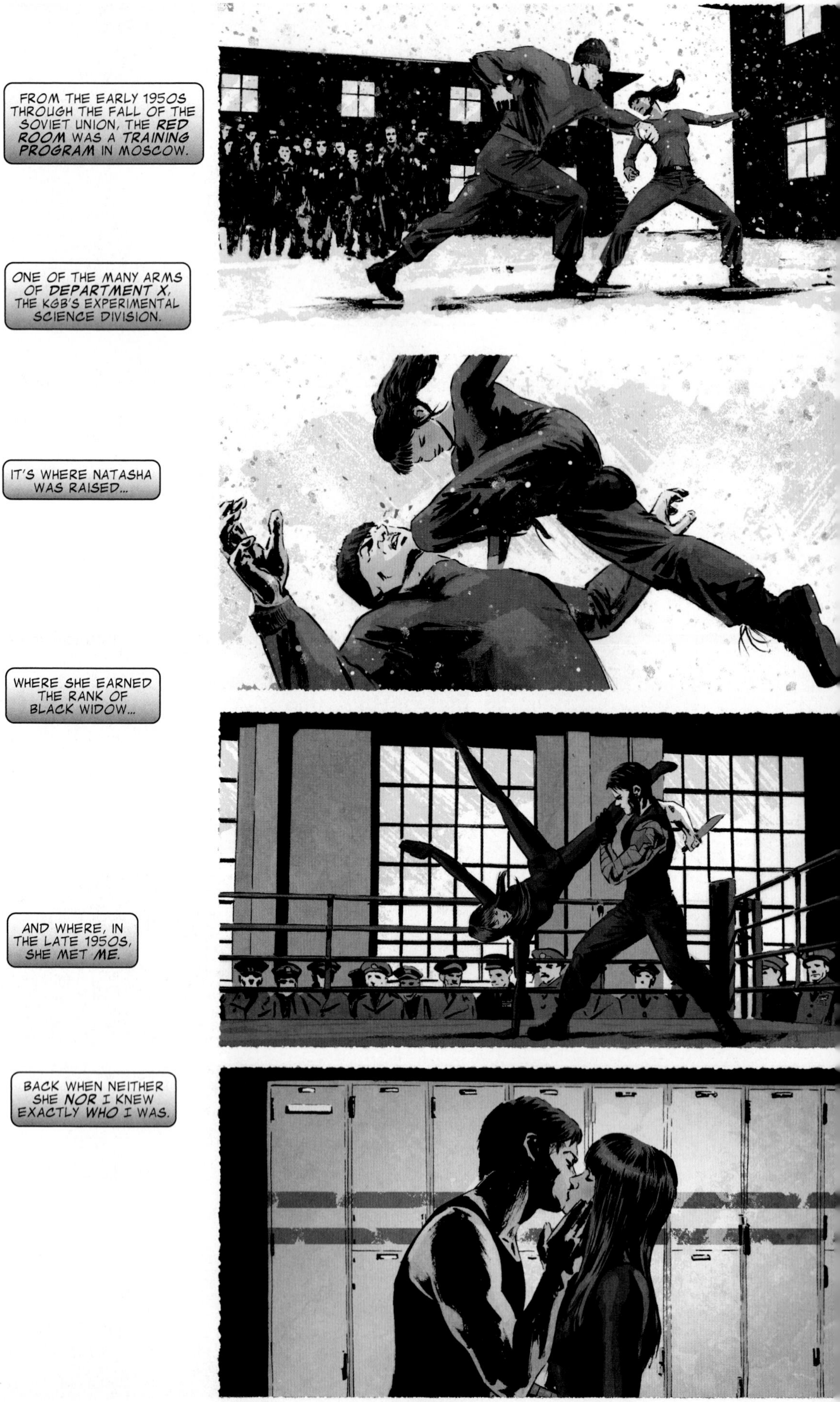
FROM THE EARLY 1950S THROUGH THE FALL OF THE SOVIET UNION, THE RED ROOM WAS A TRAINING PROGRAM IN MOSCOW.
ONE OF THE MANY ARMS OF DEPARTMENT X, THE KGB'S EXPERIMENTAL SCIENCE DIVISION.
IT'S WHERE NATASHA WAS RAISED...
WHERE SHE EARNED THE RANK OF BLACK WIDOW...
AND WHERE, IN THE LATE 1950S, SHE MET ME.
BACK WHEN NEITHER SHE NOR I KNEW EXACTLY WHO I WAS.

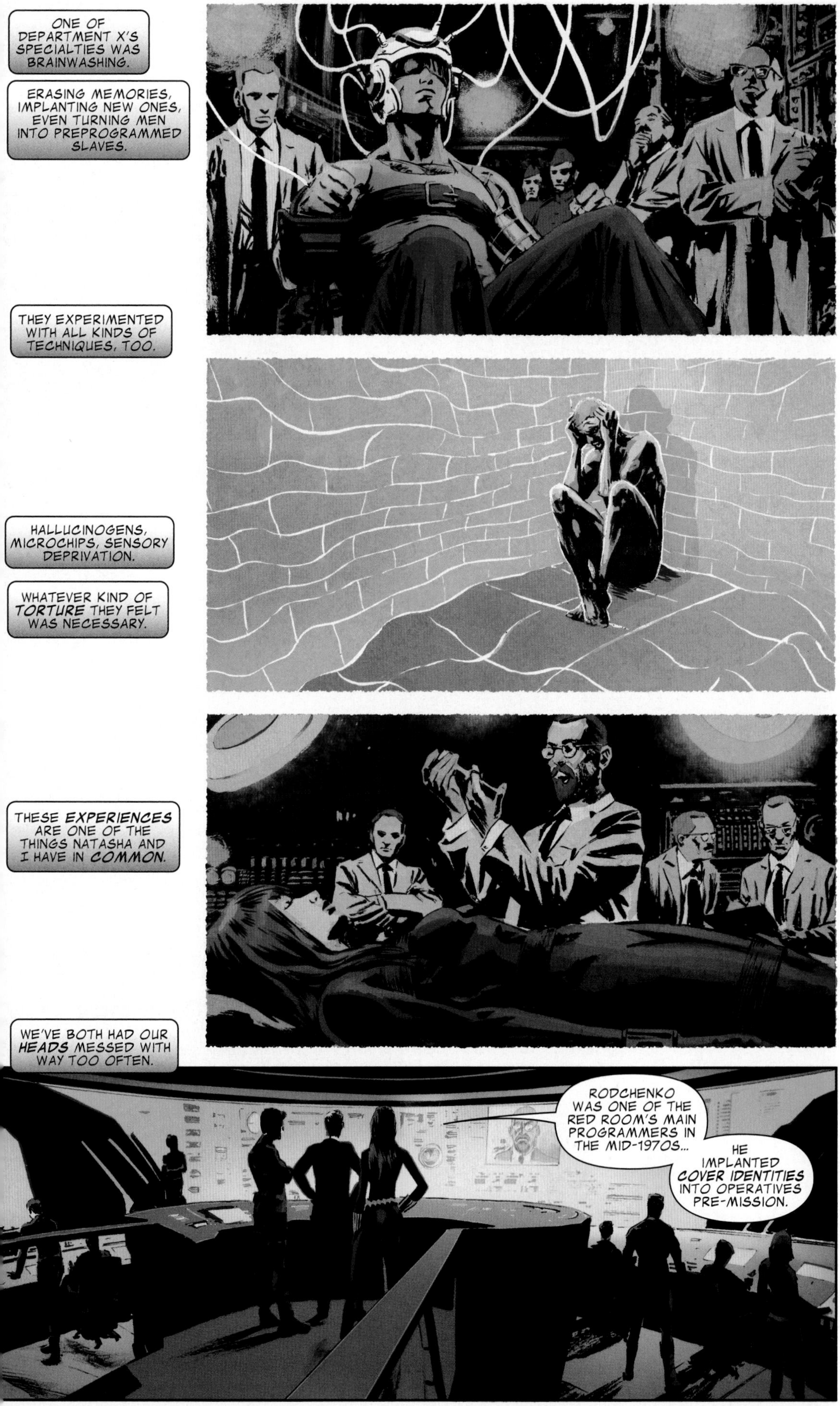
ONE OF DEPARTMENT X'S SPECIALTIES WAS BRAINWASHING.
ERASING MEMORIES, IMPLANTING NEW ONES, EVEN TURNING MEN INTO PREPROGRAMMED SLAVES.
THEY EXPERIMENTED WITH ALL KINDS OF TECHNIQUES, TOO.
HALLUCINOGENS, MICROCHIPS, SENSORY DEPRIVATION.
WHATEVER KIND OF TORTURE THEY FELT WAS NECESSARY.
THESE EXPERIENCES ARE ONE OF THE THINGS NATASHA AND I HAVE IN COMMON.
WE'VE BOTH HAD OUR HEADS MESSED WITH WAY TOO OFTEN.
RODCHENKO WAS ONE OF THE RED ROOM'S MAIN PROGRAMMERS IN THE MID-1970S...
HE IMPLANTED COVER IDENTITIES INTO OPERATIVES PRE-MISSION.

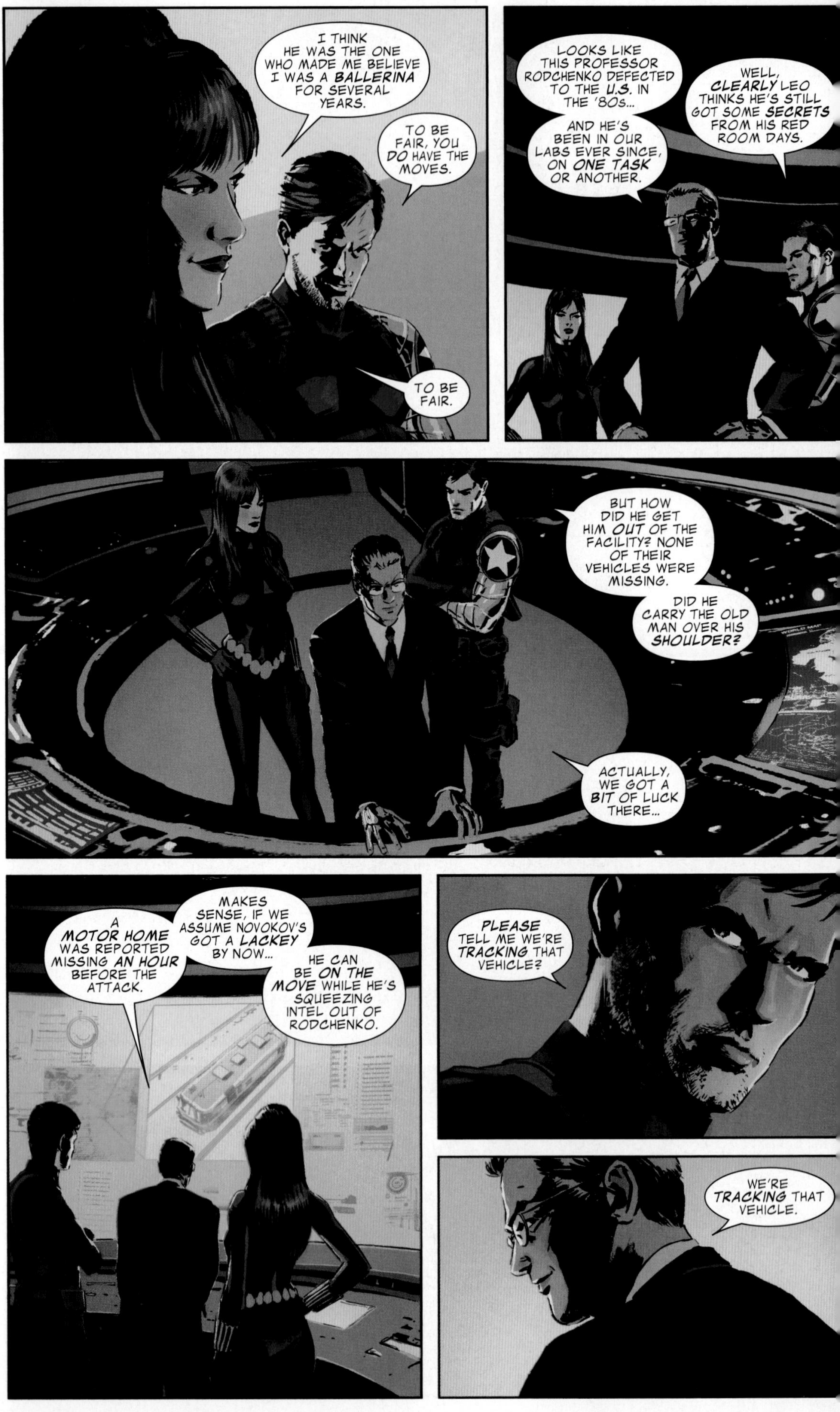
I THINK HE WAS THE ONE WHO MADE ME BELIEVE I WAS A BALLERINA FOR SEVERAL YEARS.
TO BE FAIR, YOU DO HAVE THE MOVES.
TO BE FAIR.
LOOKS LIKE THIS PROFESSOR RODCHENKO DEFECTED TO THE U.S. IN THE '80s...
AND HE'S BEEN IN OUR LABS EVER SINCE, ON ONE TASK OR ANOTHER.
WELL, CLEARLY LEO THINKS HE'S STILL GOT SOME SECRETS FROM HIS RED ROOM DAYS.
BUT HOW DID HE GET HIM OUT OF THE FACILITY? NONE OF THEIR VEHICLES WERE MISSING.
DID HE CARRY THE OLD MAN OVER HIS SHOULDER?
ACTUALLY, WE GOT A BIT OF LUCK THERE...
A MOTOR HOME WAS REPORTED MISSING AN HOUR BEFORE THE ATTACK.
MAKES SENSE, IF WE ASSUME NOVOKOV'S GOT A LACKEY BY NOW...
HE CAN BE ON THE MOVE WHILE HE'S SQUEEZING INTEL OUT OF RODCHENKO.
PLEASE TELL ME WE'RE TRACKING THAT VEHICLE?
WE'RE TRACKING THAT VEHICLE.

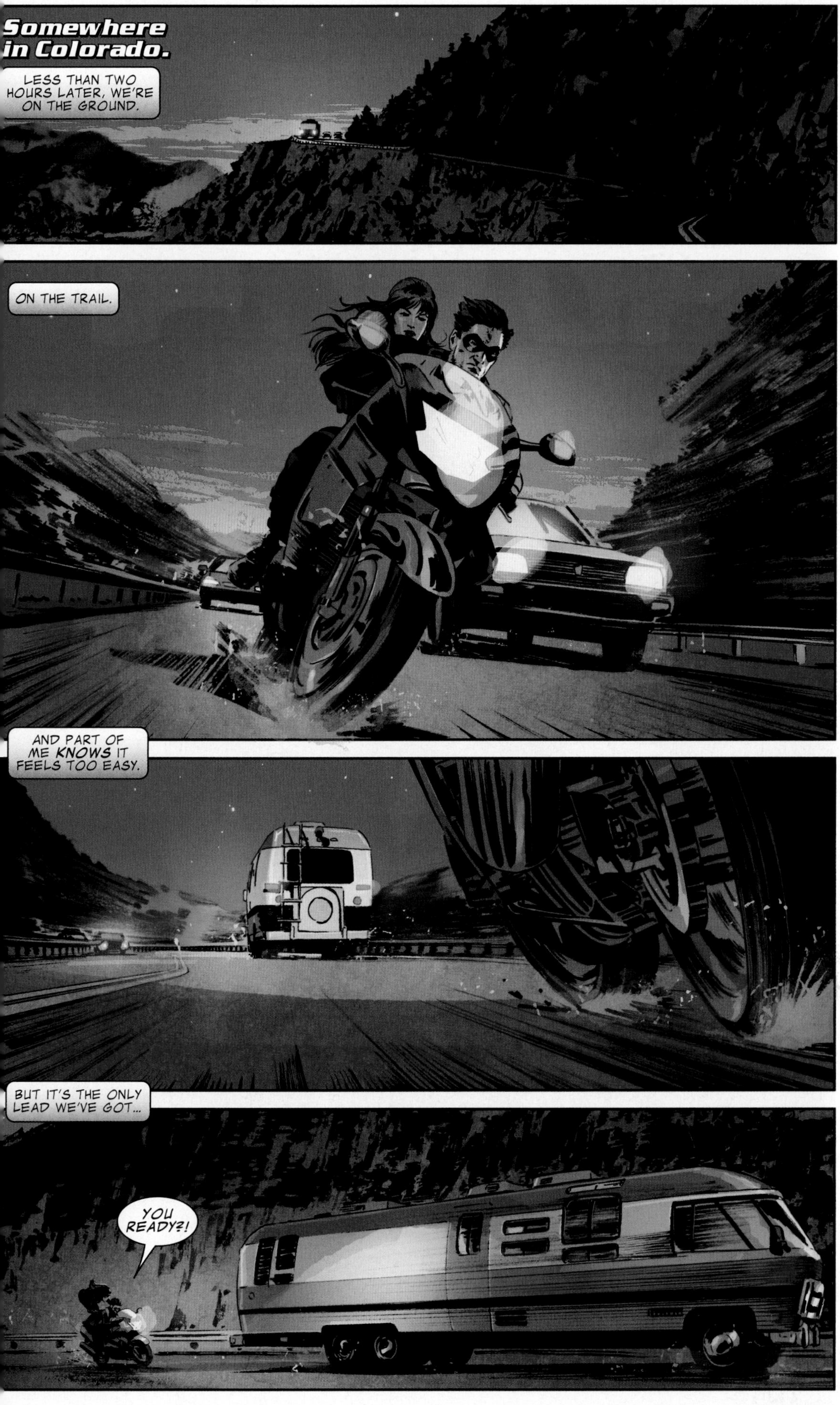
Somewhere in Colorado.
LESS THAN TWO HOURS LATER, WE'RE ON THE GROUND.
ON THE TRAIL.
AND PART OF ME KNOWS IT FEELS TOO EASY.
BUT IT'S THE ONLY LEAD WE'VE GOT...
YOU READY?!

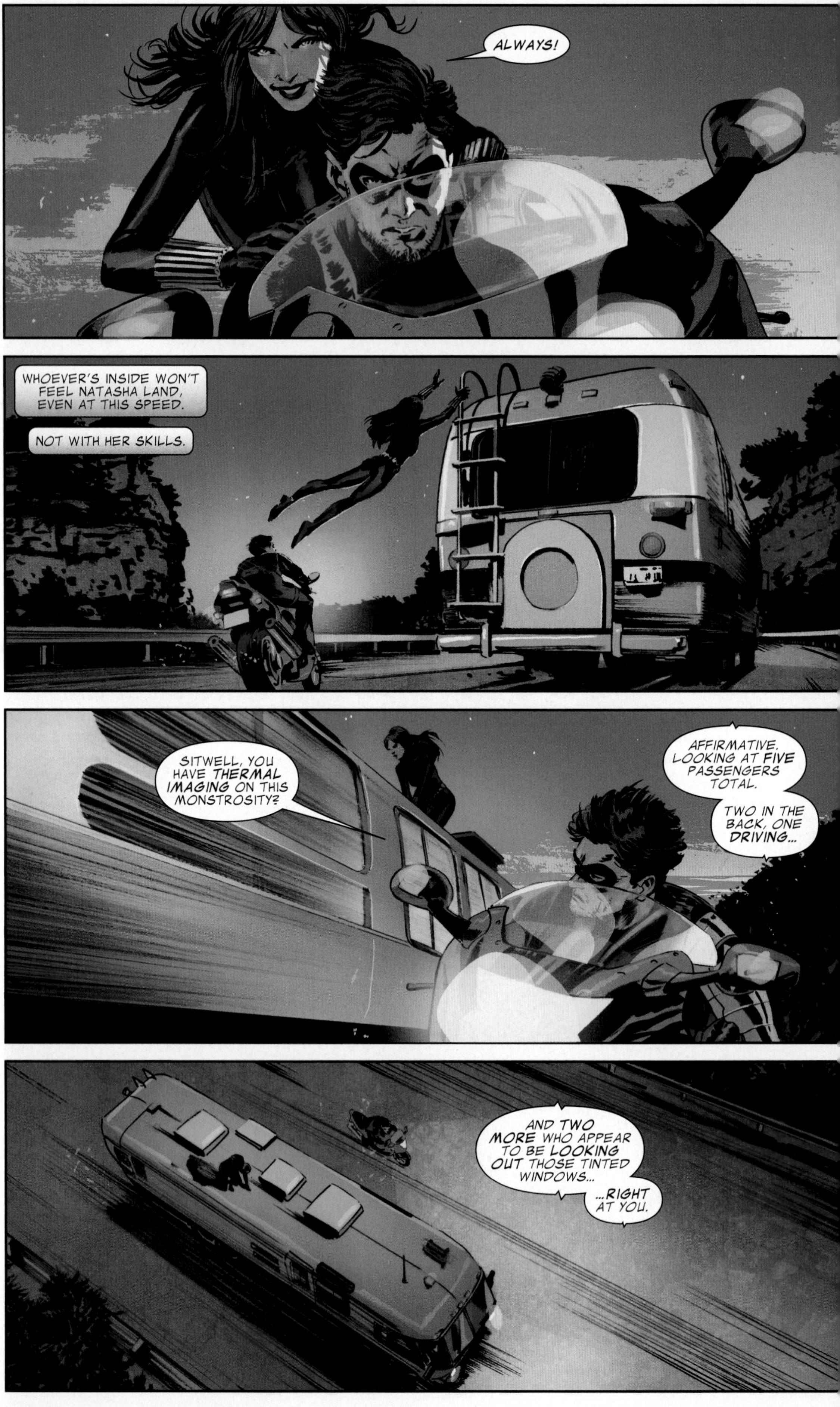
ALWAYS!
WHOEVER'S INSIDE WON'T FEEL NATASHA LAND, EVEN AT THIS SPEED.
NOT WITH HER SKILLS.
SITWELL, YOU HAVE THERMAL IMAGING ON THIS MONSTROSITY?
AFFIRMATIVE. LOOKING AT FIVE PASSENGERS TOTAL.
TWO IN THE BACK, ONE DRIVING...
AND TWO MORE WHO APPEAR TO BE LOOKING OUT THOSE TINTED WINDOWS...
...RIGHT AT YOU.

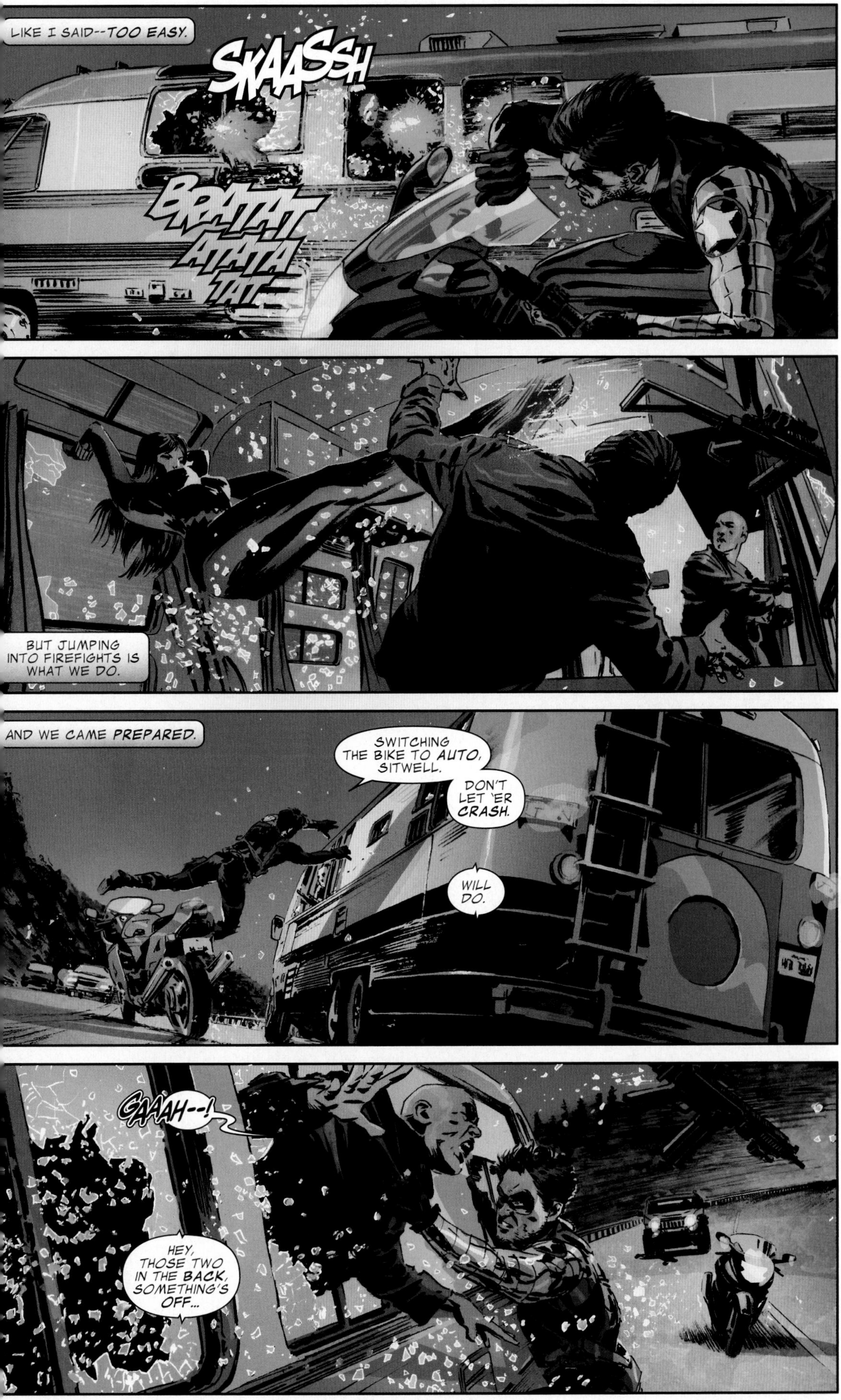
LIKE I SAID--TOO EASY.
SKAASSH
BRATAT ATATA TAT
BUT JUMPING INTO FIREFIGHTS IS WHAT WE DO.
AND WE CAME PREPARED.
SWITCHING THE BIKE TO AUTO, SITWELL.
DON'T LET 'ER CRASH.
WILL DO.
GAAAH--!
HEY, THOSE TWO IN THE BACK, SOMETHING'S OFF...

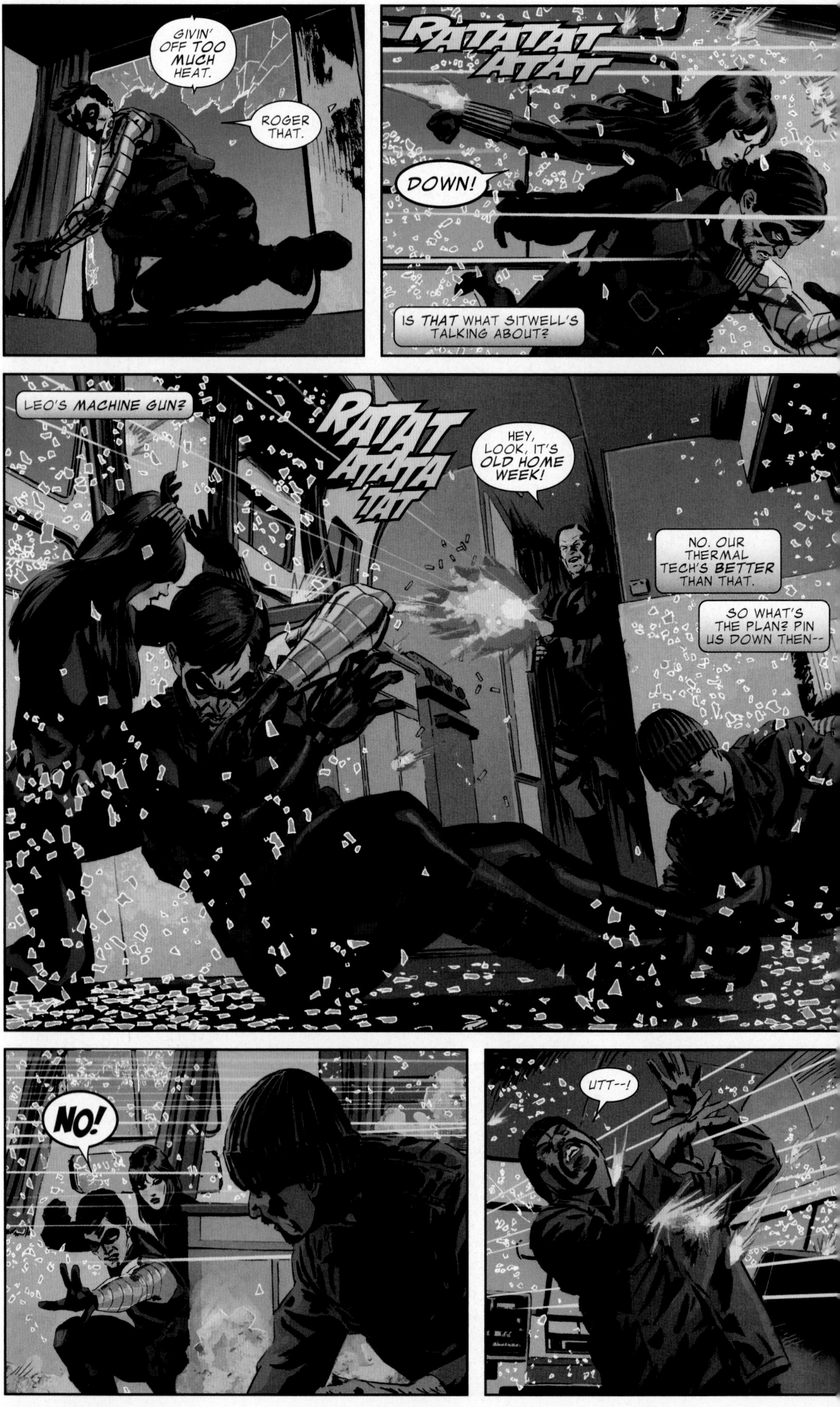
GIVIN' OFF TOO MUCH HEAT.
ROGER THAT.
RATATAT ATAT
DOWN!
IS THAT WHAT SITWELL'S TALKING ABOUT?
LEO'S MACHINE GUN?
RATAT ATATA TAT
HEY, LOOK, IT'S OLD HOME WEEK!
NO. OUR THERMAL TECH'S BETTER THAN THAT.
SO WHAT'S THE PLAN? PIN US DOWN THEN--
NO!
UTT--!

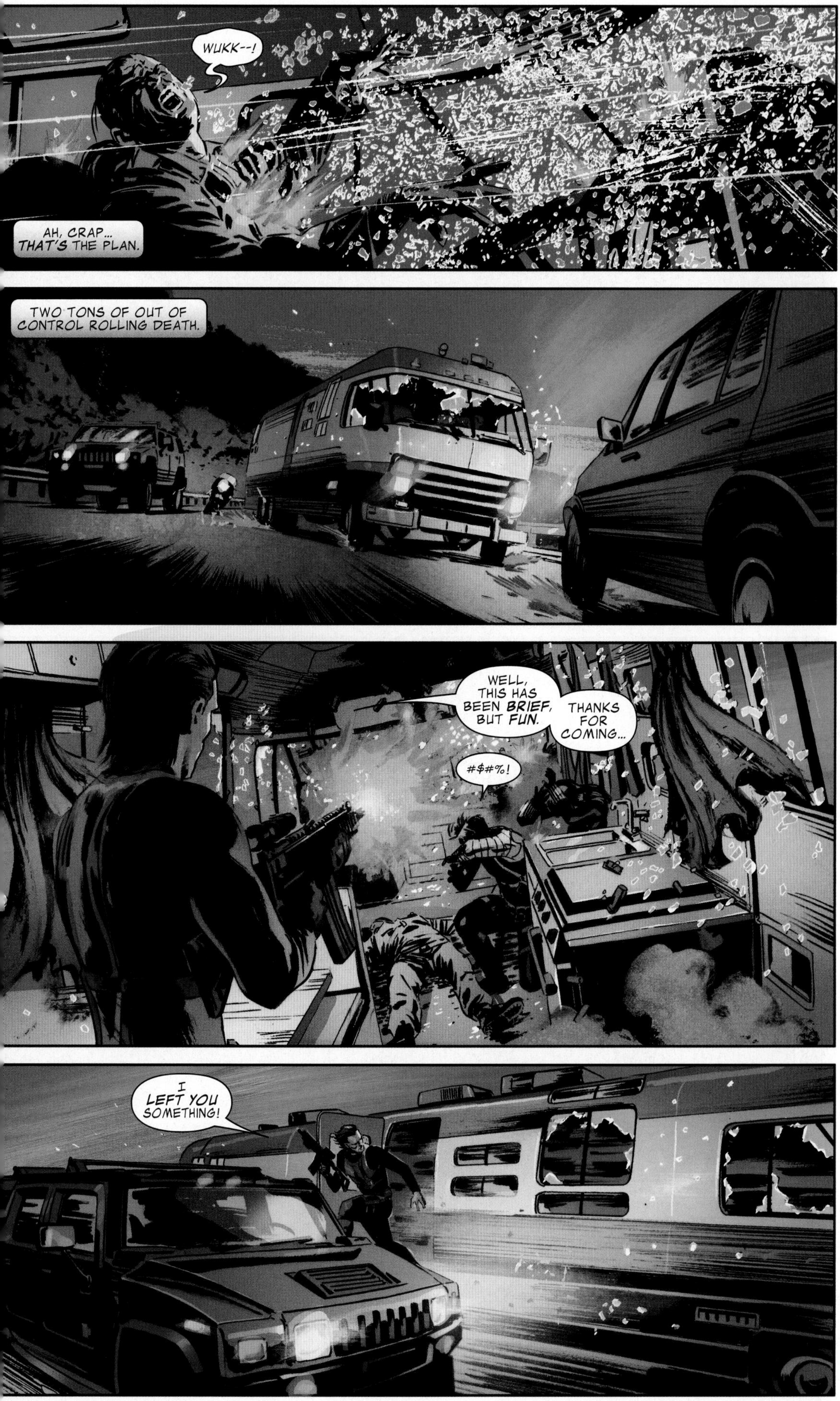

WUKK--!
AH, CRAP... THAT'S THE PLAN.
TWO TONS OF OUT OF CONTROL ROLLING DEATH.
WELL, THIS HAS BEEN BRIEF, BUT FUN.
THANKS FOR COMING...
#$#%!
I LEFT YOU SOMETHING!

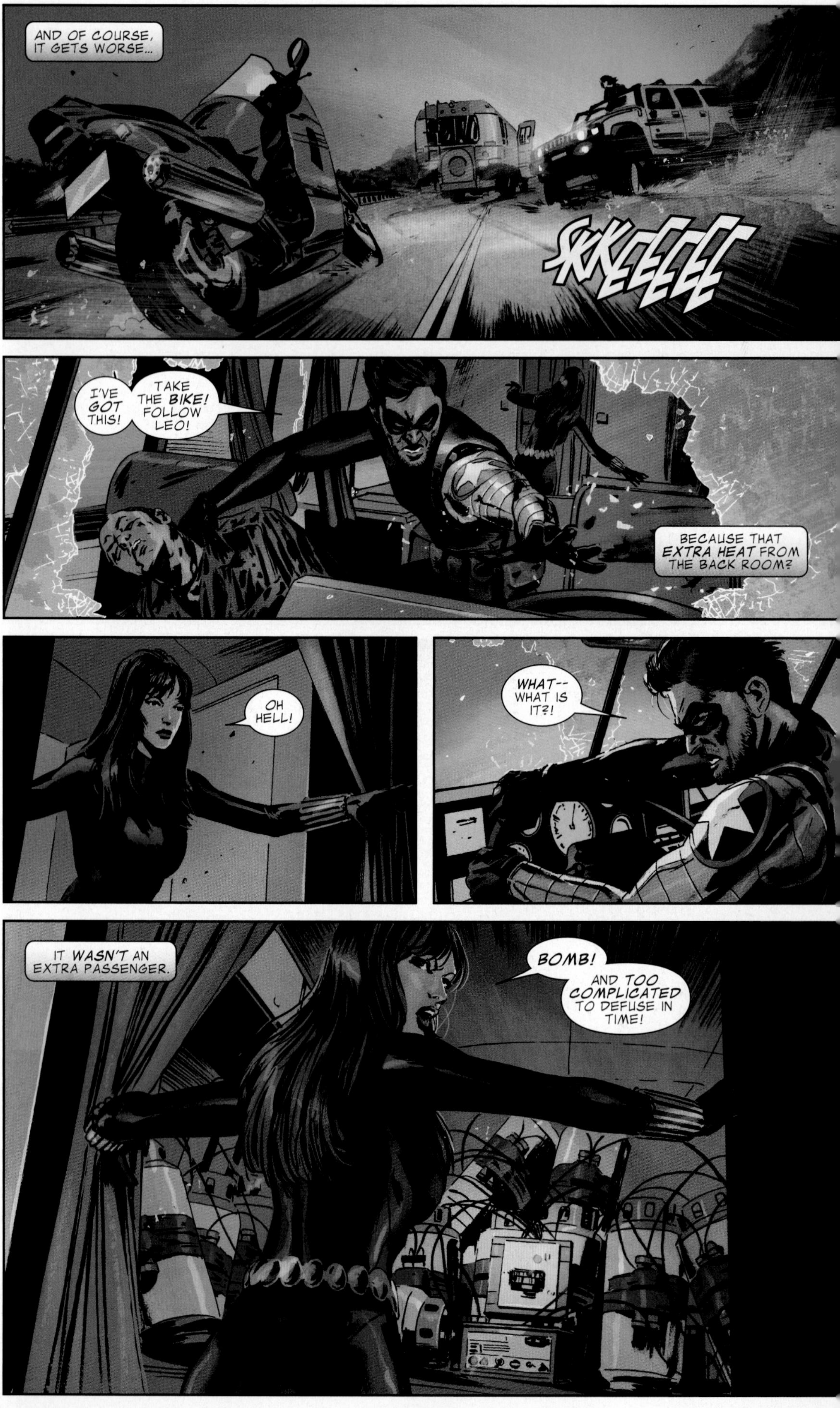
AND OF COURSE, IT GETS WORSE...
SKKEEEEEE
I'VE GOT THIS!
TAKE THE BIKE! FOLLOW LEO!
BECAUSE THAT EXTRA HEAT FROM THE BACK ROOM?
OH HELL!
WHAT-- WHAT IS IT?!
IT WASN'T AN EXTRA PASSENGER.
BOMB!
AND TOO COMPLICATED TO DEFUSE IN TIME!

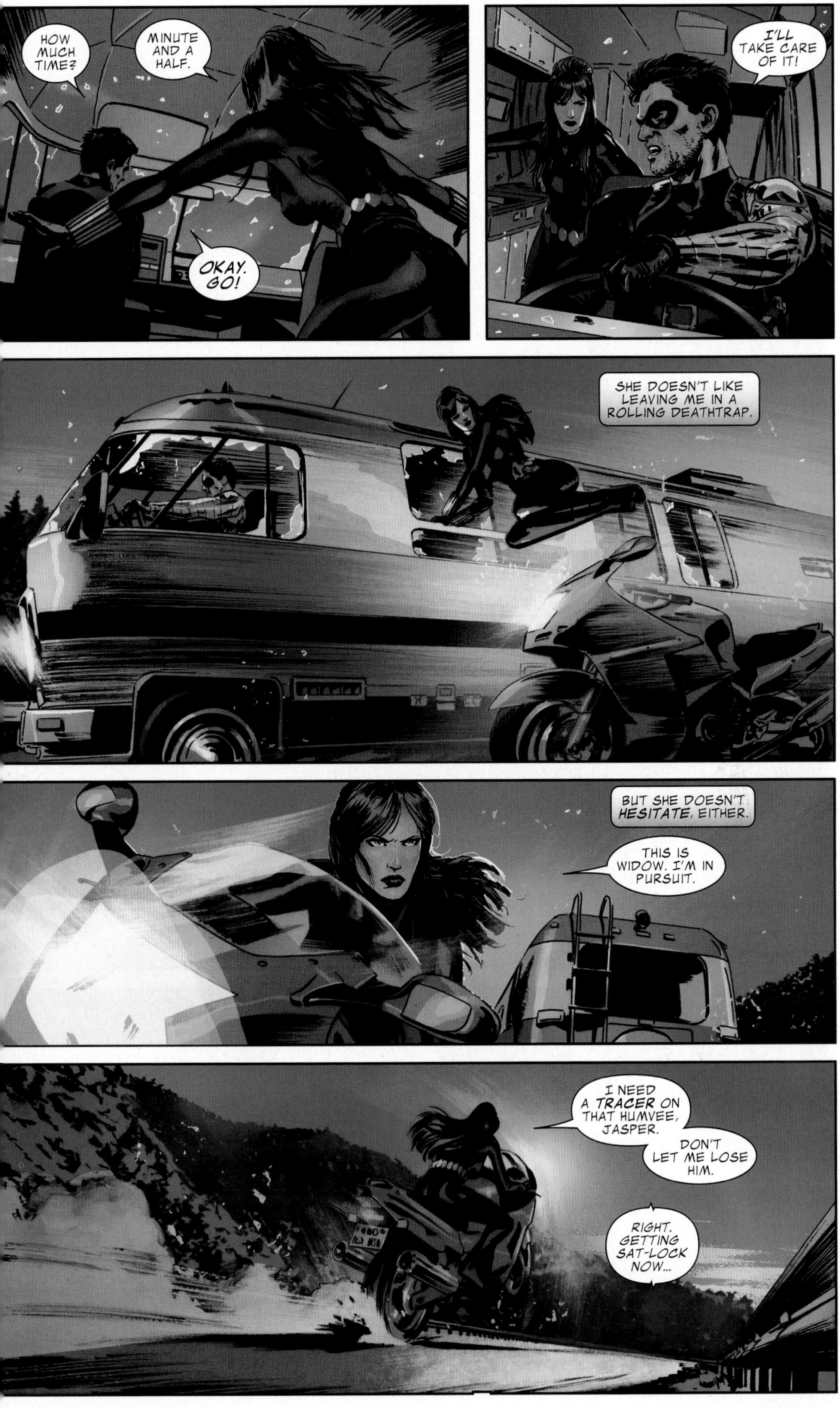
HOW MUCH TIME?
MINUTE AND A HALF.
OKAY. GO!
I'LL TAKE CARE OF IT!
SHE DOESN'T LIKE LEAVING ME IN A ROLLING DEATHTRAP.
BUT SHE DOESN'T HESITATE, EITHER.
THIS IS WIDOW. I'M IN PURSUIT.
I NEED A TRACER ON THAT HUMVEE, JASPER.
DON'T LET ME LOSE HIM.
RIGHT. GETTING SAT-LOCK NOW...

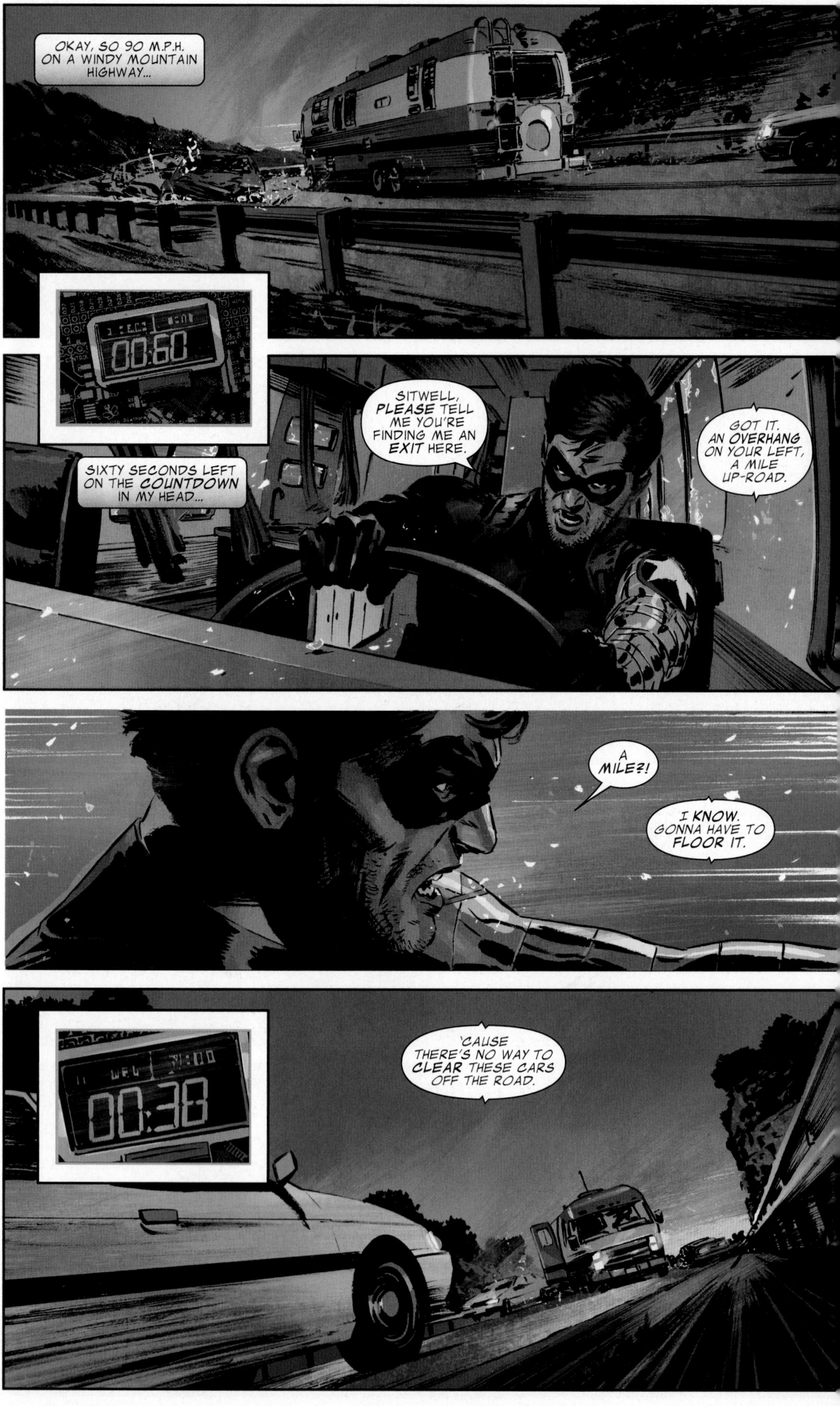
OKAY, SO 90 M.P.H. ON A WINDY MOUNTAIN HIGHWAY...
00:60
SITWELL, PLEASE TELL ME YOU'RE FINDING ME AN EXIT HERE.
GOT IT. AN OVERHANG ON YOUR LEFT, A MILE UP-ROAD.
SIXTY SECONDS LEFT ON THE COUNTDOWN IN MY HEAD...
A MILE?!
I KNOW. GONNA HAVE TO FLOOR IT.
00:38
'CAUSE THERE'S NO WAY TO CLEAR THESE CARS OFF THE ROAD.

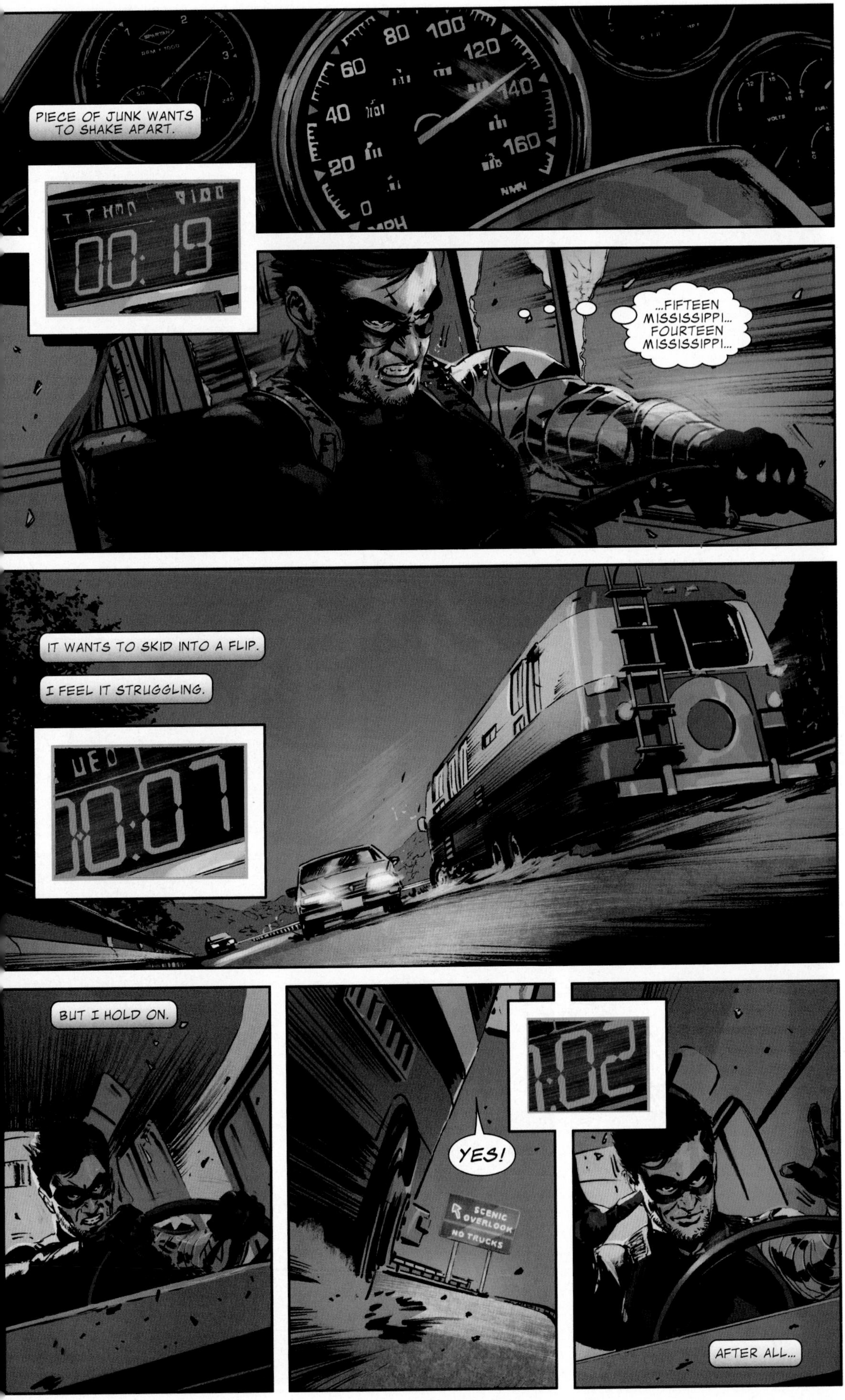

PIECE OF JUNK WANTS TO SHAKE APART.
00:13
...FIFTEEN MISSISSIPPI... FOURTEEN MISSISSIPPI...
IT WANTS TO SKID INTO A FLIP.
I FEEL IT STRUGGLING.
00:07
BUT I HOLD ON.
YES!
SCENIC OVERLOOK
NO TRUCKS
AFTER ALL...

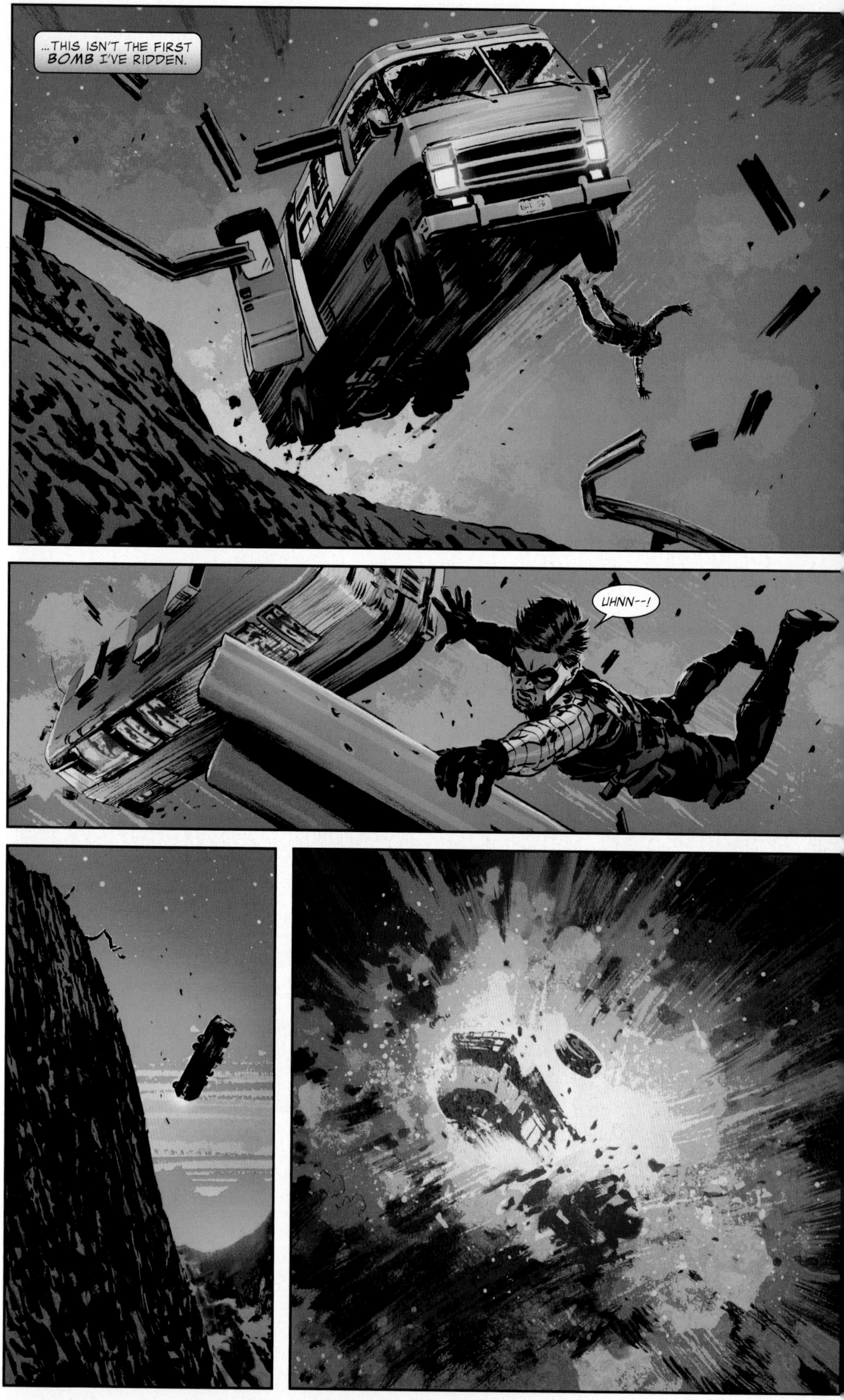
...THIS ISN'T THE FIRST BOMB I'VE RIDDEN.
UHNN--!

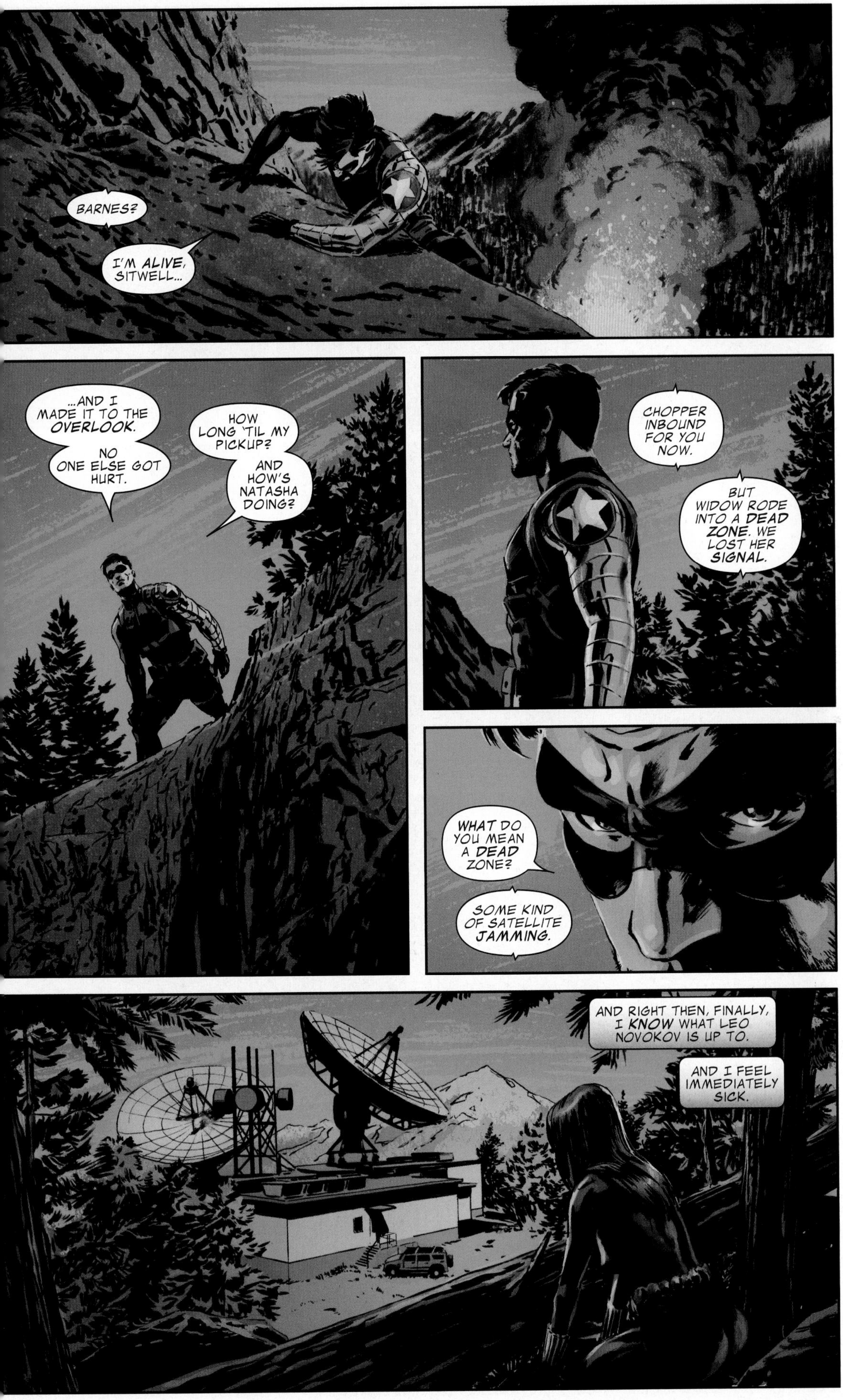

BARNES?
I'M ALIVE, SITWELL...
...AND I MADE IT TO THE OVERLOOK.
NO ONE ELSE GOT HURT.
HOW LONG 'TIL MY PICKUP?
AND HOW'S NATASHA DOING?
CHOPPER INBOUND FOR YOU NOW.
BUT WIDOW RODE INTO A DEAD ZONE. WE LOST HER SIGNAL.
WHAT DO YOU MEAN A DEAD ZONE?
SOME KIND OF SATELLITE JAMMING.
AND RIGHT THEN, FINALLY, I KNOW WHAT LEO NOVOKOV IS UP TO.
AND I FEEL IMMEDIATELY SICK.

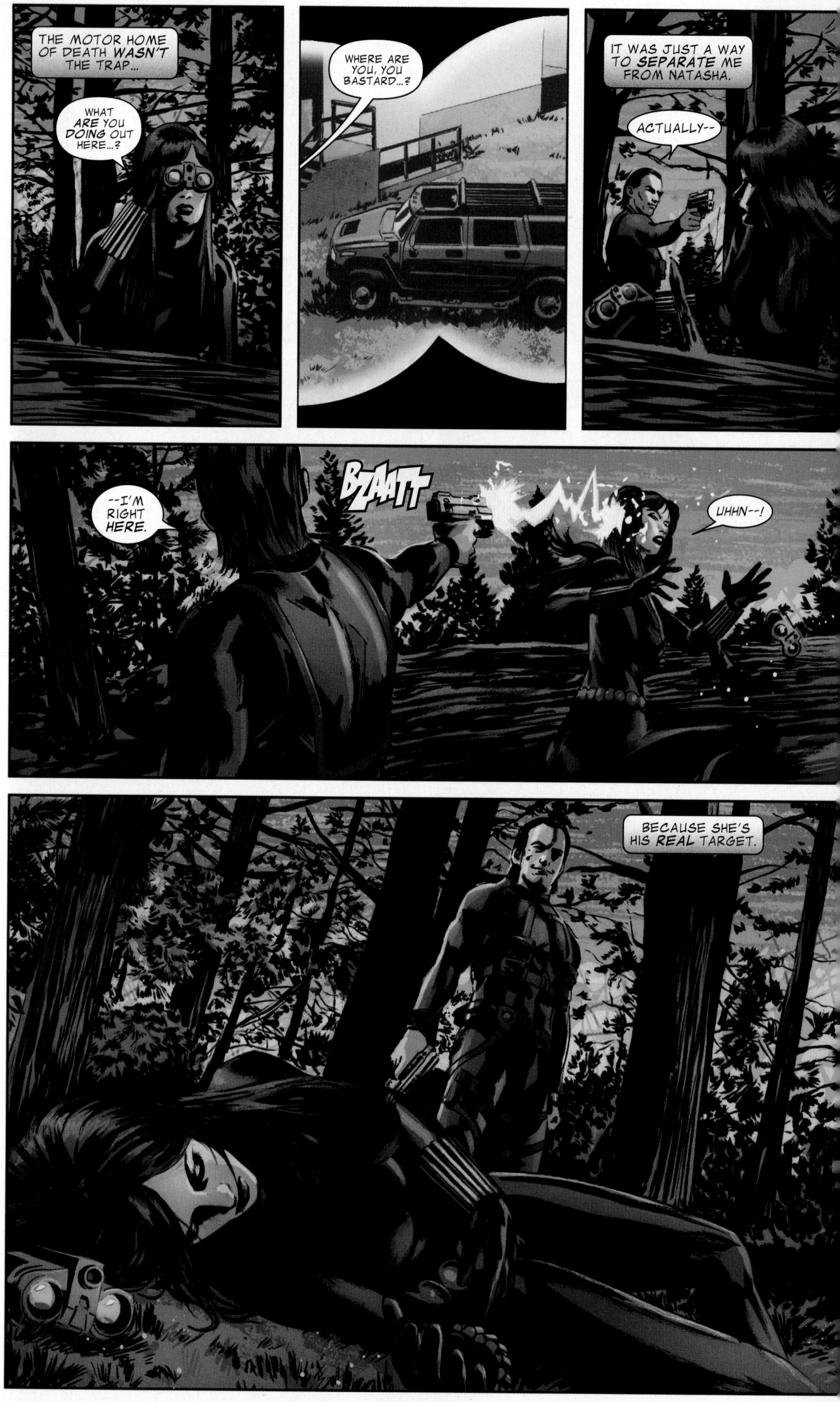
THE MOTOR HOME OF DEATH WASN'T THE TRAP...
WHAT ARE YOU DOING OUT HERE...?
WHERE ARE YOU, YOU BASTARD...?
IT WAS JUST A WAY TO SEPARATE ME FROM NATASHA.
ACTUALLY--
--I'M RIGHT HERE.
BZAATT
UHHN--!
BECAUSE SHE'S HIS REAL TARGET.

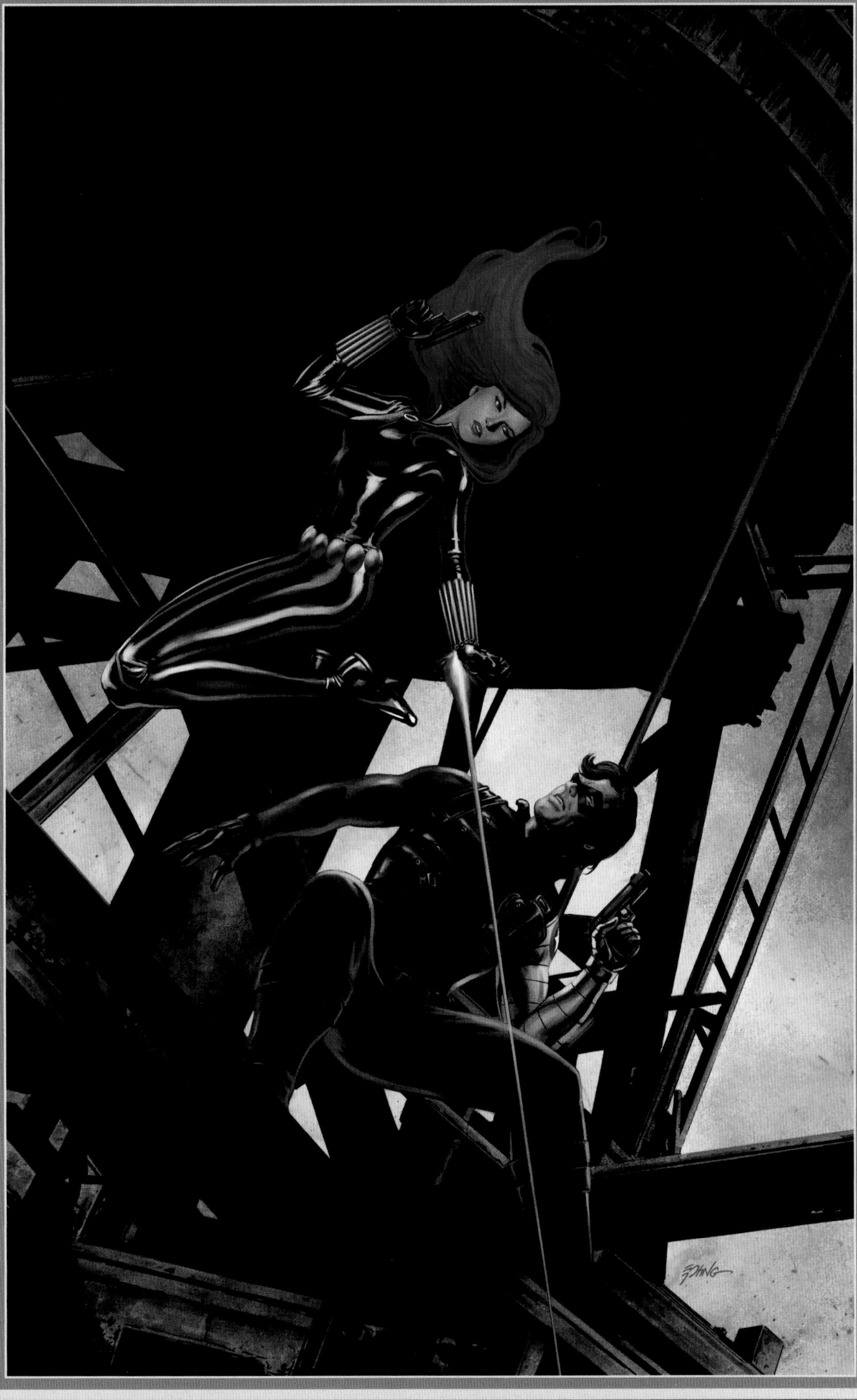

EIGHT

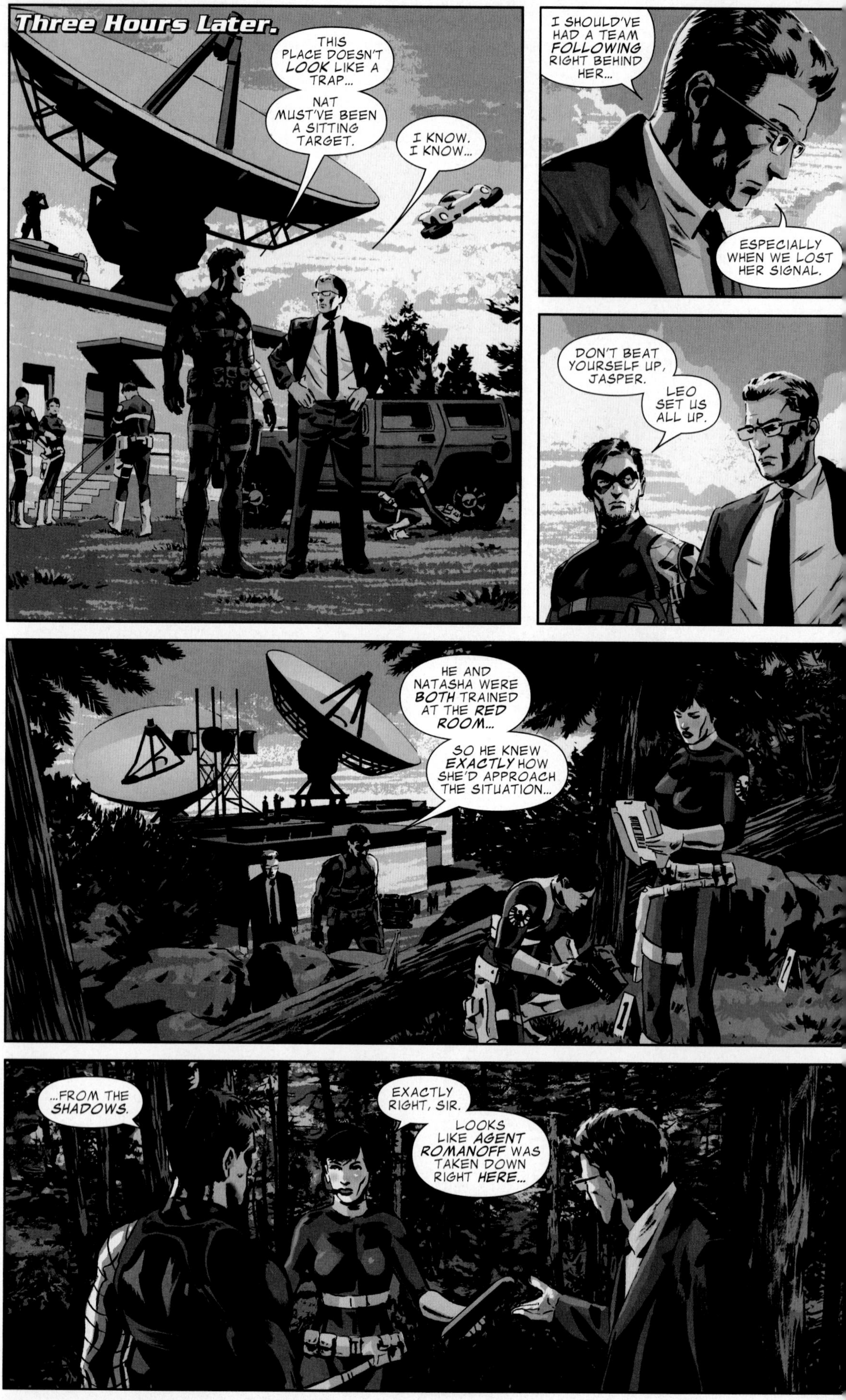
Three Hours Later.
THIS PLACE DOESN'T LOOK LIKE A TRAP...
NAT MUST'VE BEEN A SITTING TARGET.
I KNOW. I KNOW...
I SHOULD'VE HAD A TEAM FOLLOWING RIGHT BEHIND HER...
ESPECIALLY WHEN WE LOST HER SIGNAL.
DON'T BEAT YOURSELF UP, JASPER.
LEO SET US ALL UP.
HE AND NATASHA WERE BOTH TRAINED AT THE RED ROOM...
SO HE KNEW EXACTLY HOW SHE'D APPROACH THE SITUATION...
...FROM THE SHADOWS.
EXACTLY RIGHT, SIR.
LOOKS LIKE AGENT ROMANOFF WAS TAKEN DOWN RIGHT HERE...

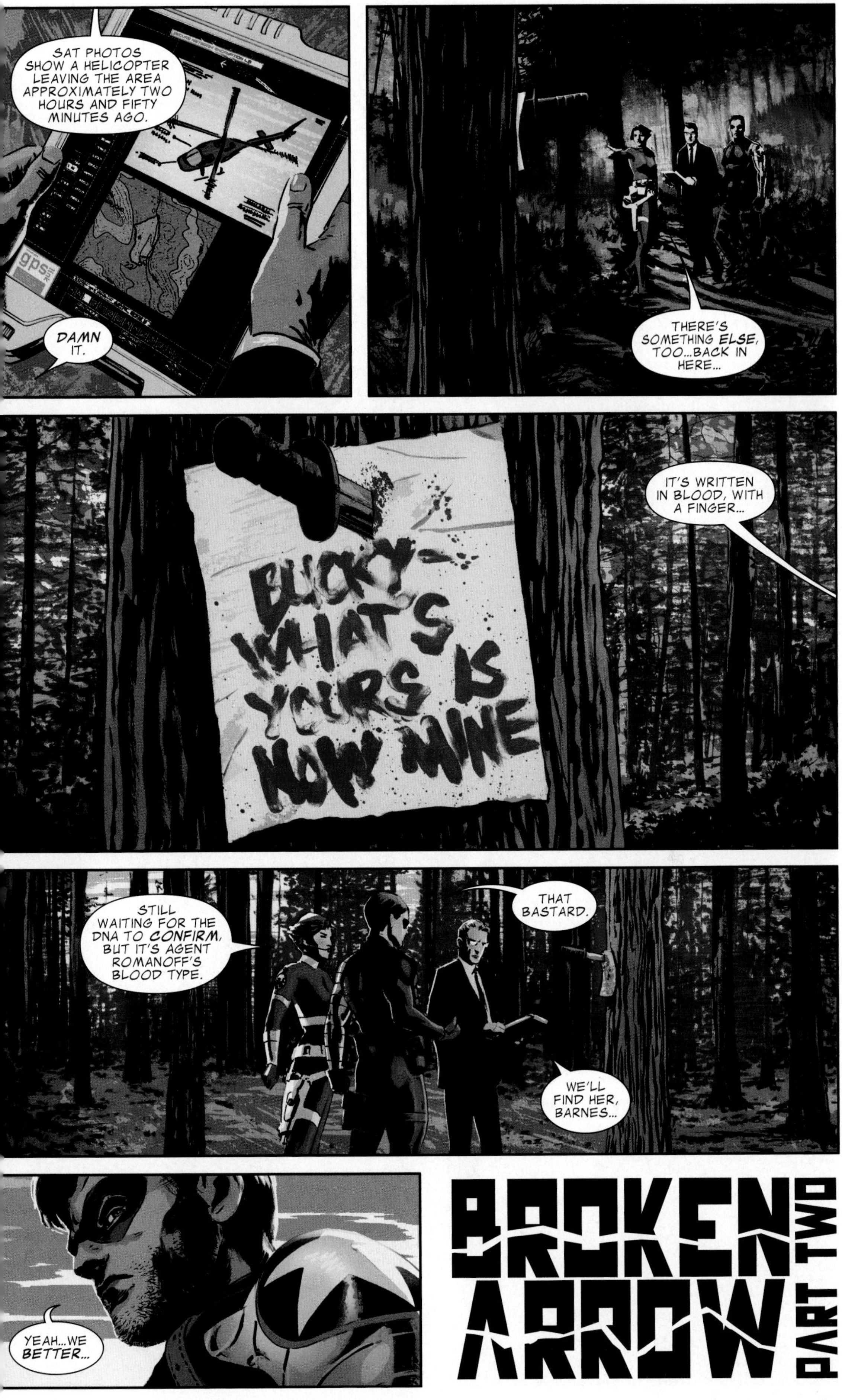

SAT PHOTOS SHOW A HELICOPTER LEAVING THE AREA APPROXIMATELY TWO HOURS AND FIFTY MINUTES AGO.
gps
DAMN IT.
THERE'S SOMETHING ELSE, TOO...BACK IN HERE...
BUCKY--
WHAT'S
YOURS IS
NOW MINE
IT'S WRITTEN IN BLOOD, WITH A FINGER...
STILL WAITING FOR THE DNA TO CONFIRM, BUT IT'S AGENT ROMANOFF'S BLOOD TYPE.
THAT BASTARD.
WE'LL FIND HER, BARNES...
YEAH...WE BETTER...
BROKEN ARROW
PART TWO

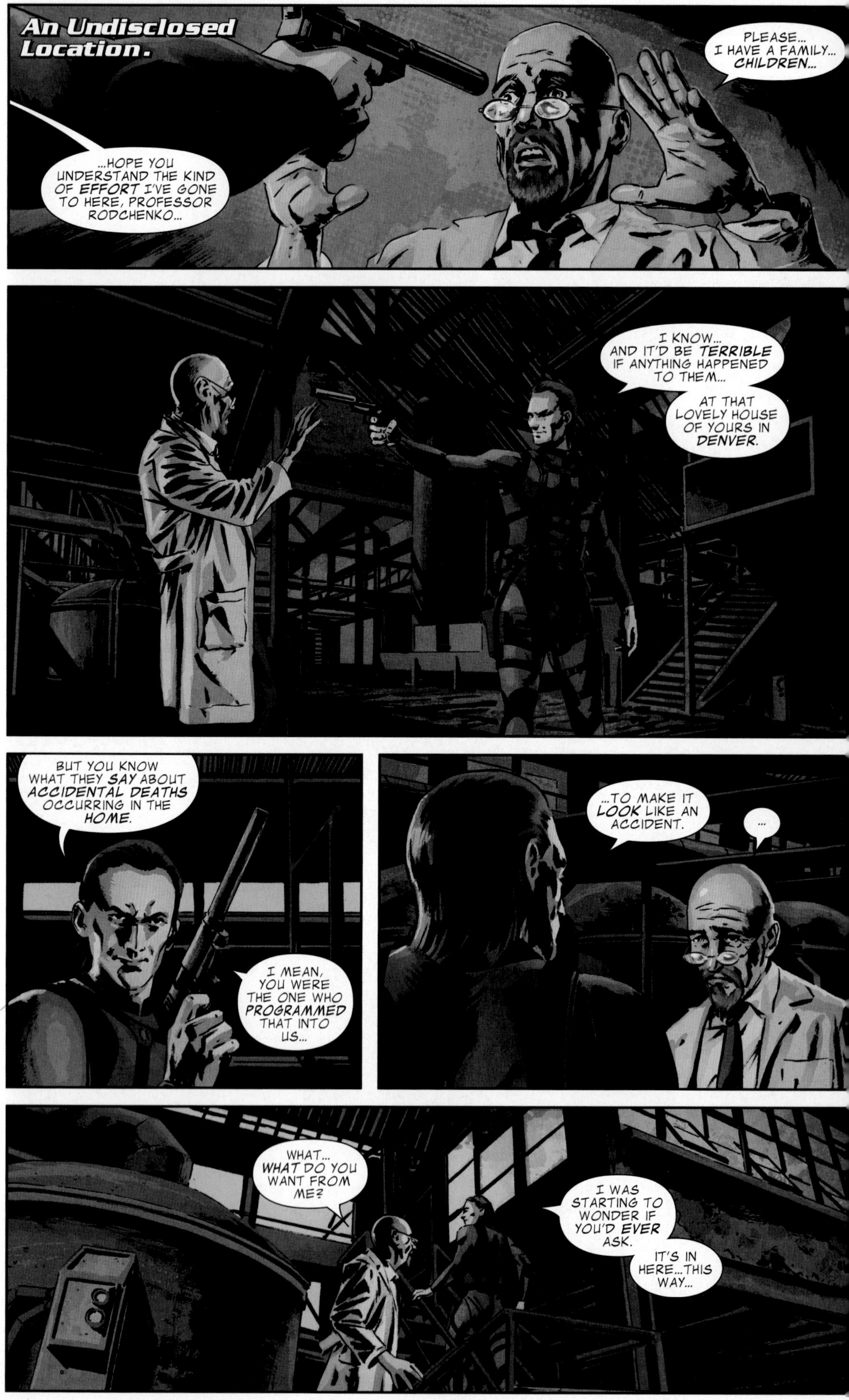
An Undisclosed Location.
PLEASE... I HAVE A FAMILY... CHILDREN...
...HOPE YOU UNDERSTAND THE KIND OF EFFORT I'VE GONE TO HERE, PROFESSOR RODCHENKO...
I KNOW... AND IT'D BE TERRIBLE IF ANYTHING HAPPENED TO THEM...
AT THAT LOVELY HOUSE OF YOURS IN DENVER.
BUT YOU KNOW WHAT THEY SAY ABOUT ACCIDENTAL DEATHS OCCURRING IN THE HOME.
I MEAN, YOU WERE THE ONE WHO PROGRAMMED THAT INTO US...
...TO MAKE IT LOOK LIKE AN ACCIDENT.
...
WHAT... WHAT DO YOU WANT FROM ME?
I WAS STARTING TO WONDER IF YOU'D EVER ASK.
IT'S IN HERE...THIS WAY...

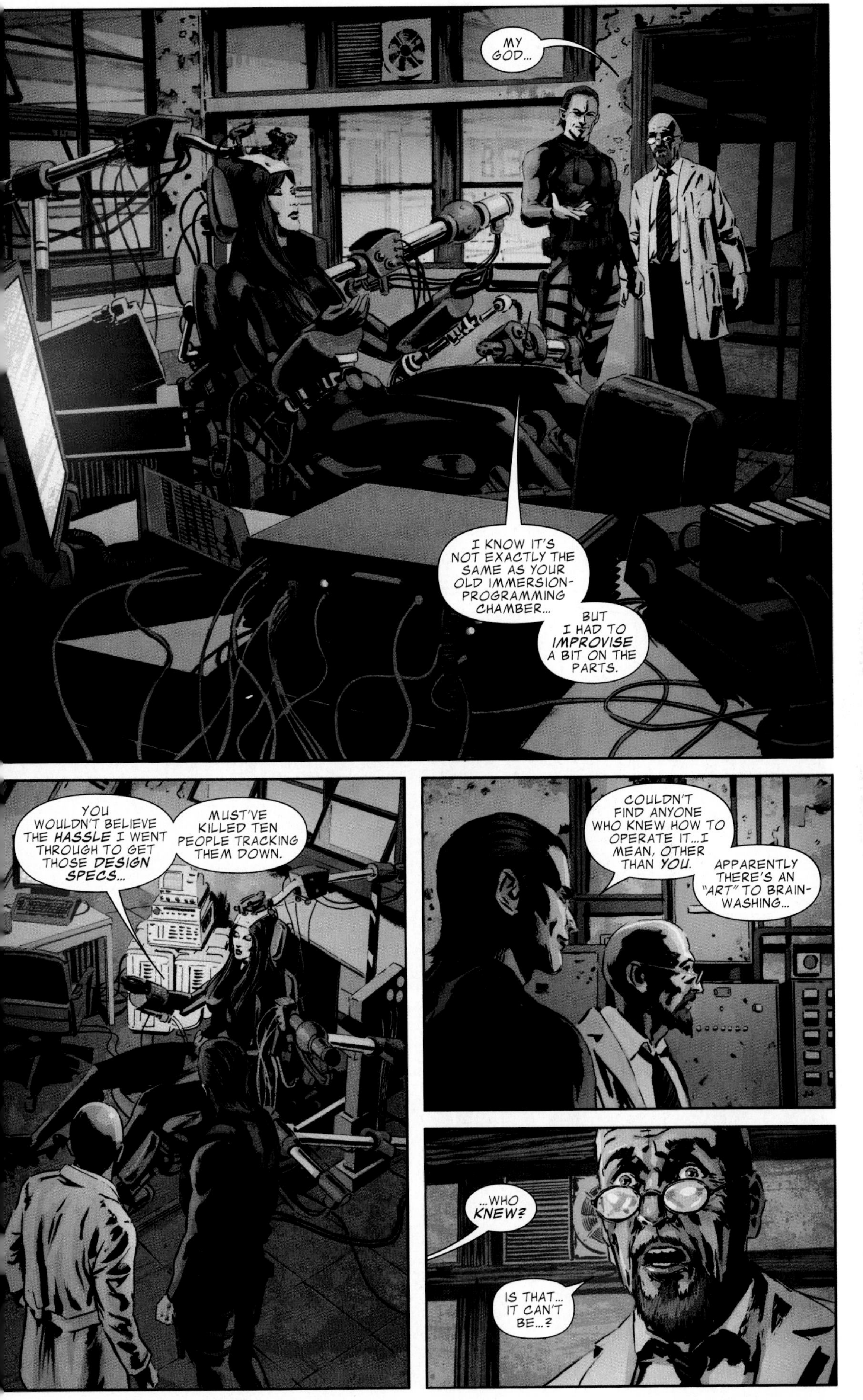
MY GOD...
I KNOW IT'S NOT EXACTLY THE SAME AS YOUR OLD IMMERSION-PROGRAMMING CHAMBER...
BUT I HAD TO IMPROVISE A BIT ON THE PARTS.
YOU WOULDN'T BELIEVE THE HASSLE I WENT THROUGH TO GET THOSE DESIGN SPECS...
MUST'VE KILLED TEN PEOPLE TRACKING THEM DOWN.
COULDN'T FIND ANYONE WHO KNEW HOW TO OPERATE IT...I MEAN, OTHER THAN YOU.
APPARENTLY THERE'S AN "ART" TO BRAIN-WASHING...
...WHO KNEW?
IS THAT... IT CAN'T BE...?

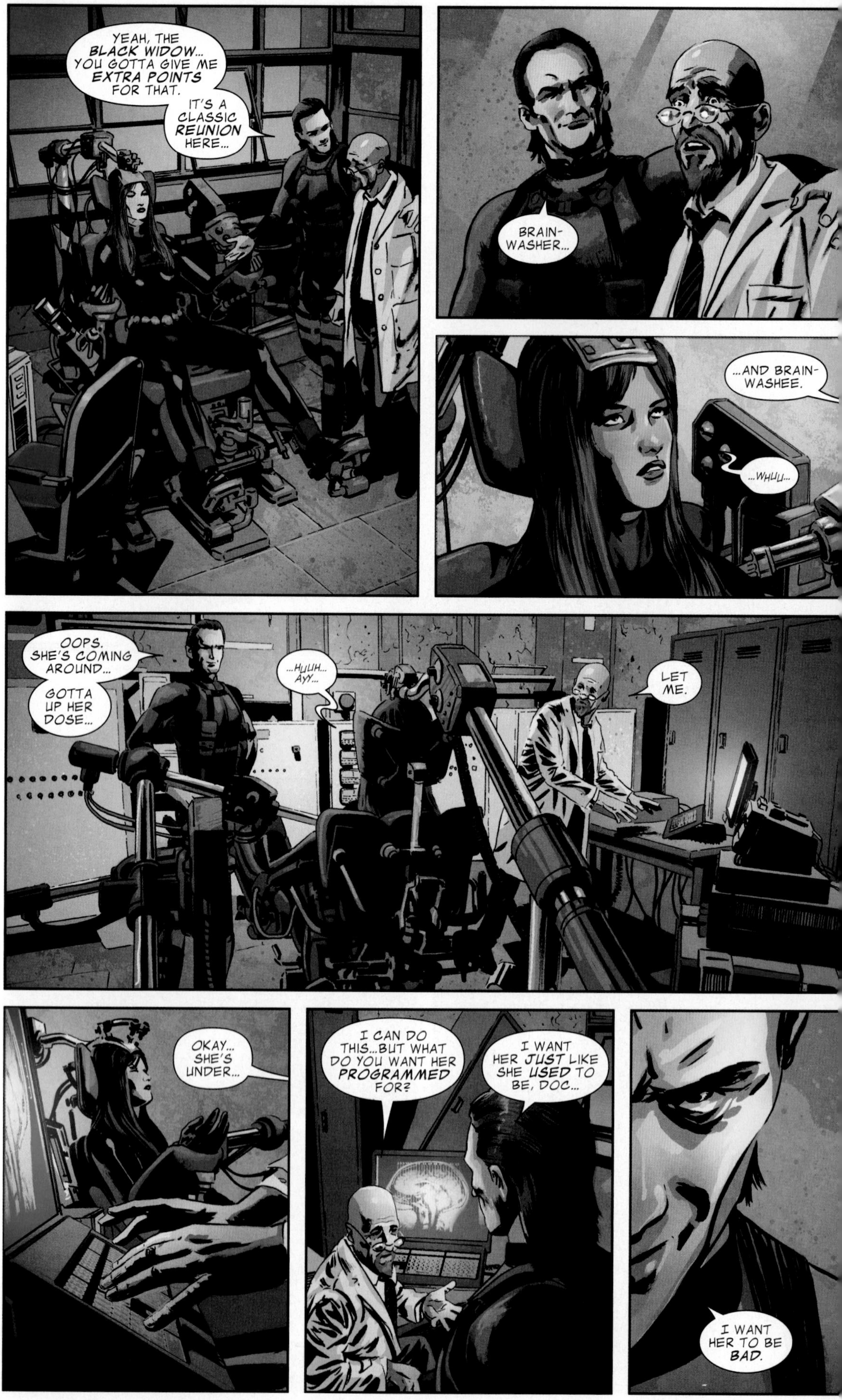
YEAH, THE BLACK WIDOW... YOU GOTTA GIVE ME EXTRA POINTS FOR THAT.
IT'S A CLASSIC REUNION HERE...
BRAIN-WASHER...
...AND BRAIN-WASHEE.
...WHUU...
OOPS. SHE'S COMING AROUND...
GOTTA UP HER DOSE...
...HUUH... AYY...
LET ME.
OKAY... SHE'S UNDER...
I CAN DO THIS...BUT WHAT DO YOU WANT HER PROGRAMMED FOR?
I WANT HER JUST LIKE SHE USED TO BE, DOC...
I WANT HER TO BE BAD.

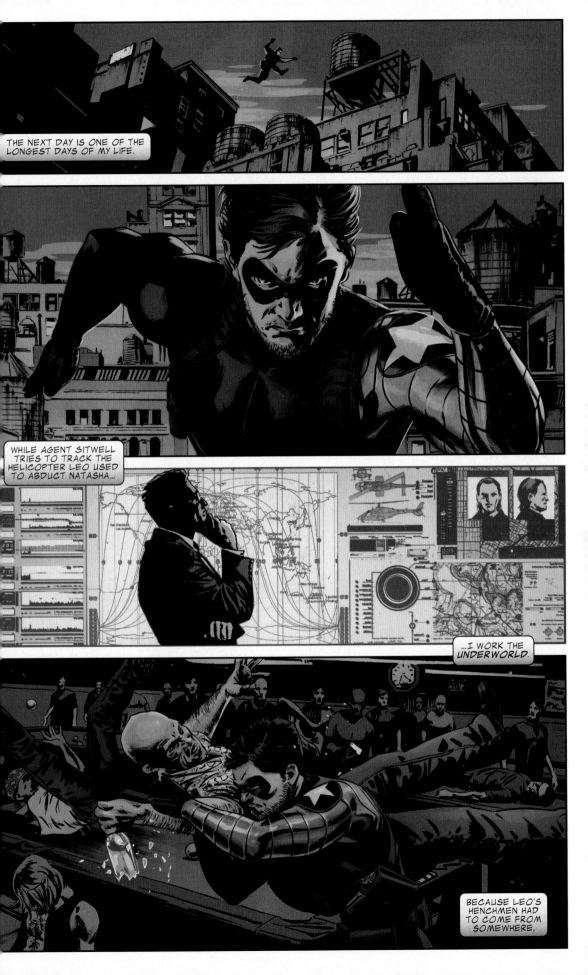

THE NEXT DAY IS ONE OF THE LONGEST DAYS OF MY LIFE.

WHILE AGENT SITWELL TRIES TO TRACK THE HELICOPTER LEO USED TO ABDUCT NATASHA...

...I WORK THE UNDERWORLD.

BECAUSE LEO'S HENCHMEN HAD TO COME FROM SOMEWHERE.

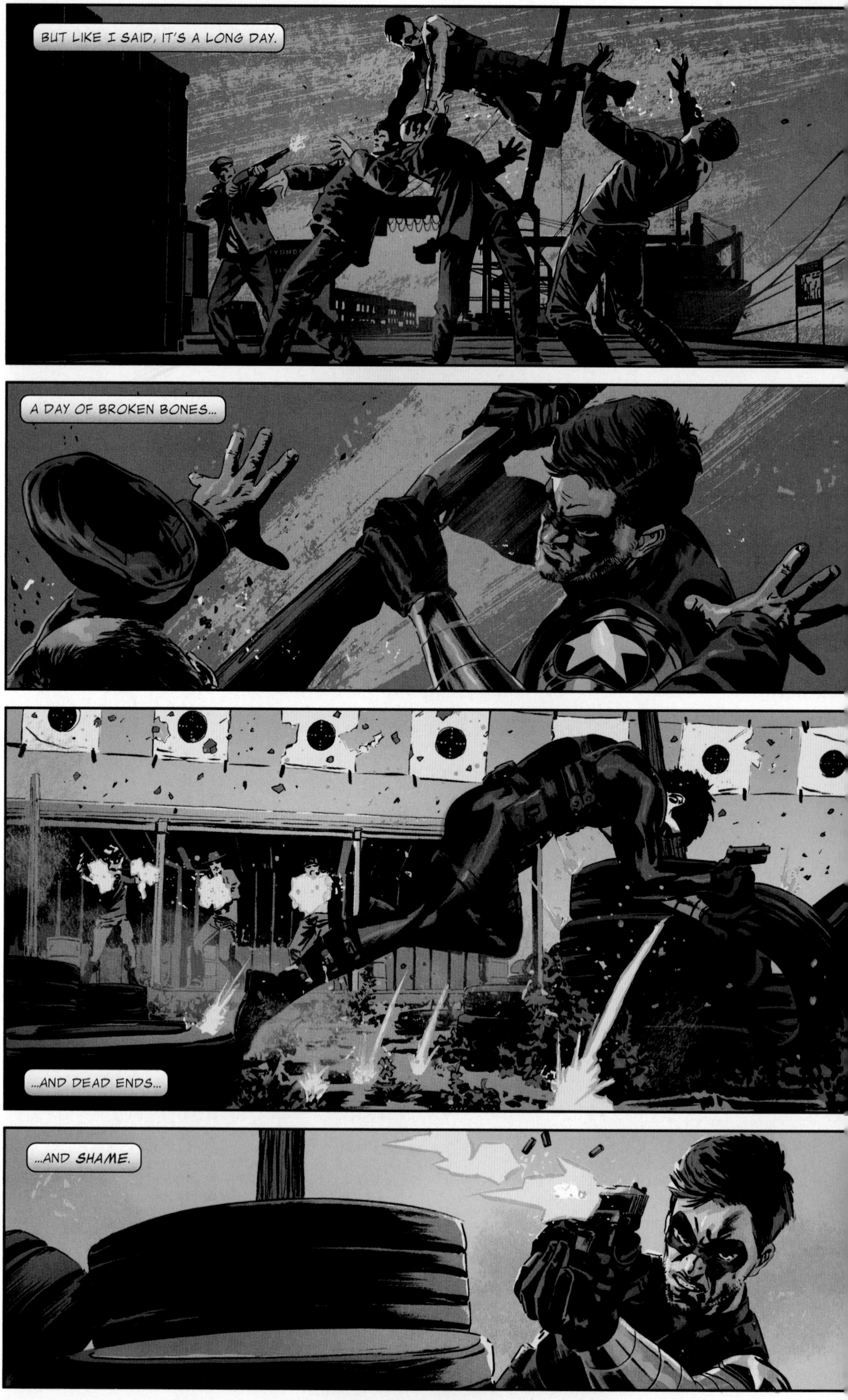
BUT LIKE I SAID, IT'S A LONG DAY.
A DAY OF BROKEN BONES...
...AND DEAD ENDS...
...AND SHAME.

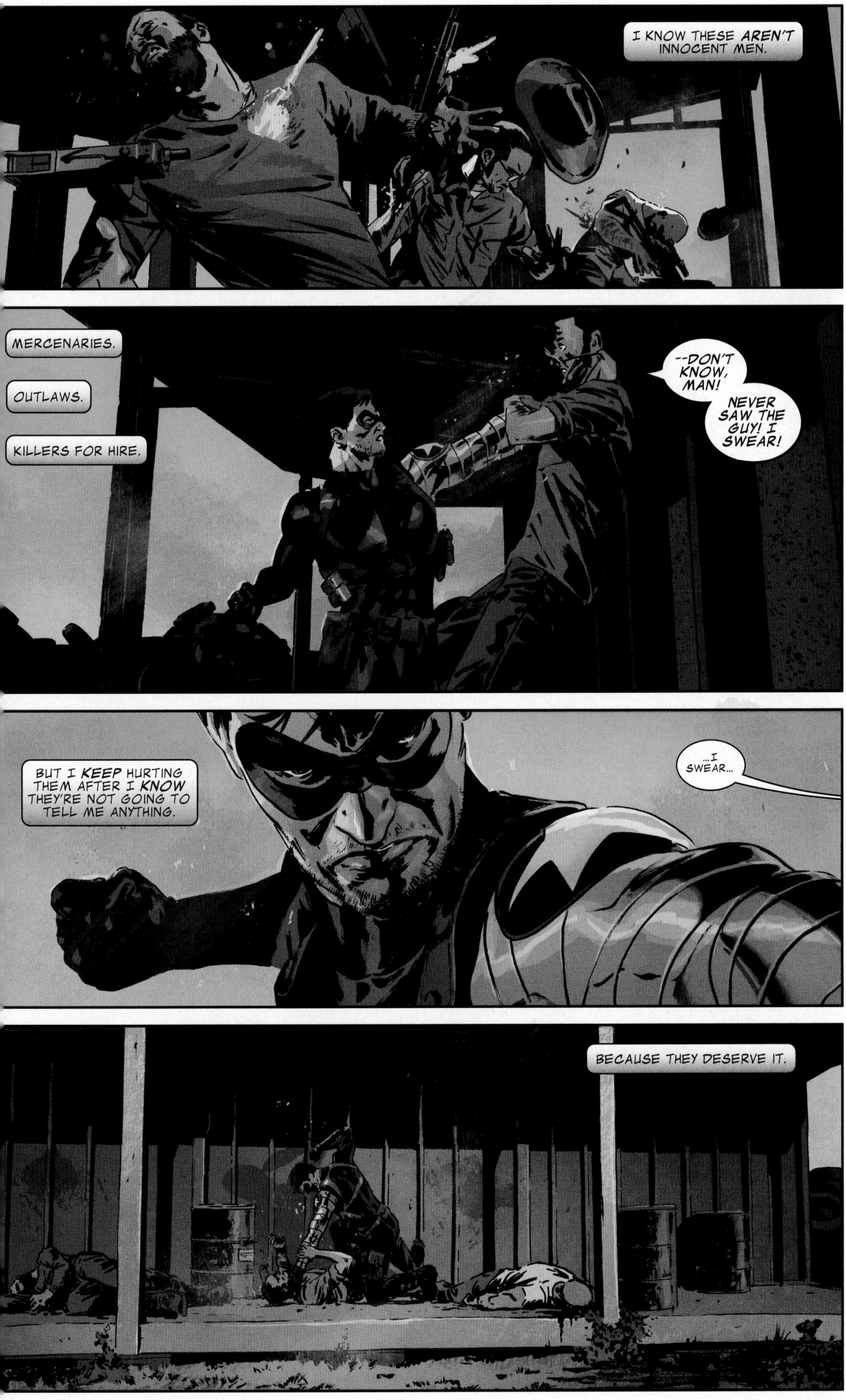
I KNOW THESE AREN'T INNOCENT MEN.
MERCENARIES.
OUTLAWS.
KILLERS FOR HIRE.
--DON'T KNOW, MAN!
NEVER SAW THE GUY! I SWEAR!
BUT I KEEP HURTING THEM AFTER I KNOW THEY'RE NOT GOING TO TELL ME ANYTHING.
...I SWEAR...
BECAUSE THEY DESERVE IT.

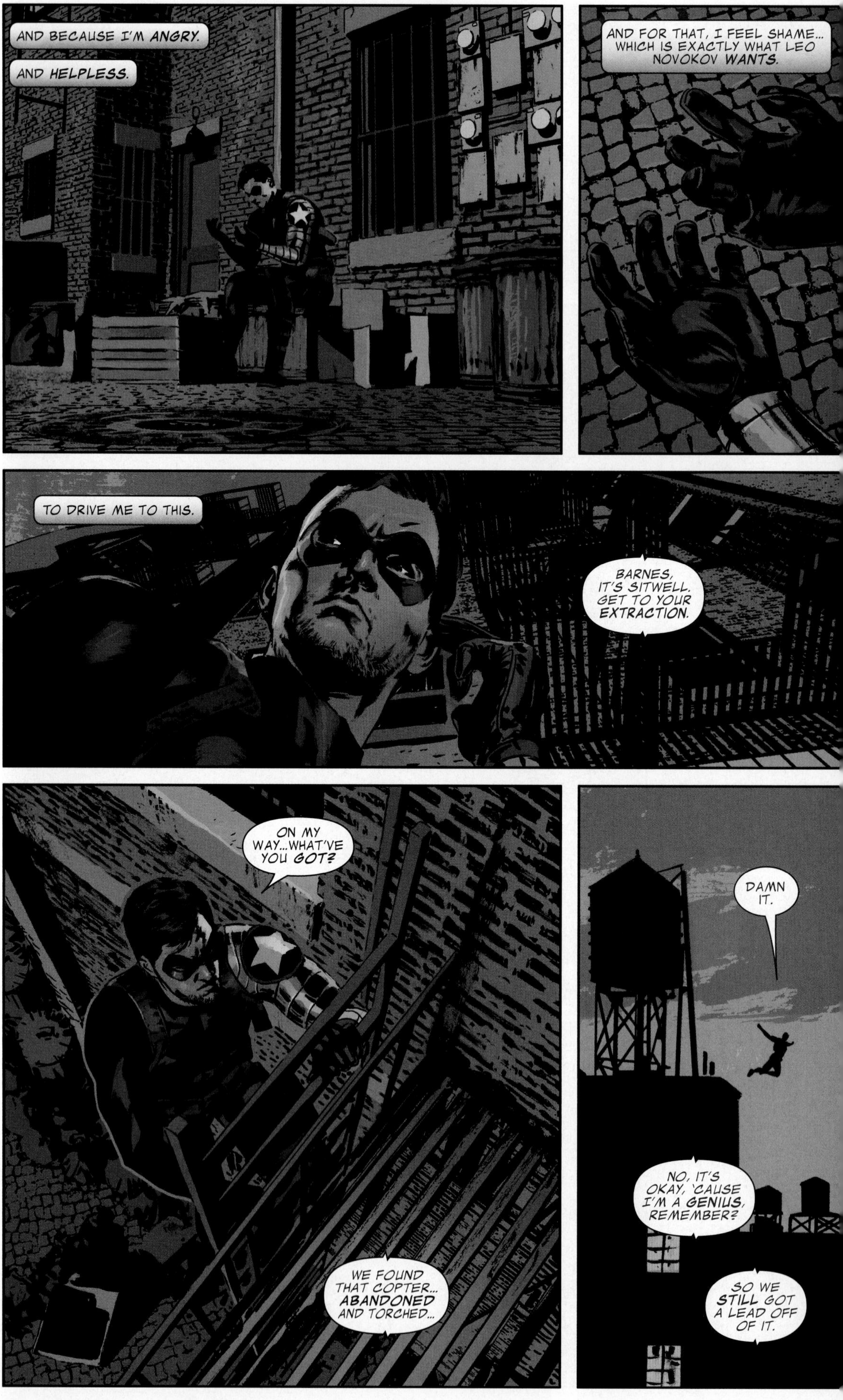
AND BECAUSE I'M ANGRY.
AND HELPLESS.
AND FOR THAT, I FEEL SHAME... WHICH IS EXACTLY WHAT LEO NOVOKOV WANTS.
TO DRIVE ME TO THIS.
BARNES, IT'S SITWELL. GET TO YOUR EXTRACTION.
ON MY WAY...WHAT'VE YOU GOT?
WE FOUND THAT COPTER... ABANDONED AND TORCHED...
DAMN IT.
NO, IT'S OKAY, 'CAUSE I'M A GENIUS, REMEMBER?
SO WE STILL GOT A LEAD OFF OF IT.

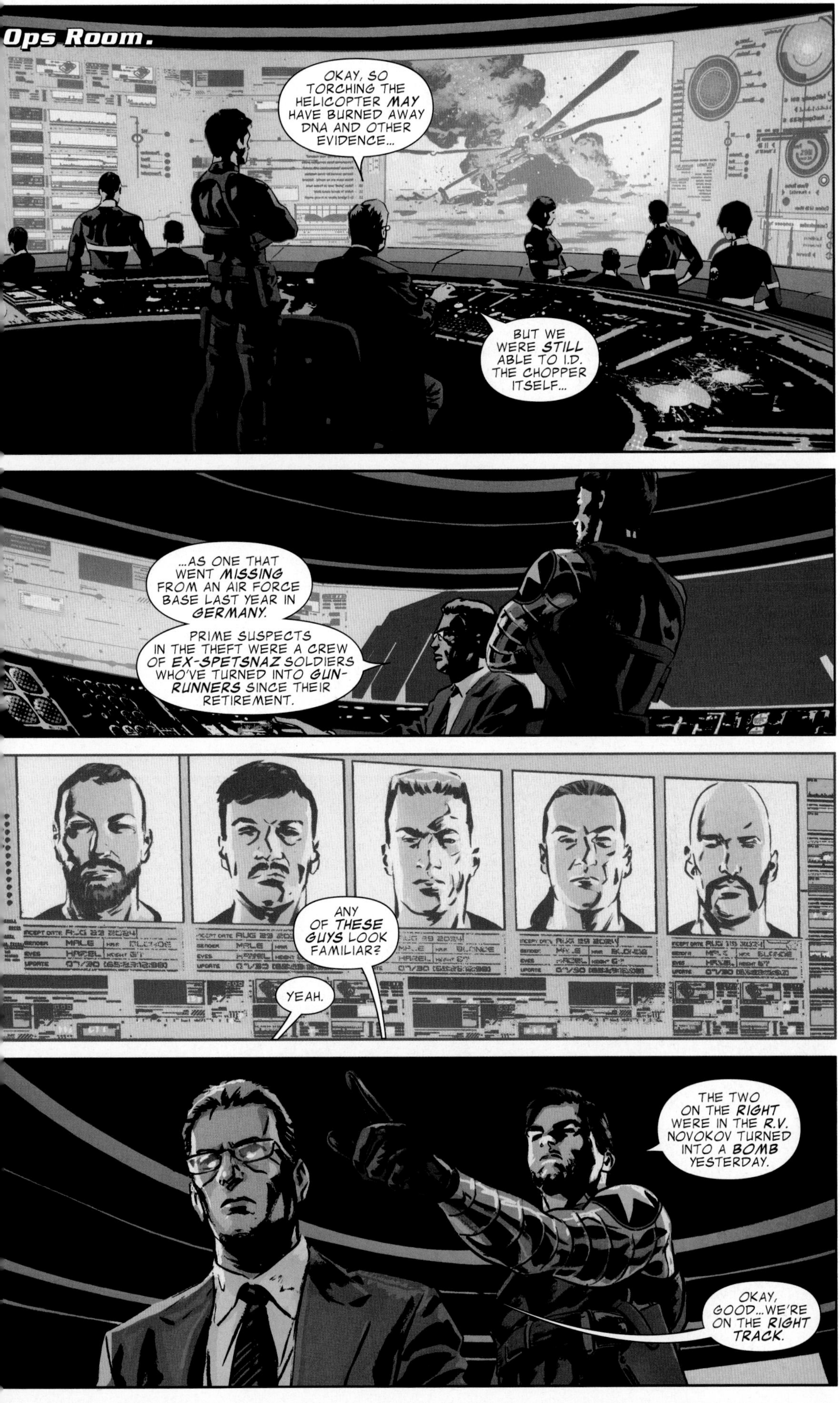

Ops Room.
OKAY, SO TORCHING THE HELICOPTER MAY HAVE BURNED AWAY DNA AND OTHER EVIDENCE...
BUT WE WERE STILL ABLE TO I.D. THE CHOPPER ITSELF...
...AS ONE THAT WENT MISSING FROM AN AIR FORCE BASE LAST YEAR IN GERMANY.
PRIME SUSPECTS IN THE THEFT WERE A CREW OF EX-SPETSNAZ SOLDIERS WHO'VE TURNED INTO GUN-RUNNERS SINCE THEIR RETIREMENT.
ANY OF THESE GUYS LOOK FAMILIAR?
YEAH.
THE TWO ON THE RIGHT WERE IN THE R.V. NOVOKOV TURNED INTO A BOMB YESTERDAY.
OKAY, GOOD...WE'RE ON THE RIGHT TRACK.

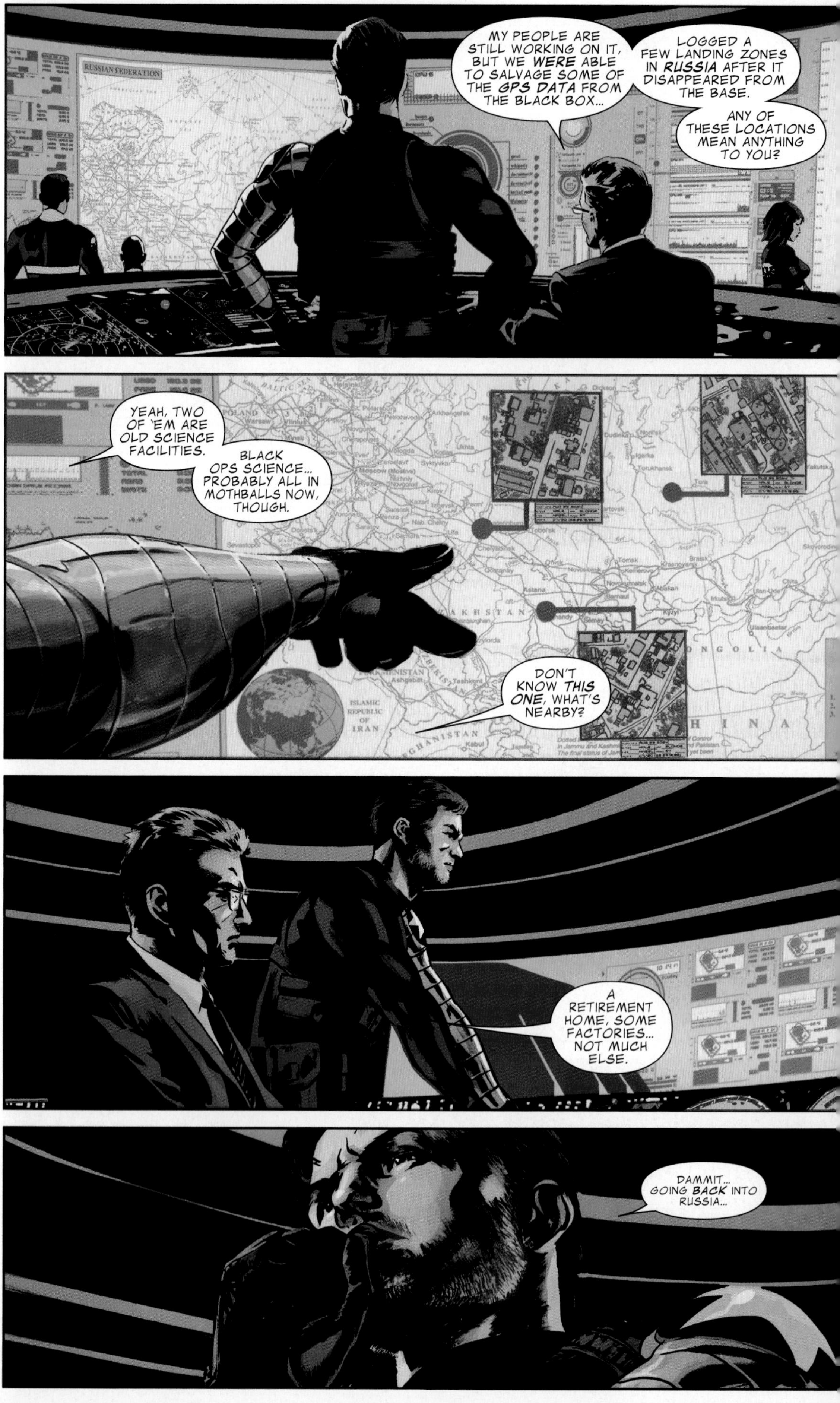
MY PEOPLE ARE STILL WORKING ON IT, BUT WE WERE ABLE TO SALVAGE SOME OF THE GPS DATA FROM THE BLACK BOX...
LOGGED A FEW LANDING ZONES IN RUSSIA AFTER IT DISAPPEARED FROM THE BASE.
ANY OF THESE LOCATIONS MEAN ANYTHING TO YOU?
RUSSIAN FEDERATION
YEAH, TWO OF 'EM ARE OLD SCIENCE FACILITIES.
BLACK OPS SCIENCE... PROBABLY ALL IN MOTHBALLS NOW, THOUGH.
DON'T KNOW THIS ONE, WHAT'S NEARBY?
A RETIREMENT HOME, SOME FACTORIES... NOT MUCH ELSE.
DAMMIT... GOING BACK INTO RUSSIA...

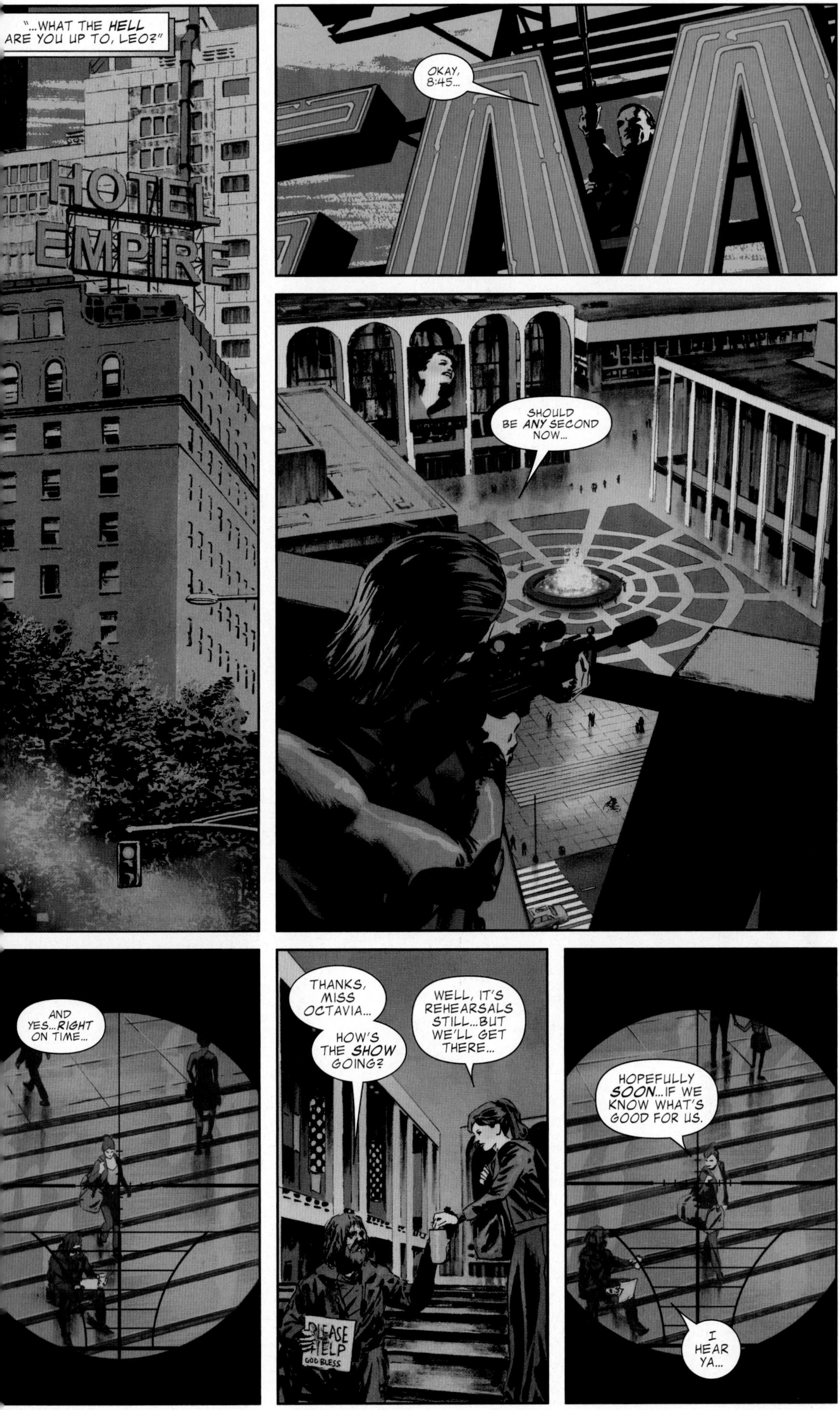
"...WHAT THE HELL ARE YOU UP TO, LEO?"
HOTEL EMPIRE
OKAY, 8:45...
SHOULD BE ANY SECOND NOW...
AND YES...RIGHT ON TIME...
THANKS, MISS OCTAVIA...
HOW'S THE SHOW GOING?
WELL, IT'S REHEARSALS STILL...BUT WE'LL GET THERE...
PLEASE HELP GOD BLESS
HOPEFULLY SOON...IF WE KNOW WHAT'S GOOD FOR US.
I HEAR YA...

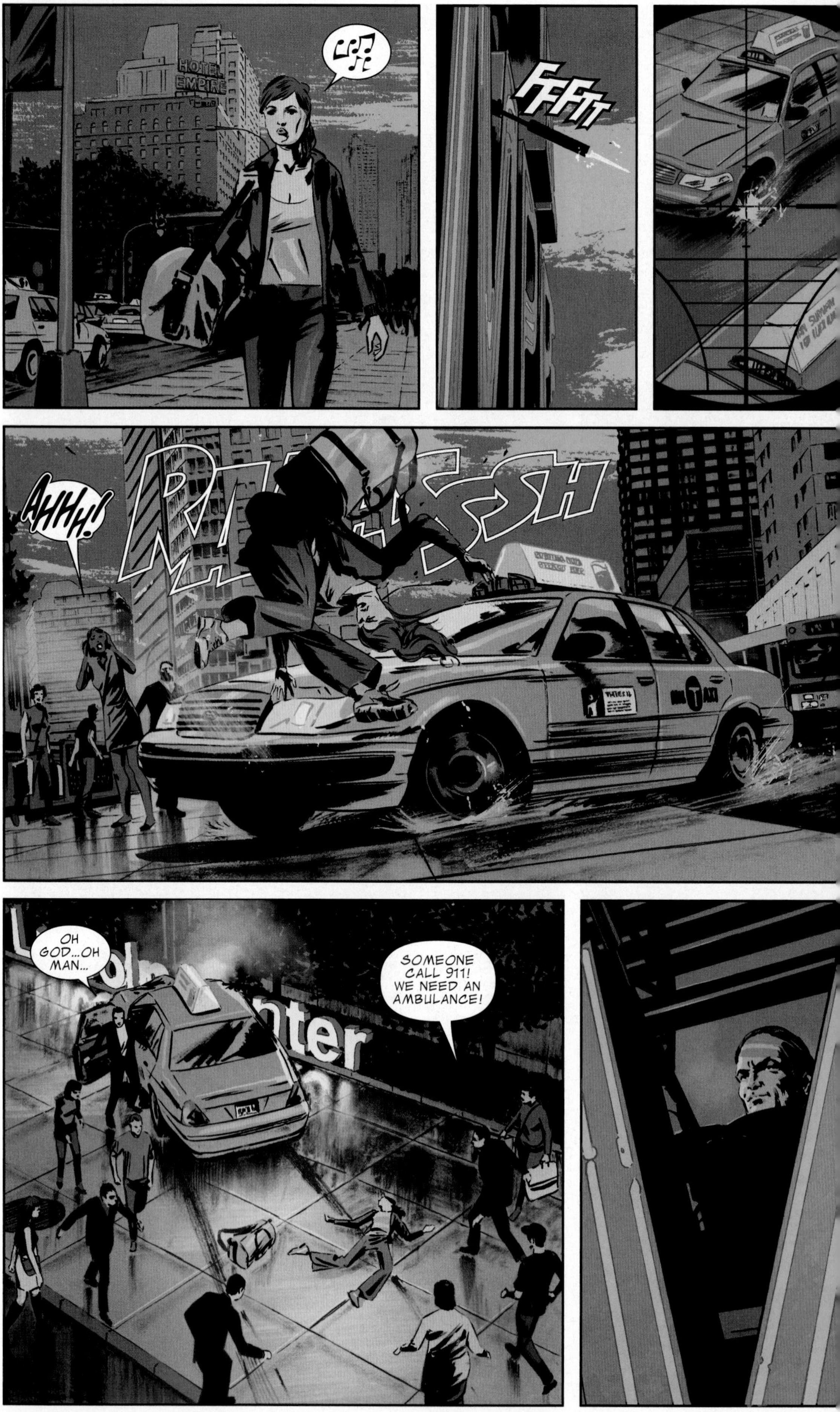

FFFTTT
AHHH!
OH GOD...OH MAN...
SOMEONE CALL 911! WE NEED AN AMBULANCE!

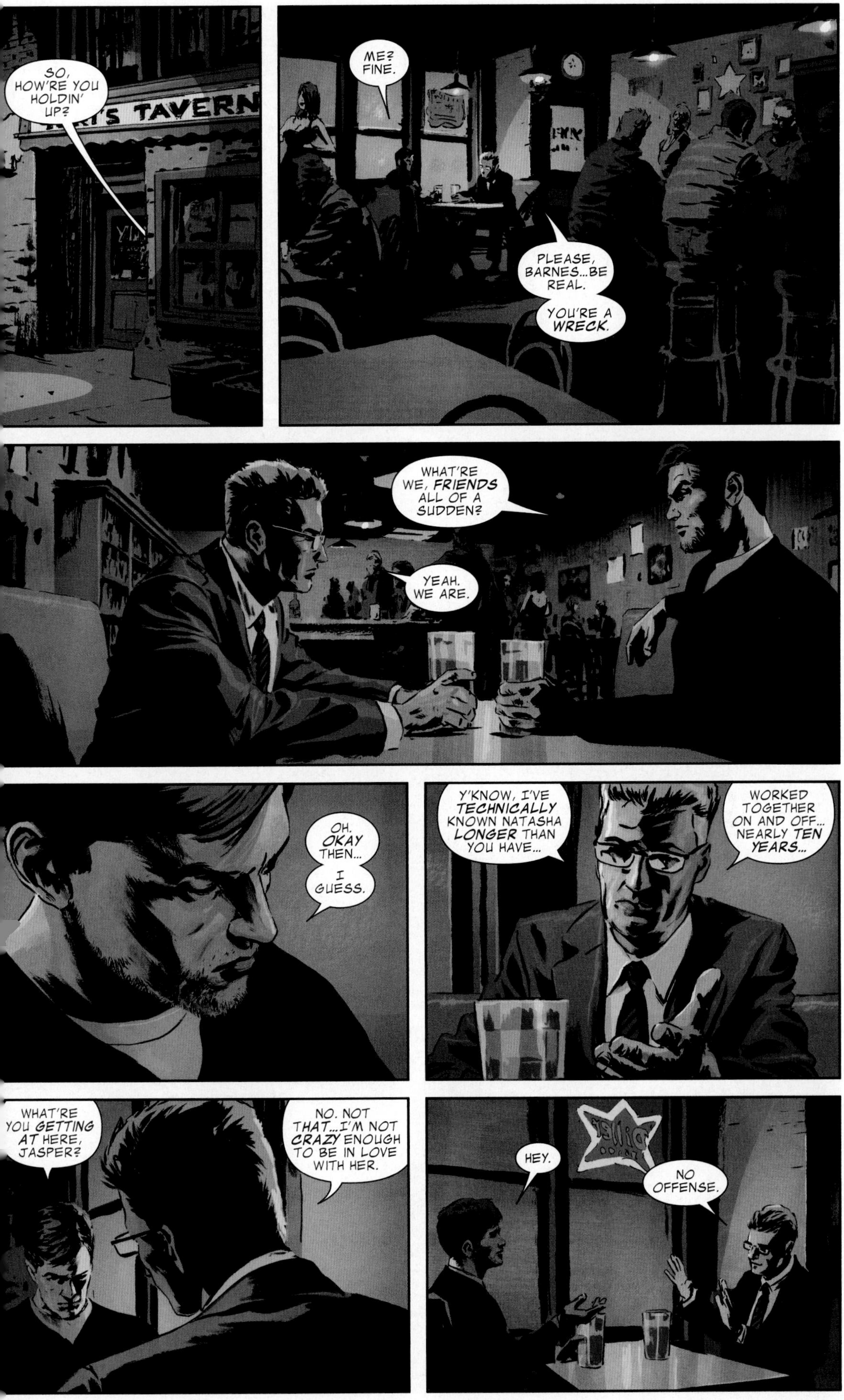
SO, HOW'RE YOU HOLDIN' UP?
ME? FINE.
PLEASE, BARNES...BE REAL.
YOU'RE A WRECK.
WHAT'RE WE, FRIENDS ALL OF A SUDDEN?
YEAH. WE ARE.
OH. OKAY THEN...
I GUESS.
Y'KNOW, I'VE TECHNICALLY KNOWN NATASHA LONGER THAN YOU HAVE...
WORKED TOGETHER ON AND OFF... NEARLY TEN YEARS...
WHAT'RE YOU GETTING AT HERE, JASPER?
NO. NOT THAT...I'M NOT CRAZY ENOUGH TO BE IN LOVE WITH HER.
HEY.
NO OFFENSE.

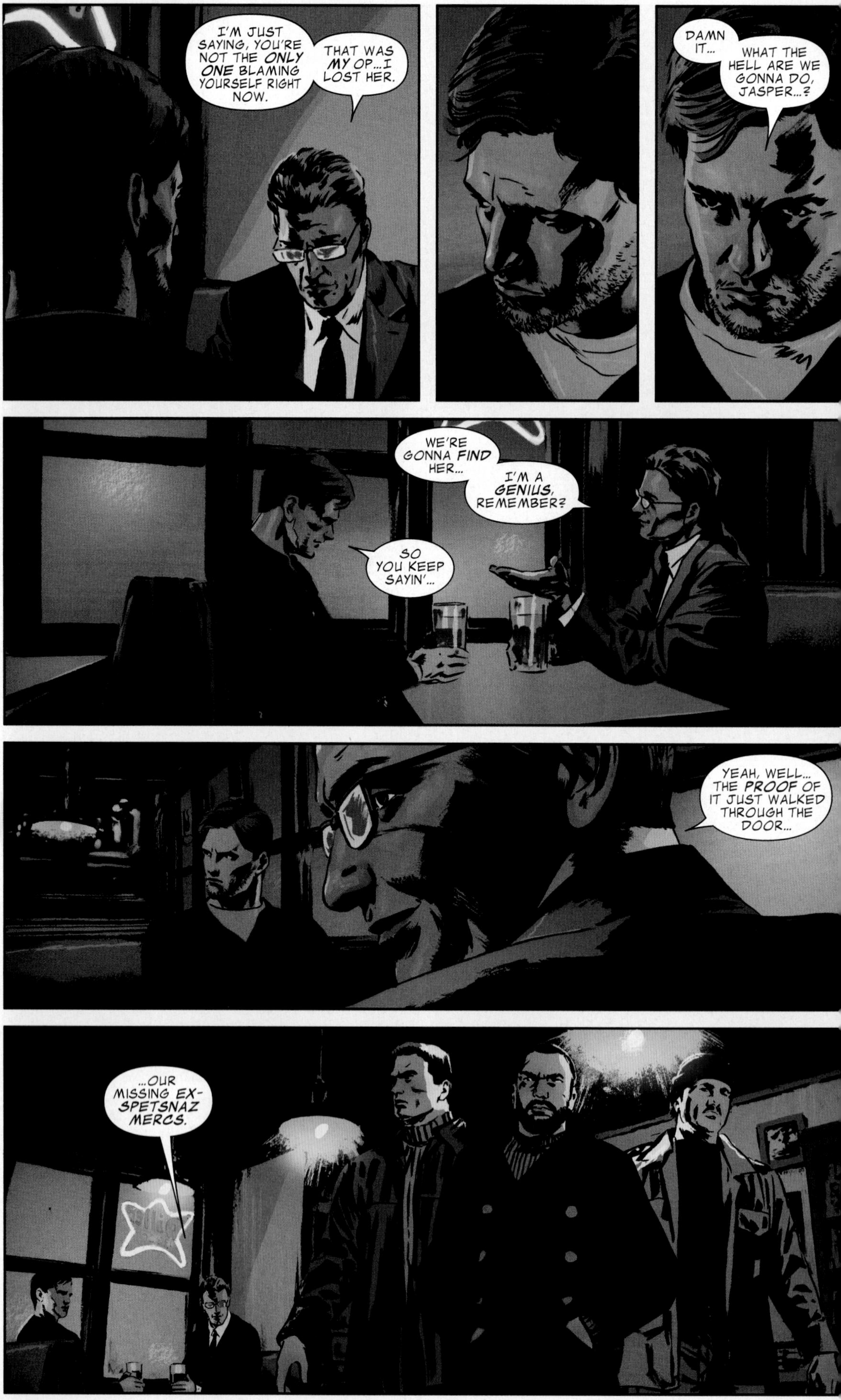
I'M JUST SAYING, YOU'RE NOT THE ONLY ONE BLAMING YOURSELF RIGHT NOW.
THAT WAS MY OP...I LOST HER.
DAMN IT...
WHAT THE HELL ARE WE GONNA DO, JASPER...?
WE'RE GONNA FIND HER...
I'M A GENIUS, REMEMBER?
SO YOU KEEP SAYIN'...
YEAH, WELL... THE PROOF OF IT JUST WALKED THROUGH THE DOOR...
...OUR MISSING EX-SPETSNAZ MERCS.

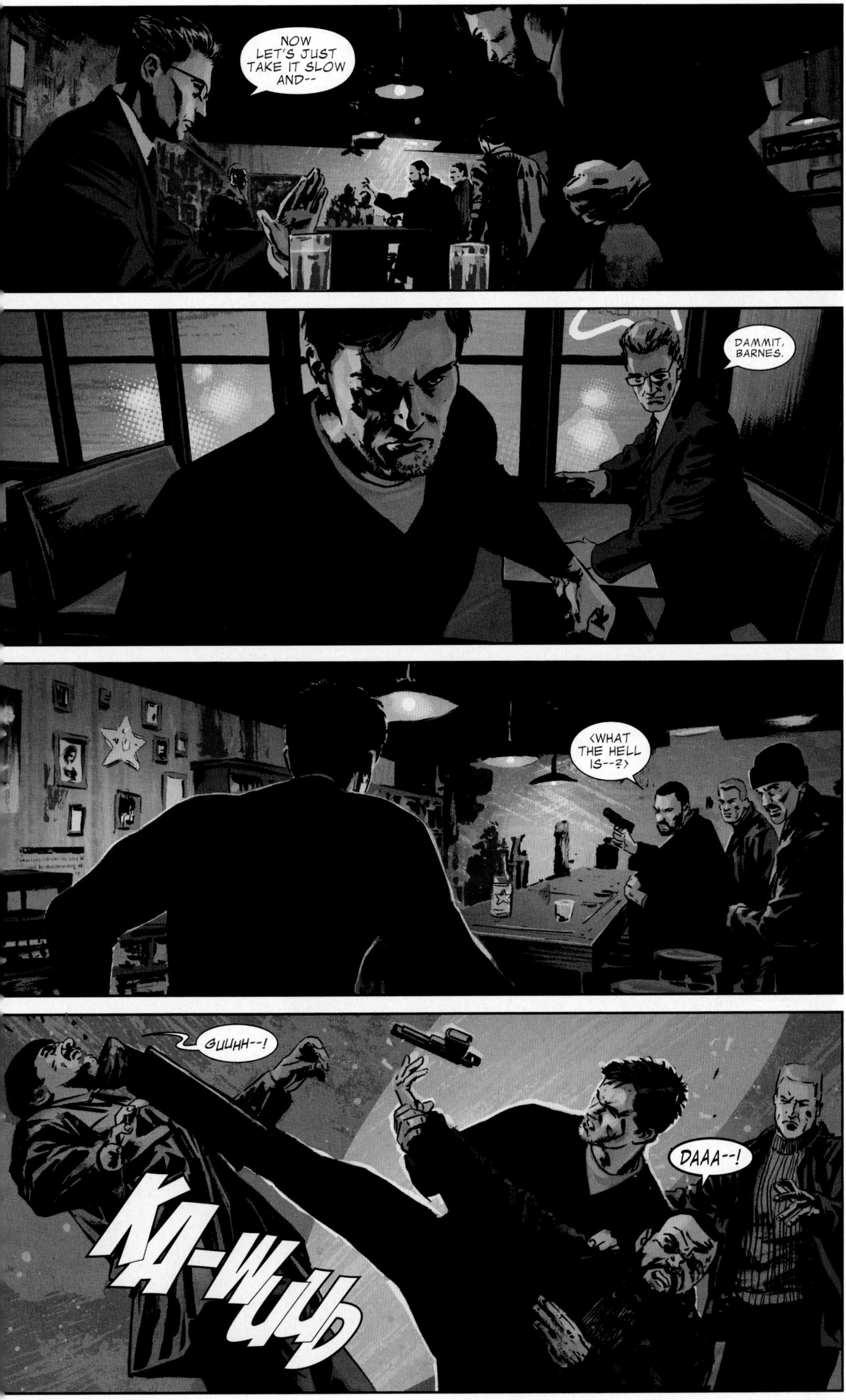
NOW LET'S JUST TAKE IT SLOW AND--
DAMMIT, BARNES.
<WHAT THE HELL IS--?>
GUUHH--!
DAAA--!
KA-WUUD

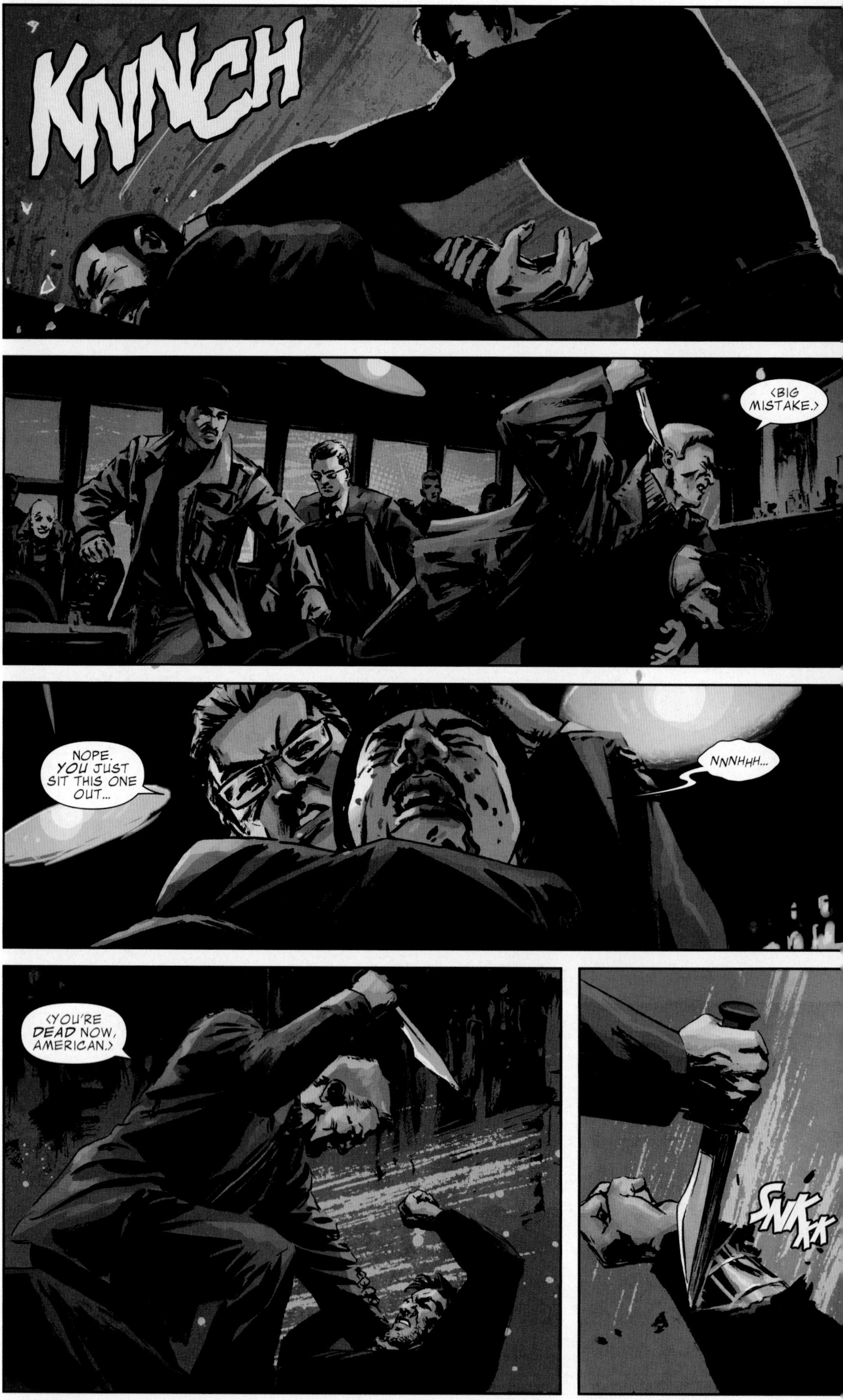
KNNCH
<BIG MISTAKE.>
NOPE. YOU JUST SIT THIS ONE OUT...
NNNHHH...
<YOU'RE DEAD NOW, AMERICAN.>
SNKXX

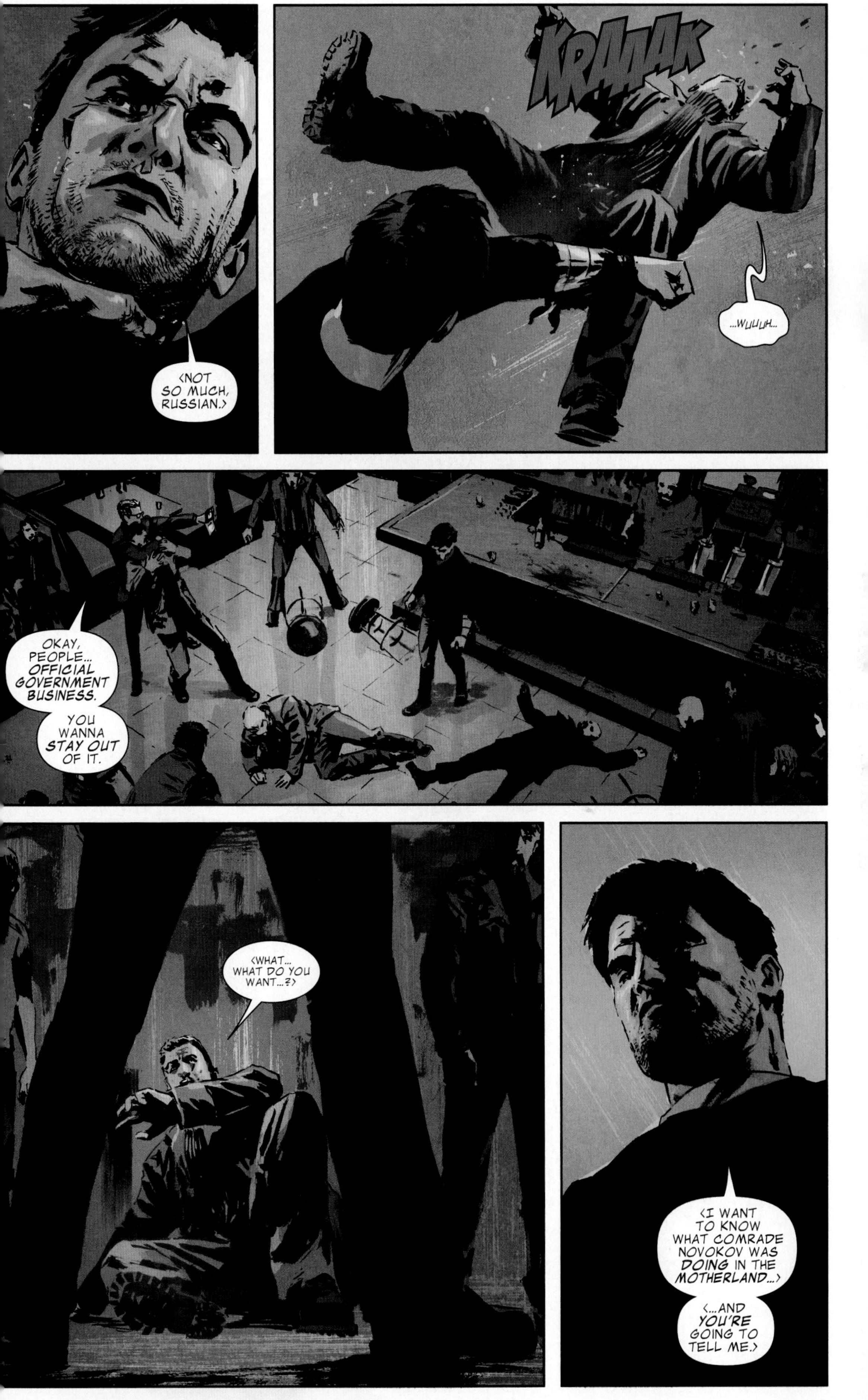

<NOT SO MUCH, RUSSIAN.>
KRAAAK
...WUUUH...
OKAY, PEOPLE... OFFICIAL GOVERNMENT BUSINESS.
YOU WANNA STAY OUT OF IT.
<WHAT... WHAT DO YOU WANT...?>
<I WANT TO KNOW WHAT COMRADE NOVOKOV WAS DOING IN THE MOTHERLAND...>
<...AND YOU'RE GOING TO TELL ME.>

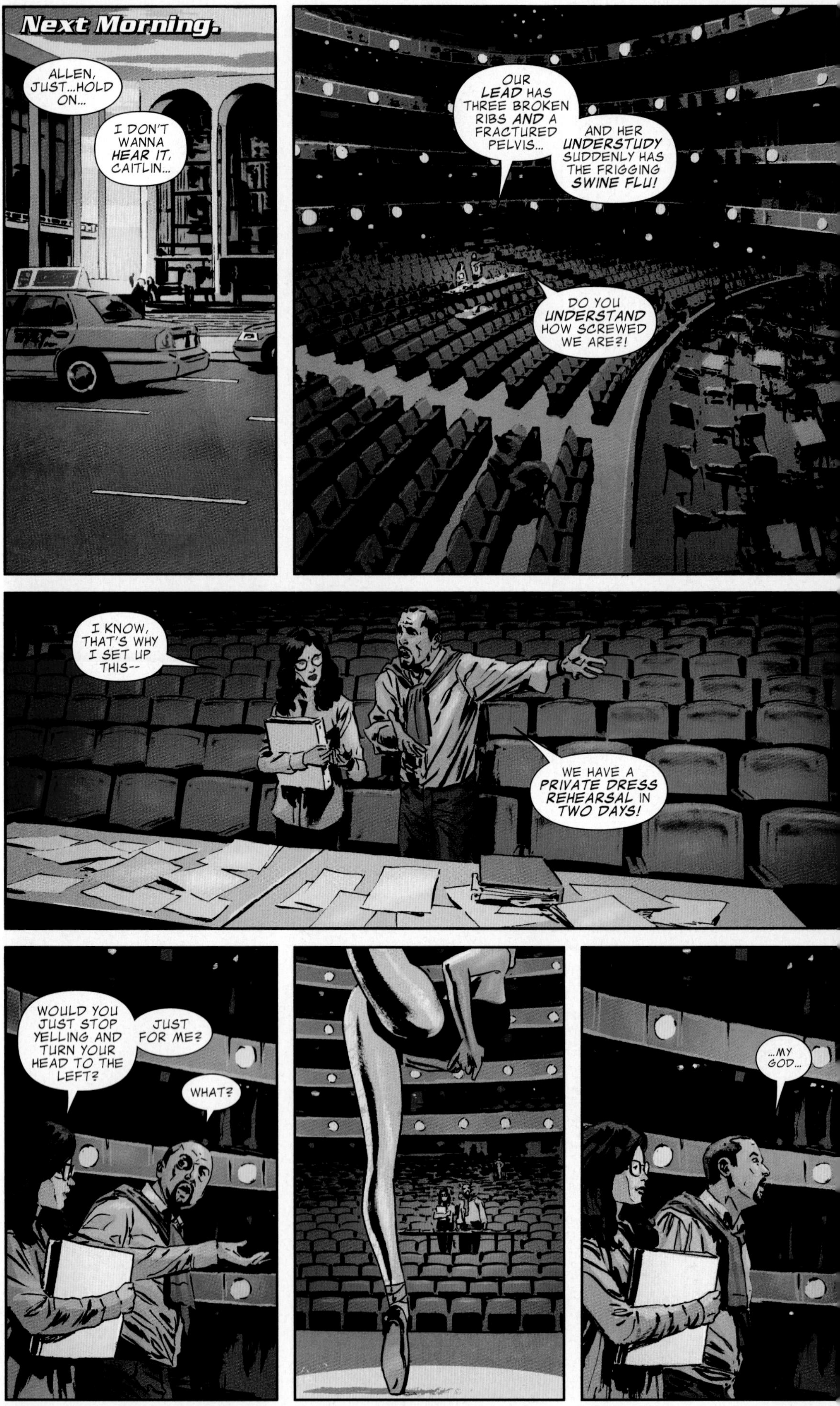
Next Morning.
ALLEN, JUST...HOLD ON...
I DON'T WANNA HEAR IT, CAITLIN...
OUR LEAD HAS THREE BROKEN RIBS AND A FRACTURED PELVIS...
AND HER UNDERSTUDY SUDDENLY HAS THE FRIGGING SWINE FLU!
DO YOU UNDERSTAND HOW SCREWED WE ARE?!
I KNOW, THAT'S WHY I SET UP THIS--
WE HAVE A PRIVATE DRESS REHEARSAL IN TWO DAYS!
WOULD YOU JUST STOP YELLING AND TURN YOUR HEAD TO THE LEFT?
JUST FOR ME?
WHAT?
...MY GOD...

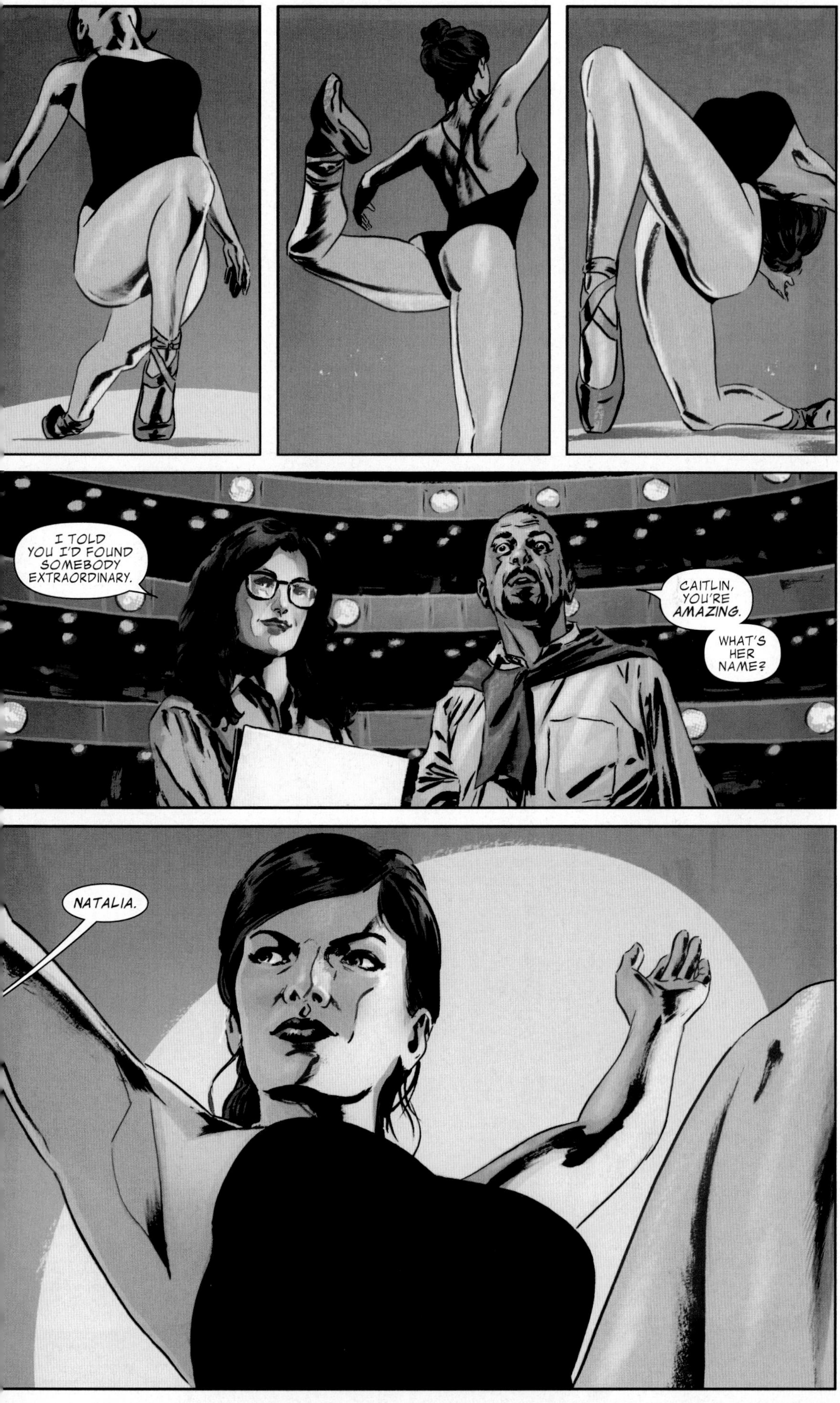
I TOLD YOU I'D FOUND SOMEBODY EXTRAORDINARY.
CAITLIN, YOU'RE AMAZING.
WHAT'S HER NAME?
NATALIA.

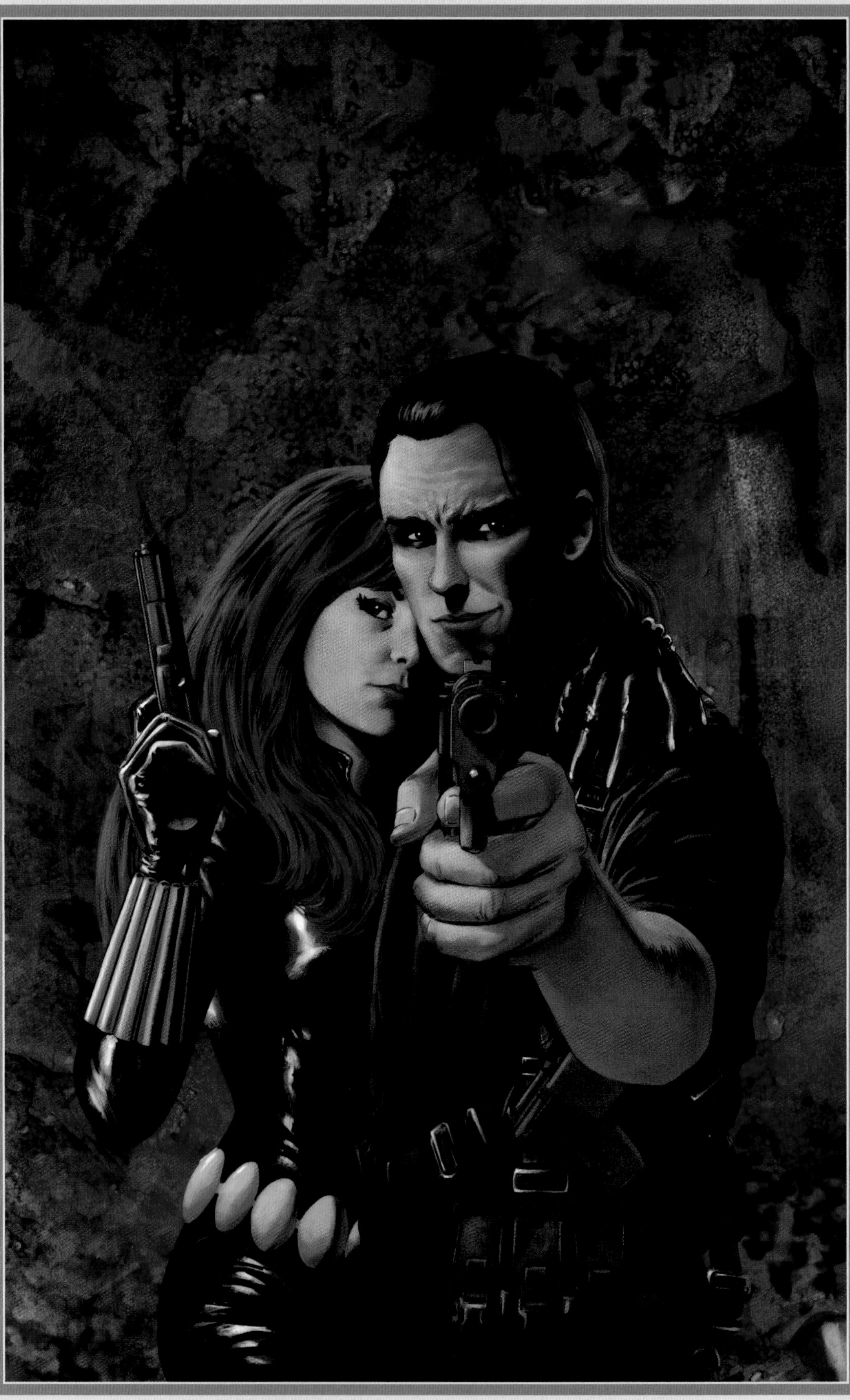

NINE

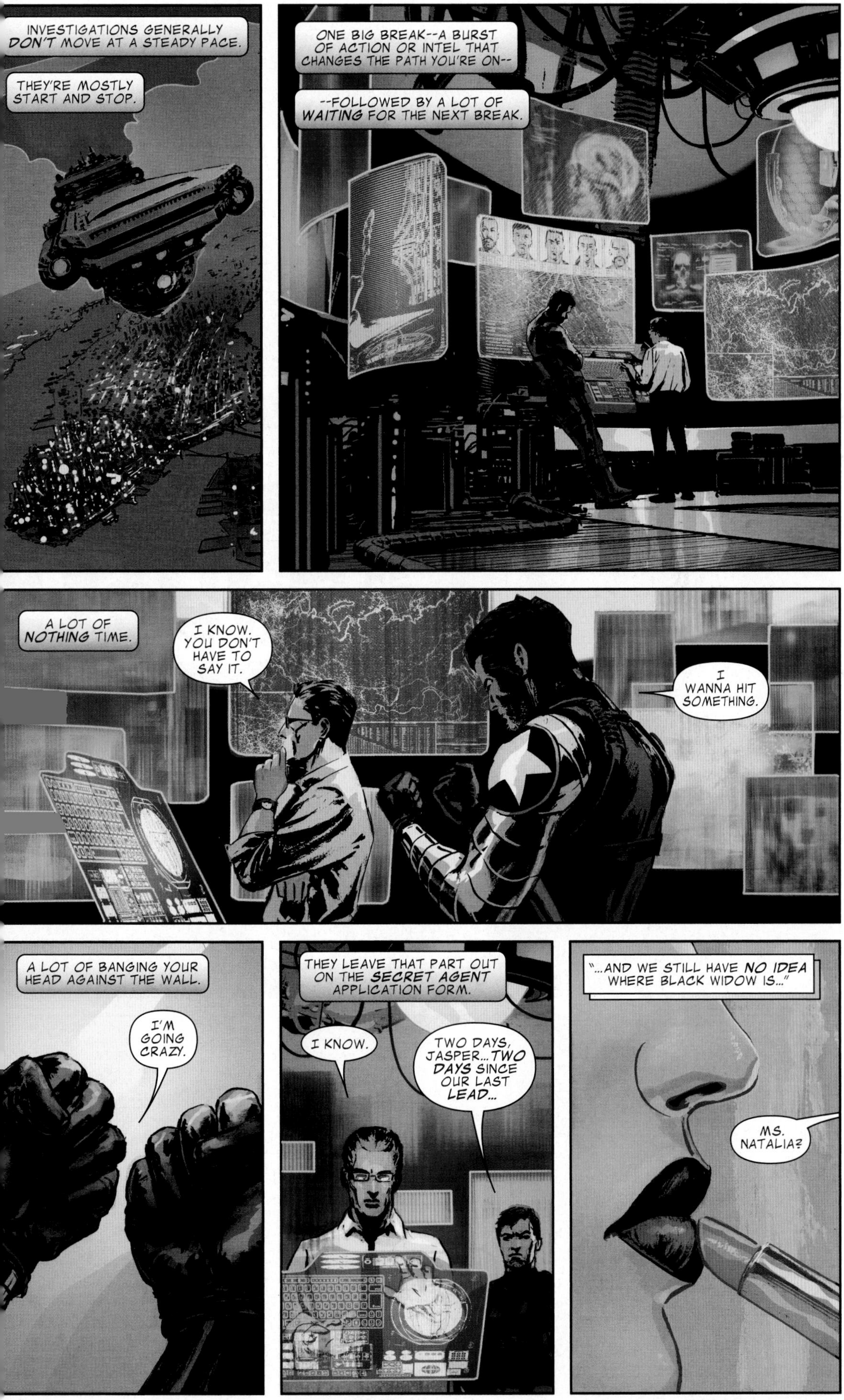
INVESTIGATIONS GENERALLY DON'T MOVE AT A STEADY PACE.
THEY'RE MOSTLY START AND STOP.
ONE BIG BREAK--A BURST OF ACTION OR INTEL THAT CHANGES THE PATH YOU'RE ON--
--FOLLOWED BY A LOT OF WAITING FOR THE NEXT BREAK.
A LOT OF NOTHING TIME.
I KNOW. YOU DON'T HAVE TO SAY IT.
I WANNA HIT SOMETHING.
A LOT OF BANGING YOUR HEAD AGAINST THE WALL.
I'M GOING CRAZY.
THEY LEAVE THAT PART OUT ON THE SECRET AGENT APPLICATION FORM.
TWO DAYS, JASPER...TWO DAYS SINCE OUR LAST LEAD...
I KNOW.
"...AND WE STILL HAVE NO IDEA WHERE BLACK WIDOW IS..."
MS. NATALIA?

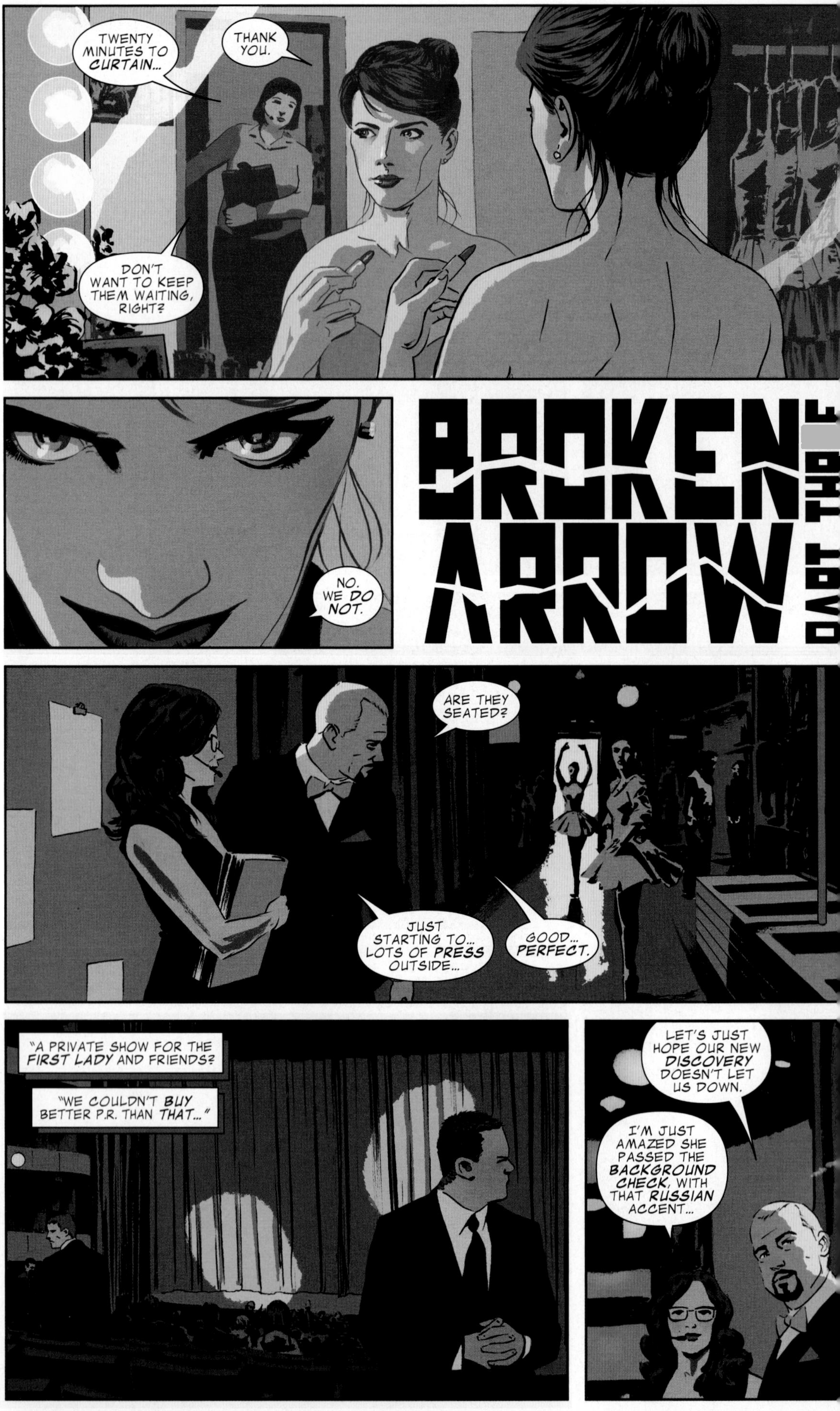
TWENTY MINUTES TO CURTAIN...
THANK YOU.
DON'T WANT TO KEEP THEM WAITING, RIGHT?
NO. WE DO NOT.
BROKEN ARROW
PART TWO
ARE THEY SEATED?
JUST STARTING TO... LOTS OF PRESS OUTSIDE...
GOOD... PERFECT.
"A PRIVATE SHOW FOR THE FIRST LADY AND FRIENDS?
"WE COULDN'T BUY BETTER P.R. THAN THAT..."
LET'S JUST HOPE OUR NEW DISCOVERY DOESN'T LET US DOWN.
I'M JUST AMAZED SHE PASSED THE BACKGROUND CHECK, WITH THAT RUSSIAN ACCENT...

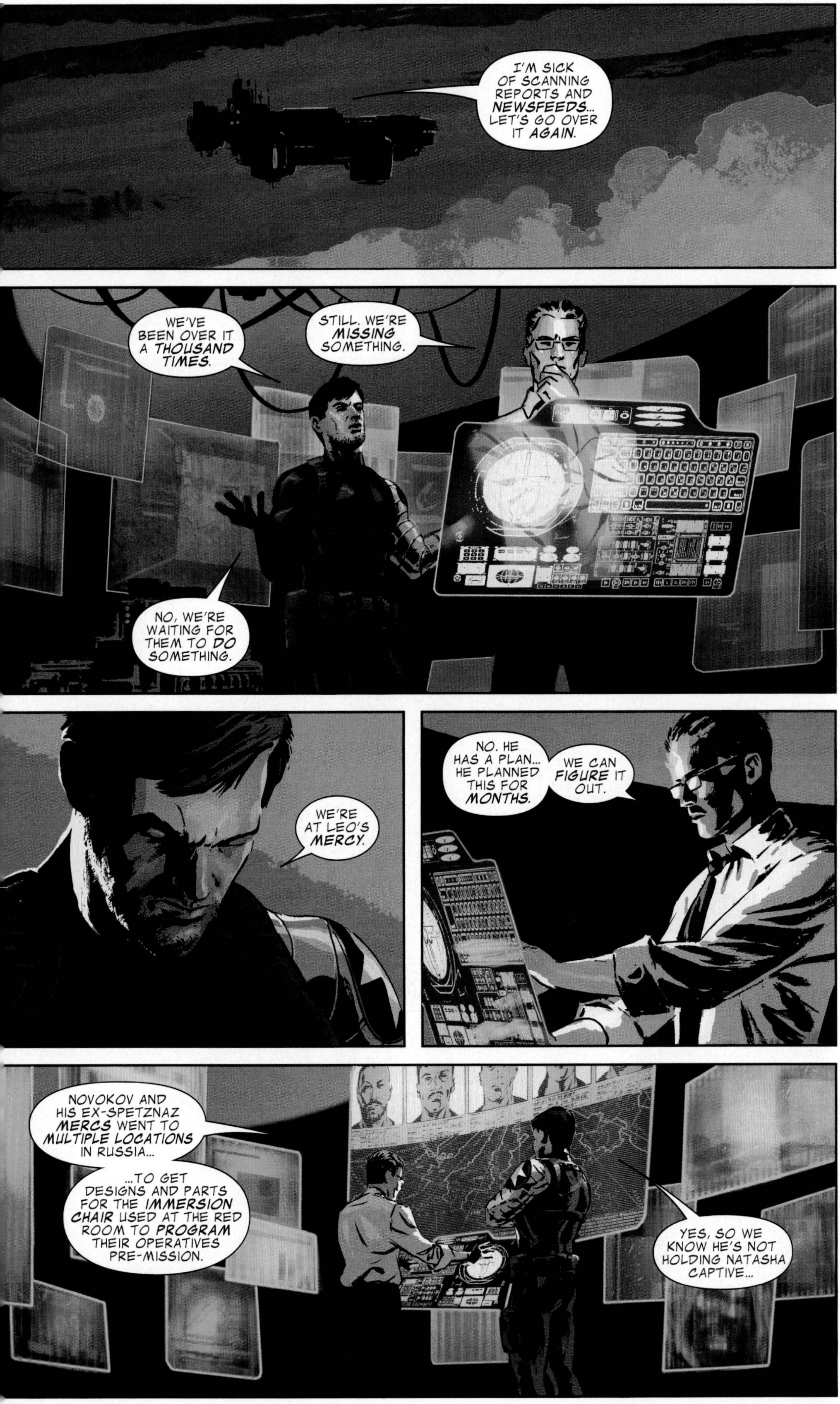
I'M SICK OF SCANNING REPORTS AND NEWSFEEDS... LET'S GO OVER IT AGAIN.
WE'VE BEEN OVER IT A THOUSAND TIMES.
STILL. WE'RE MISSING SOMETHING.
NO, WE'RE WAITING FOR THEM TO DO SOMETHING.
WE'RE AT LEO'S MERCY.
NO. HE HAS A PLAN... HE PLANNED THIS FOR MONTHS.
WE CAN FIGURE IT OUT.
NOVOKOV AND HIS EX-SPETZNAZ MERCS WENT TO MULTIPLE LOCATIONS IN RUSSIA...
...TO GET DESIGNS AND PARTS FOR THE IMMERSION CHAIR USED AT THE RED ROOM TO PROGRAM THEIR OPERATIVES PRE-MISSION.
YES, SO WE KNOW HE'S NOT HOLDING NATASHA CAPTIVE...

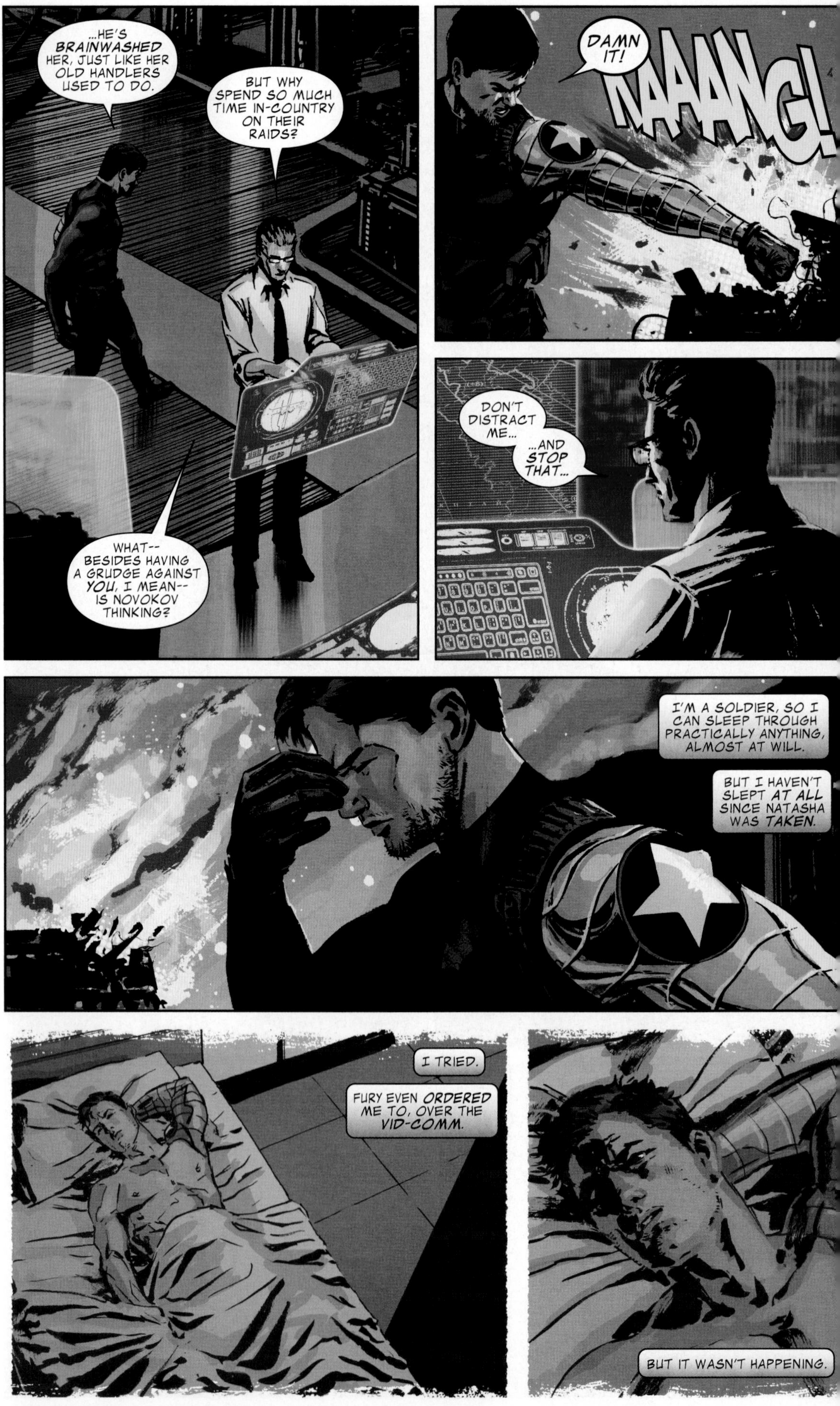
...HE'S BRAINWASHED HER, JUST LIKE HER OLD HANDLERS USED TO DO.
BUT WHY SPEND SO MUCH TIME IN-COUNTRY ON THEIR RAIDS?
WHAT-- BESIDES HAVING A GRUDGE AGAINST YOU, I MEAN-- IS NOVOKOV THINKING?
DAMN IT!
KRAAANG!
DON'T DISTRACT ME...
...AND STOP THAT...
I'M A SOLDIER, SO I CAN SLEEP THROUGH PRACTICALLY ANYTHING, ALMOST AT WILL.
BUT I HAVEN'T SLEPT AT ALL SINCE NATASHA WAS TAKEN.
I TRIED.
FURY EVEN ORDERED ME TO, OVER THE VID-COMM.
BUT IT WASN'T HAPPENING.

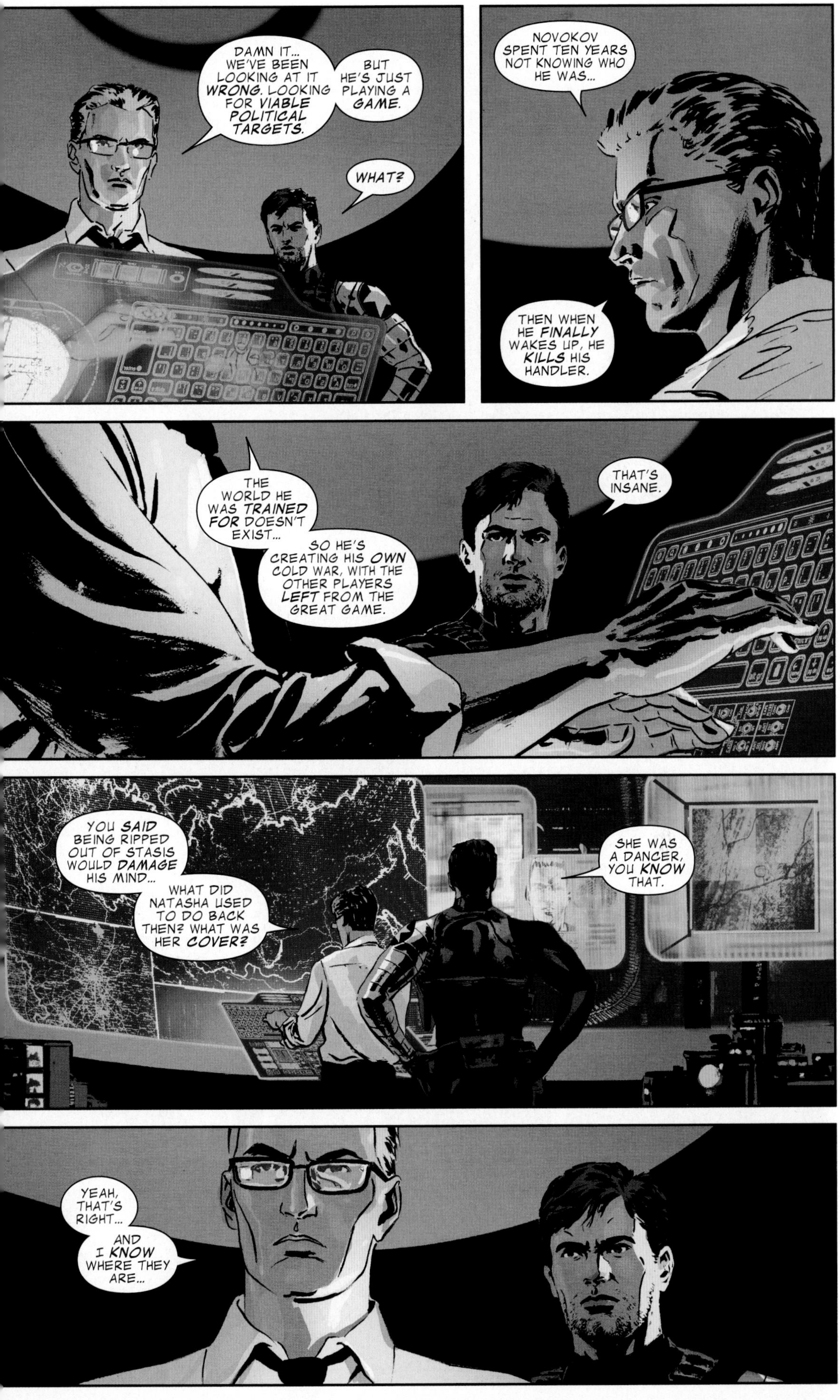
DAMN IT... WE'VE BEEN LOOKING AT IT WRONG. LOOKING FOR VIABLE POLITICAL TARGETS.
BUT HE'S JUST PLAYING A GAME.
WHAT?
NOVOKOV SPENT TEN YEARS NOT KNOWING WHO HE WAS...
THEN WHEN HE FINALLY WAKES UP, HE KILLS HIS HANDLER.
THE WORLD HE WAS TRAINED FOR DOESN'T EXIST...
SO HE'S CREATING HIS OWN COLD WAR, WITH THE OTHER PLAYERS LEFT FROM THE GREAT GAME.
THAT'S INSANE.
YOU SAID BEING RIPPED OUT OF STASIS WOULD DAMAGE HIS MIND...
WHAT DID NATASHA USED TO DO BACK THEN? WHAT WAS HER COVER?
SHE WAS A DANCER, YOU KNOW THAT.
YEAH, THAT'S RIGHT...
AND I KNOW WHERE THEY ARE...

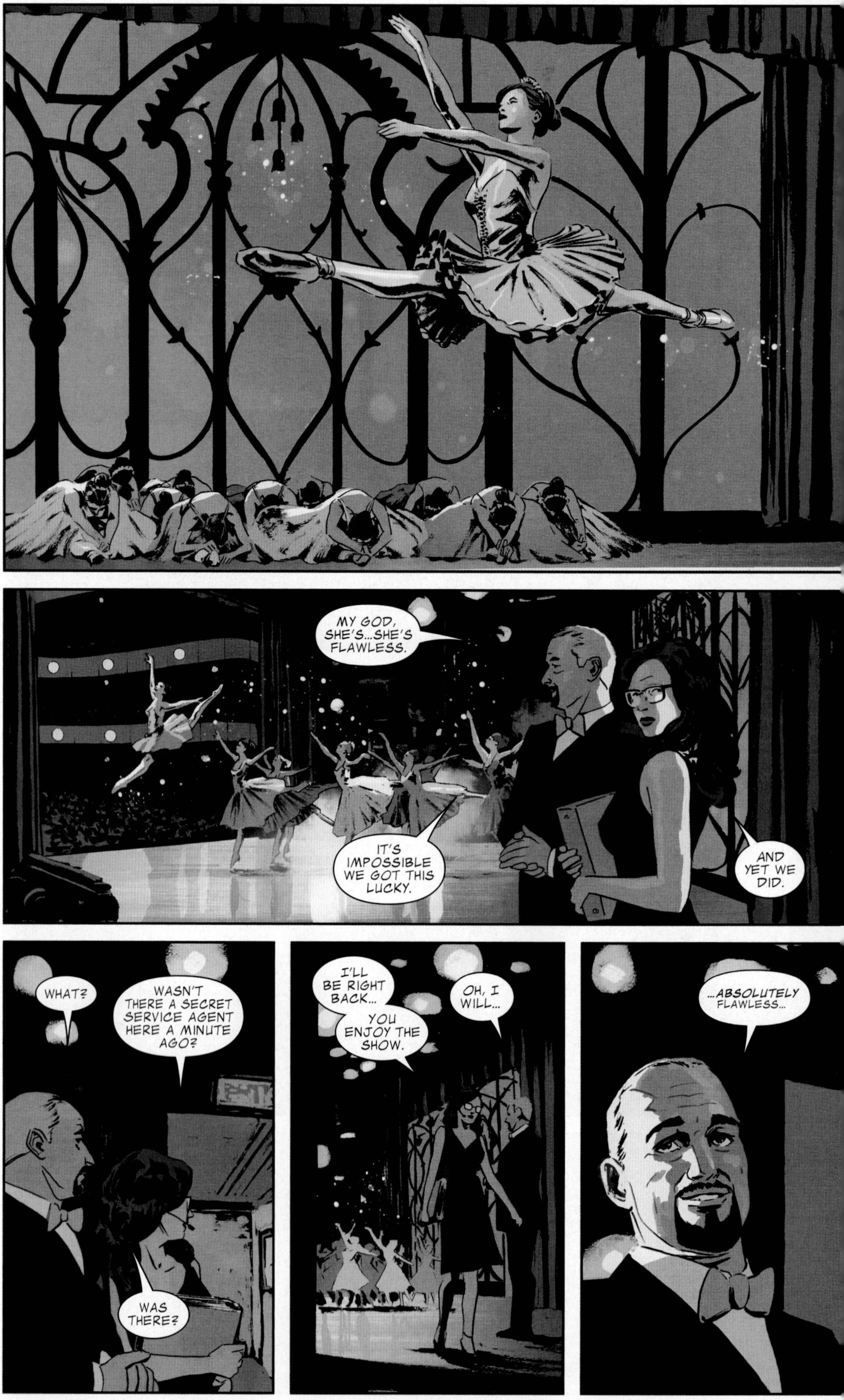
MY GOD, SHE'S...SHE'S FLAWLESS.
IT'S IMPOSSIBLE WE GOT THIS LUCKY.
AND YET WE DID.
WHAT?
WASN'T THERE A SECRET SERVICE AGENT HERE A MINUTE AGO?
WAS THERE?
I'LL BE RIGHT BACK...
YOU ENJOY THE SHOW.
OH, I WILL...
...ABSOLUTELY FLAWLESS...

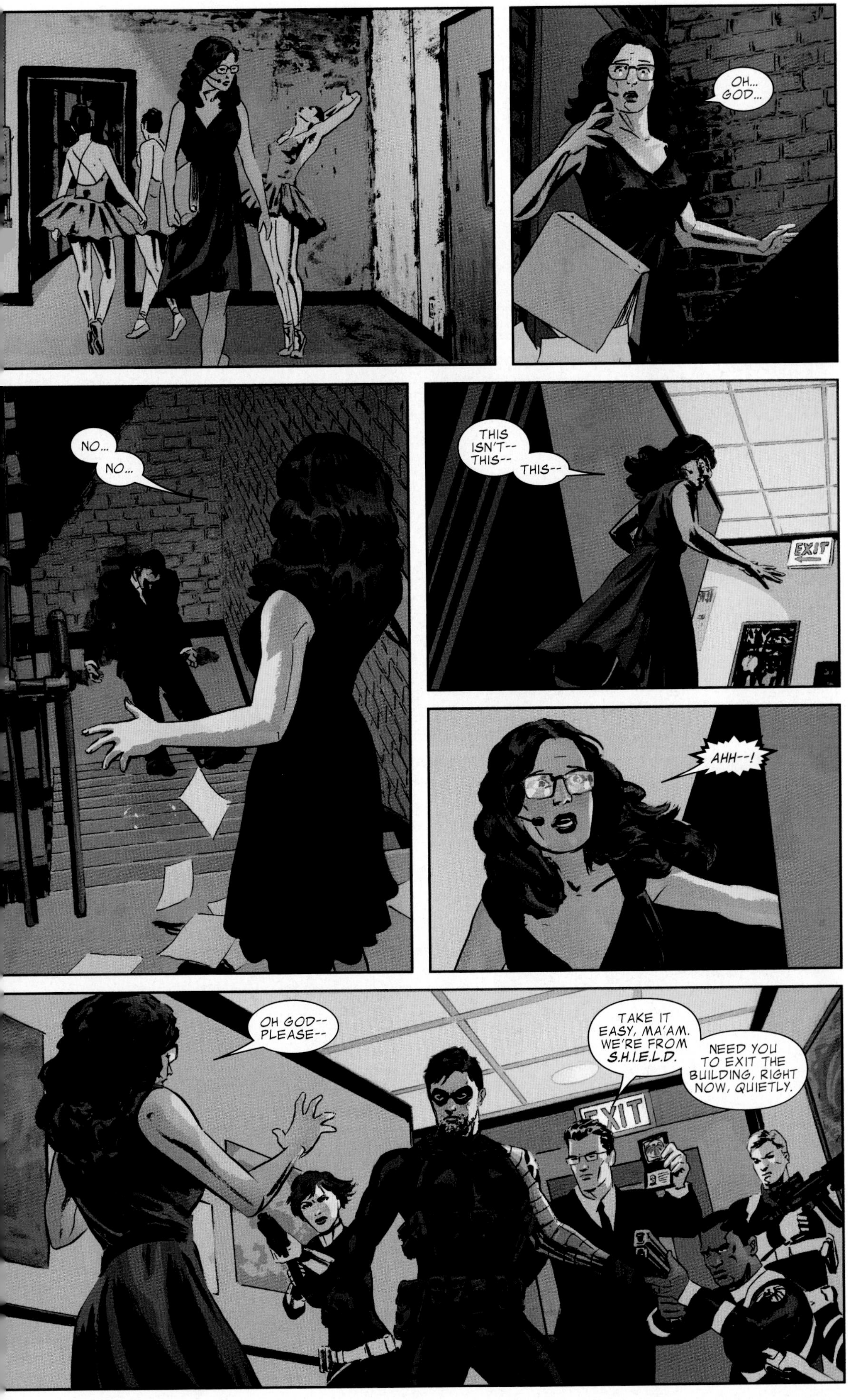

OH... GOD...
NO... NO...
THIS ISN'T-- THIS--
THIS--
AHH--!
OH GOD-- PLEASE--
TAKE IT EASY, MA'AM. WE'RE FROM S.H.I.E.L.D.
NEED YOU TO EXIT THE BUILDING, RIGHT NOW, QUIETLY.

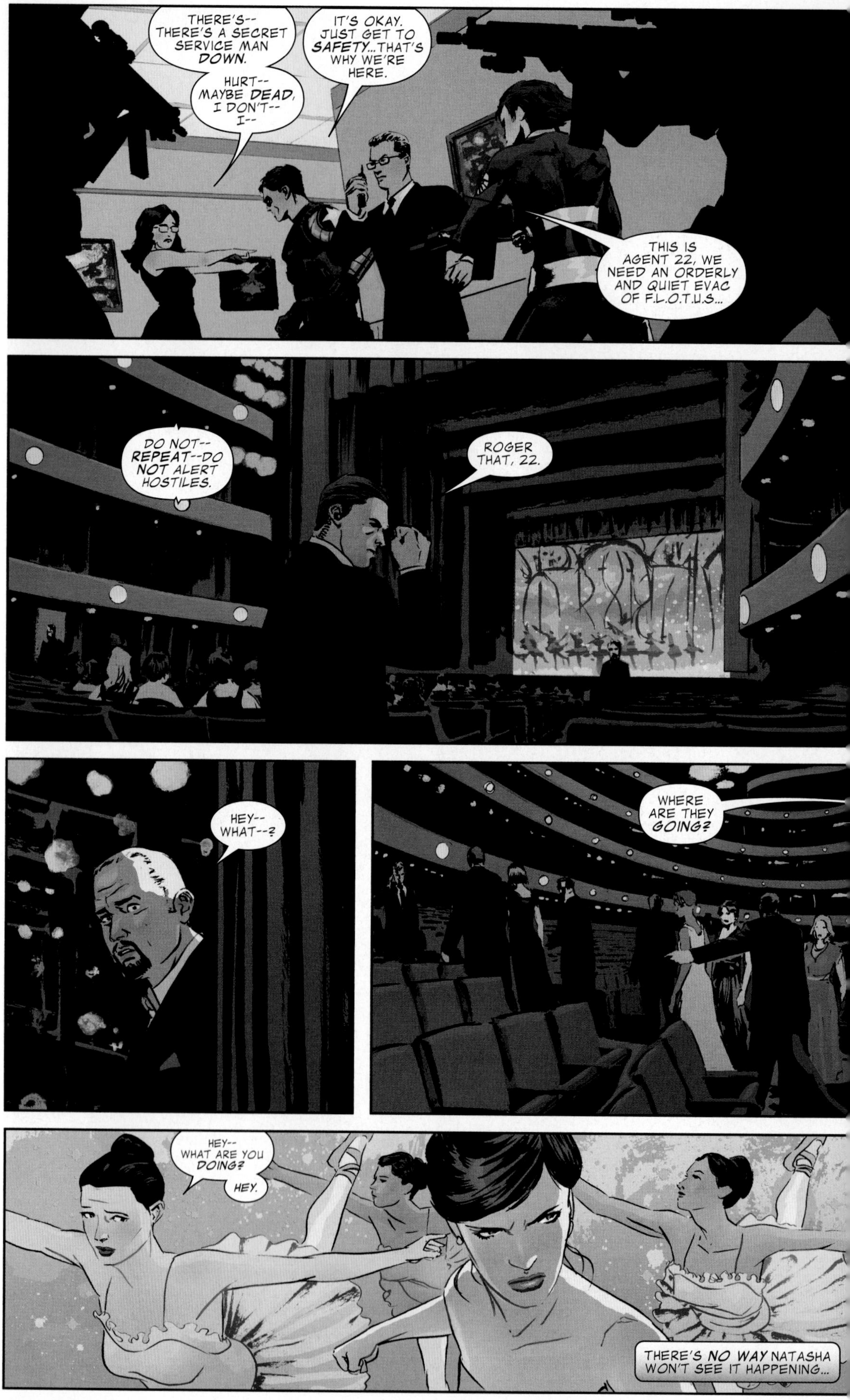
THERE'S-- THERE'S A SECRET SERVICE MAN DOWN.
HURT-- MAYBE DEAD, I DON'T-- I--
IT'S OKAY. JUST GET TO SAFETY...THAT'S WHY WE'RE HERE.
THIS IS AGENT 22, WE NEED AN ORDERLY AND QUIET EVAC OF F.L.O.T.U.S...
DO NOT-- REPEAT--DO NOT ALERT HOSTILES.
ROGER THAT, 22.
HEY-- WHAT--?
WHERE ARE THEY GOING?
HEY-- WHAT ARE YOU DOING?
HEY.
THERE'S NO WAY NATASHA WON'T SEE IT HAPPENING...

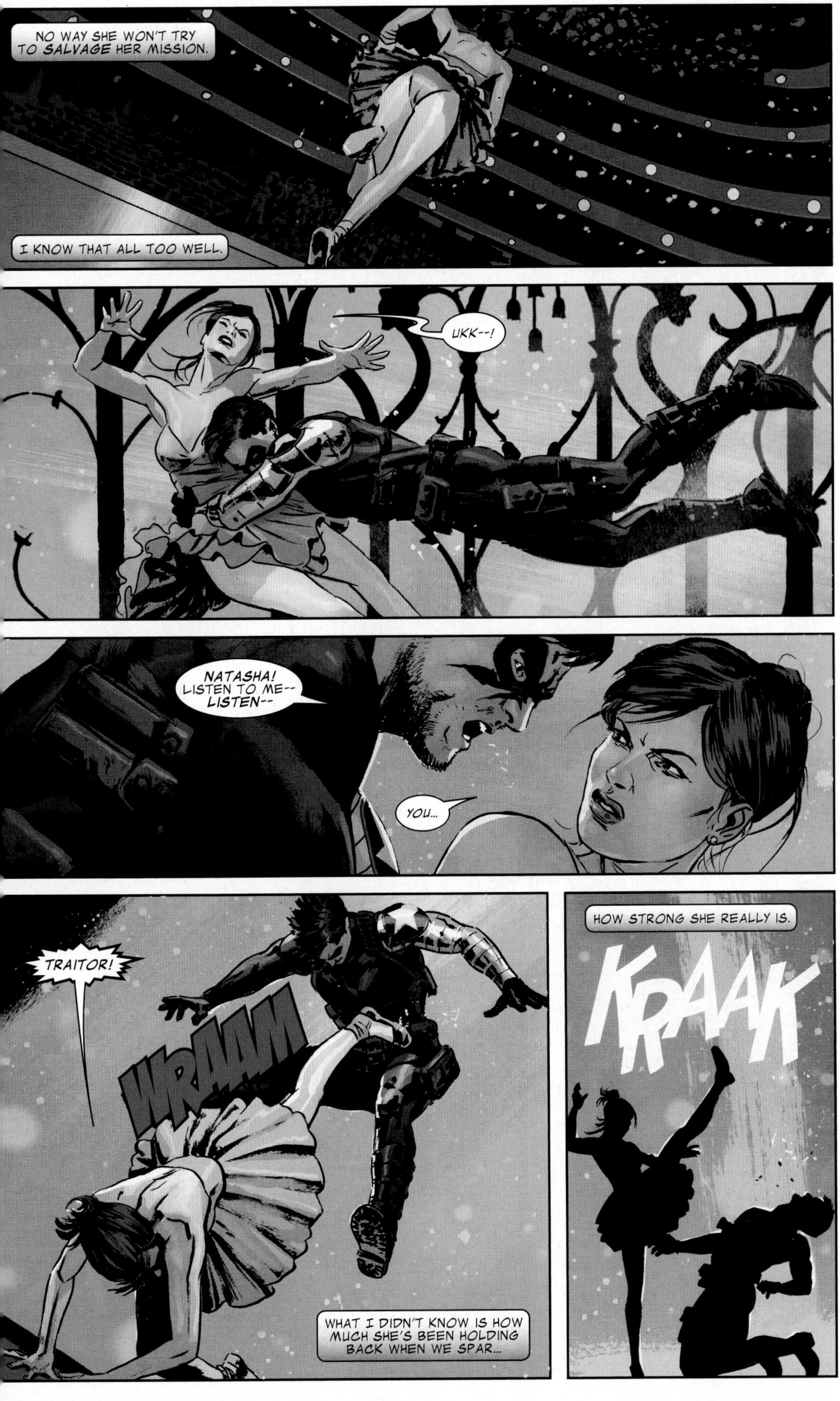
NO WAY SHE WON'T TRY TO SALVAGE HER MISSION.
I KNOW THAT ALL TOO WELL.
UKK--!
NATASHA! LISTEN TO ME-- LISTEN--
YOU...
TRAITOR!
WRAAM
WHAT I DIDN'T KNOW IS HOW MUCH SHE'S BEEN HOLDING BACK WHEN WE SPAR...
HOW STRONG SHE REALLY IS.
KRAAK

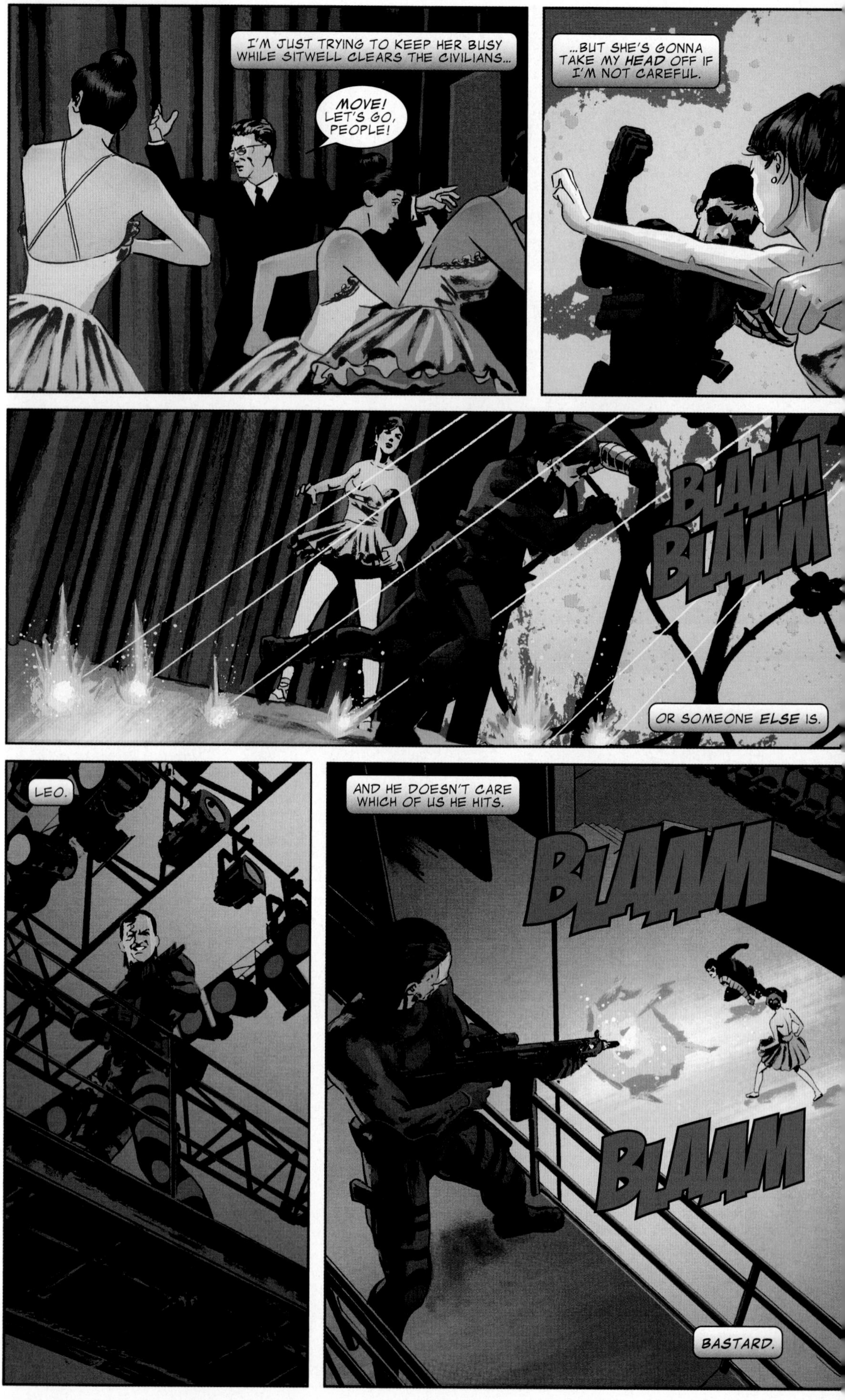
I'M JUST TRYING TO KEEP HER BUSY WHILE SITWELL CLEARS THE CIVILIANS...
MOVE! LET'S GO, PEOPLE!
...BUT SHE'S GONNA TAKE MY HEAD OFF IF I'M NOT CAREFUL.
BLAAAM
BLAAAM
OR SOMEONE ELSE IS.
LEO.
AND HE DOESN'T CARE WHICH OF US HE HITS.
BLAAAM
BLAAAM
BASTARD.

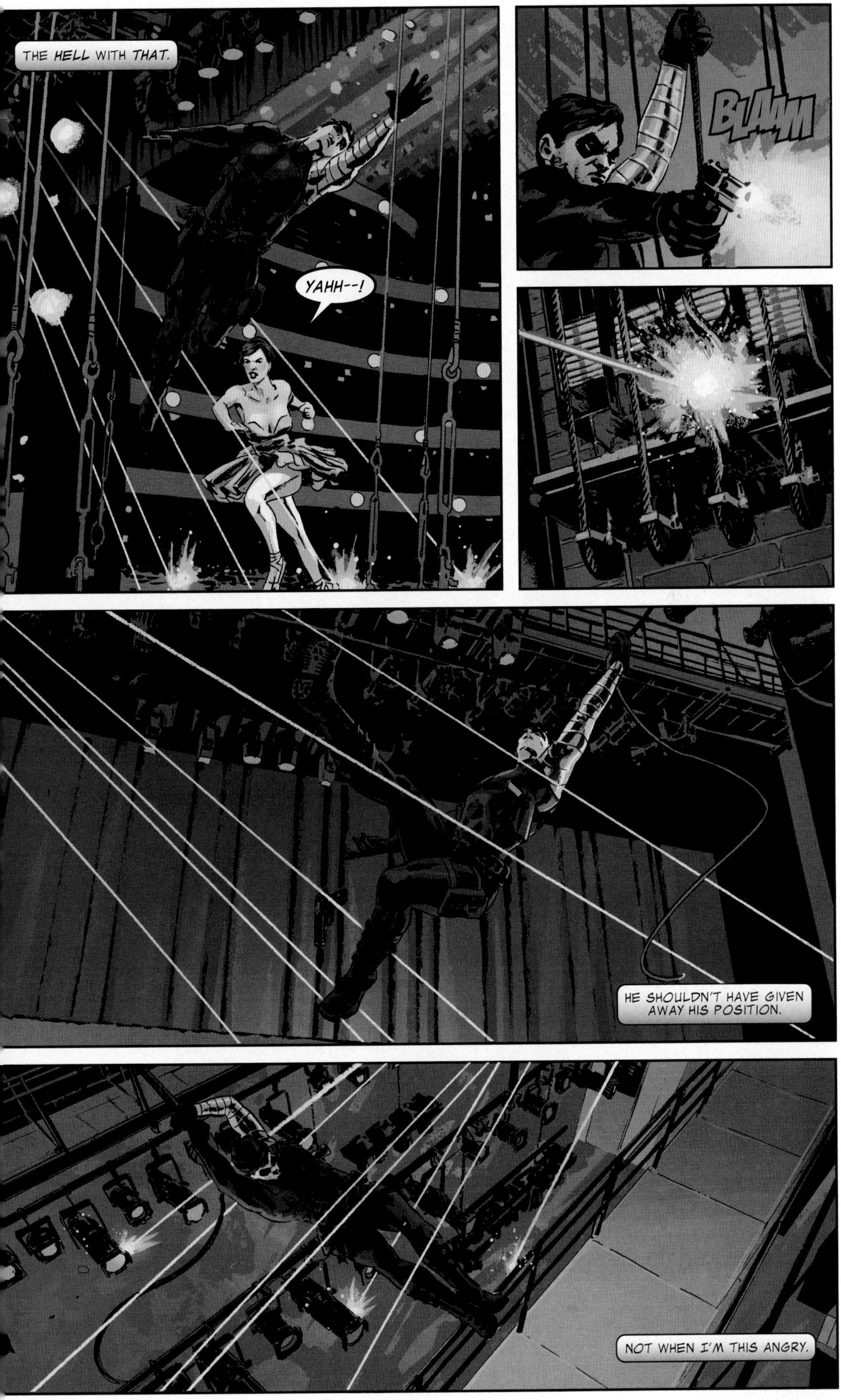
THE HELL WITH THAT.
YAHH--!
BLAAAM
HE SHOULDN'T HAVE GIVEN AWAY HIS POSITION.
NOT WHEN I'M THIS ANGRY.

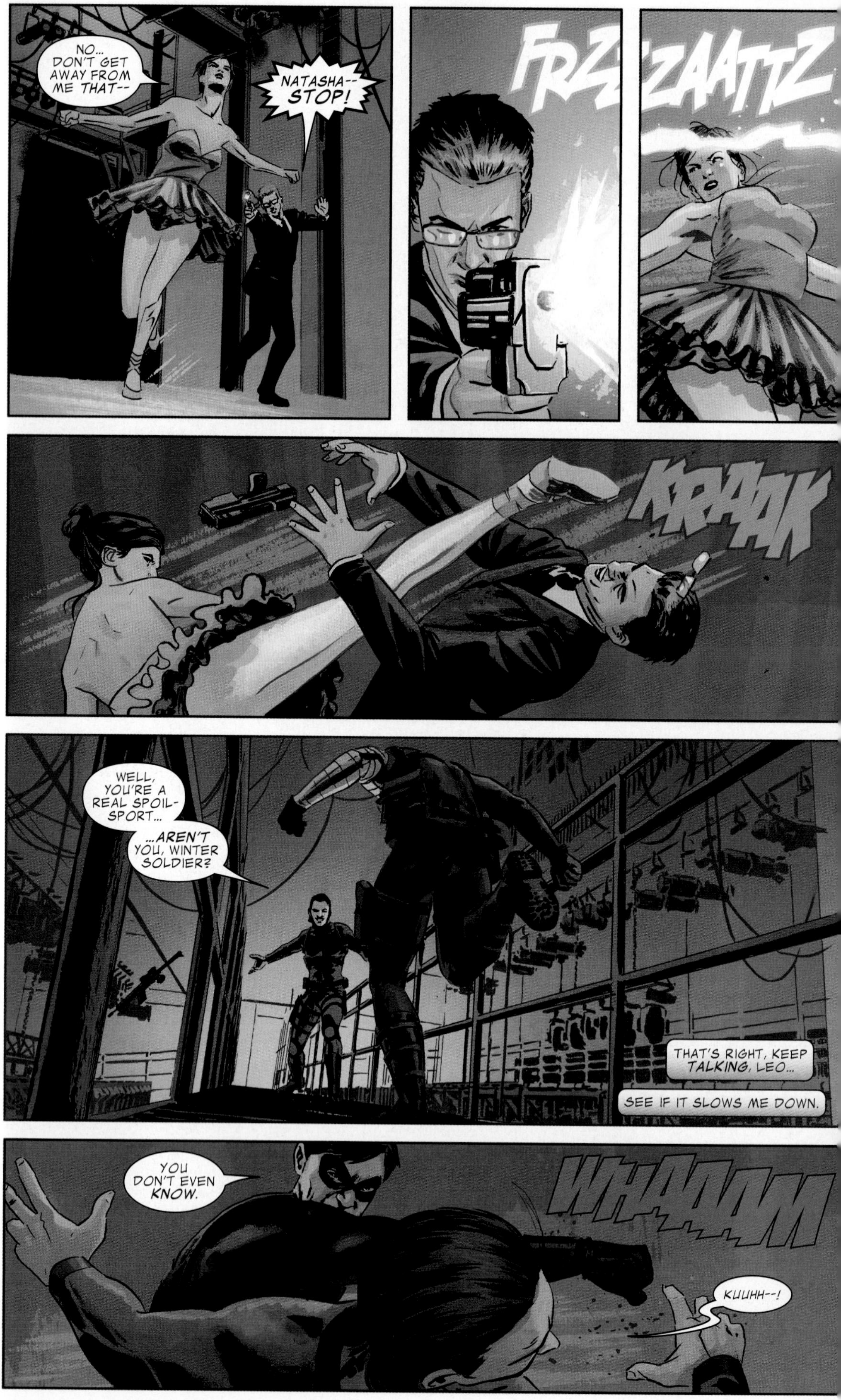
NO... DON'T GET AWAY FROM ME THAT--
NATASHA-- STOP!
FRZZZZAATTZ
KRAAAK
WELL, YOU'RE A REAL SPOIL-SPORT...
...AREN'T YOU, WINTER SOLDIER?
THAT'S RIGHT, KEEP TALKING, LEO...
SEE IF IT SLOWS ME DOWN.
YOU DON'T EVEN KNOW.
WHAAAM
KUUHH--!

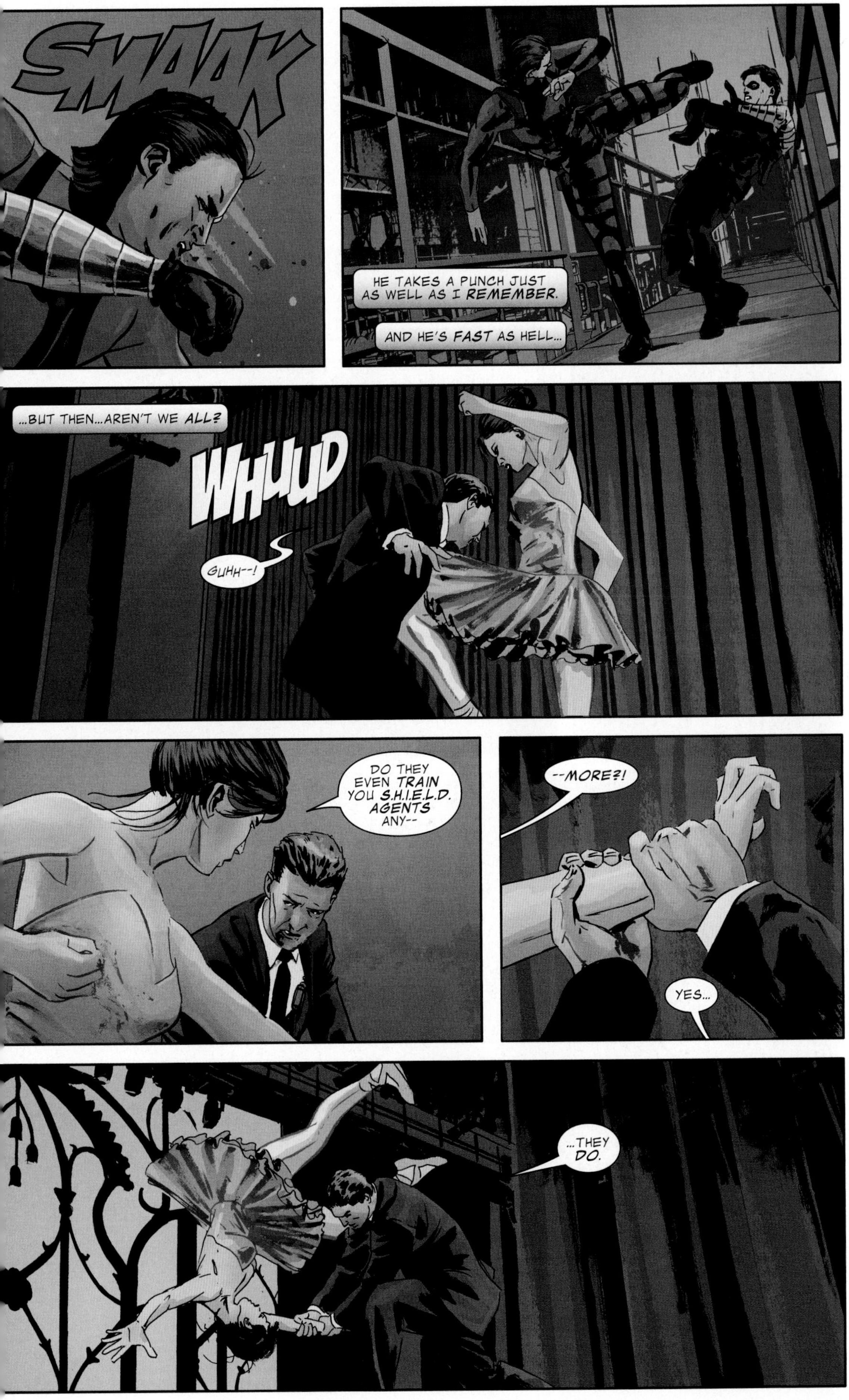
SMAAK
HE TAKES A PUNCH JUST AS WELL AS I REMEMBER.
AND HE'S FAST AS HELL...
...BUT THEN...AREN'T WE ALL?
WHUUD
GUHH--!
DO THEY EVEN TRAIN YOU S.H.I.E.L.D. AGENTS ANY--
--MORE?!
YES...
...THEY DO.

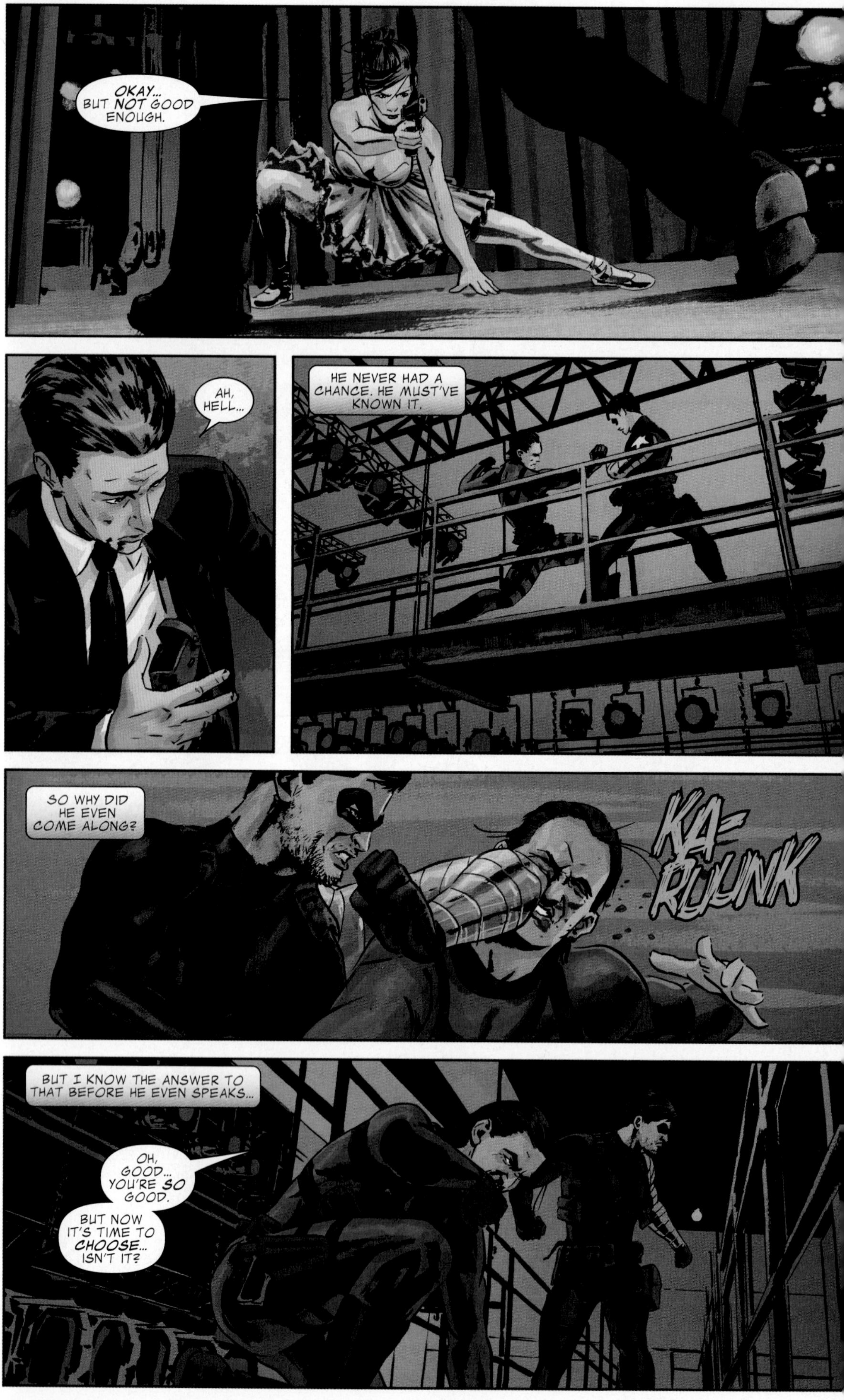
OKAY... BUT NOT GOOD ENOUGH.
AH, HELL...
HE NEVER HAD A CHANCE. HE MUST'VE KNOWN IT.
SO WHY DID HE EVEN COME ALONG?
KA-RUUNK
BUT I KNOW THE ANSWER TO THAT BEFORE HE EVEN SPEAKS...
OH, GOOD... YOU'RE SO GOOD.
BUT NOW IT'S TIME TO CHOOSE... ISN'T IT?

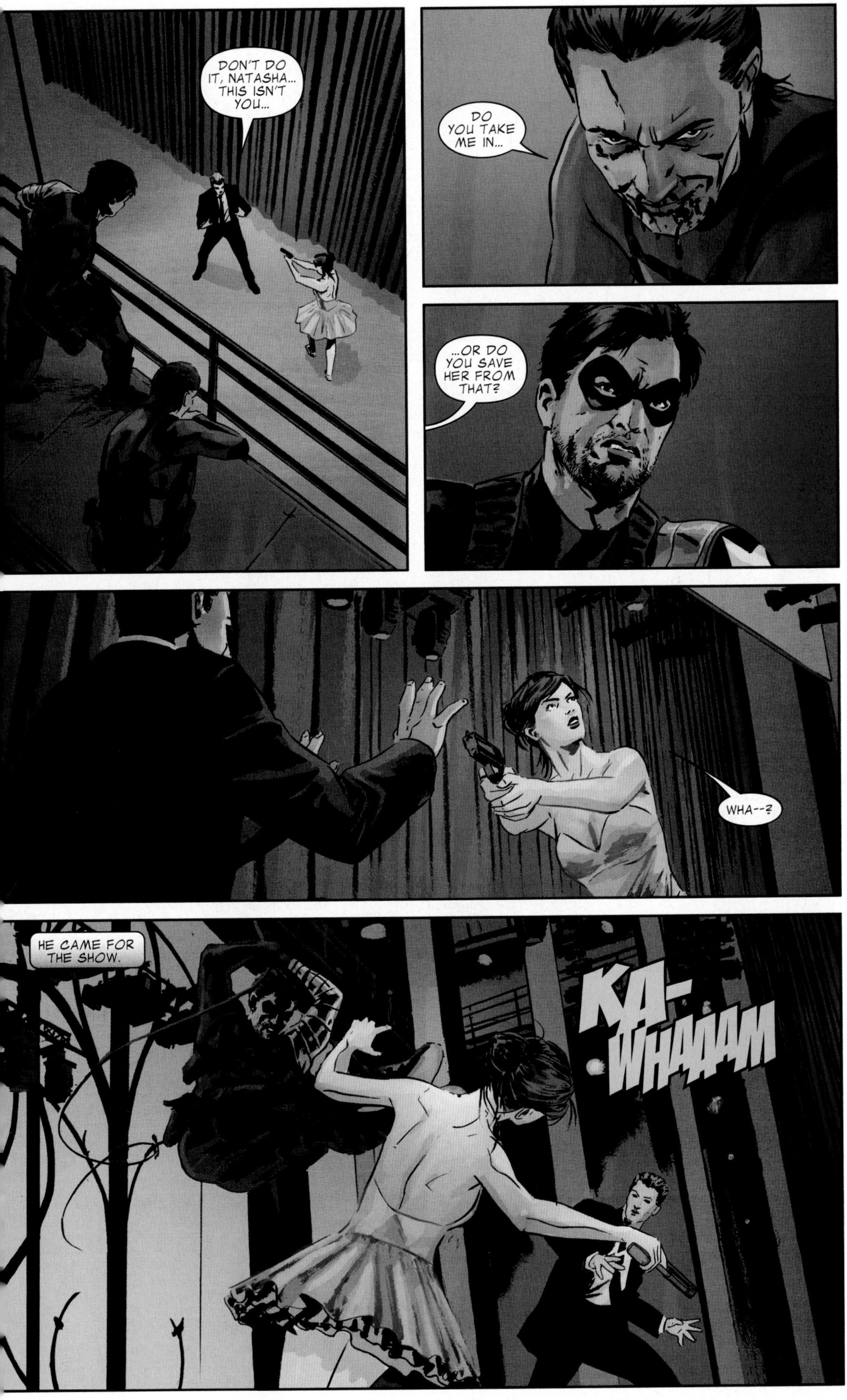
DON'T DO IT, NATASHA... THIS ISN'T YOU...
DO YOU TAKE ME IN...
...OR DO YOU SAVE HER FROM THAT?
WHA--?
HE CAME FOR THE SHOW.
KA-WHAAAM

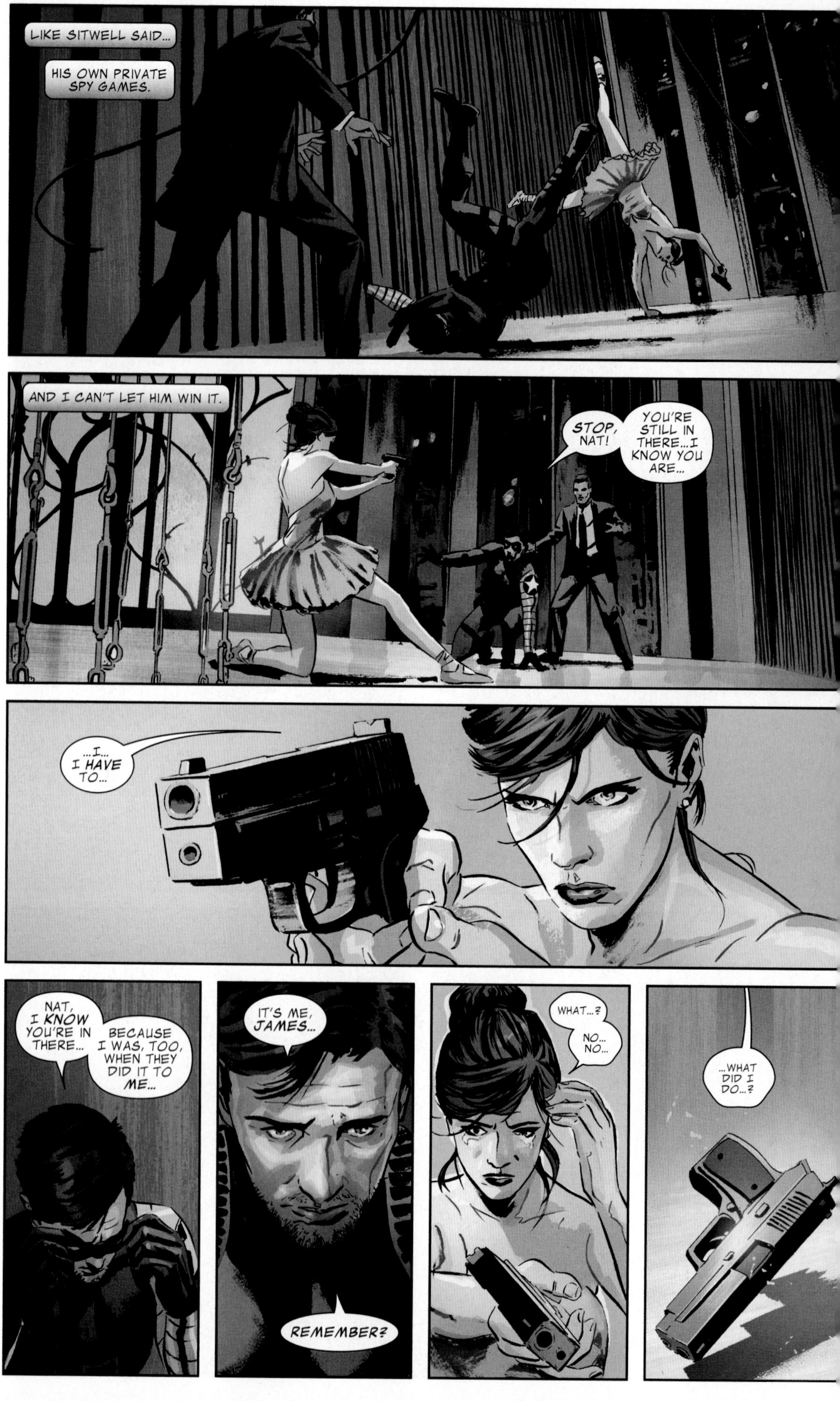
LIKE SITWELL SAID...
HIS OWN PRIVATE SPY GAMES.
AND I CAN'T LET HIM WIN IT.
STOP, NAT!
YOU'RE STILL IN THERE...I KNOW YOU ARE...
...I... I *HAVE* TO...
NAT, I *KNOW* YOU'RE IN THERE...
BECAUSE I WAS, TOO, WHEN THEY DID IT TO *ME*...
IT'S ME, *JAMES*...
REMEMBER?
WHAT...?
NO... NO...
...WHAT DID I DO...?

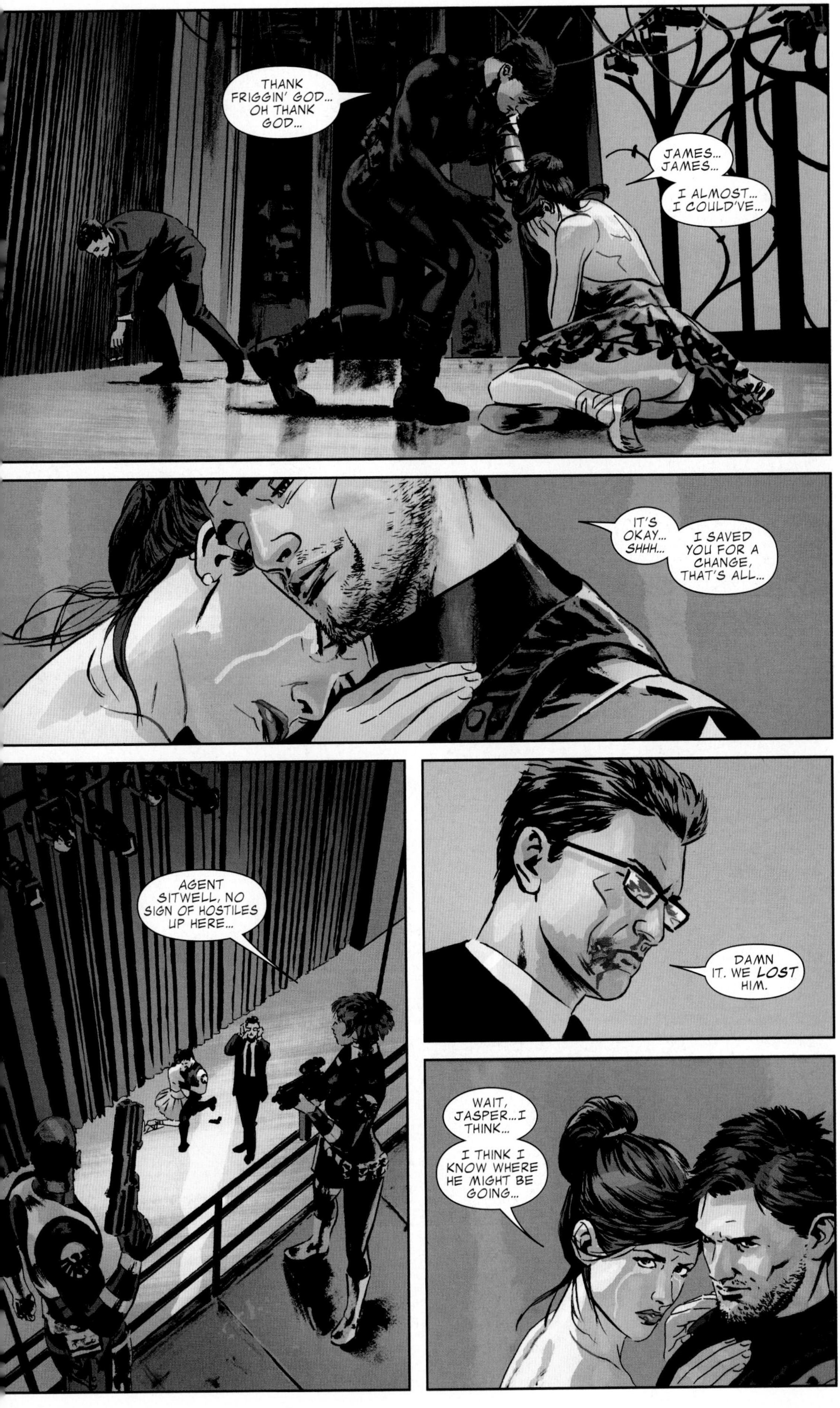

THANK FRIGGIN' GOD... OH THANK GOD...
JAMES... JAMES...
I ALMOST... I COULD'VE...
IT'S OKAY... SHHH...
I SAVED YOU FOR A CHANGE, THAT'S ALL...
AGENT SITWELL, NO SIGN OF HOSTILES UP HERE...
DAMN IT. WE LOST HIM.
WAIT, JASPER...I THINK...
I THINK I KNOW WHERE HE MIGHT BE GOING...

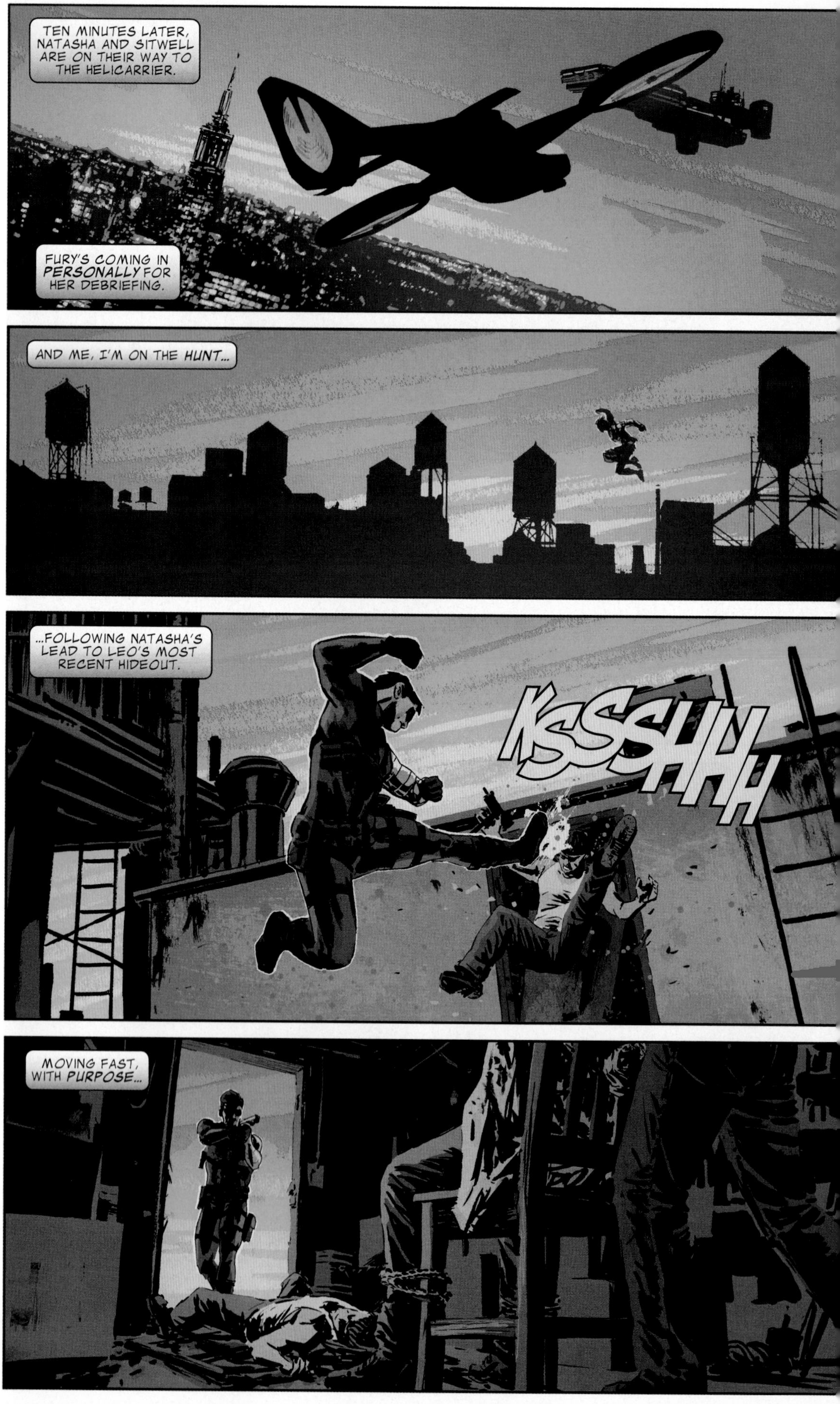
TEN MINUTES LATER, NATASHA AND SITWELL ARE ON THEIR WAY TO THE HELICARRIER.
FURY'S COMING IN *PERSONALLY* FOR HER DEBRIEFING.
AND ME, I'M ON THE *HUNT*...
...FOLLOWING NATASHA'S LEAD TO LEO'S MOST RECENT HIDEOUT.
KSSSHHH
MOVING FAST, WITH *PURPOSE*...

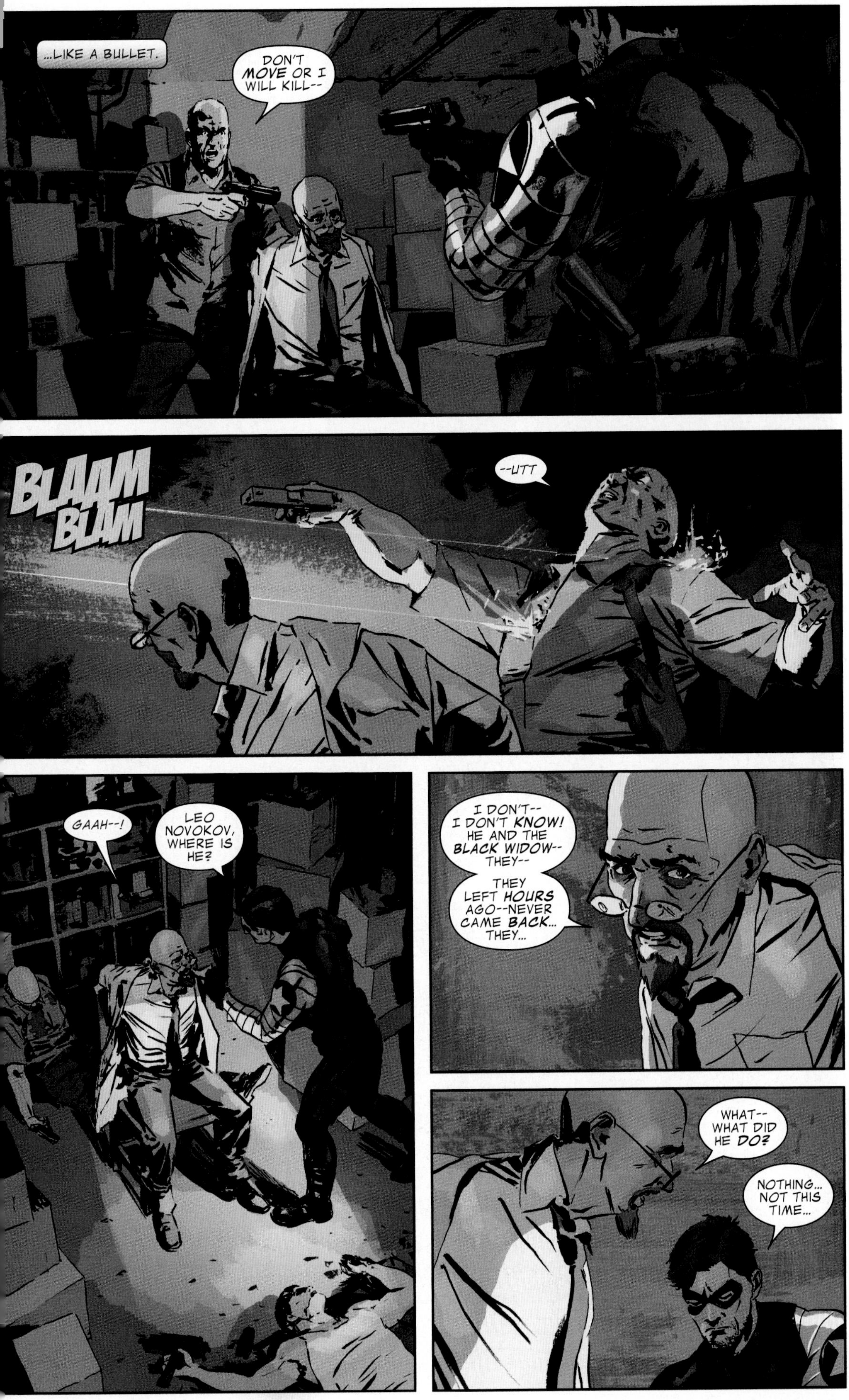
...LIKE A BULLET.
DON'T MOVE OR I WILL KILL--
BLAAM BLAM
--UTT
GAAH--!
LEO NOVOKOV, WHERE IS HE?
I DON'T-- I DON'T KNOW! HE AND THE BLACK WIDOW-- THEY--
THEY LEFT HOURS AGO--NEVER CAME BACK... THEY...
WHAT-- WHAT DID HE DO?
NOTHING... NOT THIS TIME...

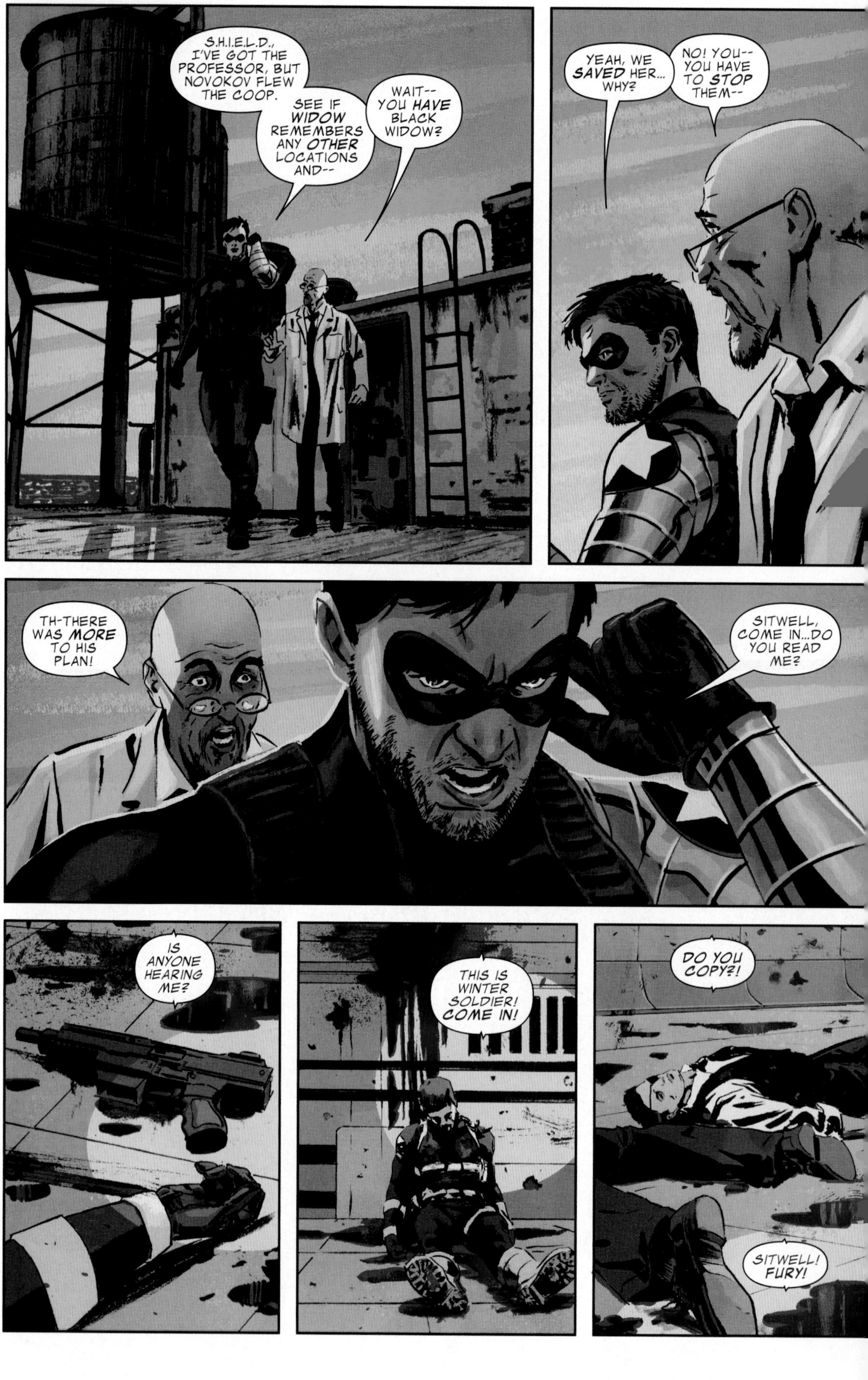
S.H.I.E.L.D., I'VE GOT THE PROFESSOR, BUT NOVOKOV FLEW THE COOP.
SEE IF WIDOW REMEMBERS ANY OTHER LOCATIONS AND--
WAIT-- YOU HAVE BLACK WIDOW?
YEAH, WE SAVED HER... WHY?
NO! YOU-- YOU HAVE TO STOP THEM--
TH-THERE WAS MORE TO HIS PLAN!
SITWELL, COME IN...DO YOU READ ME?
IS ANYONE HEARING ME?
THIS IS WINTER SOLDIER! COME IN!
DO YOU COPY?!
SITWELL! FURY!

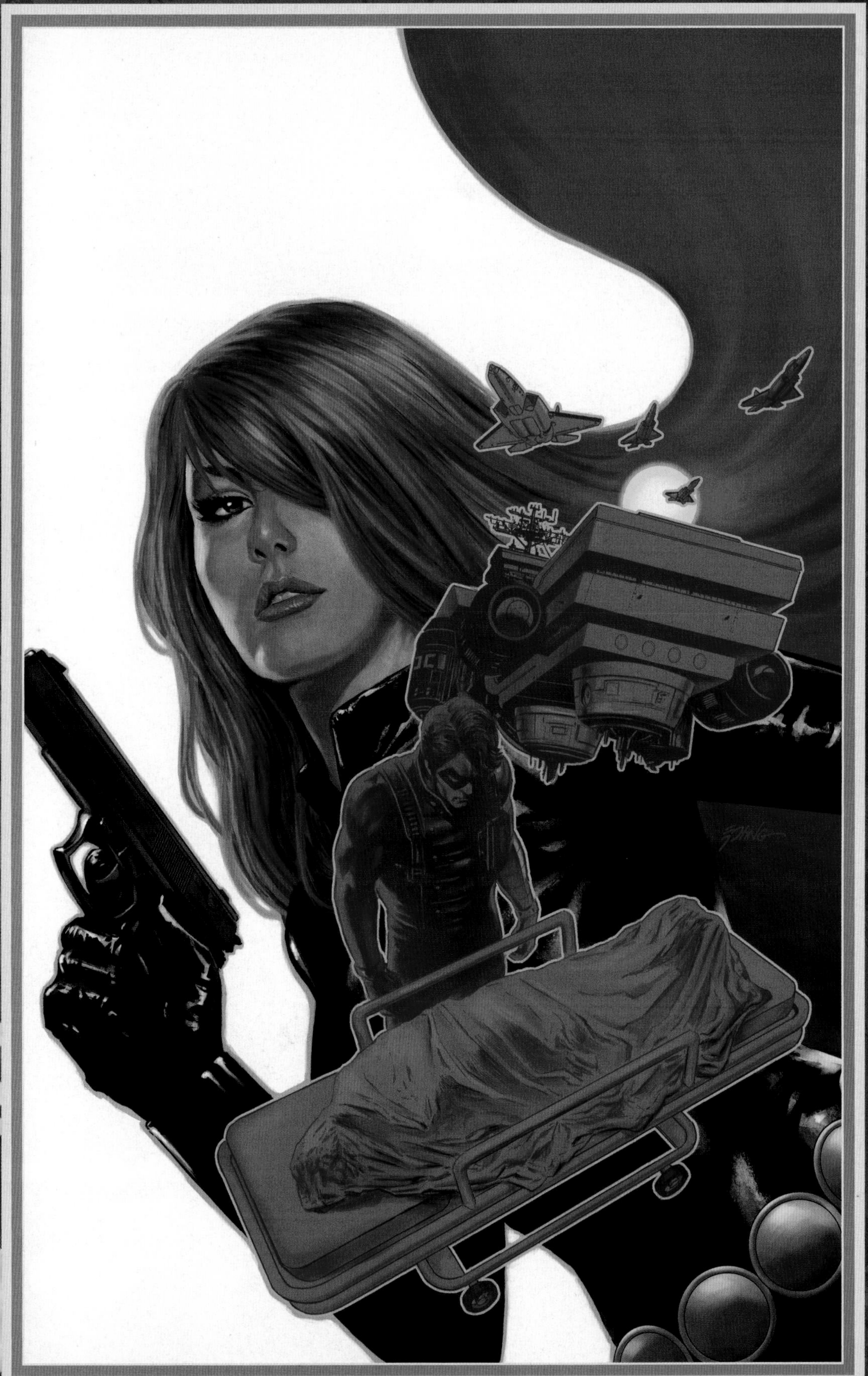

TEN

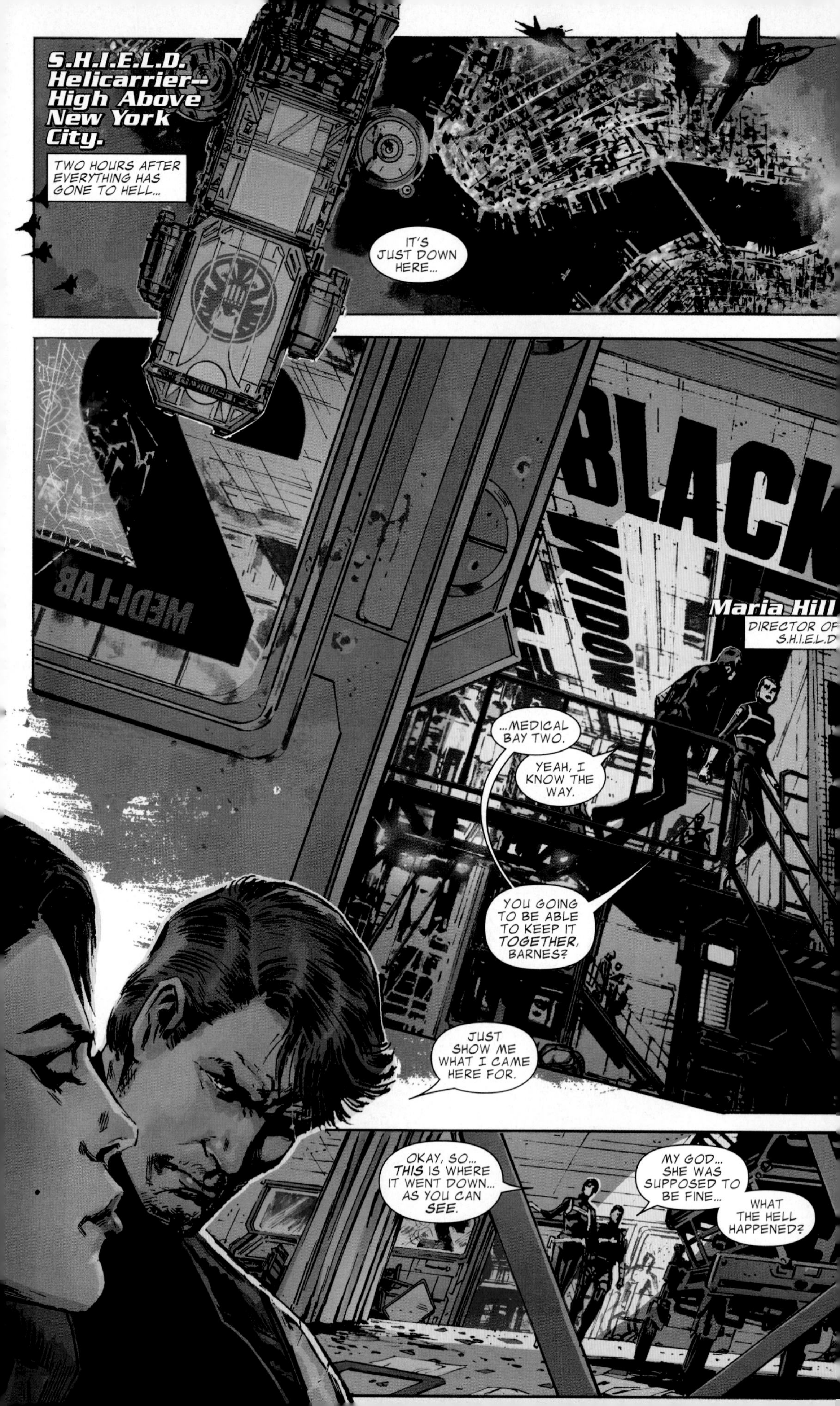

S.H.I.E.L.D. Helicarrier-- High Above New York City.
TWO HOURS AFTER EVERYTHING HAS GONE TO HELL...
IT'S JUST DOWN HERE...
MEDI-LAB
BLACK WIDOW
Maria Hill
DIRECTOR OF S.H.I.E.L.D
...MEDICAL BAY TWO.
YEAH, I KNOW THE WAY.
YOU GOING TO BE ABLE TO KEEP IT TOGETHER, BARNES?
JUST SHOW ME WHAT I CAME HERE FOR.
OKAY, SO... THIS IS WHERE IT WENT DOWN... AS YOU CAN SEE.
MY GOD... SHE WAS SUPPOSED TO BE FINE...
WHAT THE HELL HAPPENED?

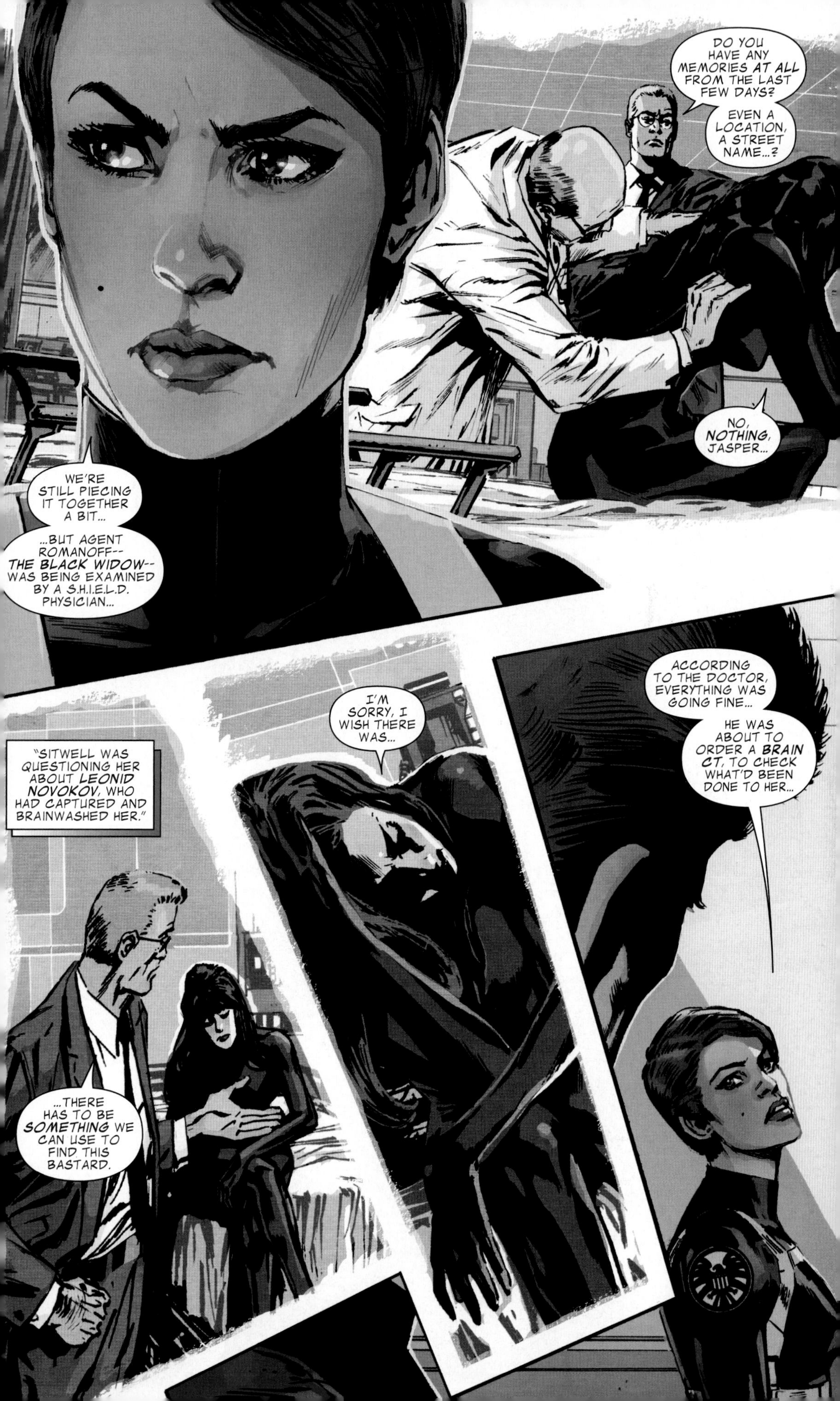

DO YOU HAVE ANY MEMORIES AT ALL FROM THE LAST FEW DAYS?
EVEN A LOCATION, A STREET NAME...?
NO, NOTHING, JASPER...
WE'RE STILL PIECING IT TOGETHER A BIT...
...BUT AGENT ROMANOFF-- THE BLACK WIDOW-- WAS BEING EXAMINED BY A S.H.I.E.L.D. PHYSICIAN...
"SITWELL WAS QUESTIONING HER ABOUT LEONID NOVOKOV, WHO HAD CAPTURED AND BRAINWASHED HER."
...THERE HAS TO BE SOMETHING WE CAN USE TO FIND THIS BASTARD.
I'M SORRY, I WISH THERE WAS...
ACCORDING TO THE DOCTOR, EVERYTHING WAS GOING FINE...
HE WAS ABOUT TO ORDER A BRAIN CT, TO CHECK WHAT'D BEEN DONE TO HER...

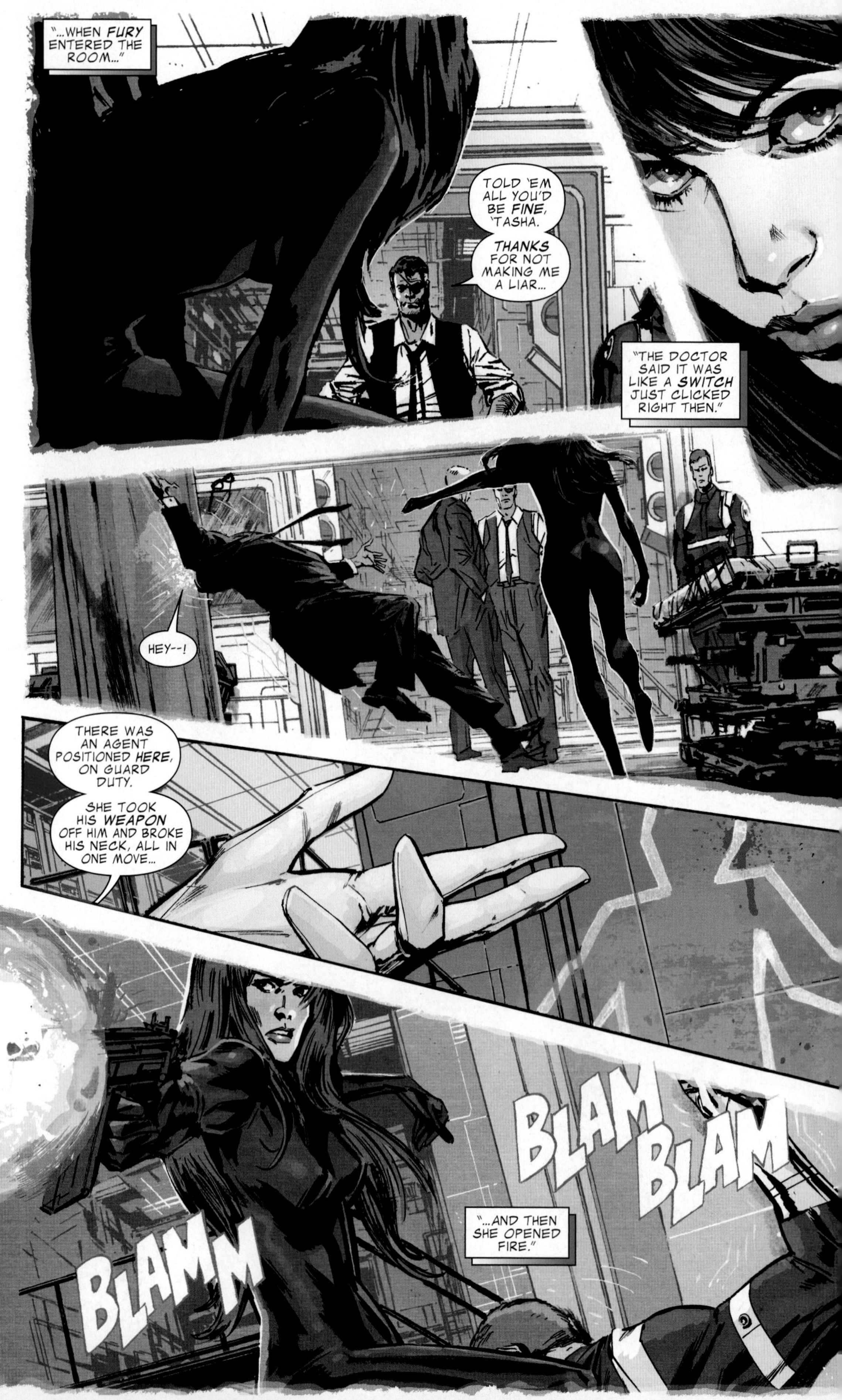

"...WHEN FURY ENTERED THE ROOM..."
TOLD 'EM ALL YOU'D BE FINE, 'TASHA.
THANKS FOR NOT MAKING ME A LIAR...
"THE DOCTOR SAID IT WAS LIKE A SWITCH JUST CLICKED RIGHT THEN."
HEY--!
THERE WAS AN AGENT POSITIONED HERE, ON GUARD DUTY.
SHE TOOK HIS WEAPON OFF HIM AND BROKE HIS NECK, ALL IN ONE MOVE...
BLAM
BLAM
"...AND THEN SHE OPENED FIRE."
BLAMM

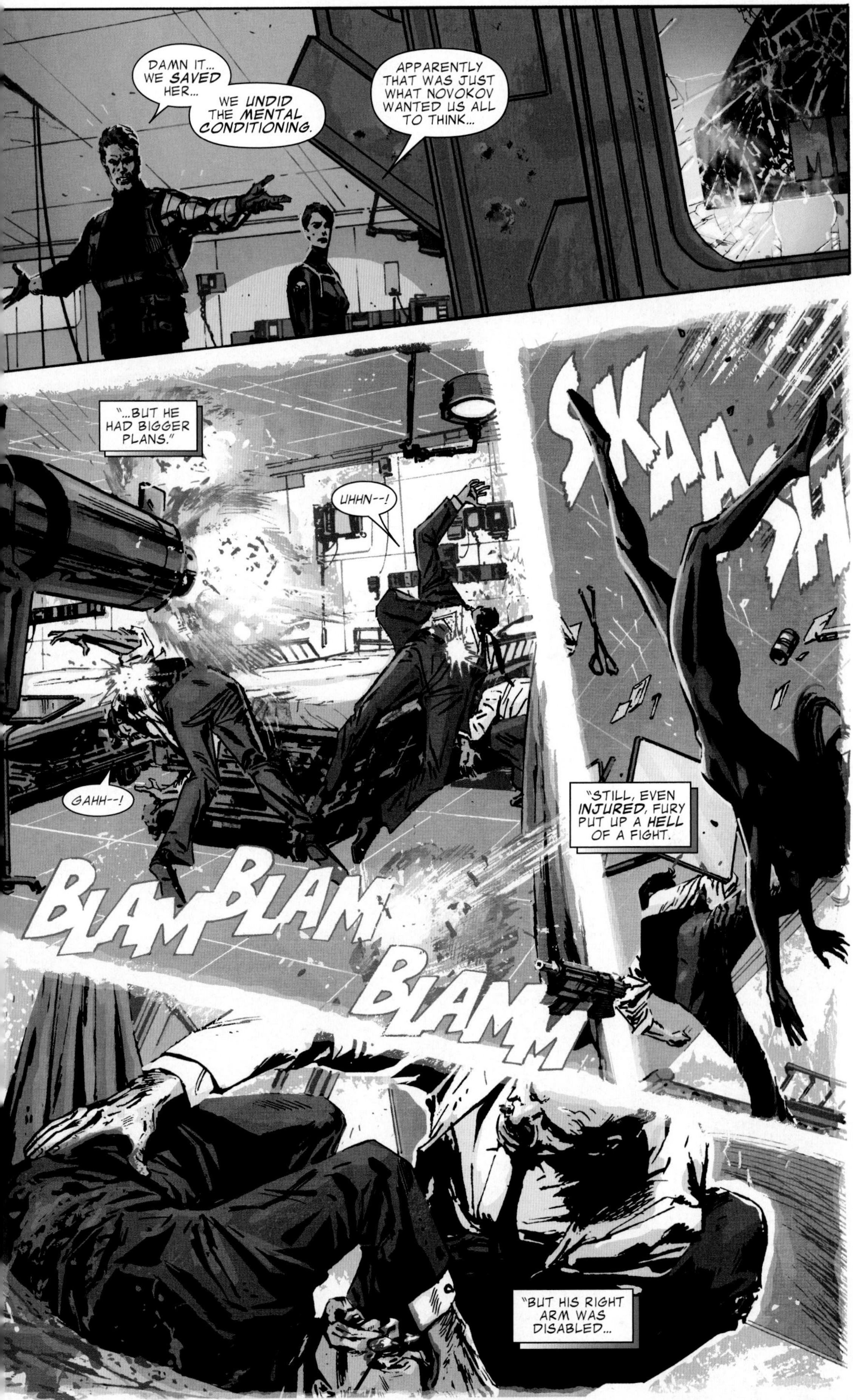
DAMN IT... WE SAVED HER...
WE UNDID THE MENTAL CONDITIONING.
APPARENTLY THAT WAS JUST WHAT NOVOKOV WANTED US ALL TO THINK...
"...BUT HE HAD BIGGER PLANS."
UHHN--!
GAHH--!
SKAAAASH
"STILL, EVEN INJURED, FURY PUT UP A HELL OF A FIGHT.
BLAM BLAM
BLAMM
"BUT HIS RIGHT ARM WAS DISABLED...

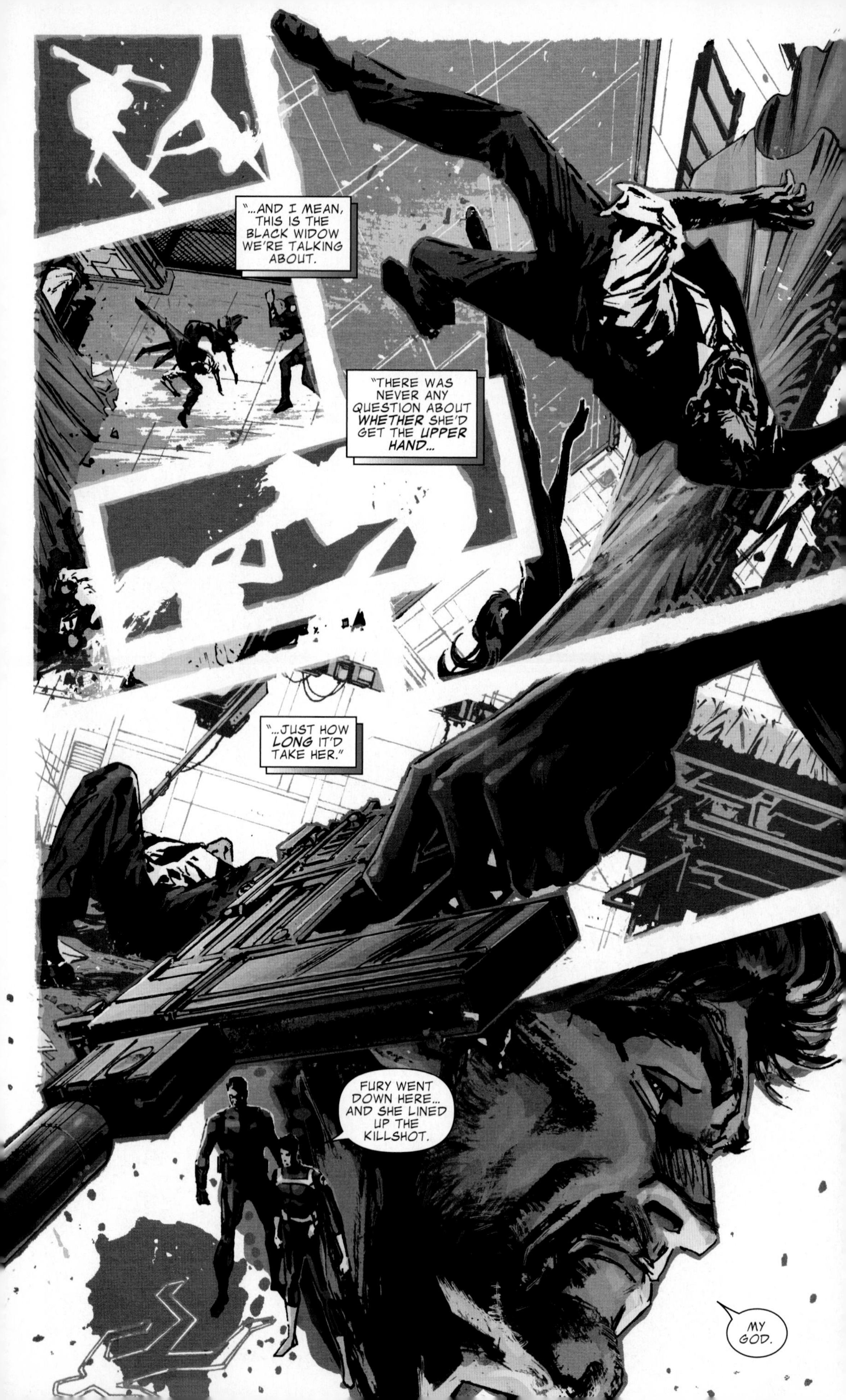
"...AND I MEAN, THIS IS THE BLACK WIDOW WE'RE TALKING ABOUT.
"THERE WAS NEVER ANY QUESTION ABOUT WHETHER SHE'D GET THE UPPER HAND...
"...JUST HOW LONG IT'D TAKE HER."
FURY WENT DOWN HERE... AND SHE LINED UP THE KILLSHOT.
MY GOD.

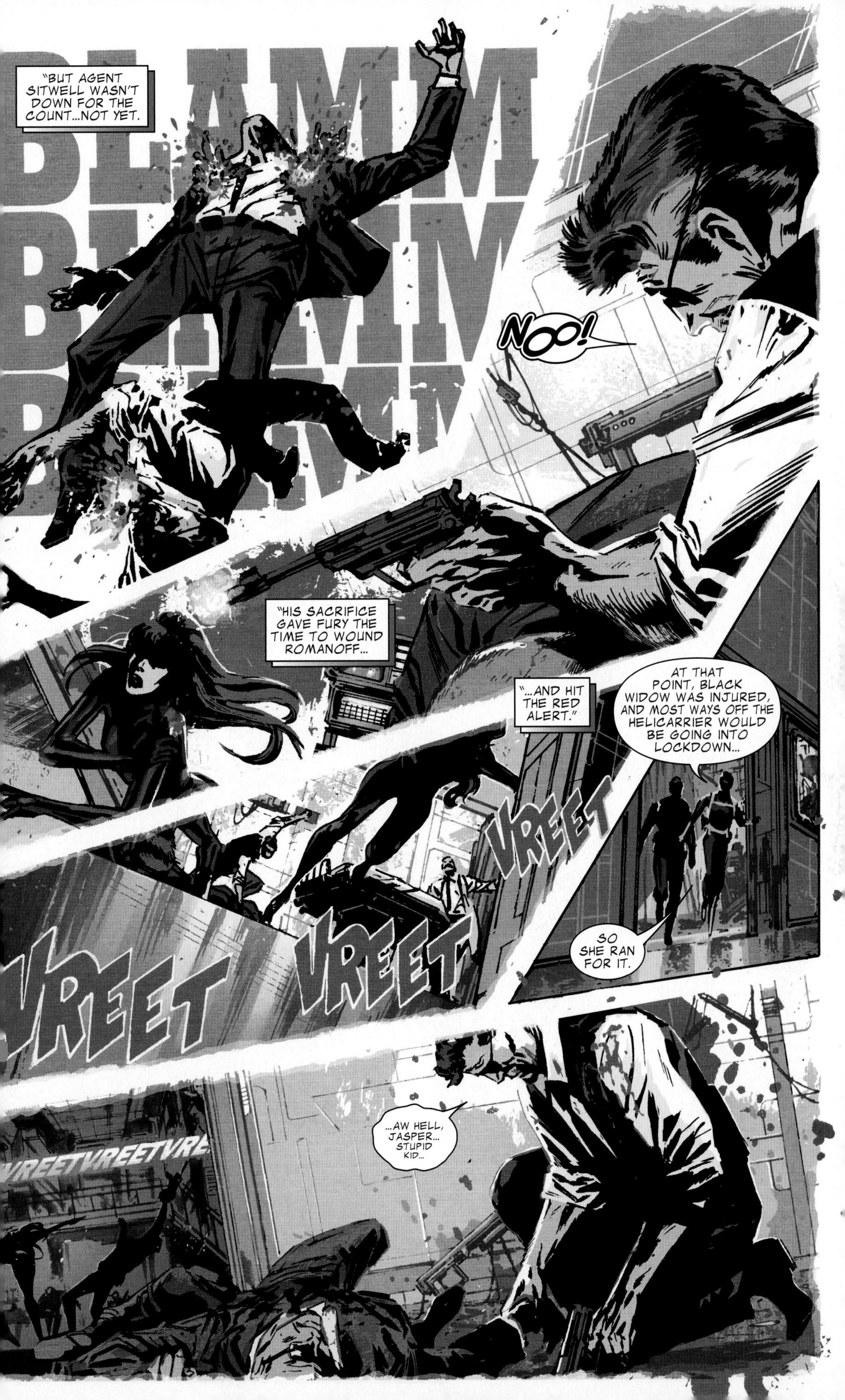
"BUT AGENT SITWELL WASN'T DOWN FOR THE COUNT...NOT YET.
BLAMM BLAMM BLAMM BLAMM
NOO!
"HIS SACRIFICE GAVE FURY THE TIME TO WOUND ROMANOFF...
"...AND HIT THE RED ALERT."
AT THAT POINT, BLACK WIDOW WAS INJURED, AND MOST WAYS OFF THE HELICARRIER WOULD BE GOING INTO LOCKDOWN...
VREET
VREET
VREET
SO SHE RAN FOR IT.
VREETVREETVRE
...AW HELL, JASPER... STUPID KID...

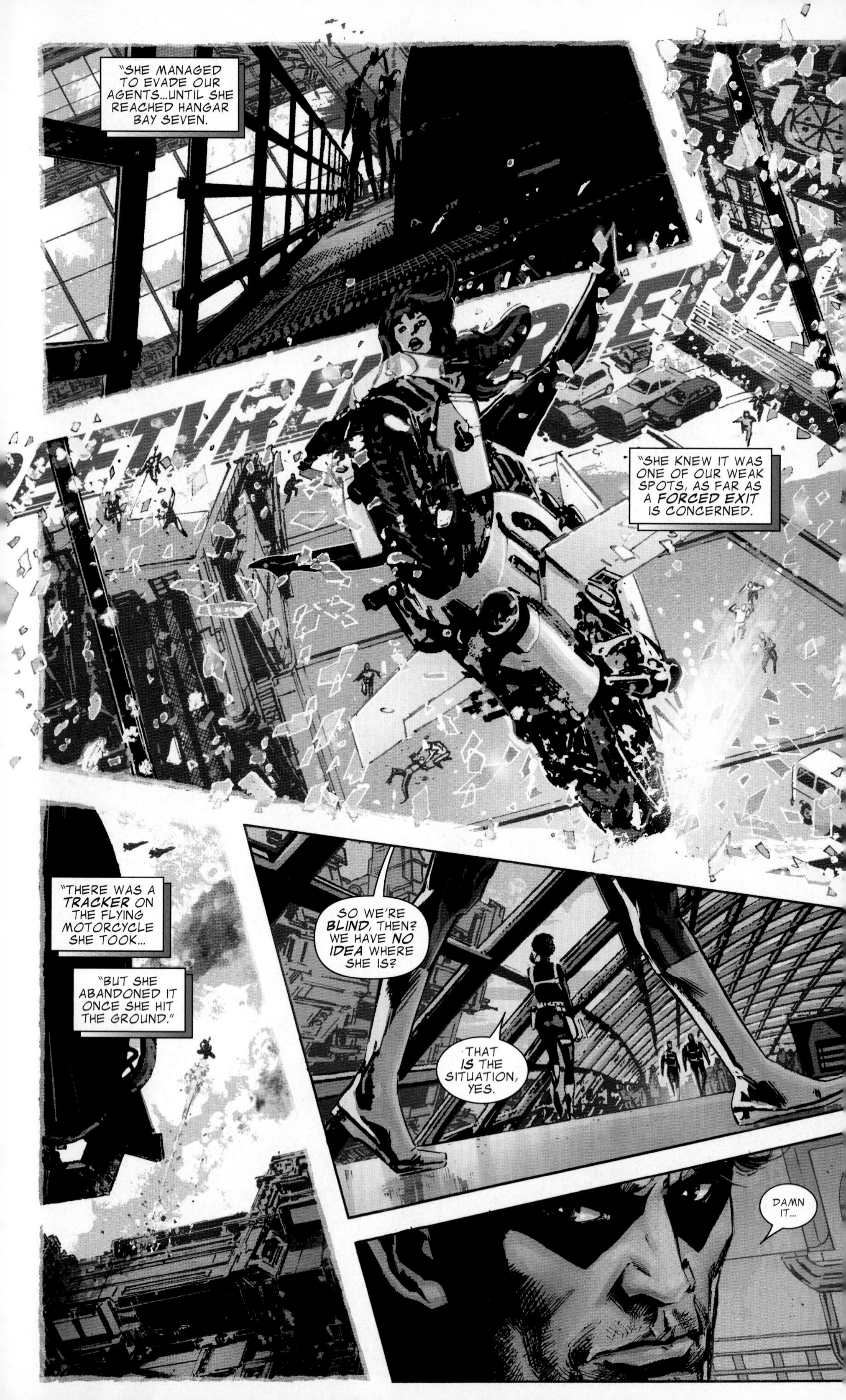
"SHE MANAGED TO EVADE OUR AGENTS...UNTIL SHE REACHED HANGAR BAY SEVEN.
"SHE KNEW IT WAS ONE OF OUR WEAK SPOTS, AS FAR AS A FORCED EXIT IS CONCERNED.
"THERE WAS A TRACKER ON THE FLYING MOTORCYCLE SHE TOOK...
"BUT SHE ABANDONED IT ONCE SHE HIT THE GROUND."
SO WE'RE BLIND, THEN? WE HAVE NO IDEA WHERE SHE IS?
THAT IS THE SITUATION, YES.
DAMN IT...

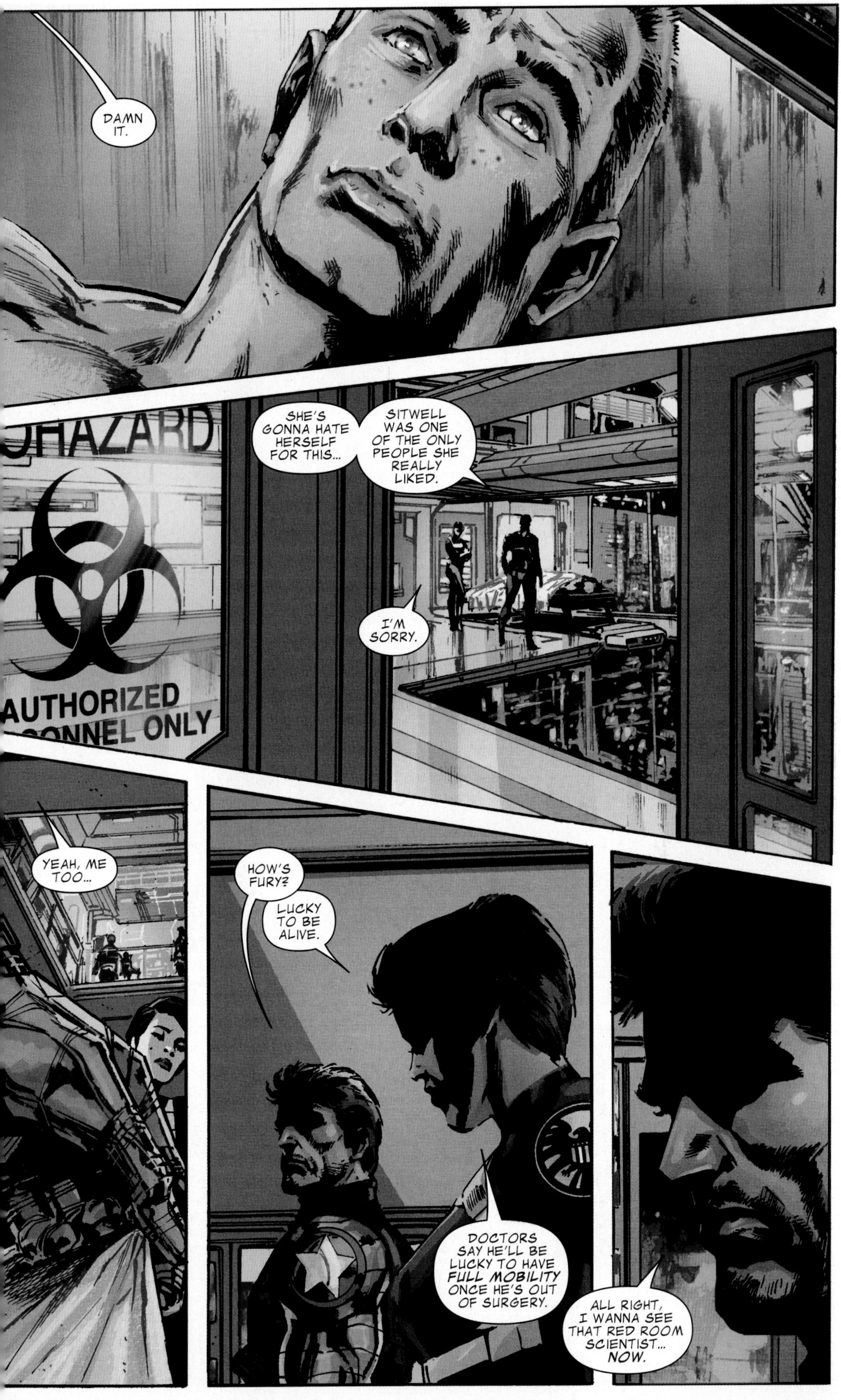
DAMN IT.
BIOHAZARD
AUTHORIZED PERSONNEL ONLY
SHE'S GONNA HATE HERSELF FOR THIS...
SITWELL WAS ONE OF THE ONLY PEOPLE SHE REALLY LIKED.
I'M SORRY.
YEAH, ME TOO...
HOW'S FURY?
LUCKY TO BE ALIVE.
DOCTORS SAY HE'LL BE LUCKY TO HAVE FULL MOBILITY ONCE HE'S OUT OF SURGERY.
ALL RIGHT, I WANNA SEE THAT RED ROOM SCIENTIST... NOW.

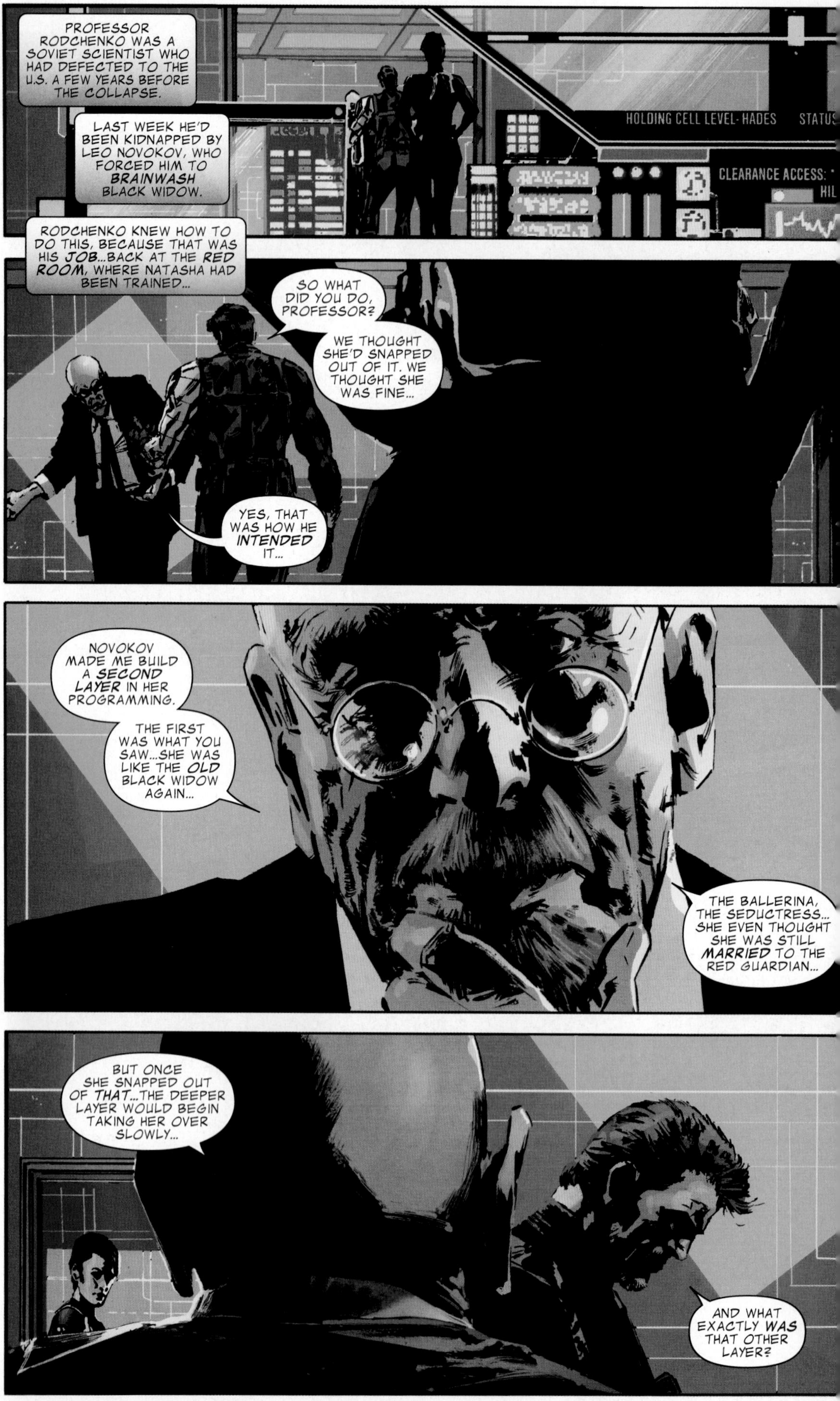
PROFESSOR RODCHENKO WAS A SOVIET SCIENTIST WHO HAD DEFECTED TO THE U.S. A FEW YEARS BEFORE THE COLLAPSE.
LAST WEEK HE'D BEEN KIDNAPPED BY LEO NOVOKOV, WHO FORCED HIM TO BRAINWASH BLACK WIDOW.
HOLDING CELL LEVEL- HADES
STATUS
CLEARANCE ACCESS:
RODCHENKO KNEW HOW TO DO THIS, BECAUSE THAT WAS HIS JOB...BACK AT THE RED ROOM, WHERE NATASHA HAD BEEN TRAINED...
SO WHAT DID YOU DO, PROFESSOR?
WE THOUGHT SHE'D SNAPPED OUT OF IT. WE THOUGHT SHE WAS FINE...
YES, THAT WAS HOW HE INTENDED IT...
NOVOKOV MADE ME BUILD A SECOND LAYER IN HER PROGRAMMING.
THE FIRST WAS WHAT YOU SAW...SHE WAS LIKE THE OLD BLACK WIDOW AGAIN...
THE BALLERINA, THE SEDUCTRESS... SHE EVEN THOUGHT SHE WAS STILL MARRIED TO THE RED GUARDIAN...
BUT ONCE SHE SNAPPED OUT OF THAT...THE DEEPER LAYER WOULD BEGIN TAKING HER OVER SLOWLY...
AND WHAT EXACTLY WAS THAT OTHER LAYER?

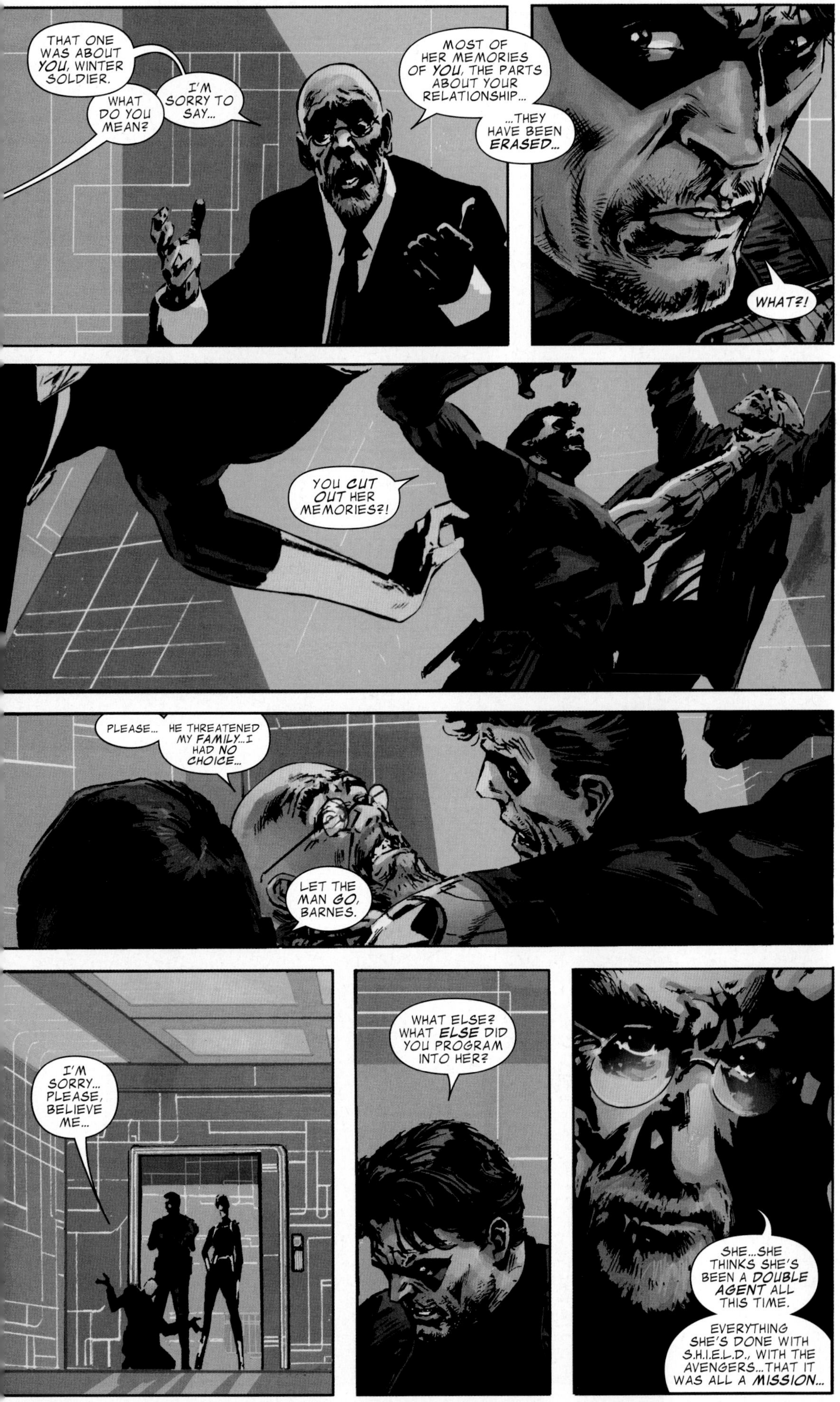
THAT ONE WAS ABOUT YOU, WINTER SOLDIER.
WHAT DO YOU MEAN?
I'M SORRY TO SAY...
MOST OF HER MEMORIES OF YOU, THE PARTS ABOUT YOUR RELATIONSHIP...
...THEY HAVE BEEN ERASED...
WHAT?!
YOU CUT OUT HER MEMORIES?!
PLEASE...
HE THREATENED MY FAMILY...I HAD NO CHOICE...
LET THE MAN GO, BARNES.
I'M SORRY... PLEASE, BELIEVE ME...
WHAT ELSE? WHAT ELSE DID YOU PROGRAM INTO HER?
SHE...SHE THINKS SHE'S BEEN A DOUBLE AGENT ALL THIS TIME.
EVERYTHING SHE'S DONE WITH S.H.I.E.L.D., WITH THE AVENGERS...THAT IT WAS ALL A MISSION...

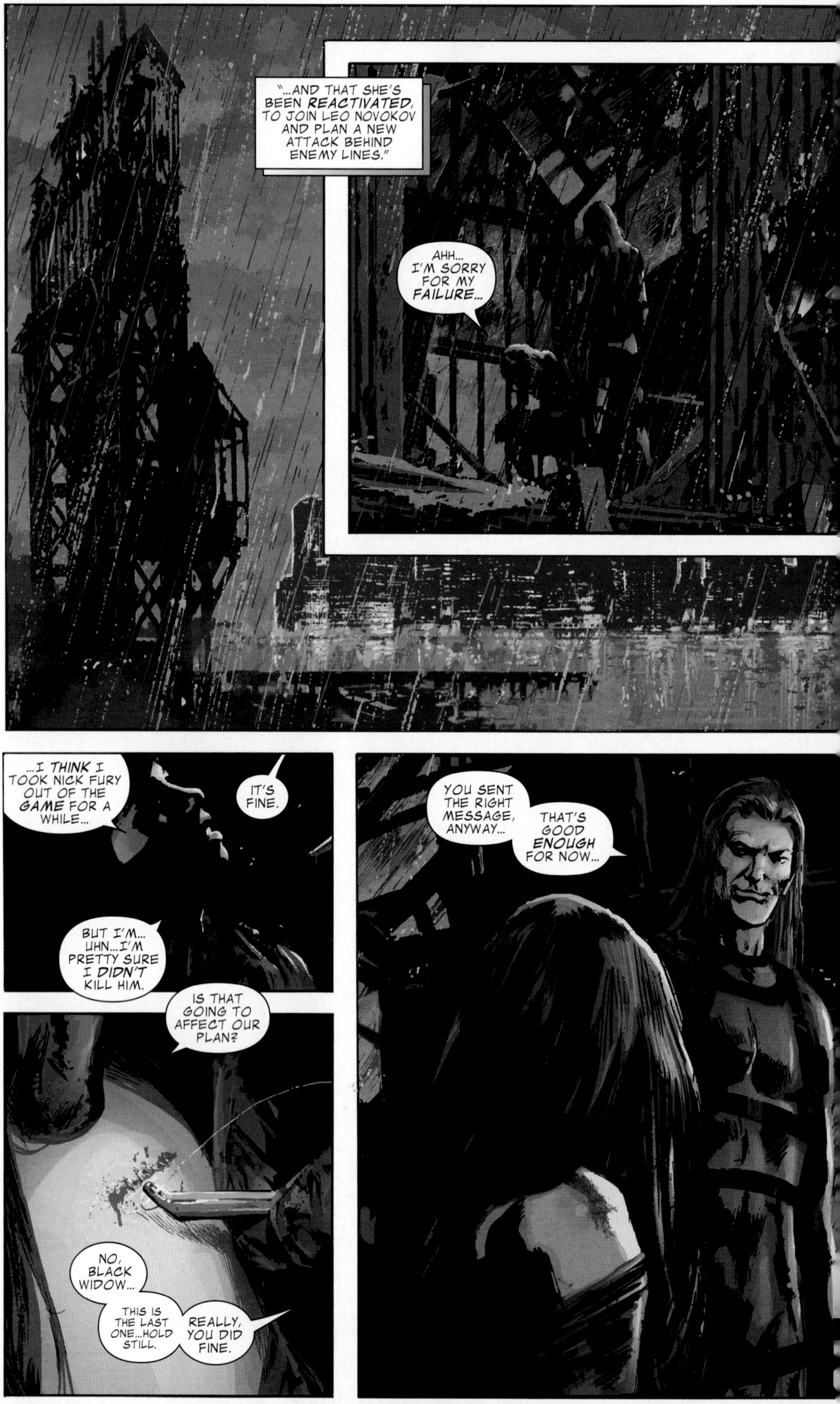
"...AND THAT SHE'S BEEN REACTIVATED, TO JOIN LEO NOVOKOV AND PLAN A NEW ATTACK BEHIND ENEMY LINES."
AHH... I'M SORRY FOR MY FAILURE...
...I THINK I TOOK NICK FURY OUT OF THE GAME FOR A WHILE...
IT'S FINE.
BUT I'M... UHN...I'M PRETTY SURE I DIDN'T KILL HIM.
IS THAT GOING TO AFFECT OUR PLAN?
NO, BLACK WIDOW...
THIS IS THE LAST ONE...HOLD STILL.
REALLY, YOU DID FINE.
YOU SENT THE RIGHT MESSAGE, ANYWAY...
THAT'S GOOD ENOUGH FOR NOW...

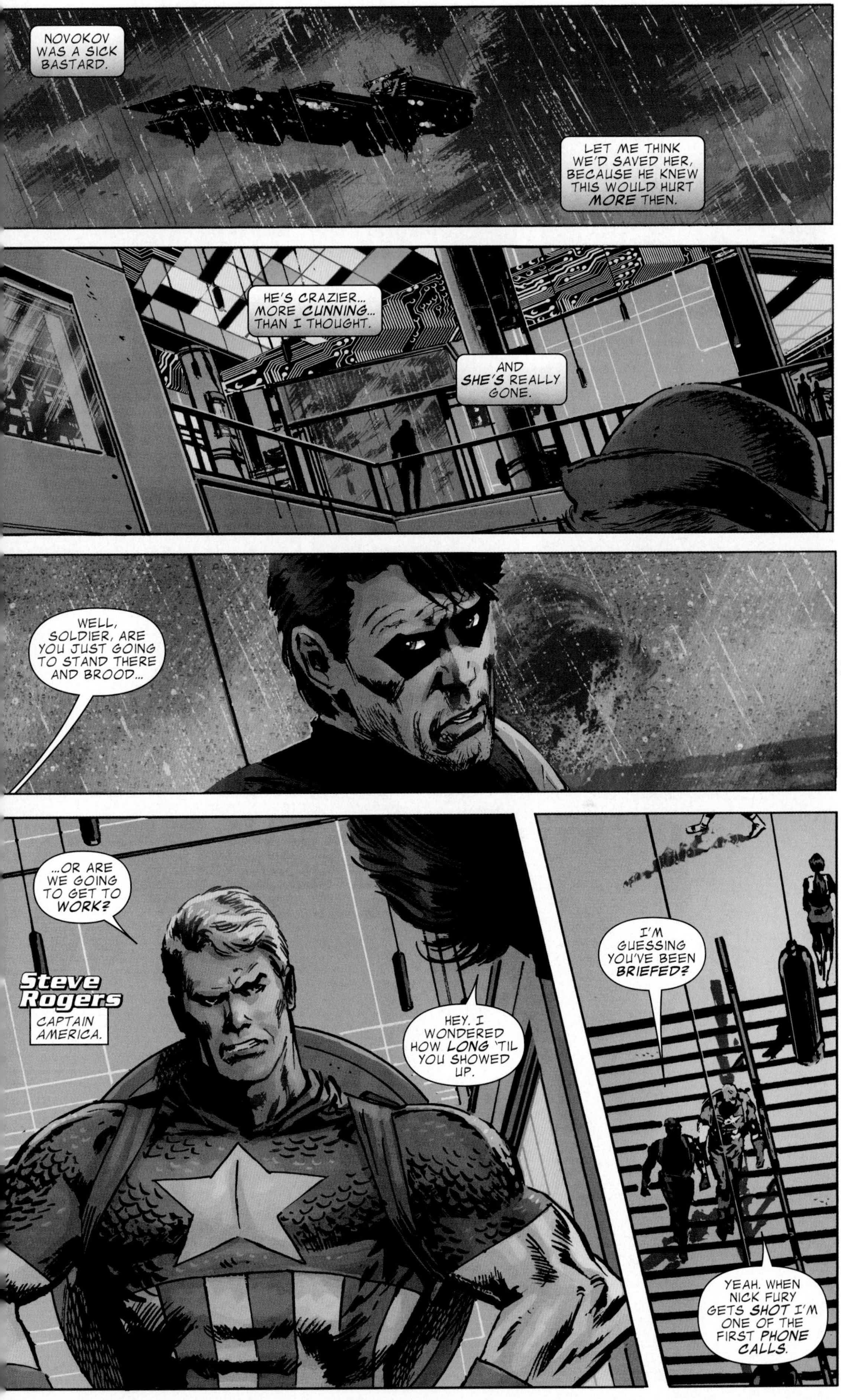
NOVOKOV WAS A SICK BASTARD.
LET ME THINK WE'D SAVED HER, BECAUSE HE KNEW THIS WOULD HURT MORE THEN.
HE'S CRAZIER... MORE CUNNING... THAN I THOUGHT.
AND SHE'S REALLY GONE.
WELL, SOLDIER, ARE YOU JUST GOING TO STAND THERE AND BROOD...
...OR ARE WE GOING TO GET TO WORK?
Steve Rogers
CAPTAIN AMERICA.
HEY. I WONDERED HOW LONG 'TIL YOU SHOWED UP.
I'M GUESSING YOU'VE BEEN BRIEFED?
YEAH. WHEN NICK FURY GETS SHOT I'M ONE OF THE FIRST PHONE CALLS.

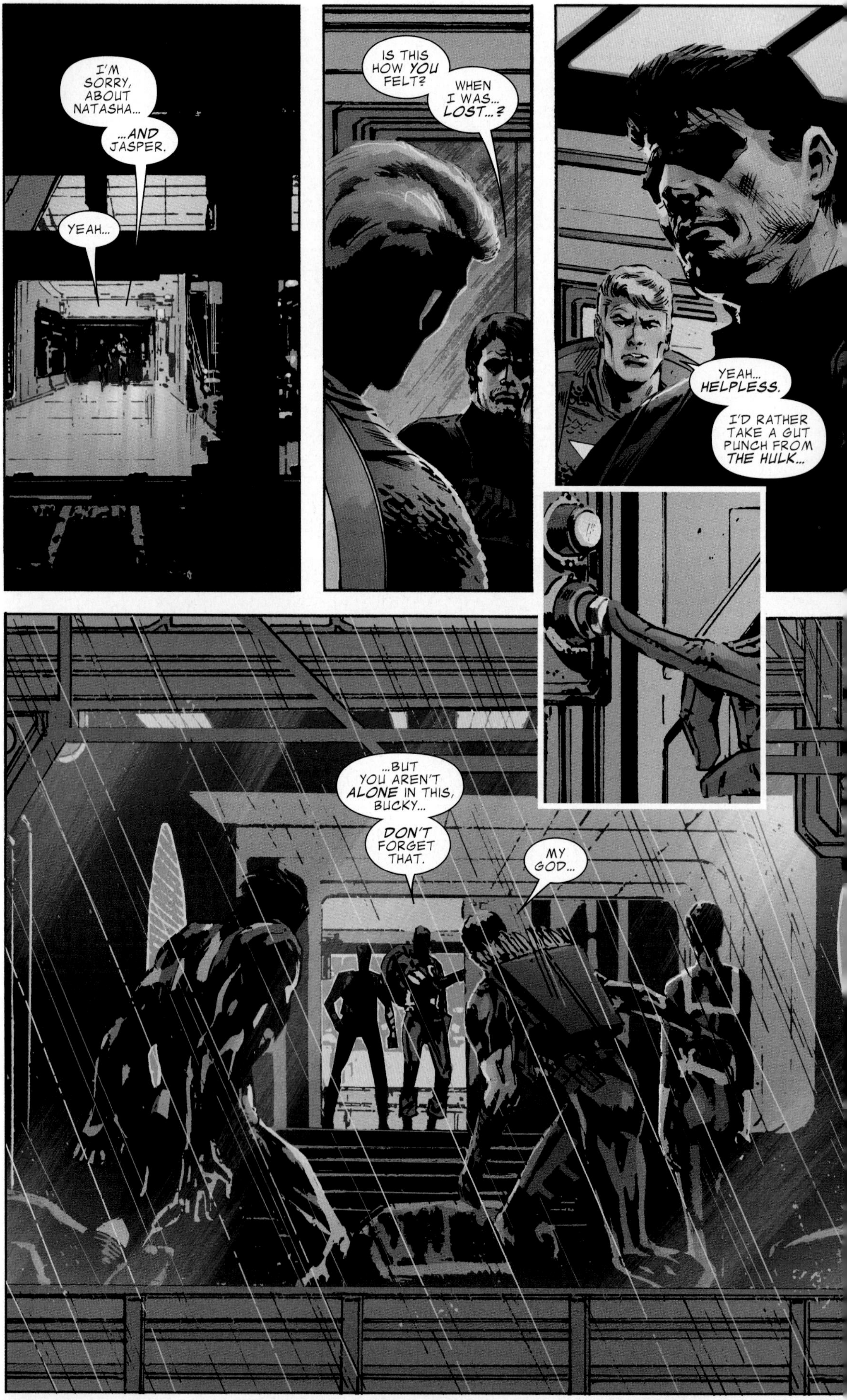
I'M SORRY, ABOUT NATASHA...
...AND JASPER.
YEAH...
IS THIS HOW YOU FELT?
WHEN I WAS... LOST...?
YEAH... HELPLESS.
I'D RATHER TAKE A GUT PUNCH FROM THE HULK...
...BUT YOU AREN'T ALONE IN THIS, BUCKY...
DON'T FORGET THAT.
MY GOD...

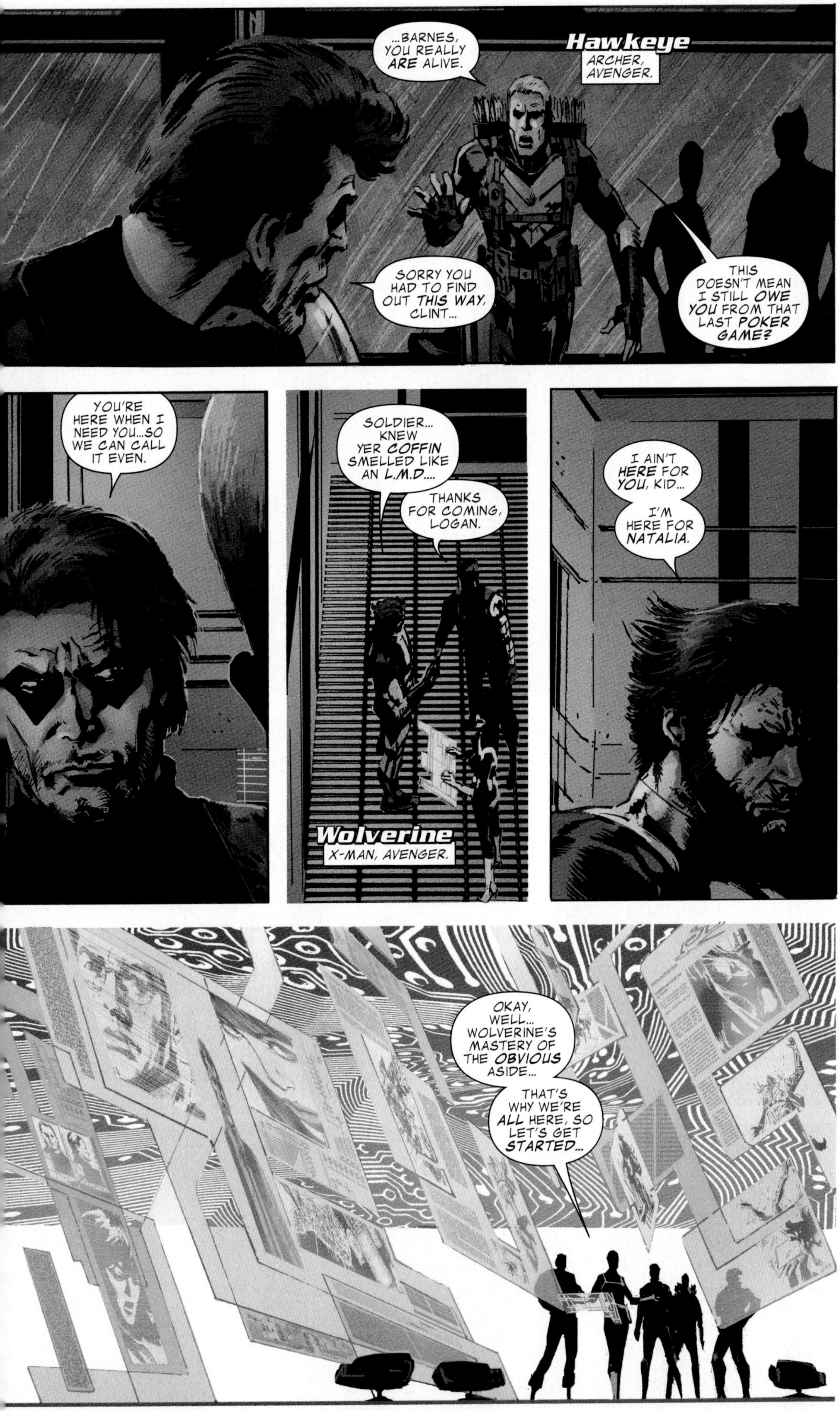

...BARNES, YOU REALLY ARE ALIVE.
Hawkeye
ARCHER, AVENGER.
SORRY YOU HAD TO FIND OUT THIS WAY, CLINT...
THIS DOESN'T MEAN I STILL OWE YOU FROM THAT LAST POKER GAME?
YOU'RE HERE WHEN I NEED YOU...SO WE CAN CALL IT EVEN.
SOLDIER... KNEW YER COFFIN SMELLED LIKE AN L.M.D....
THANKS FOR COMING, LOGAN.
Wolverine
X-MAN, AVENGER.
I AIN'T HERE FOR YOU, KID...
I'M HERE FOR NATALIA.
OKAY, WELL... WOLVERINE'S MASTERY OF THE OBVIOUS ASIDE...
THAT'S WHY WE'RE ALL HERE, SO LET'S GET STARTED...

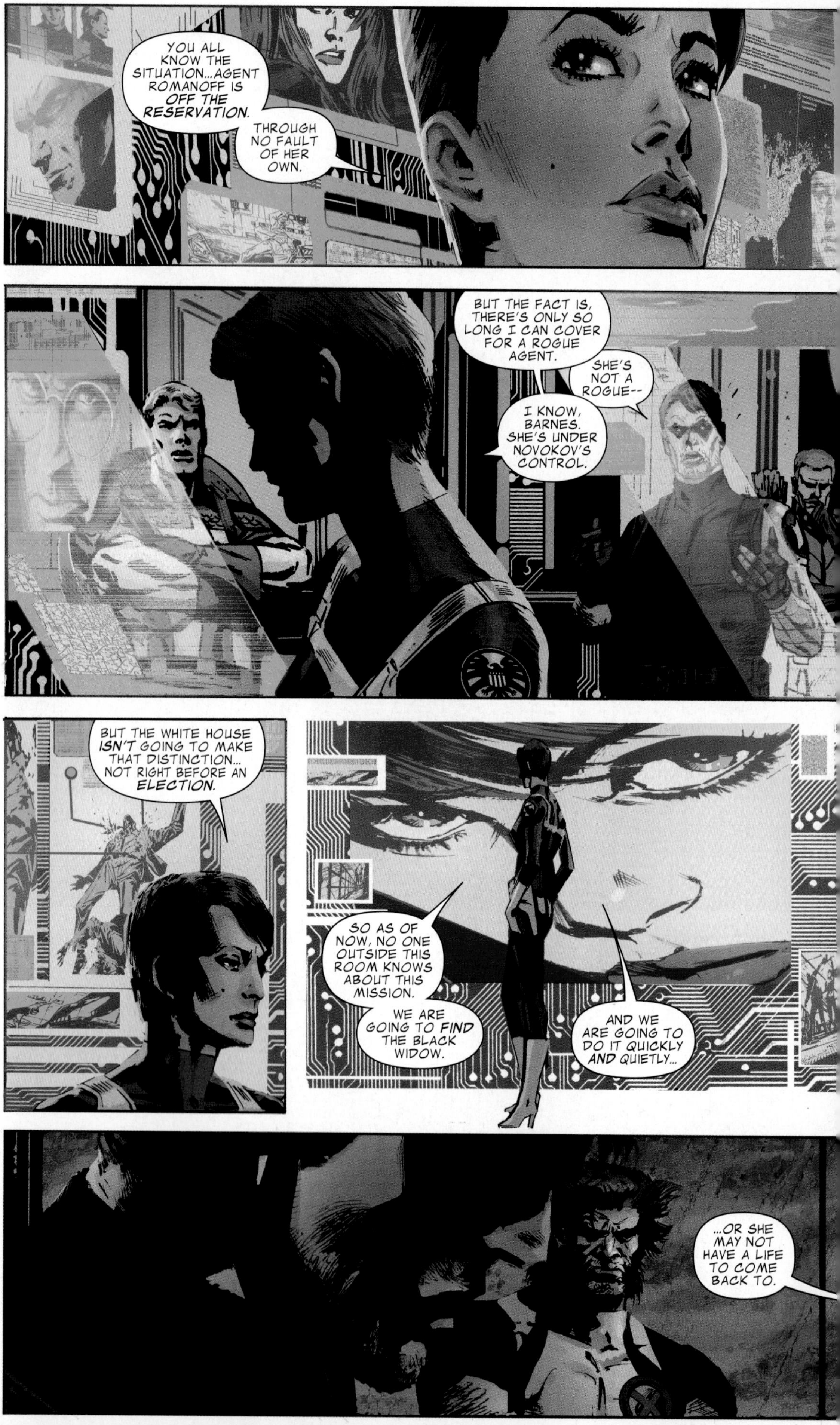
YOU ALL KNOW THE SITUATION...AGENT ROMANOFF IS OFF THE RESERVATION.
THROUGH NO FAULT OF HER OWN.
BUT THE FACT IS, THERE'S ONLY SO LONG I CAN COVER FOR A ROGUE AGENT.
SHE'S NOT A ROGUE--
I KNOW, BARNES. SHE'S UNDER NOVOKOV'S CONTROL.
BUT THE WHITE HOUSE ISN'T GOING TO MAKE THAT DISTINCTION... NOT RIGHT BEFORE AN ELECTION.
SO AS OF NOW, NO ONE OUTSIDE THIS ROOM KNOWS ABOUT THIS MISSION.
WE ARE GOING TO FIND THE BLACK WIDOW.
AND WE ARE GOING TO DO IT QUICKLY AND QUIETLY...
...OR SHE MAY NOT HAVE A LIFE TO COME BACK TO.

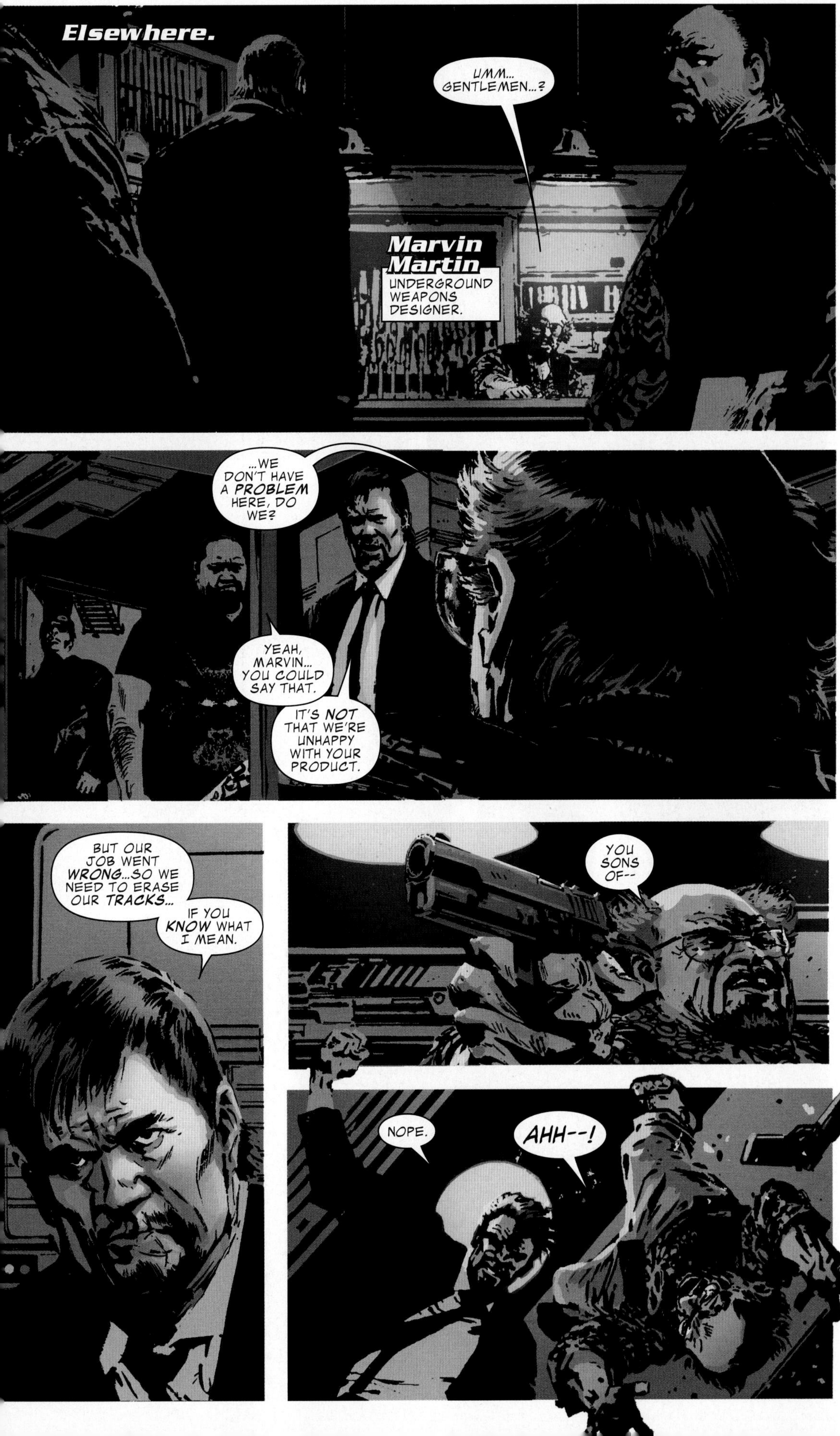
Elsewhere.
UMM... GENTLEMEN...?
Marvin Martin
UNDERGROUND WEAPONS DESIGNER.
...WE DON'T HAVE A PROBLEM HERE, DO WE?
YEAH, MARVIN... YOU COULD SAY THAT.
IT'S NOT THAT WE'RE UNHAPPY WITH YOUR PRODUCT.
BUT OUR JOB WENT WRONG...SO WE NEED TO ERASE OUR TRACKS...
IF YOU KNOW WHAT I MEAN.
YOU SONS OF--
NOPE.
AHH--!

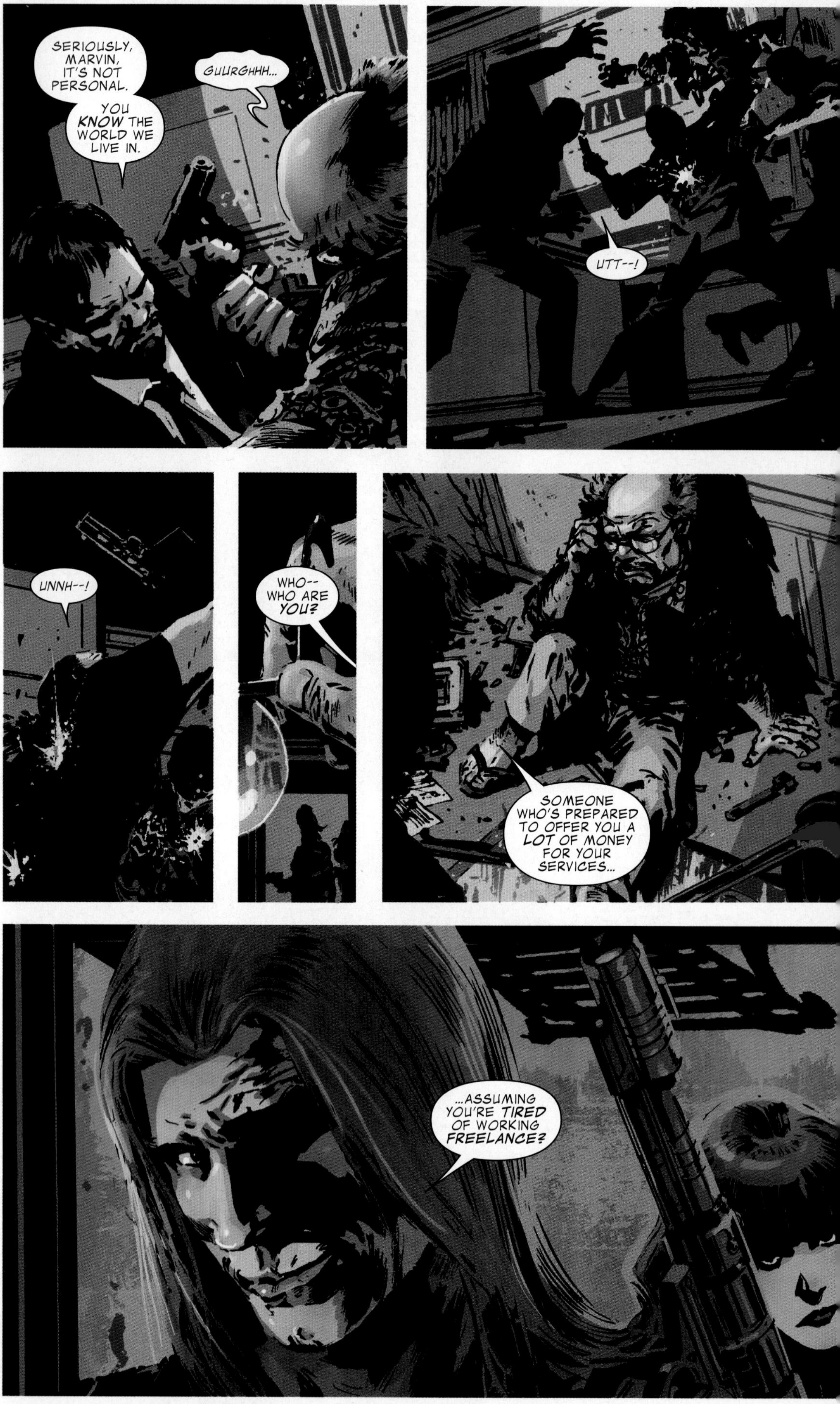
SERIOUSLY, MARVIN, IT'S NOT PERSONAL.
YOU KNOW THE WORLD WE LIVE IN.
GUURGHHH...
UTT--!
UNNH--!
WHO-- WHO ARE YOU?
SOMEONE WHO'S PREPARED TO OFFER YOU A LOT OF MONEY FOR YOUR SERVICES...
...ASSUMING YOU'RE TIRED OF WORKING FREELANCE?

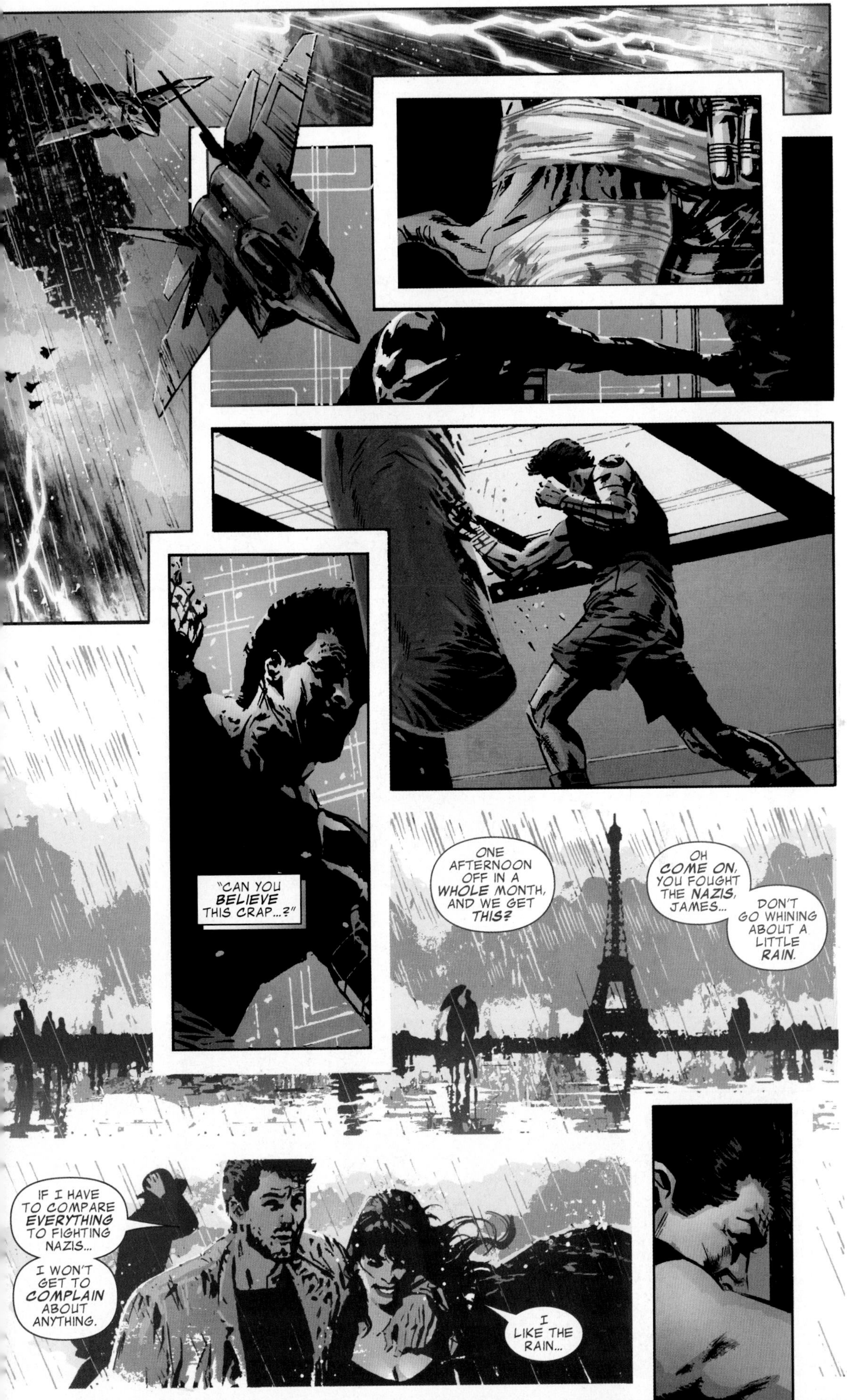
"CAN YOU BELIEVE THIS CRAP...?"
ONE AFTERNOON OFF IN A WHOLE MONTH, AND WE GET THIS?
OH COME ON, YOU FOUGHT THE NAZIS, JAMES...
DON'T GO WHINING ABOUT A LITTLE RAIN.
IF I HAVE TO COMPARE EVERYTHING TO FIGHTING NAZIS...
I WON'T GET TO COMPLAIN ABOUT ANYTHING.
I LIKE THE RAIN...

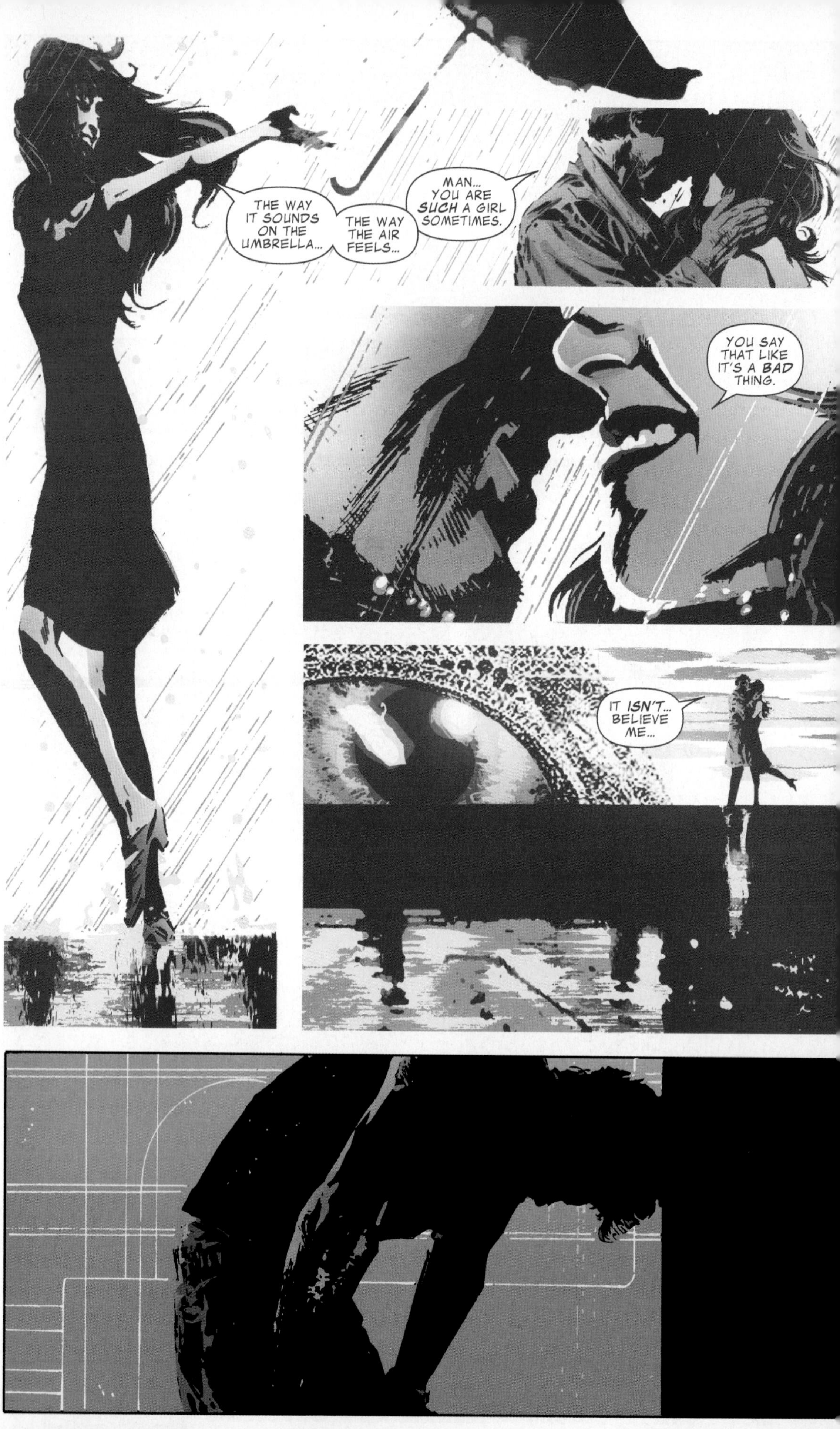
THE WAY IT SOUNDS ON THE UMBRELLA...
THE WAY THE AIR FEELS...
MAN... YOU ARE SUCH A GIRL SOMETIMES.
YOU SAY THAT LIKE IT'S A BAD THING.
IT ISN'T... BELIEVE ME...

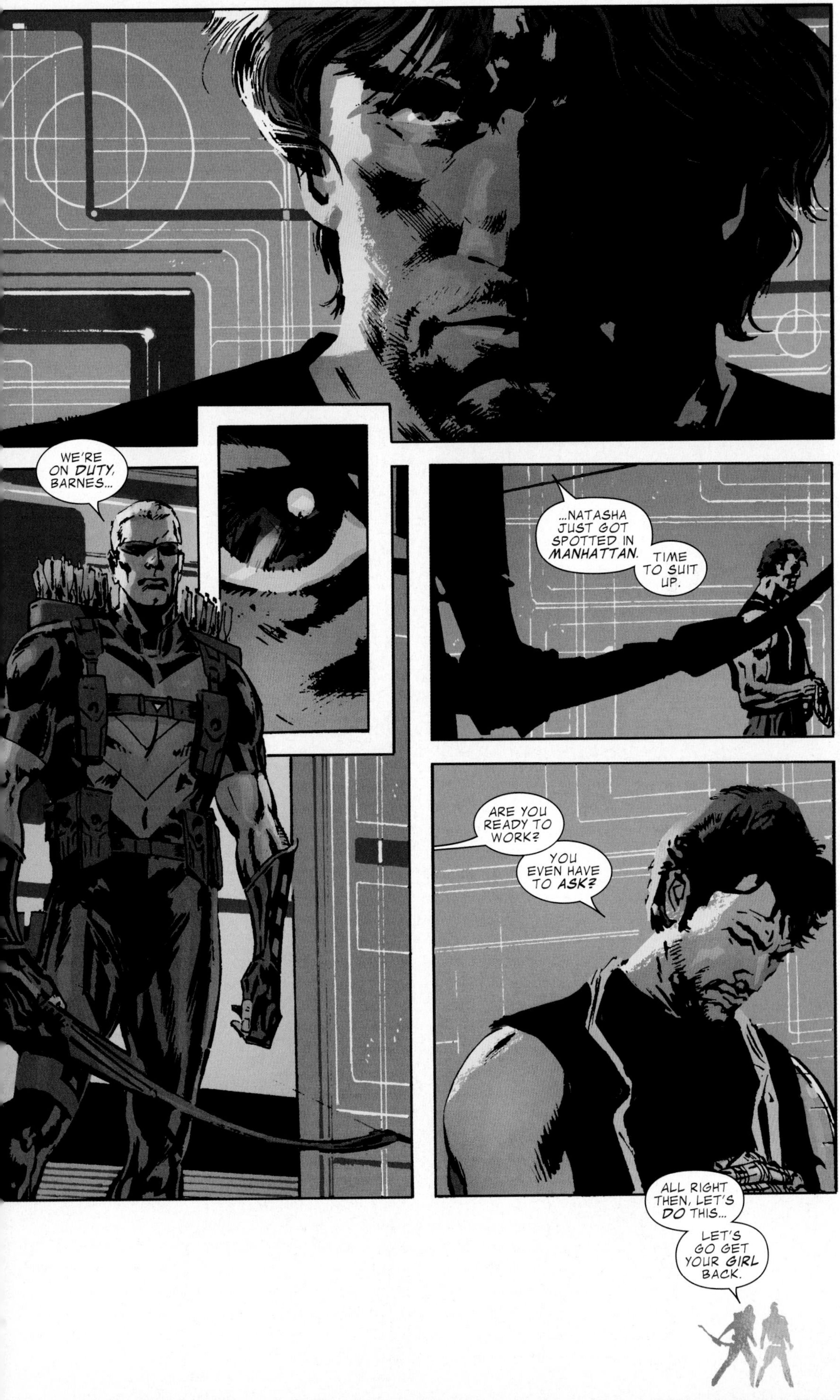
WE'RE ON DUTY, BARNES...
...NATASHA JUST GOT SPOTTED IN MANHATTAN.
TIME TO SUIT UP.
ARE YOU READY TO WORK?
YOU EVEN HAVE TO ASK?
ALL RIGHT THEN, LET'S DO THIS...
LET'S GO GET YOUR GIRL BACK.

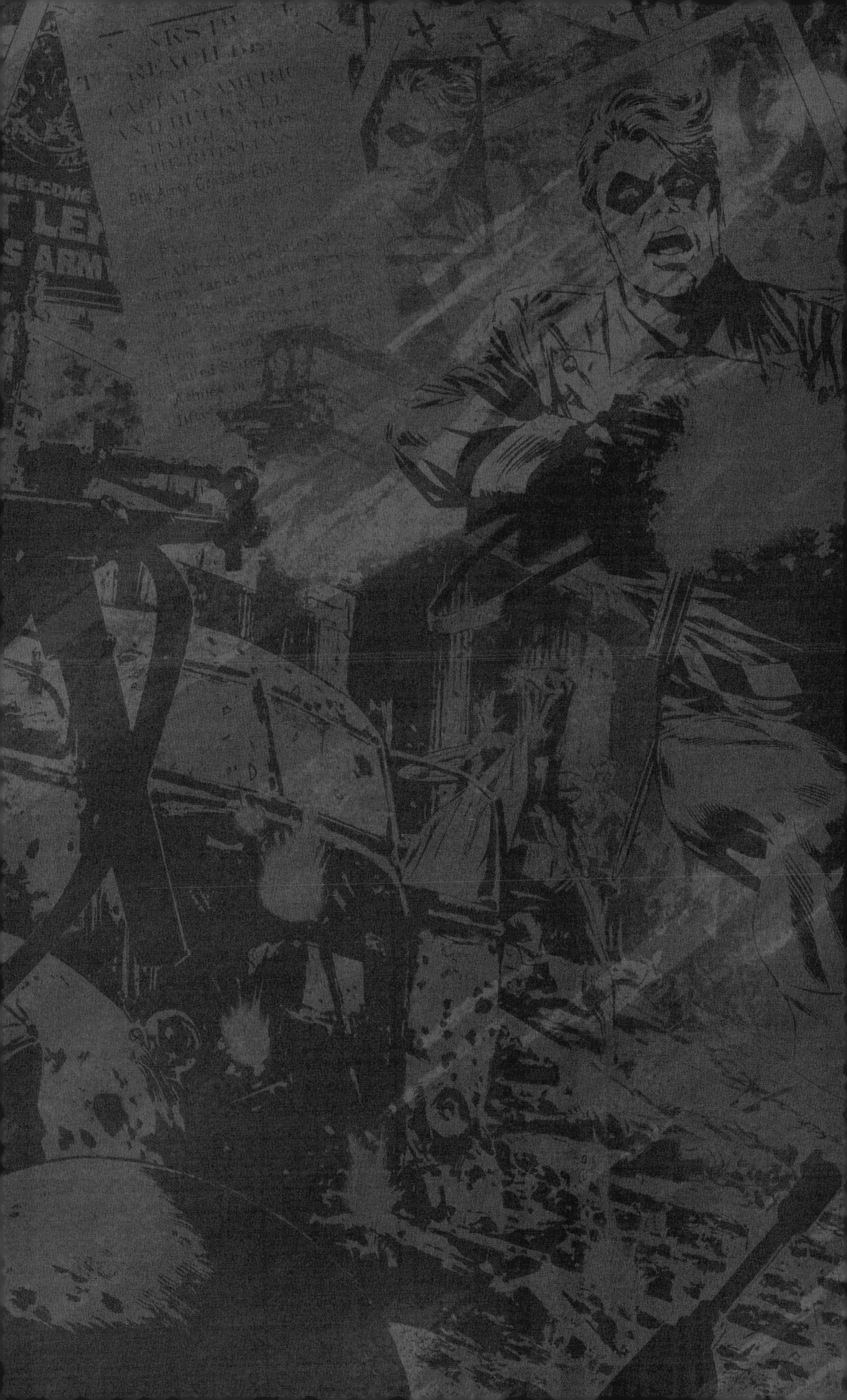

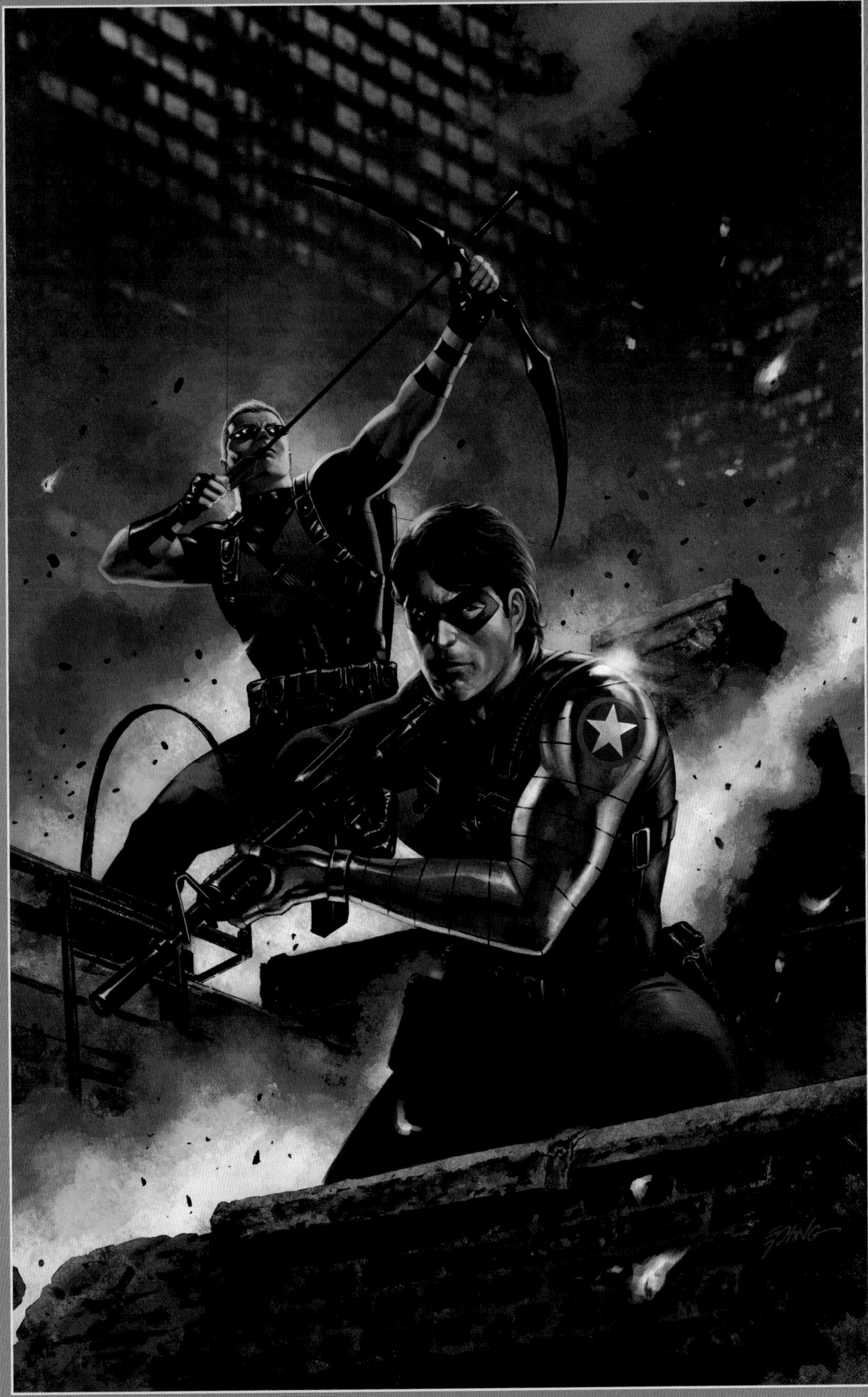

ELEVEN

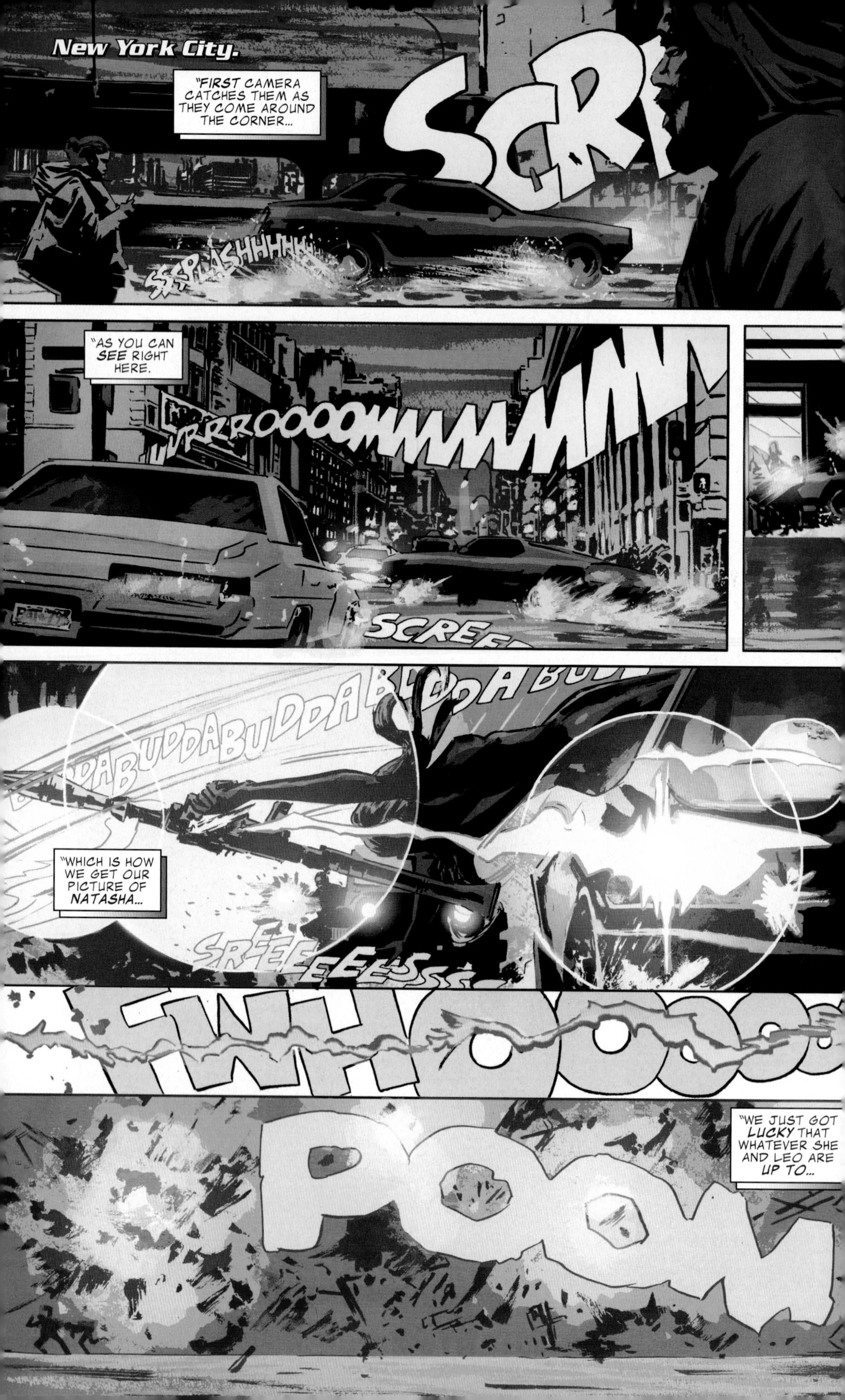
New York City.
"FIRST CAMERA CATCHES THEM AS THEY COME AROUND THE CORNER...
SCR
SSPLASHHHHH
"AS YOU CAN SEE RIGHT HERE.
VRRROOOOMMMMMM
SCREE
DDABUDDABUDDABUDDA BUDD
"WHICH IS HOW WE GET OUR PICTURE OF NATASHA...
SREEEEEESSS
TWHOOOO
"WE JUST GOT LUCKY THAT WHATEVER SHE AND LEO ARE UP TO...
POOOM

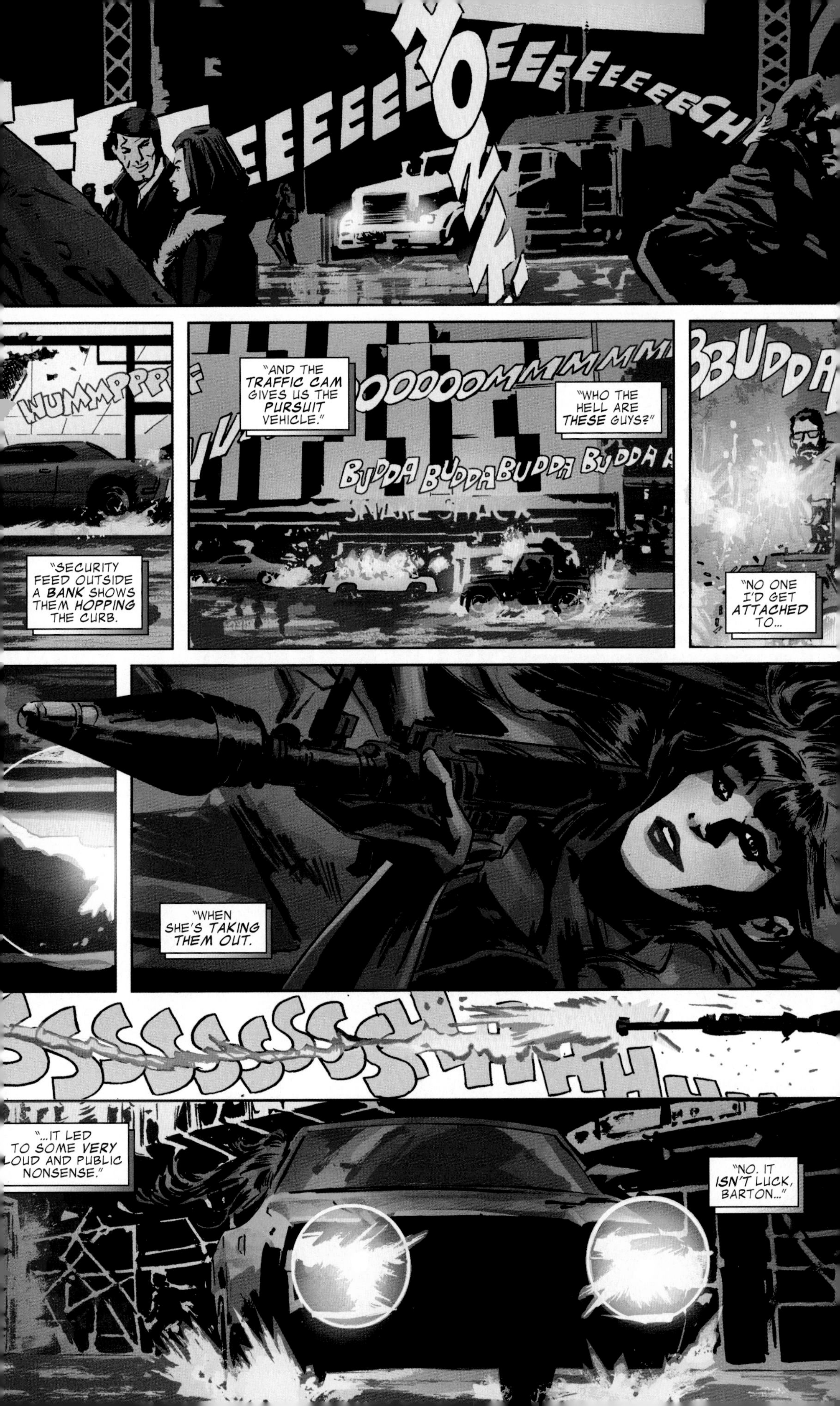
EEEEEEEEEEEEEEEEEEEECH
HONNK!
WUMMPPPF
"SECURITY FEED OUTSIDE A BANK SHOWS THEM HOPPING THE CURB.
"AND THE TRAFFIC CAM GIVES US THE PURSUIT VEHICLE."
OOOOOOMMMMMMM
"WHO THE HELL ARE THESE GUYS?"
BUDDA BUDDA BUDDA BUDDA
BBUDDA
"NO ONE I'D GET ATTACHED TO...
"WHEN SHE'S TAKING THEM OUT.
"...IT LED TO SOME VERY LOUD AND PUBLIC NONSENSE."
"NO. IT ISN'T LUCK, BARTON..."

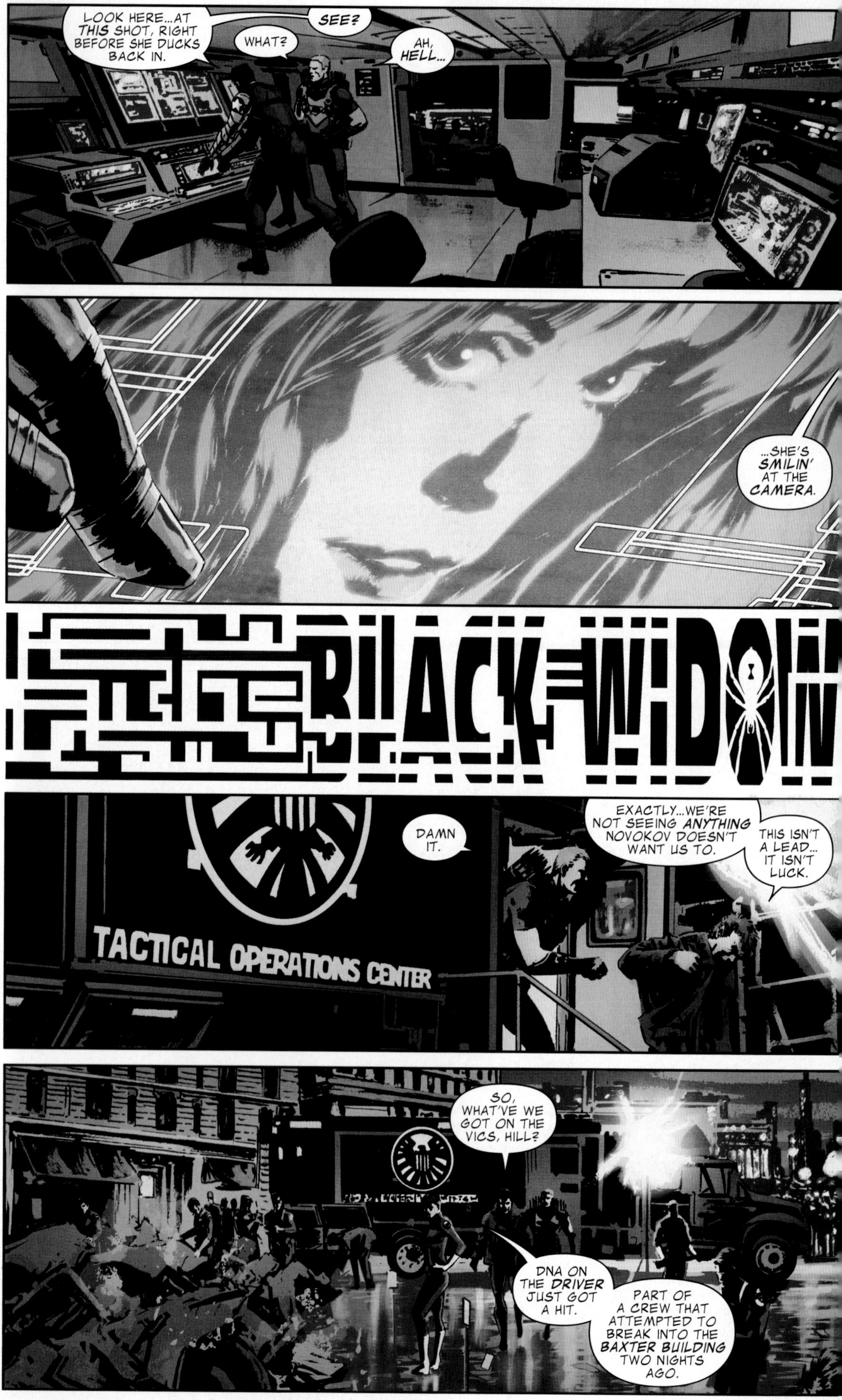

LOOK HERE...AT THIS SHOT, RIGHT BEFORE SHE DUCKS BACK IN.
WHAT?
SEE?
AH, HELL...
...SHE'S SMILIN' AT THE CAMERA.
BLACK WIDOW
DAMN IT.
EXACTLY...WE'RE NOT SEEING ANYTHING NOVOKOV DOESN'T WANT US TO.
THIS ISN'T A LEAD... IT ISN'T LUCK.
TACTICAL OPERATIONS CENTER
SO, WHAT'VE WE GOT ON THE VICS, HILL?
DNA ON THE DRIVER JUST GOT A HIT.
PART OF A CREW THAT ATTEMPTED TO BREAK INTO THE BAXTER BUILDING TWO NIGHTS AGO.

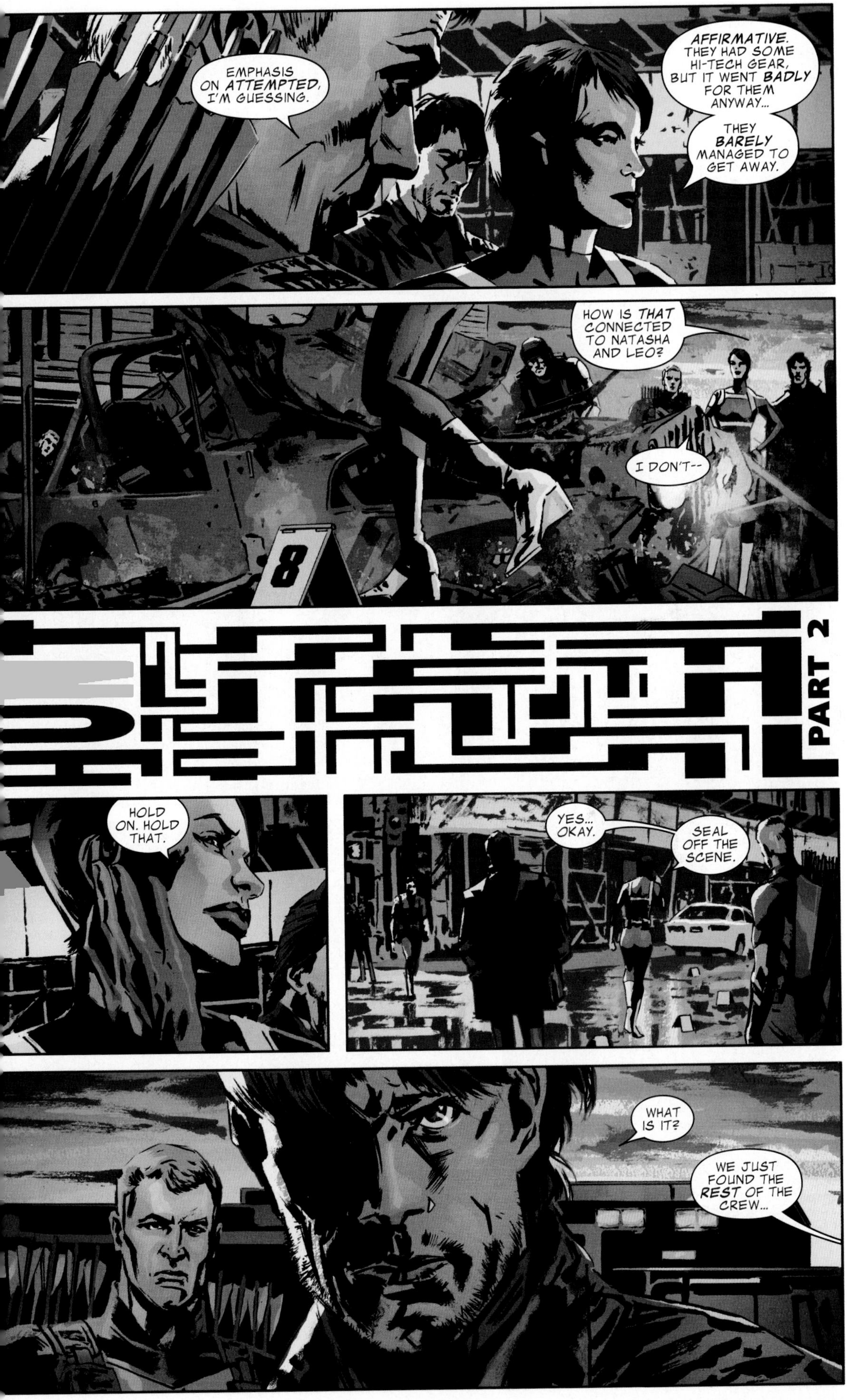
EMPHASIS ON ATTEMPTED, I'M GUESSING.
AFFIRMATIVE. THEY HAD SOME HI-TECH GEAR, BUT IT WENT BADLY FOR THEM ANYWAY...
THEY BARELY MANAGED TO GET AWAY.
HOW IS THAT CONNECTED TO NATASHA AND LEO?
I DON'T--
8
PART 2
HOLD ON. HOLD THAT.
YES... OKAY.
SEAL OFF THE SCENE.
WHAT IS IT?
WE JUST FOUND THE REST OF THE CREW...

TWO DEAD BY THE TIME OUR PEOPLE GOT HERE...

ONE STILL UNCONSCIOUS, BUT BREATHING.

I'VE SEEN THIS WORK BEFORE...THIS DESIGN.

SOME GUY WHO USED TO WORK WITH THE TINKERER SOMETIMES.

SOME GENIUS DWARF...

YES. HIS NAME'S MARVIN MARTIN.

TRIED TO CALL HIMSELF MARVELOUS MARV FOR A WHILE, BUT IT DIDN'T STICK.

CRIME SCENE · DO NOT CROSS BY ORDER OF S.H.I.E.L.

CRIME SCENE · DO NOT CROSS

CRIME SCENE · DO NOT CROSS

SO THIS WEAPONSMITH IS MISSING...

...AND LEO AND NATASHA'S CAR CHASE LED US RIGHT HERE?

YOU GOT IT.

WHEN YOU LOOK INTO THAT BAXTER BUILDING JOB, YOU'LL FIND OUT IT WENT BAD ON PURPOSE.

I'M GUESSING NOVOKOV SET IT ALL UP... SO HE COULD PLAY THE HERO HERE.

AND NOW HE'S GOT HIS OWN PRIVATE WEAPONS DESIGNER.

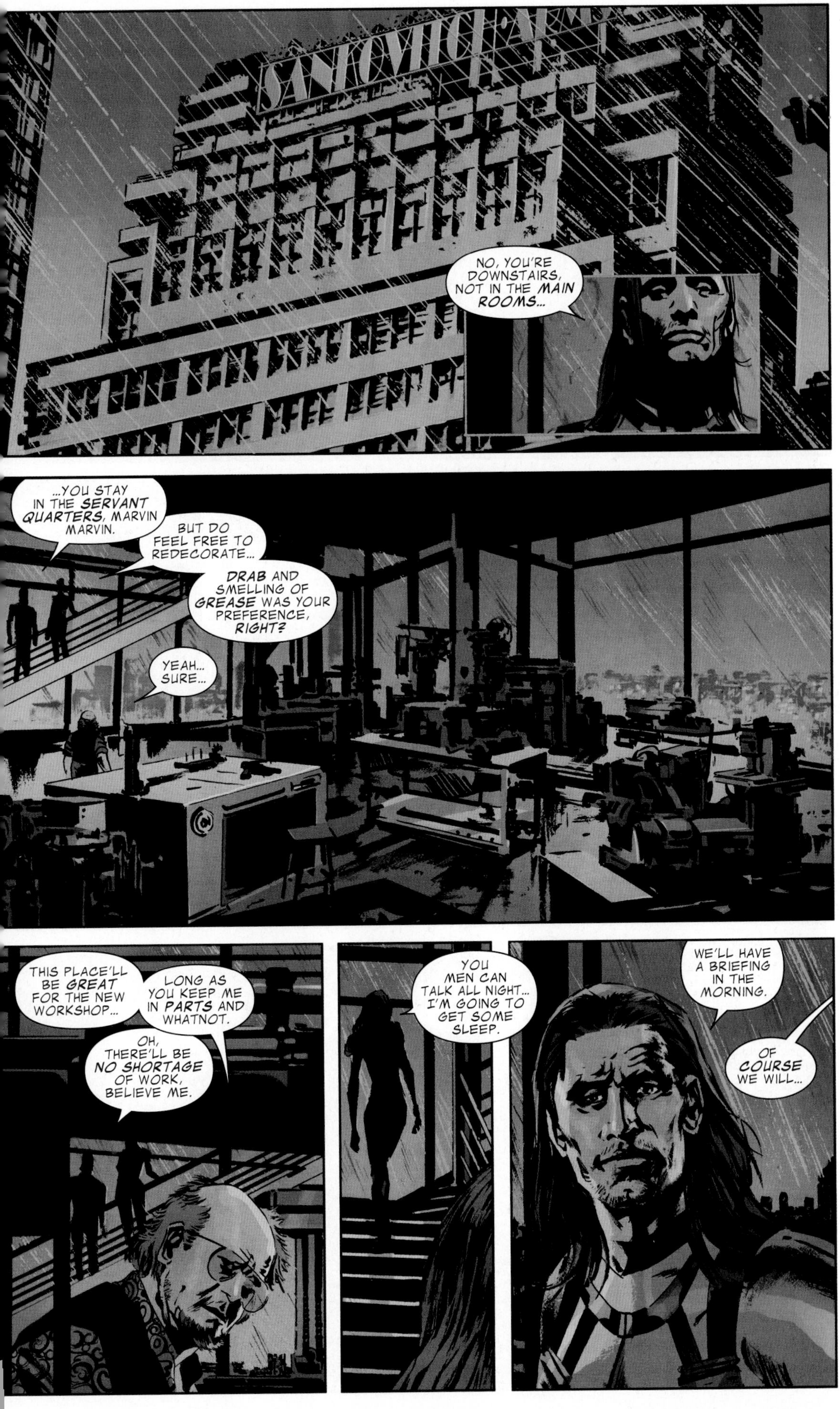
NO, YOU'RE DOWNSTAIRS, NOT IN THE MAIN ROOMS...
...YOU STAY IN THE SERVANT QUARTERS, MARVIN MARVIN.
BUT DO FEEL FREE TO REDECORATE...
DRAB AND SMELLING OF GREASE WAS YOUR PREFERENCE, RIGHT?
YEAH... SURE...
THIS PLACE'LL BE GREAT FOR THE NEW WORKSHOP...
LONG AS YOU KEEP ME IN PARTS AND WHATNOT.
OH, THERE'LL BE NO SHORTAGE OF WORK, BELIEVE ME.
YOU MEN CAN TALK ALL NIGHT... I'M GOING TO GET SOME SLEEP.
WE'LL HAVE A BRIEFING IN THE MORNING.
OF COURSE WE WILL...

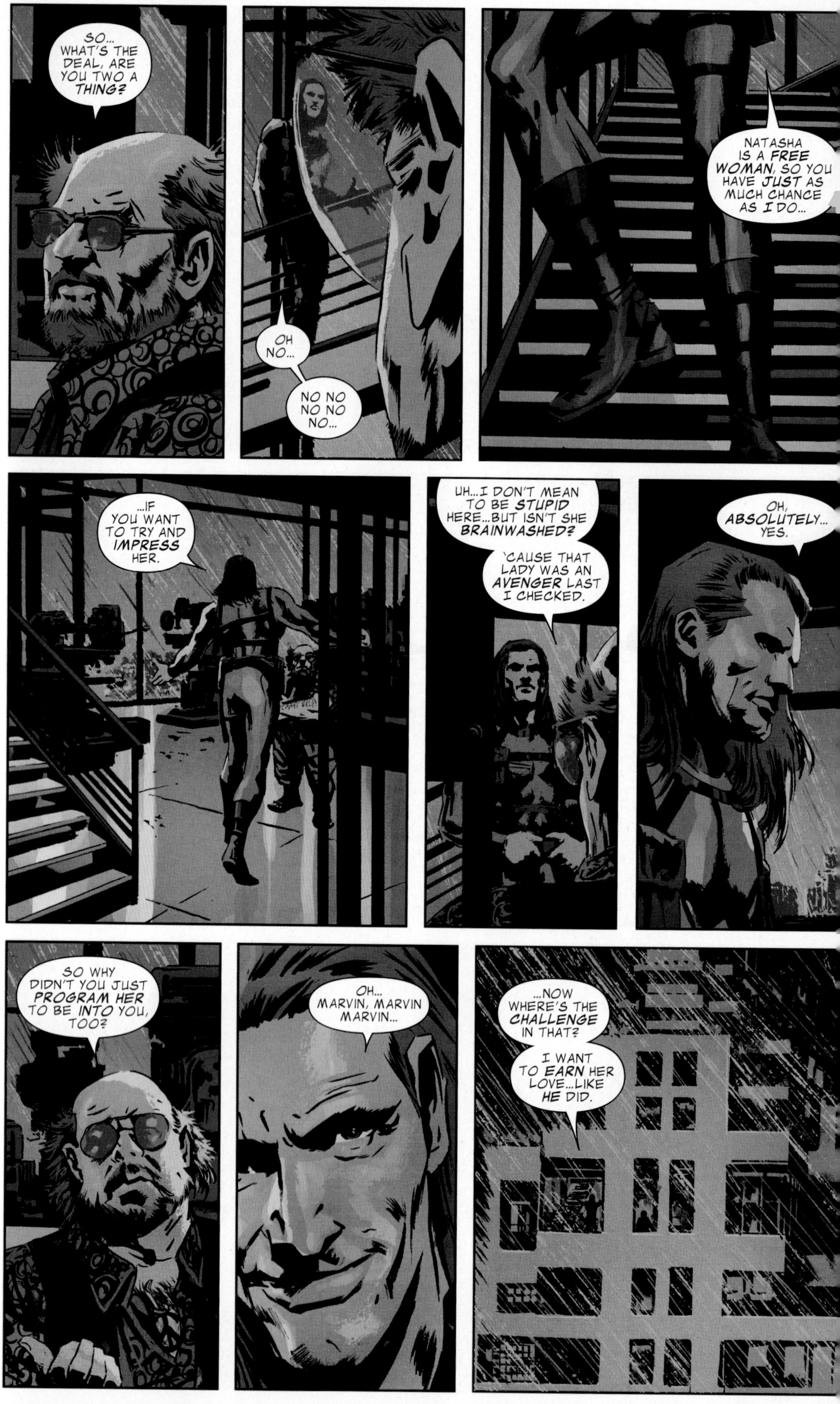
SO... WHAT'S THE DEAL, ARE YOU TWO A THING?
OH NO...
NO NO NO NO NO...
NATASHA IS A FREE WOMAN, SO YOU HAVE JUST AS MUCH CHANCE AS I DO...
...IF YOU WANT TO TRY AND IMPRESS HER.
UH...I DON'T MEAN TO BE STUPID HERE...BUT ISN'T SHE BRAINWASHED?
'CAUSE THAT LADY WAS AN AVENGER LAST I CHECKED.
OH, ABSOLUTELY... YES.
SO WHY DIDN'T YOU JUST PROGRAM HER TO BE INTO YOU, TOO?
OH... MARVIN, MARVIN MARVIN...
...NOW WHERE'S THE CHALLENGE IN THAT?
I WANT TO EARN HER LOVE...LIKE HE DID.

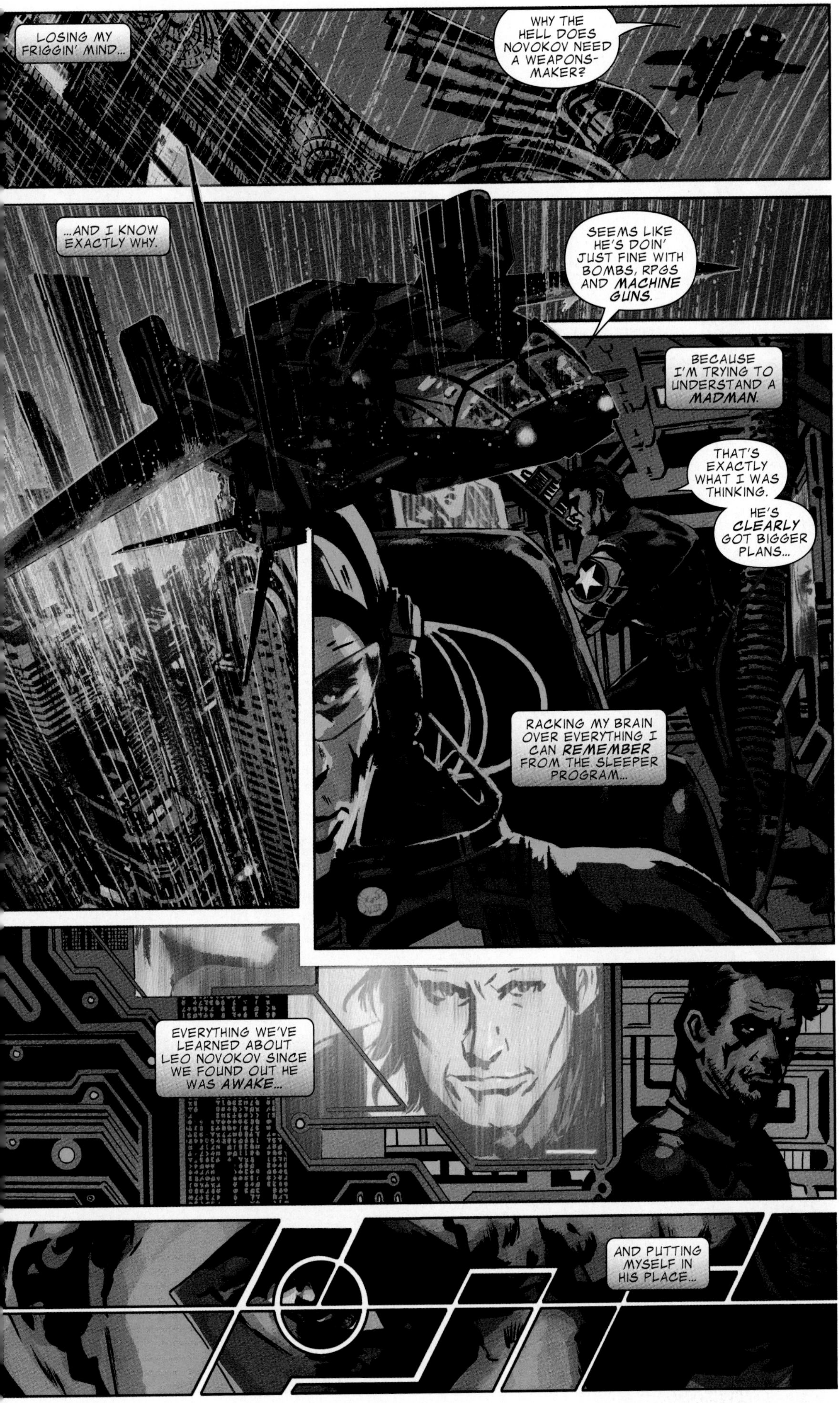
LOSING MY FRIGGIN' MIND...
WHY THE HELL DOES NOVOKOV NEED A WEAPONS-MAKER?
...AND I KNOW EXACTLY WHY.
SEEMS LIKE HE'S DOIN' JUST FINE WITH BOMBS, RPGS AND MACHINE GUNS.
BECAUSE I'M TRYING TO UNDERSTAND A MADMAN.
THAT'S EXACTLY WHAT I WAS THINKING.
HE'S CLEARLY GOT BIGGER PLANS...
RACKING MY BRAIN OVER EVERYTHING I CAN REMEMBER FROM THE SLEEPER PROGRAM...
EVERYTHING WE'VE LEARNED ABOUT LEO NOVOKOV SINCE WE FOUND OUT HE WAS AWAKE...
AND PUTTING MYSELF IN HIS PLACE...

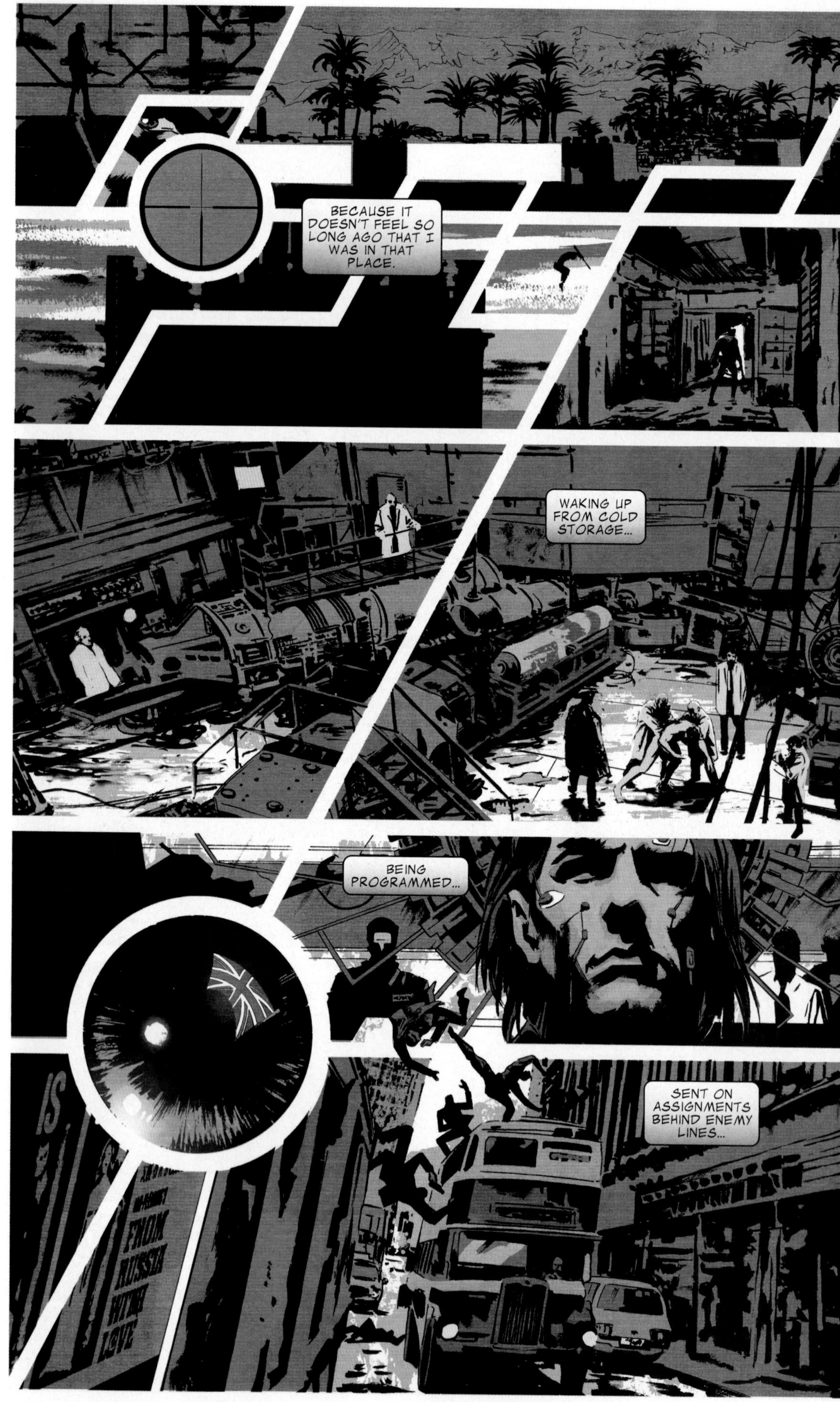
BECAUSE IT DOESN'T FEEL SO LONG AGO THAT I WAS IN THAT PLACE.
WAKING UP FROM COLD STORAGE...
BEING PROGRAMMED...
SENT ON ASSIGNMENTS BEHIND ENEMY LINES...

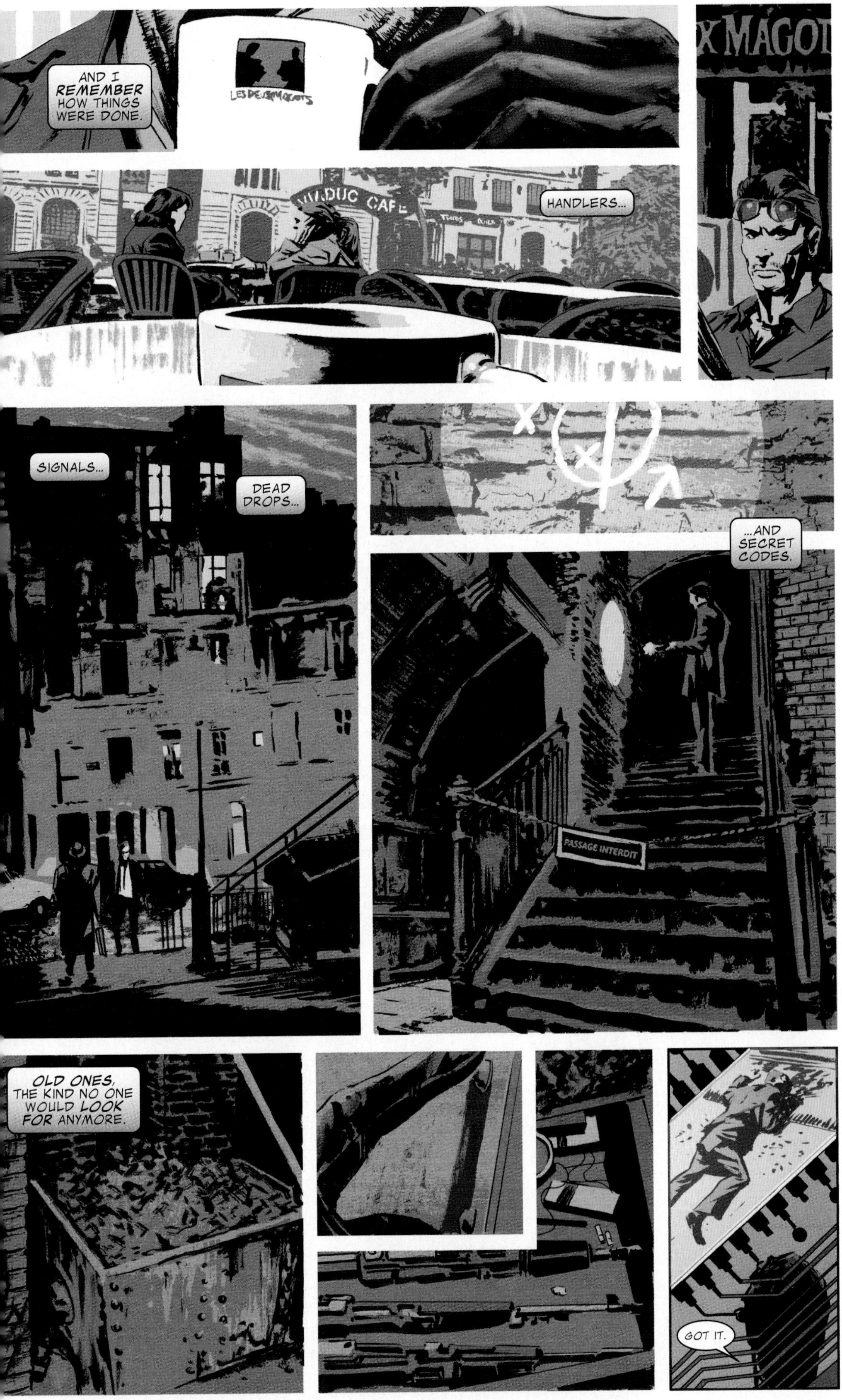

AND I REMEMBER HOW THINGS WERE DONE.
LES DEUX MAGOTS
X MAGOT
VIADUC CAFE
HANDLERS...
SIGNALS...
DEAD DROPS...
...AND SECRET CODES.
PASSAGE INTERDIT
OLD ONES, THE KIND NO ONE WOULD LOOK FOR ANYMORE.
GOT IT.

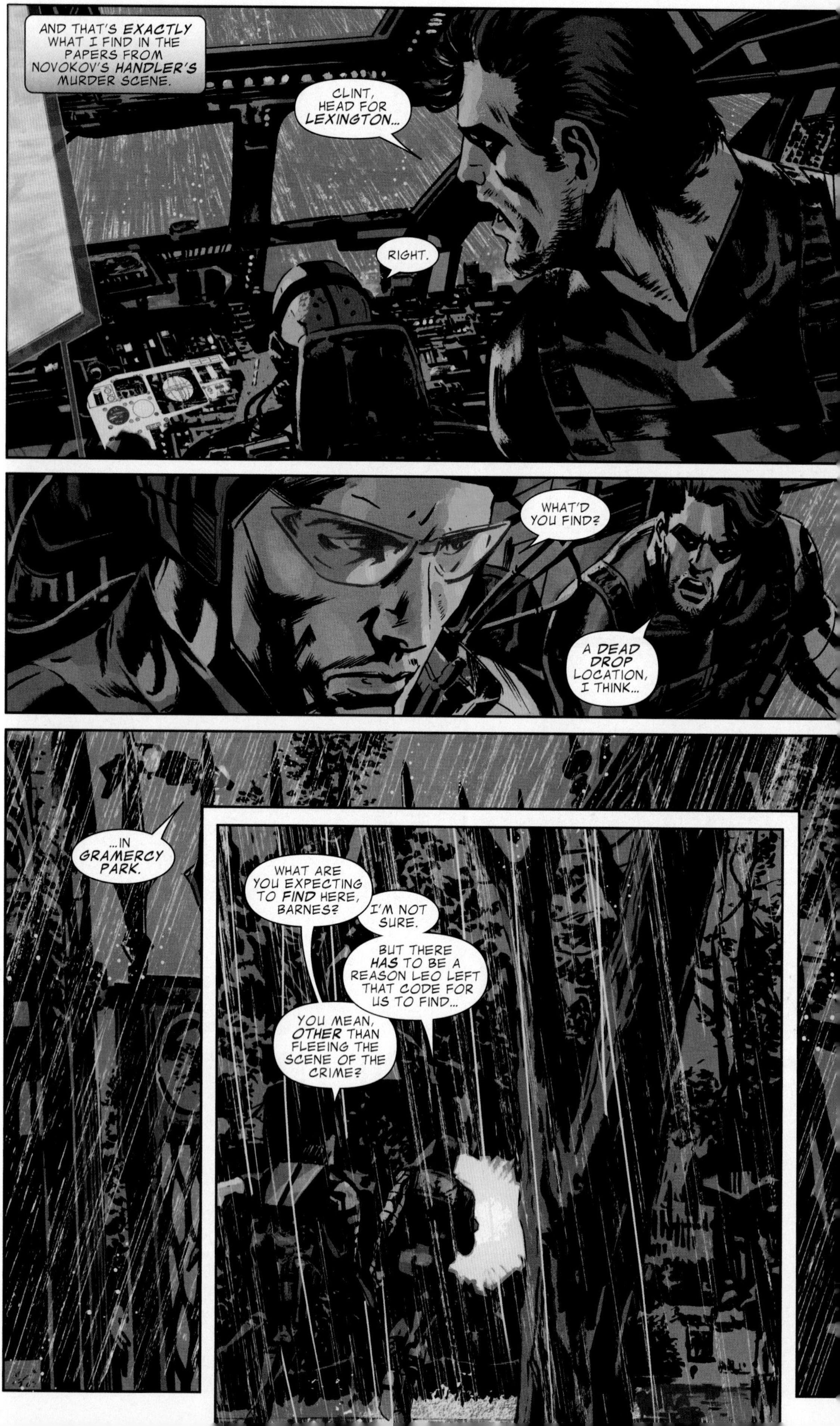
AND THAT'S EXACTLY WHAT I FIND IN THE PAPERS FROM NOVOKOV'S HANDLER'S MURDER SCENE.
CLINT, HEAD FOR LEXINGTON...
RIGHT.
WHAT'D YOU FIND?
A DEAD DROP LOCATION, I THINK...
...IN GRAMERCY PARK.
WHAT ARE YOU EXPECTING TO FIND HERE, BARNES?
I'M NOT SURE.
BUT THERE HAS TO BE A REASON LEO LEFT THAT CODE FOR US TO FIND...
YOU MEAN, OTHER THAN FLEEING THE SCENE OF THE CRIME?

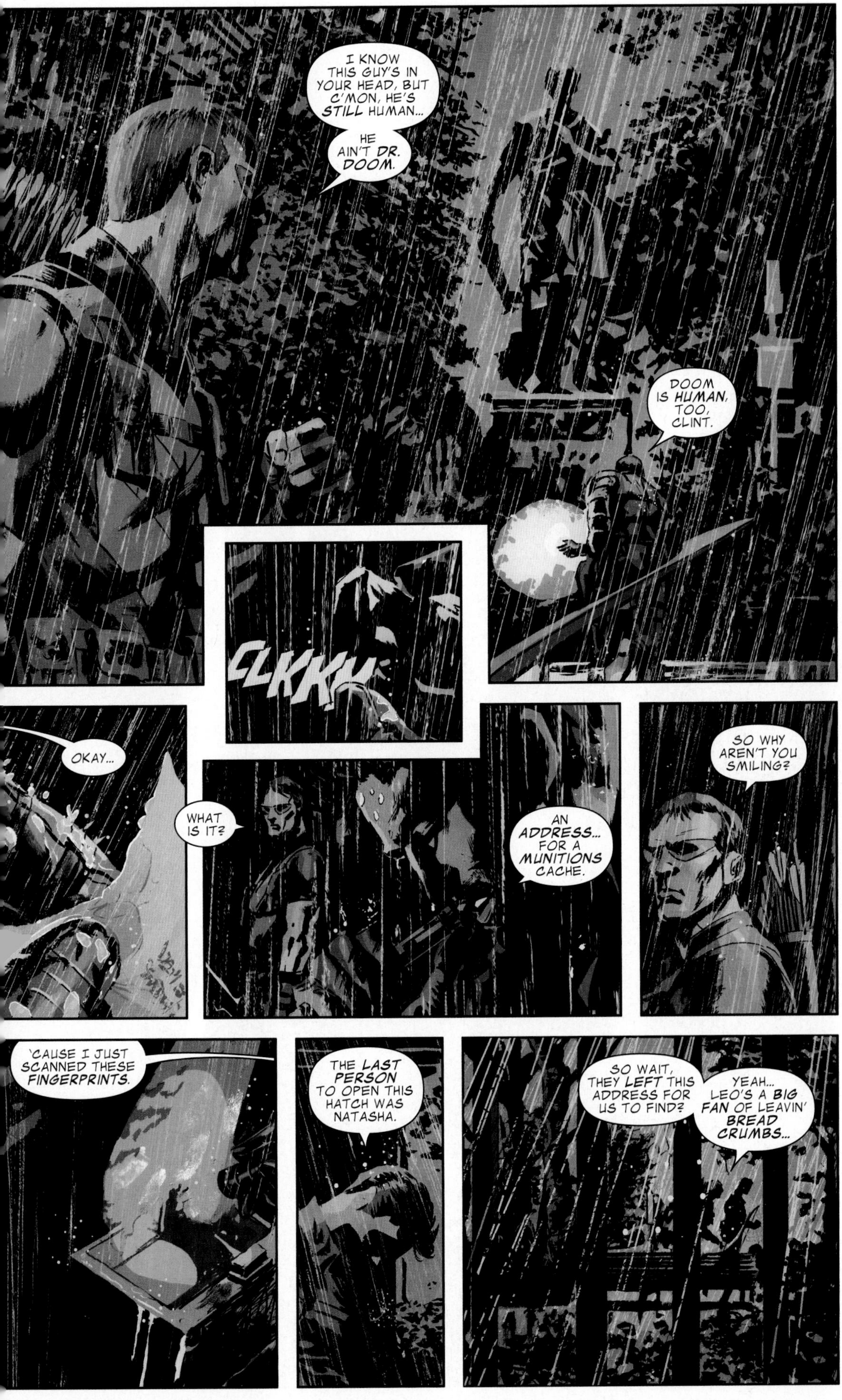
I KNOW THIS GUY'S IN YOUR HEAD, BUT C'MON, HE'S STILL HUMAN...
HE AIN'T DR. DOOM.
DOOM IS HUMAN, TOO, CLINT.
CLKKK
OKAY...
WHAT IS IT?
AN ADDRESS... FOR A MUNITIONS CACHE.
SO WHY AREN'T YOU SMILING?
'CAUSE I JUST SCANNED THESE FINGERPRINTS.
THE LAST PERSON TO OPEN THIS HATCH WAS NATASHA.
SO WAIT, THEY LEFT THIS ADDRESS FOR US TO FIND?
YEAH... LEO'S A BIG FAN OF LEAVIN' BREAD CRUMBS...

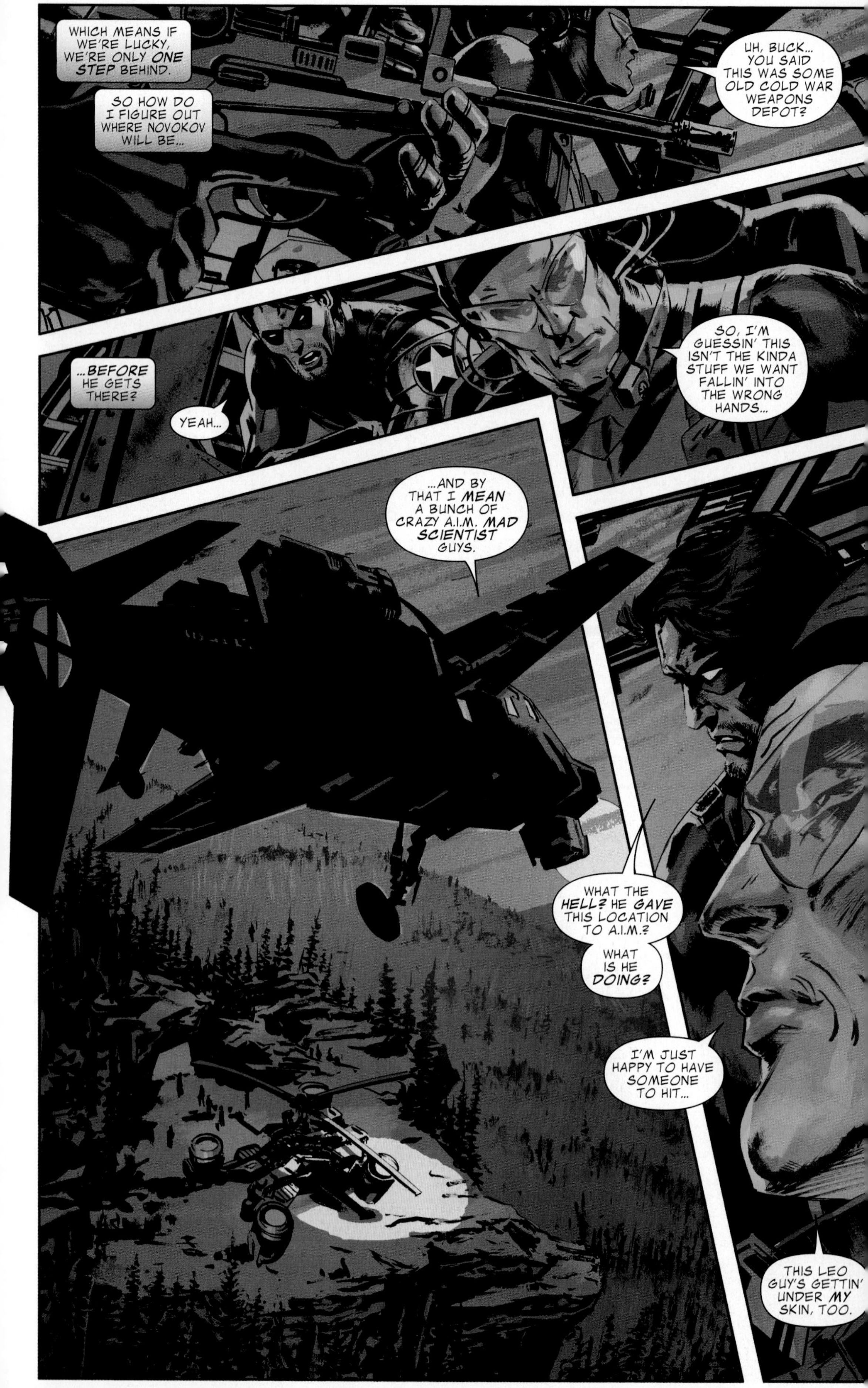
WHICH MEANS IF WE'RE LUCKY, WE'RE ONLY ONE STEP BEHIND.
SO HOW DO I FIGURE OUT WHERE NOVOKOV WILL BE...
UH, BUCK... YOU SAID THIS WAS SOME OLD COLD WAR WEAPONS DEPOT?
...BEFORE HE GETS THERE?
YEAH...
SO, I'M GUESSIN' THIS ISN'T THE KINDA STUFF WE WANT FALLIN' INTO THE WRONG HANDS...
...AND BY THAT I MEAN A BUNCH OF CRAZY A.I.M. MAD SCIENTIST GUYS.
WHAT THE HELL? HE GAVE THIS LOCATION TO A.I.M.?
WHAT IS HE DOING?
I'M JUST HAPPY TO HAVE SOMEONE TO HIT...
THIS LEO GUY'S GETTIN' UNDER MY SKIN, TOO.

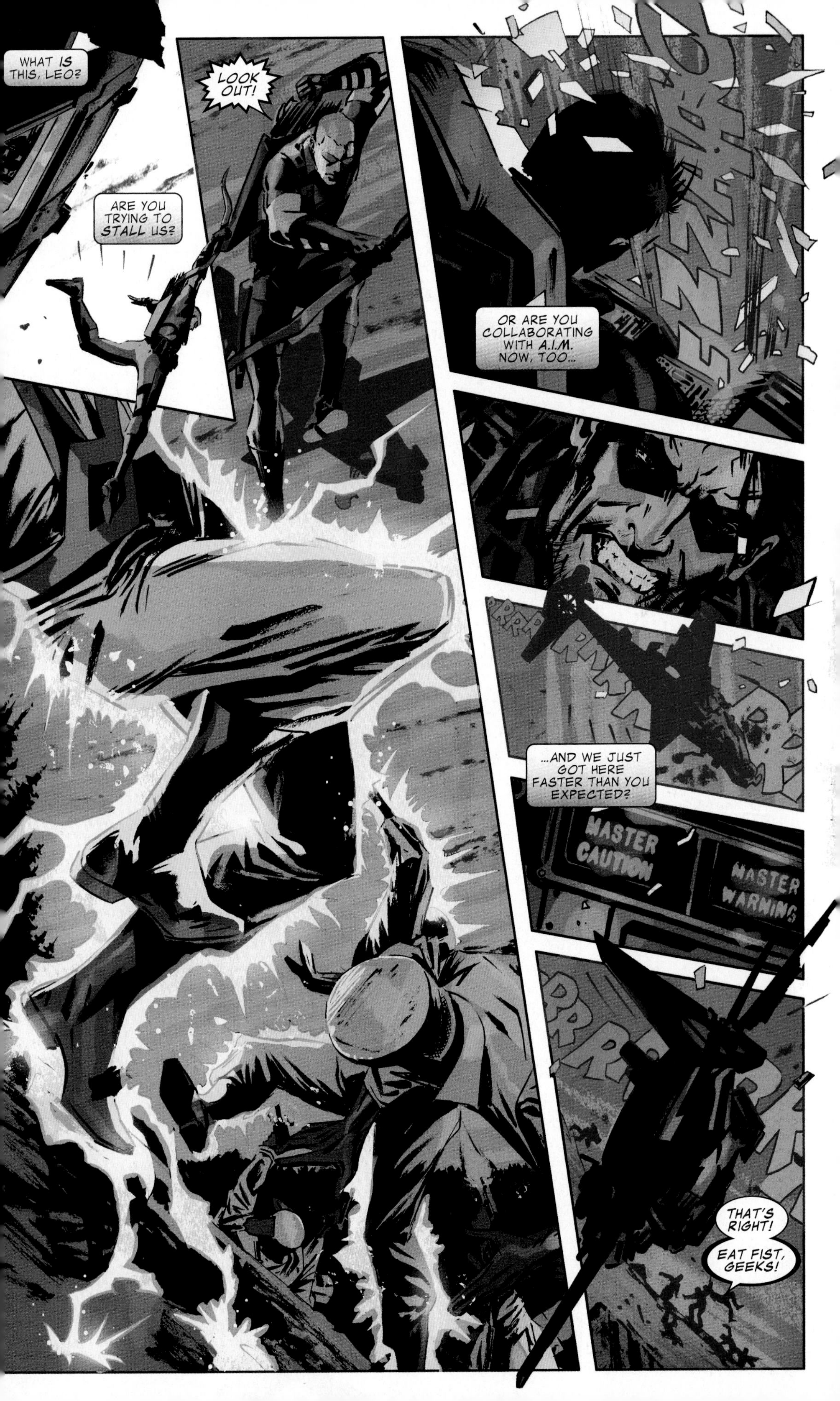
WHAT IS THIS, LEO?
LOOK OUT!
ARE YOU TRYING TO STALL US?
OR ARE YOU COLLABORATING WITH A.I.M. NOW, TOO...
...AND WE JUST GOT HERE FASTER THAN YOU EXPECTED?
MASTER CAUTION
MASTER WARNING
THAT'S RIGHT!
EAT FIST, GEEKS!

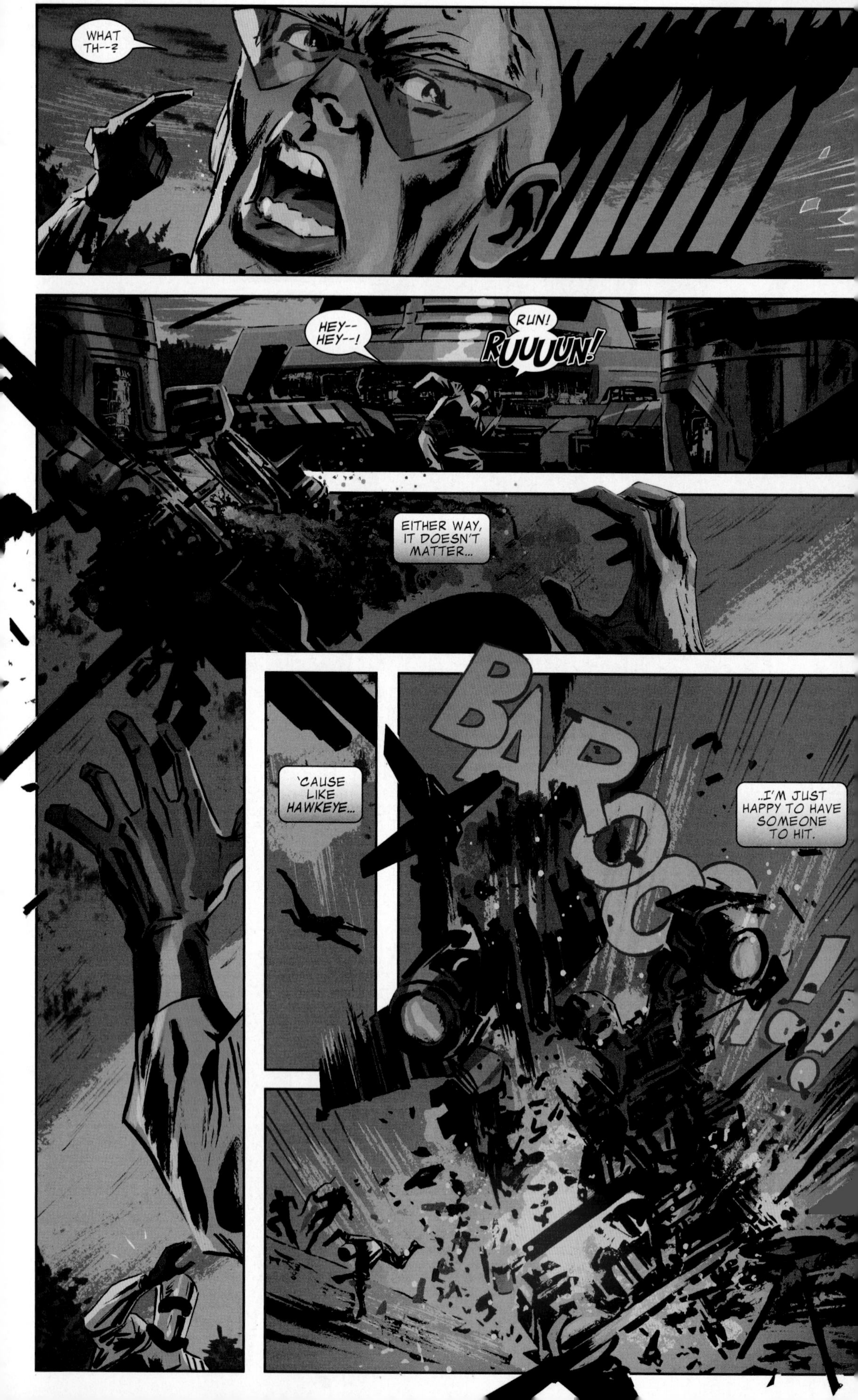
WHAT TH--?
HEY-- HEY--!
RUN!
RUUUUN!
EITHER WAY, IT DOESN'T MATTER...
'CAUSE LIKE HAWKEYE...
BAROOOOM!
..I'M JUST HAPPY TO HAVE SOMEONE TO HIT.

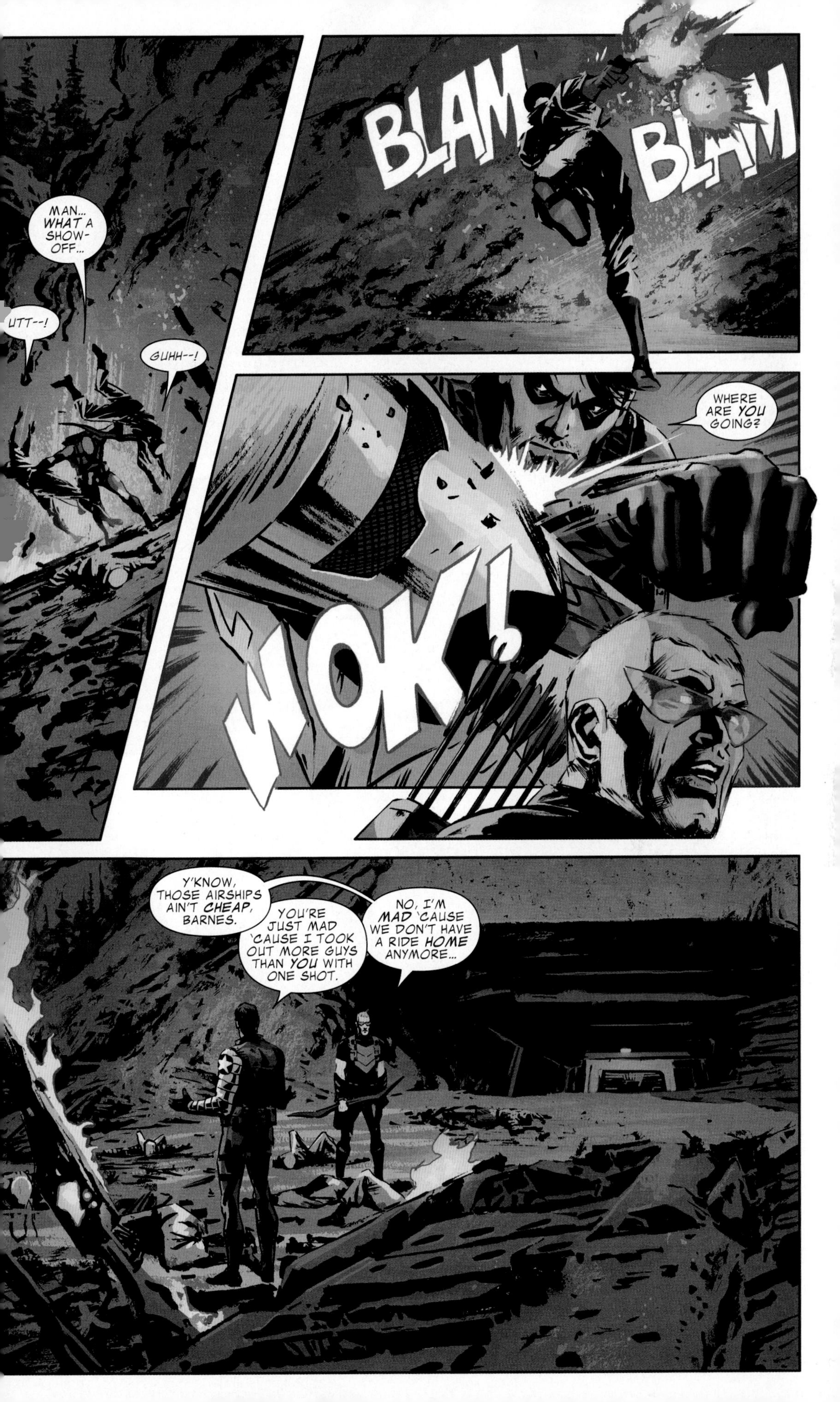
BLAM
BLAM
MAN... WHAT A SHOW-OFF...
UTT--!
GUHH--!
WHERE ARE YOU GOING?
WOK!
Y'KNOW, THOSE AIRSHIPS AIN'T CHEAP, BARNES.
YOU'RE JUST MAD 'CAUSE I TOOK OUT MORE GUYS THAN YOU WITH ONE SHOT.
NO, I'M MAD 'CAUSE WE DON'T HAVE A RIDE HOME ANYMORE...

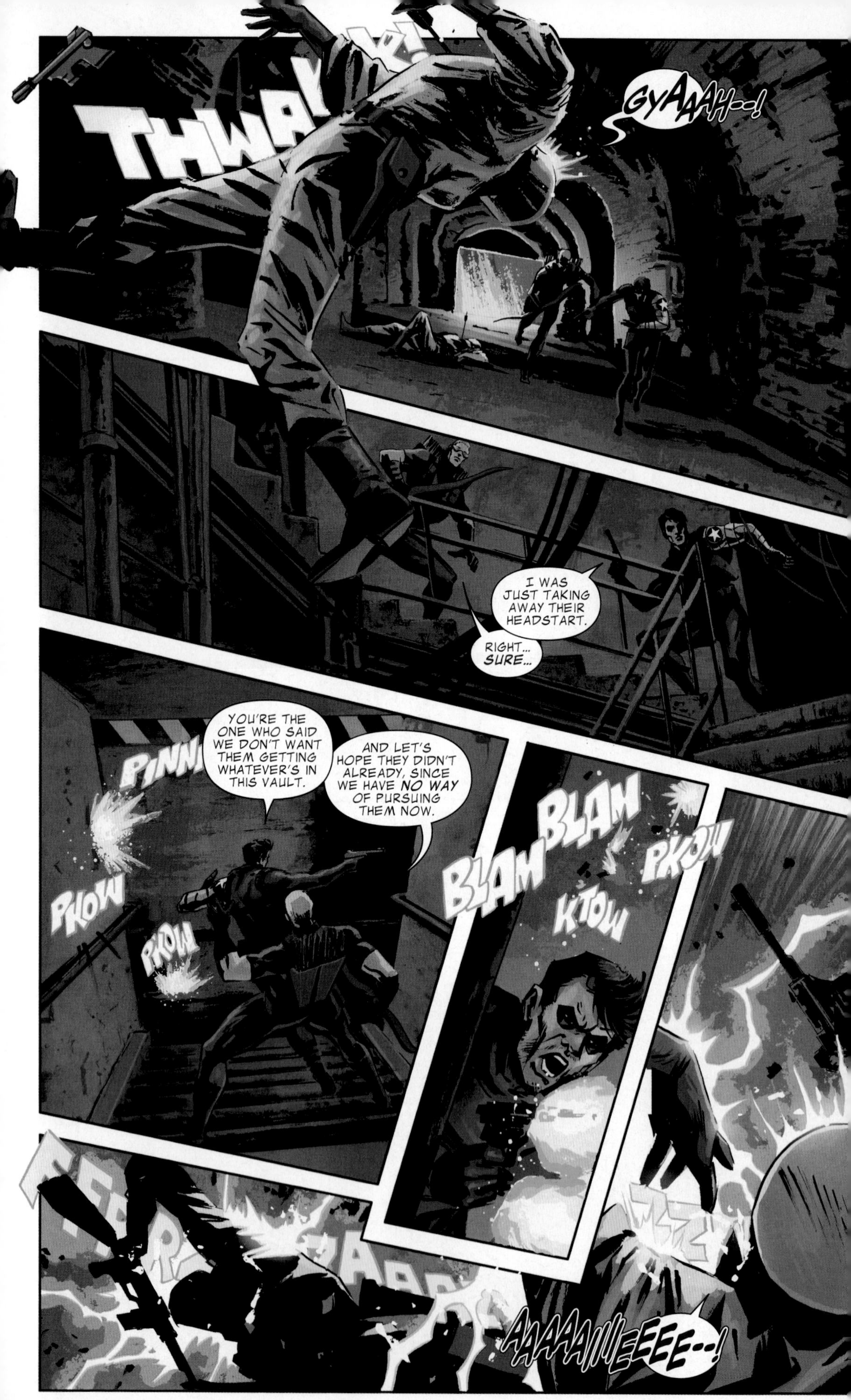

THWAK!
GYAAAH--!
I WAS JUST TAKING AWAY THEIR HEADSTART.
RIGHT... SURE...
YOU'RE THE ONE WHO SAID WE DON'T WANT THEM GETTING WHATEVER'S IN THIS VAULT.
AND LET'S HOPE THEY DIDN'T ALREADY, SINCE WE HAVE NO WAY OF PURSUING THEM NOW.
PINNG
PKOW
PKOW
BLAM
BLAM
KTOW
PKOW
AAAAAIIIEEEE--!

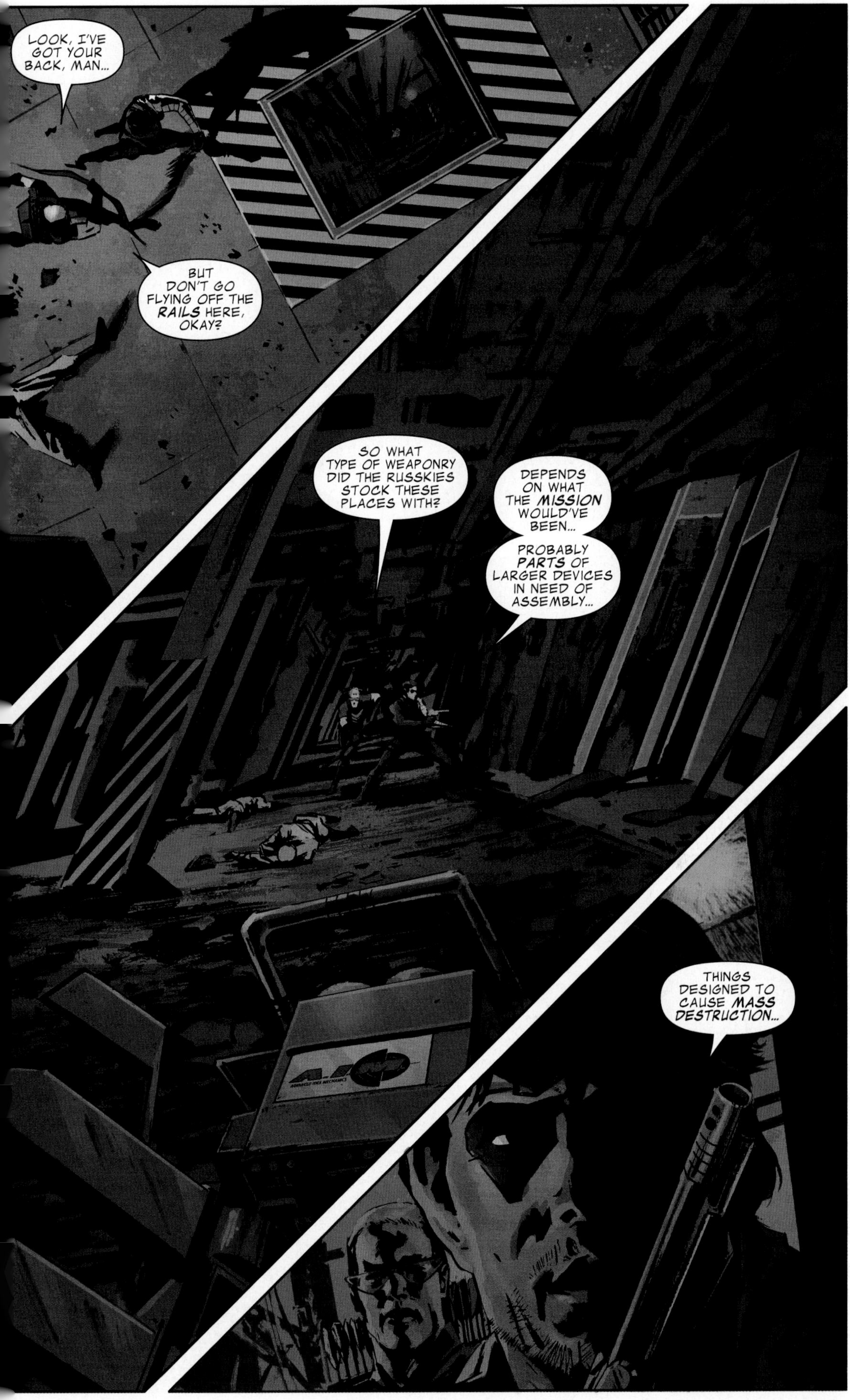
LOOK, I'VE GOT YOUR BACK, MAN...
BUT DON'T GO FLYING OFF THE RAILS HERE, OKAY?
SO WHAT TYPE OF WEAPONRY DID THE RUSSKIES STOCK THESE PLACES WITH?
DEPENDS ON WHAT THE MISSION WOULD'VE BEEN...
PROBABLY PARTS OF LARGER DEVICES IN NEED OF ASSEMBLY...
THINGS DESIGNED TO CAUSE MASS DESTRUCTION...

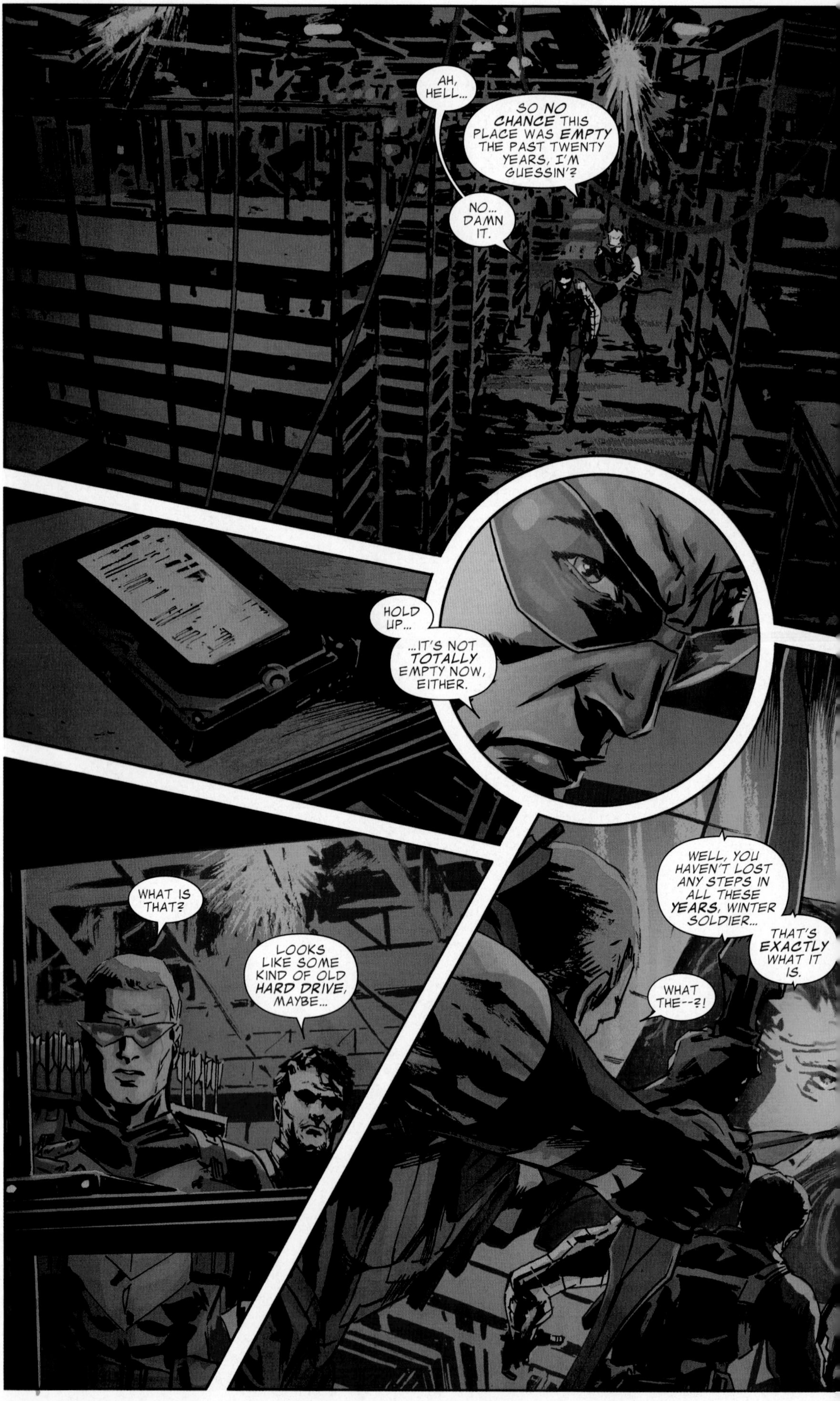

AH, HELL...
SO NO CHANCE THIS PLACE WAS EMPTY THE PAST TWENTY YEARS, I'M GUESSIN'?
NO... DAMN IT.
HOLD UP...
...IT'S NOT TOTALLY EMPTY NOW, EITHER.
WHAT IS THAT?
LOOKS LIKE SOME KIND OF OLD HARD DRIVE, MAYBE...
WELL, YOU HAVEN'T LOST ANY STEPS IN ALL THESE YEARS, WINTER SOLDIER...
THAT'S EXACTLY WHAT IT IS.
WHAT THE--?!

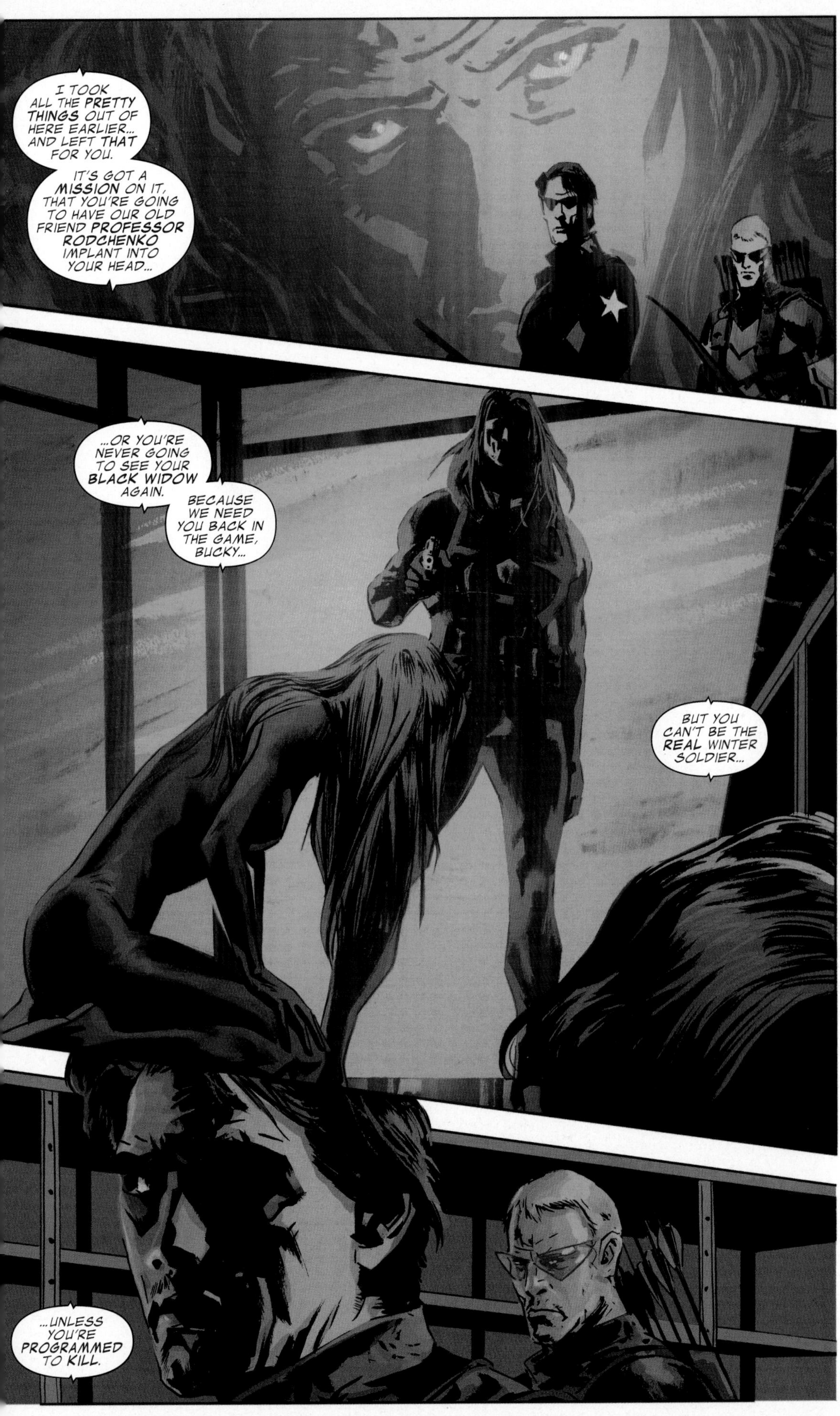
I TOOK ALL THE PRETTY THINGS OUT OF HERE EARLIER... AND LEFT THAT FOR YOU.
IT'S GOT A MISSION ON IT, THAT YOU'RE GOING TO HAVE OUR OLD FRIEND PROFESSOR RODCHENKO IMPLANT INTO YOUR HEAD...
...OR YOU'RE NEVER GOING TO SEE YOUR BLACK WIDOW AGAIN.
BECAUSE WE NEED YOU BACK IN THE GAME, BUCKY...
BUT YOU CAN'T BE THE REAL WINTER SOLDIER...
...UNLESS YOU'RE PROGRAMMED TO KILL.

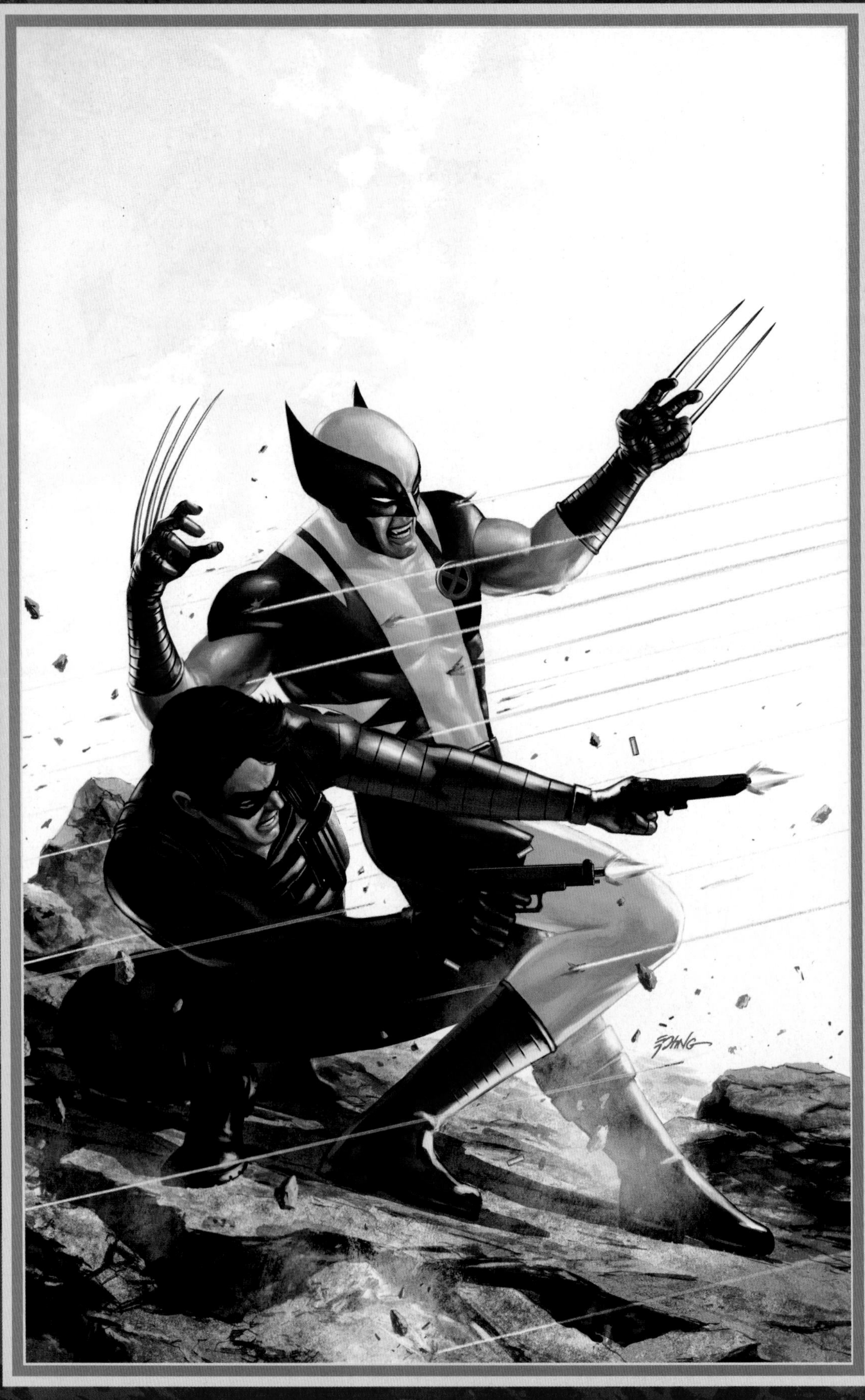

TWELVE

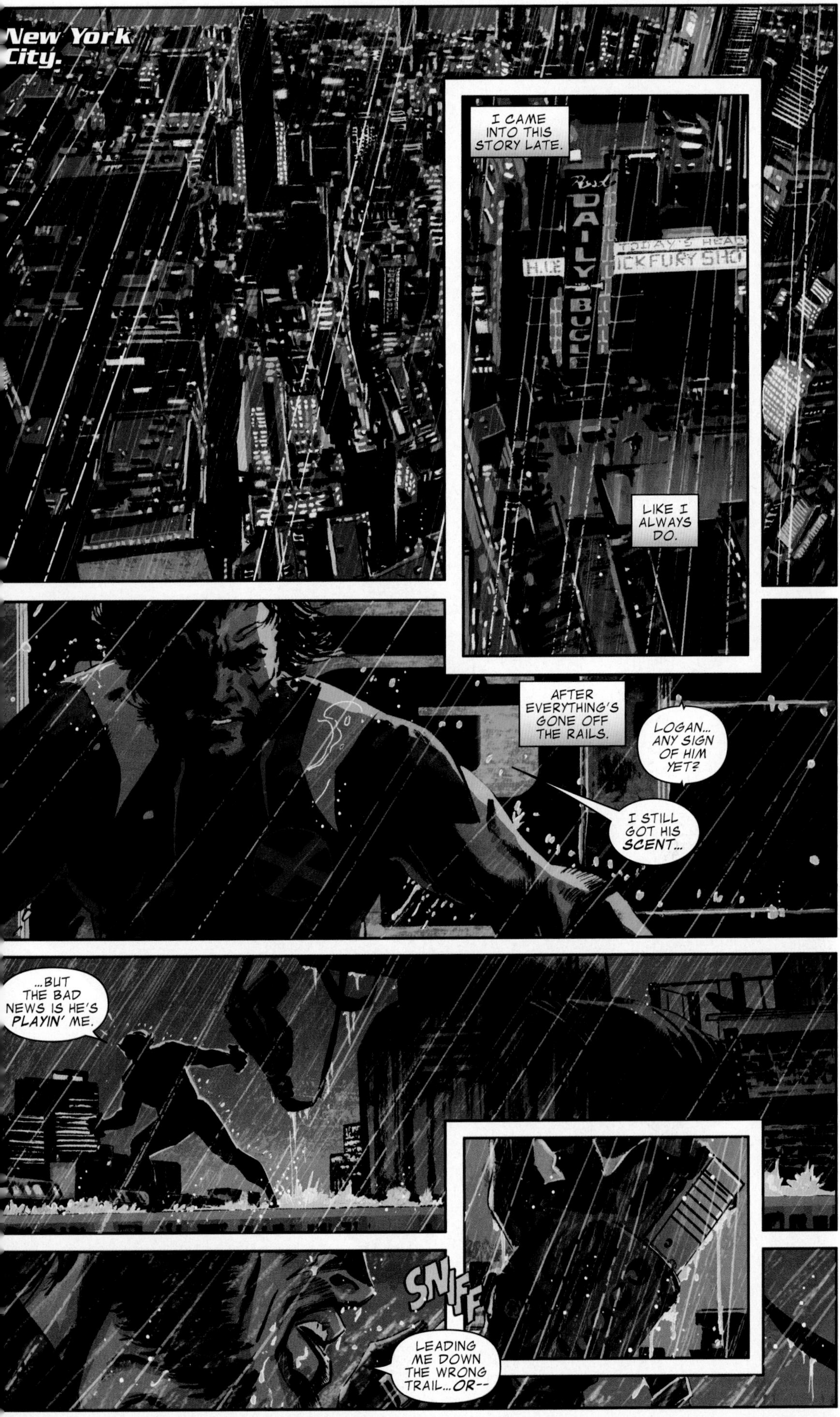
New York City.
I CAME INTO THIS STORY LATE.
DAILY BUGLE
TODAY'S HEAD
ICKFURY SHO
LIKE I ALWAYS DO.
AFTER EVERYTHING'S GONE OFF THE RAILS.
LOGAN... ANY SIGN OF HIM YET?
I STILL GOT HIS SCENT...
...BUT THE BAD NEWS IS HE'S PLAYIN' ME.
SNIFF
LEADING ME DOWN THE WRONG TRAIL...OR--

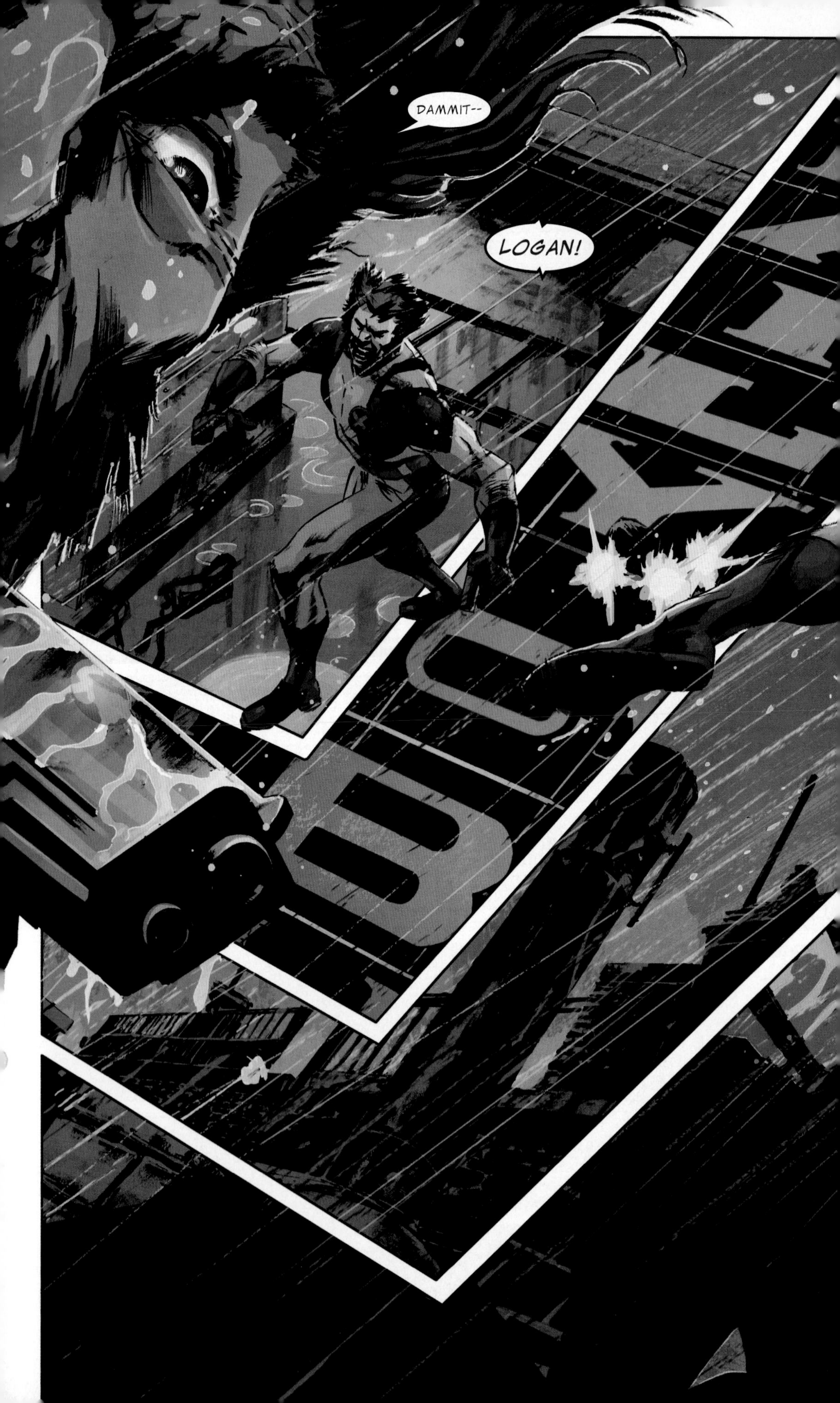
DAMMIT--
LOGAN!

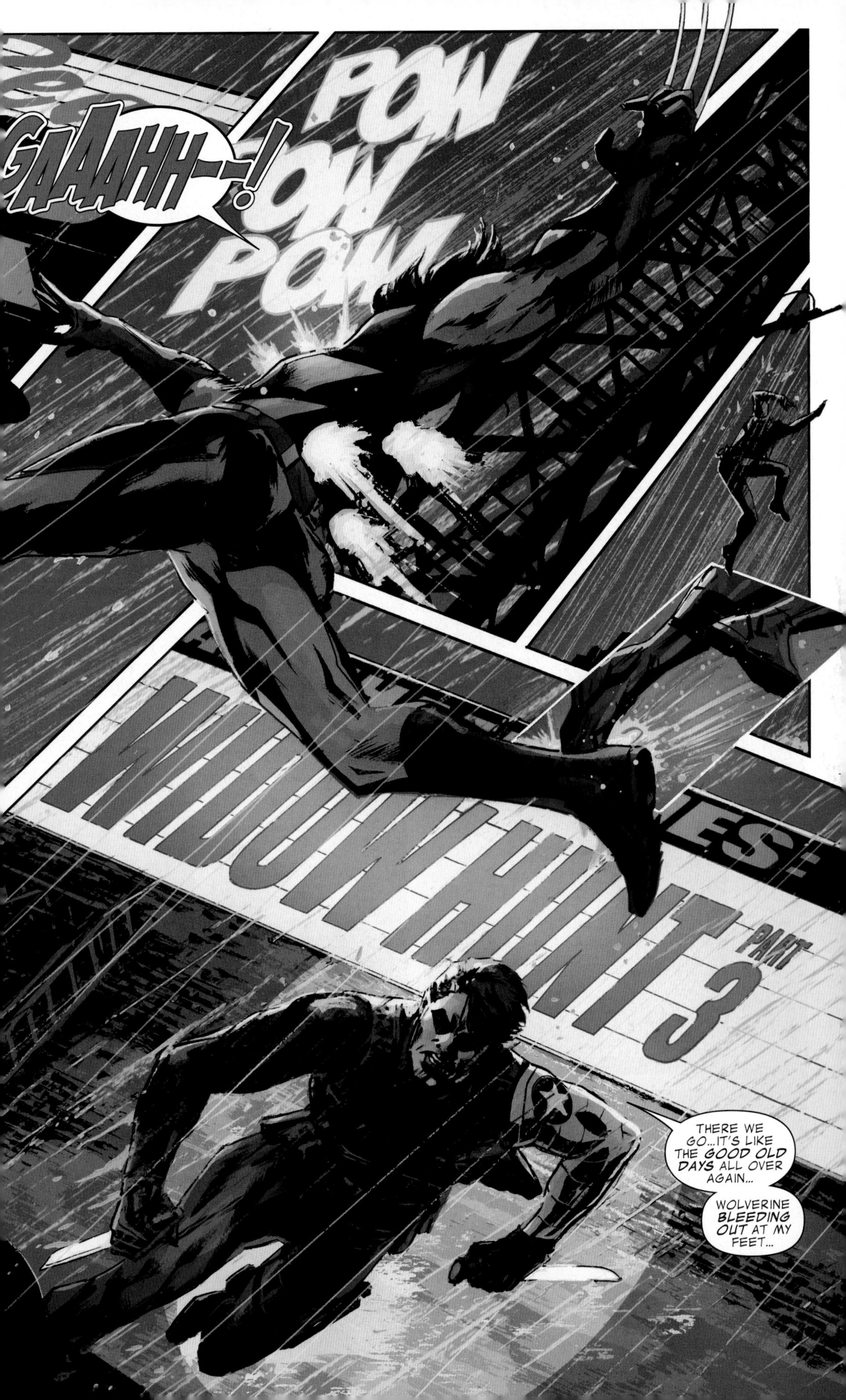
GAAAHH--!
POW POW POW
WIDOW HUNT PART 3
THERE WE GO...IT'S LIKE THE GOOD OLD DAYS ALL OVER AGAIN...
WOLVERINE BLEEDING OUT AT MY FEET...

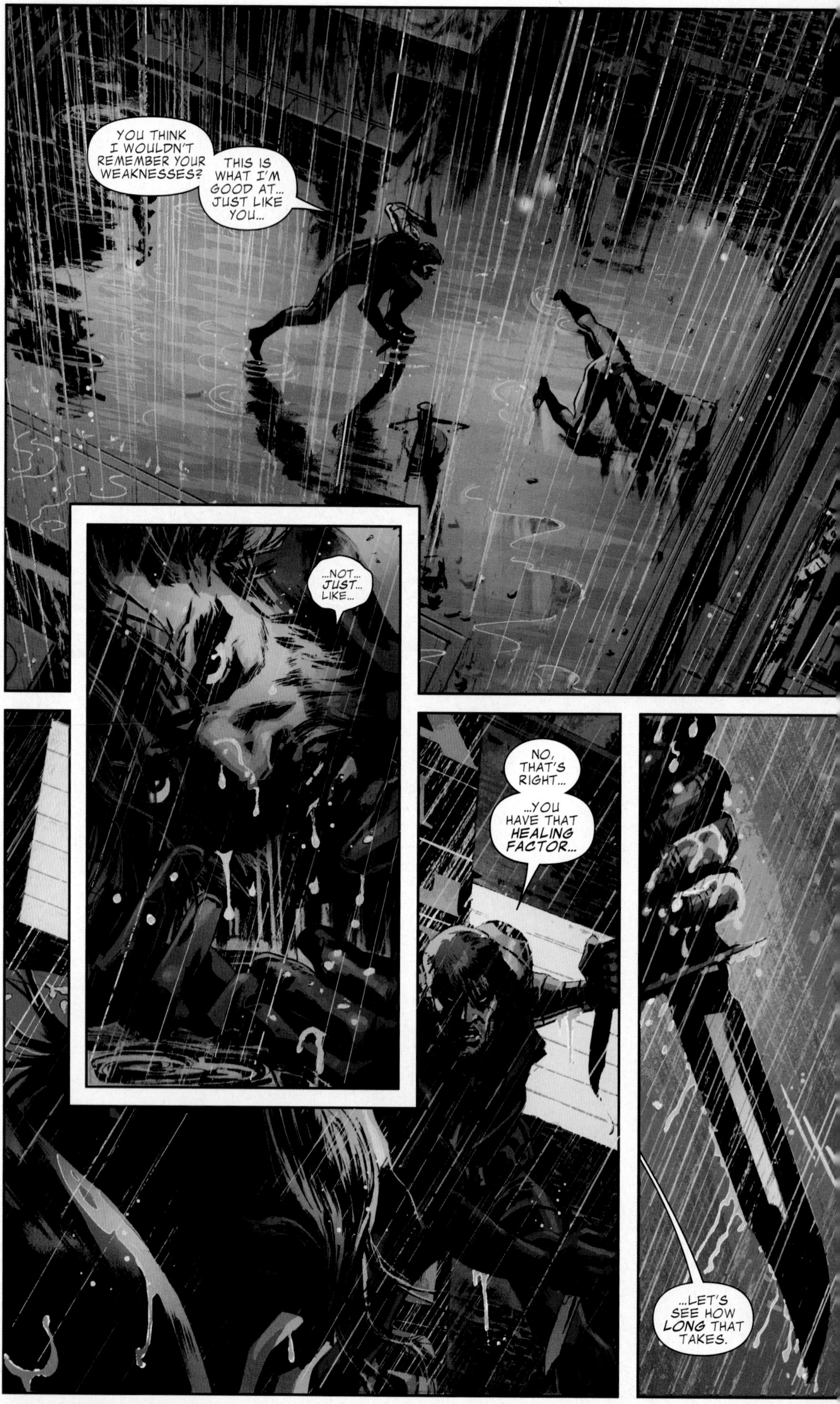
YOU THINK I WOULDN'T REMEMBER YOUR WEAKNESSES?
THIS IS WHAT I'M GOOD AT... JUST LIKE YOU...
...NOT... JUST... LIKE...
NO, THAT'S RIGHT...
...YOU HAVE THAT HEALING FACTOR...
...LET'S SEE HOW LONG THAT TAKES.

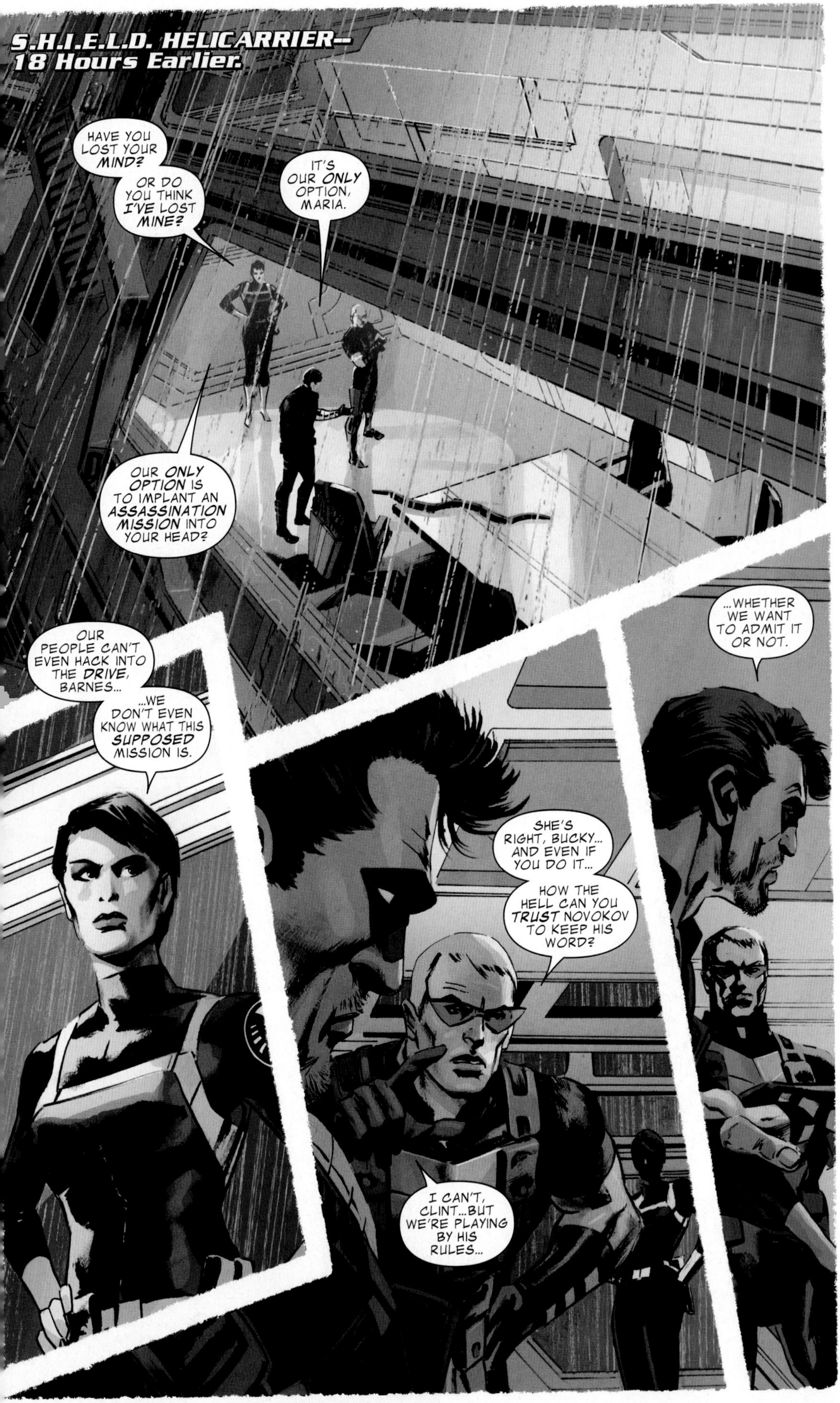
S.H.I.E.L.D. HELICARRIER-- 18 Hours Earlier.
HAVE YOU LOST YOUR MIND?
OR DO YOU THINK I'VE LOST MINE?
IT'S OUR ONLY OPTION, MARIA.
OUR ONLY OPTION IS TO IMPLANT AN ASSASSINATION MISSION INTO YOUR HEAD?
OUR PEOPLE CAN'T EVEN HACK INTO THE DRIVE, BARNES...
...WE DON'T EVEN KNOW WHAT THIS SUPPOSED MISSION IS.
SHE'S RIGHT, BUCKY... AND EVEN IF YOU DO IT...
HOW THE HELL CAN YOU TRUST NOVOKOV TO KEEP HIS WORD?
I CAN'T, CLINT...BUT WE'RE PLAYING BY HIS RULES...
...WHETHER WE WANT TO ADMIT IT OR NOT.

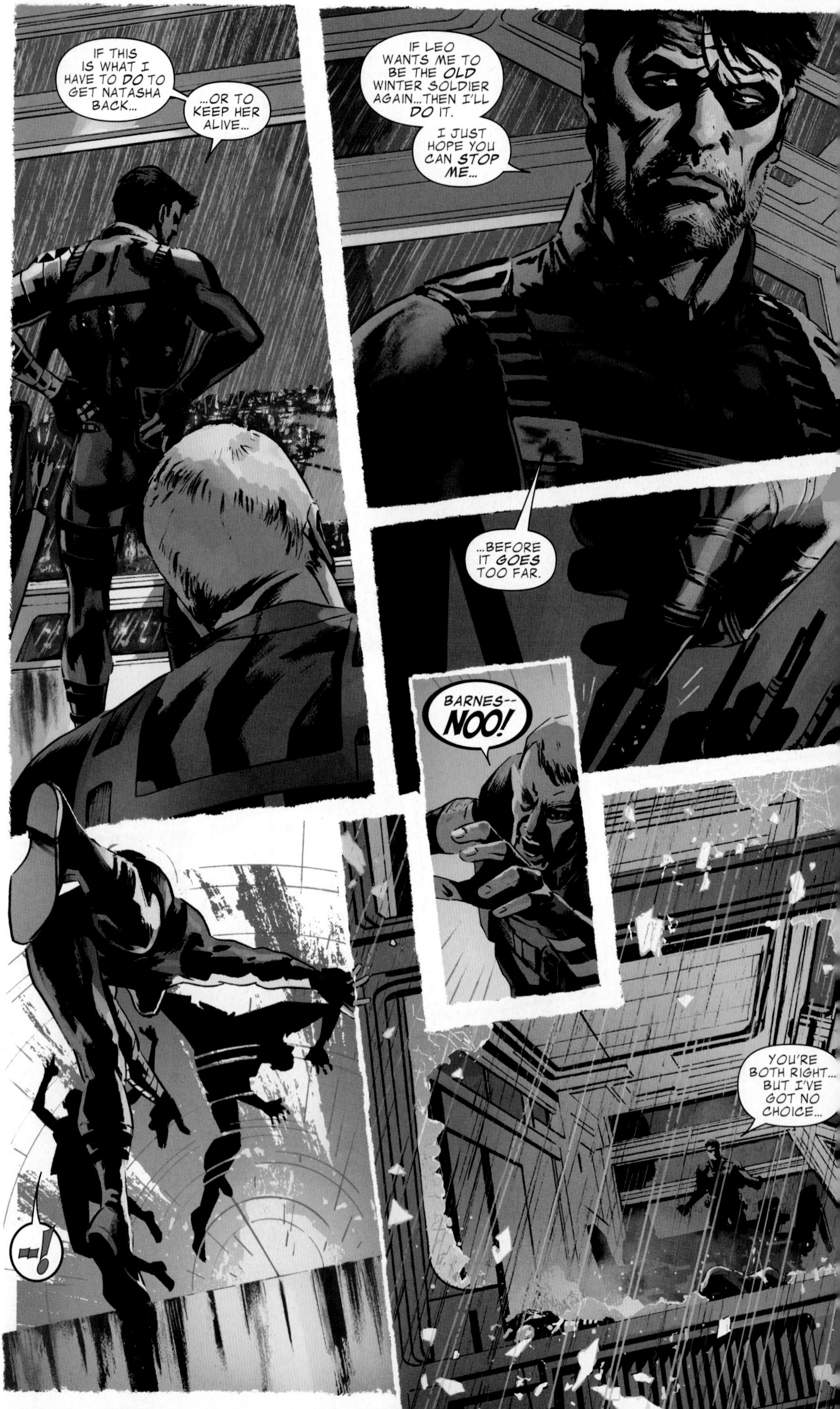
IF THIS IS WHAT I HAVE TO DO TO GET NATASHA BACK...
...OR TO KEEP HER ALIVE...
IF LEO WANTS ME TO BE THE OLD WINTER SOLDIER AGAIN...THEN I'LL DO IT.
I JUST HOPE YOU CAN STOP ME...
...BEFORE IT GOES TOO FAR.
BARNES-- NOO!
YOU'RE BOTH RIGHT... BUT I'VE GOT NO CHOICE...
!

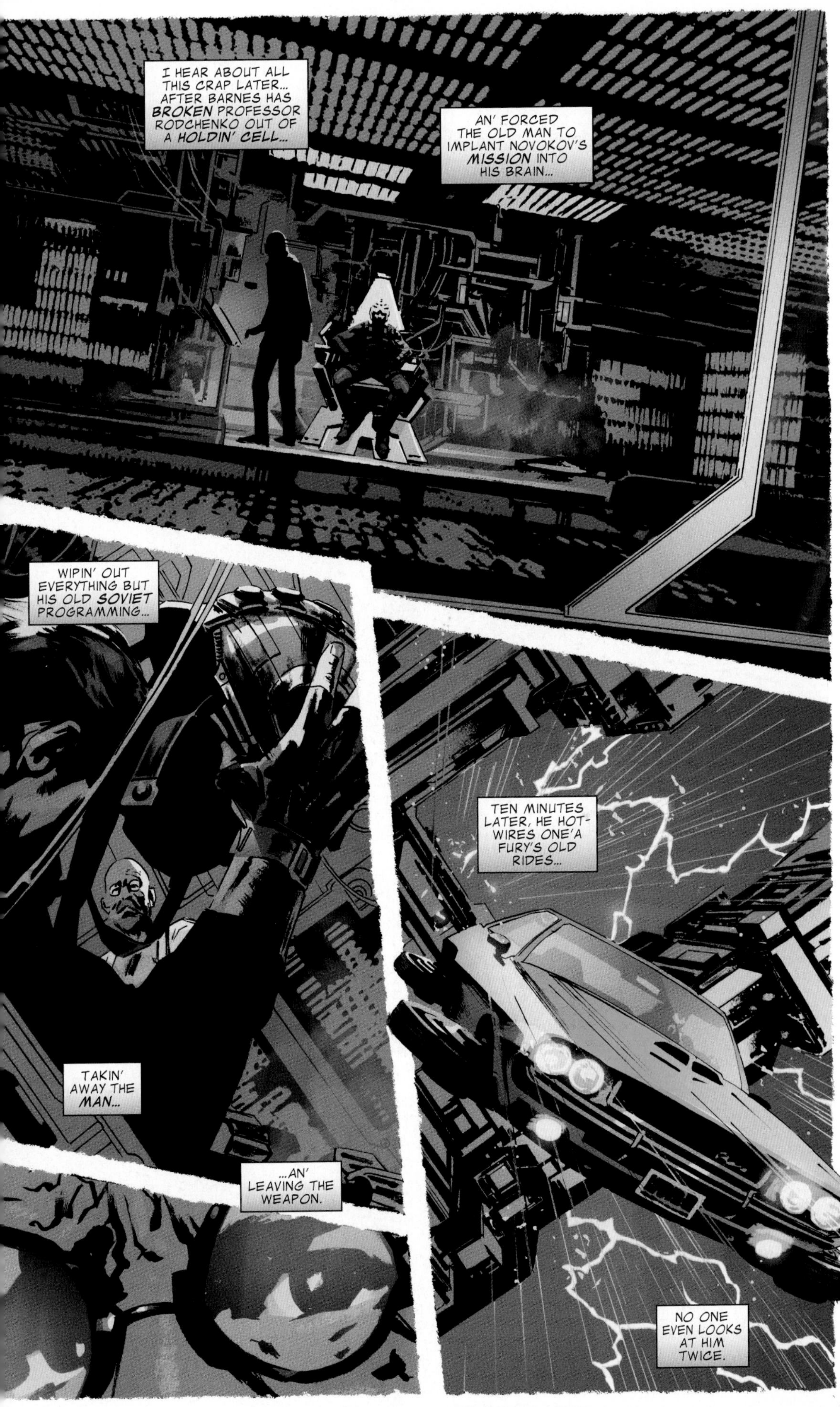
I HEAR ABOUT ALL THIS CRAP LATER... AFTER BARNES HAS BROKEN PROFESSOR RODCHENKO OUT OF A HOLDIN' CELL...
AN' FORCED THE OLD MAN TO IMPLANT NOVOKOV'S MISSION INTO HIS BRAIN...
WIPIN' OUT EVERYTHING BUT HIS OLD SOVIET PROGRAMMING...
TAKIN' AWAY THE MAN...
...AN' LEAVING THE WEAPON.
TEN MINUTES LATER, HE HOT-WIRES ONE'A FURY'S OLD RIDES...
NO ONE EVEN LOOKS AT HIM TWICE.

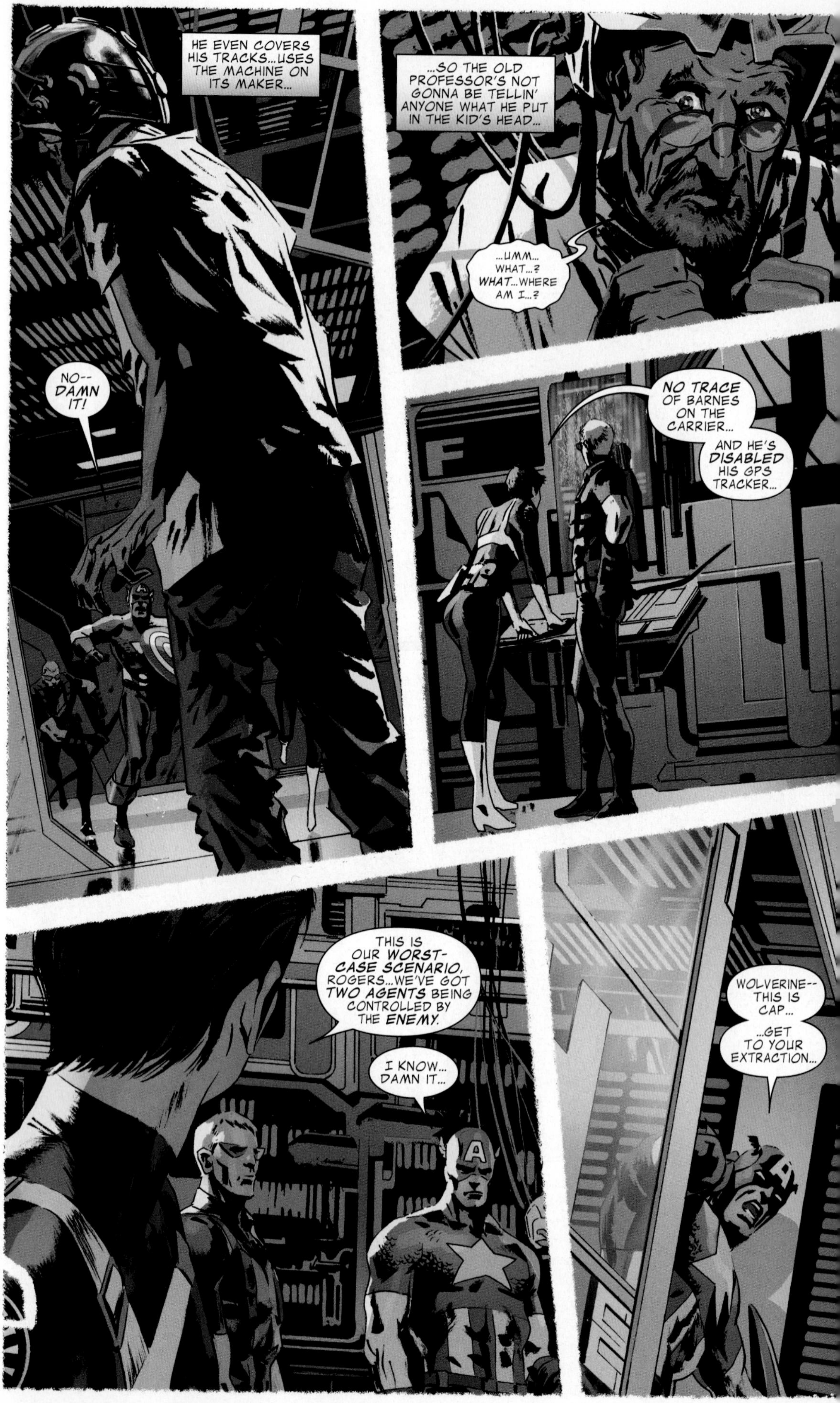
HE EVEN COVERS HIS TRACKS...USES THE MACHINE ON ITS MAKER...
NO-- DAMN IT!
...SO THE OLD PROFESSOR'S NOT GONNA BE TELLIN' ANYONE WHAT HE PUT IN THE KID'S HEAD...
...UMM... WHAT...? WHAT...WHERE AM I...?
NO TRACE OF BARNES ON THE CARRIER...
AND HE'S DISABLED HIS GPS TRACKER...
THIS IS OUR WORST-CASE SCENARIO, ROGERS...WE'VE GOT TWO AGENTS BEING CONTROLLED BY THE ENEMY.
I KNOW... DAMN IT...
WOLVERINE-- THIS IS CAP...
...GET TO YOUR EXTRACTION...

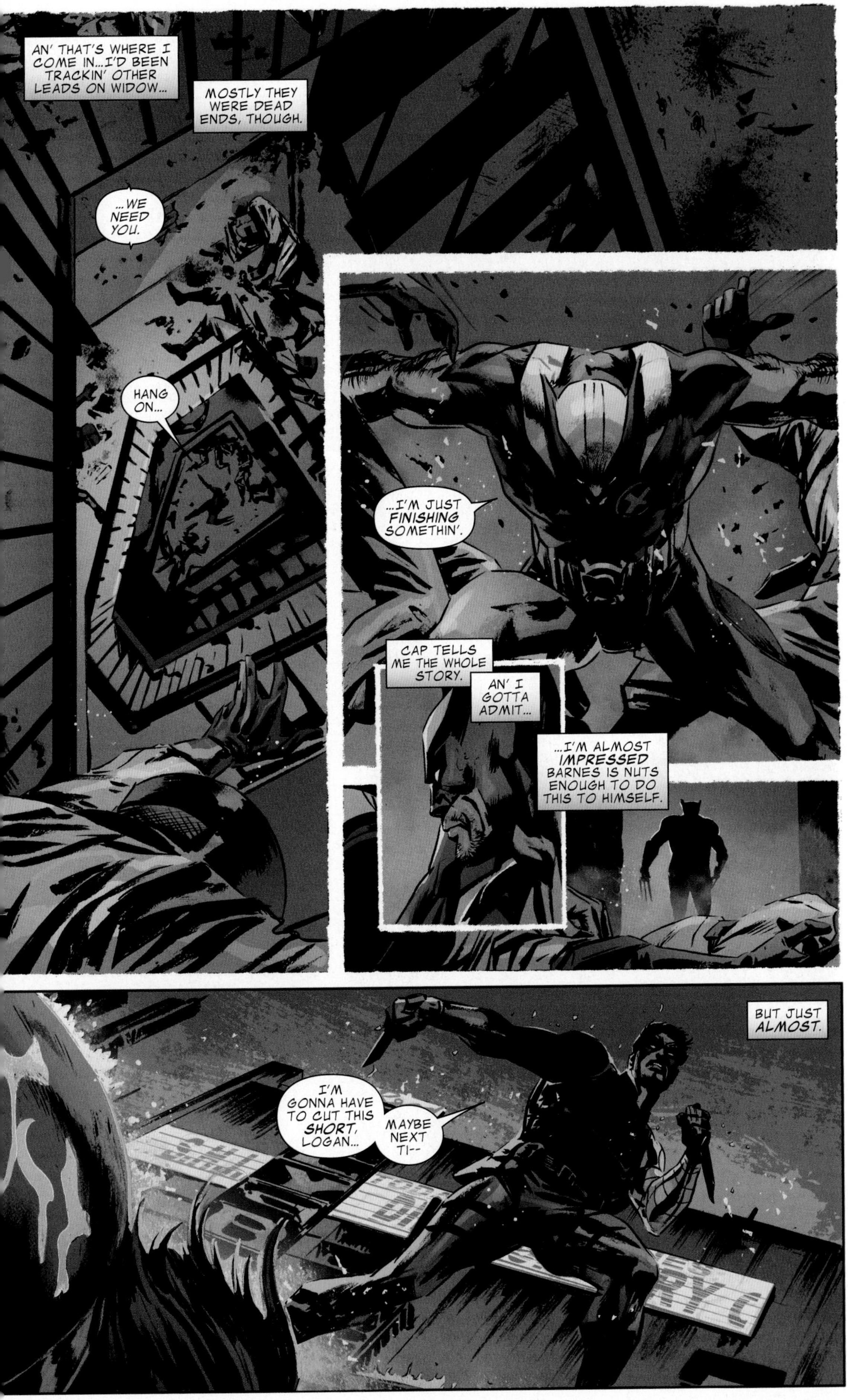
AN' THAT'S WHERE I COME IN...I'D BEEN TRACKIN' OTHER LEADS ON WIDOW...
MOSTLY THEY WERE DEAD ENDS, THOUGH.
...WE NEED YOU.
HANG ON...
...I'M JUST FINISHING SOMETHIN'.
CAP TELLS ME THE WHOLE STORY.
AN' I GOTTA ADMIT...
...I'M ALMOST IMPRESSED BARNES IS NUTS ENOUGH TO DO THIS TO HIMSELF.
BUT JUST ALMOST.
I'M GONNA HAVE TO CUT THIS SHORT, LOGAN...
MAYBE NEXT TI--

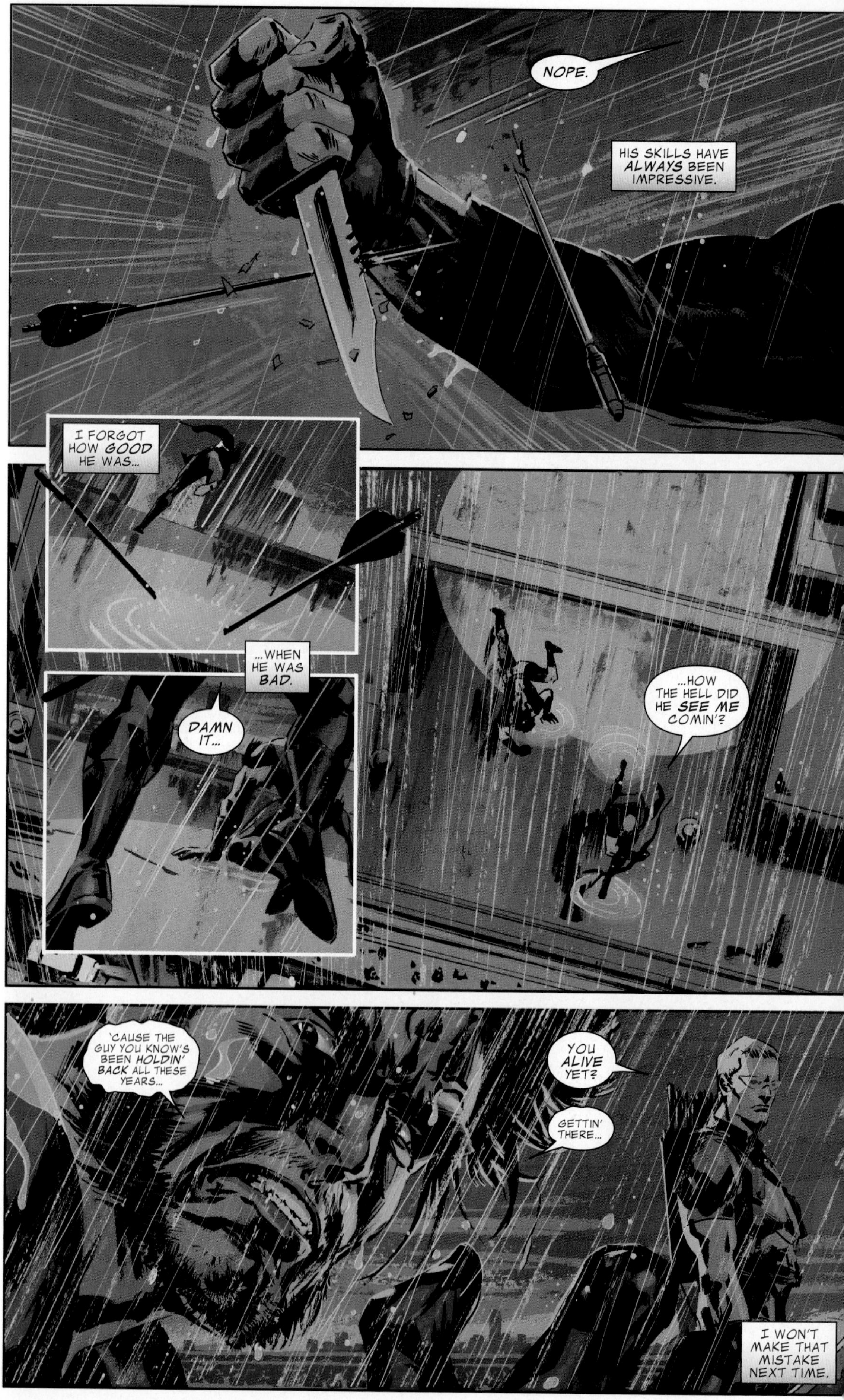
NOPE.
HIS SKILLS HAVE ALWAYS BEEN IMPRESSIVE.
I FORGOT HOW GOOD HE WAS...
...WHEN HE WAS BAD.
DAMN IT...
...HOW THE HELL DID HE SEE ME COMIN'?
'CAUSE THE GUY YOU KNOW'S BEEN HOLDIN' BACK ALL THESE YEARS...
YOU ALIVE YET?
GETTIN' THERE...
I WON'T MAKE THAT MISTAKE NEXT TIME.

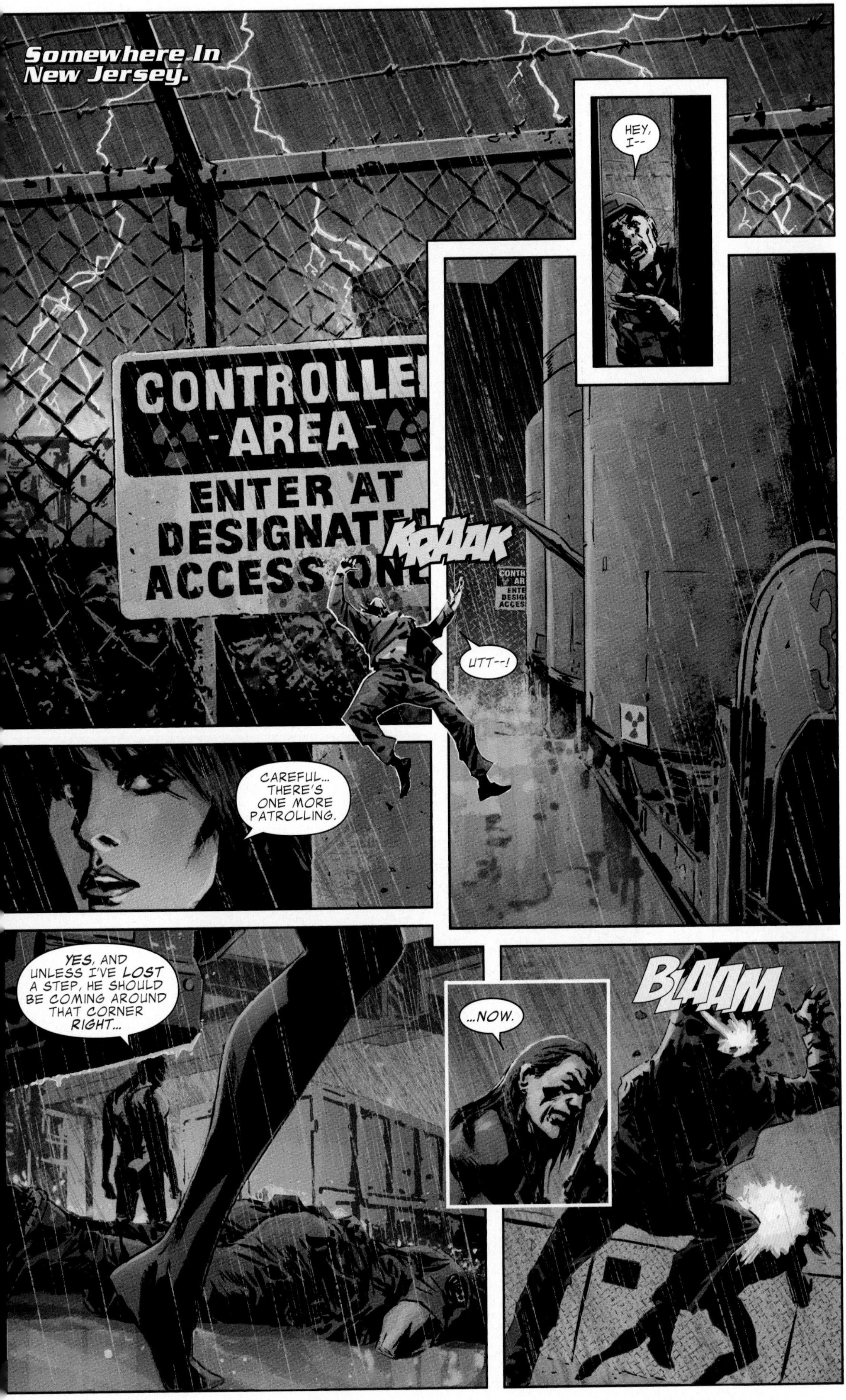

Somewhere In New Jersey.
CONTROLLE -AREA- ENTER AT DESIGNAT ACCESS
HEY, I--
KRAAK
UTT--!
CAREFUL... THERE'S ONE MORE PATROLLING.
YES, AND UNLESS I'VE LOST A STEP, HE SHOULD BE COMING AROUND THAT CORNER RIGHT...
...NOW.
BLAAM

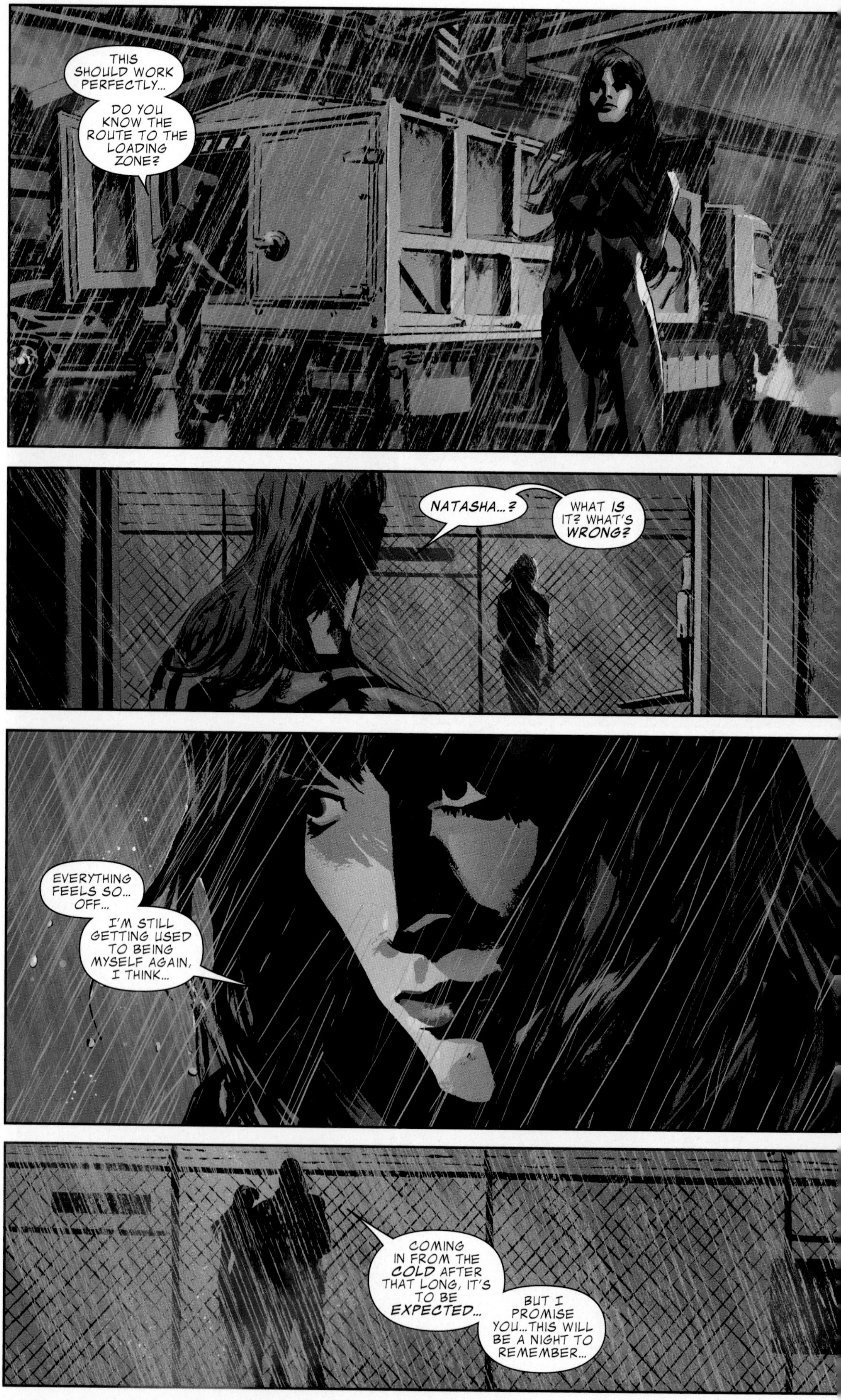
THIS SHOULD WORK PERFECTLY...
DO YOU KNOW THE ROUTE TO THE LOADING ZONE?
NATASHA...?
WHAT IS IT? WHAT'S WRONG?
EVERYTHING FEELS SO... OFF...
I'M STILL GETTING USED TO BEING MYSELF AGAIN, I THINK...
COMING IN FROM THE COLD AFTER THAT LONG, IT'S TO BE EXPECTED...
BUT I PROMISE YOU...THIS WILL BE A NIGHT TO REMEMBER...

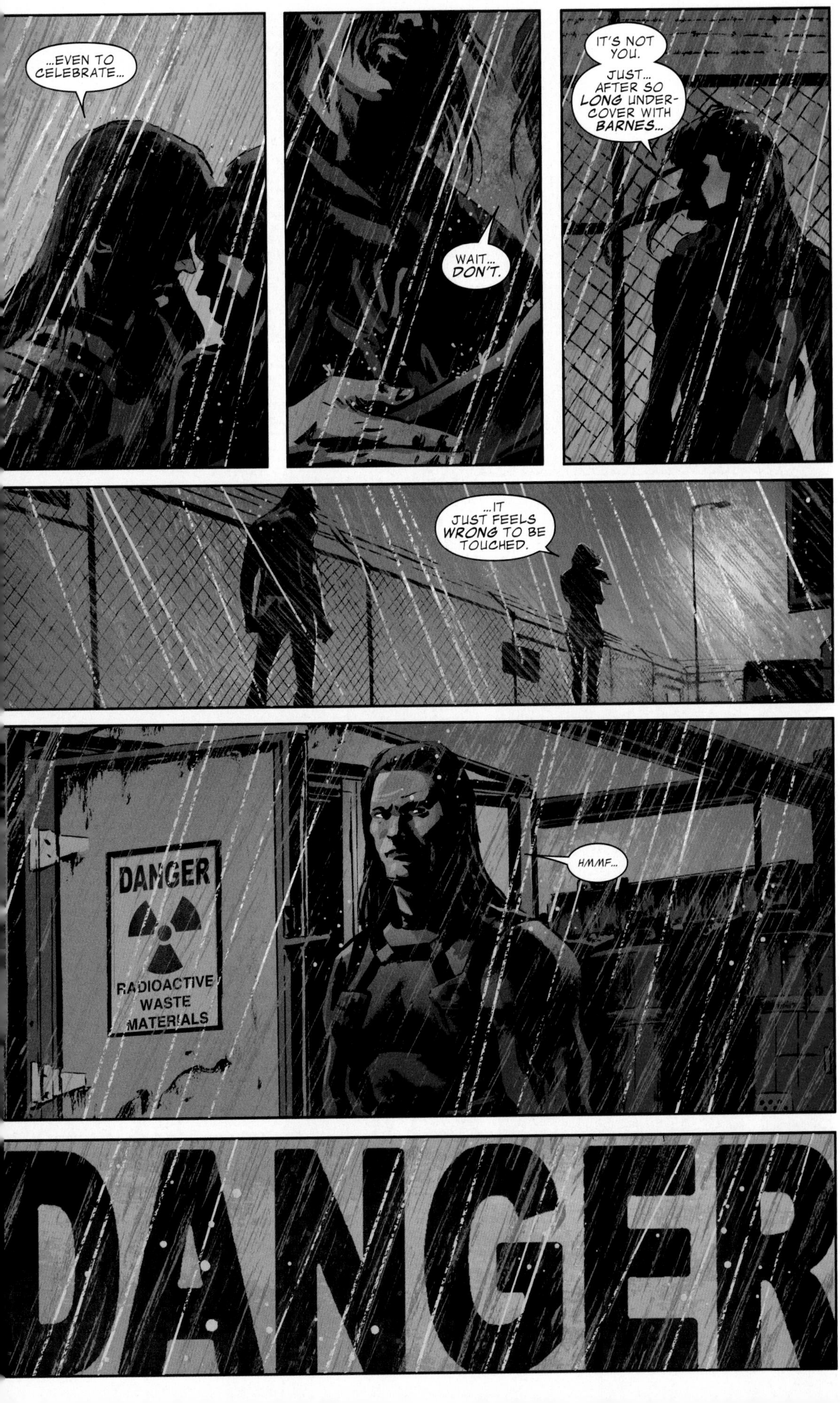
...EVEN TO CELEBRATE...
WAIT... DON'T.
IT'S NOT YOU.
JUST... AFTER SO LONG UNDER-COVER WITH BARNES...
...IT JUST FEELS WRONG TO BE TOUCHED.
DANGER
RADIOACTIVE WASTE MATERIALS
HMMF...
DANGER

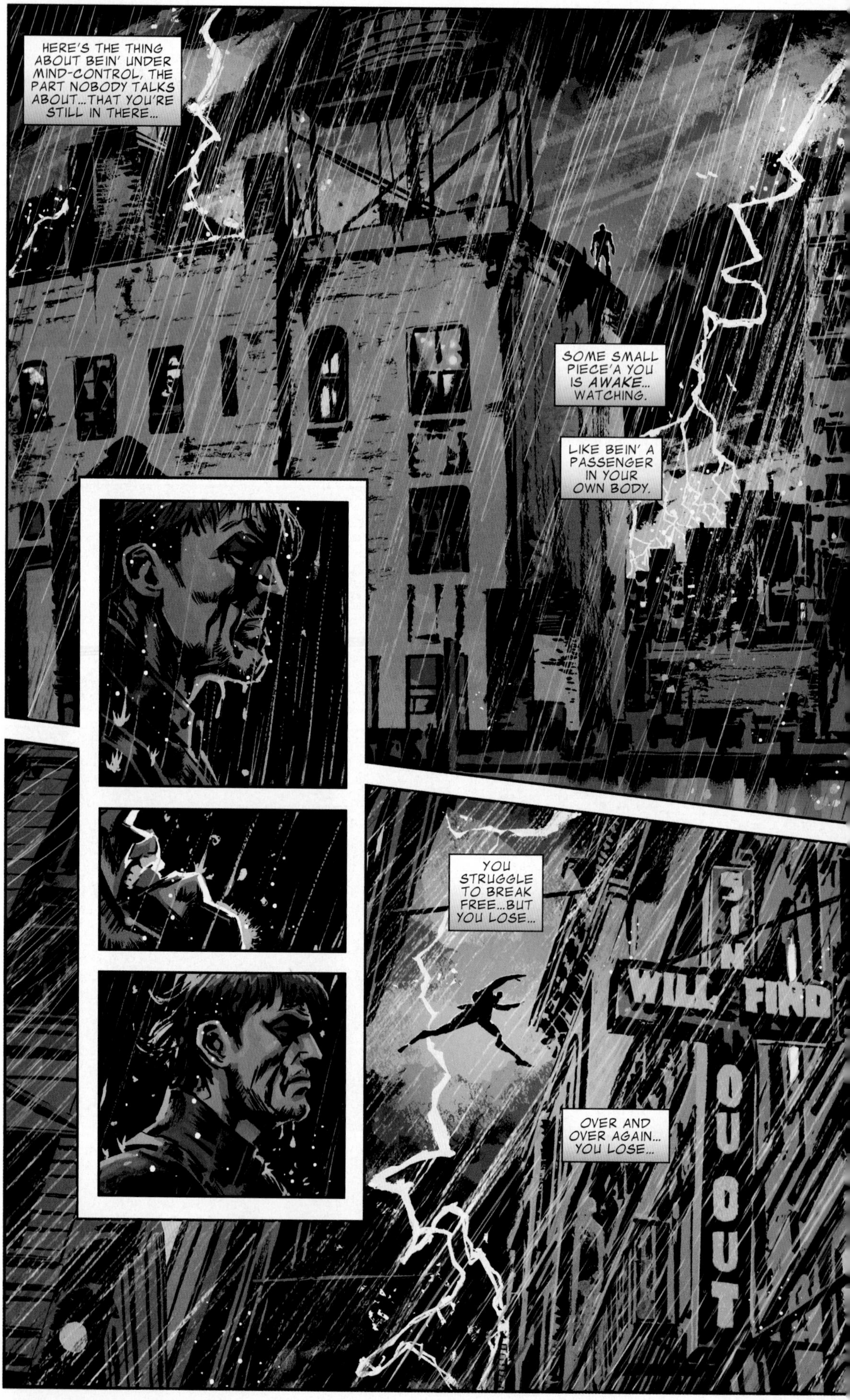

HERE'S THE THING ABOUT BEIN' UNDER MIND-CONTROL, THE PART NOBODY TALKS ABOUT...THAT YOU'RE STILL IN THERE...
SOME SMALL PIECE'A YOU IS AWAKE... WATCHING.
LIKE BEIN' A PASSENGER IN YOUR OWN BODY.
YOU STRUGGLE TO BREAK FREE...BUT YOU LOSE...
OVER AND OVER AGAIN... YOU LOSE...
FIND
OUT

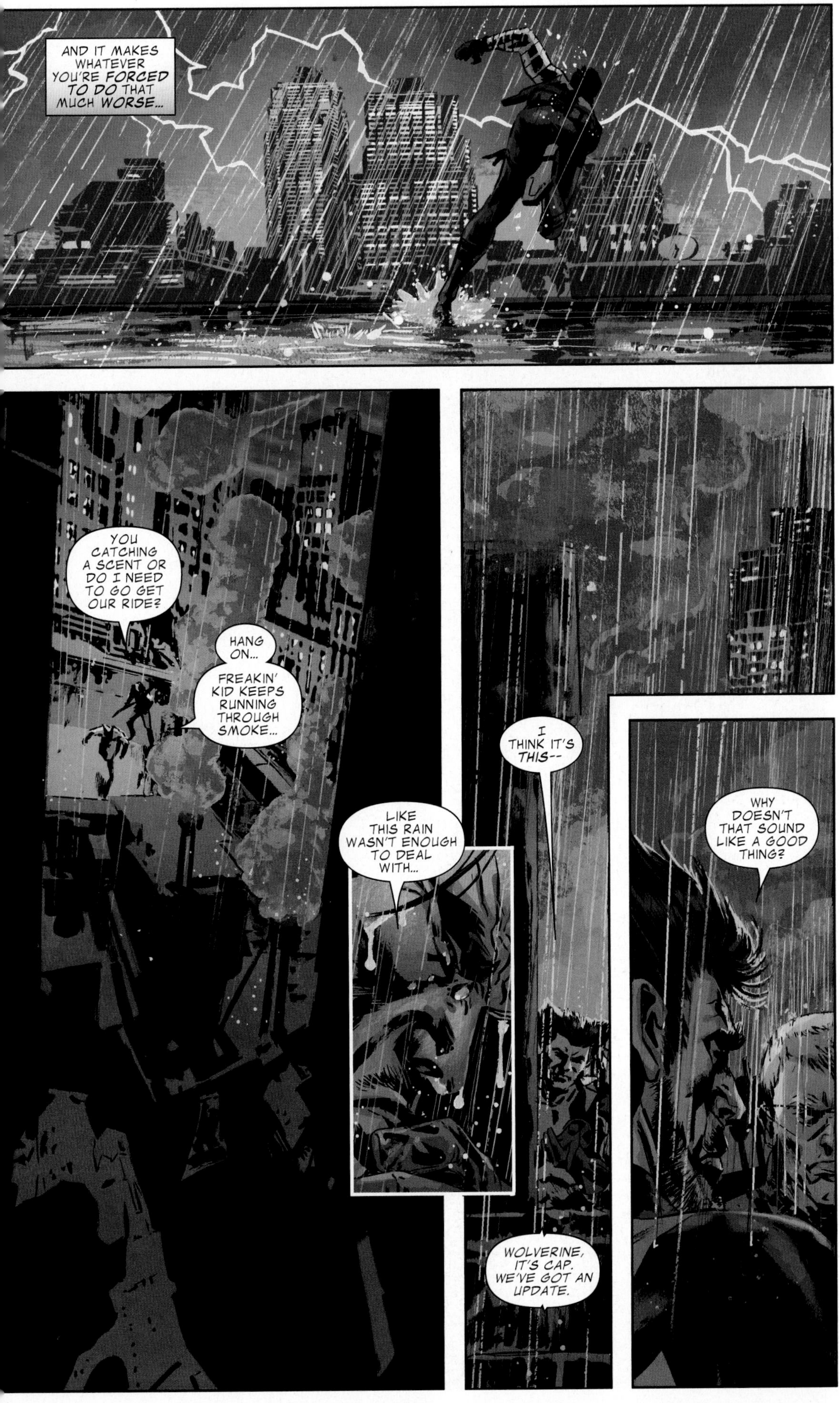

AND IT MAKES WHATEVER YOU'RE FORCED TO DO THAT MUCH WORSE...
YOU CATCHING A SCENT OR DO I NEED TO GO GET OUR RIDE?
HANG ON...
FREAKIN' KID KEEPS RUNNING THROUGH SMOKE...
LIKE THIS RAIN WASN'T ENOUGH TO DEAL WITH...
I THINK IT'S THIS--
WOLVERINE, IT'S CAP. WE'VE GOT AN UPDATE.
WHY DOESN'T THAT SOUND LIKE A GOOD THING?

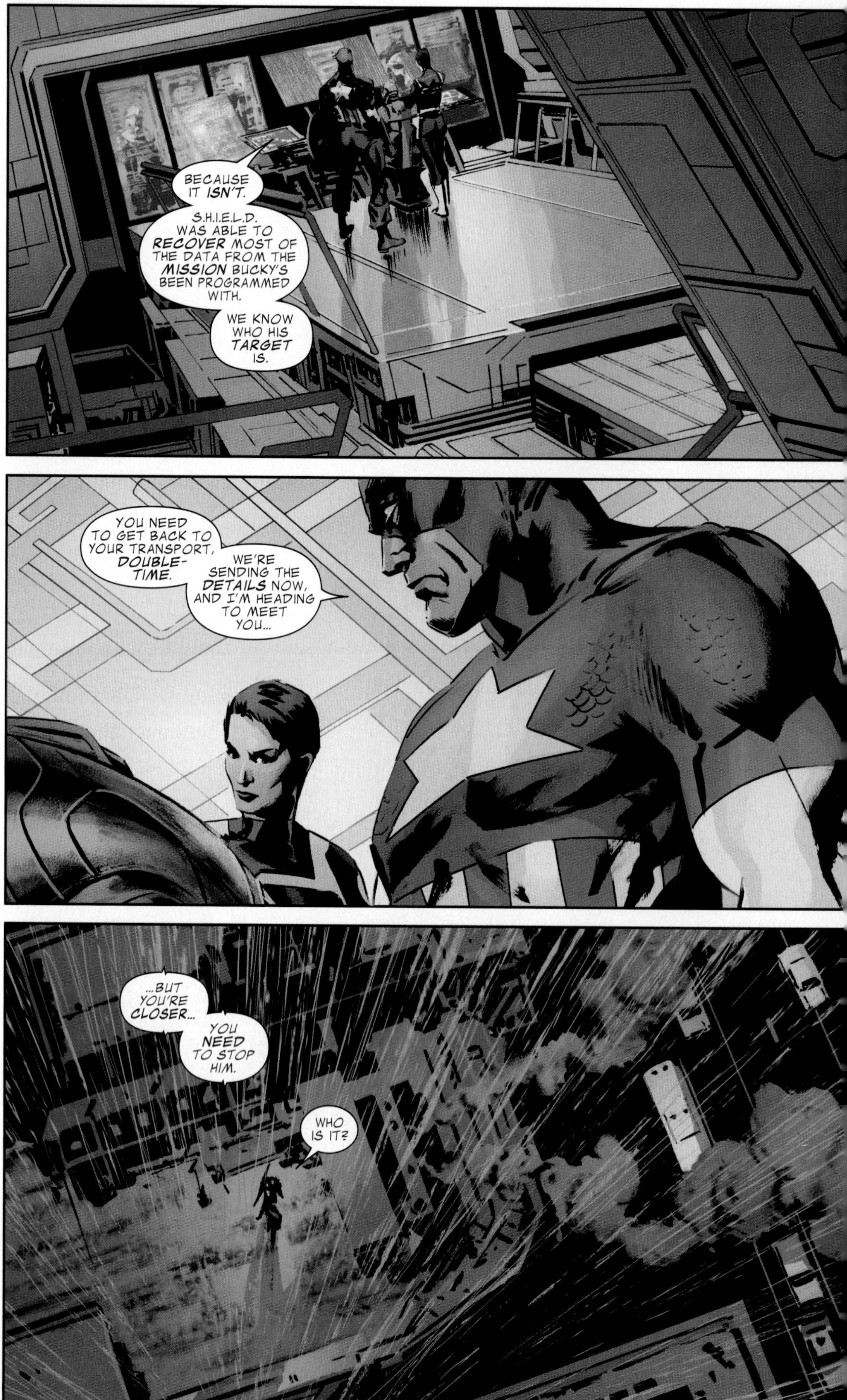
BECAUSE IT ISN'T.
S.H.I.E.L.D. WAS ABLE TO RECOVER MOST OF THE DATA FROM THE MISSION BUCKY'S BEEN PROGRAMMED WITH.
WE KNOW WHO HIS TARGET IS.
YOU NEED TO GET BACK TO YOUR TRANSPORT, DOUBLE-TIME.
WE'RE SENDING THE DETAILS NOW, AND I'M HEADING TO MEET YOU...
...BUT YOU'RE CLOSER...
YOU NEED TO STOP HIM.
WHO IS IT?

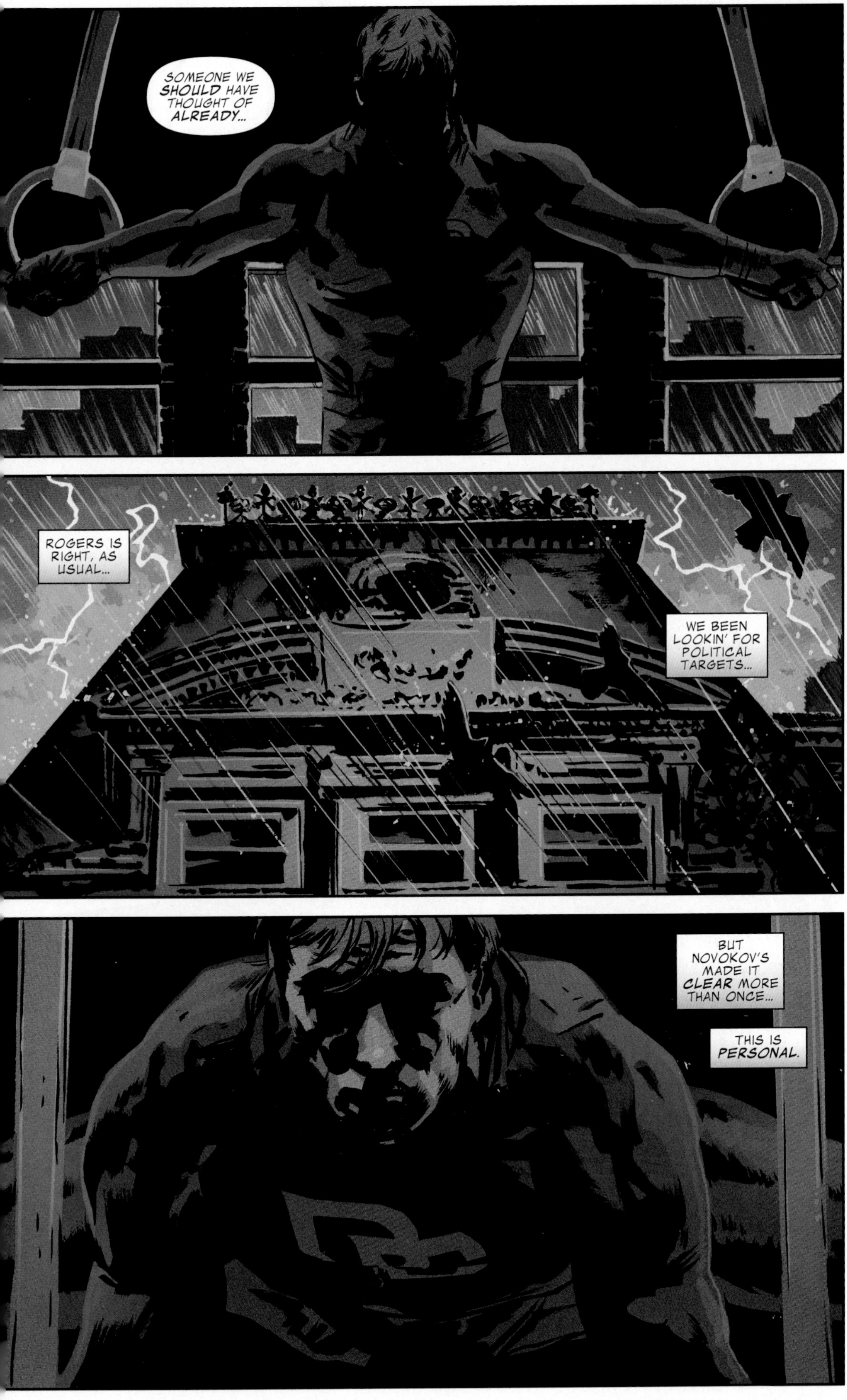
SOMEONE WE SHOULD HAVE THOUGHT OF ALREADY...
ROGERS IS RIGHT, AS USUAL...
WE BEEN LOOKIN' FOR POLITICAL TARGETS...
BUT NOVOKOV'S MADE IT CLEAR MORE THAN ONCE...
THIS IS PERSONAL.

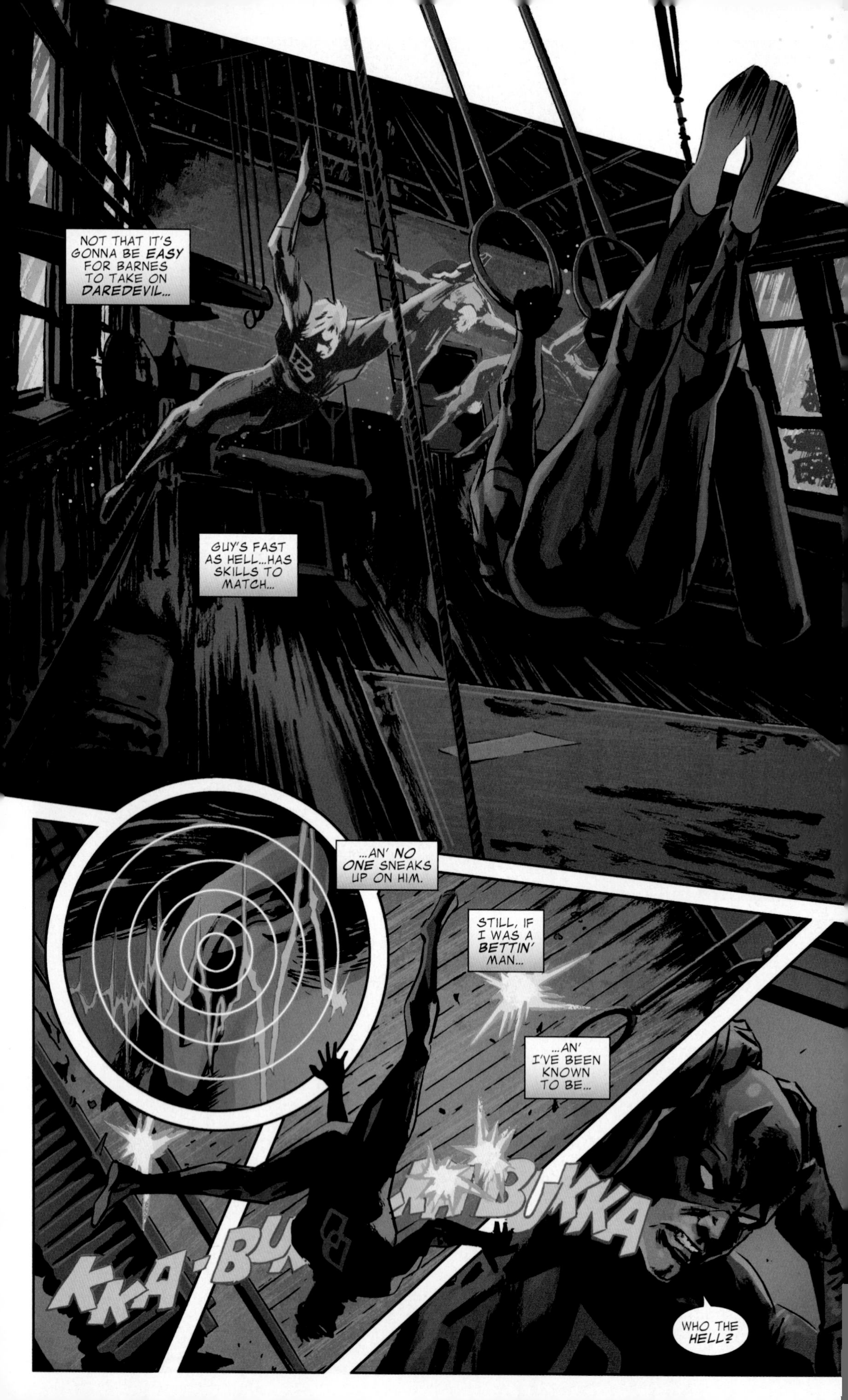
NOT THAT IT'S GONNA BE EASY FOR BARNES TO TAKE ON DAREDEVIL...
GUY'S FAST AS HELL...HAS SKILLS TO MATCH...
...AN' NO ONE SNEAKS UP ON HIM.
STILL, IF I WAS A BETTIN' MAN...
...AN' I'VE BEEN KNOWN TO BE...
KKA-BUKKA-BUKKA
WHO THE HELL?

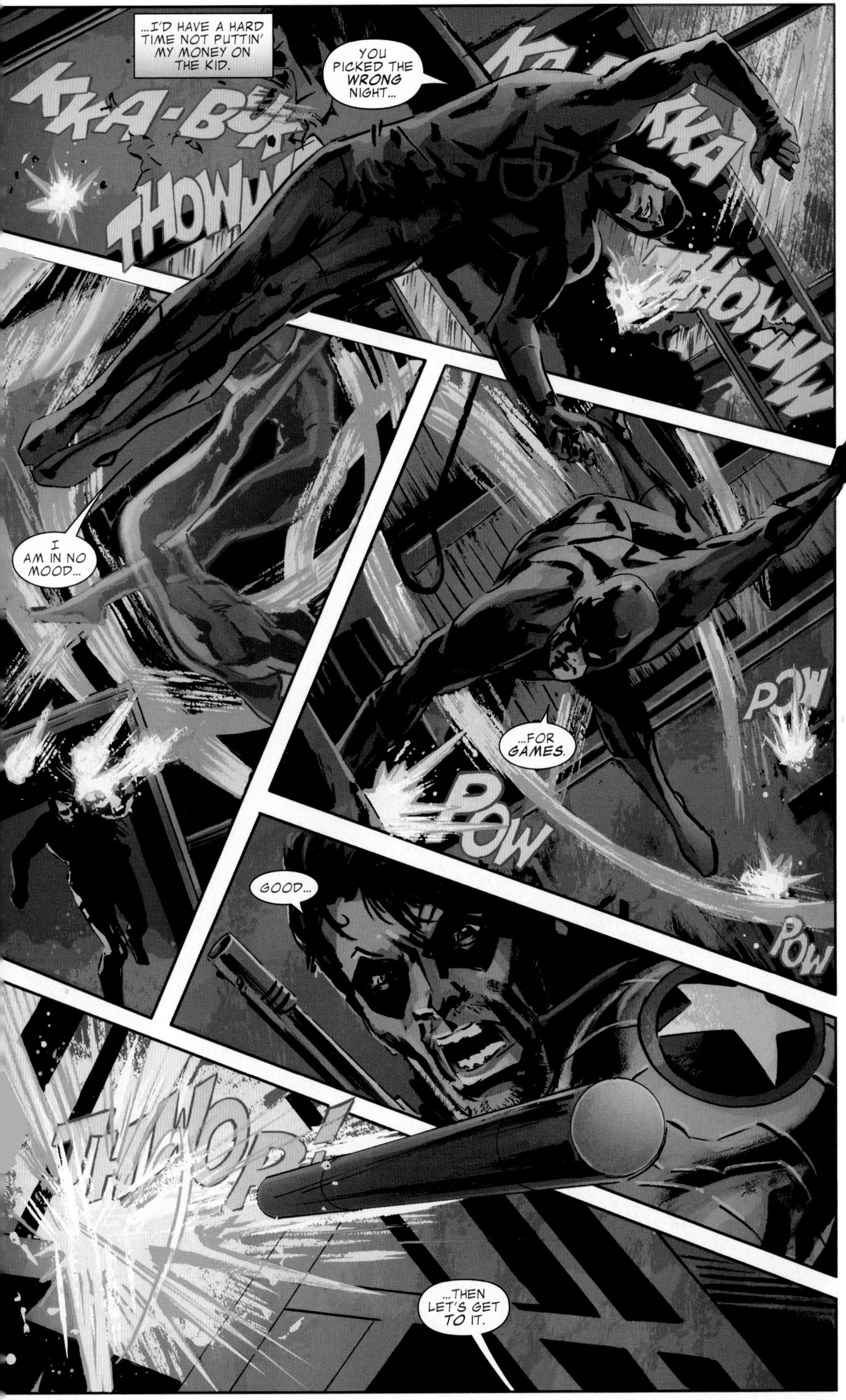

...I'D HAVE A HARD TIME NOT PUTTIN' MY MONEY ON THE KID.
YOU PICKED THE WRONG NIGHT...
THOWM
I AM IN NO MOOD...
...FOR GAMES.
POW
POW
POW
GOOD...
THWOP!
...THEN LET'S GET TO IT.

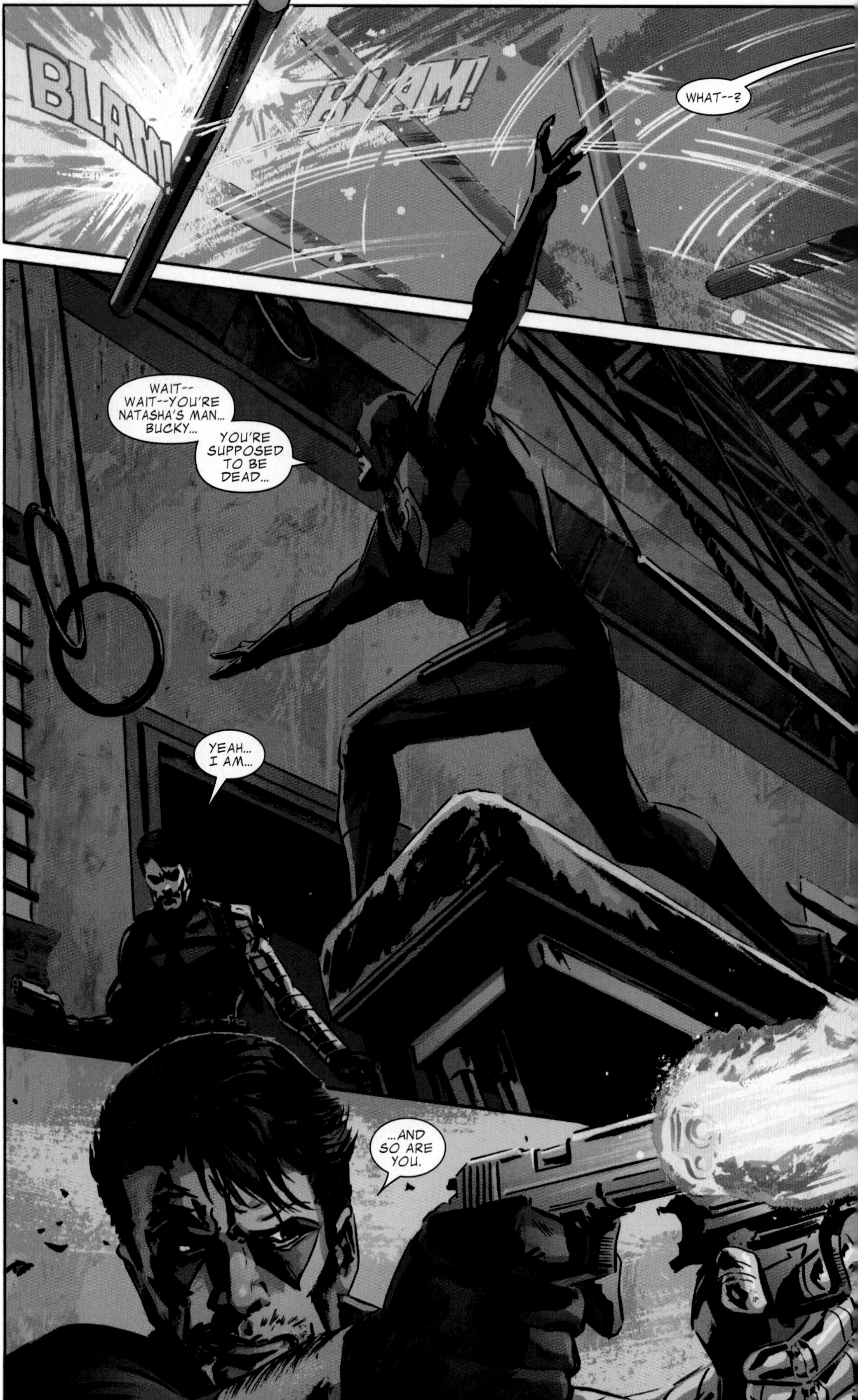
BLAM!
BLAM!
WHAT--?
WAIT--
WAIT--YOU'RE NATASHA'S MAN... BUCKY...
YOU'RE SUPPOSED TO BE DEAD...
YEAH... I AM...
...AND SO ARE YOU.

AND BUCKY REPORTED KIA

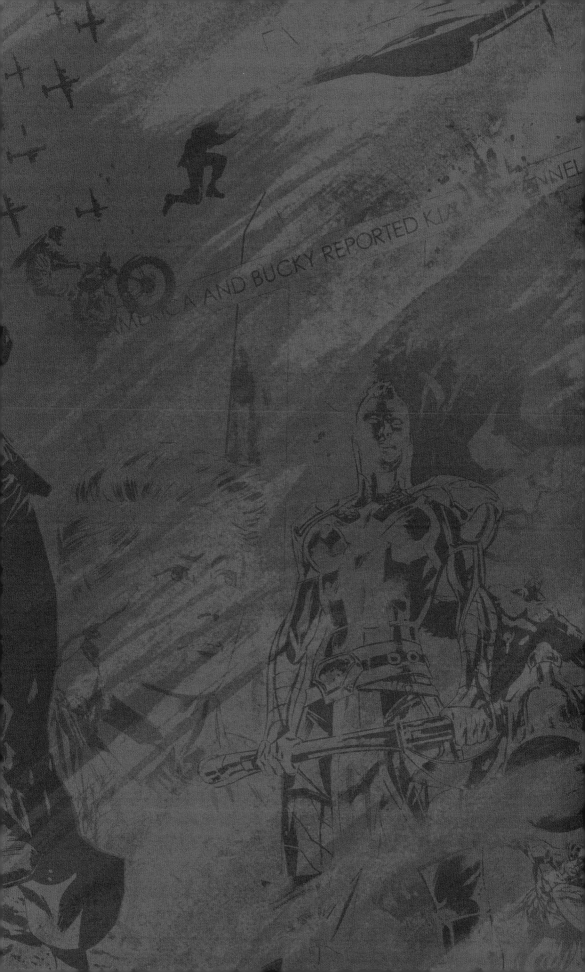

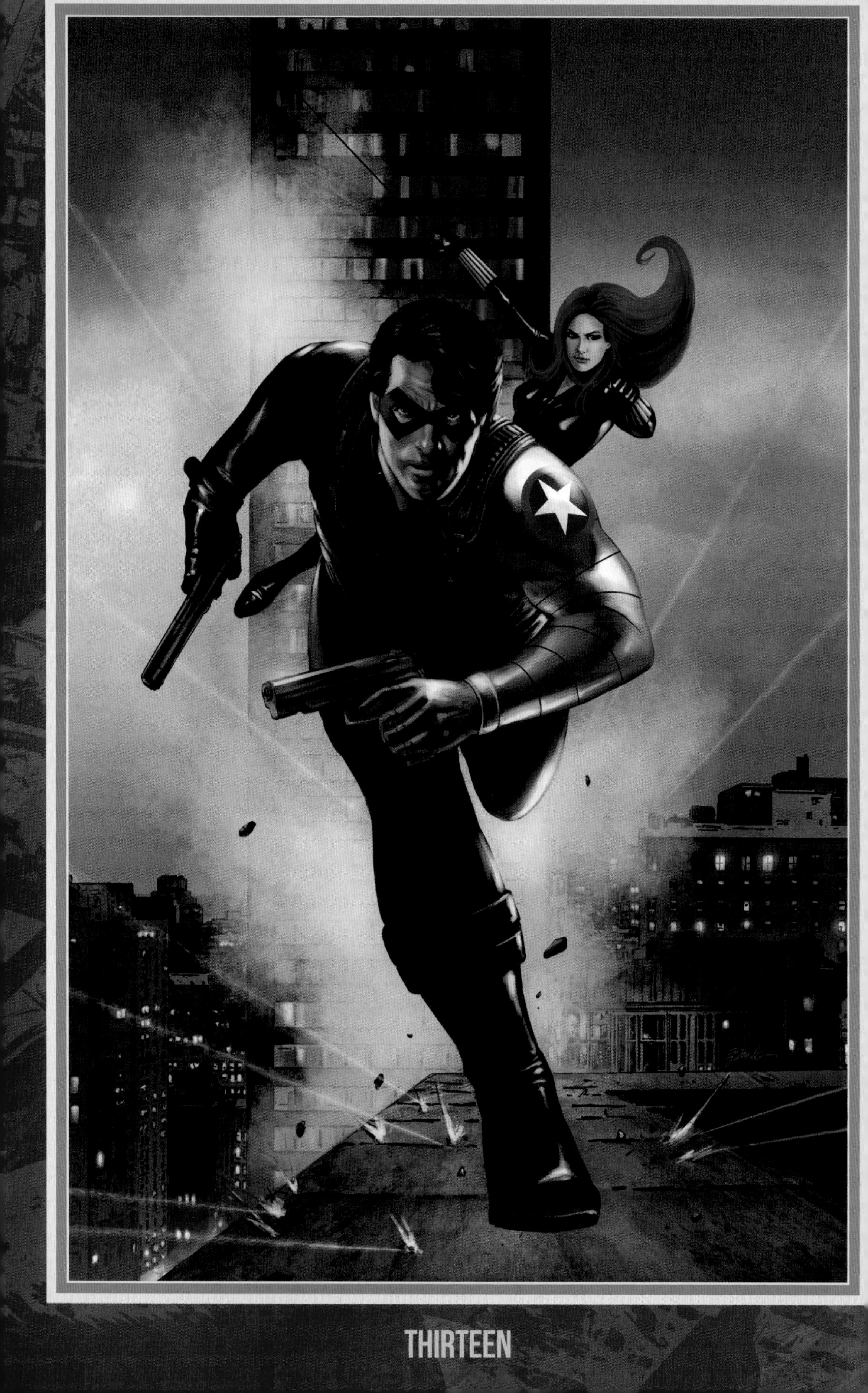

THIRTEEN

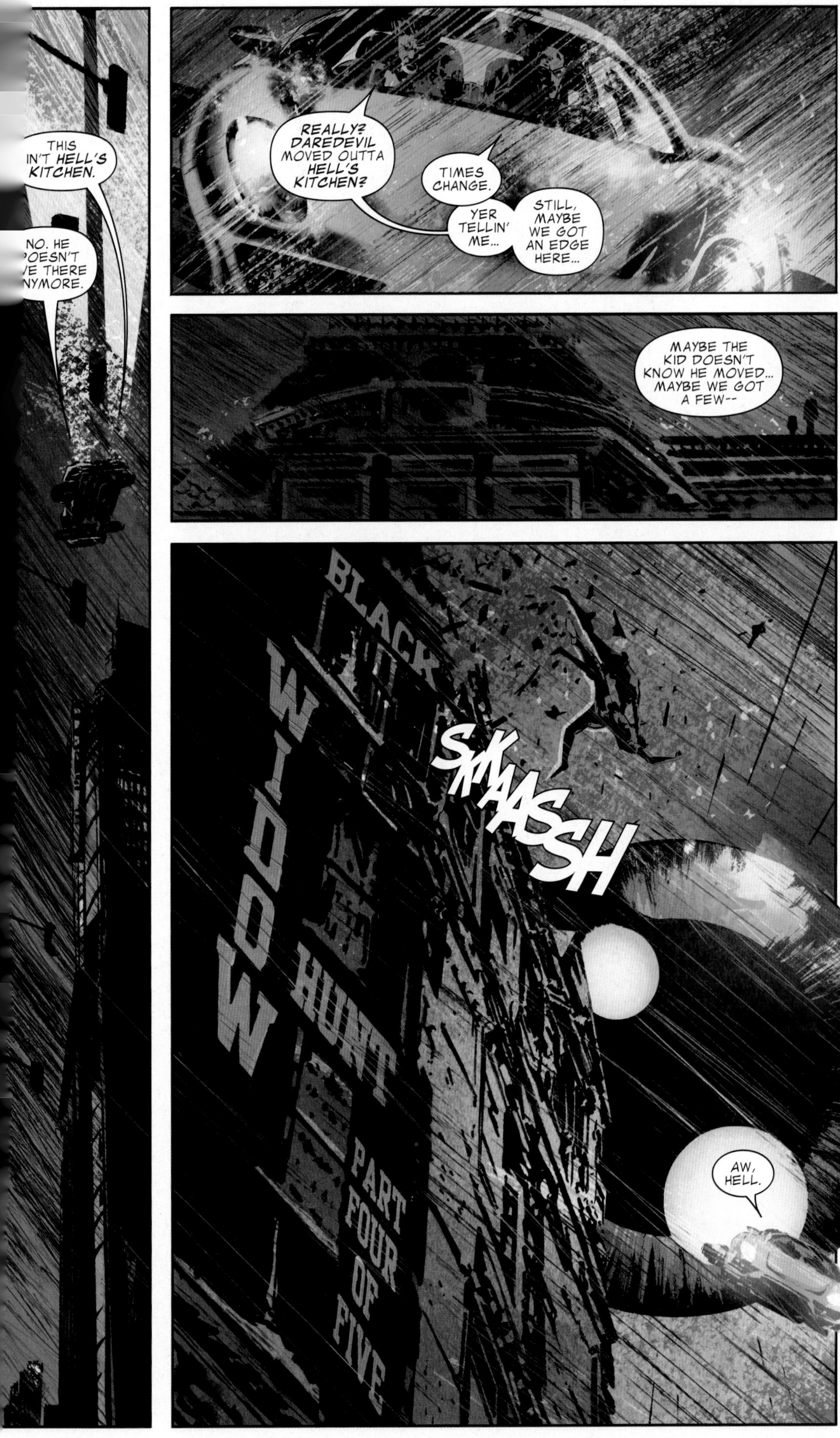
THIS ...N'T HELL'S KITCHEN.
NO. HE ...OESN'T ...E THERE ...NYMORE.
REALLY? DAREDEVIL MOVED OUTTA HELL'S KITCHEN?
TIMES CHANGE.
YER TELLIN' ME...
STILL, MAYBE WE GOT AN EDGE HERE...
MAYBE THE KID DOESN'T KNOW HE MOVED... MAYBE WE GOT A FEW--
BLACK WIDOW
HUNT
PART FOUR OF FIVE
SKAASSH
AW, HELL.

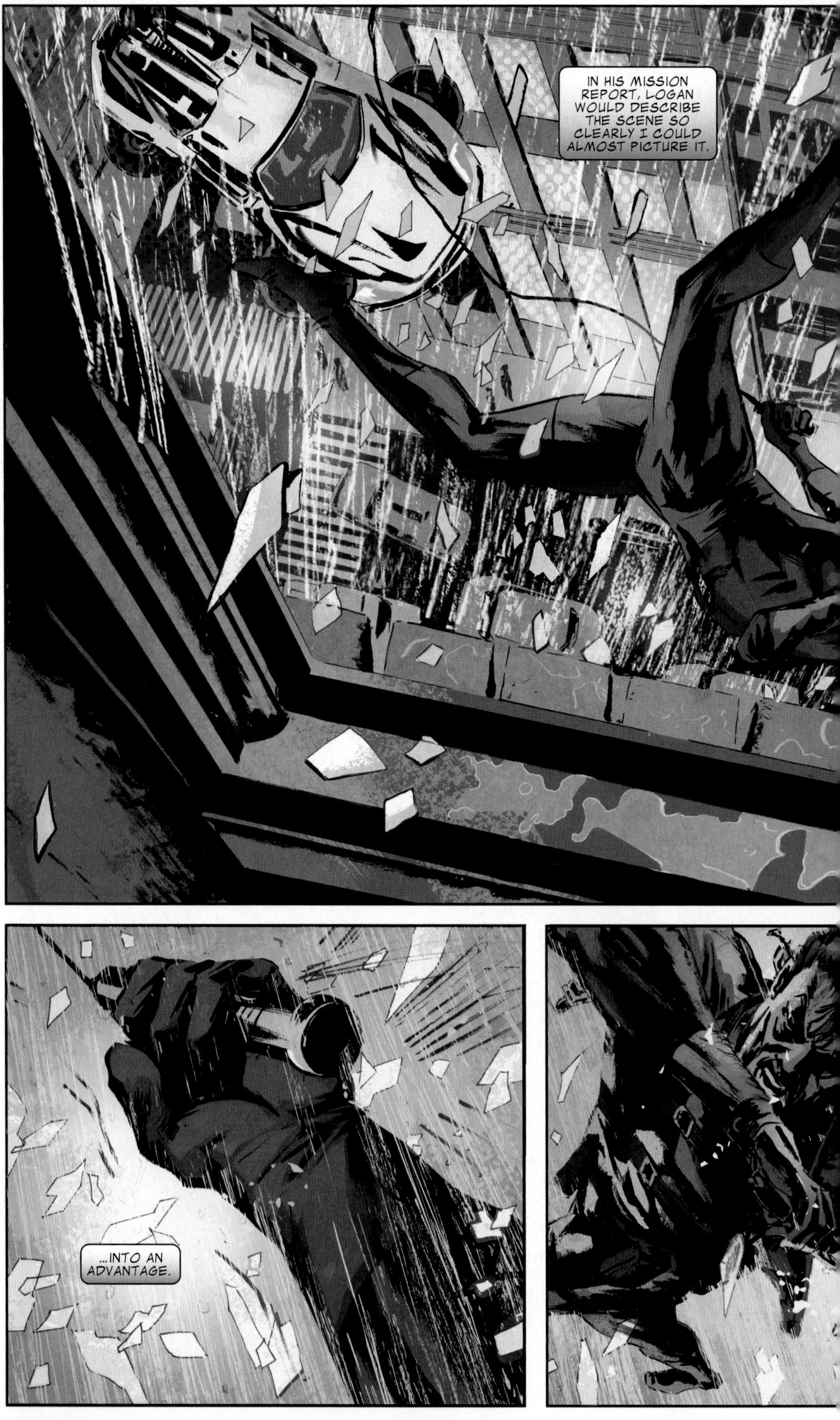
IN HIS MISSION REPORT, LOGAN WOULD DESCRIBE THE SCENE SO CLEARLY I COULD ALMOST PICTURE IT.
...INTO AN ADVANTAGE.

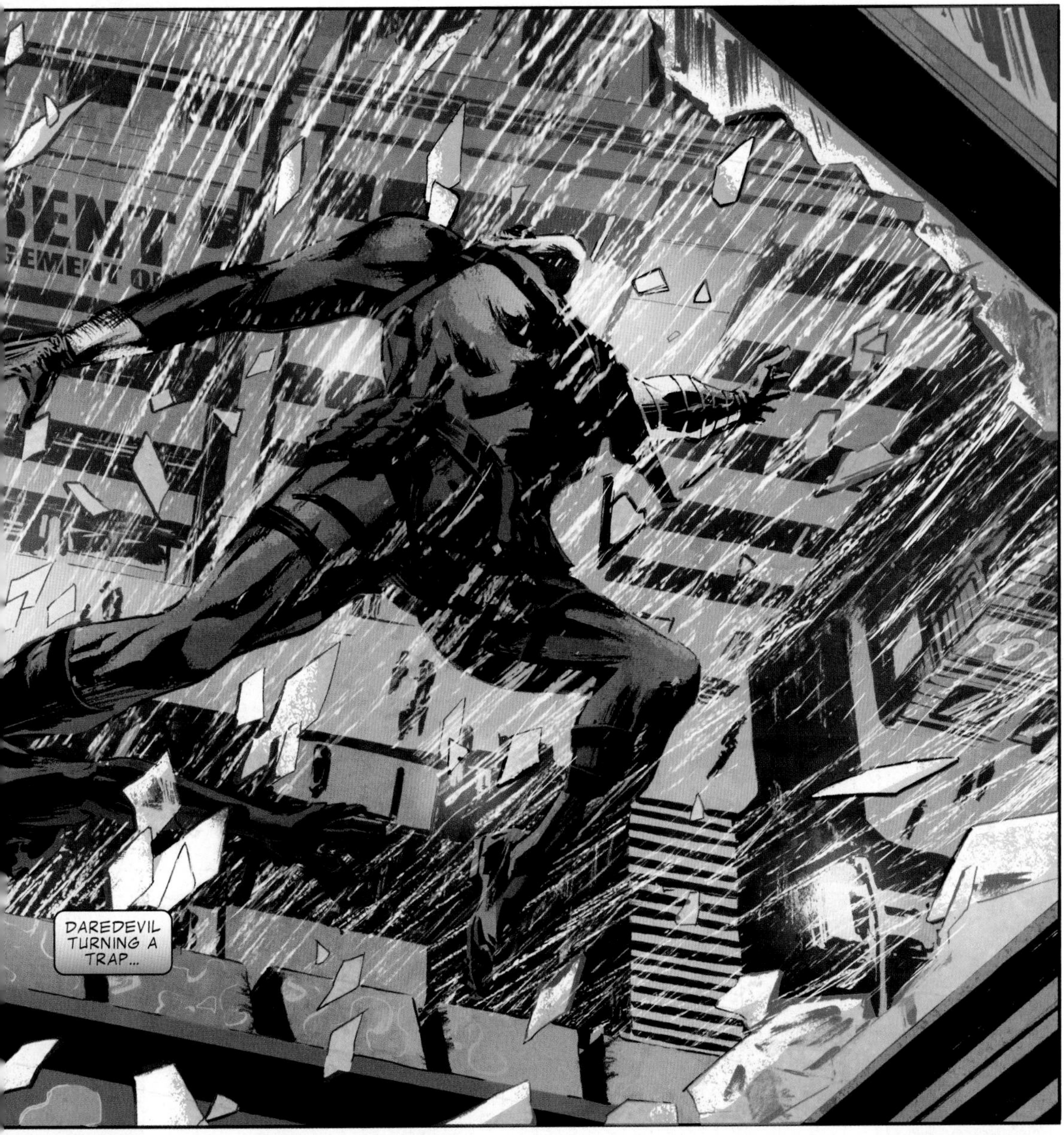
DAREDEVIL TURNING A TRAP...

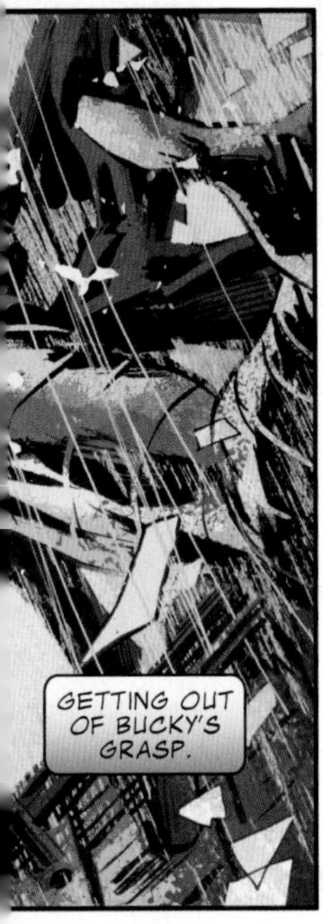
GETTING OUT OF BUCKY'S GRASP.

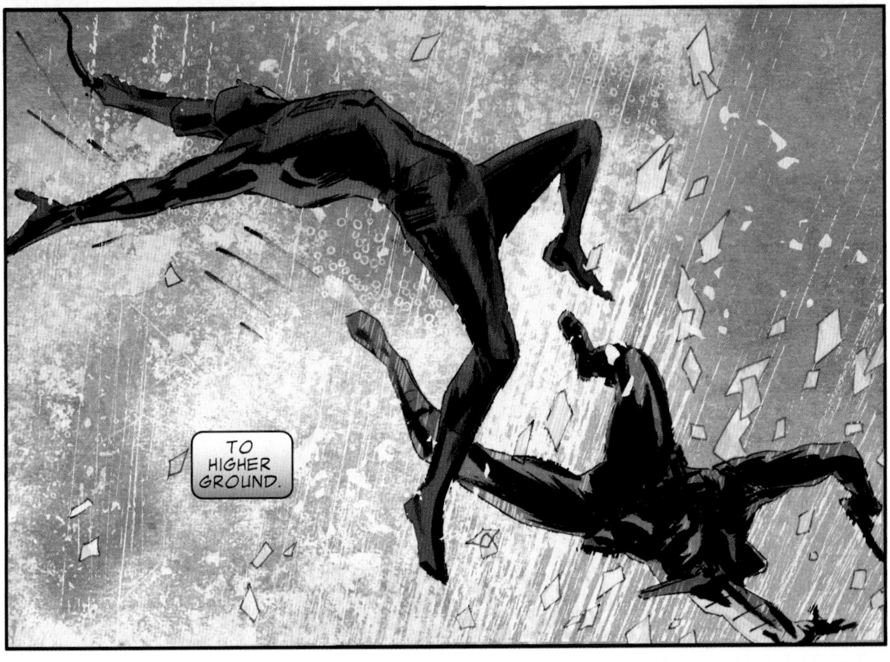
TO HIGHER GROUND.

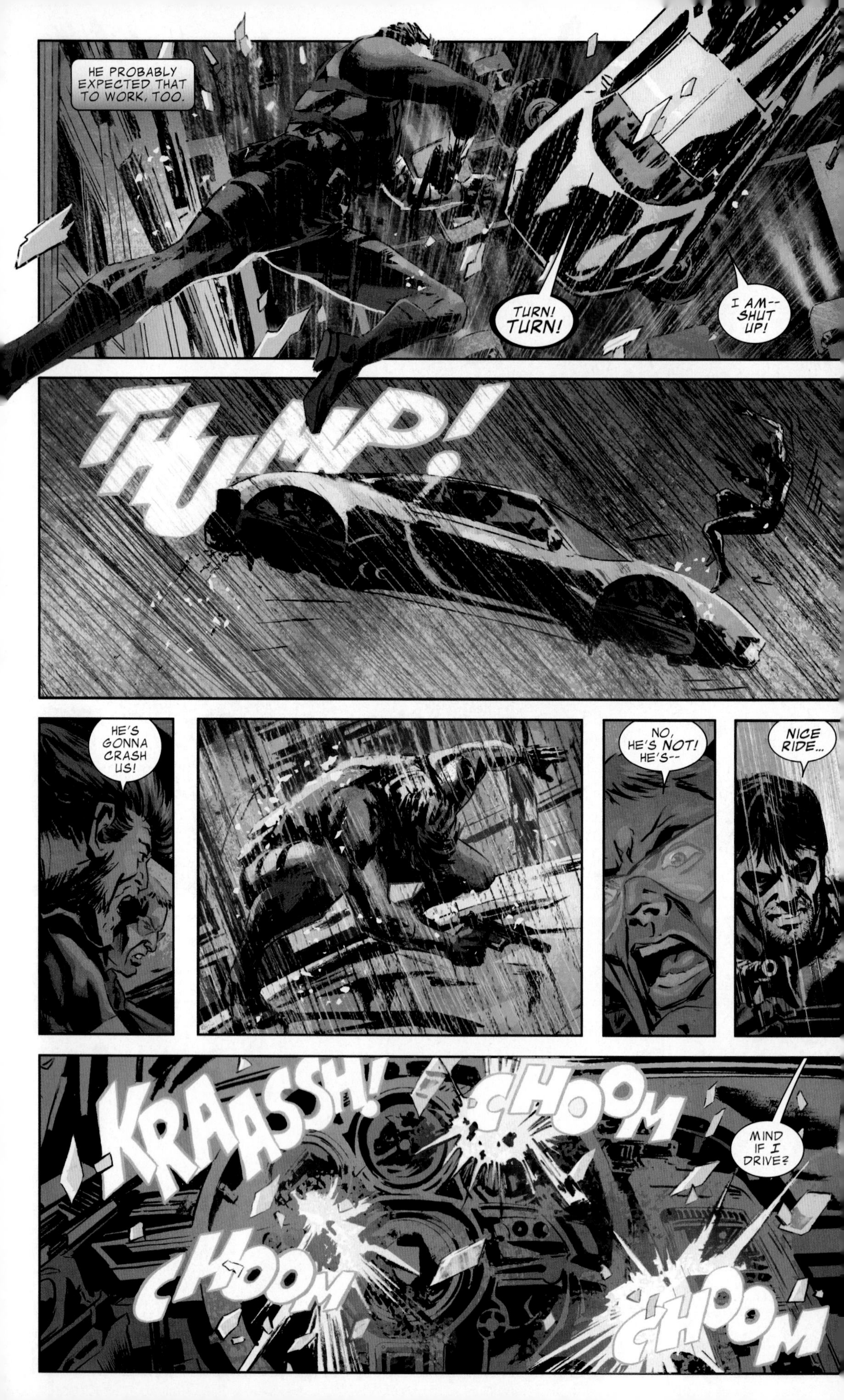
HE PROBABLY EXPECTED THAT TO WORK, TOO.
TURN! TURN!
I AM-- SHUT UP!
THUMP!
HE'S GONNA CRASH US!
NO, HE'S NOT! HE'S--
NICE RIDE...
KRAASSH!
CHOOM
MIND IF I DRIVE?
CHOOM
CHOOM

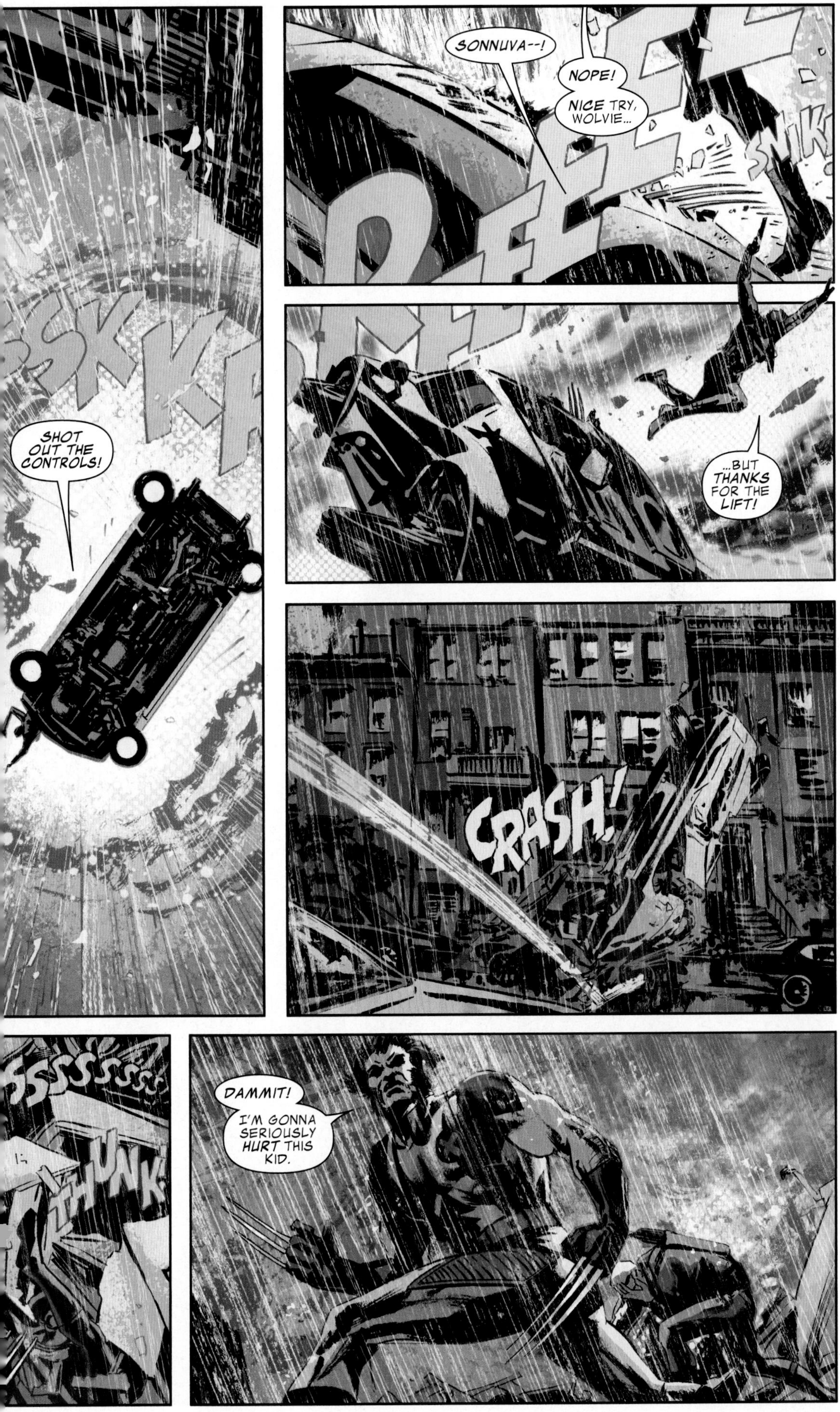
SONNUVA--!
NOPE!
NICE TRY, WOLVIE...
SSKKK
SHOT OUT THE CONTROLS!
...BUT THANKS FOR THE LIFT!
CRASH!
SSSSSSSS
THUNK
DAMMIT!
I'M GONNA SERIOUSLY HURT THIS KID.

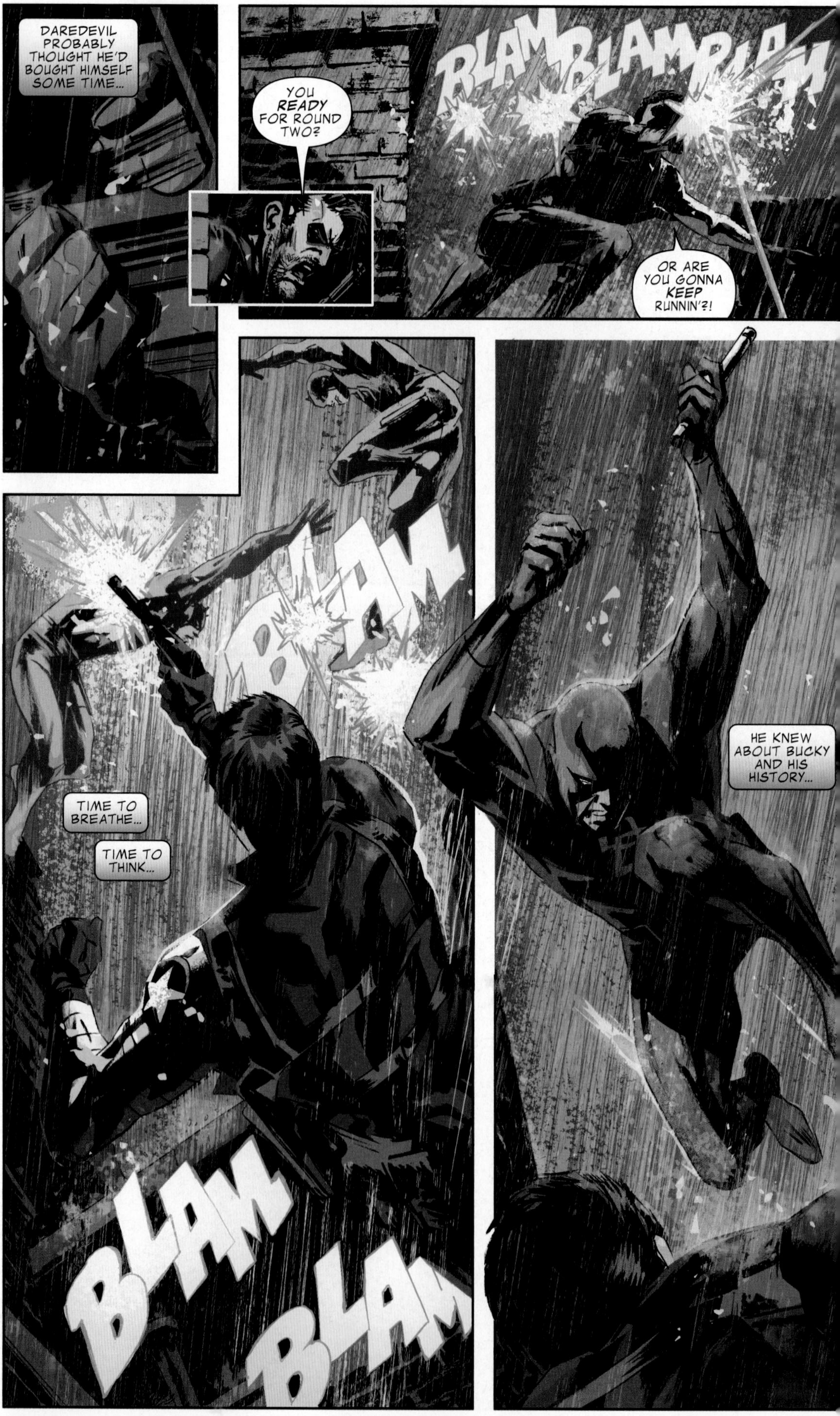
DAREDEVIL PROBABLY THOUGHT HE'D BOUGHT HIMSELF SOME TIME...
YOU READY FOR ROUND TWO?
BLAMBLAMBLAM
OR ARE YOU GONNA KEEP RUNNIN'?!
BLAM
TIME TO BREATHE...
TIME TO THINK...
HE KNEW ABOUT BUCKY AND HIS HISTORY...
BLAM
BLAM

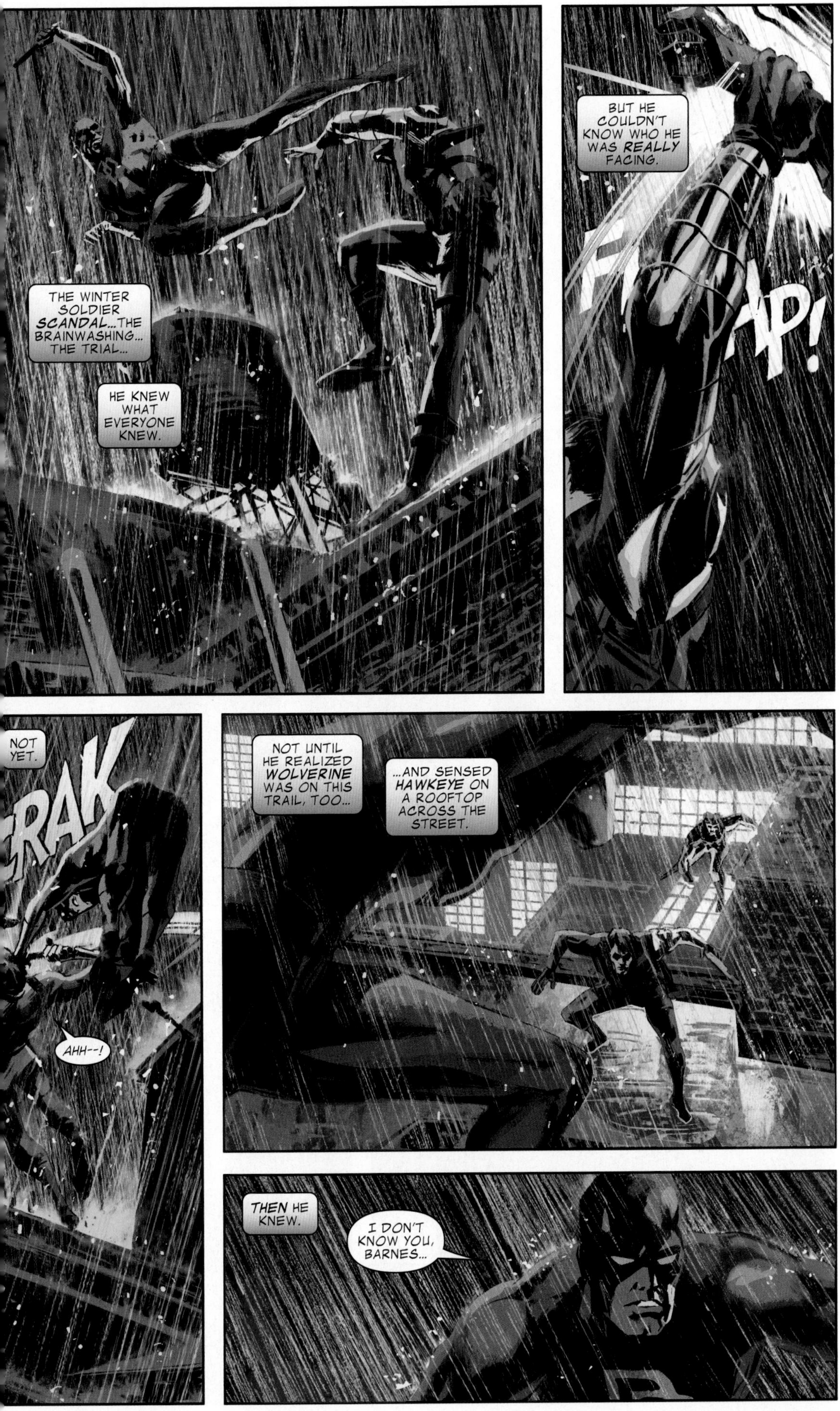
THE WINTER SOLDIER SCANDAL...THE BRAINWASHING... THE TRIAL...
HE KNEW WHAT EVERYONE KNEW.
BUT HE COULDN'T KNOW WHO HE WAS REALLY FACING.
NOT YET.
AHH--!
NOT UNTIL HE REALIZED WOLVERINE WAS ON THIS TRAIL, TOO...
...AND SENSED HAWKEYE ON A ROOFTOP ACROSS THE STREET.
THEN HE KNEW.
I DON'T KNOW YOU, BARNES...

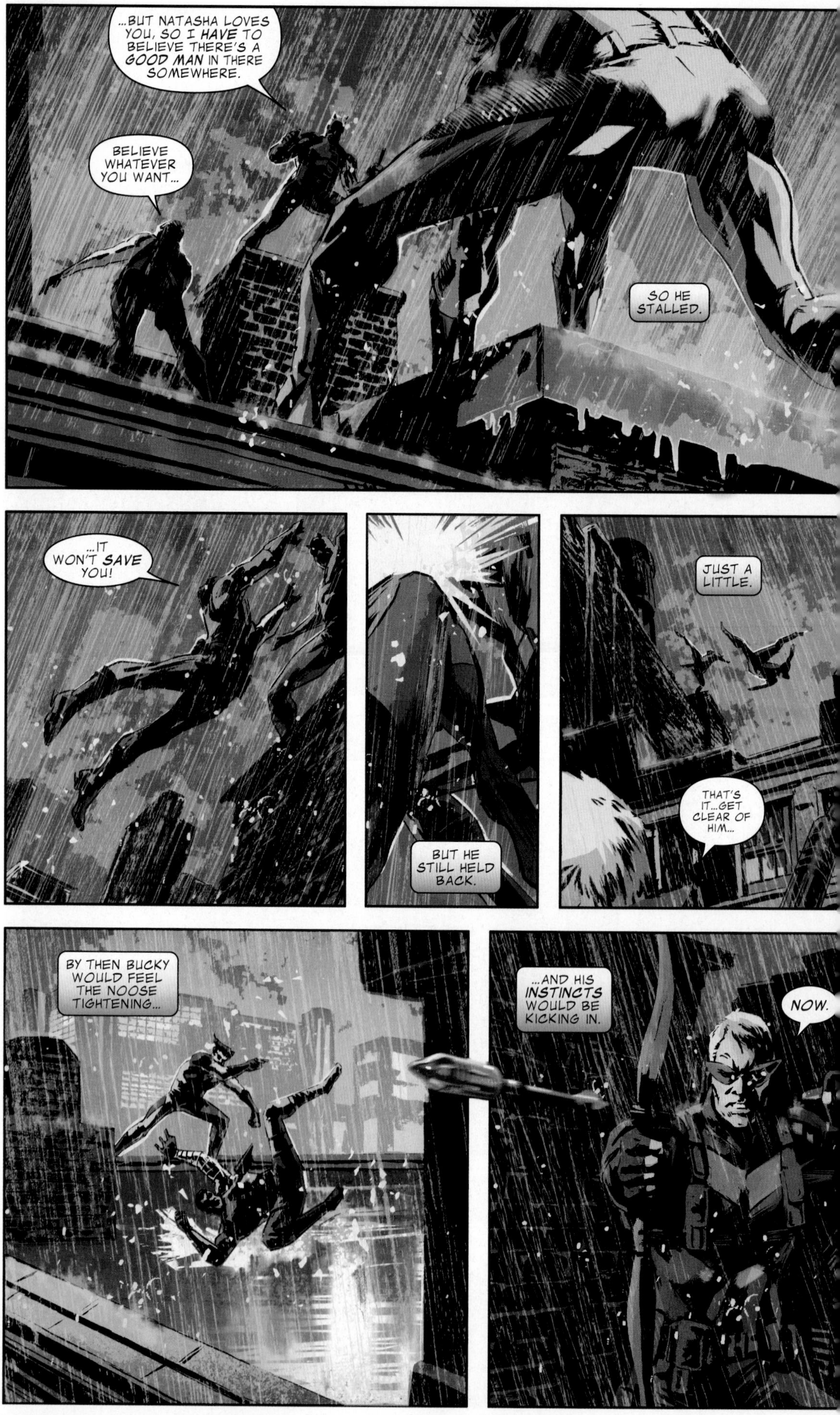

...BUT NATASHA LOVES YOU, SO I HAVE TO BELIEVE THERE'S A GOOD MAN IN THERE SOMEWHERE.
BELIEVE WHATEVER YOU WANT...
SO HE STALLED.
...IT WON'T SAVE YOU!
BUT HE STILL HELD BACK.
JUST A LITTLE.
THAT'S IT...GET CLEAR OF HIM...
BY THEN BUCKY WOULD FEEL THE NOOSE TIGHTENING...
...AND HIS INSTINCTS WOULD BE KICKING IN.
NOW.

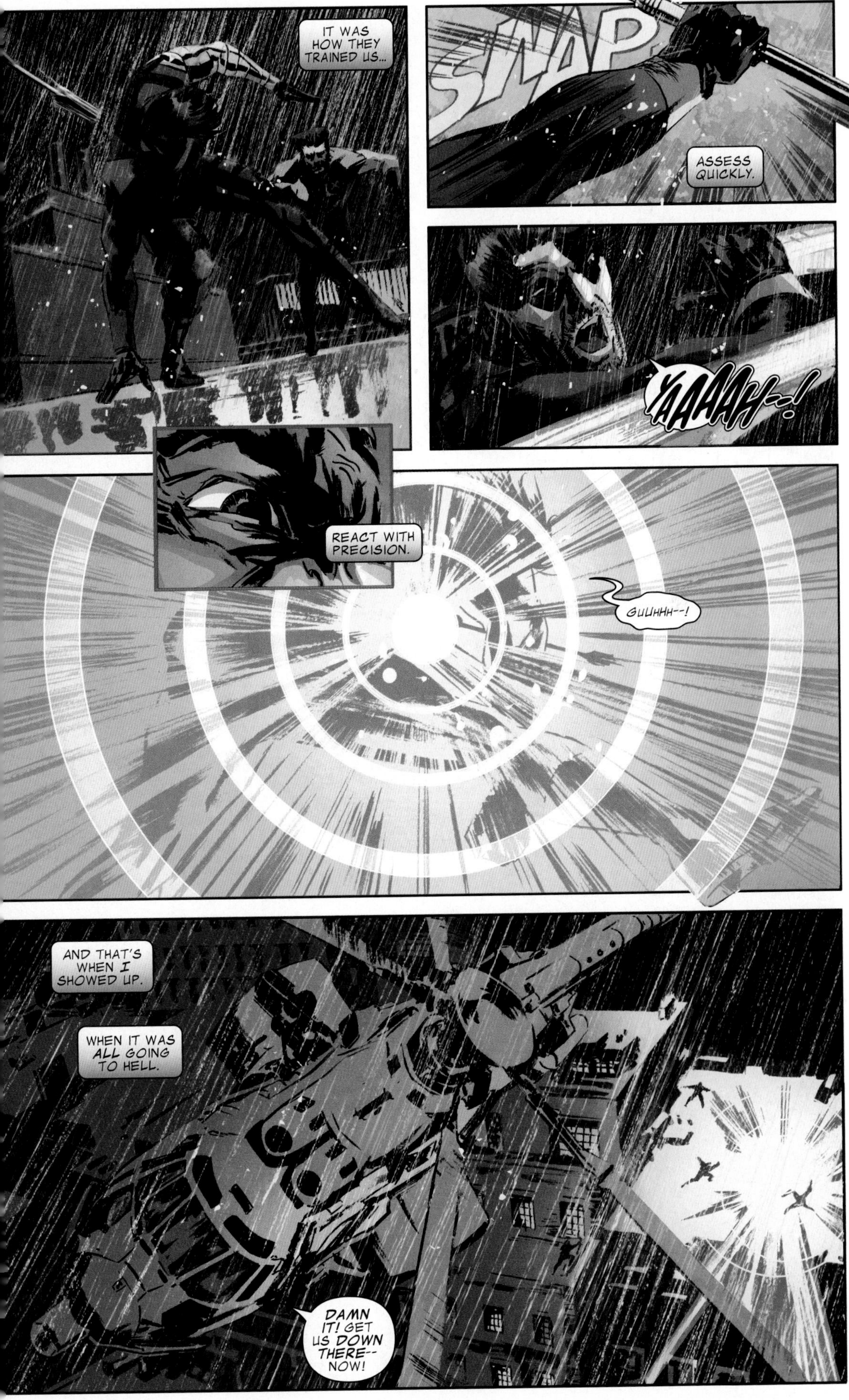
IT WAS HOW THEY TRAINED US...
SNAP
ASSESS QUICKLY.
YAAAAH--!
REACT WITH PRECISION.
GUUHHH--!
AND THAT'S WHEN I SHOWED UP.
WHEN IT WAS ALL GOING TO HELL.
DAMN IT! GET US DOWN THERE-- NOW!

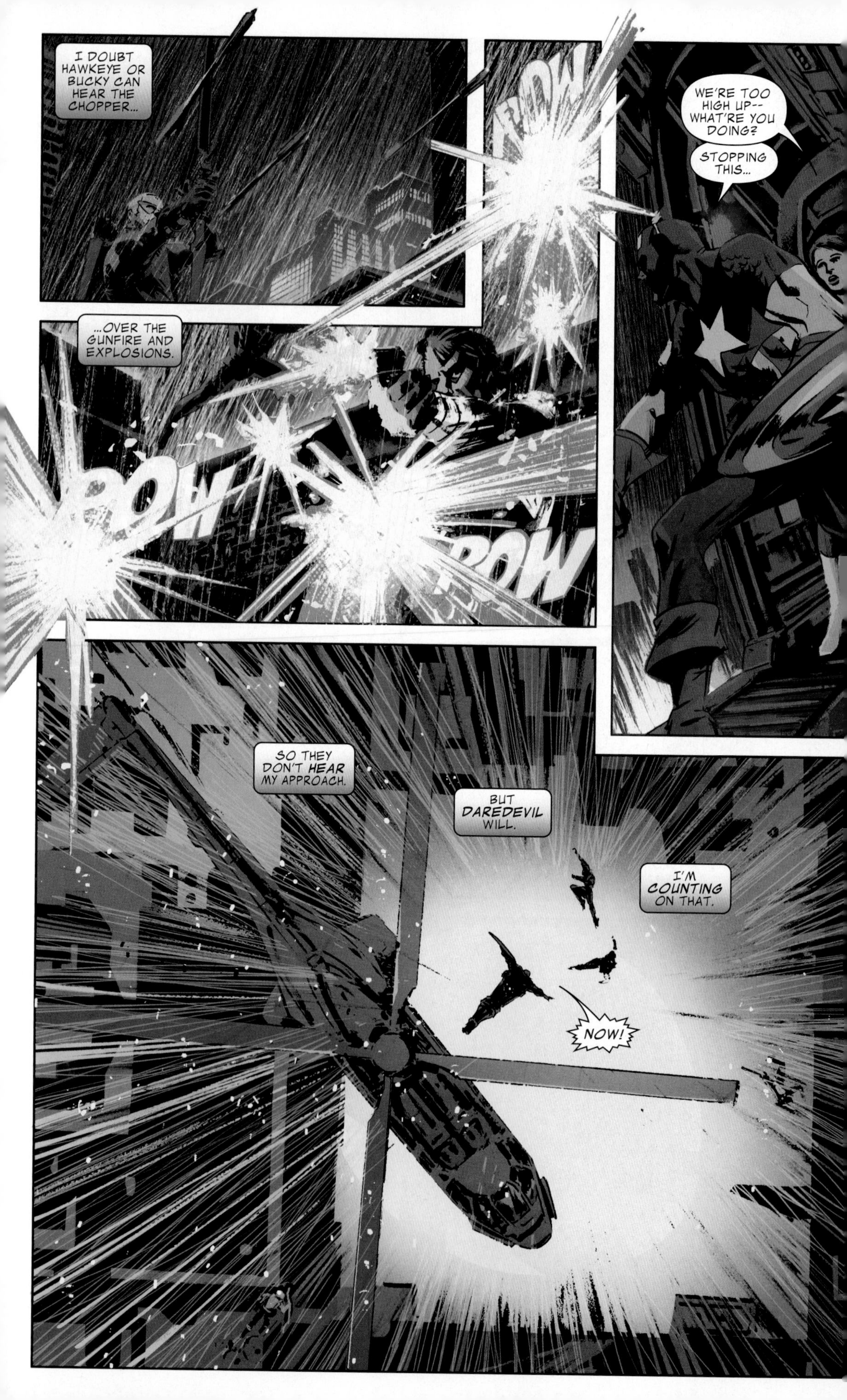
I DOUBT HAWKEYE OR BUCKY CAN HEAR THE CHOPPER...
BLAM
WE'RE TOO HIGH UP-- WHAT'RE YOU DOING?
STOPPING THIS...
...OVER THE GUNFIRE AND EXPLOSIONS.
BLAM
BLAM
SO THEY DON'T HEAR MY APPROACH.
BUT DAREDEVIL WILL.
I'M COUNTING ON THAT.
NOW!

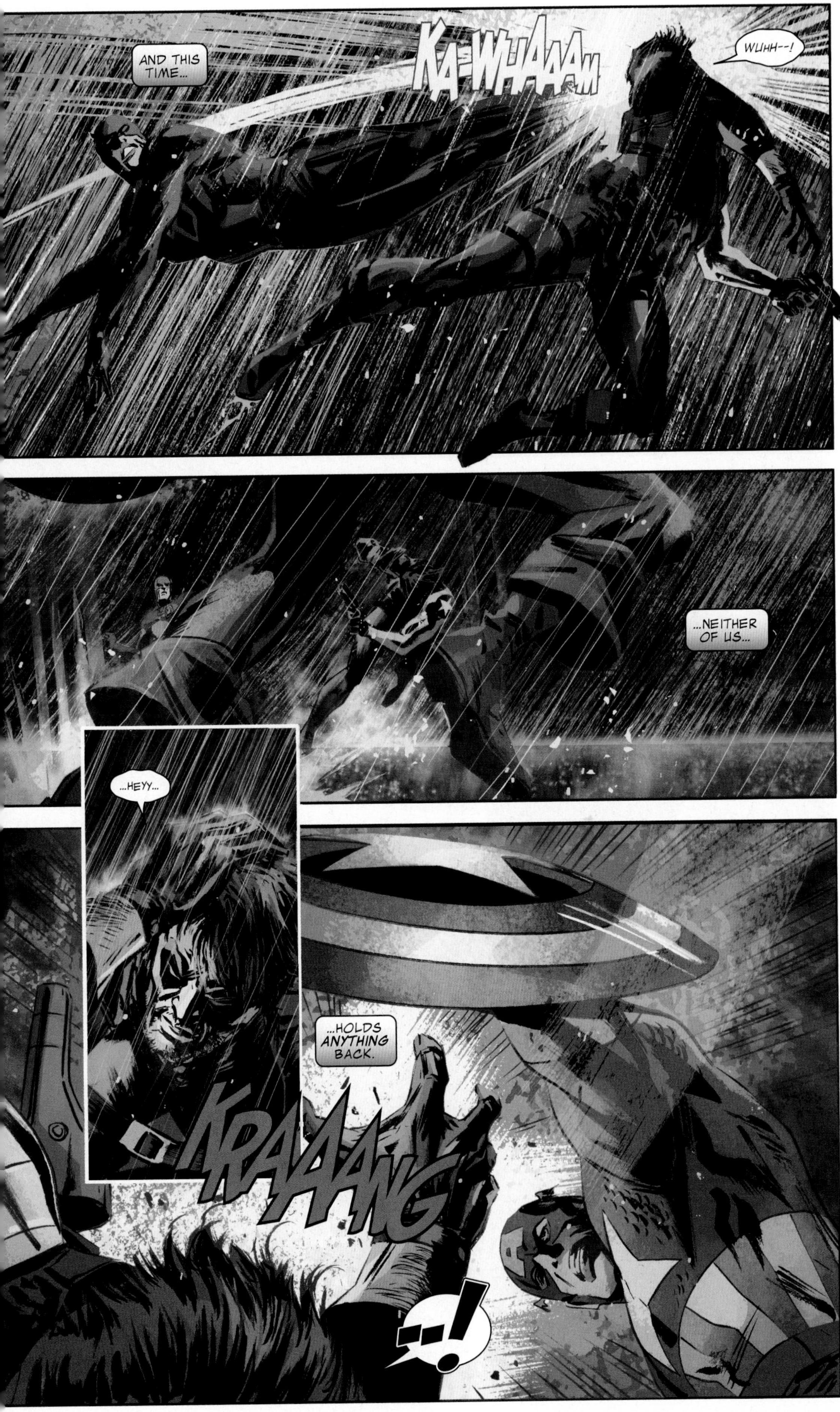
AND THIS TIME...
KA-WHAAAM
WUHH--!
...NEITHER OF US...
...HEYY...
...HOLDS ANYTHING BACK.
KRAAANG
..!

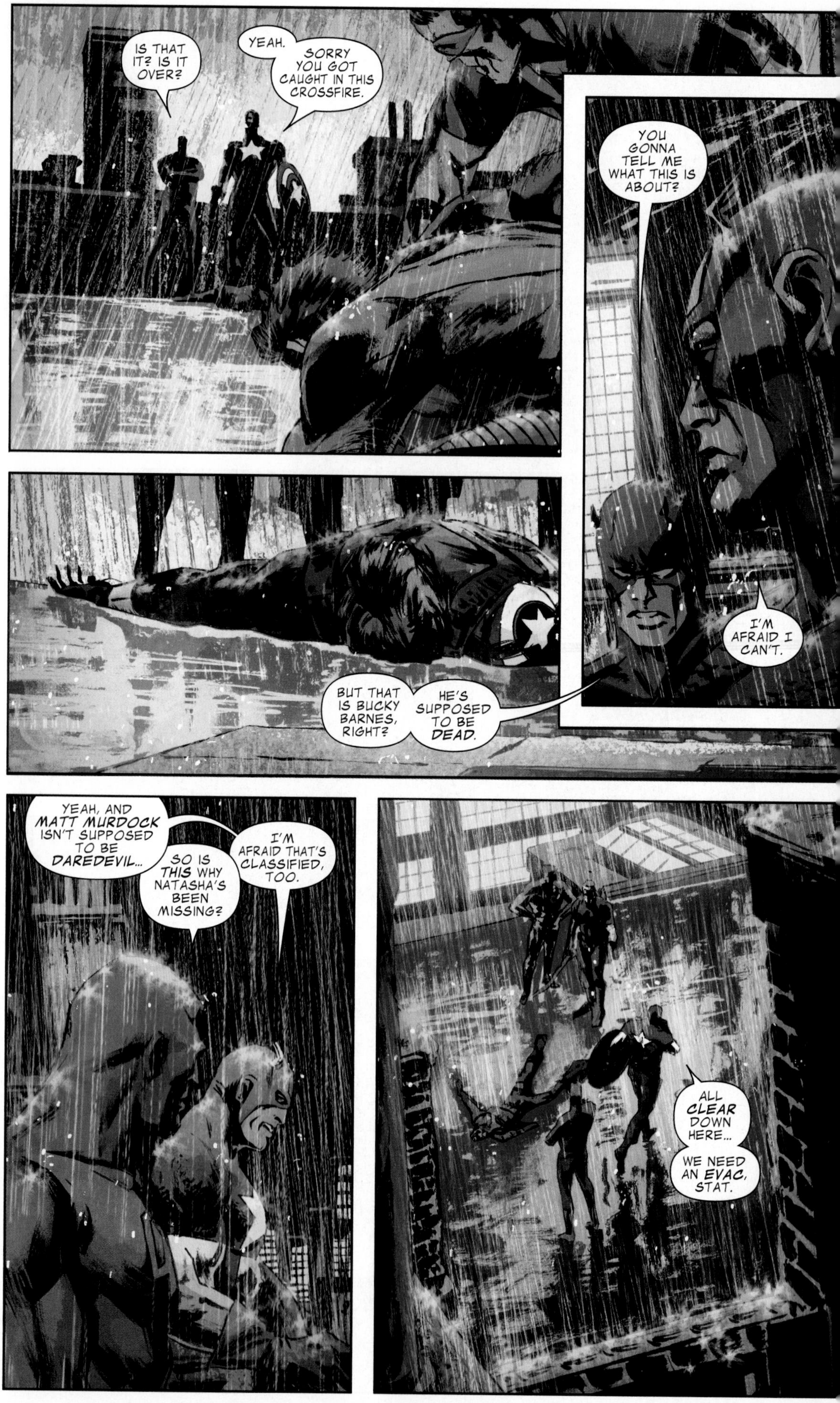
IS THAT IT? IS IT OVER?
YEAH.
SORRY YOU GOT CAUGHT IN THIS CROSSFIRE.
YOU GONNA TELL ME WHAT THIS IS ABOUT?
I'M AFRAID I CAN'T.
BUT THAT IS BUCKY BARNES, RIGHT?
HE'S SUPPOSED TO BE DEAD.
YEAH, AND MATT MURDOCK ISN'T SUPPOSED TO BE DAREDEVIL...
I'M AFRAID THAT'S CLASSIFIED, TOO.
SO IS THIS WHY NATASHA'S BEEN MISSING?
ALL CLEAR DOWN HERE...
WE NEED AN EVAC, STAT.

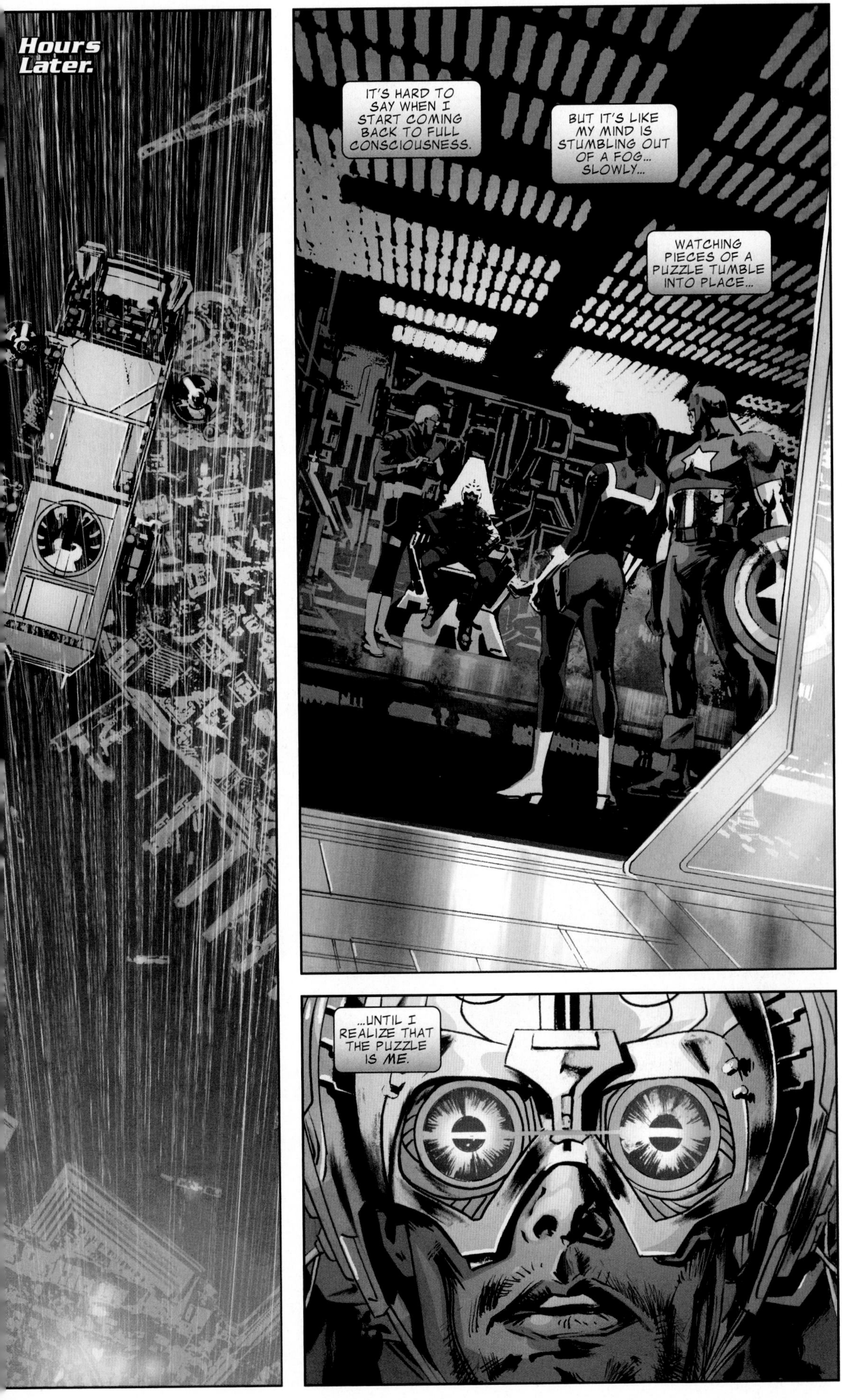
Hours Later.
IT'S HARD TO SAY WHEN I START COMING BACK TO FULL CONSCIOUSNESS.
BUT IT'S LIKE MY MIND IS STUMBLING OUT OF A FOG... SLOWLY...
WATCHING PIECES OF A PUZZLE TUMBLE INTO PLACE...
...UNTIL I REALIZE THAT THE PUZZLE IS ME.

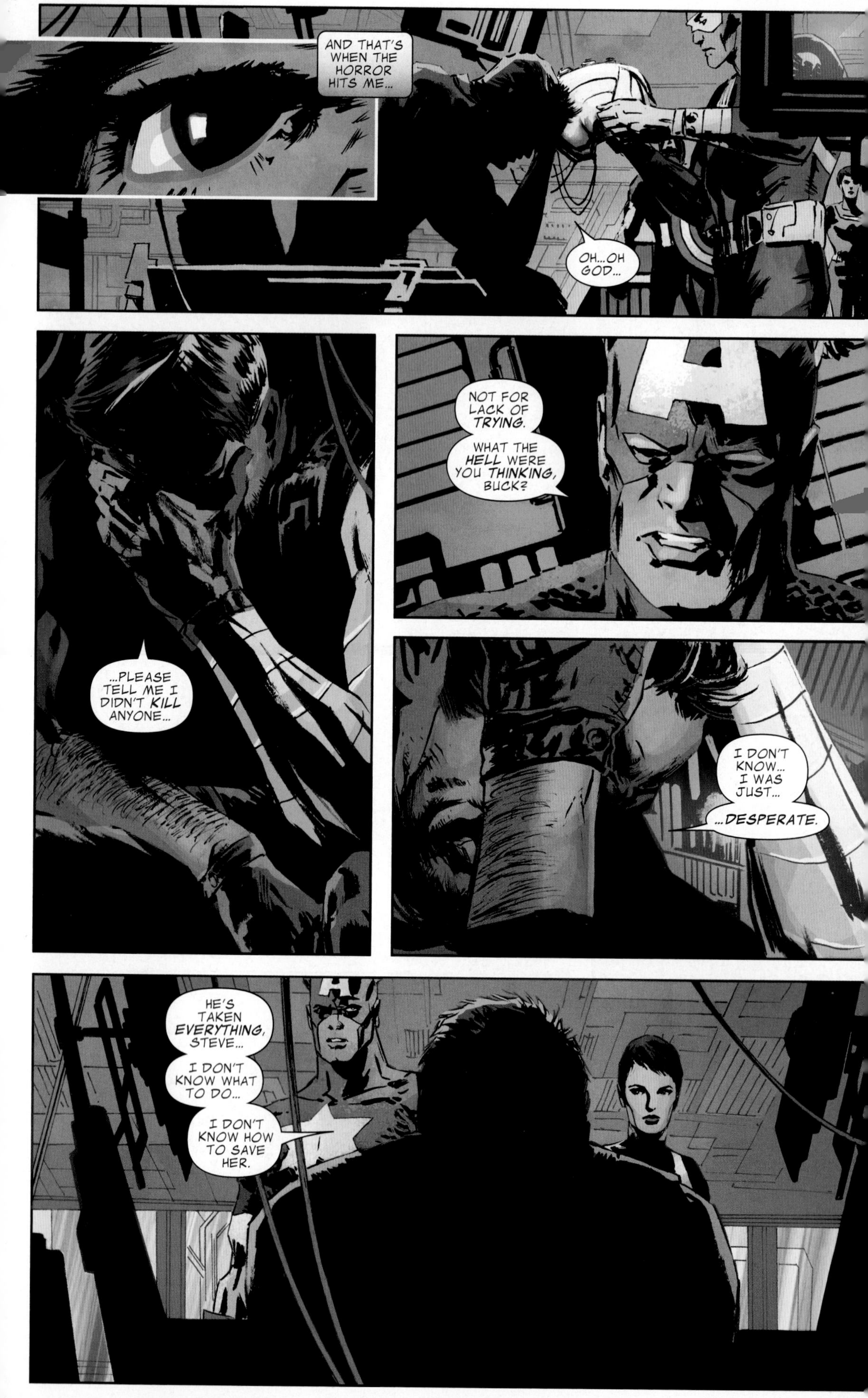

AND THAT'S WHEN THE HORROR HITS ME...
OH...OH GOD...
...PLEASE TELL ME I DIDN'T KILL ANYONE...
NOT FOR LACK OF TRYING.
WHAT THE HELL WERE YOU THINKING, BUCK?
I DON'T KNOW... I WAS JUST...
...DESPERATE.
HE'S TAKEN EVERYTHING, STEVE...
I DON'T KNOW WHAT TO DO...
I DON'T KNOW HOW TO SAVE HER.

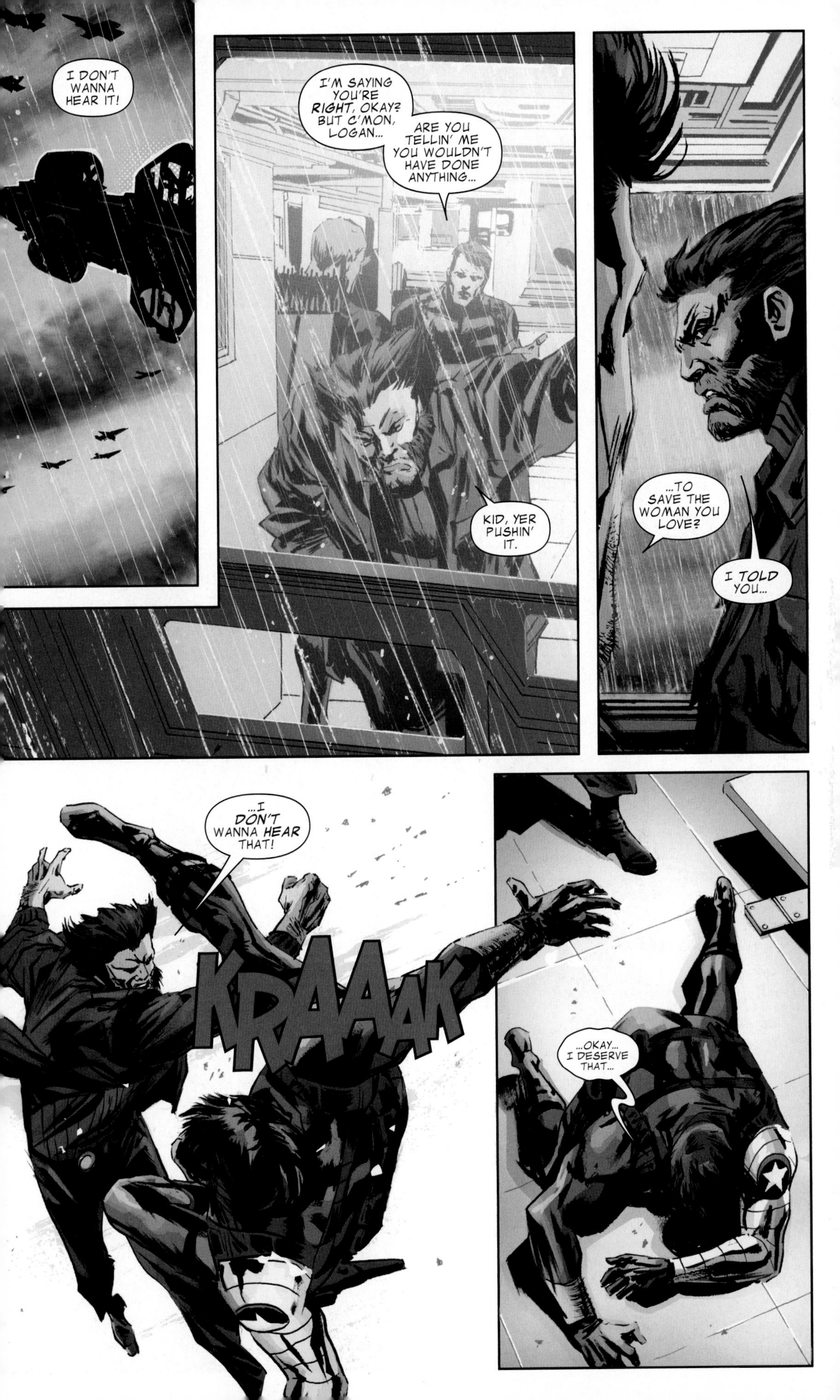

I DON'T WANNA HEAR IT!
I'M SAYING YOU'RE RIGHT, OKAY? BUT C'MON, LOGAN...
ARE YOU TELLIN' ME YOU WOULDN'T HAVE DONE ANYTHING...
KID, YER PUSHIN' IT.
...TO SAVE THE WOMAN YOU LOVE?
I TOLD YOU...
...I DON'T WANNA HEAR THAT!
KRAAAAK
...OKAY... I DESERVE THAT...

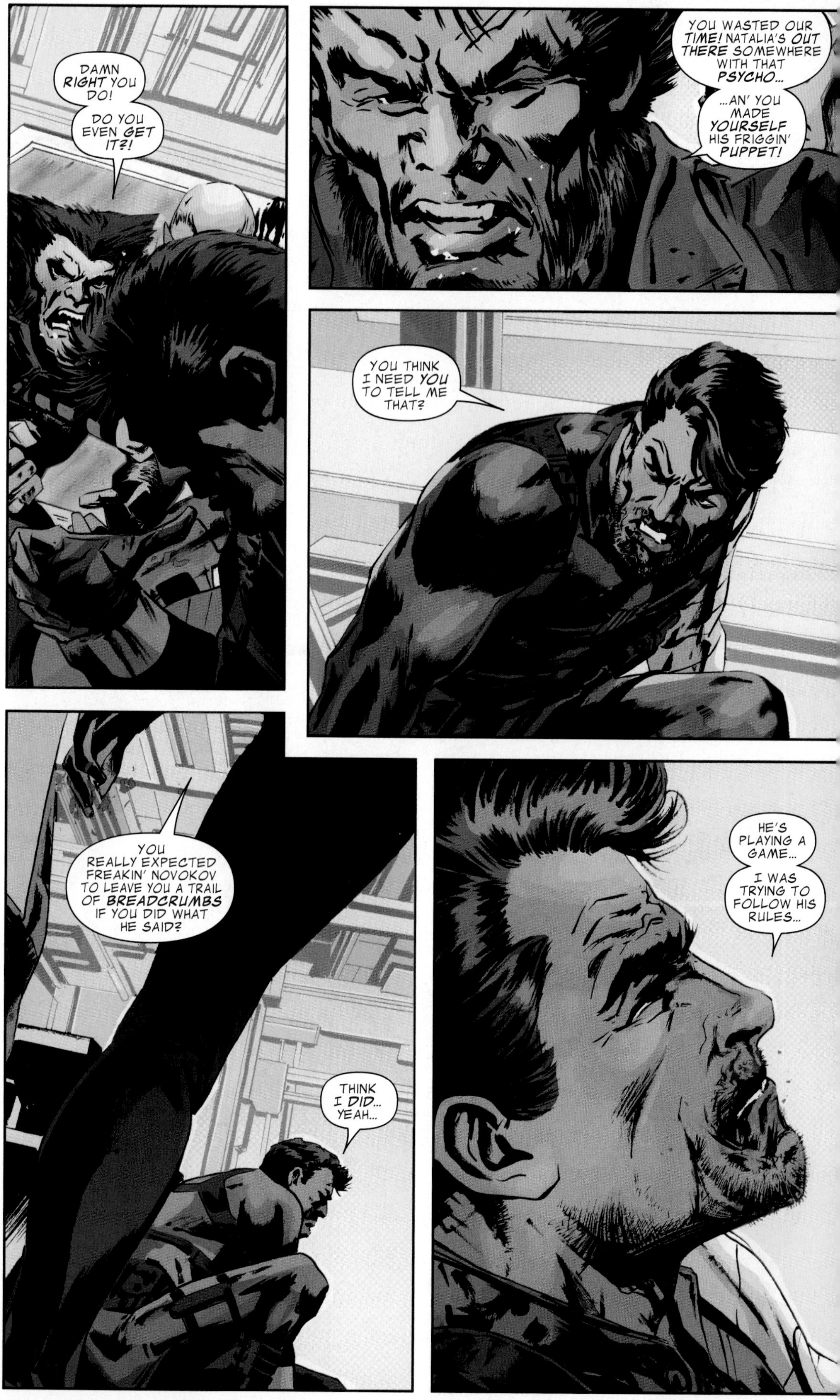
DAMN RIGHT YOU DO!
DO YOU EVEN GET IT?!
YOU WASTED OUR TIME! NATALIA'S OUT THERE SOMEWHERE WITH THAT PSYCHO...
...AN' YOU MADE YOURSELF HIS FRIGGIN' PUPPET!
YOU THINK I NEED YOU TO TELL ME THAT?
YOU REALLY EXPECTED FREAKIN' NOVOKOV TO LEAVE YOU A TRAIL OF BREADCRUMBS IF YOU DID WHAT HE SAID?
THINK I DID... YEAH...
HE'S PLAYING A GAME...
I WAS TRYING TO FOLLOW HIS RULES...

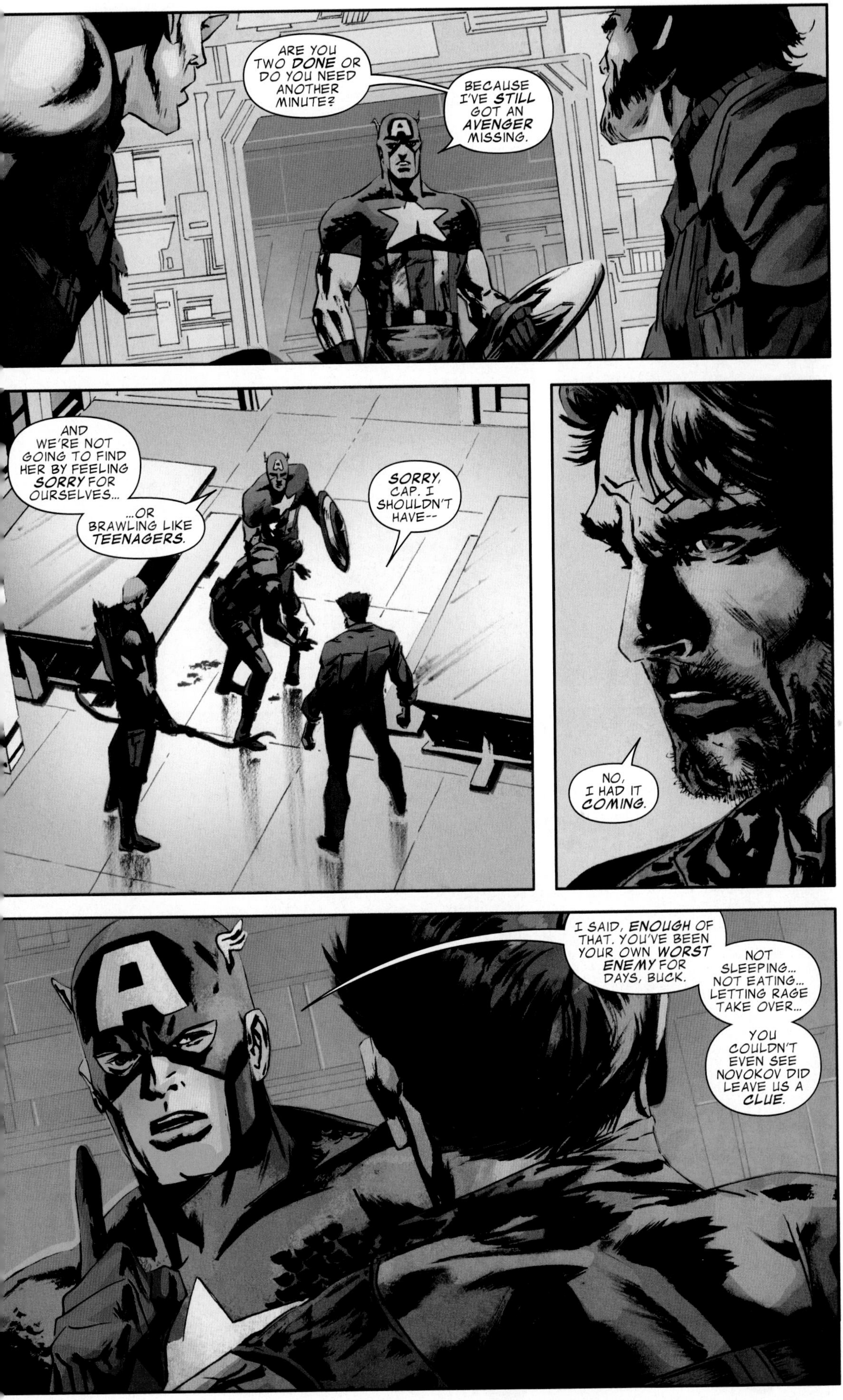
ARE YOU TWO DONE OR DO YOU NEED ANOTHER MINUTE?
BECAUSE I'VE STILL GOT AN AVENGER MISSING.
AND WE'RE NOT GOING TO FIND HER BY FEELING SORRY FOR OURSELVES...
...OR BRAWLING LIKE TEENAGERS.
SORRY, CAP. I SHOULDN'T HAVE--
NO, I HAD IT COMING.
I SAID, ENOUGH OF THAT. YOU'VE BEEN YOUR OWN WORST ENEMY FOR DAYS, BUCK.
NOT SLEEPING... NOT EATING... LETTING RAGE TAKE OVER...
YOU COULDN'T EVEN SEE NOVOKOV DID LEAVE US A CLUE.

THAT *WHOLE MISSION* YOU LET HIM *PROGRAM* INTO YOU *WAS* THE CLUE.

WHAT? WHAT'RE YOU TALKIN' ABOUT?

DAREDEVIL IS IMPORTANT TO *NATASHA*, NOT TO *YOU*.

HE WANTED YOU TO KILL SOMEONE *SHE* LOVES...SO WHAT DOES *THAT* TELL YOU?

THAT...HE'S PLANNING TO GIVE HER BACK...?

BUT ONLY WHEN THAT'LL BE *WORSE TORTURE* FOR BOTH OF YOU...

STILL, THAT MEAN WE GOT A CHANCE...

...AN' THAT'S ALL I NEED.

IF IT'S ALL WE'VE *GOT*...THEN I'LL *TAKE* IT.

LET'S GO FIND OUR GIRL.

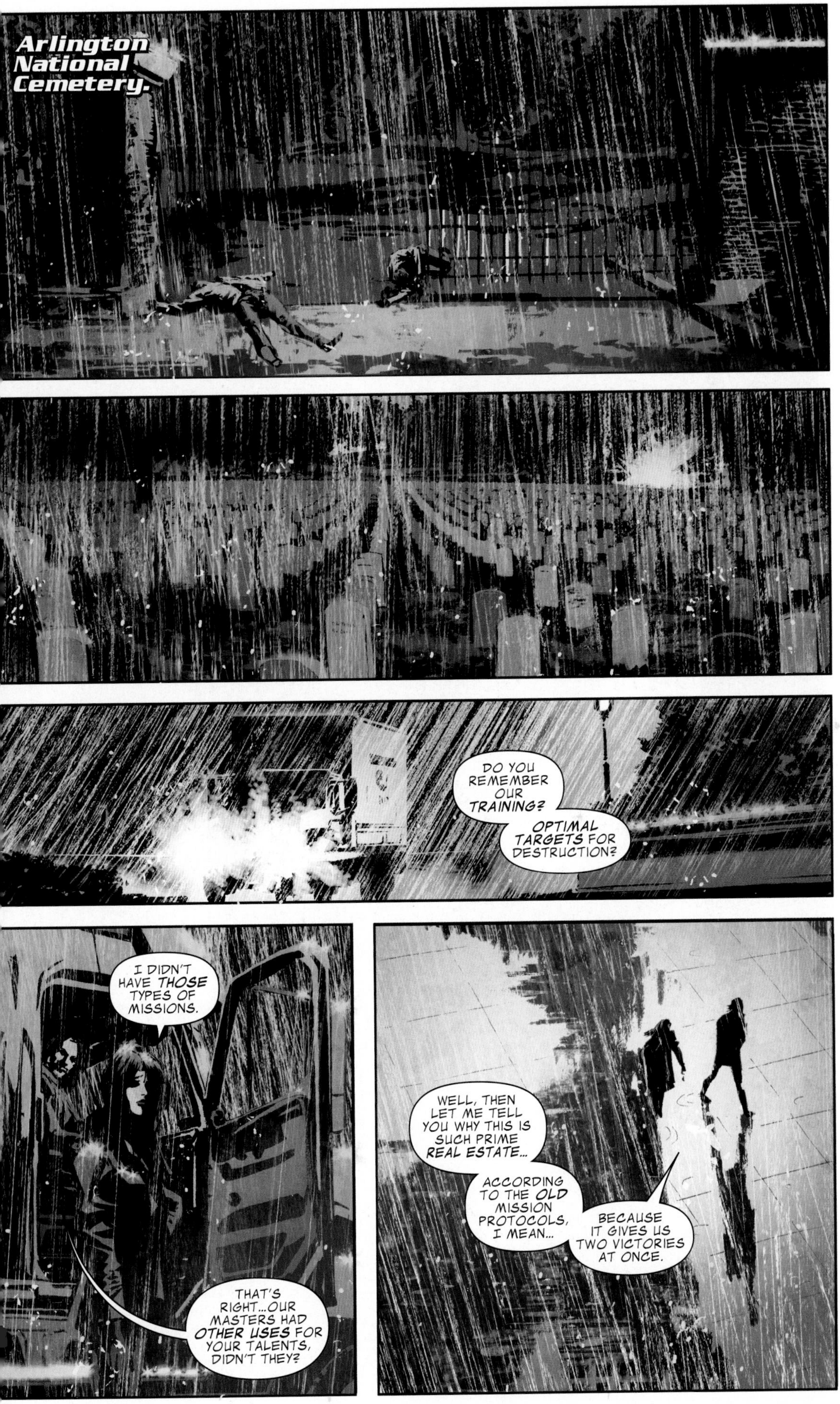
Arlington National Cemetery.
DO YOU REMEMBER OUR TRAINING?
OPTIMAL TARGETS FOR DESTRUCTION?
I DIDN'T HAVE THOSE TYPES OF MISSIONS.
THAT'S RIGHT...OUR MASTERS HAD OTHER USES FOR YOUR TALENTS, DIDN'T THEY?
WELL, THEN LET ME TELL YOU WHY THIS IS SUCH PRIME REAL ESTATE...
ACCORDING TO THE OLD MISSION PROTOCOLS, I MEAN...
BECAUSE IT GIVES US TWO VICTORIES AT ONCE.

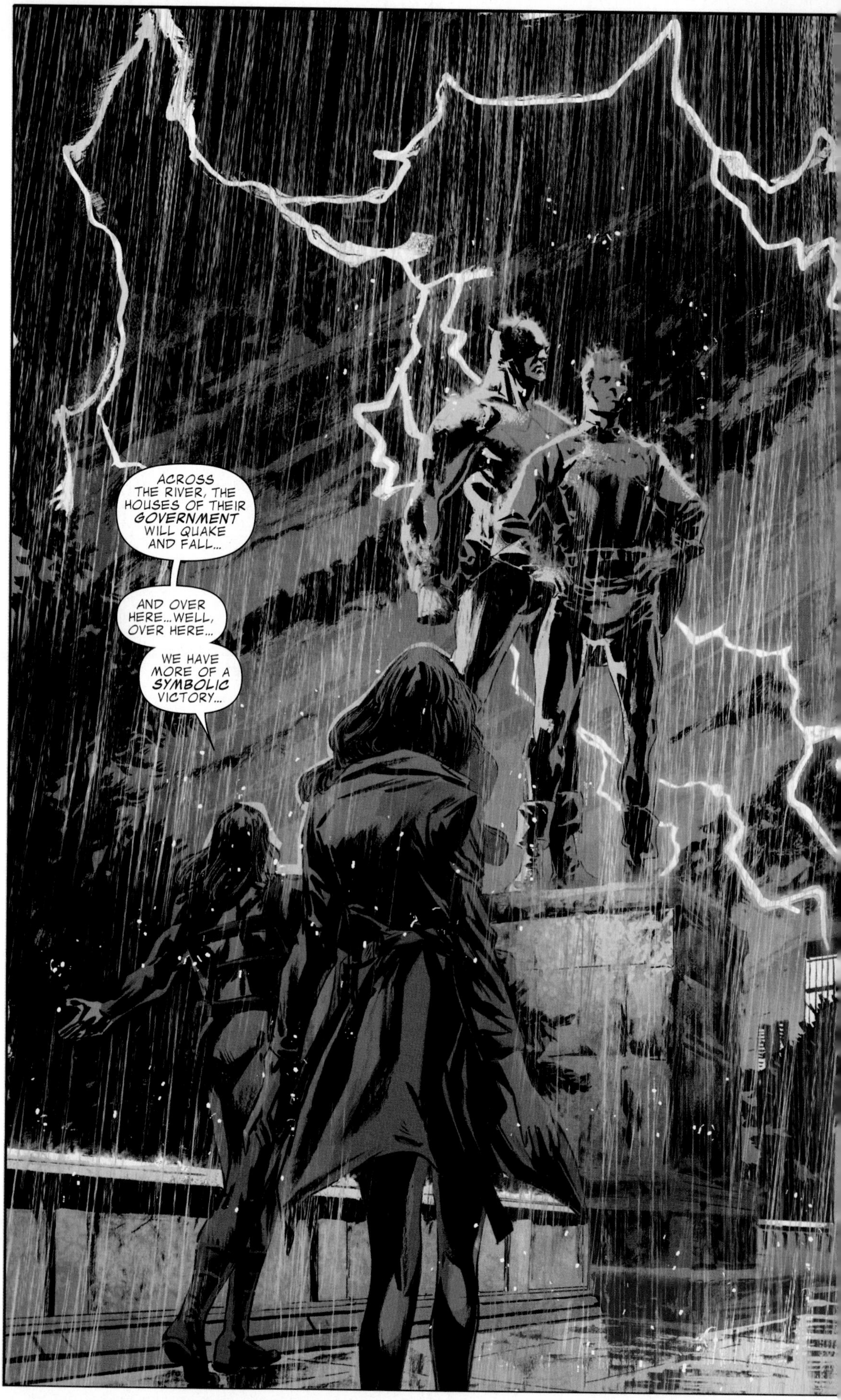
ACROSS THE RIVER, THE HOUSES OF THEIR *GOVERNMENT* WILL QUAKE AND FALL...
AND OVER HERE...WELL, OVER HERE...
WE HAVE MORE OF A *SYMBOLIC* VICTORY...

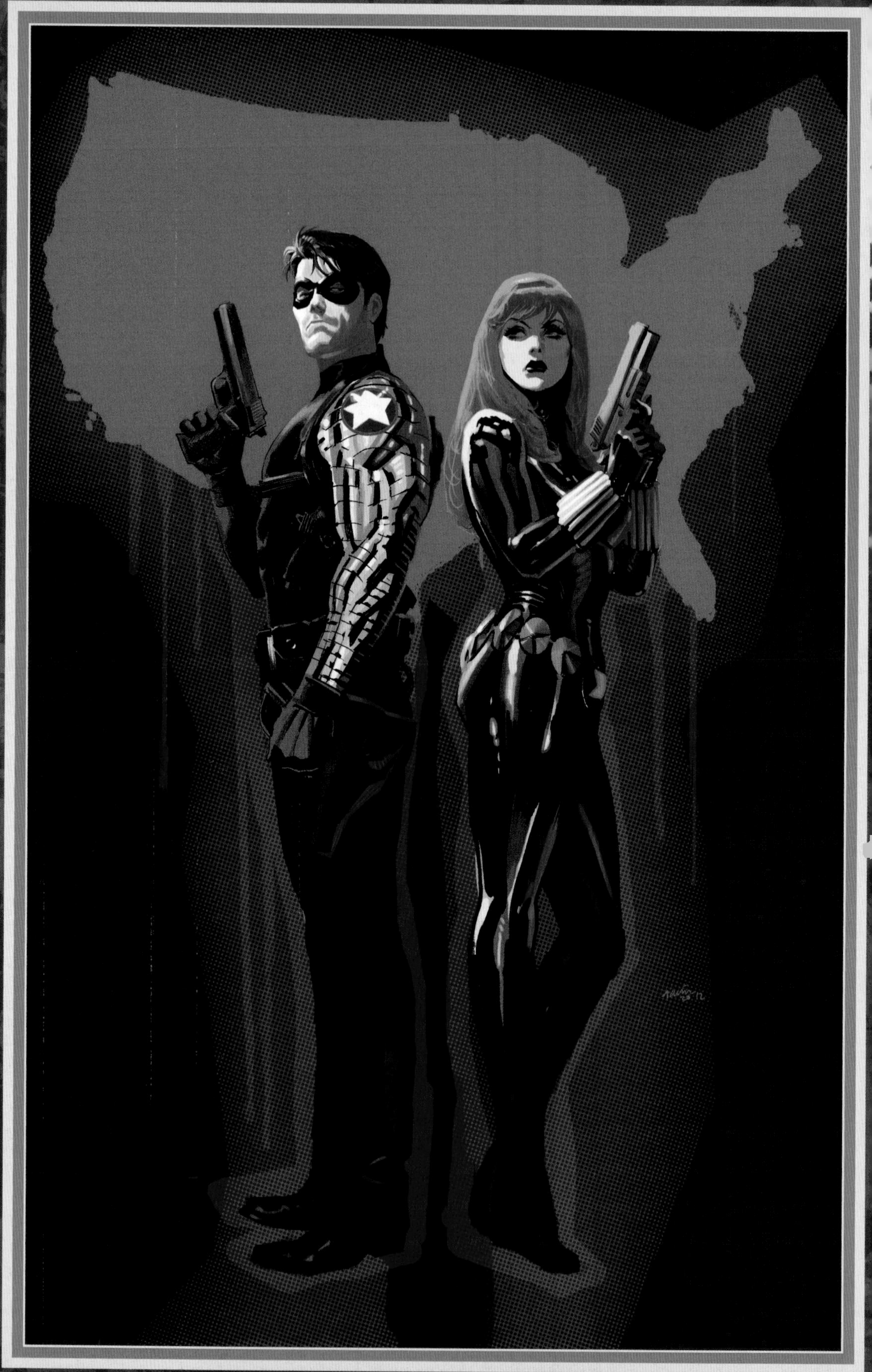

FOURTEEN

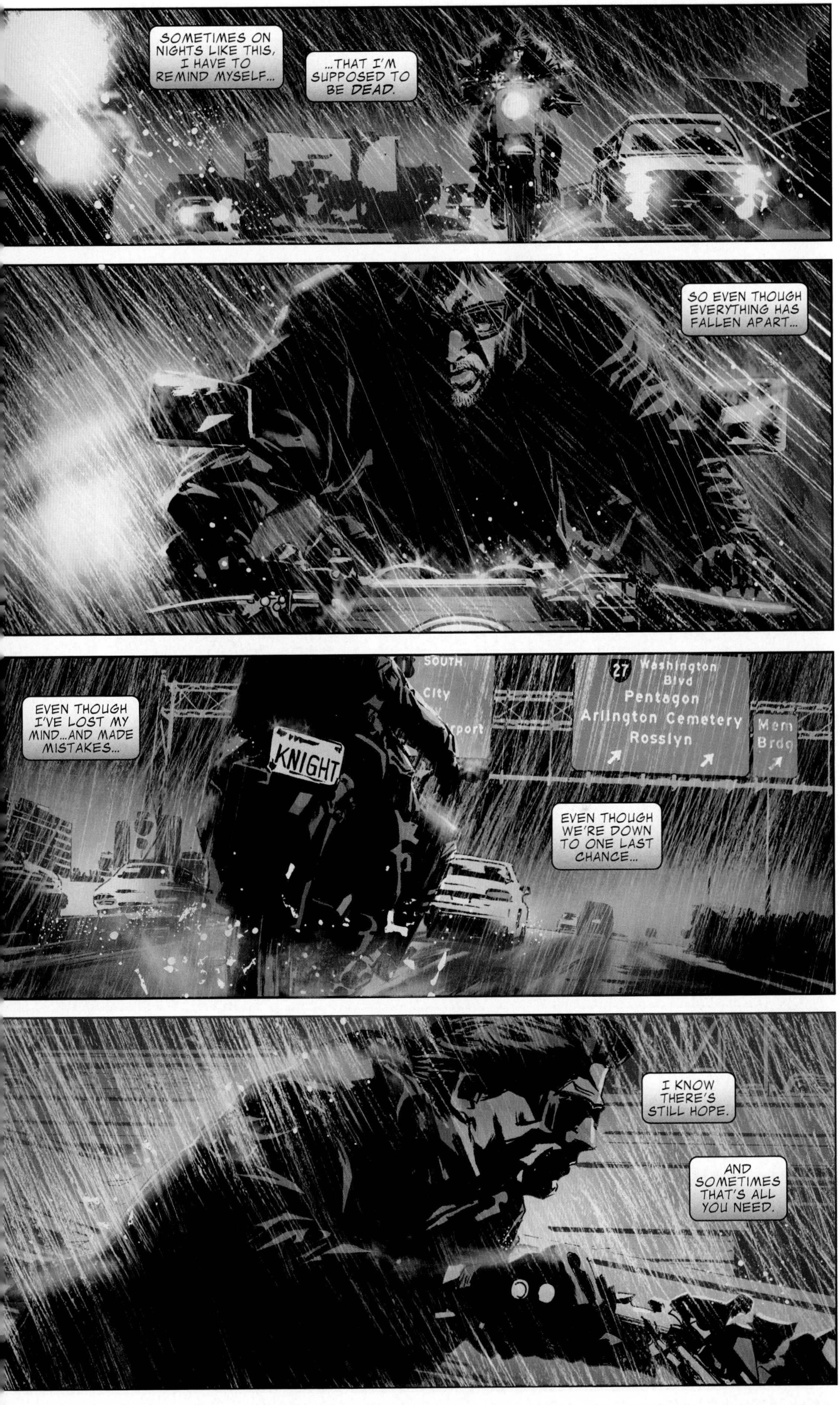
SOMETIMES ON NIGHTS LIKE THIS, I HAVE TO REMIND MYSELF...
...THAT I'M SUPPOSED TO BE *DEAD*.
SO EVEN THOUGH EVERYTHING HAS FALLEN APART...
SOUTH
City
27 Washington Blvd
Pentagon
Arlington Cemetery
Rosslyn
Mem Brdg
KNIGHT
EVEN THOUGH I'VE LOST MY MIND...AND MADE MISTAKES...
EVEN THOUGH WE'RE DOWN TO ONE LAST CHANCE...
I KNOW THERE'S STILL HOPE.
AND SOMETIMES THAT'S ALL YOU NEED.

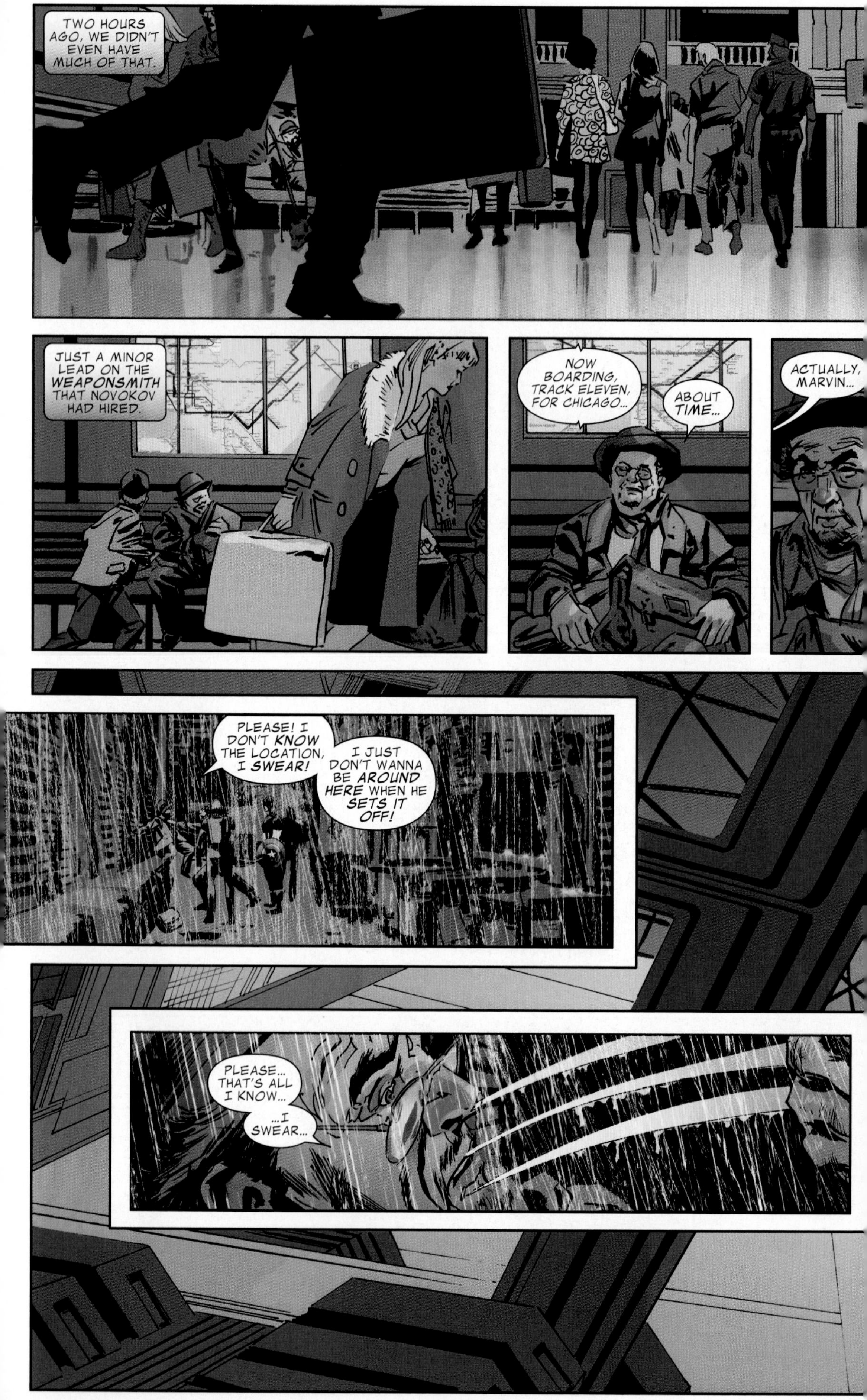

TWO HOURS AGO, WE DIDN'T EVEN HAVE MUCH OF THAT.
JUST A MINOR LEAD ON THE WEAPONSMITH THAT NOVOKOV HAD HIRED.
NOW BOARDING, TRACK ELEVEN, FOR CHICAGO...
ABOUT TIME...
ACTUALLY, MARVIN...
PLEASE! I DON'T KNOW THE LOCATION, I SWEAR!
I JUST DON'T WANNA BE AROUND HERE WHEN HE SETS IT OFF!
PLEASE... THAT'S ALL I KNOW...
...I SWEAR...

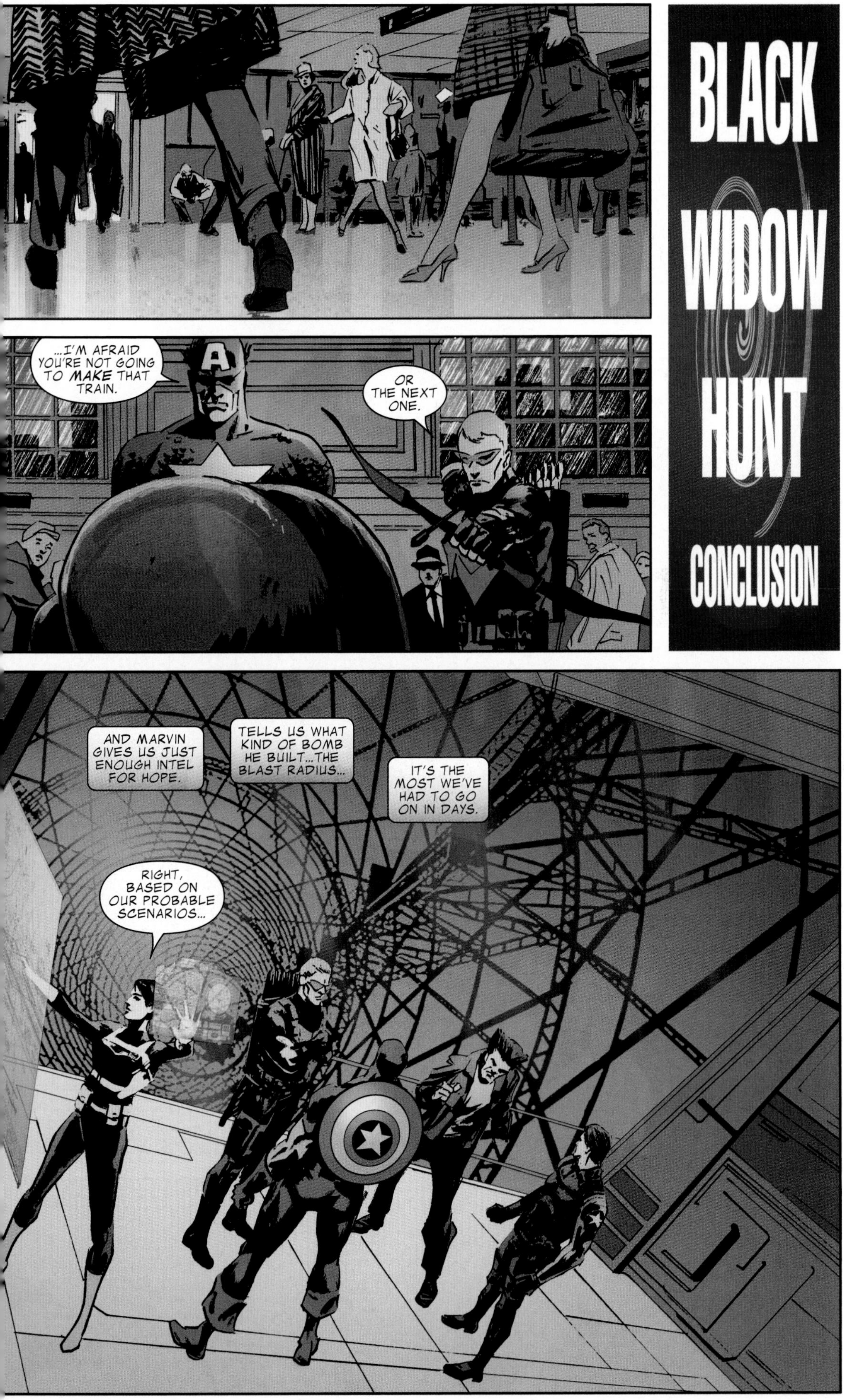
BLACK WIDOW HUNT
CONCLUSION
...I'M AFRAID YOU'RE NOT GOING TO MAKE THAT TRAIN.
OR THE NEXT ONE.
AND MARVIN GIVES US JUST ENOUGH INTEL FOR HOPE.
TELLS US WHAT KIND OF BOMB HE BUILT...THE BLAST RADIUS...
IT'S THE MOST WE'VE HAD TO GO ON IN DAYS.
RIGHT, BASED ON OUR PROBABLE SCENARIOS...

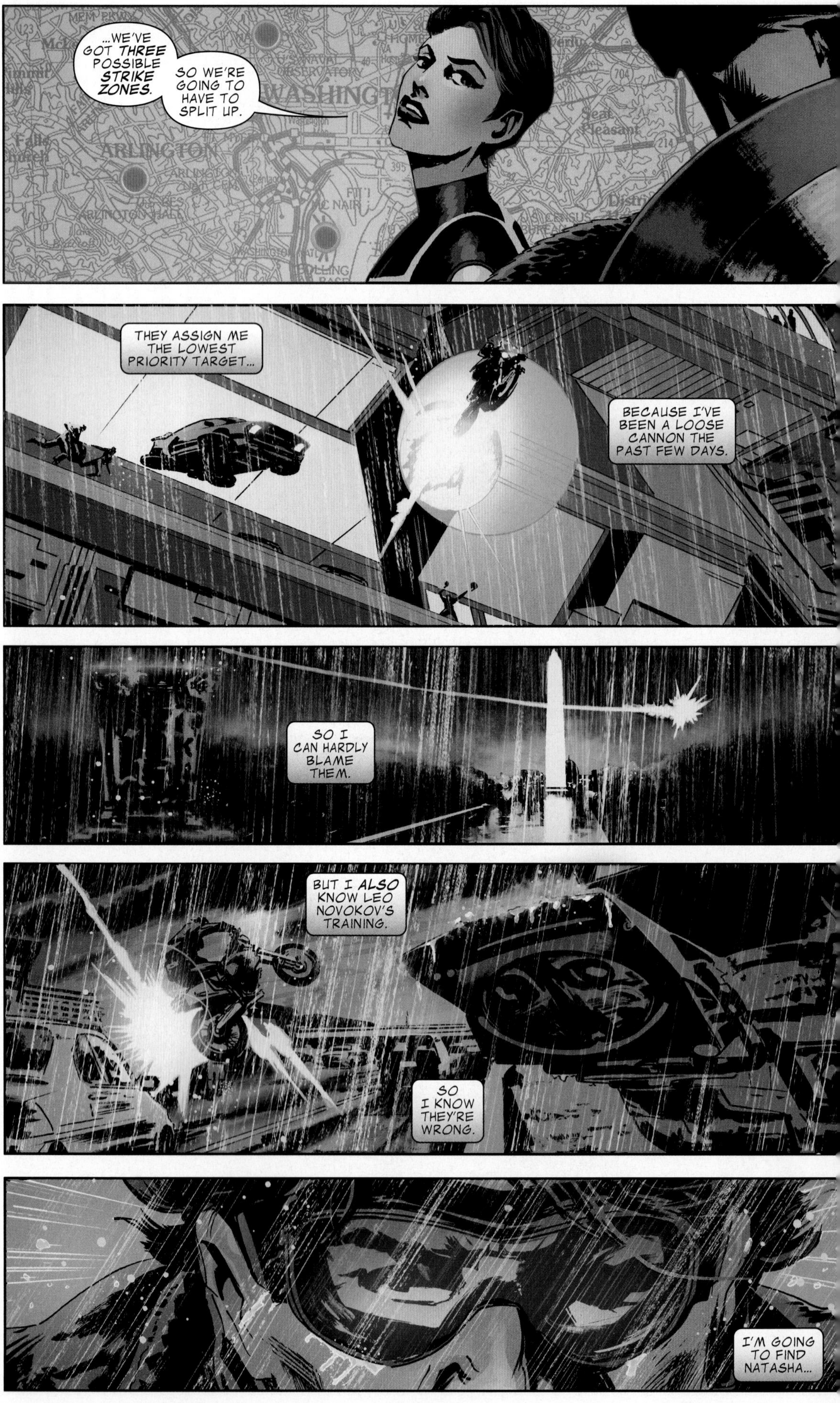
...WE'VE GOT THREE POSSIBLE STRIKE ZONES.
SO WE'RE GOING TO HAVE TO SPLIT UP.
WASHINGT
ARLINGTON
THEY ASSIGN ME THE LOWEST PRIORITY TARGET...
BECAUSE I'VE BEEN A LOOSE CANNON THE PAST FEW DAYS.
SO I CAN HARDLY BLAME THEM.
BUT I ALSO KNOW LEO NOVOKOV'S TRAINING.
SO I KNOW THEY'RE WRONG.
I'M GOING TO FIND NATASHA...

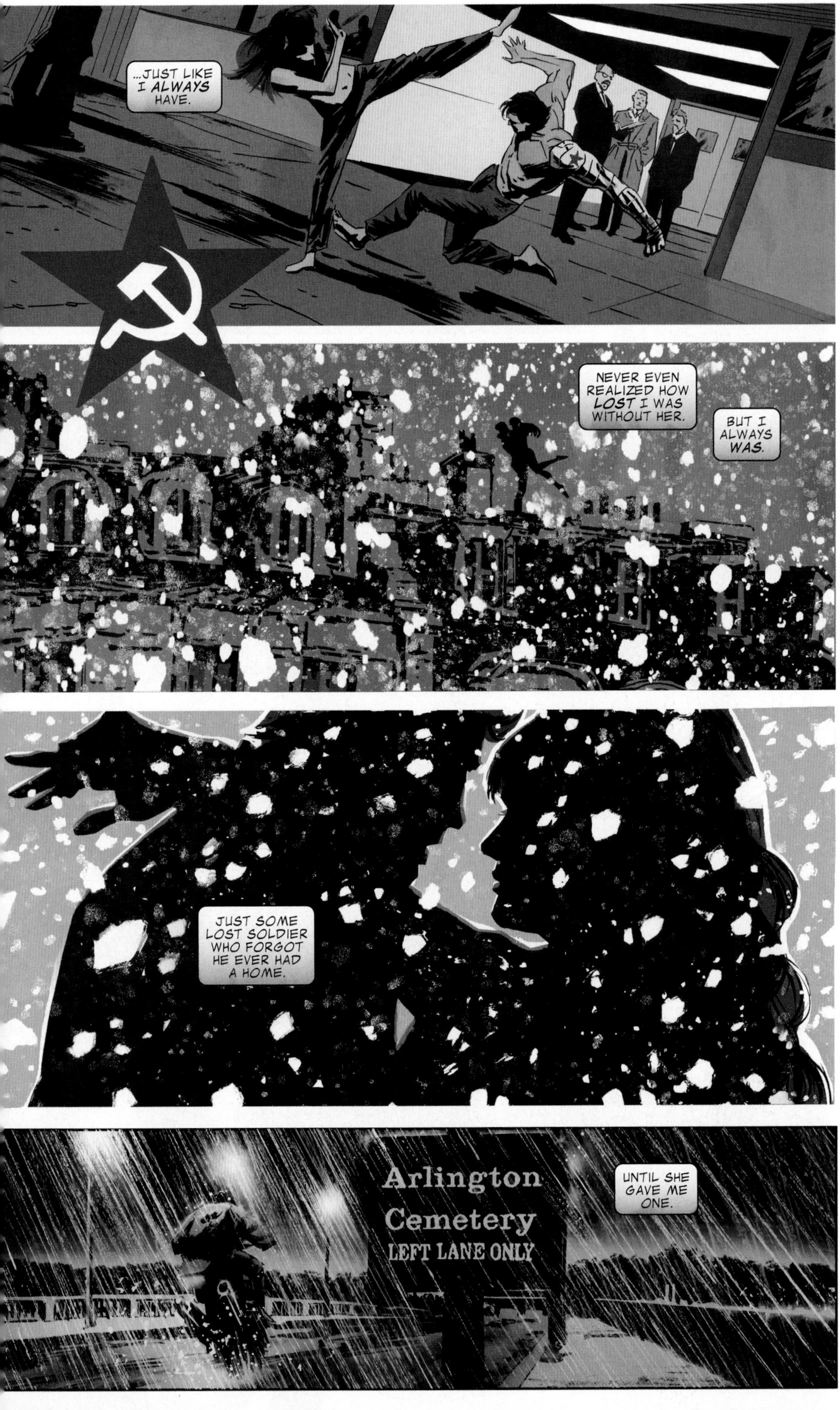
...JUST LIKE I ALWAYS HAVE.
NEVER EVEN REALIZED HOW LOST I WAS WITHOUT HER.
BUT I ALWAYS WAS.
JUST SOME LOST SOLDIER WHO FORGOT HE EVER HAD A HOME.
Arlington Cemetery LEFT LANE ONLY
UNTIL SHE GAVE ME ONE.

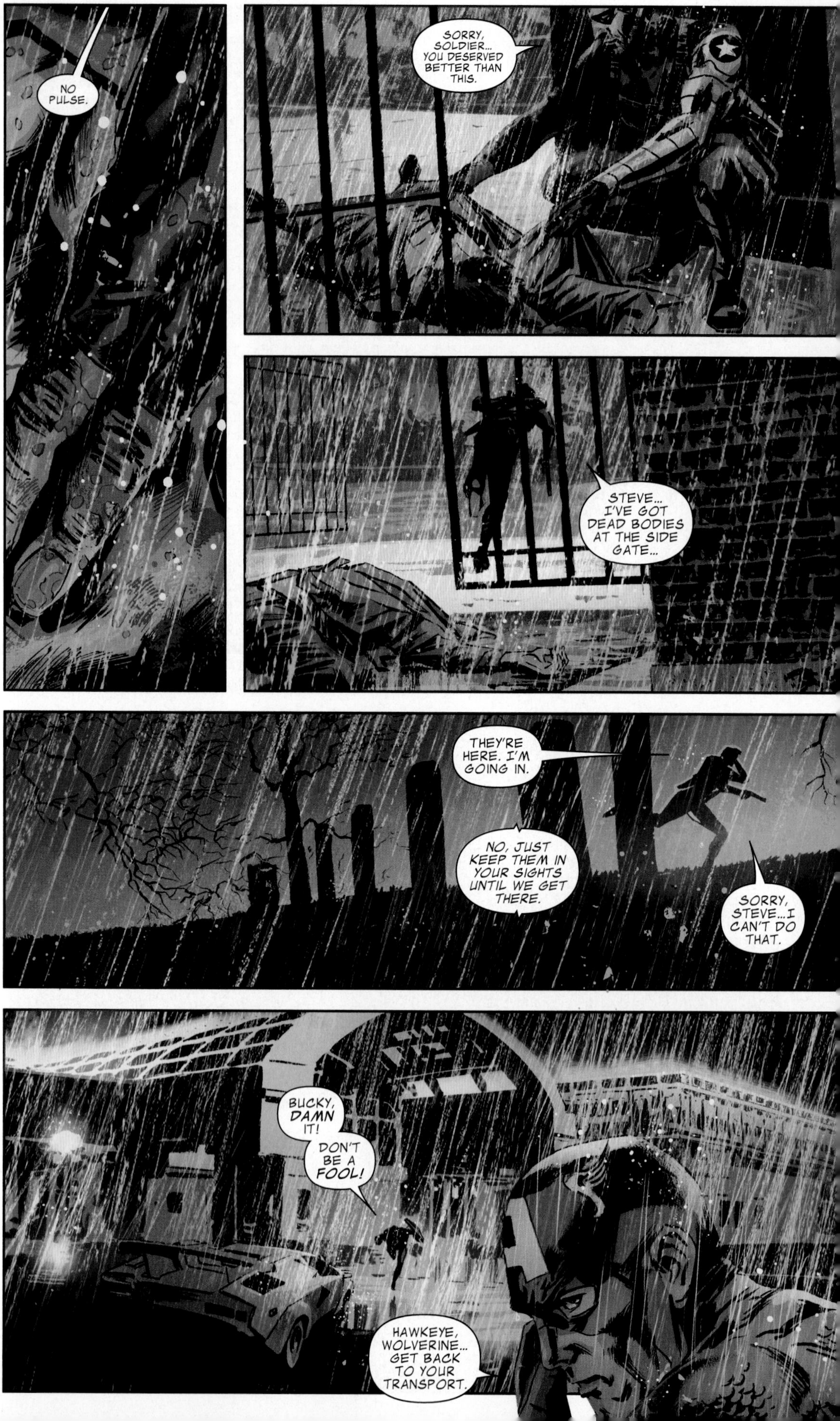
NO PULSE.
SORRY, SOLDIER... YOU DESERVED BETTER THAN THIS.
STEVE... I'VE GOT DEAD BODIES AT THE SIDE GATE...
THEY'RE HERE. I'M GOING IN.
NO, JUST KEEP THEM IN YOUR SIGHTS UNTIL WE GET THERE.
SORRY, STEVE...I CAN'T DO THAT.
BUCKY, DAMN IT!
DON'T BE A FOOL!
HAWKEYE, WOLVERINE... GET BACK TO YOUR TRANSPORT.

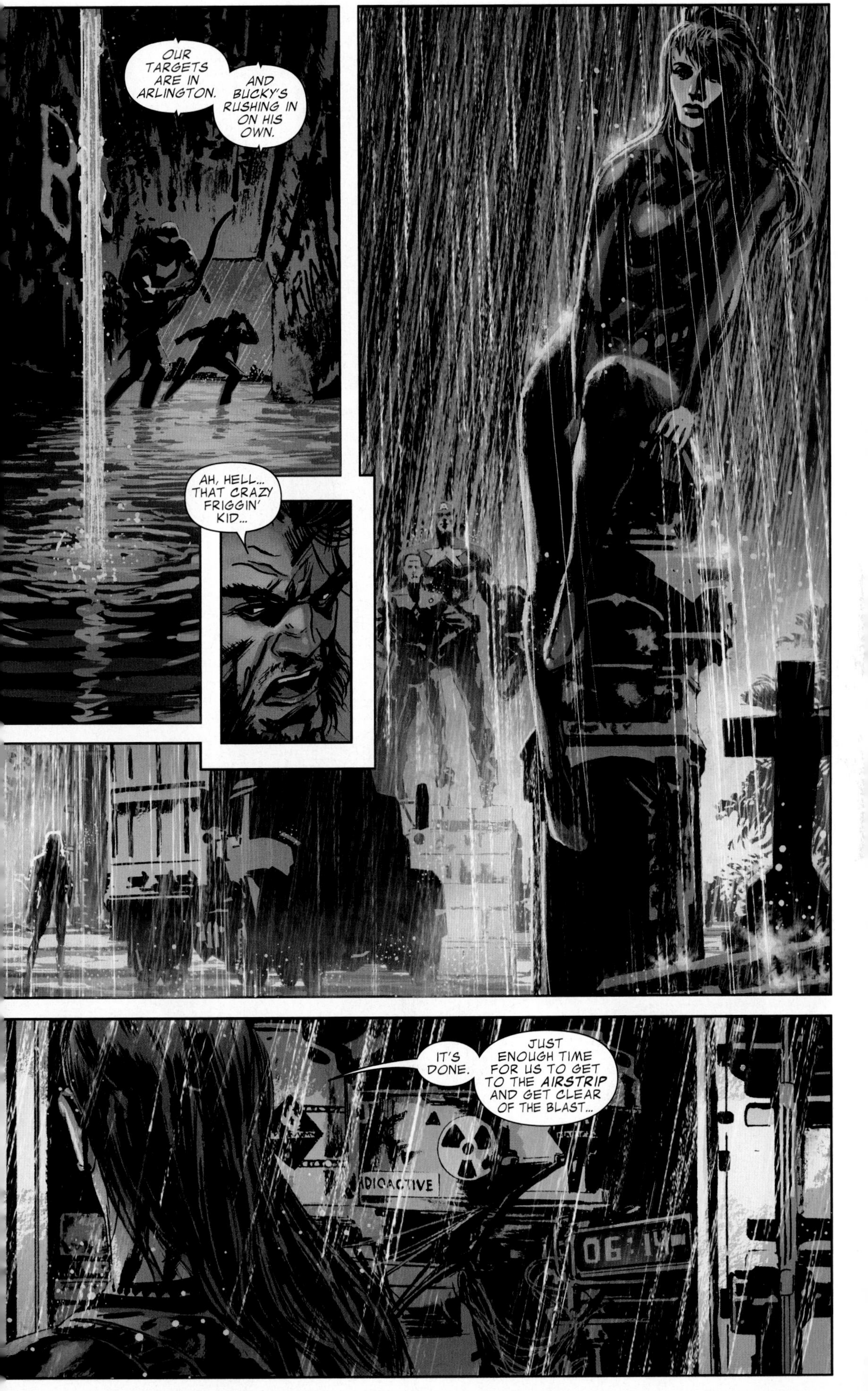
OUR TARGETS ARE IN ARLINGTON.
AND BUCKY'S RUSHING IN ON HIS OWN.
AH, HELL... THAT CRAZY FRIGGIN' KID...
IT'S DONE.
JUST ENOUGH TIME FOR US TO GET TO THE AIRSTRIP AND GET CLEAR OF THE BLAST...
DIOACTIVE
06:14

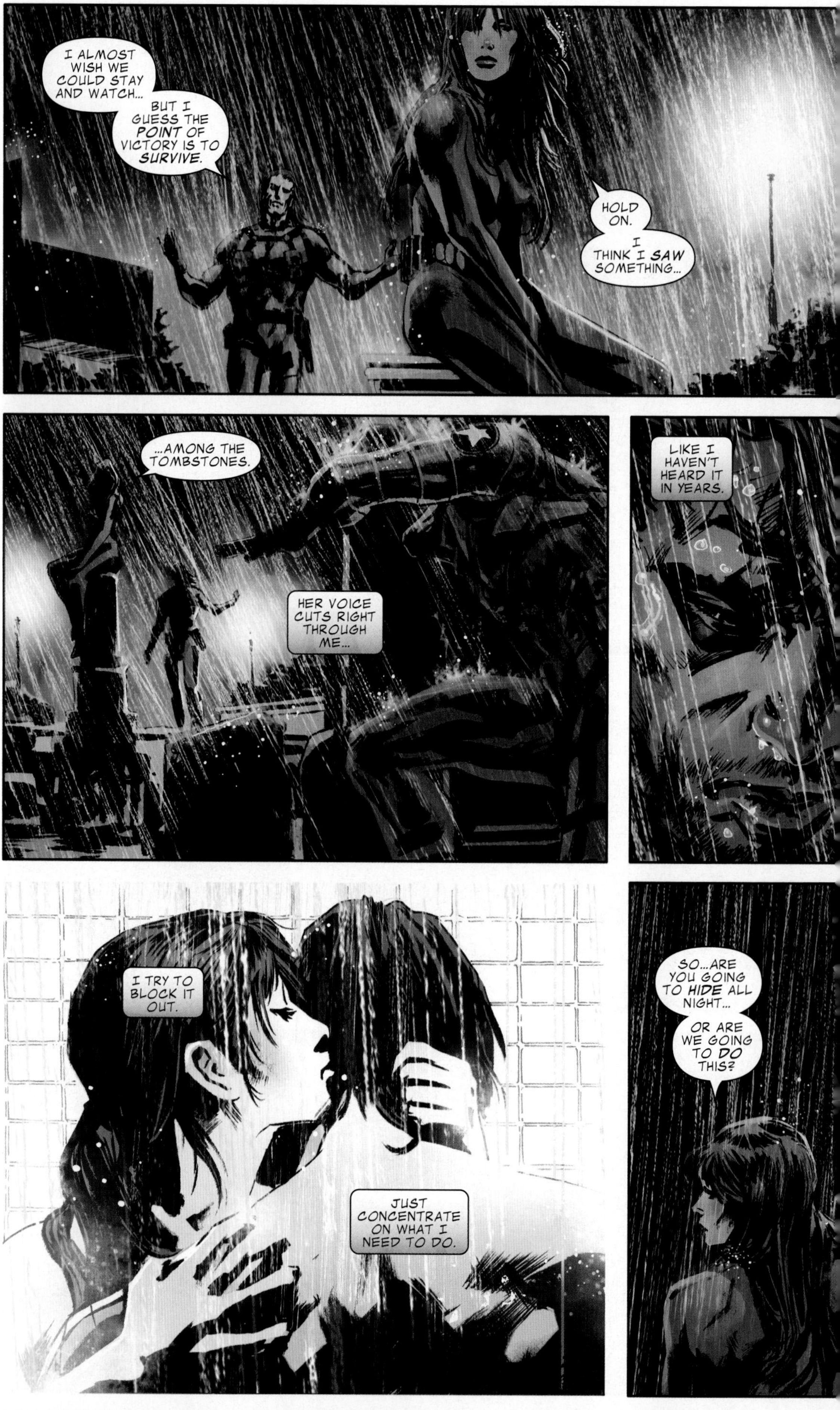
I ALMOST WISH WE COULD STAY AND WATCH...
BUT I GUESS THE *POINT* OF VICTORY IS TO ***SURVIVE***.
HOLD ON.
I THINK I **SAW** SOMETHING...
...AMONG THE TOMBSTONES.
HER VOICE CUTS RIGHT THROUGH ME...
LIKE I HAVEN'T HEARD IT IN YEARS.
I TRY TO BLOCK IT OUT.
JUST CONCENTRATE ON WHAT I NEED TO DO.
SO...ARE YOU GOING TO ***HIDE*** ALL NIGHT...
OR ARE WE GOING TO ***DO*** THIS?

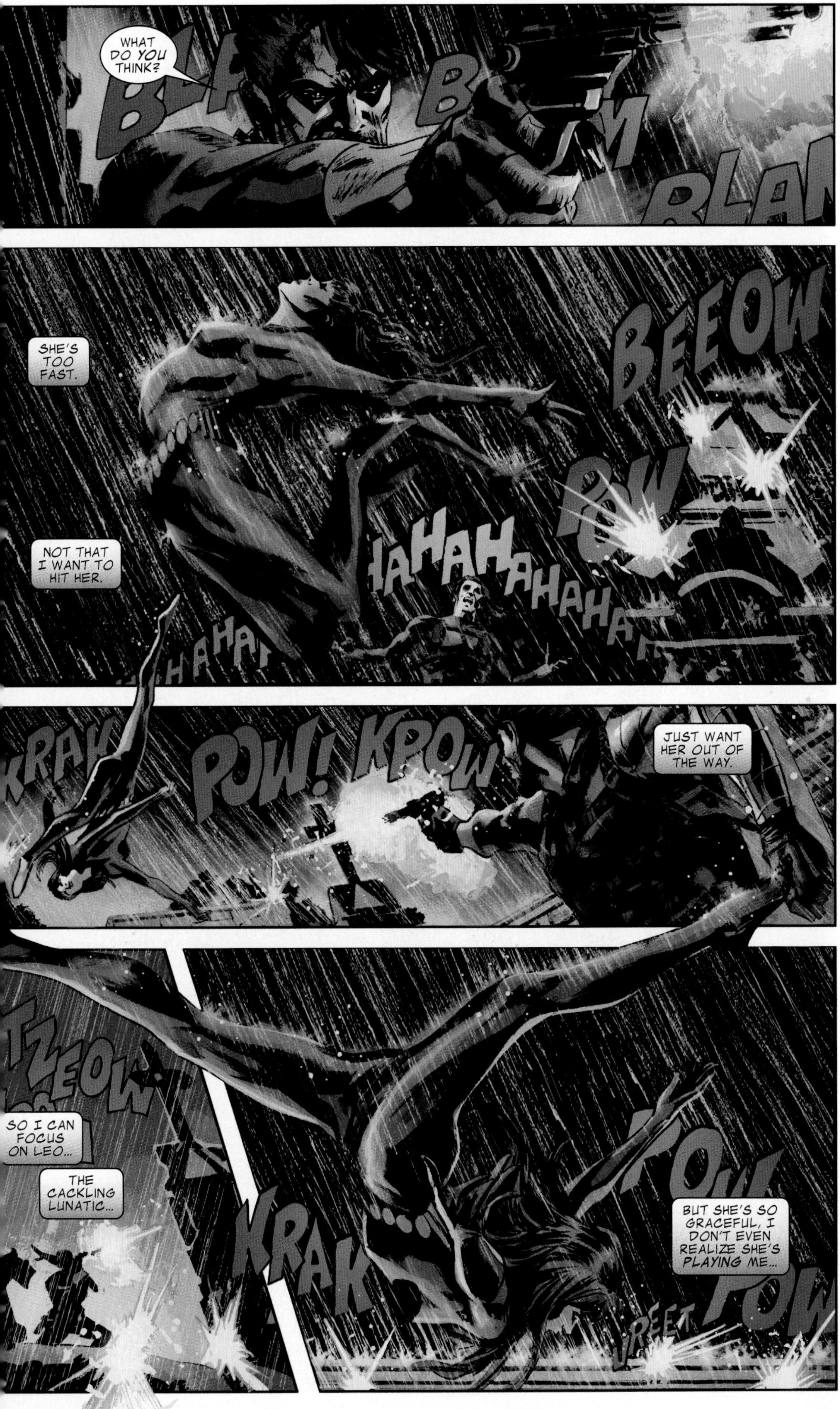
WHAT DO YOU THINK?
BLAM
BLAM
SHE'S TOO FAST.
BEEOW
POW
NOT THAT I WANT TO HIT HER.
HAHAHAHAHAH
KRAK
POW! KPOW
JUST WANT HER OUT OF THE WAY.
TZEOW
SO I CAN FOCUS ON LEO...
THE CACKLING LUNATIC...
KRAK
POW
BUT SHE'S SO GRACEFUL, I DON'T EVEN REALIZE SHE'S PLAYING ME...
REET
POW

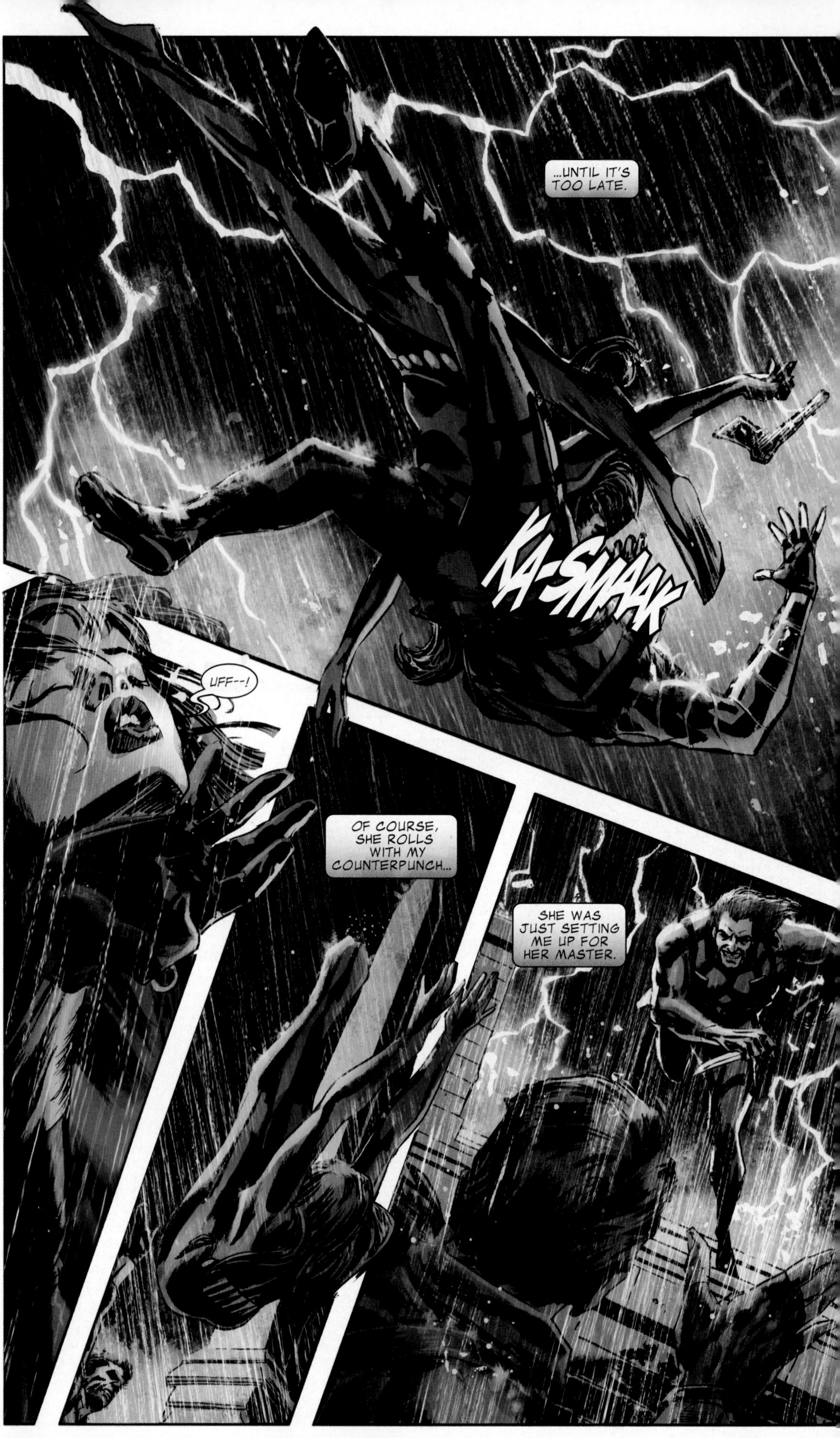
...UNTIL IT'S TOO LATE.
KA-SMAAK
UFF--!
OF COURSE, SHE ROLLS WITH MY COUNTERPUNCH...
SHE WAS JUST SETTING ME UP FOR HER MASTER.

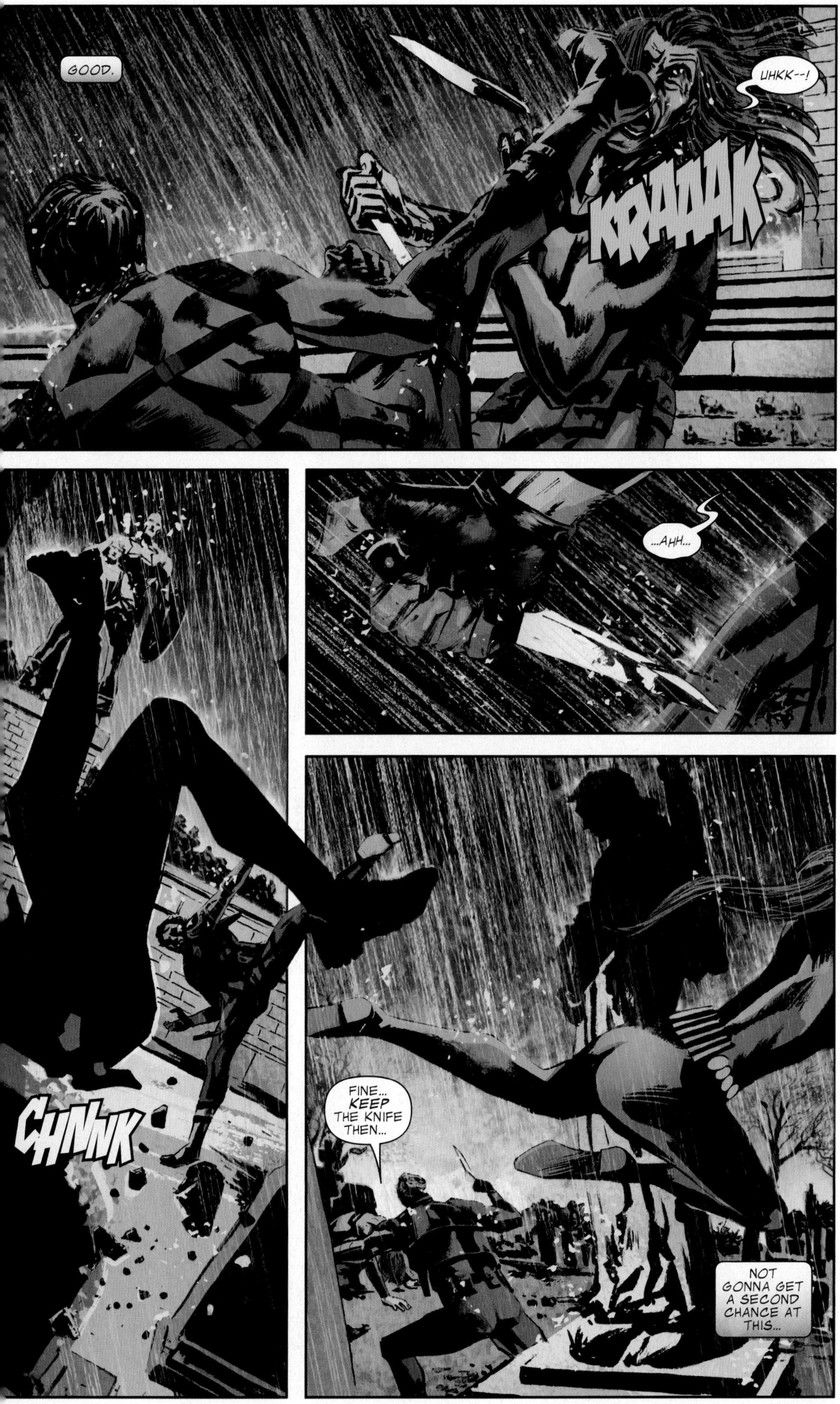
GOOD.
UHKK--!
KRAAAK
...AHH...
CHNNK
FINE... KEEP THE KNIFE THEN...
NOT GONNA GET A SECOND CHANCE AT THIS...

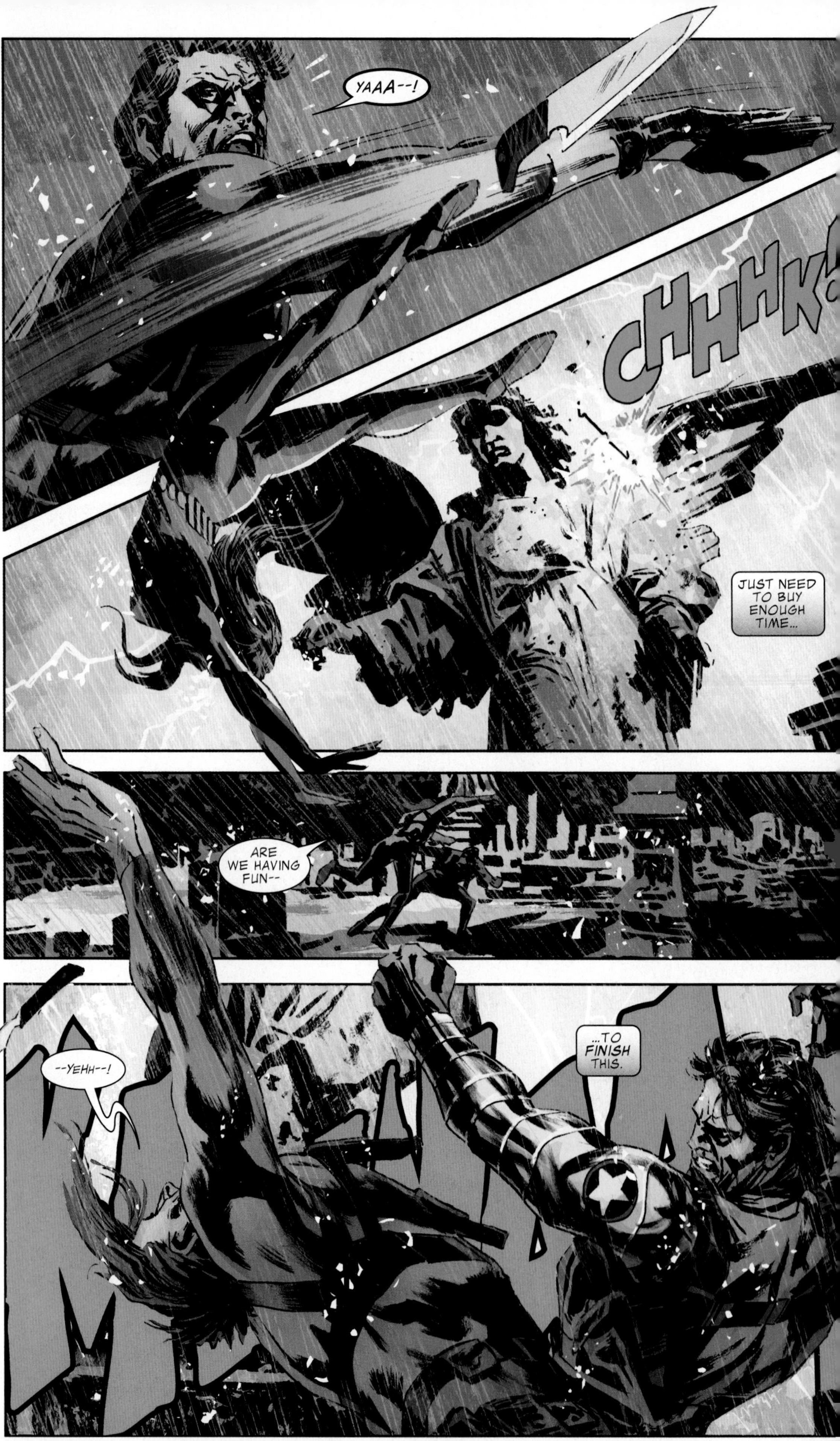
YAAA--!
CHHHK!
JUST NEED TO BUY ENOUGH TIME...
ARE WE HAVING FUN--
--YEHH--!
...TO FINISH THIS.

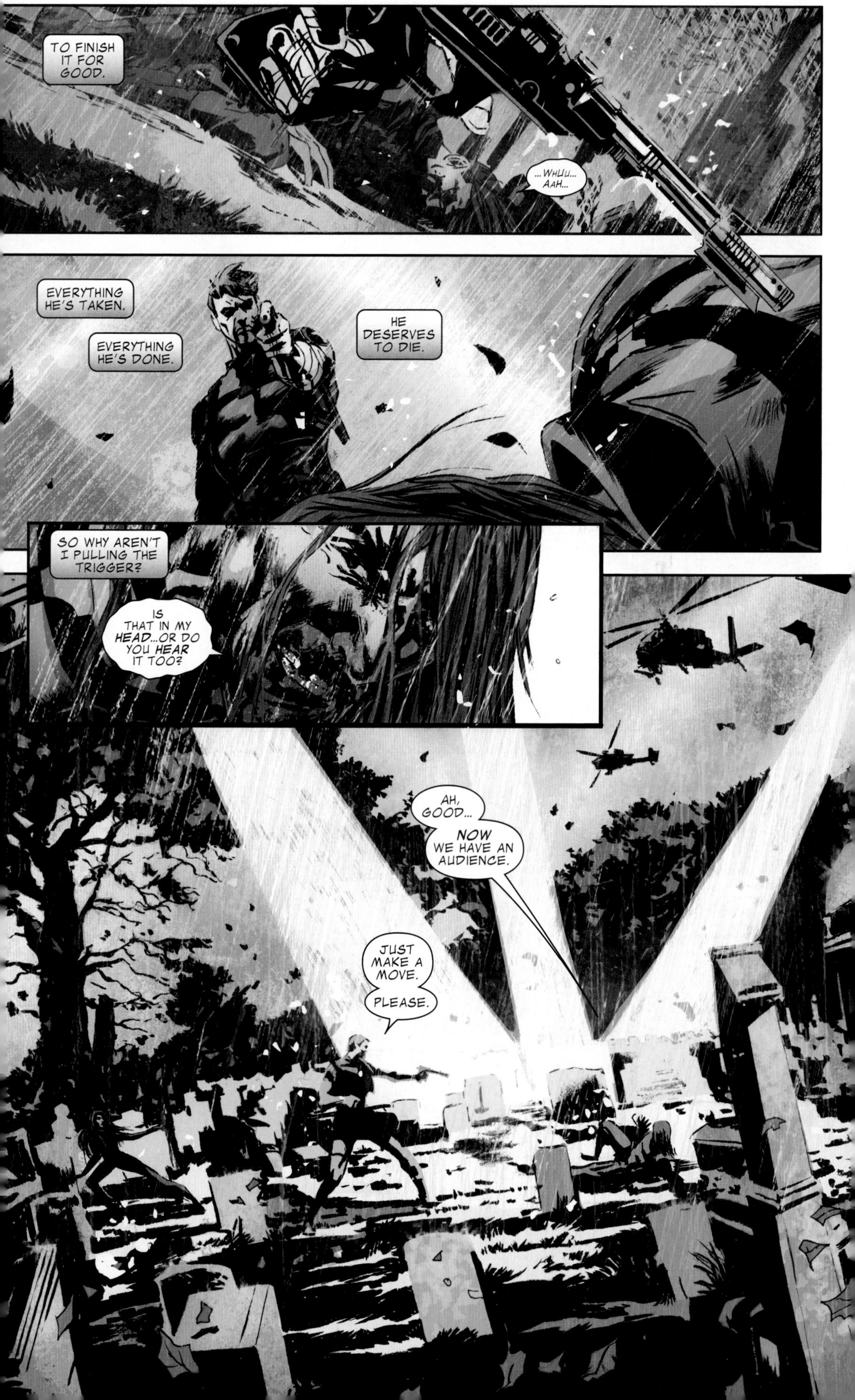
TO FINISH IT FOR GOOD.
...WHUU... AAH...
EVERYTHING HE'S TAKEN.
EVERYTHING HE'S DONE.
HE DESERVES TO DIE.
SO WHY AREN'T I PULLING THE TRIGGER?
IS THAT IN MY HEAD...OR DO YOU HEAR IT TOO?
AH, GOOD...
NOW WE HAVE AN AUDIENCE.
JUST MAKE A MOVE.
PLEASE.

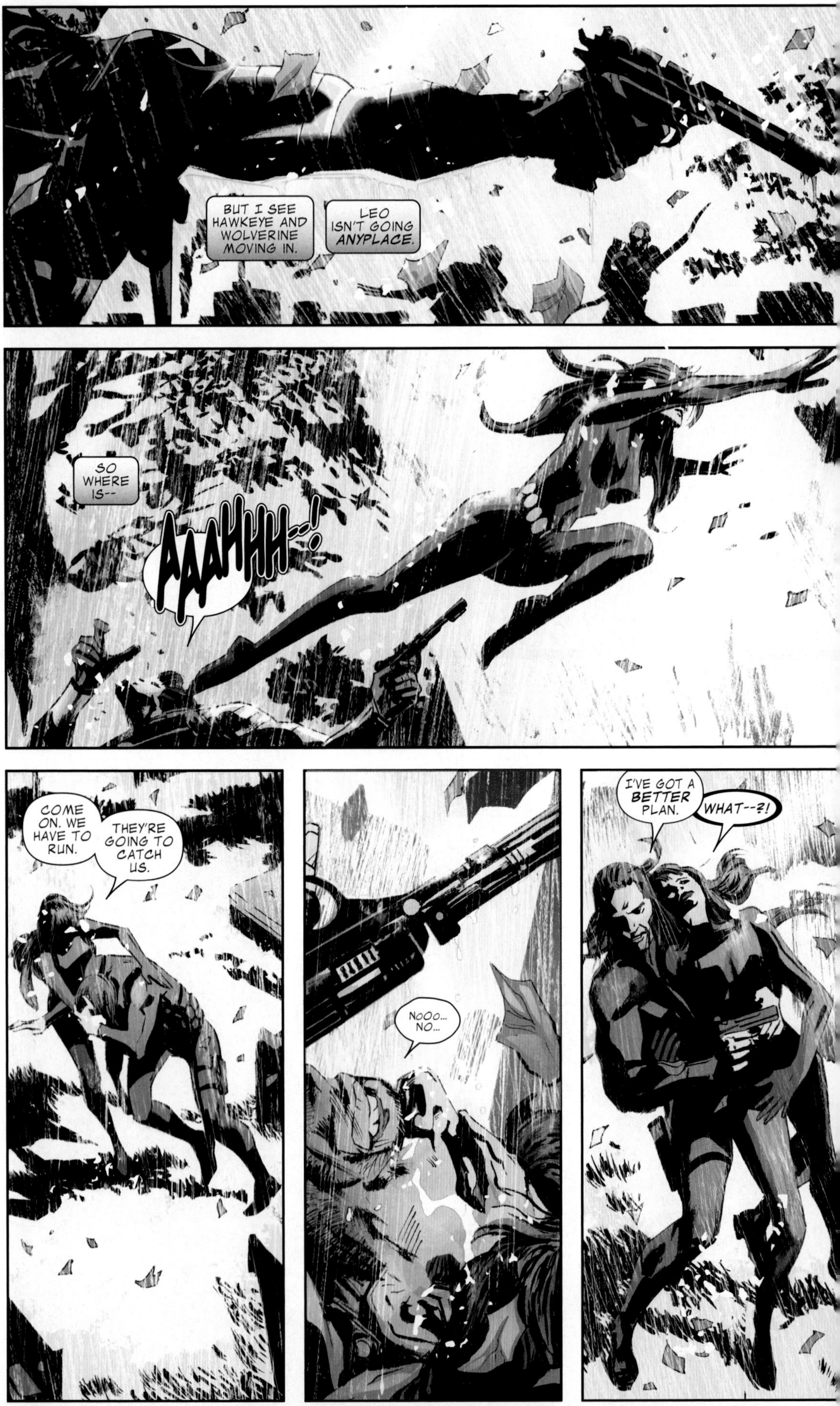

BUT I SEE HAWKEYE AND WOLVERINE MOVING IN.
LEO ISN'T GOING ANYPLACE.
SO WHERE IS--
AAAHHH--!
COME ON. WE HAVE TO RUN.
THEY'RE GOING TO CATCH US.
NOOO... NO...
I'VE GOT A BETTER PLAN.
WHAT--?!

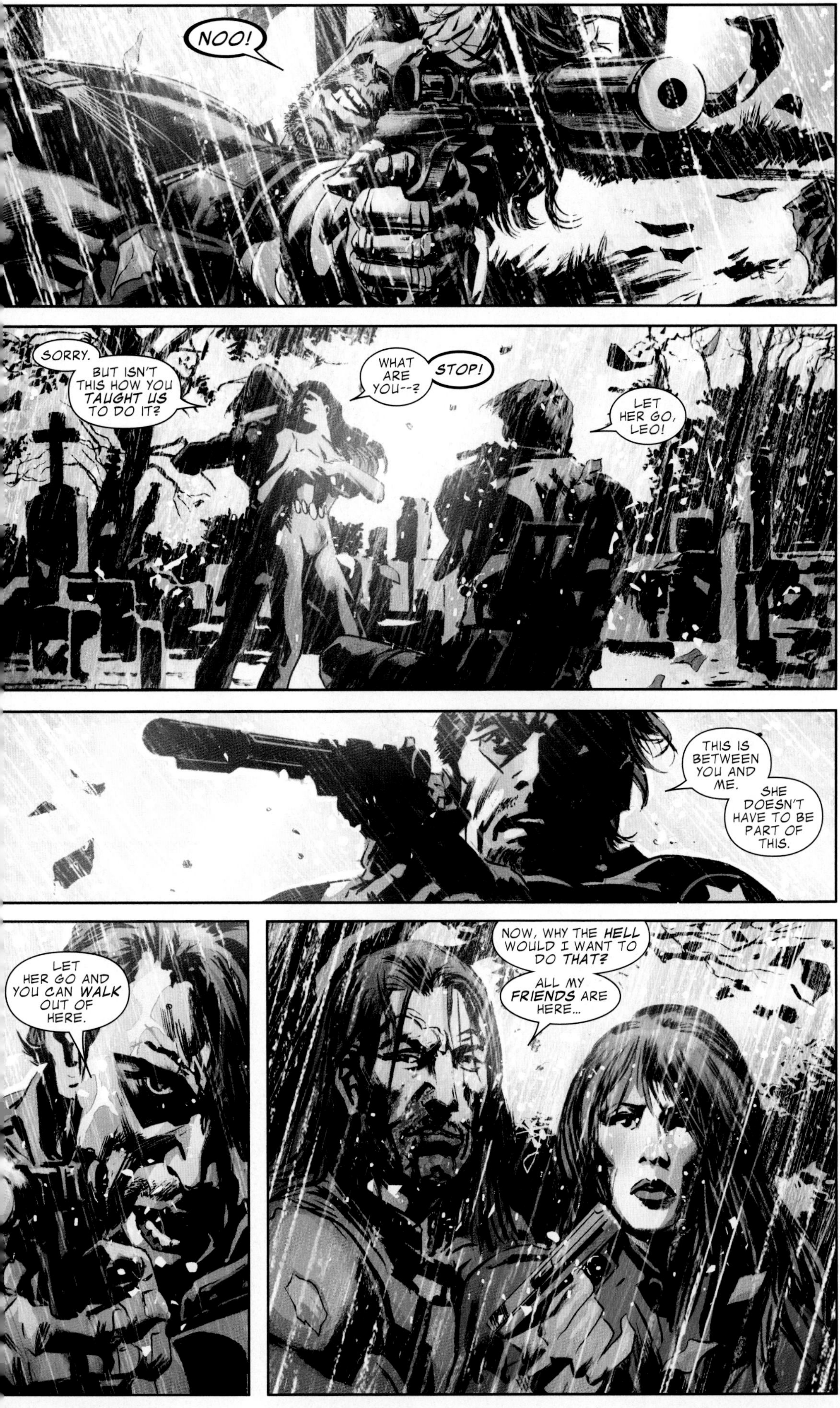
NOO!
SORRY.
BUT ISN'T THIS HOW YOU TAUGHT US TO DO IT?
WHAT ARE YOU--?
STOP!
LET HER GO, LEO!
THIS IS BETWEEN YOU AND ME.
SHE DOESN'T HAVE TO BE PART OF THIS.
LET HER GO AND YOU CAN WALK OUT OF HERE.
NOW, WHY THE HELL WOULD I WANT TO DO THAT?
ALL MY FRIENDS ARE HERE...

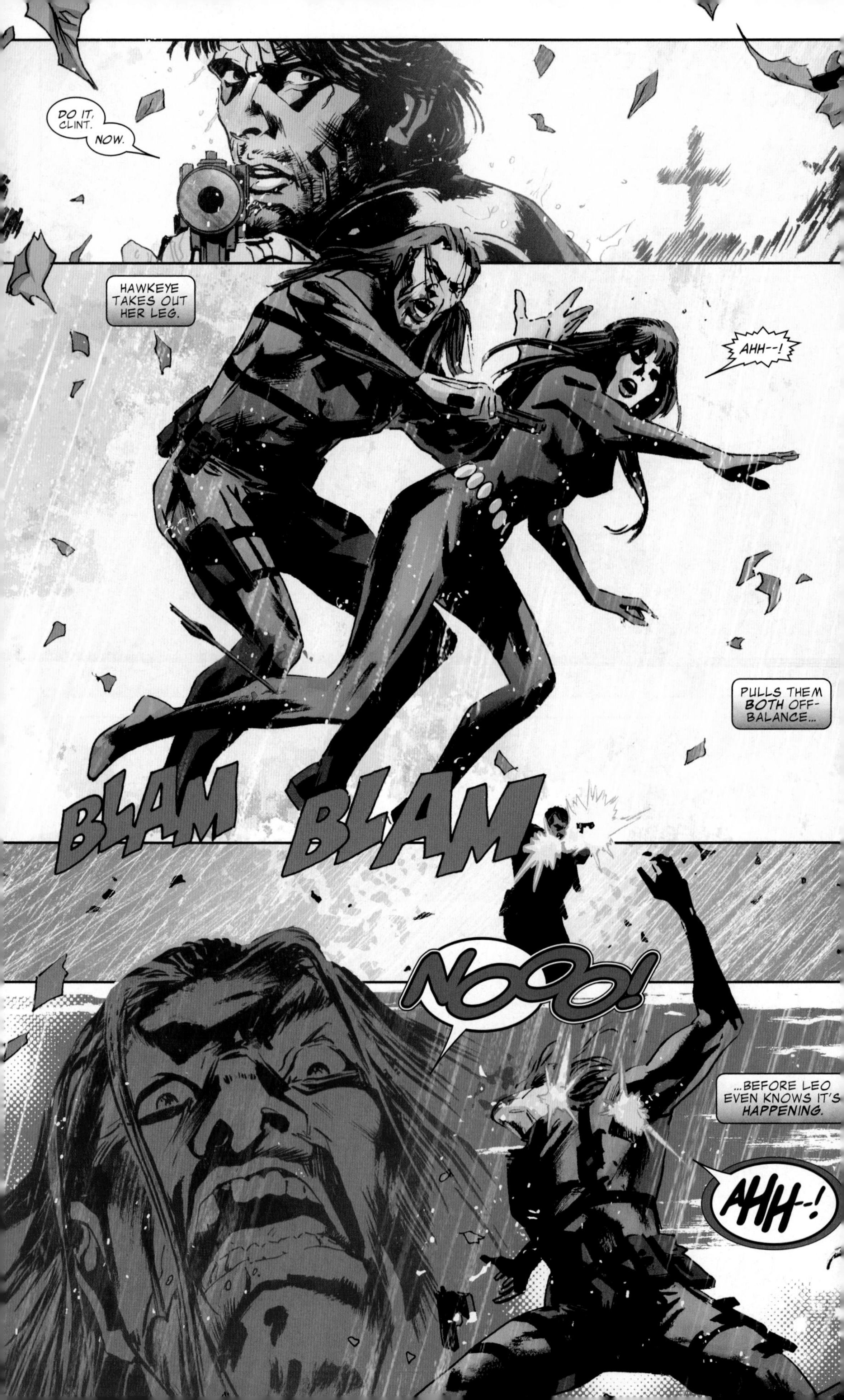
DO IT, CLINT.
NOW.
HAWKEYE TAKES OUT HER LEG.
AHH--!
PULLS THEM BOTH OFF-BALANCE...
BLAM BLAM
NOOO!
...BEFORE LEO EVEN KNOWS IT'S HAPPENING.
AHH--!

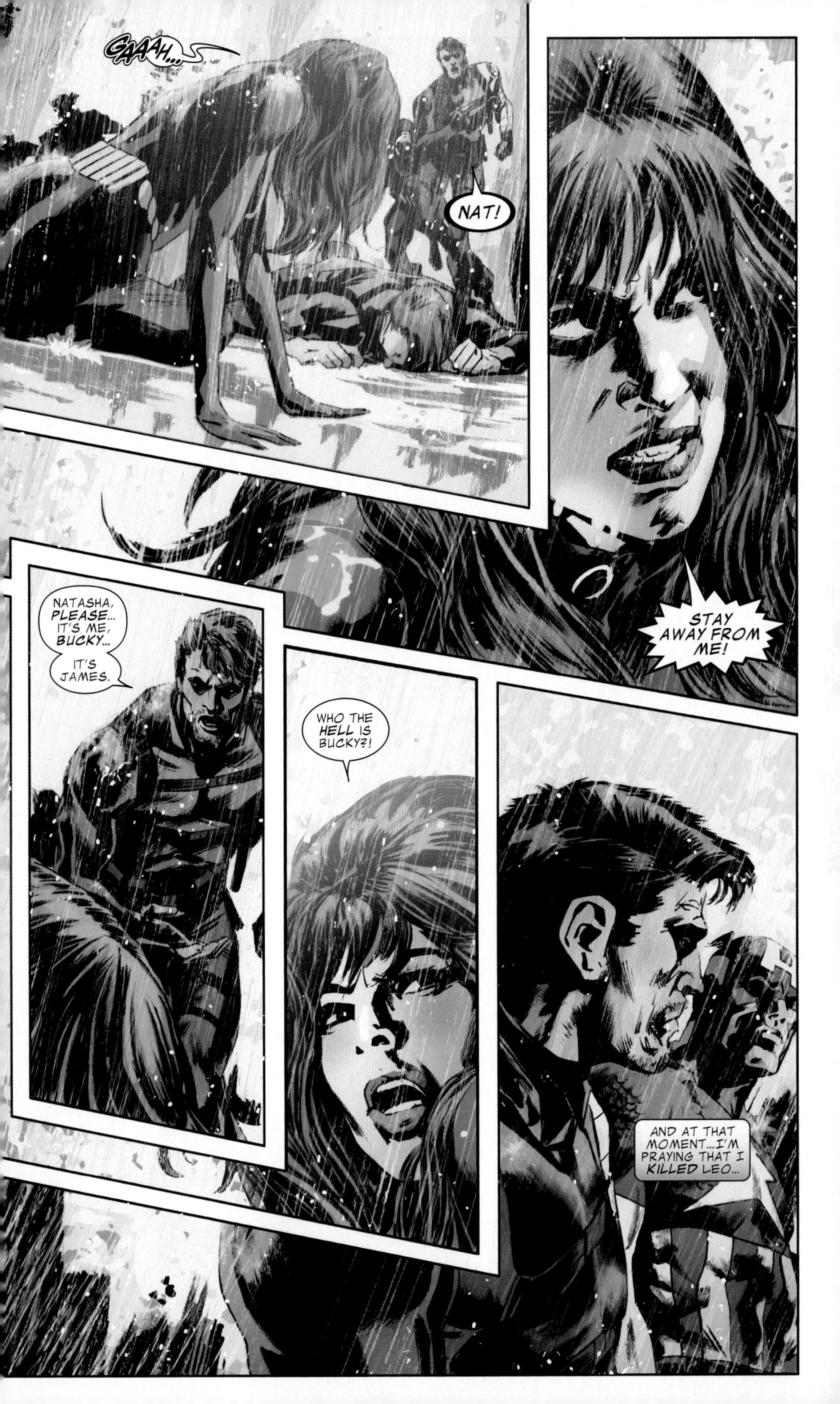
GAAAH...
NAT!
STAY AWAY FROM ME!
NATASHA, PLEASE... IT'S ME, BUCKY...
IT'S JAMES.
WHO THE HELL IS BUCKY?!
AND AT THAT MOMENT...I'M PRAYING THAT I KILLED LEO...

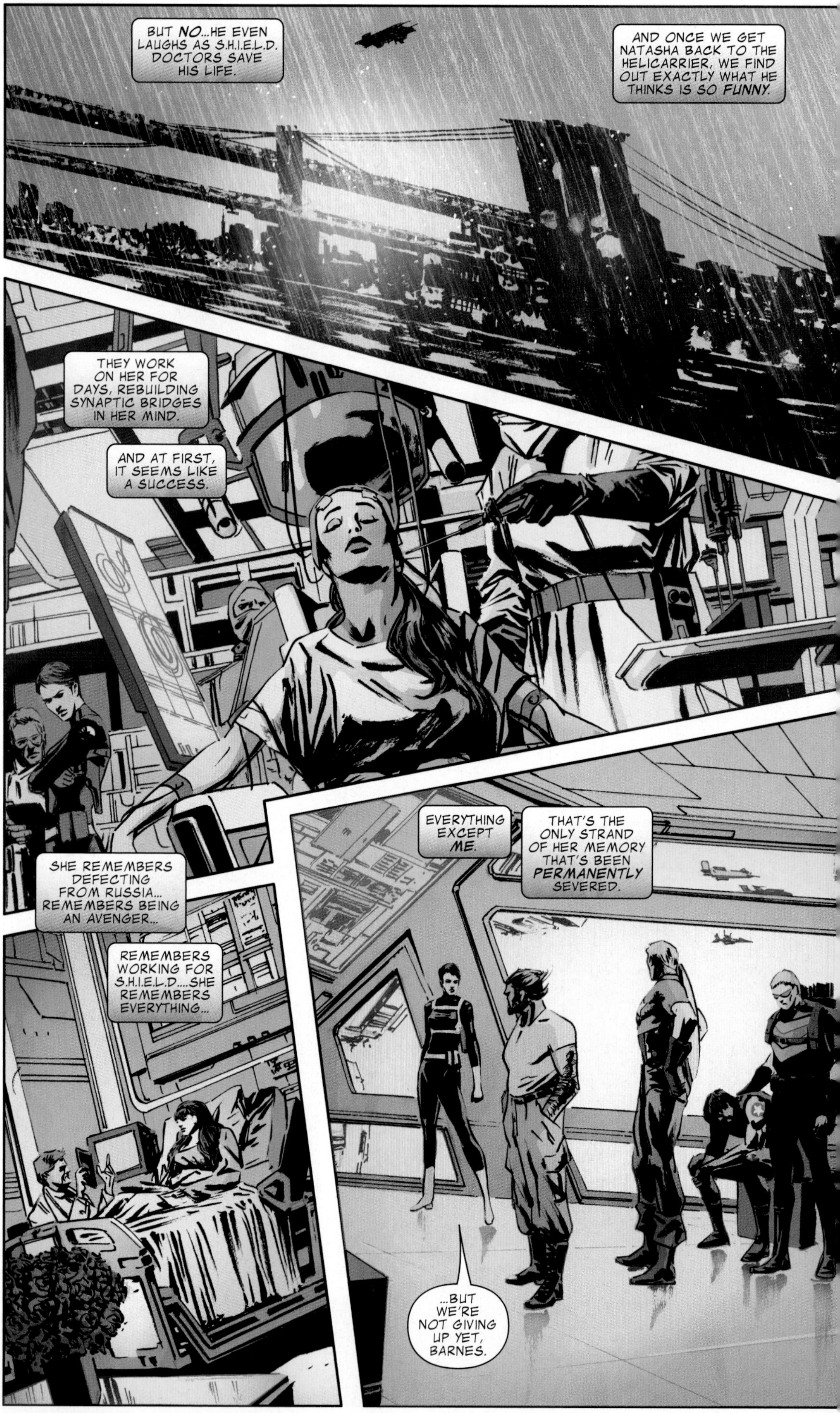
BUT NO...HE EVEN LAUGHS AS S.H.I.E.L.D. DOCTORS SAVE HIS LIFE.
AND ONCE WE GET NATASHA BACK TO THE HELICARRIER, WE FIND OUT EXACTLY WHAT HE THINKS IS SO FUNNY.
THEY WORK ON HER FOR DAYS, REBUILDING SYNAPTIC BRIDGES IN HER MIND.
AND AT FIRST, IT SEEMS LIKE A SUCCESS.
SHE REMEMBERS DEFECTING FROM RUSSIA... REMEMBERS BEING AN AVENGER...
REMEMBERS WORKING FOR S.H.I.E.L.D....SHE REMEMBERS EVERYTHING...
EVERYTHING EXCEPT ME.
THAT'S THE ONLY STRAND OF HER MEMORY THAT'S BEEN PERMANENTLY SEVERED.
...BUT WE'RE NOT GIVING UP YET, BARNES.

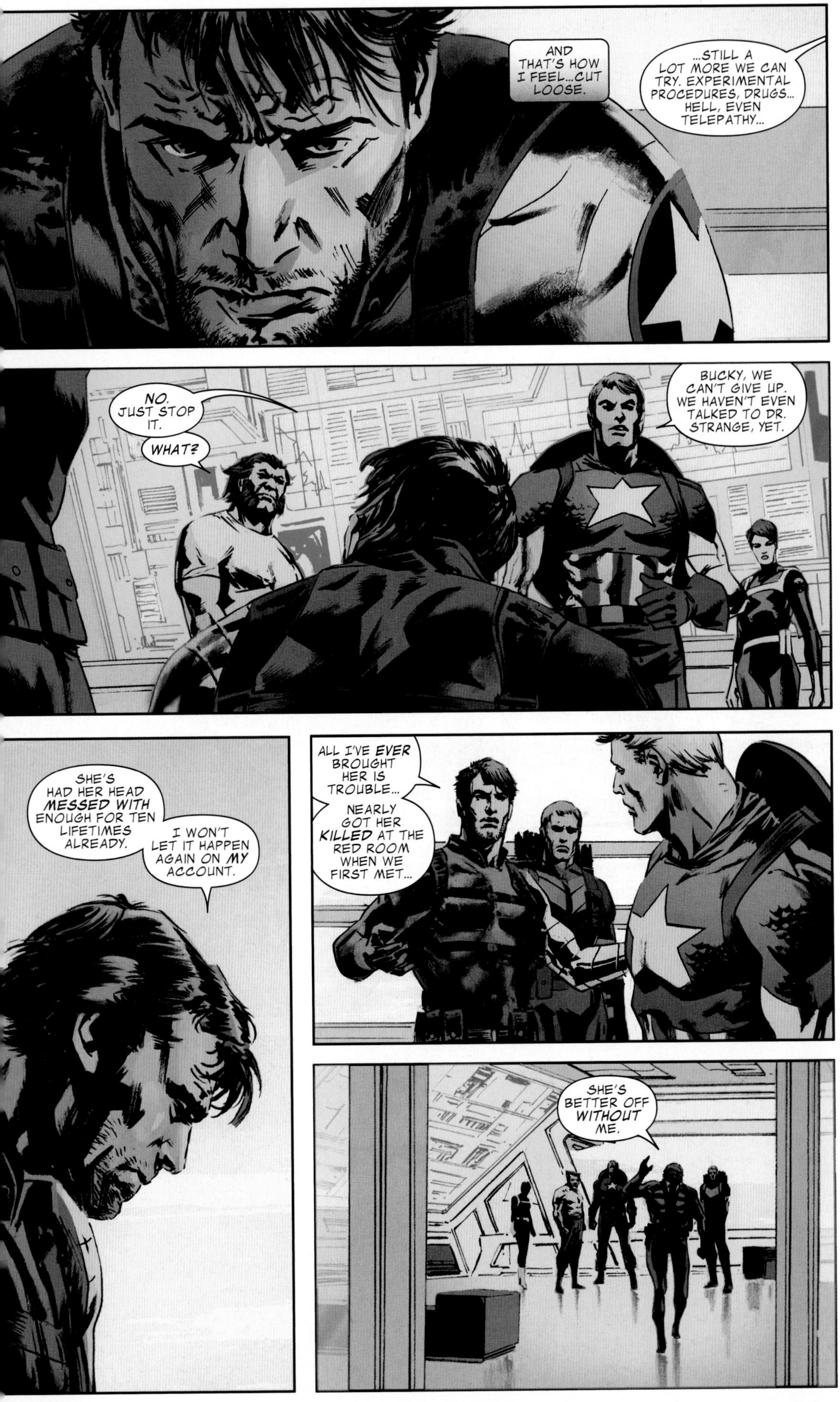
AND THAT'S HOW I FEEL...CUT LOOSE.
...STILL A LOT MORE WE CAN TRY. EXPERIMENTAL PROCEDURES, DRUGS... HELL, EVEN TELEPATHY...
BUCKY, WE CAN'T GIVE UP. WE HAVEN'T EVEN TALKED TO DR. STRANGE, YET.
NO. JUST STOP IT.
WHAT?
SHE'S HAD HER HEAD MESSED WITH ENOUGH FOR TEN LIFETIMES ALREADY.
I WON'T LET IT HAPPEN AGAIN ON MY ACCOUNT.
ALL I'VE EVER BROUGHT HER IS TROUBLE...
NEARLY GOT HER KILLED AT THE RED ROOM WHEN WE FIRST MET...
SHE'S BETTER OFF WITHOUT ME.

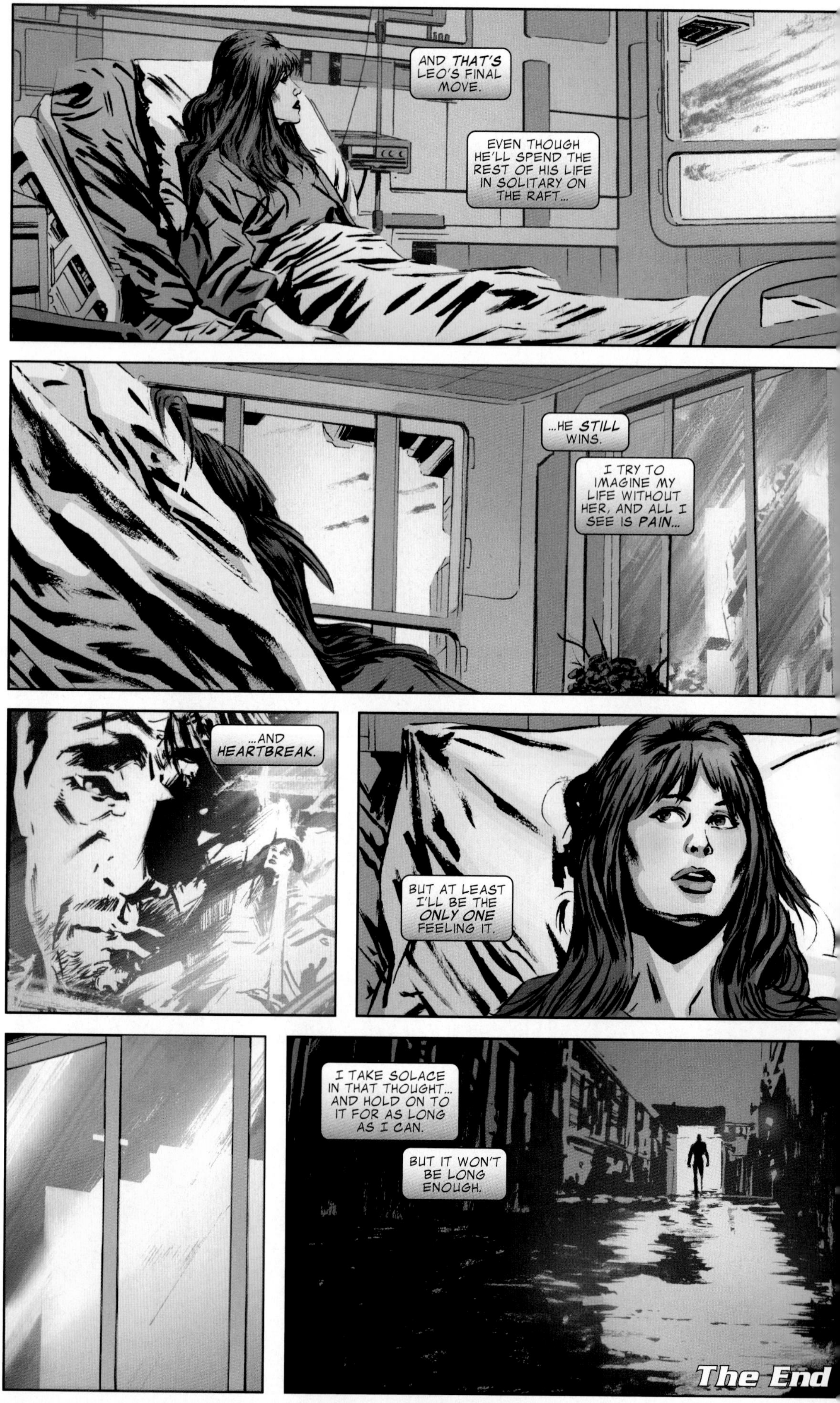
AND THAT'S LEO'S FINAL MOVE.
EVEN THOUGH HE'LL SPEND THE REST OF HIS LIFE IN SOLITARY ON THE RAFT...
...HE STILL WINS.
I TRY TO IMAGINE MY LIFE WITHOUT HER, AND ALL I SEE IS PAIN...
...AND HEARTBREAK.
BUT AT LEAST I'LL BE THE ONLY ONE FEELING IT.
I TAKE SOLACE IN THAT THOUGHT... AND HOLD ON TO IT FOR AS LONG AS I CAN.
BUT IT WON'T BE LONG ENOUGH.
The End

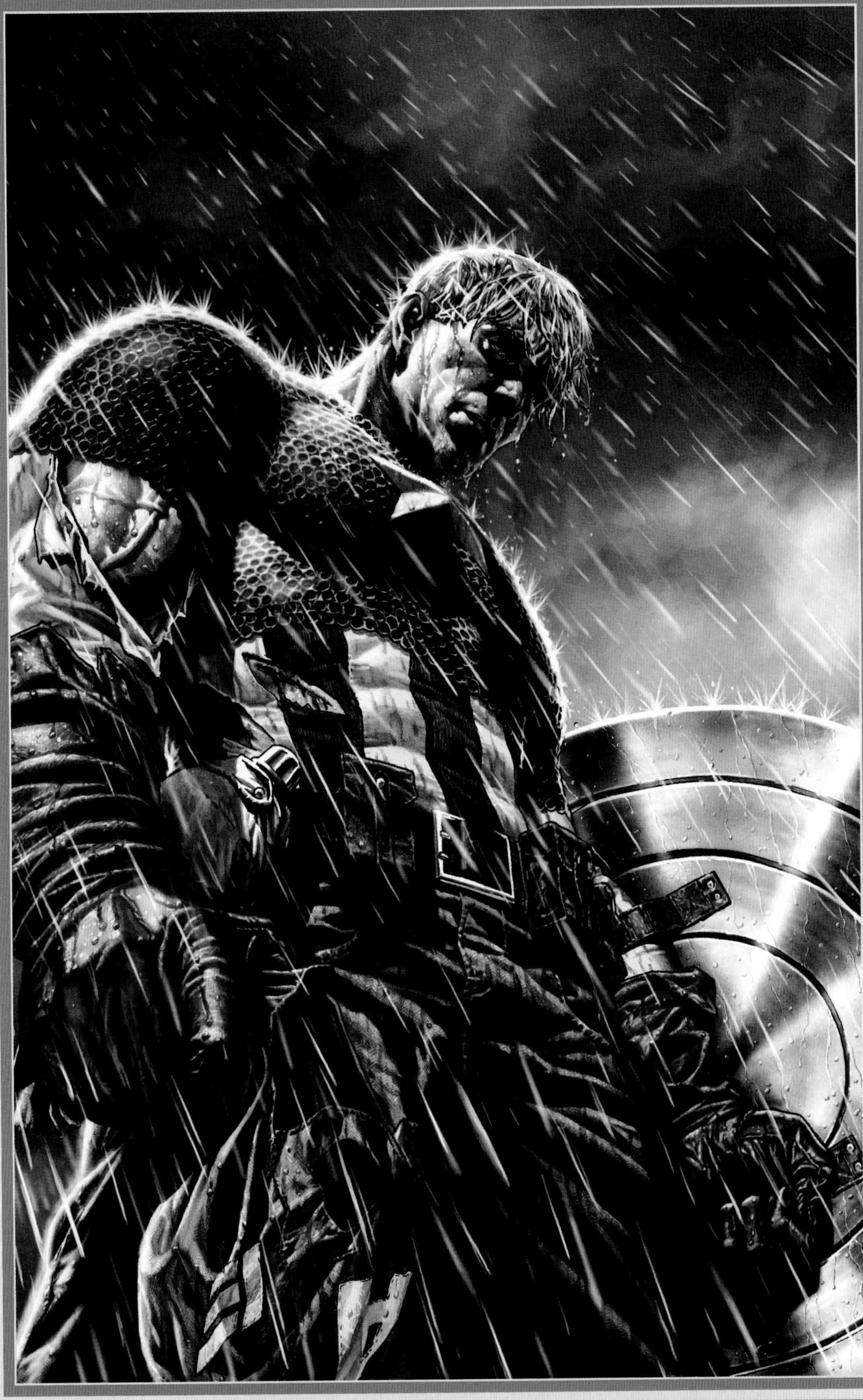

FEAR ITSELF #7.1: CAPTAIN AMERICA VARIANT BY LEE BERMEJO

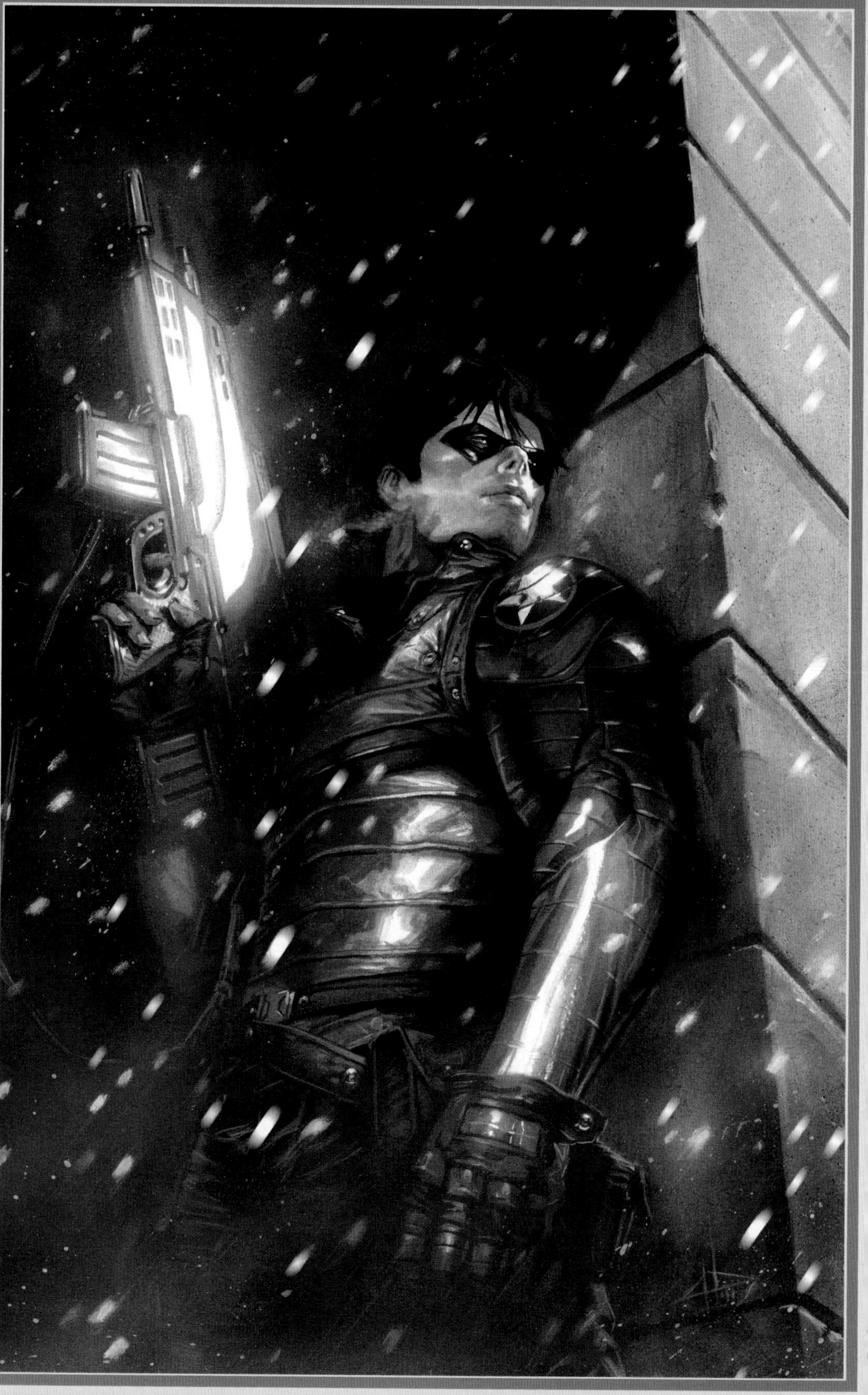

ONE VARIANT BY GABRIELE DELL'OTTO

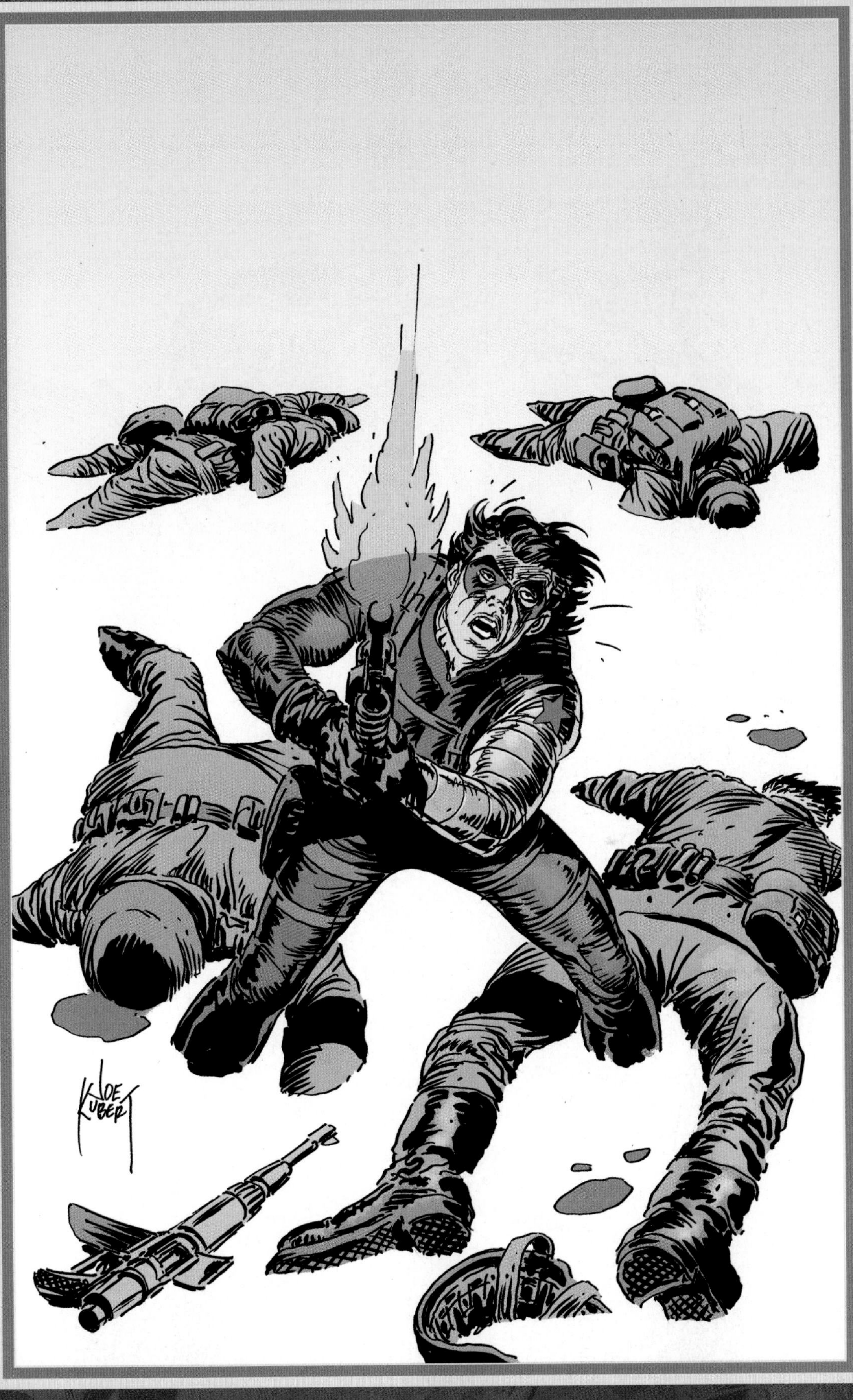
JOE KUBERT

ONE VARIANT BY JOE KUBERT

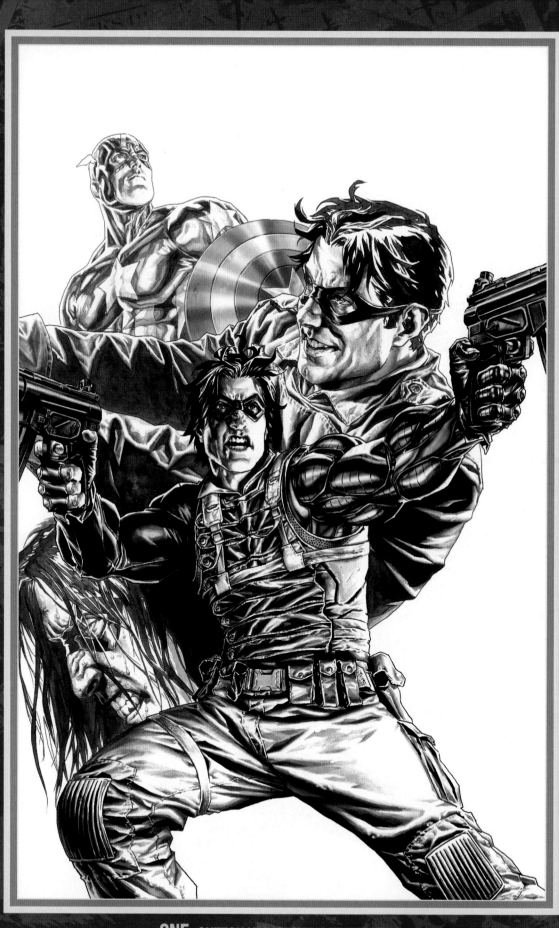

ONE SKETCH VARIANT BY LEE BERMEJO

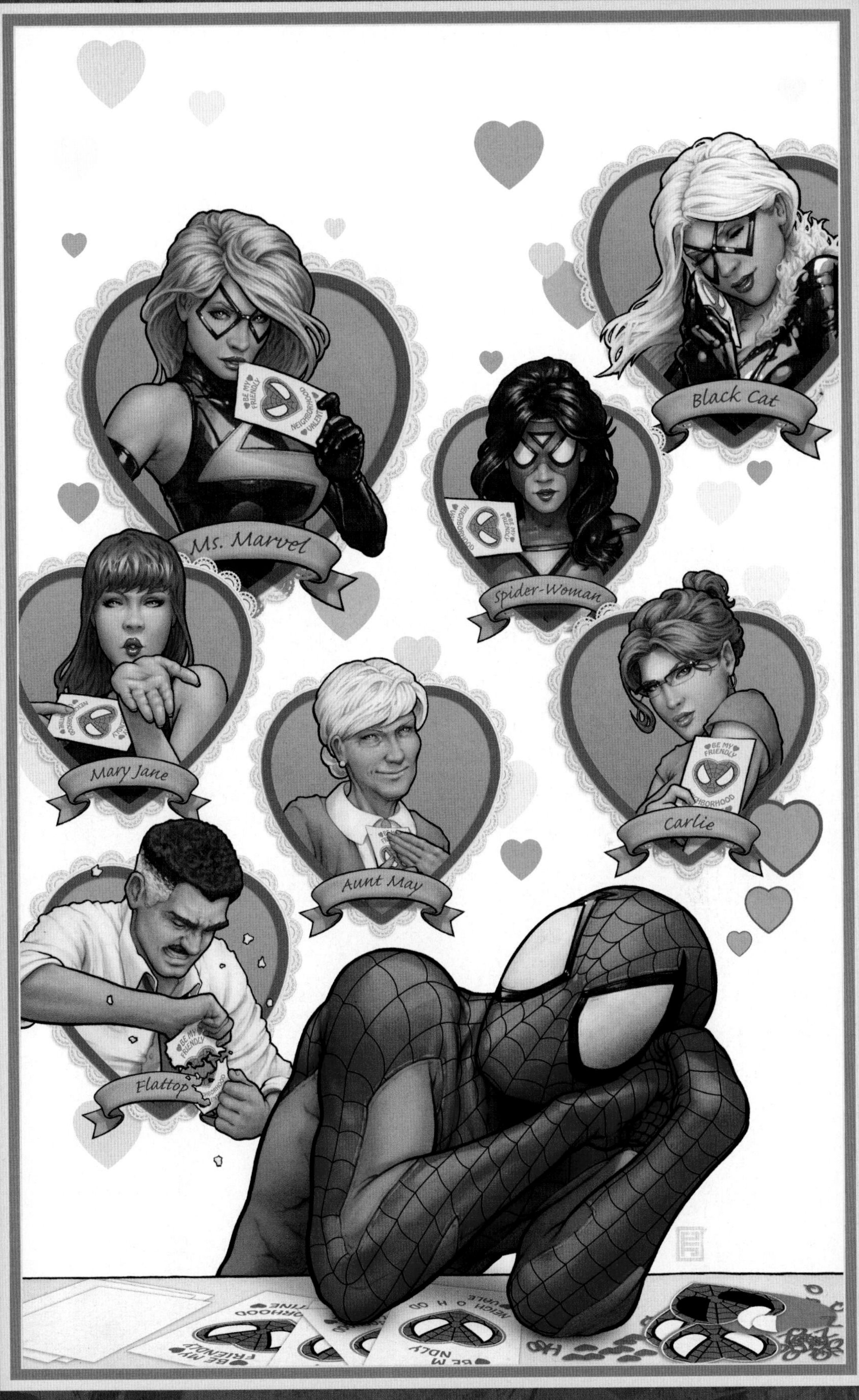
Black Cat
BE MY FRIENDLY
NEIGHBORHOOD
Ms. Marvel
Spider-Woman
Mary Jane
Carlie
Aunt May
Flattop

TWO AMAZING SPIDER-MAN ANNIVERSARY VARIANT BY BUTCH GUICE & BETTY BREITWEISER

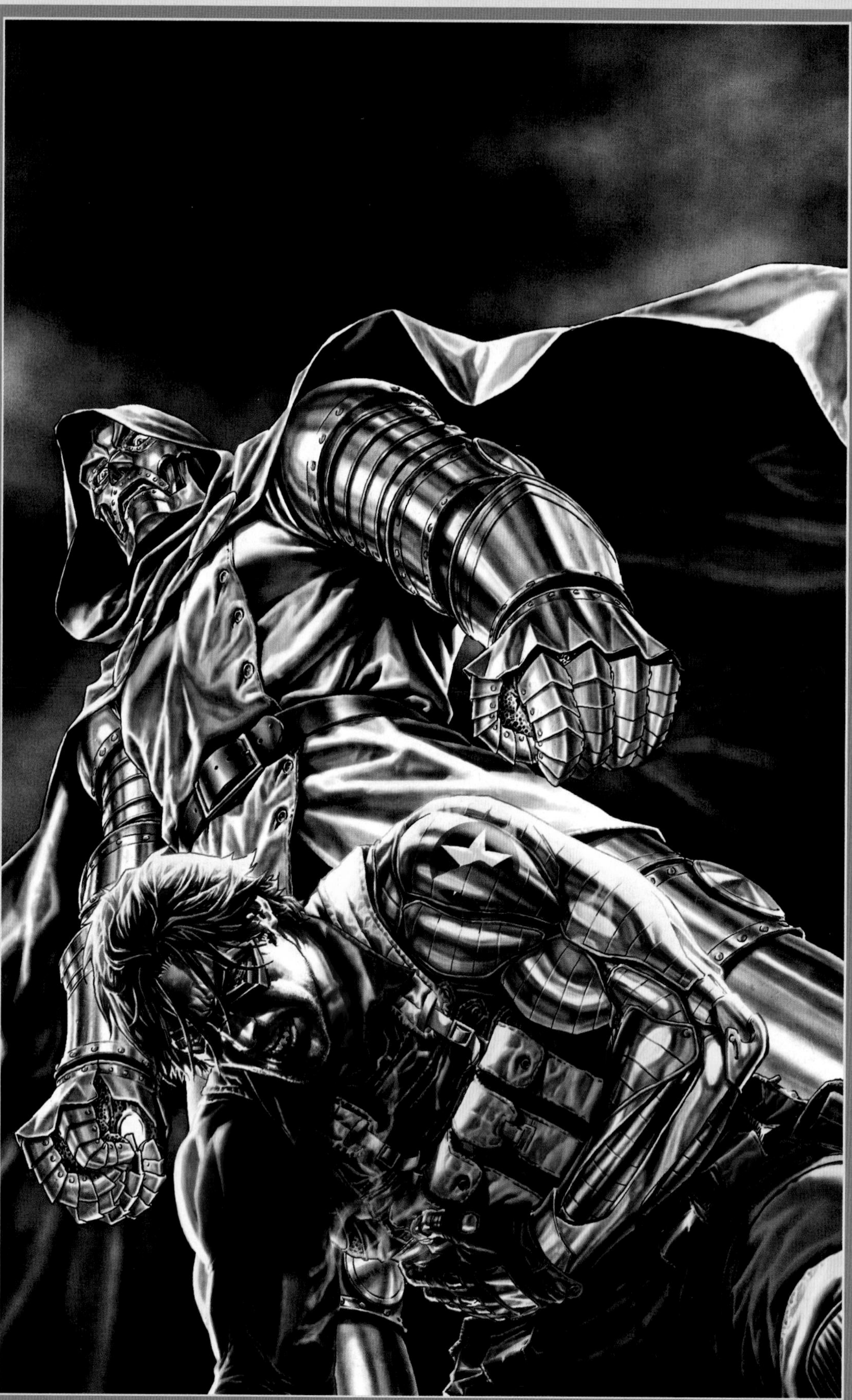

THREE 2ND-PRINTING VARIANT BY LEE BERMEJO

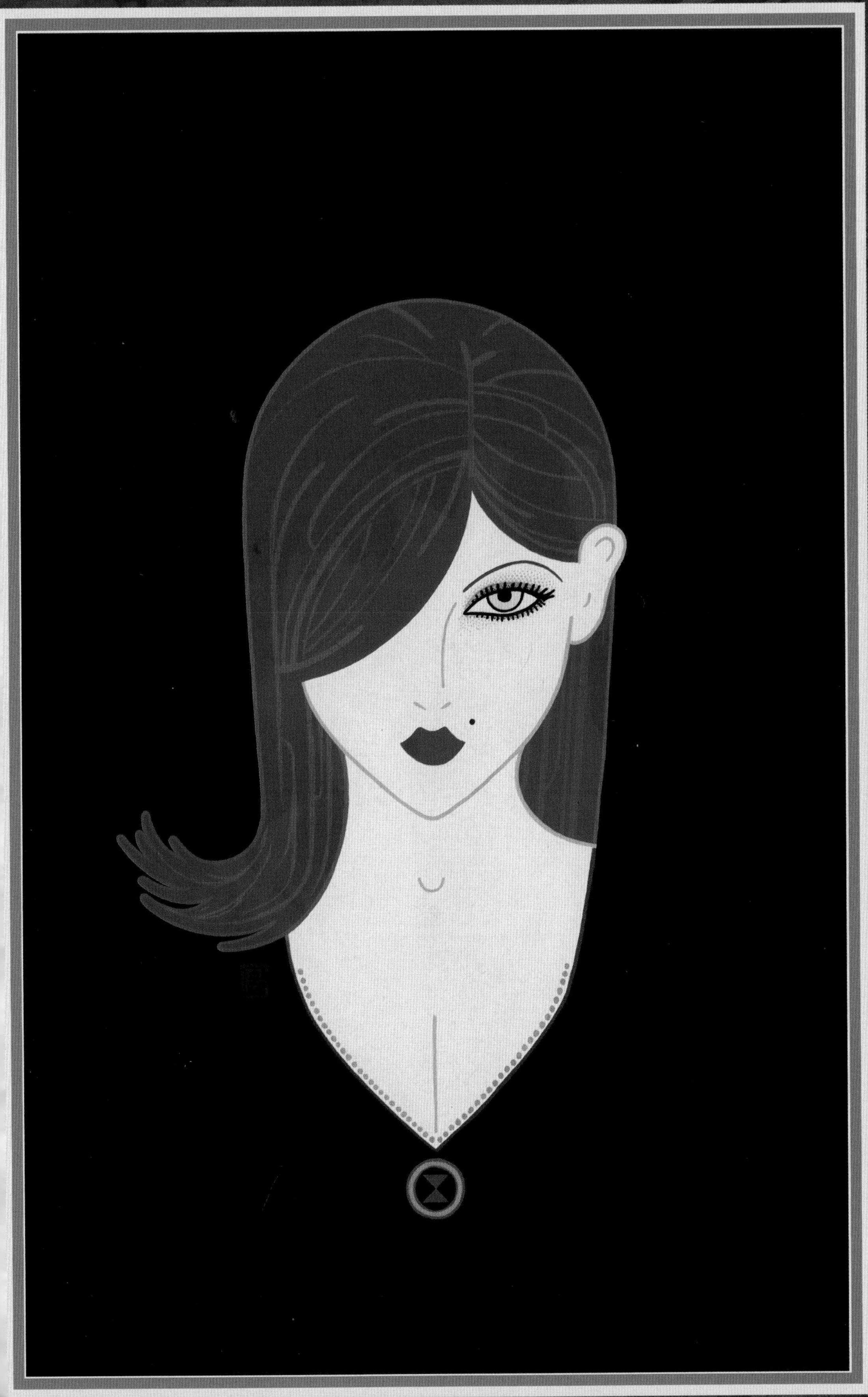

FOUR ART APPRECIATION VARIANT BY JOHN TYLER CHRISTOPHER

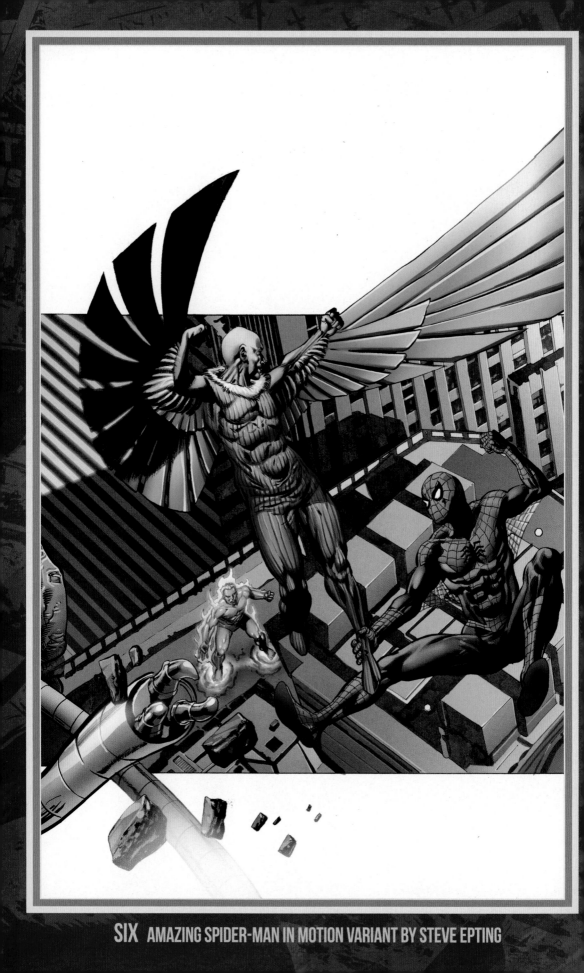

SIX AMAZING SPIDER-MAN IN MOTION VARIANT BY STEVE EPTING

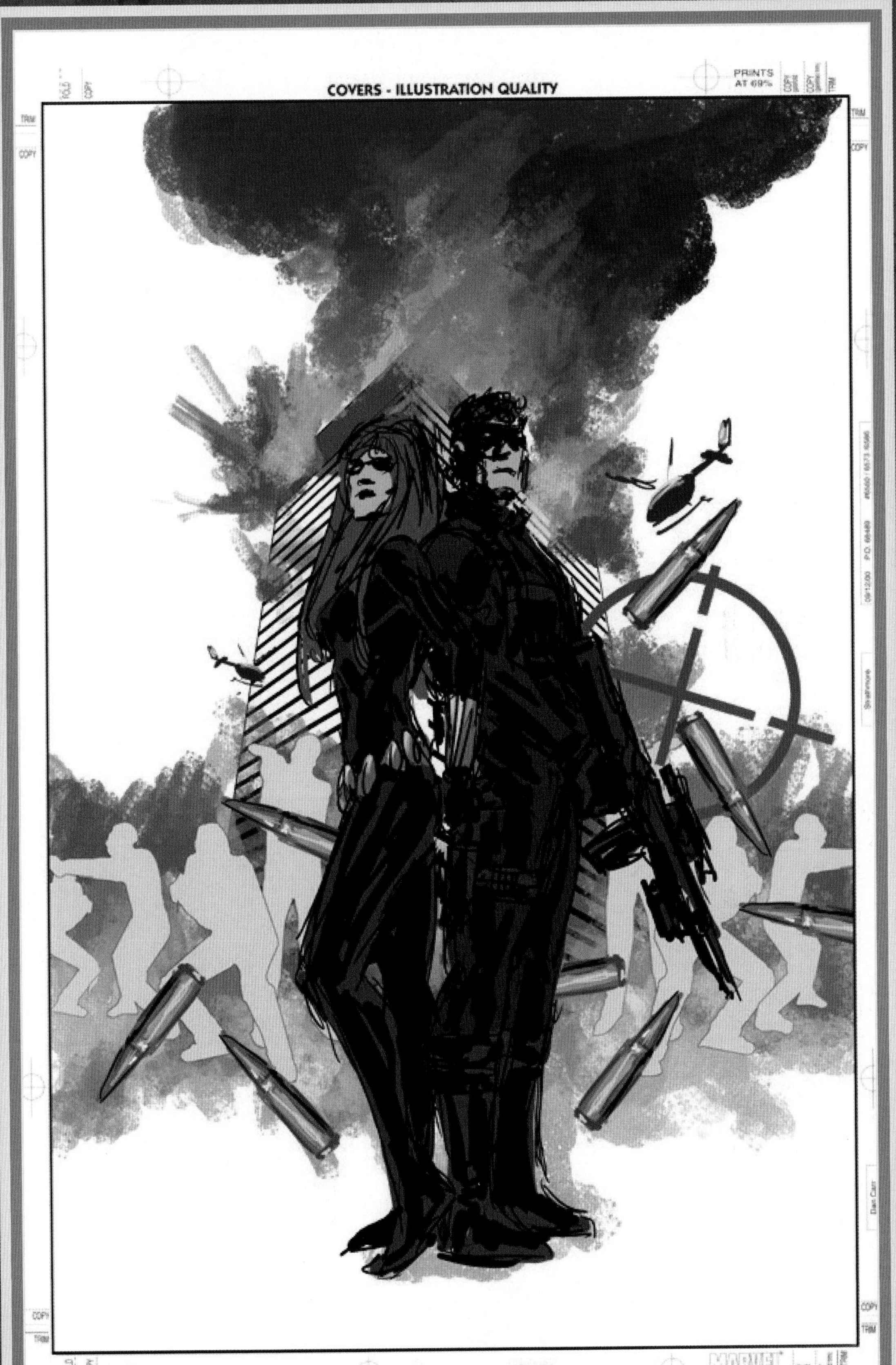
COVERS - ILLUSTRATION QUALITY
PRINTS AT 69%
TITLE
#
MONTH
ARTIST STEVE EPTING
MARVEL COMICS

SEVEN COVER LAYOUT BY STEVE EPTING

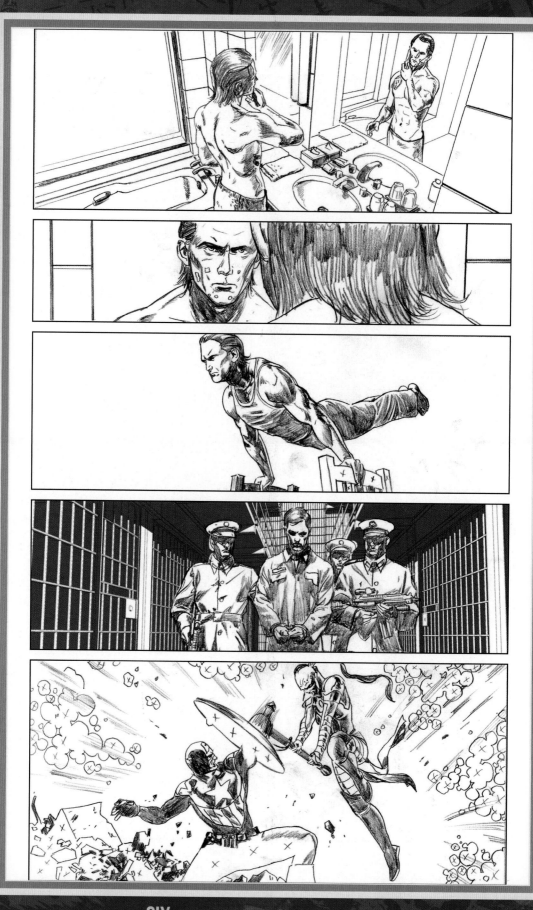

SIX PAGE 14 PENCILS BY MICHAEL LARK

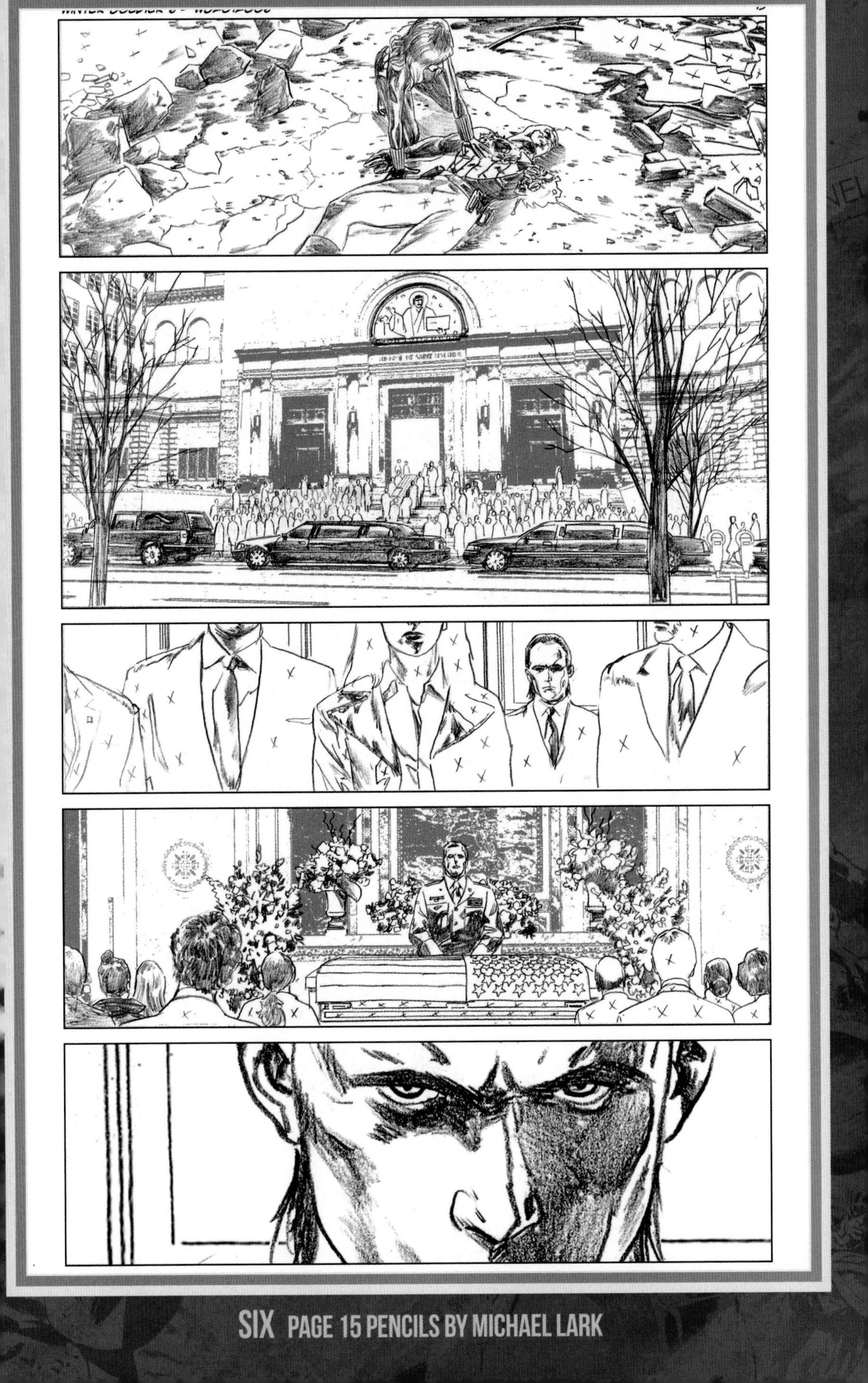

SIX PAGE 15 PENCILS BY MICHAEL LARK

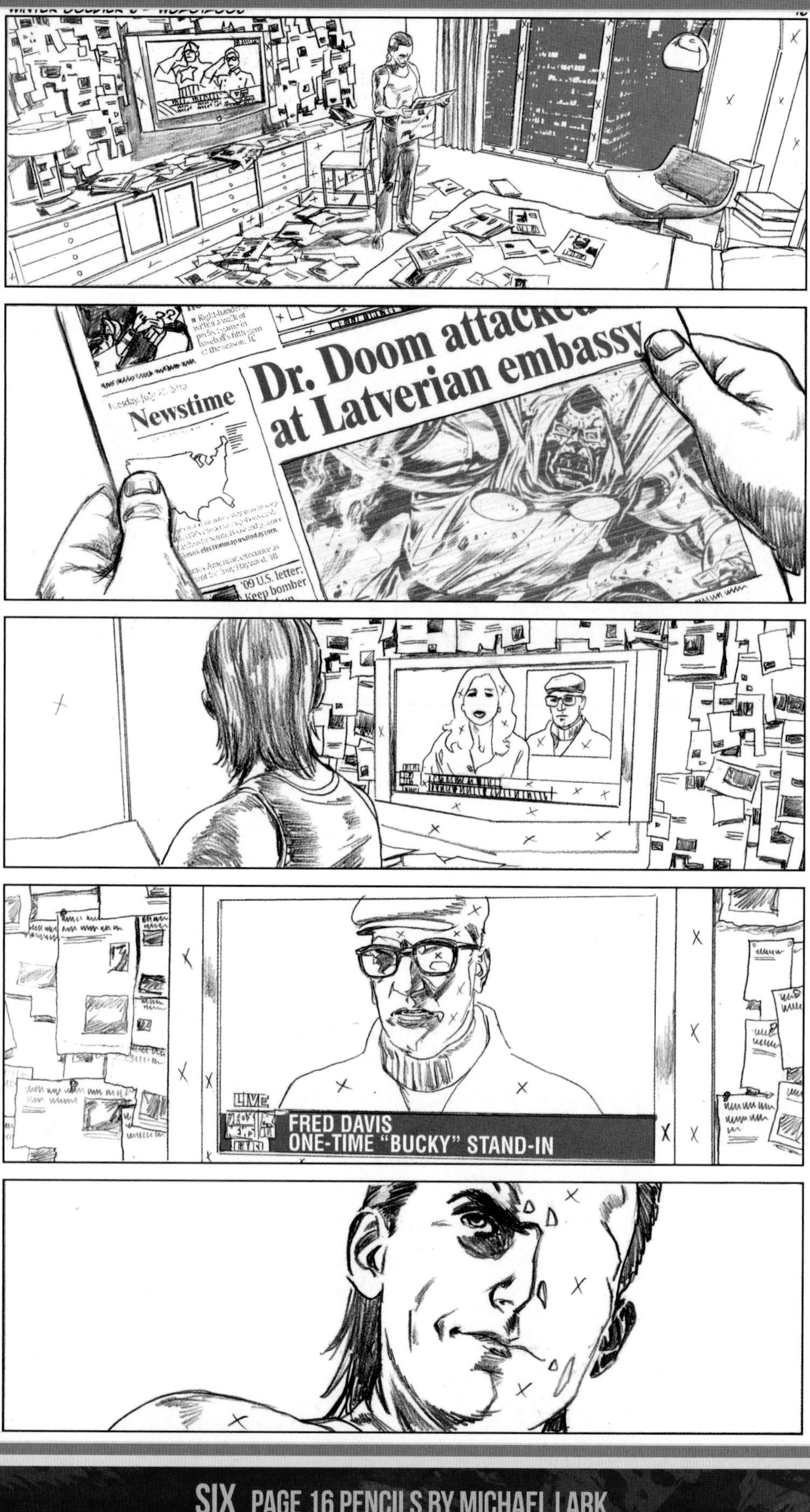

Dr. Doom attacked
at Latverian embassy
Newstime
LIVE
FRED DAVIS
ONE-TIME "BUCKY" STAND-IN

SIX PAGE 16 PENCILS BY MICHAEL LARK

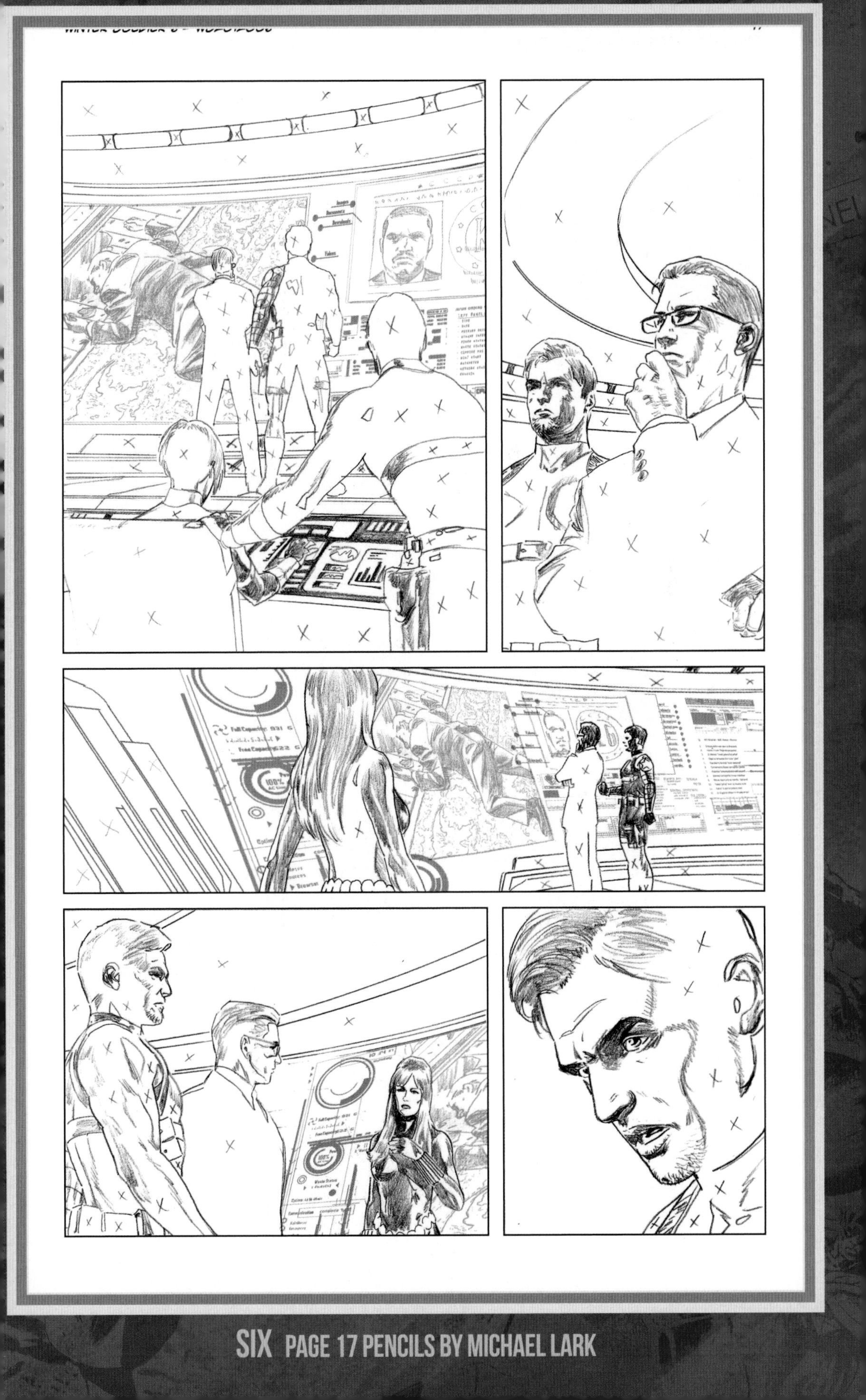

SIX PAGE 17 PENCILS BY MICHAEL LARK

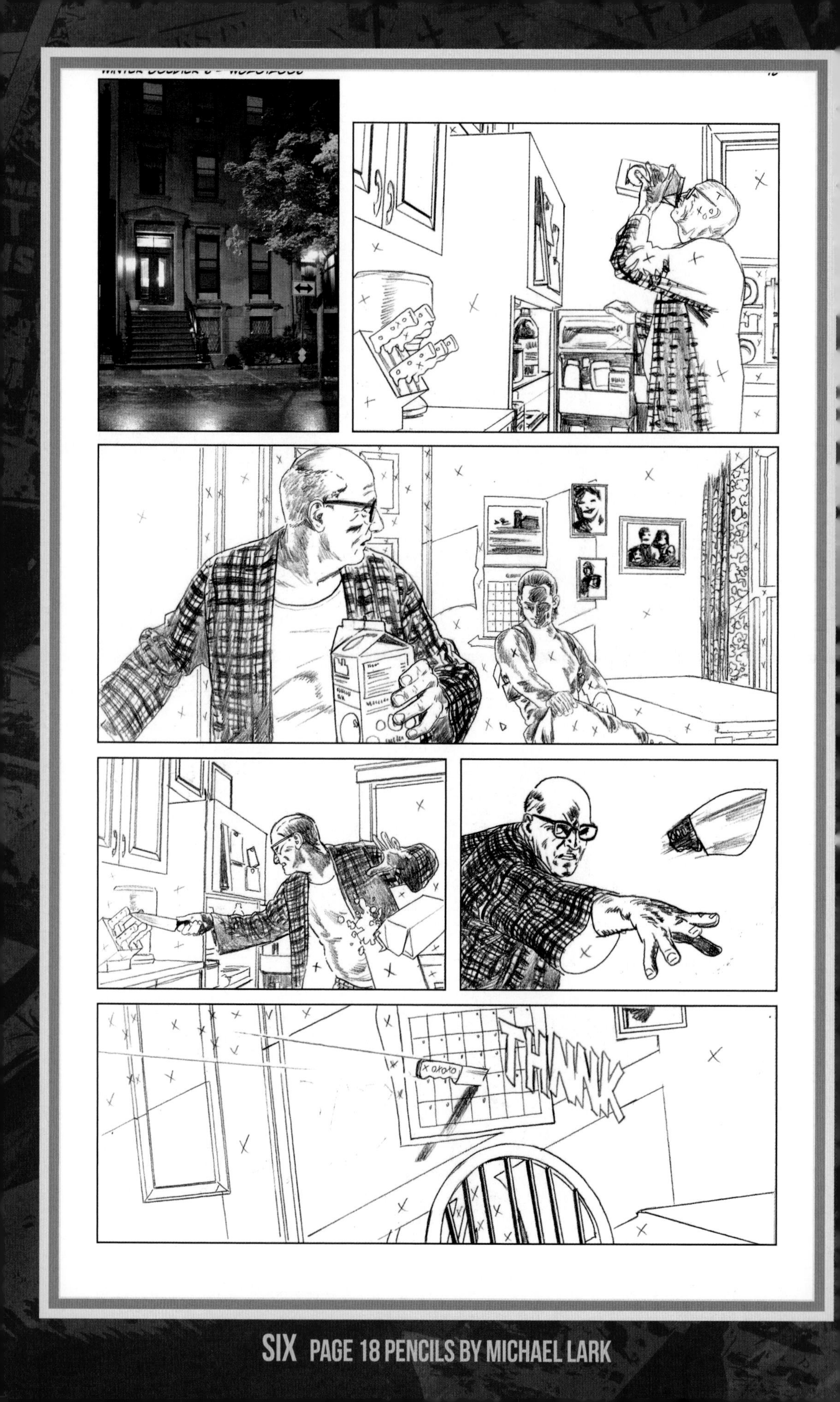
THNNK

SIX PAGE 18 PENCILS BY MICHAEL LARK

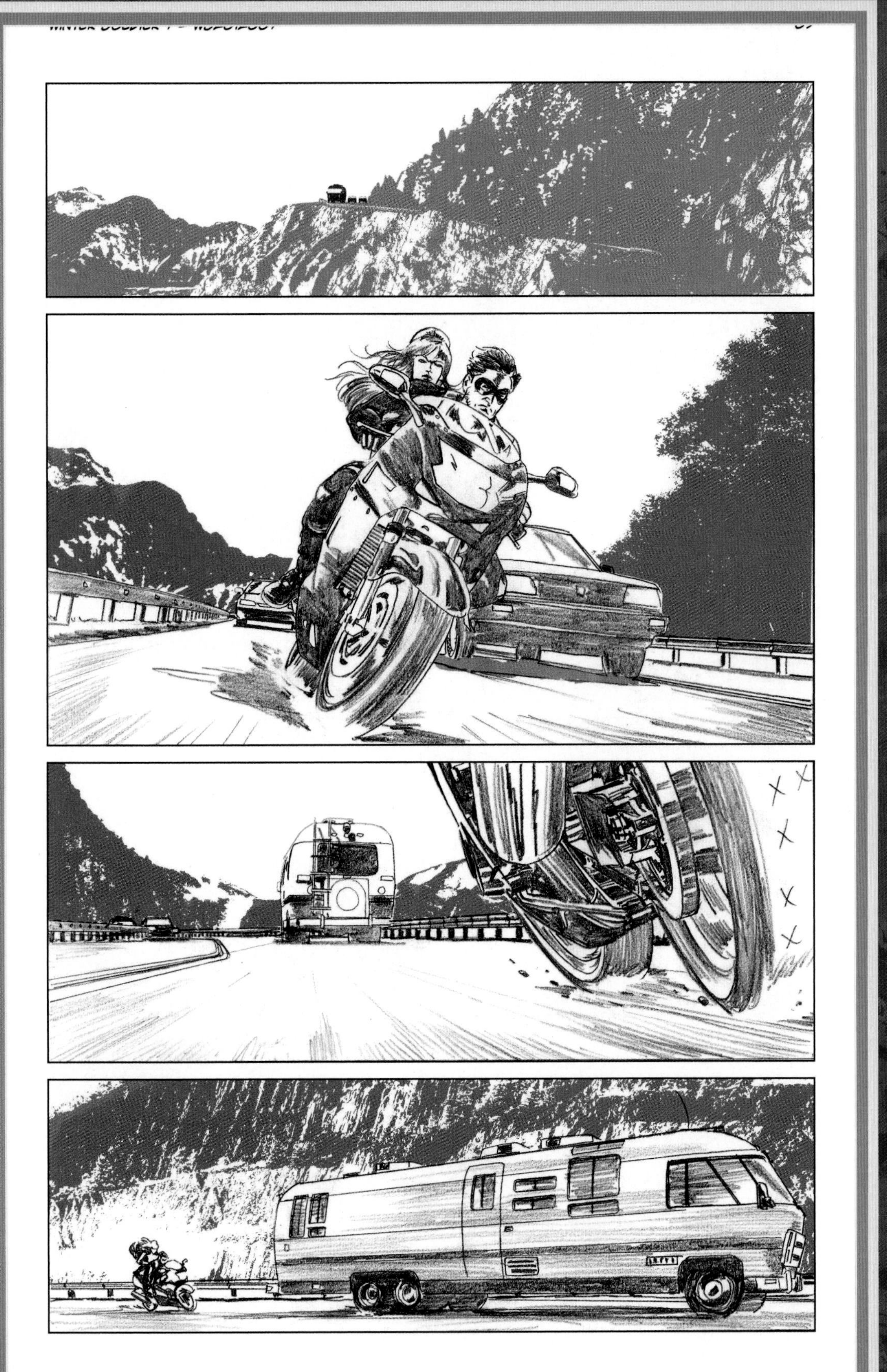

SEVEN PAGE 9 PENCILS BY MICHAEL LARK

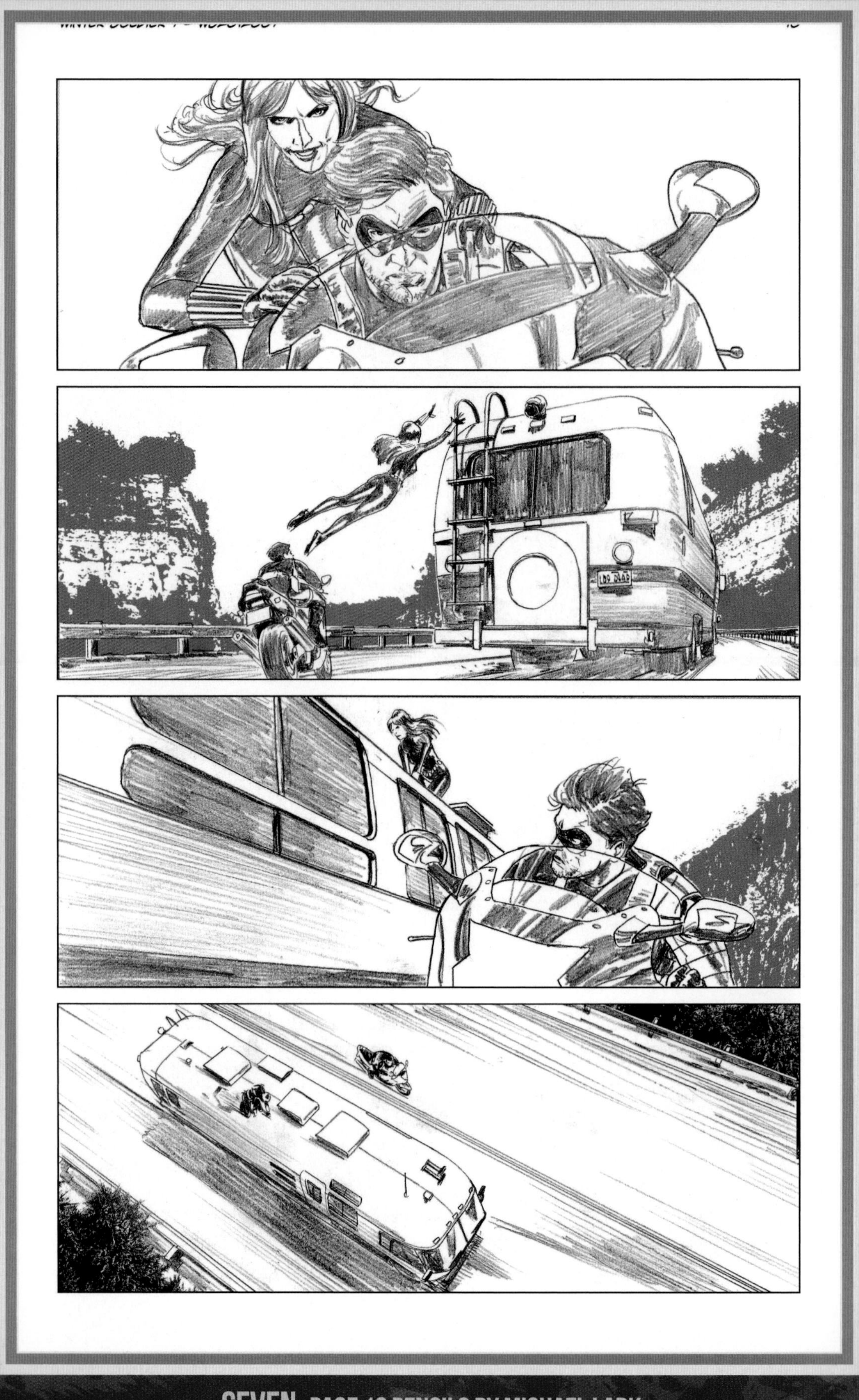

SEVEN PAGE 10 PENCILS BY MICHAEL LARK

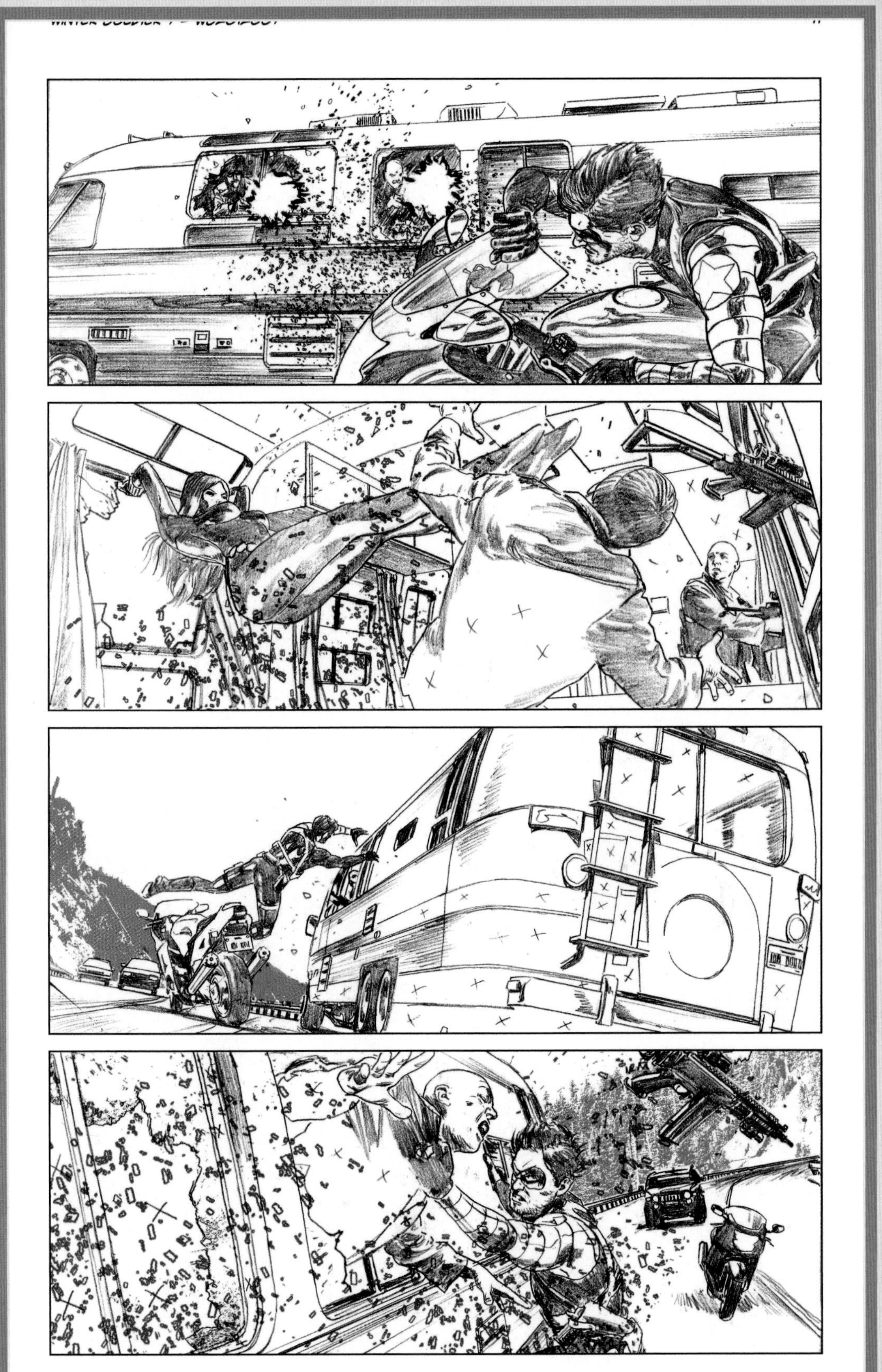

SEVEN PAGE 11 PENCILS BY MICHAEL LARK

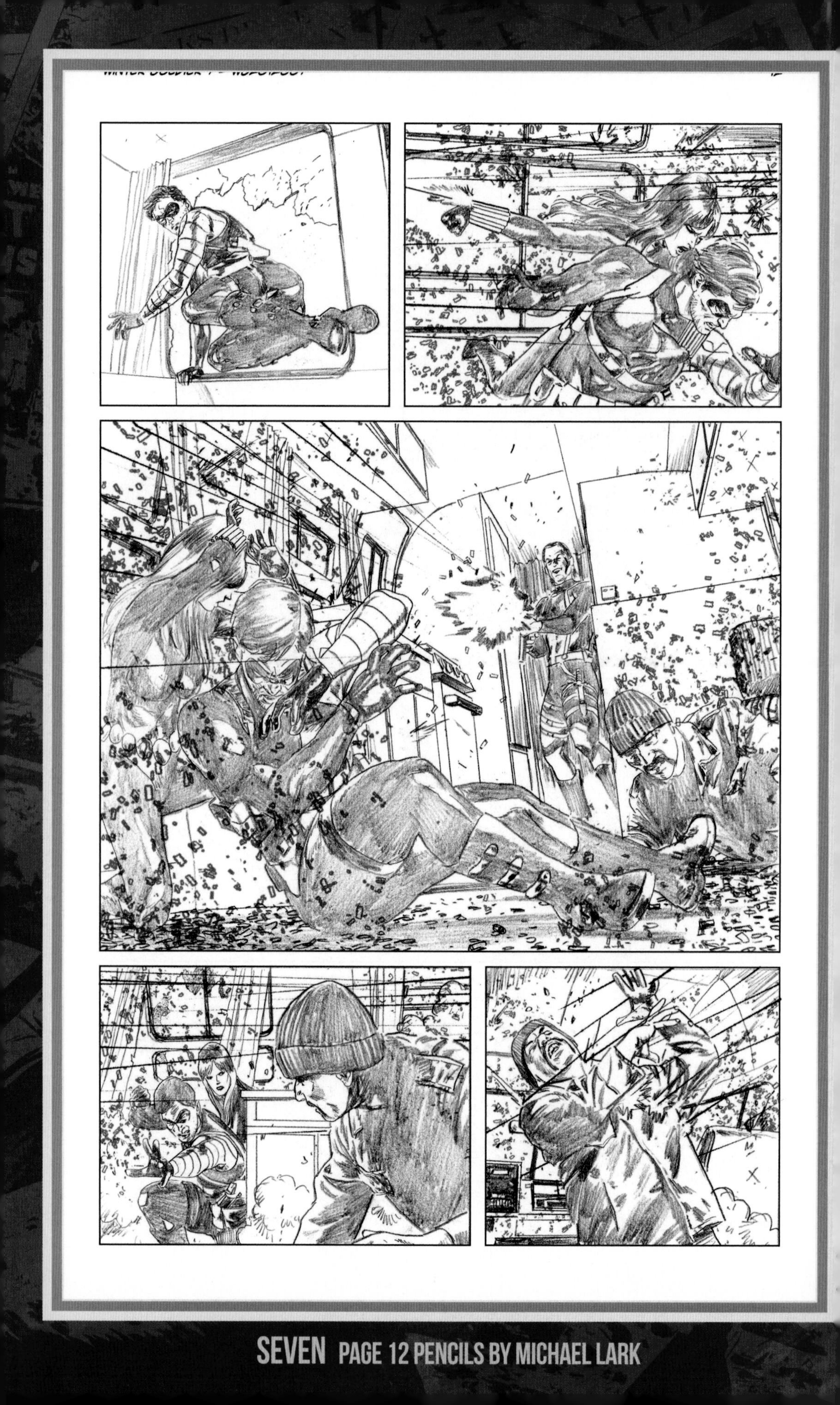

SEVEN PAGE 12 PENCILS BY MICHAEL LARK

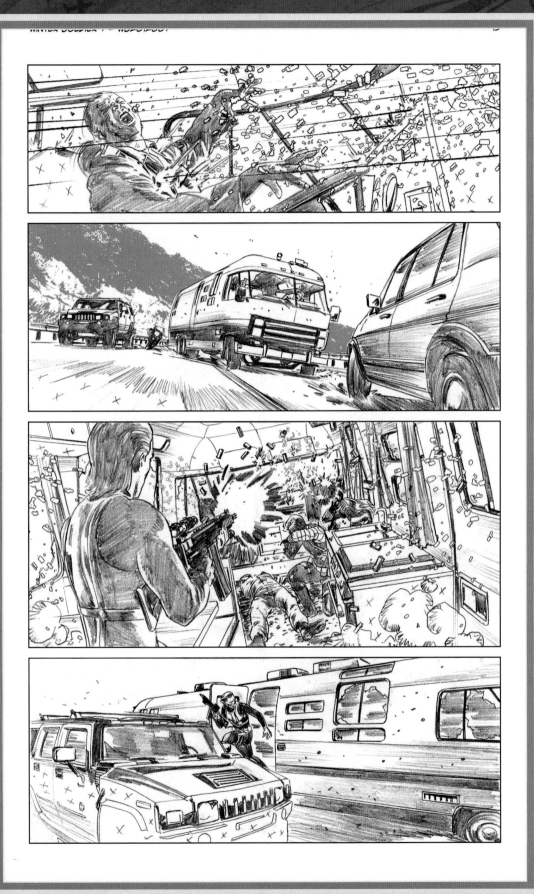

SEVEN PAGE 13 PENCILS BY MICHAEL LARK

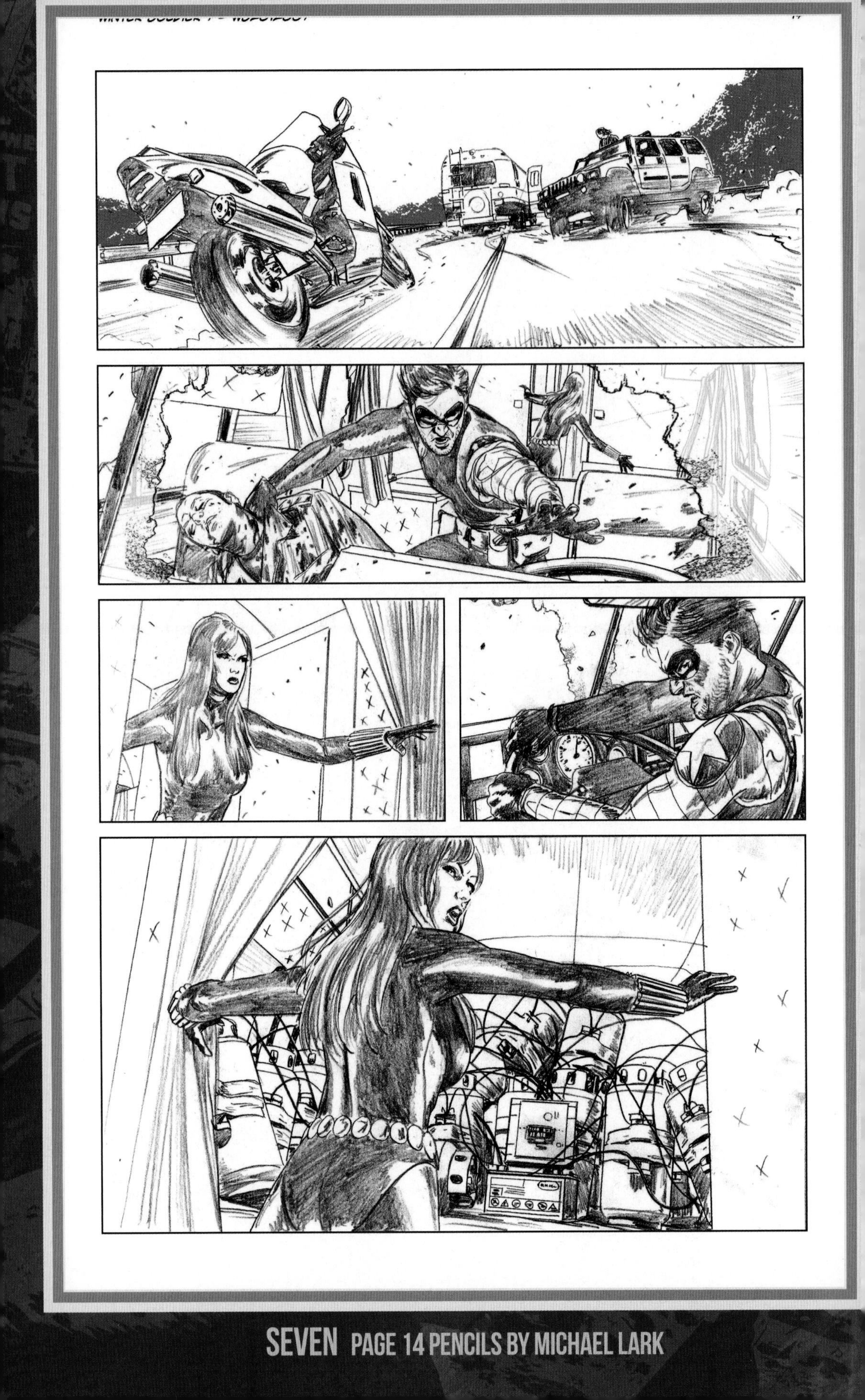

SEVEN PAGE 14 PENCILS BY MICHAEL LARK

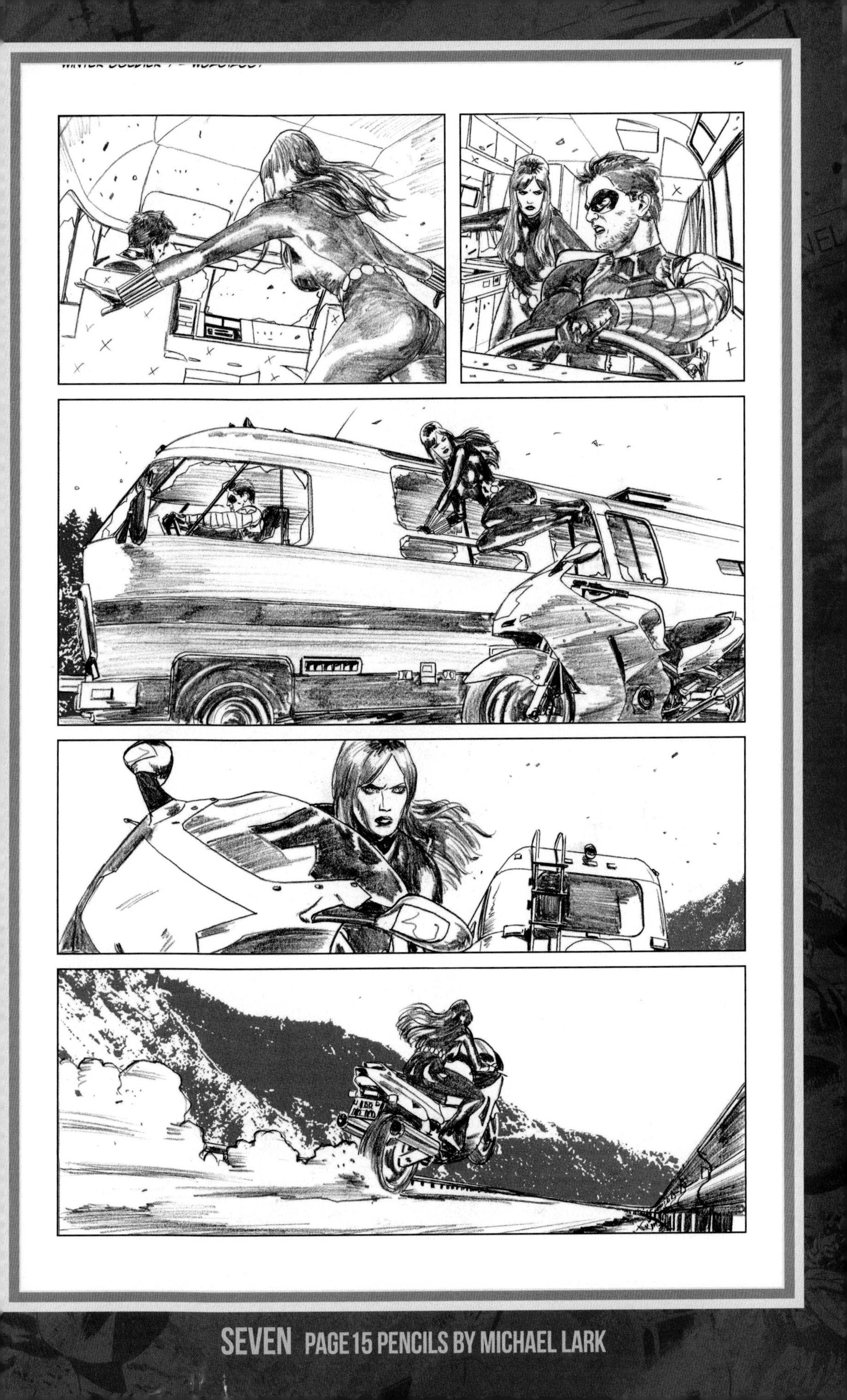

SEVEN PAGE 15 PENCILS BY MICHAEL LARK

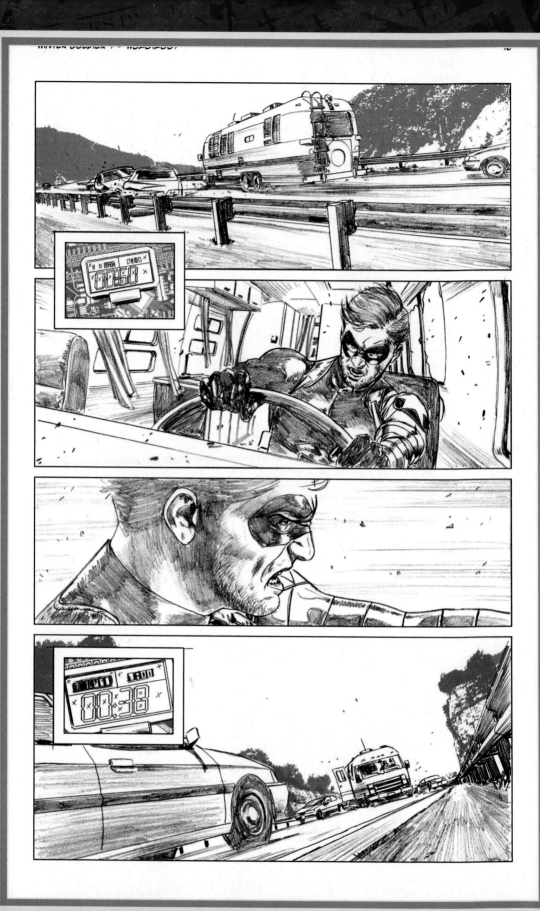

SEVEN PAGE 16 PENCILS BY MICHAEL LARK